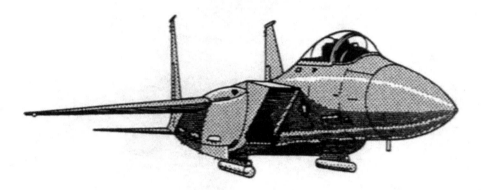

McDonnell Douglas F-15E Strike Eagle
Pilot's Flight Operating Instructions

by United States Air Force

This manual is sold for historic research purposes only, as an entertainment.
It is not intended to be used as part of an actual flight training program. No
book can substitute for flight training by an authorized instructor. The licensing
of pilots is overseen by organizations and authorities such as the FAA and CAA.
Operating an aircraft without the proper license is a federal crime.

FLIGHT MANUAL

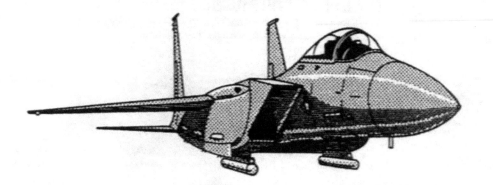

USAF SERIES
F-15E AIRCRAFT

McDonnell Aircraft
F33657-86-C-2001
F33657-89-C-2000

AIR FORCE: 22, 05, 91 1720

C 15 AUGUST 1990
CHANGE 2 - 15 MARCH 1991

LIST OF EFFECTIVE PAGES

Insert latest changed pages; dispose of superseded pages in accordance with applicable regulations.

Dates of issue for original and changed pages:

Original .... 0 ..... 15 Aug 90   Change .... 1 ..... 15 Dec 90   Change .... 2 ..... 15 Mar 91

Total number of pages in this publication is 652 consisting of the following:

Page No.	#Change No.	Page No.	#Change No.	Page No.	#Change No.	Page No.	#Change No.
Title	2	1-26	2	1-62A	2	1-98	2
A	2	1-27	2	1-62B blank	2	1-99	2
B	2	1-28	2	1-63	2	1-100	2
C	2	1-28A	2	1-64	0	1-101	2
i	2	1-28B blank	2	1-65	2	1-102	0
ii blank	2	1-29	0	1-66	2	1-103	0
iii	0	1-30	0	1-67	2	1-104	2
iv	2	1-31	2	1-68	2	1-105	2
v	0	1-32	2	1-69	2	1-106	2
vi	2	1-33	2	1-70	2	1-107	2
vii	0	1-34	2	1-71	2	1-108	2
viii	2	1-34A	2	1-72	2	1-108A	2
ix	2	1-34B blank	2	1-73	2	1-108B	2
x	0	1-35	0	1-74	2	1-108C	2
1-1	2	1-36	2	1-75	2	1-108D	2
1-2	2	1-37	2	1-76	2	1-108E	2
1-3	2	1-38	2	1-77	2	1-108F	2
1-4	2	1-39	2	1-78	2	1-109	0
1-5	2	1-40	0	1-79	2	1-110	0
1-6	2	1-41	0	1-80	2	1-111	2
1-7	2	1-42	2	1-81	2	1-112	2
1-8	2	1-43	2	1-82	2	1-113	2
1-8A	2	1-44	2	1-83	2	1-114	2
1-8B	2	1-44A	2	1-84	2	1-115	2
1-9	0	1-44B	2	1-85	2	1-116	2
1-10	2	1-45	0	1-86	2	1-116A	2
1-11	2	1-46	0	1-86A	2	1-116B	2
1-12	2	1-47	0	1-86B	2	1-117	0
1-13	2	1-48	0	1-86C	2	1-118	0
1-14	0	1-49	0	1-86D blank	2	1-119	0
1-15	0	1-50	0	1-87	0	1-120	0
1-16	2	1-51	0	1-88	2	1-121	0
1-17	2	1-52	0	1-89	2	1-122	0
1-18	2	1-53	0	1-90	2	1-123	0
1-18A	2	1-54	0	1-90A	2	1-124	0
1-18B blank	2	1-55	0	1-90B blank	2	1-125	2
1-19	0	1-56	0	1-91	0	1-126	0
1-20	0	1-57	0	1-92	0	1-127	0
1-21	2	1-58	0	1-93	2	1-128	0
1-22	2	1-59	0	1-94	2	1-129	0
1-23	2	1-60	2	1-95	2	1-130	2
1-24	2	1-61	2	1-96	2	1-131	2
1-25	2	1-62	2	1-97	2	1-132	2

#Zero in this column indicates an original page.

Page No.	#Change No.	Page No.	#Change No.	Page No.	#Change No.	Page No.	#Change No.
1-132A	2	2-12	2	3-28A	2	5-32 blank	2
1-132B blank	2	2-12A	2	3-28B blank	2	6-1	2
1-133	0	2-12B	2	3-29	2	6-2	0
1-134	0	2-12C	2	3-30	0	6-3	2
1-135	0	2-12D blank	2	3-31	0	6-4	2
1-136	0	2-13	2	3-32	2	6-5	2
1-137	0	2-14	0	3-33	0	6-6	2
1-138	0	2-15	0	3-34	2	6-6A	2
1-139	0	2-16	2	3-35	0	6-6B blank	2
1-140	2	2-17	2	3-36	0	6-7	0
1-141	0	2-18	2	3-37	2	6-8	0
1-142	0	2-18A	2	3-38	2	6-9	2
1-143	0	2-18B blank	2	3-39	0	6-10	0
1-144	0	2-19	2	3-40	0	7-1	0
1-145	0	2-20	2	3-41	0	7-2	0
1-146	2	2-21	0	3-42	0	7-3	0
1-147	0	2-22	2	3-43	0	7-4	0
1-148	0	2-23	0	3-44	0	7-5	0
1-149	2	2-24	2	3-45	2	7-6 blank	0
1-150	2	2-25	2	3-46	0	A-1	2
1-151	2	2-26	2	3-47	0	A-2 blank	2
1-152	2	2-27	2	3-48	0	A1-1	0
1-152A	2	2-28	2	3-49	0	A1-2	0
1-152B	2	3-1	2	3-50	2	A1-3	0
1-152C	2	3-2	2	3-51	0	A1-4	0
1-152D blank	2	3-2A	2	3-52	0	A1-5	0
1-153	0	3-2B blank	2	3-53	0	A1-6	2
1-154	0	3-3	2	3-54	0	A1-7	0
1-155	2	3-4	0	4-1	0	A1-8	0
1-156	2	3-5	2	4-2 blank	0	A1-9	0
1-157	0	3-6	0	5-1	0	A1-10	0
1-158	2	3-7	1	5-2	0	A1-11	0
1-158A	2	3-8	2	5-3	2	A1-12	0
1-158B blank	2	3-8A deleted	2	5-4	2	A1-13	0
1-159	0	3-8B deleted	2	5-5	2	A1-14	0
1-160	0	3-9	2	5-6	0	A1-15	0
1-161	0	3-10	2	5-7	2	A1-16	0
1-162	0	3-11	2	5-8	2	A1-17	0
1-163	2	3-12	2	5-9	2	A1-18	0
1-164	2	3-13	2	5-10	2	A1-19	0
1-165	0	3-14	2	5-11	2	A1-20 blank	0
1-166	0	3-15	2	5-12	2	A2-1	0
1-167	0	3-16	2	5-13	2	A2-2 blank	0
1-168	0	3-17	2	5-14	2	A3-1	0
2-1	2	3-18	2	5-15	2	A3-2	0
2-2	1	3-19	2	5-16	0	A3-3	0
2-2A	1	3-20	2	5-17	0	A3-4	0
2-2B blank	1	3-20A	2	5-18	0	A3-5	0
2-3	1	3-20B	2	5-19	2	A3-6	0
2-4	2	3-20C	2	5-20	2	A3-7	0
2-4A deleted	2	3-20D	2	5-21	2	A3-8	0
2-4B deleted	2	3-21	2	5-22	2	A3-9	0
2-5	2	3-22	0	5-23	2	A3-10	0
2-6	2	3-23	2	5-24	2	A3-11	0
2-7	2	3-24	2	5-25	2	A3-12	0
2-8	2	3-24A	2	5-26	2	A3-13	0
2-9	2	3-24B blank	2	5-27	2	A3-14	0
2-10	2	3-25	0	5-28	2	A3-15	0
2-10A deleted	2	3-26	2	5-29	2	A3-16	0
2-10B deleted	2	3-27	0	5-30	2	A3-17	0
2-11	2	3-28	2	5-31	2	A3-18	0

#Zero in this column indicates an original page.

Page No.	#Change No.	Page No.	#Change No.	Page No.	#Change No.	Page No.	#Change No.
A3-19	0	A6-4	0	A9-31	0	B4-2	2
A3-20	0	A6-5	0	A9-32	0	B5-1	2
A3-21	0	A6-6	0	A9-33	0	B5-2	2
A3-22	0	A7-1	0	A9-34	0	B5-3	2
A3-23	0	A7-2	0	A9-35	0	B5-4	2
A3-24	0	A7-3	0	A9-36	0	B6-1	2
A3-25	0	A7-4	0	A9-37	0	B6-2	2
A3-26	0	A7-5	0	A9-38	0	B6-3	2
A3-27	0	A7-6	0	A9-39	0	B6-4 blank	2
A3-28 blank	0	A8-1	0	A9-40	0	B7-1	2
A4-1	0	A8-2	0	A9-41	0	B7-2 blank	2
A4-2	0	A8-3	0	A9-42	0	B8-1	2
A4-3	0	A8-4	0	A9-43	0	B8-2	2
A4-4	0	A8-5	0	A9-44	0	B8-3	2
A4-5	0	A8-6	0	A9-45	0	B8-4	2
A4-6	0	A8-7	0	A9-46	0	B8-5	2
A4-7	0	A8-8	0	A9-47	0	B8-6	2
A4-8	0	A8-9	0	A9-48	0	B8-7	2
A4-9	0	A8-10 blank	0	A9-49	0	B8-8	2
A4-10	0	A9-1	0	A9-50	0	B8-9	2
A5-1	0	A9-2	0	A9-51	0	B8-10 blank	2
A5-2	0	A9-3	0	A9-52	0	B9-1	2
A5-3	0	A9-4	0	A9-53	0	B9-2	2
A5-4	0	A9-5	0	A9-54	0	B9-3	2
A5-5	0	A9-6	0	A9-55	0	B9-4	2
A5-6	0	A9-7	0	A9-56	0	B9-5	2
A5-7	0	A9-8	0	A9-57	0	B9-6	2
A5-8	0	A9-9	0	A9-58	0	F/O 1	0
A5-9	0	A9-10	0	A9-59	0	F/O 2 blank	0
A5-10	0	A9-11	0	A9-60	0	F/O 3	0
A5-11	0	A9-12	0	A9-61	0	F/O 4 blank	0
A5-12	0	A9-13	0	A9-62 blank	0	F/O 5	2
A5-13	0	A9-14	0	B-1	2	F/O 6 blank	2
A5-14	0	A9-15	0	B-2 blank	2	F/O 7	2
A5-15	0	A9-16	0	B1-1	2	F/O 8 blank	2
A5-16	0	A9-17	0	B1-2	2	F/O 9	0
A5-17	0	A9-18	0	B1-3	2	F/O 10 blank	0
A5-18	0	A9-19	0	B1-4	2	F/O 11	2
A5-19	0	A9-20	0	B1-5	2	F/O 12 blank	2
A5-20	0	A9-21	0	B1-6	2	F/O 13	0
A5-21	0	A9-22	0	B1-7	2	F/O 14 blank	0
A5-22	0	A9-23	0	B1-8	2	F/O 15	2
A5-23	0	A9-24	0	B1-9	2	F/O 16 blank	2
A5-24	0	A9-24A	2	B1-10	2	F/O 17	0
A5-25	0	A9-24B	2	B1-11	2	F/O 18 blank	0
A5-26	0	A9-24C	2	B1-12	2	F/O 19	0
A5-27	0	A9-24D	2	B1-13	2	F/O 20 blank	0
A5-28	0	A9-24E	2	B1-14	2	F/O 21	0
A5-29	0	A9-24F	2	B1-15	2	F/O 22 blank	0
A5-30	0	A9-24G	2	B1-16 blank	2	F/O 23	0
A5-31	0	A9-24H	2	B2-1	2	F/O 24 blank	0
A5-32	0	A9-24J	2	B2-2 blank	2	F/O 25	2
A5-33	0	A9-24K	2	B3-1	2	F/O 26 blank	2
A5-34	0	A9-24L	2	B3-2	2	Glossary 1	2
A5-35	0	A9-24M blank	2	B3-3	2	Glossary 2	2
A5-36	0	A9-25	0	B3-4	2	Glossary 3	2
A5-37	0	A9-26	0	B3-5	2	Glossary 4	2
A5-38	0	A9-27	0	B3-6	2	Index 1	2
A6-1	0	A9-28	0	B3-7	2	Index 2	2
A6-2	0	A9-29	0	B3-8	2	Index 3	2
A6-3	0	A9-30	0	B4-1	2	Index 4	2

#Zero in this column indicates an original page.

TABLE OF CONTENTS

SECTION	TITLE	PAGE
SECTION I	DESCRIPTION	1-1
SECTION II	NORMAL PROCEDURES	2-1
SECTION III	EMERGENCY PROCEDURES AND ABNORMAL OPERATIONS	3-1
SECTION IV	CREW DUTIES	4-1
SECTION V	OPERATING LIMITATIONS	5-1
SECTION VI	FLIGHT CHARACTERISTICS	6-1
SECTION VII	ADVERSE WEATHER OPERATION	7-1
APPENDIX A	PERFORMANCE DATA WITH F100-PW-220 ENGINES	A-1
APPENDIX B	PERFORMANCE DATA WITH F100-PW-229 ENGINES	B-1
	FOLDOUT ILLUSTRATIONS	FO-1
	GLOSSARY	Glossary 1
	ALPHABETICAL INDEX	Index 1

INTRODUCING THE F-15E

SCOPE. This manual contains the necessary information for safe and efficient operation of your aircraft. These instructions provide you with a general knowledge of the aircraft and its characteristics and specific normal and emergency operating procedures. Your experience is recognized; therefore, basic flight principles are avoided. This manual provides the best possible operating instructions under most circumstances. Multiple emergencies, adverse weather, terrain, etc. may require modification of the procedures.

PERMISSIBLE OPERATIONS. The flight manual takes a positive approach, and normally states only what you can do. Unusual operations or configurations are prohibited unless specifically covered herein. Clearance must be obtained before any questionable operation, which is not specifically permitted in this manual, is attempted.

HOW TO BE ASSURED OF HAVING LATEST DATA. Refer to TO 0-1-1-4 for a listing of all current flight manuals, safety supplements, operational supplements, and checklists. Also, check the flight manual cover page, the title block of each safety and operational supplement, and all status pages contained in the flight manual or attached to formal safety and operational supplements. Clear up all discrepancies before flight.

ARRANGEMENT. The manual is divided into seven fairly independent sections to simplify reading it straight through or using it as a reference manual.

SAFETY SUPPLEMENTS. Information involving safety will be promptly forwarded to you in a safety supplement. Supplements covering loss of life will get to you within 48 hours by teletype, and supplements covering serious damage to equipment within 10 days by mail. The cover page of the flight manual and the title block of each safety supplement should be checked to determine the effect they may have on existing supplements.

OPERATIONAL SUPPLEMENTS. Information involving changes to operating procedures will be forwarded to you by operational supplements. The procedure for handling operational supplements is the same as for safety supplements.

CHECKLISTS. The flight manual contains itemized procedures with necessary amplifications. The checklist contains itemized procedures without the amplification. Primary line items in the flight manual and checklist are identical. If a formal safety or operational supplement affects your checklist, the affected checklist page will be attached to the supplement. Cut it out and insert it over the affected page but never discard the checklist page in case the supplement is rescinded and the page is needed.

HOW TO GET PERSONAL COPIES. Each flight crewmember is entitled to personal copies of the flight manual, safety supplements, operational supplements, and checklists. The required quantities should be ordered before you need them to assure their prompt receipt. Check with your publication distribution officer - it is his job to fulfill your TO requests. Basically, you must order the required quantities on the appropriate Numerical Index and Requirement Table (NIRT). TO 00-5-1 and TO 00-5-2 give detailed information for properly ordering these publications. Make sure a system is established at your base to deliver these publications to the flight crews immediately upon receipt.

FLIGHT MANUAL BINDERS. Looseleaf binders and sectionalized tabs are available for use with your manual. They are obtained through local purchase procedures and are listed in the Federal Supply Schedule (FSC Group 75, Office Supplies, Part 1). Check with your supply personnel for assistance in procuring these items.

CHANGE SYMBOL. The change symbol, as illustrated by the black line in the margin of this paragraph, indicates text and tabular illustration changes made to the current issue. Changes to illustrations (except tabular and performance data in appendix A) are indicated by a changed area box located at the upper right side of the illustration. The box is divided into eight equal parts which represent eight proportional areas of the illustration. The shaded area of the box represents the area of the illustration which contains a change. An unshaded box indicates no change. The word "NEW" will appear in the box for new illustrations.

NOTE

Throughout the manual, retrofit (TCTO) effectivities are presented in abbreviated form. Refer to the Technical Order Summary at the front of the manual for detailed production/retrofit effectivites.

WARNINGS, CAUTIONS, AND NOTES.

The following definitions apply to Warnings, Cautions, and Notes found throughout the manual.

WARNING

Operating procedures, techniques, etc., which will result in personal injury or loss of life if not carefully followed.

CAUTION

Operating procedures, techniques, etc., which will result in damage to equipment if not carefully followed.

NOTE

An operating procedure, technique, etc., which is considered essential to emphasize.

SHALL, SHOULD, MAY, AND WILL.

The following definitions apply to Shall, Will, May and Should found throughout the manual. The word "shall" is used to express a mandatory requirement. The word "should" is used to express nonmandatory provisions. The word "may" is used to express permissiveness. The word "will" is used only to indicate futurity.

ILLUSTRATIONS

The illustrations used throughout Section 1 of the manual are intended to be used as examples. The specific situation may not be exactly as shown.

YOUR RESPONSIBILITY - TO LET US KNOW.

Review conferences with operating personnel and a constant review of accident and flight test reports assure inclusion of the latest data in the manual. In this regard, it is essential that you do your part. Comments, corrections, and questions regarding this manual or any phase of the Flight Manual program are welcomed. Corrections shall be submitted on AFTO Form 847 and forwarded through your Command Headquarters to Aeronautical Systems Division Wright-Patterson AFB, OH 45433-6503, ATTN: ASD/VFT

INTERIM SAFETY/OPERATIONAL SUPPLEMENT SUMMARY

The following list contains the previously cancelled or incorporated Safety/Operational Supplements; the outstanding Safety/Operational Supplements, if any; and the Safety/Operational Supplements incorporated in this issue. In addition, space is provided to list those Operational Supplements received since the latest issue.

NUMBER	PURPOSE	DISPOSITION/ INCORPORATION DATE
1F-15E-1S-1	Flight Clearance for carriage, jettison and release of SUU-20B/A	Change 1, 15 June 88
1F-15E-1S-2	Flight Clearance for carriage, jettison and release of 610 gallon fuel tank with/without the SUU-20B/A w/BDU-33 or MK-106	Change 1, 15 June 88
1F-15E-1S-3	Flight Clearance for carriage, jettison and release of CATM-9 with/without CFT or LANTIRN pods	Change 1, 15 June 88
1F-15E-1SS-4	WFOV HUD instrument flight considerations	Rev B, 1 Feb 89
1F-15E-1S-5	Operating limitations - CFTs must be installed when LANTIRN pods are carried	Rev B, 1 Feb 89
1F-15E-1S-6	Possible RPM fluctuations during air starts	Rev B, 1 Feb 89
1F-15E-1S-7	CG Limitations	Change 1, 1 May 89
1F-15E-1S-8	Maximum allowable gross weight	Change 1, 1 May 89
1F-15E-1SS-9	To advise pilots of restricted use of emergency landing gear system with normal utility A hydraulic pressure	Change 1, 1 May 89
1F-15E-1S-10	Limited 9g capability	Change 1, 1 May 89
1F-15E-1S-11	Operating limitations with AGM-65/MK82 LDGP/MK82 air munitions	Change 1, 1 May 89
1F-15E-1S-12	Operating Limitations with LANTIRN NAVpods for manual, unarmed, terrain following	Change 2, 15 Aug 89
1F-15E-1S-13	Operating Limitations - External Stores	Change 2, 15 Aug 89
1F-15E-1S-14	AIM-9 Missile carriage and employment limitations	Change 2, 15 Aug 89
1F-15E-1S-15	AIM-7 Incorporation and Limitations Chart updates	Change 3, 15 Nov 89
1F-15E-1SS-16	Stores Limitation Chart update	Change 3, 15 Nov 89
1F-15E-1SS-17	Design anomaly in the MPDP operation	Change 3, 15 Nov 89
1F-15E-1S-18	Updated stores capabilites (CBU-52, 58 or 71)	Change 3, 15 Nov 89

INTERIM SAFETY/OPERATIONAL SUPPLEMENT SUMMARY

The following list contains the previously cancelled or incorporated Safety/Operational Supplements; the outstanding Safety/Operational Supplements, if any; and the Safety/Operational Supplements incorporated in this issue. In addition, space is provided to list those Operational Supplements received since the latest issue.

1F-15E-1S-19	Updated stores capabilites (GBU-1UC/B's)	Change 3, 15 Nov 89
1F-15E-1S-20	Clarify external stores limitations (note #11 pg 5-17)	Change 3, 15 Nov 89
1F-15E-1S-21	Updated stores capabilities (CBU-52, 58 or 71)	Change 3, 15 Nov 89
1F-15E-1S-22	Add GBU-10C/D. Restrict TF operation. Update various store limits.	Rev. C, 15 Aug 90
1F-15E-1S-23	Updated Stores	Rescinded by TO1F-15E-1S-26
1F-15E-1S-24	Updated Stores	Rescinded by TO1F-15E-1S-26
1F-15E-1S-25	Updated Stores	Rescinded by TO1F-15E-1S-26
1F-15E-1S-26	Combined supplements 23, 24 and 25 into one supplement for Updated stores	Change 2, 15March 1991

TECHNICAL ORDER SUMMARY

The Technical Order Summary lists only those technical orders which affect this manual.

Technical Order	ECP	Title	Production Effectivity	Retrofit Effectivity
	1656	F110 Compatible Fuselage Incorporating BLATS and 9G Capability	86-0184 andup	
	1661-M6	Countermeasures Dispenser Switch	86-0185 and up	
	1839-0	Additional JFS Accumulator Power-Source For Emergency Landing Gear Extension	86-0183 and up	
TO 1F-15E-501	1851	Expanded AFT FIRE BURN THRU Detection System	87-0201 and up	
	1873-V	JFS/AMAD/Engine Bay Pneumatic Fire Detection System	86-0185 and up	
	1886	Central Computer OFP Modification	87-0189 and up	86-0183 thru 87-0188
	1887-0	CFT Fuel Transfer Pump Monitoring	86-0185 and up	
	1935	Installation of Have Quick II Radio	87-0189 and up	
TO 1F-15E-542	1967	Removal of Lead Computing Gyro	88-1667 and up	86-0186 thru 87-0210
	2009	Incorporation of Maintenance Diagnostic Panel	88-1667 and up	
TO 1F-15E-506	2018	Pitch, Roll and Yaw Trim Excitation Switchover from Main 28VDC to ESS 28 VDC Bus	87-0181 and up	86-0186 thru 87-0180

TECHNICAL ORDER SUMMARY (CONT)
The Technical Order Summary lists only those technical orders which affect this manual.

Technical Order	ECP	Title	Production Effectivity	Retrofit Effectivity
TO 1F-15E-552	2191	Redundant Ejection Seat System	89-0477 and up	86-0183 thru 89-0476
TO 1F-15E-582		Incorporation of Emergency Manual Chute Handle	89-0489 and up	86-0183 thru 89-0488
	2297-C	MPCD Power Source Change	89-0497 and up	
TO 1F-15E-602	2306-M	F-15E Modification for Aircrew Eye/Respiratory Protection (AERP)	Selected aircraft of the 4th Tactical Fighter Wing, Seymour-Johnson AFB	
	1955	Installation of F100-PW-229 Engines	90-0233 and up	
	1955-S4	Addition of Asymmetric Thrust Departure Prevention System(ATDPS)	90-0233 and up	
TO 1F-15E-561	1975-R1	Installation of Molecular Sieve Oxygen Generating System (MSOGS)	90-0233 and up	86-0183 thru 90-0232

BLOCK NUMBERS

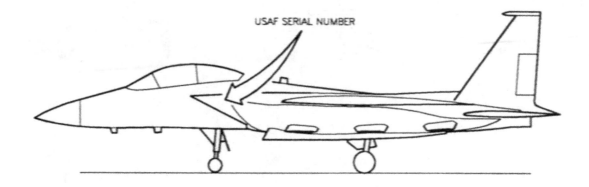

USAF SERIAL NUMBER

BLOCK 41
86-0183 AND 86-0184

BLOCK 42
86-0185 THRU 86-0190

BLOCK 43
87-0169 THRU 87-0189

BLOCK 44
87-0190 THRU 87-0210

BLOCK 45
88-1667 THRU 88-1687

BLOCK 46
88-1688 THRU 88-1708

BLOCK 47
89-0471 THRU 89-0488

BLOCK 48
89-0489 THRU 89-0506

BLOCK 49
90-0227 THRU 90-0244

15E-1-(19-1)21-CATI

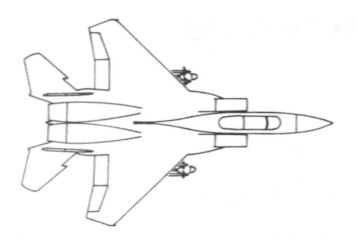

F - 15E

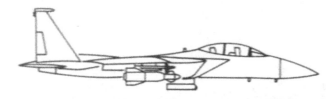

15E-1-(20)A

x

SECTION I

DESCRIPTION

TABLE OF CONTENTS

Aircraft...1-1
Engines 1-2
Asymmetric Thrust Departure
Prevention System (ATDPS) 1-6
Engine Controls and Indicators 1-6
Fire Warning/Extinguishing System 1-8A
Secondary Power System.........................1-9
Aircraft Fuel System 1-10
Electrical Power Supply System...............1-17
Hydraulic Power Supply System..............1-20
Landing Gear System 1-21
Nose Gear Steering System 1-21
Brake System...1-22
Arresting Hook System 1-23
Flap System 1-23
Speed Brake System...............................1-23
Flight Control System 1-24
Automatic Flight Control System (AFCS) ...1-28A
Overload Warning System (OWS)..............1-35
Warning/Caution/Advisory Lights 1-37
Audio Warning System 1-38
Built-In-Test (BIT) System 1-39
Central Computer (CC) 1-42
Multiplex Bus (MUX BUS) 1-42
Avionics Interface Units (AIU) 1-42
Data Transfer Module Set (DTMS) 1-44
Front Cockpit Controls............................1-45
Rear Cockpit Controls 1-53
Upfront Controls (UFC) 1-60
Head-Up Display (HUD) 1-68
Multipurpose Display Processor (MPDP)....1-82
Multipurpose Display/
Multipurpose Color Display (MPD/MPCD) ...1-83
Instruments...1-86
Navigation Displays 1-99
Tactical Situation Display (TSD)...............1-113
Intercom System 1-124
UHF Communications System..................1-124
Secure Speech System (KY-58) 1-128
Have Quick System 1-128
Have Quick II System 1-129
Identification System Friend or Foe (IFF) ...1-130
Air Data Computer (ADC) 1-132
Inertial Navigation System (INS) 1-135

Attitude Heading Reference Set (AHRS) 1-141
Tacan (Tactical Air Navigation) System............1-142
Instrument Landing System (ILS) 1-144
Video Tape Recorder Set (VTRS) 1-146
Lighting Equipment 1-149
Oxygen System (F-15E 86-0183 THRU
90-0232 BEFORE TO1F-15E-561) 1-151
Molecular Sieve Oxygen Generating
System (MSOGS)(F-15E 90-0233 AND UP
AND F-15E 86-0183 THRU 90-0232
AFTER TO 1F-15E-561).................................1-152
Environmental Control System (ECS)............ 1-152C
Boarding Steps 1-155
Canopy System..1-155
Ejection Seat System....................................1-158
Stores Jettison Systems 1-163
Programmable Armament
Control Set (PACS) 1-164
Tactical Electronic Warfare
System (TEWS) 1-164
Interference Blanker System (IBS) 1-164
Radar System 1-164
LANTIRN Navigation Pod (NAV Pod) 1-164
LANTIRN Targeting Pod (TGT Pod) 1-164
Weapon Systems 1-164
Servicing Diagram 1-168

AIRCRAFT

The F-15E is a high-performance, supersonic, all-weather, dual role fighter built by McDonnell Aircraft Company. In the air superiority role, its primary weapons are radar guided and infrared homing air-to-air missiles and a 20 MM gun. In the interdiction role, the aircraft carries LANTIRN targeting and navigation pods on dedicated sensor stations under the left and right engine inlets and can carry a variety of guided and unguided air-to-ground weapons. The aircraft is powered by two Pratt and Whitney F-100-PW-220 or -229 turbofan engines. Aircraft appearance is characterized by a high-mounted swept-back wing and twin vertical stabilizers. The cockpits are elevated to enhance visibility. Conformal fuel tanks with tangential carriage of air-to-air and air-to-ground weapons will be installed. A jet fuel starter (JFS) provides self-starting of the engines. Aircraft systems are designed and located for high maintainability and reliability. Refer to foldout section for general arrangement illustration

DIMENSIONS

The approximate overall dimensions of the aircraft are:

Span — 42 feet, 10 inches
Length — 63 feet, 9 inches
Height — top of vertical tail —18 feet, 8 inches
top of closed canopy — 12 feet
Distance between main landing gear — 9 feet

WEIGHTS

The following weights are approximate to the nearest 500 pounds and shall not be used for computing aircraft performance or for any type operation.

W/O CFTs pounds	Configuration	With CFTs pounds
32,500	Operating weight (basic weight plus crew)	37,000
53,000	Takeoff gross weight (operating weight plus full internal fuel, full centerline fuel tank, ammunition, LANTIRN Pods, wing pylons and 4 LAU-114 missile racks)	66,500
61,500	Takeoff gross weight as above plus 2 full external wing fuel tanks	75,000
81,000	Maximum gross weight	81,000

ENGINES

The aircraft is powered by two Pratt and Whitney F100-PW-220 or -229 turbofan engines with afterburners. The -220 engines are installed on F-15E 86-0183 THRU 90-0232. The -229 are installed on F-15E 90-0233 AND UP. All further references will be made using "-220 engines" or "-229 engines". The -220 engine is controlled by a full authority digital electronic engine control (DEEC). The -229 engine is controlled by an improved digital electronic engine control (IDEEC). The DEEC/IDEEC automatically trims to maintain performance as the engine deteriorates. In the remaining text the DEEC/IDEEC will be referred to generically as the DEEC unless specifically referring to either the -220 engine or the -229 engine.

ENGINE STARTING SYSTEM

A self contained jet fuel starter (JFS) is used to crank the engines for starting. The JFS is a small jet engine mounted on the central gearbox and along with the Airframe Mounted Accessory Drive (AMAD), provides rotation and initial electrical power for start. The JFS itself is started by accumulated hydraulic pressure. External power is not required during engine start. The JFS provides the only means of engine rotation for start.

ENGINE AIR INDUCTION SYSTEM

The two independent air induction systems consist of three variable ramps, a variable diffuser ramp, and a variable bypass door. Refer to figure 1-1.

Variable Ramps

The variable ramps provide air, at optimum subsonic flow, to the face of the engine fan inlet throughout a wide range of aircraft speeds. Ramp position is controlled by the air inlet controller.

Bypass Door

The bypass door automatically relieves excess pressure in the inlet duct. The air inlet controller positions the bypass door.

Air Inlet Controller

An air inlet controller (AIC), one for each inlet, uses angle of attack, aircraft Mach number and other air data system outputs to automatically schedule the ramps and bypass door throughout the aircraft envelope. The first ramp is locked in the up position until the engine is started.

Inlet Ramp Switch

An inlet ramp switch for each inlet is in the front cockpit on the miscellaneous control panel. The switch is lever locked, and has positions of AUTO and EMERG.

ENGINE AIR INDUCTION SYSTEM

Figure 1-1

AUTO	The AIC automatically controls the air inlet system. This is the normal position.
EMERG	Removes electrical power from the ramp and bypass door actuators, causing them to move hydraulically to the emergency (ramps locked up and bypass door closed) positions. If hydraulic pressure fails, airloads will force the ramps and bypass door to the emergency position.

ENGINE OIL SYSTEM

Each engine is equipped with a completely self-contained oil system. Oil is supplied to the main pump element by gravity feed. Return of the engine oil to the pump reservoir is severely limited during 0 or negative G flight. Refer to Servicing Diagram, this section, for oil specifications.

ENGINE FUEL SYSTEM

Refer to foldout section for airplane and engine fuel system illustration.

IGNITION SYSTEM

The ignition system contains an independent engine mounted generator and four igniter plugs (two for the engine and two for the afterburner). During engine start, moving the throttle from OFF to IDLE causes the engine igniter plugs to discharge. Ignition then remains continuous during engine operation. When the throttle is moved into afterburner, afterburner ignition is activated for approximately 1-1/2 seconds. Ignition is automatically recycled, up to 3 times, in the event of a no-light or blowout, without retarding the throttle to MIL.

ENGINE CONTROL SYSTEM

-220 ENGINES

The engine control consists primarily of a hydromechanical main fuel control (MFC), afterburner fuel control (AFC) and a full authority Digital Electronic Engine Control (DEEC).

-229 ENGINES

The engine control uses a digital primary control (PRI) with a backup hydrometrical secondary control (SEC). The secondary mode can be achieved either by an automatic primary mode fault action or by the pilot manually selecting OFF on the cockpit ENG CONTR switch. During SEC mode operation, A/B is inhibited and engine thrust is limited to approximately 70% of primary mode MIL power. The pilot can attempt to restore primary mode operation by cycling the ENG CONTR switch; if the fault that caused the transfer has cleared, the engine will return to primary mode.

Digital Electronic Engine Control (DEEC) -220 ENGINES

The DEEC contains the engine operating schedules for automatic control from IDLE to MAX A/B, and is powered by the engine alternator. The DEEC schedules engine and afterburner fuel flows, compressor inlet variable vanes (CIVV), rear compressor variable vanes (RCVV), start bleed position, anti-ice and nozzle position. The DEEC controls engine performance by scheduling engine fuel flow to control airflow and nozzle position to control engine pressure ratio (EPR). EPR is the ratio between engine exhaust pressure and engine inlet pressure. By controlling airflow and EPR the engine performance is maintained consistent for a new or deteriorated engine until the FTIT limit is reached. If the DEEC detects a failure that prevents it from safely controlling the engine it will automatically switch to the secondary mode, the same as ENG CONTR switch OFF. In this mode afterburner operation is inhibited, thrust is limited, the CIVV are in the fully closed position, the nozzle is closed to the minimum area (less than 5%) and the L or R ENG CONTR caution is displayed. The RCVV, start bleeds and engine fuel flow are scheduled by the MFC. The engine will remain in this mode until the failure clears and the L or R ENG CONTR switch is cycled. The engine can be started with the L or R ENG CONTR switch ON or OFF. If the start is made with the switches ON they should be left ON for at least 1 minute or the DEEC will revert to the secondary mode If the start is made with the switches OFF or the DEEC reverts to the secondary mode, ground starting time will be longer.

Improved Digital Electronic Engine Control (IDEEC) -229 ENGINES

The IDEEC contains the engine operating schedules for the same automatic control from start through MAX A/B as provided by the -220 engine. The -229 IDEEC includes a ground idle thrust setting to maintain equivalent -220 engine taxi performance. Ground idle thrust requires both an airframe request (automatic) and engine authorization (based on gear handle position, Mach number and throttle position). Acceleration from ground IDLE to MIL will be approximately 1 second longer than from approach or flight idle.

After a snap decel, engine rpm will initially decrease to approximately 79% rpm, then if the throttle is not advanced for 20 seconds, rpm will further decrease to the normal flight idle rpm. This control feature extends engine life and improves bodie (MAX-IDLE-MAX and MIL-IDLE-MIL) response times.

Engine Control Switches

The L and R ENG CONTR (engine control) switches are located in the front cockpit on the engine control panel. The switches have two positions ON and OFF.

ON	DEEC provides normal engine control.
OFF	Engine control is transferred to secondary mode (hydromechanical MFC). Afterburner inhibited, engine thrust reduced to 70-80% MIL, and exhaust nozzle will remain closed with gear handle down.

Main Fuel Control

The main fuel control (MFC) houses the hydromechanical components that are controlled by the DEEC in the ENG CONTR ON mode. If the DEEC is transferred to the secondary mode or the ENG CONTR switch is OFF the MFC schedules the engine fuel flow, start bleed position and RCVV position hydromechanically in response to throttle movement, inlet static pressure and engine inlet total temperature.

ENGINE MONITORING SYSTEM

The engine incorporates an engine monitoring system which consists of the DEEC and the engine diagnostic unit (EDU). The DEEC and EDU continuously monitor electrical control components and engine operation to detect engine failures. Abnormal engine operation and either intermittent or hard failures of components are detected and flagged for maintenance. During abnormal engine operation or component failure, the EDU will record engine and aircraft data as an aid to maintenance troubleshooting. The EDU also maintains engine life cycle information. Airframe mounted LEFT or RIGHT ENGINE and L or R ENG MON SYS fail indicators, located on the avionics status panel in the nose wheelwell, are latched if a fault is detected which requires maintenance attention.

AFTERBURNER SYSTEM

-220 ENGINES
The afterburner has five stages that are progressively selected as the throttle is moved from MIL to MAX. In the upper left corner of the engine envelope stages 2 thru 5 may be inhibited.

-229 ENGINES
The afterburner has 11 segments that are progressively selected as the throttle is advanced from MIL to MAX. The number of selectable afterburner segments is automatically reduced as the aircraft moves

towards the upper left corner of the afterburner operating envelope. During snap accelerations the first segment of the afterburner may, depending on flight condition, light at just above IDLE rpm and the succeeding segments will light as speed approaches MIL rpm.

The engine (-220 or -229) uses a light-off detector (LOD) to signal the DEEC if a light-off occurs. The DEEC then schedules the AFC fuel flow for the remaining segments. If the LOD does not sense a light-off or a blowout occurs, the DEEC automatically resets the MFC to MIL, terminates afterburner fuel flow and a check of the LOD is performed. If the LOD checks good, the DEEC will automatically attempt two more relights. If the afterburner still fails to light, retarding the throttle to MIL or below will reset the DEEC and the system will operate normally when afterburner is reselected. If the LOD checks failed, the DEEC will attempt one relight, bypassing the LOD, using tailpipe pressure to verify an afterburner light-off. Afterburner light-off may take longer and appear to hesitate if the LOD is failed. Afterburner is inhibited in the ENG CONTR OFF mode.

VARIABLE AREA EXHAUST NOZZLE

The engine has a convergent-divergent nozzle system which is continuously variable between minimum and maximum opening. The nozzle is positioned pneumatically by engine bleed air.

Exhaust Nozzle Control

-220 ENGINES

The nozzle is controlled by throttle position and landing gear handle position. With the gear handle down, throttle in IDLE and the DEEC on, the nozzle will be approximately 80% open. As the throttle is advanced, the nozzle closes to near minimum area. With the landing gear handle up, the nozzle is near minimum area at all times except at MIL or above. At MIL the nozzle indicators will show the nozzles slightly open (5 - 10%). As the throttle is advanced in the afterburner range the nozzles will schedule further open to compensate for increasing afterburner fuel flow. With the DEEC off or in secondary mode, nozzle position will be closed to near the minimum area in flight or on the ground. This will result in higher idle thrust and taxi speeds.

-229 ENGINES

The exhaust nozzle is used to control engine pressure ratio (EPR) in response to throttle position and landing gear handle inputs. With the gear handle down, throttle in IDLE and the IDEEC ON, the nozzle will be approximately 90-100% open. As the throttle is advanced, the nozzles close to near minimum area. With the landing gear handle UP, the nozzle is near minimum area (10%) at all times except at MIL or above. At MIL the nozzle indicator will show the nozzle slightly open (6-20%). As the throttle is advanced in the afterburner range, the nozzle will schedule further open to compensate for increasing afterburner fuel flow. During SEC mode operation, nozzle position will be closed to near the minimum area ($\leq$5%) inflight or on the ground. This will result in higher idle thrust and taxi speeds.

ENGINE ANTI-ICE

The engine anti-ice system is comprised of the inlet ice detector and the engine anti-ice valve. The engine anti-ice valve and the inlet ice detector are functionally unrelated. The detector only senses engine inlet ice build up and turns on the INLET ICE caution. The engine heat switch, on the front cockpit ECS panel, controls the engine anti-ice airflow to the engine nose cone and stationary inlet guide vanes and electrically heats the inlet pressure probe. The DEEC will automatically shut off the engines anti-ice when the altitude is above 30,000 feet or the engine inlet temperature is above 15°C (60°F) regardless of switch position.

Engine ANTI-ICE Switch

The engine ANTI-ICE switch is a three position switch. The functions are described below.

ON	Activates the engine anti-ice system.
OFF	Deactivates the engine anti-ice system.
TEST	Checks detector operation, and turns on the INLET ICE caution.

INLET ICE Caution

The INLET ICE caution indicates an ice build up on the engine inlet ice probe located in the left engine inlet duct. The INLET ICE caution remains on as long as the icing condition exists and will not be extinguished by activating the engine anti-ice system.

ASYMMETRIC THRUST DEPARTURE PREVENTION SYSTEM (ATDPS)

On F-15E 90-0233 AND UP, the ATDPS prevents aircraft damage or loss in the event of augmentor loss while operating at high dynamic pressures. In the event of a large thrust loss on one engine in a critical flight region, the system automatically commands both engines to secondary (SEC) mode to quickly equalize thrust from both engines. After the aircraft exits the critical region, ATDPS will automatically enable primary operation of both engines.

ENGINE CONTROLS AND INDICATORS

ENGINE MASTER SWITCHES

Two guarded engine master switches are in the front cockpit on the engine control panel. Placing either switch to ON (with electrical power available), opens its corresponding airframe mounted engine fuel shutoff valve and directs power to the fuel transfer pumps. The engine master switch must be ON before the corresponding engine can be coupled to the JFS. Placing the switch OFF decouples the engine from the JFS. If engine control/essential power is not available, placing an engine master switch OFF will not shut off its airframe mounted engine fuel shutoff valve.

VMAX Switch -220 ENGINES

Use of the VMAX switch is prohibited in peace time. The Vmax switch is below the front cockpit left canopy sill. The switch has a guard which is wired down. When the wire is broken and the guard raised, the switch may be placed to Vmax which arms the system. With the system armed, the throttle in MAX AB, and airspeed above MACH 1.1, the engine control schedules a 22°C increase in FTIT and a 2% increase in rpm. Main engine and afterburner fuel flow is increased about 4% and thrust is increased about 4%,

maximum continuous time in Vmax is 6 minutes. Each use of Vmax must be reported so that a hot section borescope inspection may be performed. Maximum total Vmax time before engine overhaul is 60 minutes.

VMAX Switch -229 ENGINES

The PW-229 does not respond to changes in the VMAX switch position.

THROTTLE QUADRANTS

The front throttle quadrant contains the front throttles, finger lifts, friction adjusting lever, rudder trim switch and flap switch. Additionally, the throttle grips contain switches to provide various system controls without moving the left hand from the grips. The rear throttle quadrant contains the rear throttles and rudder trim switch. The rear right throttle grip provides control switches for the microphone and speed brake. Refer to figure 1-2. A detailed description of switch functions is in Front Cockpit Controls or Rear Cockpit Controls, this section or in the individual systems in this manual and TO 1F-15E-34-1-1.

Throttles

Movement of the throttle is transmitted by mechanical linkage to the main fuel control. A friction adjusting lever is mounted adjacent to the front cockpit right throttle. Finger lifts on the front cockpit throttles couple the JFS to the engine during starting; they must also be lifted to move the throttles below IDLE and must then be released to move the throttles to OFF. Advancing the throttle from OFF to IDLE (during engine start) opens the main fuel shutoff valve in the fuel control and turns on engine ignition. Movement of the throttles from IDLE to OFF closes the main fuel shutoff valve in the fuel control, stopping fuel flow to the engine. Afterburner light-off is initiated by advancing the throttle forward of the afterburner detent.

THROTTLE QUADRANT
(FRONT COCKPIT)

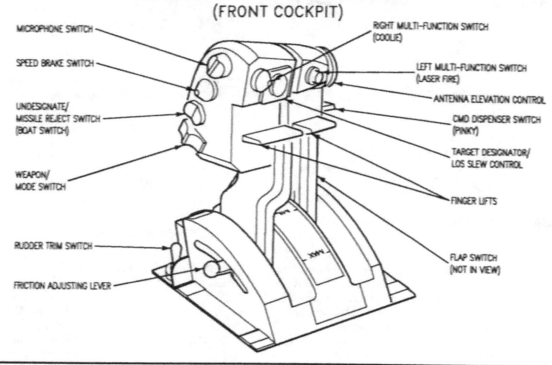

MICROPHONE SWITCH

SPEED BRAKE SWITCH

UNDESIGNATE/
MISSILE REJECT SWITCH
(BOAT SWITCH)

WEAPON/
MODE SWITCH

RUDDER TRIM SWITCH

FRICTION ADJUSTING LEVER

RIGHT MULTI-FUNCTION SWITCH
(COOLIE)

LEFT MULTI-FUNCTION SWITCH
(LASER FIRE)

ANTENNA ELEVATION CONTROL

CMD DISPENSER SWITCH
(PINKY)

TARGET DESIGNATOR/
LOS SLEW CONTROL

FINGER LIFTS

FLAP SWITCH
(NOT IN VIEW)

(REAR COCKPIT)

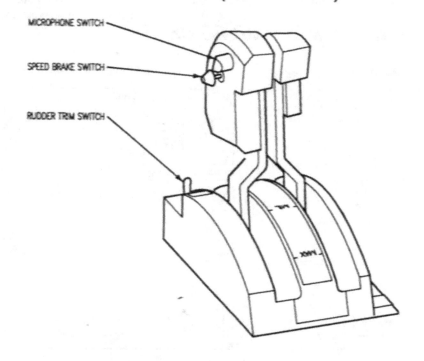

MICROPHONE SWITCH

SPEED BRAKE SWITCH

RUDDER TRIM SWITCH

15E-1-(255-1)21-CAT

Figure 1-2

ENGINE MONITOR DISPLAY

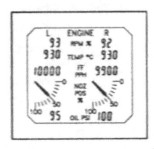

15E-1-(248-1)12-CATI

Figure 1-3

ENGINE MONITOR DISPLAY (EMD)

The engine monitor display (EMD) located on the front cockpit lower main instrument panel has a left and right liquid crystal display for rpm, temperature, fuel flow, nozzle position, and oil pressure (figure 1-3). During engine starts without external electrical power or when airborne and both main generators are off line and the emergency generator is on line, only rpm and temperature will be displayed until one main generator comes on line. With one main generator on line or external electrical power on, all engine data will be displayed. If the engine data exceeds the range

of a parameter, that parameter will go blank until it is within the display range.

RPM %	Displays compressor rpm from 0 to 110% in 1% increments.
TEMP °C	Displays FTIT from 200 to 1400°C in 10°C increments.
FF PPH	Displays main engine fuel flow from 0 to 99,900 pounds per hour in 100 pph increments.
NOZ POS %	Displays exhaust nozzle position from 0 to 100% open in 10% increments.
OIL PSI	Displays oil pressure from 0 to 100 psi in 5 psi increments.

MPD/MPCD ENGINE DISPLAY

The MPD/MPCD engine display format provides an alternate source for engine data displayed on the EMD by displaying data on selected multi-purpose display/multi-purpose color display (MPD/MPCD). Refer to figure 1-4. The display is selected by pressing the ENG button on the MENU display. If engine data exceeds the range of a parameter the maximum or minimum limit will be displayed, on an MPCD the parameter will be displayed in yellow and boxed. If on the MPD, they are displayed at a greater intensity

ENGINE MONITOR FORMAT

(-220 ENGINES INSTALLED)

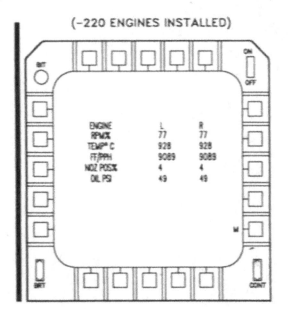

(-229 ENGINES INSTALLED)

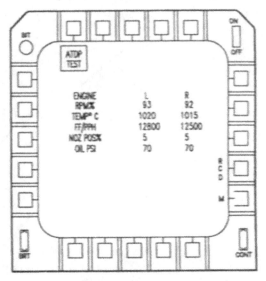

15E-1-(3-1)21-CATI

Figure 1-4

level and boxed. If any engine data is invalid or no signal is received, OFF will be displayed for that engine parameter.

On F-15E 90-0233 AND UP, an additional test is available for the ATDPS. The ATDPS can only be tested during low speed ground operation. When ATDP TEST is selected (from the MPD/MPCD engine display format), switching one engine control to OFF will result in both engines transferring to secondary mode. The engines will return to primary mode only after engine control switches are set to ON and ATDP TEST is deselected.

RPM %	Compressor rpm from 0 to 110% in 1% increments.
TEMP °C	FTIT from 100 to 1375°C in 1°C increments.
FF/PPH	Main engine fuel flow from 0 to 150,000 pph in 10 pph increments.
NOZ POS	Exhaust nozzle position from 0 to 100% open in 1% increments.
OIL PSI	Oil pressure from 0 to 100 psi in 1 psi increments.

ENGINE CAUTION LIGHTS

The ENGINE caution light is in the front cockpit on the caution lights panel and in the rear cockpit on the warning/caution/advisory light panel. The ENGINE caution light, MASTER CAUTION light and MPD/MPCD caution come on when any of the following cautions are activated: L INLET, R INLET, L ENG CONTR, R ENG CONTR, L OIL PRESS, R OIL PRESS, INLET ICE, FIRE SENSOR, FUEL HOT, L BST PUMP, R BST PUMP, L BLEED AIR, R BLEED AIR or, on F-15E 90-0233 AND UP, ATDP. The light remains on until the problem is corrected.

L/R INLET Cautions

The L or R INLET caution comes on with left or right engine inlet controller failure.

L/R Engine Control Cautions

The L or R ENG CONTR caution comes on with left or right DEEC failure, loss of Mach number signal, afterburner inhibit (either the last 3 segments or a total afterburner inhibit), or switch off.

L/R OIL Pressure Cautions

The L or R OIL PRESS caution comes on with a low left or right engine oil pressure (less than or equal to 8 psi).

FUEL HOT Caution

The FUEL HOT caution is displayed when the engine fuel inlet temperature is too high

L/R BOOST PUMP Cautions

Two boost pump cautions are used. These cautions are; L BST PMP (for left main boost pump) and R BST PMP (for right main boost pump) and are displayed if the associated boost output pressure is low.

L/R BLEED AIR Cautions

These cautions come on when there is a left/right bleed air leak or overtemperature.

ATDP Caution

The ATDP caution comes on when system operating mode is other than commanded or when air data is invalid.

FIRE WARNING/EXTINGUISHING SYSTEM

The fire warning and extinguisher system consists of three illuminating pushbutton switches, one fire extinguisher bottle, a discharge/test switch, and fire sensors located in the engine and AMAD compartments, and various warning/caution lights. The system provides engine and AMAD fire warning, emergency engine and JFS shutdown, and selective fire extinguishing. The extinguisher is a gaseous system which provides one-shot, one-compartment extinguishing capability. The gas is non-toxic, non-corrosive and will not damage aircraft components. Electrical power is required to operate the fire warning and extinguisher system. During JFS operation, before the emergency generator comes on the line, only the AMAD system is operative.

FIRE LIGHTS

Three fire lights on the fire warning/extinguishing panel in the front cockpit are combination warning lights and fire extinguisher arming buttons. Two fire warning lights in rear cockpit provide warning of L FIRE and R FIRE but have no extinguisher function. The three lights in the front cockpit are labeled AMAD FIRE PUSH, L ENG FIRE PUSH and R ENG FIRE PUSH. The appropriate fire light(s) comes on when a fire or overheat condition exists. After first lifting a spring loaded metal guard, pressing the L ENG FIRE PUSH or R ENG FIRE PUSH light shuts off bleed air from, and fuel flow to, the corresponding engine, and arms the extinguisher bottle for release into the selected engine compartment. After the L or R ENG FIRE PUSH light is pressed, the engine decelerates but may continue running at sub-idle rpm for up to 120 seconds until the fuel is consumed downstream of the airframe mounted fuel shutoff valve. After first lifting a spring loaded metal guard, pressing the AMAD FIRE PUSH light arms the extinguisher bottle for release into the AMAD/JFS compartment but will not prevent normal JFS operation. When arm is selected, approximately 1/8 inch of yellow and black stripes will be visible around the outer edges of the light(s). The fire lights must be pressed again to dearm the extinguisher and restore the selected system to normal operation. On aircraft 87-0201 AND UP, the front cockpit firewarning/extinguisher panel contains left and right AFTER-BURNER BURNTHRU warning lights. The respective light comes on to indicate a fire. Refer to Voice Warning System, this section, for voice warning associated with FIRE lights.

FIRE VOICE WARNINGS

-220 ENGINES
The fire voice warning system is activated when either or both engines FTIT exceed 1000°C (overheat), or a fire condition exists.

-229 ENGINES
The fire voice warning system is activated when either or both engines FTIT exceed 1107°C (overheat), or a fire condition exists. .

-220 or -229 ENGINES
For an FTIT overtemperature condition the voice warning states:

WARNING, OVERTEMP LEFT or WARNING OVERTEMP RIGHT, pauses then repeats the warning again. For an engine/AMAD fire condition the voice warning states: WARNING, ENGINE FIRE LEFT or WARNING, ENGINE FIRE RIGHT or WARNING, AMAD FIRE pauses, then repeats the warning again. For a single-point burn through or overtemperature condition in the afterburner section the voice warning states: AB BURN THRU LEFT or AB BURN THRU RIGHT, pauses then repeats the warning again.

FIRE TEST/EXTINGUISHER SWITCH

A discharge/test switch is located on the fire warning/extinguishing panel in the front cockpit.

OFF	System provides normal fire warning.
TEST	Turns on the three fire lights (only the AMAD light if the JFS is providing electrical power) and the left/right AB BURN THRU lights, indicating the fire sensors are operational. Also turns on rear cockpit lights. Each fire light has four sections with an individual light bulb in each section. The top two bulbs of the AMAD light are associated with the AMAD fire sensor loop and the bottom two bulbs with the JFS fire sensor loop. The top bulbs of the engine fire lights are associated with the forward transponder loop of the corresponding engine, and the bottom two bulbs with the aft transponder loop. Failure of any of the above pairs of lights to come on during test indicates failure of the corresponding sensor loop. Switch is spring loaded to OFF.
DIS-CHARGE	Momentary contact immediately discharges the extinguisher into the selected compartment. If the AMAD circuit was selected, the discharge switch also shuts off fuel flow to the JFS. The switch is lever-locked from OFF to DIS-CHARGE and is spring loaded to OFF.

FIRE SENSOR CAUTION

Appearance of the FIRE SENSOR caution on the MPD/MPCD indicates one or more fire sensors have failed. The MASTER CAUTION and ENGINE caution also come on.

SECONDARY POWER SYSTEM

The secondary power system provides power for starting the aircraft engines and transmits power from the engine to the aircraft accessories. It consists of an accumulator-powered hydraulic motor, central gearbox (CGB), JFS, and left and right AMAD gearboxes.

CENTRAL GEARBOX (CGB)

During JFS start, the CGB provides the mechanical connection between the hydraulic motor and the JFS. After the JFS is started, the CGB then provides the gearing and clutching functions necessary to transmit power from the JFS to the left or right AMAD gearboxes.

AIRFRAME MOUNTED ACCESSORY DRIVE (AMAD)

The left and right AMAD gearboxes are directly connected to their respective engine, utility hydraulic pump, power control (PC) hydraulic pump, and integrated drive generator (IDG). During engine start, power is transmitted from the JFS through the CGB and through the applicable AMAD gearbox to the engine. Once the engine is started, the CGB decouples from the AMAD gearbox and the engine then drives the AMAD gearbox and its associated accessories. The accessories on either AMAD gearbox are sufficient to support the aircraft systems if one engine or its associated AMAD gearbox fails. Refer to figure 1-5.

JET FUEL STARTER (JFS)

A JFS, mounted on the central gearbox, is used for engine starting. It can start either engine, but not both simultaneously. JFS operation is controlled by the JFS starter switch and the JFS control handle; fuel is provided by the main aircraft fuel system. JFS ignition and electrical power are provided by the JFS generator (permanent magnet). Starting power to the JFS is provided by a hydraulic motor that is driven by hydraulic pressure accumulators. The accumulators are charged automatically by circuit B of the utility hydraulic system, or manually by hand pump. The JFS automatically shuts down when the second

SECONDARY POWER SYSTEM

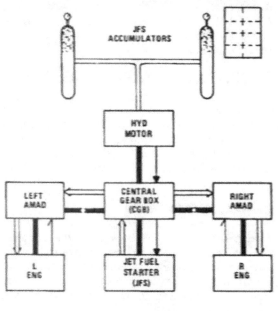

CECOUPLER
- ▶ DRIVE TRAIN FOR JFS START (HYD POWER)
⟹ DRIVE TRAIN FOR ENG START (JFS POWER)
→ DRIVE TRAIN FOR ACCESSORIES (ENG POWER)

15E—1—(22)

Figure 1-5

engine reaches approximately 50% rpm. The JFS may be used inflight to perform a JFS Assisted Restart, refer to section III.

JFS Starter Switch

The JFS starter switch is in the front cockpit on the right console engine control panel. It has positions of ON and OFF. During engine start, the JFS is automatically shut down after both engines are started; however, it can be shut down at any time by placing the switch OFF.

NOTE

On aircraft 86-0183 thru 87-0200, a manual JFS shutdown may result in the CAS and MPDP temporarily dropping of the line.

JFS Ready Light

The JFS ready light is in the front cockpit on the right console engine control panel. The light indicates the JFS is ready to be engaged. The light goes out when the JFS shuts down.

JFS Control Handle

The JFS control handle is in the front cockpit on the lower right corner of the main instrument panel. Pulling the handle straight out discharges one JFS accumulator. Rotating the handle 45° counterclockwise (CCW) and pulling discharges both accumulators, or the remaining accumulator if one has already been discharged. The handle is spring loaded to return to its normal position.

JFS LOW Caution

The JFS LOW caution is displayed if either JFS accumulator pressure is low.

AIRCRAFT FUEL SYSTEM

Refer to foldout section for airplane and engine fuel system illustration. Fuel is carried internally in four interconnected fuselage tanks, and two internal (wet) wing tanks. External fuel can be carried in three external tanks and two conformal fuel tanks. The external tanks are mounted on the centerline and inboard wing station pylons and are completely interchangeable. Conformal fuel tanks (CFT) are mounted on the outboard side of each engine nacelle. All tanks may be refueled on the ground through a single pressure refueling point, airborne they can be refueled through the aerial refueling receptacle. External tanks may be individually fueled through external filler points. The internal wing tanks and tank 1 are transfer tanks. Tank 1 consists of one main tank and a right auxiliary tank. The tanks are so arranged that all internal fuel will transfer even if the transfer pumps fail. CFT fuel is transferred by transfer pumps to any internal tank that will accept it. Regulated engine bleed air pressure transfers fuel from the external tanks to any internal tank that will accept it and also provides a positive pressure on all internal fuel tanks. Each CFT is pressurized by a self-contained ram air pressurization and vent system. Float type fuel level control valves control fuel level during refueling or fuel transfer operations. All internal, CFT and external fuel (except engine feed tanks) may be dumped overboard from an outlet at the trailing edge of the right wing tip. All internal fuel tanks are vented through the vent outlets at each wing trailing edge. The external tanks are vented through the vent outlets in their individual pylons. Each CFT is vented through its vent outlet near the back of the CFT. The fuel quantity indicating system provides fuel quantity, in pounds, of all internal, CFT and external fuel. Refer to Servicing Diagram, this section, for fuel grade and specifications.

SURVIVABILITY

The internal fuel tanks, all of which are located forward of the engines, contain foam for fire/explosion protection. The feed tanks are self-sealing. Fuel lines are routed inside tanks where possible, and most have self-sealing protection when outside the tanks. All CFT compartments incorporate explosion suppression foam slabs for enhanced survivability. Dry bay areas (voids) around fuel cells on the sides and bottom of fuselage fuel tanks are filled with explosion suppression polyether foam.

FUEL TRANSFER SYSTEM

The fuel transfer system provides for internal fuel transfer and external fuel transfer. Internal fuel consists of L and R internal wing tanks, L and R engine feed tanks, right aux tank, and tank 1. External fuel consists of L and R CFT, L and R external wing tanks, and the external centerline tank. Any sustained fuel imbalance greater than 200 pounds between internal wing tanks or 1000 pounds between CFT lasting over 5 minutes should be reported on AFTO Form 781.

Internal Fuel Transfer

Internal fuel transfer is accomplished by three electric transfer pumps (L and R internal wing tanks and tank 1) and one fuel ejector pump (right aux tank). The electric pumps automatically transfer internal wing and tank 1 fuel to the engine feed tanks when the level control valve(s) in either of the two feed tanks is open. The transfer pumps run continuously when electrical power is applied to the aircraft and an engine master switch is on. However, tank 1 transfer pump will not run unless the slipway switch is in CLOSE even if the FUEL LOW light is on. During normal operation 200 pounds of tank 1 fuel will transfer before the internal wing tanks start transferring. This is called CG kick and is done in order to get the aircraft CG moving aft. Once the internal wings start feeding, they will simultaneously transfer along with tank 1 to the engine feed tanks. This is true during all engine operations both on the ground or in flight. Although tank 1 fuel quantity is initially higher

(approximately 550 ±200 pounds) than either internal wing tank, the transfer rate of tank 1 and the internal wing tanks is designed so that tank 1 and the wing tanks empty within 200 pounds of each other. If the electric transfer pumps fail, fuel from all internal tanks will gravity transfer at a reduced rate to the engine feed tanks. Check valves prevent fuel flow from the feed tanks to the transfer tanks. The fuel ejector pump in the right auxiliary tank automatically transfers fuel to main tank 1 when its transfer pump is operating. If the ejector pump or tank 1 transfer pump fails, fuel will gravity transfer (through the open ejector pump) at a reduced rate as the level of main tank 1 decreases.

External Wing and Centerline Tank Transfer

External wing and centerline fuel is transferred by engine bleed air pressure providing the landing gear handle is UP. External fuel will not transfer with the landing gear handle down or with the slipway switch in OPEN unless the FUEL LOW light comes on. If a complete electrical failure occurs, the external fuel will still transfer. There is no backup provision for the external fuel transfer system. External fuel will normally transfer before the internal tanks start to deplete. External wing tank fuel may not transfer at the same rate or even together, but will normally transfer before centerline fuel. Internal and all external tanks can deplete simultaneously whenever engine fuel consumption exceeds transfer capability.

CFT Transfer

Each CFT contains two transfer pumps, one in the center compartment sump and one in the aft compartment sump. The sumps are connected by a float controlled interconnect valve which isolates the sumps until the aft compartment is almost empty or the aft transfer pump fails. Each CFT also contains an ejector pump that transfers fuel from the forward compartment to the center compartment. The center pump transfers forward/center compartment fuel and the aft pump transfers aft compartment fuel. When the aft compartment fuel level drops below an interconnect float valve level, the interconnect valve opens connecting the two sumps. The CFT transfer pumps run continuously when electrical power is applied to the aircraft, an engine master switch is on, and the slipway switch is in CLOSE. Fuel transfer within the CFT is sequenced to automatically maintain the aircraft center of gravity within limits.

External Transfer Switch

The external transfer switch has switch positions of WING/CTR and CONF TANK. The switch is provided to select the transfer sequence of the external fuel. Whichever tank is selected, the opposite tank position will not transfer unless the selected tank position transfer rate is insufficient to maintain full internal fuel or the fuel in the selected tanks is depleted. If the transfer rate of the selected tanks is insufficient to maintain full internal tanks, all the external tanks (wing, centerline and CFT) will transfer simultaneously until the internal tanks are full. Once full, the simultaneous transfer will cease until the transfer rate of the selected tank again fails to keep the internal tanks full. If CFT are installed and external wing tanks are not installed but the external transfer switch is placed in the WING/CTR position, cyclic CFT transfer will occur. Internal fuel will deplete by approximately 3000 pounds before the CFT will transfer. Once the internal tanks are full, CFT transfer will cease until internals are again depleted by about 3000 pounds. This same cyclic action will occur if the opposite is true; external wing tanks installed, no CFT installed, and external transfer switch in CONF TANK position. On the ground, since external wing and centerline tanks are depressurized, CFT fuel (if installed) will transfer to maintain the internal tanks full regardless of the external transfer switch position.

Fuel Control Switches

Three fuel control switches, labeled WING (external wing tanks), CTR (centerline tank), and CONF TANK are on the fuel control panel.

NORM	Provides normal transfer and refuel of corresponding tanks.
STOP TRANS	Stops transfer from corresponding tanks, including automatic external transfer, unless FUEL LOW light is on, in which case fuel will transfer regardless of position of this switch.
STOP REFUEL	Will prevent filling of the tank(s) selected.

CFT Emergency Transfer Switch

The conformal tank emergency transfer switch, located on the fuel control panel has positions of NORM, L, and R. This switch should be in NORM with or without conformal tanks installed. When operating on the emergency generator, selecting either L or R will deactivate all aircraft pitot heaters, and activate the selected (L or R) CFT center sump transfer pump. Selecting L or R will deactivate the aircraft pitot heaters even if the CFT are not installed. If the external transfer switch is not set to CONF this cycling will continue until the conformal tanks are empty.

FUEL FEED SYSTEM

There are two separate fuel feed systems, one for each engine. During normal operation, fuel temperature is controlled by fuel recirculation to the internal wing tanks. The internal wing tanks act as a heat exchanger to lower the fuel temperature before it again transfers to the feed tanks. Baffles in the feed tanks provide limited fuel supply for the left and right main boost pumps during negative g or inverted flight. During normal operation, the right main boost pump supplies fuel to the right engine only, and the left main boost pump supplies fuel to the left engine only. Below 1000 pounds total feed tank fuel, feed tanks may not feed simultaneously. The main boost pumps are capable of providing pressurized fuel flow to the engines at all power settings throughout the flight envelope. If either or both main boost pumps fail or, either or both main generators are inoperative or both main transformer-rectifiers fail, the emergency boost pump is activated and a system of tank interconnect and crossfeed valves allows the remaining operating pump(s) to supply all usable fuel in the feed tanks to both engines. With one main boost pump and the emergency boost pump operating, pressurized fuel is supplied to both engines at all non-afterburner power settings throughout the entire flight envelope. With double boost pump failure (any two), the remaining pump is capable of supplying fuel to both engines at all non-afterburner power settings from sea level to 30,000 feet. If both main boost pumps and the emergency boost pump are inoperative, fuel is available to the engines by suction feed only. Under most flight conditions the engine requires pressurized (boosted) fuel to preclude fuel vaporization. Therefore, loss of both main pumps and the emergency boost pump may cause dual engine flameout. During single-engine operation, the feed tank of the inoperative engine will not feed to the operative engine until the fuel level of the good engine feed tank is well below FUEL LOW light activation.

L/R BOOST PUMP Cautions

The L and R Boost Pump cautions are displayed on the MPD/MPCD if the associated boost output pressure is low.

EMERGENCY BOOST PUMP ON Caution

The EMER BST ON caution, on both the caution light panel, and the MPD/MPCD come on any time the emergency generator is operating and sufficient emergency boost pump output pressure is available.

BOOST SYSTEM MALFUNCTION Caution

The BST SYS MAL caution on both the caution light panel and the MPD/MPCD come on any time the emergency fuel boost pump output is insufficient.

TRANSFER PUMP Caution

The XFER pump caution is displayed on the MPD/MPCD and comes on when a failure of a CFT or a wing fuel transfer pump occurs. There is no differentiation between left or right transfer pump or between external wing tanks and CFT.

TRANSFER PUMP Voice Warning

Failure of the CFT or wing fuel transfer pump will activate the transfer voice warning. When a failure is detected the voice warning states: "WARNING TRANSFER PUMP" pauses, then repeats the warning.

FUEL TANK PRESSURIZATION AND VENT

The pressurization and vent system provides regulated engine bleed air pressure to all internal tanks to prevent fuel boil-off at altitude and to the external tanks for fuel transfer. The system also provides pressure relief of the fuel tanks during climbs, and vacuum relief of the fuel tanks, as required, during descents. The internal and external tanks are pressurized when the landing gear handle is UP. Internal and external tanks are depressurized when the landing gear handle is DOWN.

The pressurization and vent system is self-contained for each CFT. Each CFT provides regulated ram air pressure (from a flush inlet on the side of the CFT) to all three compartments to maintain positive tank pressures. The system also provides pressure relief of the CFT through the overboard vents during climb and air refueling, and vacuum relief during ground operation.

FUEL QUANTITY INDICATING SYSTEM

The fuel quantity indication system provides readings, in pounds, of usable internal, CFT and external fuel. Refer to figure 1-6. The system components include the fuel quantity indicator, a built-in test (BIT), a BINGO caution display, and an independent FUEL LOW caution light.

Fuel Quantity Indicator

A combination pointer-counter fuel quantity indicator is on the lower right side of the main instrument panel. Refer to figure 1-6. The pointer indicates total internal fuel (with readings multiplied by 1000). The upper counter marked TOTAL LBS indicates total internal fuel plus CFT and external fuel. The two lower counters, marked LEFT and RIGHT, and a selector switch provide individual tank monitoring and a check of the indicator. An OFF flag will be displayed if no electrical power is available. Erroneous fuel indications resulting from fuel slosh will occur during and immediately following maneuvering flight.

FUEL QUANTITIES

(F-15E)

TANK	GALLONS	USABLE FUEL			
		JP–4		JP–8	JP–5
		POUNDS AT 6.5 LB/GAL	POUNDS AT 6.3 LB/GAL	POUNDS AT 6.7 LB/GAL	POUNDS AT 6.8 LB/GAL
TANK 1	604	3,900 ±150	3,800 ±150	4,050 ±150	4,100 ±150
RIGHT ENG FEED (TANK 2)	234	1,500 ±100	1,450 ±100	1,550 ±100	1,590 ±100
LEFT ENG FEED (TANK 3)	189	1,250 ±100	1,150 ±100	1,250 ±100	1,290 ±100
INTERNAL WING TANKS L	496	3,200 ±250	3,150 ±250	3,300 ±250	3,370 ±250
INTERNAL WING TANKS R	496	3,200 ±250	3,150 ±250	3,300 ±250	3,370 ±250
INTERNAL FUEL LESS CONFORMAL TANKS	2,019	13,100 ±500	12,700 ±500	13,550 ±500	13,750 ±500
EXTERNAL WING TANKS L	610	3,950 ±300	3,800 ±300	4,100 ±300	4,150 ±300
EXTERNAL WING TANKS R	610	3,950 ±300	3,800 ±300	4,100 ±300	4,150 ±300
INT FUEL PLUS EXT WING TANKS LESS CONFORMAL TANKS	3,239	21,050 ±850	20,400 ±850	21,700 ±850	22,000 ±850
EXTERNAL ₵ TANK	610	3,950 ±300	3,800 ±300	4,100 ±300	4,150 ±300
INT FUEL PLUS EXT ₵ TANK LESS CONFORMAL TANKS	2,629	17,100 ±750	16,550 ±750	17,600 ±750	17,900 ±750
INT FUEL PLUS 3 EXT TANKS LESS CONFORMAL TANKS	3,849	25,000 ±950	24,250 ±950	25,800 ±950	26,150 ±950
CONFORMAL TANKS L	728	4,750 ±300	4,600 ±300	4,900 ±300	4,950 ±300
CONFORMAL TANKS R	728	4,750 ±300	4,600 ±300	4,900 ±300	4,950 ±300
INTERNAL FUEL PLUS CONFORMAL TANKS	3,475	22,600 ±900	21,900 ±900	23,300 ±900	23,650 ±900
INT FUEL PLUS EXT WING TANKS AND CONFORMAL TANKS	4,695	30,500 ±1050	29,600 ±1050	31,450 ±1050	31,950 ±1050
INT FUEL PLUS EXT ₵ TANK AND CONFORMAL TANKS	4,085	26,550 ±950	25,750 ±950	27,350 ±950	27,800 ±950
MAX FUEL LOAD–INT FUEL PLUS 3 EXT TANKS AND CONFORMAL TANKS	5,305	34,500 ±1150	33,400 ±1150	35,550 ±1150	36,100 ±1150

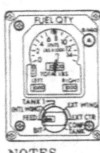

NOTES

- THE FUEL QUANTITIES, IN POUNDS, ARE ROUNDED OFF TO READABLE VALUES OF COUNTER PORTION OF THE FUEL QUANTITY INDICATOR; THEREFORE, THE ACTUAL GALLONS TIME 6.5, 6.3, 6.7 OR 6.8 WILL NOT NECESSARILY AGREE WITH THE POUNDS COLUMN.

- FUEL WEIGHTS ARE BASED ON JP–5 AT 6.8, JP–8 AT 6.7 AND JP–4 AT 6.5 AND 6.3 POUNDS PER GALLON (DIFFERENCES ARE DUE TO MANUFACTURERS ALLOWABLE TOLERANCES) AND 65 DEGREES FAHRENHEIT.

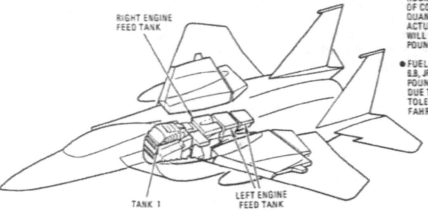

RIGHT ENGINE FEED TANK

TANK 1

LEFT ENGINE FEED TANK

15E-1-(21)03

Figure 1-6

Fuel Quantity Selector Knob

FEED	The fuel remaining in the respective engine feed tanks will be displayed.
INT WING	The fuel remaining in the respective internal wing tanks will be displayed.
TANK 1	The fuel remaining in tank 1 will be displayed in the LEFT counter (RIGHT will indicate zero).
EXT WING	The fuel remaining in the respective external wing tanks will be displayed.
EXT CTR	The fuel remaining in the external centerline tank will be displayed in the LEFT counter (RIGHT will indicate zero).
CONF TANK	The fuel remaining in the respective conformal tank will be displayed.
BIT	A spring-loaded position that will drive the internal (pointer) and total (counter) indicators to 6000 pounds, and the LEFT and RIGHT (counters) to 600 pounds indicating the fuel quantity indicator is operating normally.

FUEL LOW Caution

A FUEL LOW caution, on the MPD/MPCD display, warns the aircrew of a low fuel level in one or both engine feed tanks. The FUEL LOW caution is completely independent of the fuel quantity indicating system and is controlled by a sensor in each feed tank. The sensor in the right feed tank is located at the 960 pound level and the sensor in the left feed tank is located at the 540 pound level. If either sensor is exposed (regardless of the combined indicated fuel quantity) the FUEL LOW caution will come on. The caution normally comes on at 1500 ± 200 pounds total internal fuel remaining. The FUEL LOW caution may come on with more than 1500 pounds of fuel remaining if fuel transfer falls behind engine fuel consumption because of transfer system failure or sustained high speed afterburner usage. The FUEL LOW caution activates automatic transfer of fuel from the CFT's and external tanks regardless of cockpit fuel switch positions. Transfer will stop as soon as feed tanks refill to the sensor levels and will reactivate when the fuel level again drops below the

sensors. FUEL LOW activation will not turn on the tank 1 or CFT transfer pumps if the slipway switch is in OPEN or ORIDE.

FUEL LOW Voice Warning

The FUEL LOW voice warning is activated in conjunction with the FUEL LOW caution. When a low fuel condition exists, the voice warning states: "WARNING, FUEL LOW" pauses, then repeats the warning.

BINGO FUEL Caution

A BINGO fuel caution on MPD/MPCD comes on at a preset value, controlled by the aircrew. An adjustable index (bug) on the face of the indicator may be set to any internal fuel quantity by turning the bingo knob. If the bingo index is set above 6000 pounds, the BINGO caution will come on when the BIT check is made. The bingo caution circuit may be used to automatically terminate fuel dumping.

BINGO FUEL Voice Warning

The bingo fuel voice warning is activated in conjunction with the bingo fuel caution. When a bingo fuel condition exists, the voice warning states: "BINGO FUEL" pauses, then repeats the warning.

FUEL DUMP SYSTEM

All fuel except engine feed tank fuel may be dumped by placing the dump switch, on the fuel control panel, to DUMP. With the landing gear handle DOWN, external fuel cannot be dumped. Internal and/or CFT fuel is not dependent on the landing gear handle position. The fuel dump switch is spring-loaded to the lever-locked NORM position and is electrically held in the DUMP position (with BINGO caution off). When DUMP is selected, a motor-operated dump valve in the right internal wing tank opens. With the dump valve open, the transfer pumps in tank 1 and each internal wing tank force fuel out the right wing dump mast. Conformal fuel tanks and/or external fuel tanks transfer into tank 1 and the wing tanks and is then dumped. Dumping will continue until STOP TRANS is selected or in the case of the external tanks, the landing gear handle is moved to DN. If the tank 1 and internal transfer pumps fail, external fuel passes through a check valve and is dumped. Dumping will continue until:

a. Norm is selected on the dump switch.

b. The BINGO caution comes on, at which time the dump switch automatically returns to NORM terminating fuel dumping.

c. Only feed tank fuel remains. This can occur if the BINGO bug is set below approximately 2700 pounds.

The approximate fuel dumping rates are: right internal wing tank 390 PPM, left internal wing tank 260 PPM, and tank 1, 260 PPM for a total of 910 PPM. The uneven dump rates of the internal wing tanks produce a fuel imbalance (left wing heavy) of approximately 130 pounds per minute up to a maximum of approximately 1100 pounds of wing fuel asymmetry. Wing fuel asymmetry will remain until all the fuel in the internal wing tanks is depleted.

EXTERNAL TANK JETTISON

The external fuel tanks may be jettisoned individually or simultaneously. See Stores Jettison Systems , this section.

AIR REFUELING SYSTEM

The air refueling system has a fixed receptacle, a slipway control switch, a hydraulically operated slipway door, two slipway lights, a receptacle flood-light, a signal amplifier, a READY light, an air refueling release button, an air refuel pressure switch, and an emergency slipway door actuating system. For CG control, a float switch in tank 1 prevents external tank refueling until tank 1 fuel quantity is above approximately 1,560 pounds. The CFTs start filling immediately (regardless of tank 1 fuel quantity) with CG being maintained by the sequence in which the CFT compartments are filled. For normal and emergency air refueling procedures refer to F-15 Flight Crew Air Refueling Procedures (TO 1-1C-1-25).

> **CAUTION**
>
> During refueling of external tanks or CFTs, a sudden fuel valve closure could occur which may shatter the pylon standpipe, causing fuel to flow overboard. If fuel valves manufactured by Dolphin/Autovalve (Part Number 60486-1) are installed in the CFT or external fuel tank pylons, restrict the rate of flow for refueling (after internal fuel is full) to less than 150 gpm (gallons per minute). Valves manufactured by JC Carter are not restricted.

Slipway Switch

The three position slipway switch is located on the fuel control panel.

CLOSE   Closes the slipway door, turns on tank 1 and CFT transfer pump(s), reestablishes external fuel tank pressurization, and fuel sequencing.

OPEN   Shuts off tank 1 transfer pump, CFT transfer pumps (if operating) opens the slipway door and, providing the slipway door has opened,
     a. Depressurizes the external fuel tanks if FUEL LOW light not on.
     b. Turns on the receptacle lights.
     c. Turns on the READY light indicating the system is ready for boom engagement.

ORIDE   Accomplishes the same function as in OPEN above plus the following:
     a. Allows boom locking, but the tanker disengage feature (both automatic and manual) is lost.
     b. The receiver must initiate all disconnects.
     c. Bypasses tank 1 float switch and external tanks may be refueled regardless of fuel tank 1.

NOTE

- With the slipway switch in OPEN or ORIDE and the slipway door open, the external tanks are depressurized and descent rate should not exceed 10,000 feet per minute.

- To prevent an undesirable CG condition when using ORIDE position, STOP REFUEL should be selected for the external tanks and CFT until tank 1 fuel quantity is above 1560 pounds.

- FUEL LOW caution activation will not turn on the tank 1 transfer pump if the slipway switch is in OPEN or ORIDE.

Fuel Control Switches

The three fuel control switches, on the fuel control panel, provide an option of refueling the external/conformal tanks. If the switches are in NORM, the external/conformal tanks will fill during refueling. If any or all switches are in STOP REFUEL, the corresponding external/conformal tank(s) will not fill during refueling.

Air Refuel Pressure Switch

The air refuel pressure switch prevents the aircraft fuel system from becoming over-pressurized during refueling by unlatching the receptacle from the air refueling boom if fuel pressure exceeds approximately 80psi.

Air Refueling Release Button

The auto acquisition button is used as an air refueling release button. When the button is depressed, the receptacle unlatches from the boom.

Emergency Air Refueling Switch

The slipway door can be opened by placing the emergency air refueling switch to OPEN. Pyrotechnic devices powered by the emergency essential 28 volt dc bus open the door which cannot then be closed in flight. Normal slipway lighting will be available but the READY light will not go out during refueling nor will the boom lock in the receptacle. External fuel tank pressurization can be restored by placing the slipway door switch to CLOSE.

GROUND REFUELING

All internal, CFT and external fuel tanks are pressure fueled through a single point receptacle. However, the external tanks may be fueled through individual filler points. No external power is required for single point refueling.

CFT Manual Precheck Valve

The manual precheck valve, located on the forward end of the CFT, has two positions.

PRECHECK   Prevents ground refueling.

LOCK   Allows ground refueling of the CFT.

CAUTION

If the fuel dump valve(s) was/were open when electrical power was removed from the aircraft, they/it will remain open until power is reapplied. Fuel will be dumped during refueling if the dump valve(s) is/are open.

ELECTRICAL POWER SUPPLY SYSTEM

The electrical power supply system consists of two main AC generators, three transformer-rectifiers, an emergency AC/DC generator, and a power distribution (bus) system. External electrical power can be applied to the bus system on the ground, and the JFS generator provides electrical power to part of the bus system during an engine start without external power. Refer to foldout section for electrical system simplified schematic.

AC ELECTRICAL POWER

Two AC generators are the primary source of electrical power. The two generators are connected for split bus nonsynchronized operation. This means that with both generators operating each generator supplies power independently to certain aircraft buses. If one generator fails, it drops off the line; and at the same time, power from the remaining generator is provided to the buses of the failed (or turned off) generator. Current limiters are provided to prevent a fault in one generator system from shutting down both generators. Either generator is capable of supplying power to the entire system. Each generator is activated auto-matically when its control switch is in the ON posi-tion, and the generator is connected to its buses when voltage and frequency are within prescribed limits (approximately 56% engine rpm). A protection sys-tem within the generator control unit protects against damage due to undervoltage, overvoltage, over and under frequency, feeder faults, and generator locked rotor. If a fault or malfunction occurs, the generator control unit removes the affected generator from its buses. Except for an under frequency condition, the control switch of the affected generator must be cycled to bring the generator back on the line after the fault or out-of-tolerance condition clears. If the generator drops off the line due to under frequency and the prescribed frequency is restored, the genera-tor will come back on the line automatically. A generator may be removed from its buses at any time by placing the generator control switch to OFF. Indicator lights, labeled L GEN and R GEN, are on both caution light panels. These lights come on when-ever their respective generator drops off the line with power available on the essential 115 VAC bus to illuminate the lights.

Generator Control Switches

Two generator control switches, one for each genera-tor, are on the engine control panel. They are two-position toggle switches with positions of OFF and ON. The switches are lever-lock type and must be raised up before they are moved to a new position.

DC ELECTRICAL POWER

Three transformer-rectifiers (TR) are provided. The outputs of the left and right transformer-rectifiers are connected in parallel; however, protection is provided so that a short on a bus of one TR will not affect the other TR. Also, if either the right or the left TR fails, the other TR will power the entire DC system. A third TR is provided, the essential TR, which operates independently of the other two. No cockpit warning of single TR failure is provided.

EMERGENCY GENERATOR

A utility hydraulic motor-driven emergency AC/DC generator is provided. The emergency electrical sys-tem is separate from the primary electrical system. If either or both main generators are inoperative or both the left and right transformer-rectifiers fail, or some combination of faults occur, or if either or both main fuel boost pumps fail, the emergency generator is activated. If only one generator is inoperative or

either or both main fuel boost pumps fail, the emer-gency generator powers the emergency/essential buses only (emergency fuel boost pump, arresting hook, emergency air refueling door open and AFCS/CAS). If both generators are inoperative or both right and left transformer-rectifiers fail, the emergency generator supplies the essential AC/DC buses, the emergency/essential buses and the ground power switch number 1 28 volt dc bus. With aircraft on the ground and the emergency generator switch in AUTO during engine start without external electrical power, the emergency generator automatically shuts off 30 seconds after first main generator comes on the line. The purpose of shutting down the emergency gener-ator is to limit operation on the ground. The 30 second delay is to allow time to check the emergency generator/emergency boost pump system. For engine start using external power, the emergency generator or emergency boost pump will not operate as long as external power is connected. With the emergency generator switch in AUTO on the ground, except with external power connected, both the EMER BST ON and BST SYS MAL lights come on in situations (single engine taxi, first engine start, etc.) where a main generator is off the line. The lights will go out when the second main generator comes on the line.

Emergency Generator Control Switch

The emergency generator control switch, on the engine control panel, is a three-position toggle switch with positions of AUTO, MAN, and ISOLATE. The switch is electrically held in the ISOLATE position.

AUTO	Provides automatic activation of the emergency generator if either or both main generators are inop-erative, both left and right transformer-rectifiers fail, or either or both main fuel boost pumps fail. Also provides auto-matic shutdown of the emergency generator 30 seconds after the first main generator comes on the line after a ground start without external power. For starts with external power the emergency generator will not operate as long as external power is connected.
MAN	Provides manual activation of the emergency generator.

ISOLATE   Restricts the emergency generator to powering the emergency fuel boost pump, the arresting hook and provides power from the emergency/essential 28 volt dc bus to the emergency air refueling switch to open the slipway door. It also provides power to the ground power switch number 1 28 volt dc bus for operation of the engine monitor indicator. Power and intercom are removed from the rear cockpit. In the event of a complete electrical failure, an attempt to restore the emergency generator may be made by cycling the switch to ISOLATE and back to MAN.

EMER BST ON/ SYSTEM MALFUNCTION Caution

The EMER BST ON and BST SYS MAL cautions provide indication of the status of both the emergency fuel boost pump system and the emergency generator system. A single caution or combination of cautions indicate the following:

EMER BST ON	BST SYS MAL	STATUS
ON	OFF	Emergency fuel boost pump pressure normal and pump powered by emergency generator.
OFF	ON	Emergency fuel boost pump failed.
ON	ON	Emergency fuel boost pump pressure normal but powered by abnormal electrical source.

JFS GENERATOR

The JFS generator provides JFS ignition and control, and, with the JFS READY light on, intercom, front utility light, and AMAD fire warning. These items are powered by the JFS generator until JFS shutdown. If the

GROUND POWER CONTROL PANEL & PLACARD

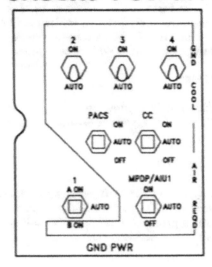

GND PWR		
SW 1	**SW 2**	**SW 3**
HYD PRESS	AHRS	ADC
FUEL FLOW	STBY ATT	EAIC
ENG MON	MAD	AOA
FUEL QTY IND		VVI
LDG GR		IBS
FLAPS		VTRS
EXTONCE CNTR		
SPD BK		**SW 4**
AFCS		ILSR
POS A		AIU NO. 2
ALL EXCEPT		TACAN
AFCS		RMR
POS B		
ALL		

15E-1-(33-1)04-CAT)

Figure 1-7

JFS start switch is used for shutdown, the AMAD fire warning remains powered for a short time during JFS rundown.

EXTERNAL ELECTRICAL POWER

External electrical power may be connected to the aircraft through an external electrical power receptacle near the nose gear wheelwell. The aircraft buses are energized by external power in the same manner as if a main generator were operating. The exceptions to this are those buses which furnish power to systems which do not have on-off control switches and/or require cooling air. Power can be applied to these buses by the use of ground power switches. With external power on the airplane, if the left engine is started first, the complete electrical system automatically switches to internal power when the left generator comes on the line. If the right engine is started first, the right generator, when it comes on the line, energizes only the buses it normally feeds. The buses normally energized by the left generator remain on external power (except those buses energized by the JFS generator) until the external power is removed or the left engine is started and the left generator comes on the line.

External Power Control Switch

The external power control switch, on the engine control panel, controls application of external power to the aircraft electrical buses. An external power monitor will prevent faulty external power from being connected to the aircraft system.

NORM   Allows the aircraft electrical buses to be energized by external power if no aircraft generators are operating.

RESET   Will establish external power if it is not on the line. The RESET position is spring-loaded to NORM.

OFF   Disconnects external power from the aircraft.

Ground Power Switches

Seven ground power switches are provided on the ground power panel (figure 1-7) on the left console. Each controls a group of systems and/or instruments and will prevent unnecessary operation of the systems/instruments on ground power. Switches 2, 3, and 4 have two positions. The CC switch, PACS switch, switch 1 and MPDP A1U 1 switch have three positions.

AUTO — System/instrument can only be energized by aircraft generator power.

ON — System/instrument can be energized by external power.

OFF — CC, PACS or MPDP/AIU 1 are de-energized regardless of power source.

Ground cooling air is required except for switch 1 (A or AUTO).

NOTE

With the ECS caution on because of a low avionics cooling air flow condition, all ground power switches become inoperative as a means of applying external power to their applicable equipment. Should any of the switches be set to the ON position when a low avionics cooling air condition occurs, the switch(es) will remain in the ON position although the power to their equipment will be shut off.

CIRCUIT BREAKERS

Circuit breakers for the AFCS, pitot heat, speed brake, flaps, landing gear, and nosewheel steering are provided on the lower center instrument panel in the front cockpit. Two circuit breaker panels are in the rear cockpit below the right and left consoles. All other circuit breakers are inaccessible to the flight crew.

HYDRAULIC POWER SUPPLY SYSTEM

Hydraulic power is supplied by three separate systems with each system divided into two or more circuits. Reservoir level sensing (RLS) is employed in all three systems for the purpose of isolating a leak.

When a leak develops in a circuit a valve senses the reservoir level and shuts off the affected circuit. Through this method the maximum number of circuits remain operable. Refer to Hydraulic Flow Diagram, section III and the hydraulic systems foldout for a description of what each system powers.

PC SYSTEMS

PC1 pump and PC2 pump operate at a pressure of 3000 psi. Each PC system is divided into a circuit A and a circuit B.

UTILITY SYSTEM

The utility system has a left pump which operates at a pressure of 3000 psi and a right pump which operates at a pressure of 2775 psi. The utility system is divided into a circuit A, circuit B, and a non-RLS circuit.

RESERVOIR LEVEL SENSING (RLS)

If a leak occurs in any circuit, the reservoir level of that system (PC1, PC2 or utility) drops and circuit A is shut off. If the leak is in circuit B the reservoir level continues to drop causing circuit A to be restored and circuit B is shut off. In the case of the utility system with a non-RLS circuit leak, circuit A is shut off then restored as circuit B is shut off; however, if flight is continued, a complete utility failure will eventually occur as indicated by zero pressure on the utility hydraulic gage.

HYDRAULIC PRESSURE INDICATORS

Three hydraulic pressure gages on the upper right corner of the instrument panel display PC1, PC2 and utility hydraulic system pressures.

HYDRAULIC SYSTEMS CAUTION LIGHTS

An amber HYD light on the caution light panel and the MASTER CAUTION light come on when any hydraulic systems caution exists. The appropriate caution display: PC1 A, PC1 B, PC2 A, PC2 B, UTL A and UTL B will be displayed on the MPD/MPCD when their respective RLS valve actuates to shut off that circuit. The L PUMP or R PUMP caution is also displayed on the MPD/MPCD when the respective utility hydraulic pump output pressure is low. An indication of a PC pump failure or low pressure is displayed on the MPD/MPCD. Resetting the MASTER CAUTION light will not extinguish the HYD light or the associated caution on the MPD/MPCD.

LANDING GEAR SYSTEM

The gear is electrically controlled and hydraulically operated. While weight is on the gear, the gear cannot be retracted. When the main and nose gear are extended, the forward door(s) will be closed.

LANDING GEAR CONTROL HANDLE

The landing gear is controlled by a wheel shaped handle located on the lower left side of the main instrument panel, and has two positions.

DOWN   Extends landing gear.
(DN)

UP   Retracts landing gear.

Landing Gear Warning/UNSAFE Lights and Warning Tone

A red warning light in the front cockpit landing gear control handle and the rear cockpit UNSAFE light on the left lower main instrument panel come on when any landing gear is not locked in the selected position. A low pitch (250 Hz) warning tone will be activated ten seconds after the landing gear control handle is placed down and will remain activated until all gear are down and locked. The red warning lights will also illuminate due to an unlocked gear door when the landing gear control handle is up. These lights are independent of the three green landing gear position lights. The lights will illuminate and the warning tone will sound whenever the following conditions exist simultaneously: aircraft altitude is below 10,000 feet, airspeed is below 200 knots, rate of descent greater than 250 fpm and the gear handle is not down. In addition, the lights will illuminate and a warning tone will sound when the Air Data Computer (ADC) becomes inoperative, regardless of altitude, airspeed, or rate of descent. The warning tone may be silenced by depressing the warning tone silence button adjacent to the landing gear control handle. If the landing gear is up and locked and then the landing gear control circuit power fails (e.g., circuit breaker popped), the warning lights will illuminate; however, the warning tone will not come on.

Landing Gear Position Lights

There are three green landing gear position lights marked NOSE, LEFT, and RIGHT located on the left lower main instrument panel in each cockpit. Each light will illuminate when its respective gear is down and locked.

EMERGENCY LANDING GEAR HANDLE

An EMERG LG handle is located on the left main instrument panel in both cockpits. Emergency gear extension is accomplished by pulling either the front or rear cockpit EMERG LG handle full travel and ensuring the handle is locked in the extend (full travel) position. This bypasses normal hydraulic and electrical controls and hydraulically (JFS accumulator) releases the doors and landing gear. The landing gear then free falls to the down and locked position. The landing gear doors will remain open. The emergency landing gear handle in the forward cockpit can be reset by rotating the handle 45° clockwise and pushing forward. The handle in the rear cockpit must be pulled completely out and locked and once pulled and locked, cannot be reset from the rear seat.

NOSE GEAR STEERING SYSTEM

Nose gear steering is a full time mechanically controlled (front and rear cockpit rudder pedals) hydraulically powered (UTL A pressure) system that features dual authority steering ranges consisting of a normal (15° maximum left or right) range and a maneuvering (45° left or right) range. The steering system automatically engages whenever the nose gear strut is compressed by the weight of the aircraft and provides normal steering authority range. The maneuvering range is selected by pressing the nose gear steering button on the front cockpit control stick. The nose gear steering system may be disengaged from either cockpit by pressing and holding the paddle switch on the control stick. With the system disengaged, the nose wheel becomes free swiveling and may be swiveled 360°. When the paddle switch is released, the system will not re-engage if the nose gear has rotated more than approximately 56°. However if the steering is engaged with the nose gear rotated beyond 45°, the nose wheel will be immediately driven back to the 45° position. During taxi, when centering action reduces the angle below approximately 45°, the nose gear steering system will re-engage. On takeoff, nose gear steering is disengaged when the nose gear strut extends.

Emergency Steering

Emergency power for the nose gear steering is selected by pulling the front or rear cockpit emergency brake/steering handle located on the lower center of the main instrument panel. Pulling the handle selects JFS hydraulic accumulator pressure to power the nose gear steering. With an emergency brake/steering handle pulled, both nose gear steering ranges are available and cannot be disengaged with the paddle switches. If UTL A is operating, the nose gear steering may not shift to the JFS hydraulic accumulator pressure or may only partially shift which can cause loss of, or reduced steering rate (sluggish) that may appear as loss of steering. Pressing and holding the paddle switch will remove UTL A from the system and ensure that the nose gear steering shifts fully to JFS hydraulic accumulator pressure. If UTL A is available the normal steering system can be restored by resetting the emergency brake/steering handle and releasing the paddle switches. If the JFS LOW caution is on, the emergency steering system is not reliable for taxi since accumulator pressure can no longer be monitored.

Emergency Brake/Steering Handle

For location and use of the emergency/brake steering handle, refer to Emergency Steering and Emergency Brakes narrative this section.

BRAKE SYSTEM

The main landing gear wheels are equipped with hydraulic powered brakes operated by toe action on the rudder pedals. An anti-skid system is incorporated in the normal brake system to provide maximum deceleration with controlled wheel skid. An emergency brake system provides JFS hydraulic accumulator pressure to power the brake system in the event of loss of UTL A which normally powers the system. Anti-skid protection is not available on the emergency brake system. A holding brake relieves the aircrew from maintaining pressure on the brake pedals when the aircraft is stopped for long periods of time.

Anti-Skid System

The anti-skid system is electronically controlled by a three position switch in the front cockpit on the miscellaneous control panel. An ANTI-SKID caution and the MASTER CAUTION light will come on whenever the landing gear is down and a system failure is detected. A touchdown protection circuit (with anti-skid on) prevents hydraulic pressure from being applied to the brakes until both main wheels spin up. The brake pulser provides main tire skid control in the event anti-skid braking is not available. Skid control effectiveness deteriorates below 30 knots; therefore, heavy braking below 30 knots may

result in locked wheels. The pulser may also be selected manually by use of the three position anti-skid switch. When the pulser system is activated, applied brake pressure is repeatedly interrupted to the wheel brakes. This provides pulsating braking action which reduces the probability of tire blow-out from locked wheels. This also prevents bringing the aircraft to a complete stop on the brake pulser. After touchdown, the ARI will be disengaged by the anti-skid wheel spin up signal. With the anti-skid switch in OFF or PULSER, the ARI will be disengaged anytime the landing gear handle is down. When the anti-skid is inoperative and for some anti-skid detected malfunctions, the ARI will remain engaged at wheel spin-up, adversely affecting crosswind landing characteristics. Placing the anti-skid switch to OFF or PULSER will ensure ARI disengagement. The MASTER CAUTION light and ANTI-SKID caution do not depend on the position of the landing gear circuit breaker in the front cockpit. However, if the landing gear circuit breaker is pulled or popped, the automatic selection of the brake pulser is disabled and PULSER must be manually selected in order to obtain pulser and disengage ARI.

NORM	The anti-skid is on when the gear is down. However, illumination of the ANTI-SKID caution activates the brake pulser and ARI is disengaged with the gear down.
PULSER	Turns off normal anti-skid protection, turns on the ANTI-SKID caution and MASTER CAUTION, and activates the brake pulser. The ARI is disengaged with the gear handle down.
OFF	Turns off the normal anti-skid and brake pulser systems. Disengages ARI with the gear handle down.

Emergency Brake System

Emergency brake system pressure is supplied by the JFS accumulator and actuated by pulling the emergency brake/steering handle in either cockpit. If UTL B is operating, the accumulator will be continuously replenished. If not, sufficient braking should be available to stop the aircraft. Emergency brakes may feel more sensitive than normal brakes because anti-skid protection is not available. If UTL A pressure is available, the normal brake system can be restored by resetting the emergency brake/steering handle.

Holding Brake

The holding brake is electrically controlled by a two position toggle switch located in the front cockpit on the lower main instrument panel. The switch is electrically held in the ON position and automatically switches off when a throttle is moved above IDLE, the aircraft is weight off wheels or electrical power is removed. The holding brake 'ON' signal is used by the INS to reenter alignment after interrupted alignment occurs. The holding brake should not be placed to ON while the aircraft is moving but must be ON during AFCS BIT.

ON   Holding brake is on, hydraulic system pressure (3000 PSI) is supplied to brakes.

OFF   Holding brake is off, normal brake system operation is restored.

ARRESTING HOOK SYSTEM

A retractable arresting hook is in the underside of the aft fuselage. It is electrically controlled, extended by gravity and a hydraulic dashpot, and retracted by utility hydraulic pressure.

Arresting Hook Switch

The arresting hook control switches are two position switches located on the front and rear cockpit left sub panels.

UP   Hook is retracted.

DOWN   Hook is extended.

ARRESTING HOOK Caution

Any time the arresting hook is not up and locked the MASTER CAUTION and HOOK caution come on.

FLAP SYSTEM

Each wing has a two position trailing edge flap. The flaps are electrically controlled and hydraulically operated. When the flaps are down, they are protected from structural damage by a blow up airspeed switch. The switch is set to automatically retract the flaps at approximately 250 knots. At approximately 240 knots, the flaps will automatically return to the down position, providing the flap control switch is in the down position.

Flap Control Switch

The flap control switch is a two position switch located on the throttle quadrant.

UP   Retracts the flaps.

DOWN (DN)   Extends the flaps.

Flap Position Lights

The flap position lights are on the left sub panel. The YELLOW light indicates the flaps are in transit. A GREEN light indicates the flaps are down.

SPEED BRAKE SYSTEM

A speed brake is located on the upper surface of the center fuselage just aft of the canopy. It is electrically controlled and hydraulically operated. The speed brake can be positioned to any intermediate position between fully retracted and fully extended with AOA below approximately 25 units. If AOA is above 25 units, the speed brake will not extend when selected. If the speed brake is extended, it will automatically retract, when AOA increases through 25 units.

NOTE

If the CC detects a failure in the AOA system (AOA Fail displayed on MPCD), the ground to the speed brake switch is broken and the speed brake, if extended, will retract. If the AOA failure occurs with the speed brake closed, it cannot be extended.

Following automatic retraction of the speed brake, when AOA is reduced, the speed brake will automatically extend provided the speed brake switch is in the OUT position.

Speed Brake Switch

The speed brake switch has three positions and is located on the inboard throttle. The switch will remain in any selected position.

CENTER	Stops the speed brake in any intermediate position.
AFT	Extends the speed brake.
FORWARD	Retracts the speed brake.

The rear cockpit speed brake switch will override any position selected by the front cockpit. It is spring-loaded to the hold (centered) position. When the rear cockpit switch is released to hold, control is returned to the front cockpit.

FLIGHT CONTROL SYSTEM

The aircraft primary flight control surfaces consist of conventional ailerons, twin rudders and stabilators (which are capable of symmetrical or differential movement). Hydraulic actuators are used to position the control surfaces. The inputs to the hydraulic actuators are from a hydromechanical system and an electrical system called the control augmentation system (CAS). The hydromechanical system and the CAS normally work together, but either system alone is capable of providing sufficient aircraft control for flight. Spring cartridges provide simulated aerodynamic forces to the control stick and rudder pedals. The spring cartridges have trim actuators which actually move the neutral positions and thus the control surfaces. Refer to foldout section for the flight control schematic.

Control Stick

The front cockpit control stick consists of a stick grip and force transducer, and contains seven controls: an autopilot/nose gear steering disengage switch (paddle switch), nose gear steering/weapons button, a trigger, a weapon release button, a trim switch, an auto acquisition button and a castle switch. The rear cockpit control stick consists of a stick grip and force transducer and contains four controls: an autopilot/nose gear steering disengage switch (paddle switch), a weapon release button, a trim switch and an air refueling release button. The rear cockpit trigger is non-functional. Refer to figure 1-8. A detailed description of switch functions is in Front Cockpit Controls or Rear Cockpit Controls, this section, or in the description of individual systems in this manual and TO 1F-15E-34-1-1.

Rudder Pedals

The rudder pedals operate conventionally and are adjustable. The rudder pedals are also used for the brakes and nose gear steering.

Rudder Pedal Adjust Knob

Pulling the rudder pedal adjust knob located on the instrument panel releases both rudder pedals. The pedals are then forced aft by spring pressure or pushed forward by foot pressure to achieve the desired adjustment.

NOTE

With the rudder pedal adjust knob extended, aircraft steering or braking is not possible.

T/O Trim Button and Light

The T/O trim button, on the CAS control panel, when pressed, drives the stick and rudder pedals to the takeoff position which, in turn, drives the aileron, rudder and stabilator actuators to the takeoff position. The T/O trim light will then come on. The departure warning tone will sound after the T/O trim button has been pressed and takeoff trim is within limits. The T/O trim light will go out and the tone will cease when the button is released. The stick takeoff position produces a slight nose up trim position which, in turn, drives the pitch trim compensator (PTC) to the full nose up limit of its authority (stabilator leading edge down). This provides maximum nose up stabilator authority for takeoff. The pitch trim compensator will continue to drive the stabilator leading edge down after the button is released.

HYDROMECHANICAL FLIGHT CONTROL SYSTEM

The hydromechanical flight control system uses mechanical linkages and hydraulic actuators to position the flight control surfaces.

LONGITUDINAL CONTROL

Longitudinal stick motion positions the stabilators symmetrically to provide pitch control. The ratio of symmetrical stabilator motion to longitudinal stick motion (pitch ratio) is automatically adjusted for altitude and speed. This provides the same pitch response (constant g) for a given stick deflection regardless of airspeed. The ratio is high (greatest stabilator authority) at low speeds, and low at high speeds at low altitude. If hydraulic pressure is lost the pitch ratio will drive to an intermediate position and lock. If the mechanical linkage becomes jammed, mechanical longitudinal control is lost; however, the CAS can provide enough stabilator control for moderate flight maneuvers and landing.

CONTROL STICK
(FRONT COCKPIT)

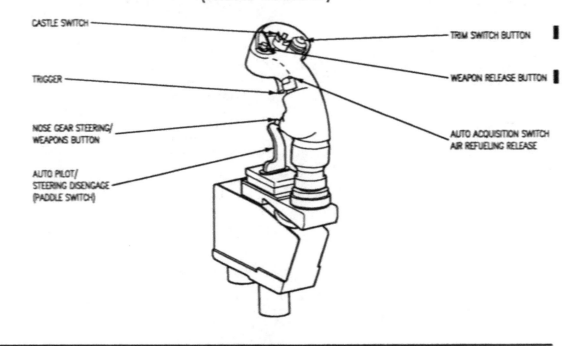

CASTLE SWITCH

TRIGGER

NOSE GEAR STEERING/
WEAPONS BUTTON

AUTO PILOT/
STEERING DISENGAGE
(PADDLE SWITCH)

TRIM SWITCH BUTTON

WEAPON RELEASE BUTTON

AUTO ACQUISITION SWITCH
AIR REFUELING RELEASE

(REAR COCKPIT)

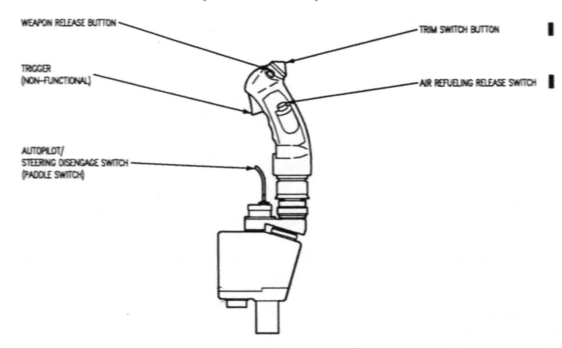

WEAPON RELEASE BUTTON

TRIGGER
(NON-FUNCTIONAL)

AUTOPILOT/
STEERING DISENGAGE SWITCH
(PADDLE SWITCH)

TRIM SWITCH BUTTON

AIR REFUELING RELEASE SWITCH

15E-1-(2)54-1(2)21-CAT1

Figure 1-8

Longitudinal Trim/Feel System

The longitudinal control system includes a manual trim and an automatic trim. The manual trim is controlled by the trim button on the stick. The manual trim actuator changes the neutral position of the longitudinal feel spring cartridge to reposition neutral stick position and thus neutral stabilator position. When airborne, the flight control system automatically trims the stabilator without affecting stick position to compensate for changes in trim caused by such things as changing speed, operating flaps or speed brake, or store separations. On the ground, the PTC slowly trims the stabilator to either the extreme forward or aft limit of its authority as the stick is positioned forward or aft of the neutral stick position. This stick positioning can take place by manual stick inputs or by manual trim.

Pitch Ratio Switch

The pitch ratio switch is on the main instrument panel.

AUTO	Provides normal system functions.
EMERG	Removes hydraulic pressure from the hydromechanical pitch control system which causes the pitch ratio and the PTC to drive to a midrange position and lock. Mechanical aileron rudder interconnect (ARI) is also disabled.

Pitch Ratio Indicator

The pitch ratio indicator on the main instrument panel shows the ratio of symmetrical stabilator motion to longitudinal stick motion. For a given stick motion, the stabilators move most at a pitch ratio of 1.0 and least at zero. The ratio should be 1.0 at slow speeds and near zero at .9 mach near sea level. The indicator will show 0.3 to 0.5 if the pitch ratio switch is placed in EMERG or hydraulic pressure is lost.

PITCH RATIO Caution

The PITCH RATIO caution comes on if hydraulic pressure is lost to the control stick boost/pitch compensator (CSBPC), the pitch ratio switch is in the EMERG position, or the pitch ratio versus airspeed is incorrect below 20,000 feet. However, with the gear down and airspeed above 220 knots the PITCH

RATIO caution may come on until the pitch ratio drives to above 0.9. This condition is normal and should be disregarded.

LATERAL CONTROL

Lateral stick motion positions the ailerons, rudders and stabilators to provide roll control. The ratio of aileron/differential stabilator deflection to lateral stick motion (roll ratio) is adjusted automatically for different airspeeds, longitudinal stick position and gear position. Aileron and differential stabilator deflection are washed out to prevent adverse yaw when longitudinal stick deflection is combined with lateral stick deflection. At subsonic speeds, the roll ratio is high; at supersonic speeds the roll ratio is reduced. Additional roll ratio reductions also occur as the stick is moved forward or aft. With the landing gear down, full aileron/differential stabilator is available at any longitudinal stick position. If UTL A and PC2A hydraulic pressures are lost or the roll ratio switch is in EMER, the roll ratio drives to mid-range and locks. A spin recovery aid provides full lateral control authority, regardless of longitudinal stick position, when the yaw rate exceeds 41.5° per second and remains greater than 30° per second for 5 seconds. The spin recovery aid is discontinued (normal control authority) when the yaw rate drops below 30° per second.

Mechanical ARI

The mechanical ARI adjusts the control system such that lateral stick motion results in varying rudder deflection dependent on longitudinal stick position. With the control stick aft of neutral, lateral stick motion causes rudder deflection in the same direction as stick motion. With the control stick forward of neutral, lateral stick motion causes rudder deflection in the opposite direction of the stick motion. With the flaps down, the point where longitudinal stick position causes opposite rudder motion with a lateral input is shifted forward of neutral. This position shift causes the amount of rudder deflection for lateral input to increase with aft stick movement.

The ARI is disengaged at supersonic speeds and on landing. If the anti-skid system detects a malfunction, or the landing gear circuit breaker is OUT, the ARI may remain engaged at wheel spin up, adversely affecting crosswind landing characteristics. Turning the anti-skid switch OFF or PULSER will insure ARI disengagement. If UTL A and PC2A hydraulic pressures are lost or either the Pitch or Roll Ratio switch is in EMER, the ARI is inoperative. If the mechanical system is inoperative, the differential stabilators (through roll CAS) will provide lateral control for moderate maneuvers including landing.

Lateral Trim/Feel System

The aircraft is trimmed laterally using the trim button on the stick. The trim actuator changes the neutral position of the lateral feel spring cartridge to reposition neutral stick position and thus neutral aileron/differential stabilator position.

Roll Ratio Switch

The roll ratio switch is on the miscellaneous control panel.

AUTO	Provides normal system functions.
EMERG	Removes hydraulic pressure from the hydromechanical roll control system which causes the roll ratio to drive to a midrange and lock. Mechanical ARI is also disabled.

ROLL RATIO Caution

The ROLL RATIO caution comes on if hydraulic pressure is lost, the roll ratio switch is in EMERG, the landing gear control handle is DOWN without full roll authority available, or the landing gear control handle is UP with full roll authority available or if roll authority is not commanded to 2/3 of maximum roll authority above Mach 1.0. The ROLL RATIO caution above Mach 1.0 may also indicate the mechanical ARI has not been commanded OFF.

YAW CONTROL

Rudder pedal motion positions the rudders to provide yaw control. If the rudder linkage jams, safety spring cartridges allow the rudder pedals to move to permit nose wheel steering. The rudders are still actuated through the CAS (CAS alone provides only about half rudder deflection). If the nose gear steering jams, similar devices permit rudder operations.

Yaw Trim/Feel System

The aircraft yaw is trimmed using the trim switch on the throttle quadrant. The trim actuator changes the neutral position of the rudder feel spring cartridges to reposition neutral rudder pedal position and also neutral rudder position.

Rudder Travel Limiter

The rudder travel limiter system is completely automatic. When aircraft speed reaches approximately 1.5 mach, rudder pedal movement is mechanically limited. As the airspeed decreases through 1.5 Mach, the limiter retracts and full rudder pedal movement is restored.

RUDDER TRAVEL LIMITER Light Caution

The RUDR LMTR caution comes on when the rudder pedal limiter is not engaged above 1.5 Mach or is engaged below 1.5 Mach.

AOA TONE

The gear-down AOA tone is a high pitch (1600 Hz) beeping tone which starts at approximately 30 units AOA. The beep rate increases as AOA increases. The tone may be eliminated by decreasing AOA.

HIGH ANGLE OF ATTACK WARNING

A high angle of attack warning is provided. This gear-up AOA tone is a medium pitch (900 Hz) tone which starts at approximately 28 units AOA, depending on aircraft configuration. The landing gear handle must be up and the external stores configuration must be set correctly in the PACS for the AOA warning to function correctly. The tone (at a 4hz rate) come on at 28 units AOA. At 30 units AOA a 10Hz (beep) rate is heard, and at 33 units AOA a steady tone will be heard. The AOA must decrease by 1 unit before the warning level transitions to the next lower state. The high AOA warnings pertain to all external stores configurations unless configured with only air-to-air stores. In addition, if the aircraft is loaded exclusively with SUU-20B/A dispensers on stations 2 and/or 8, the above limits are increased by 5 units AOA and consequently the warning tones will be triggered at 33, 35 and 38 units AOA respectively.

NOTE

This high angle of attack warning tone uses the same tones as used by the OWS aural warnings.

DEPARTURE WARNING

With the landing gear up, a medium pitch (900 Hz) beeping tone sounds when the yaw rate reaches 30° per second. As the yaw rate increases the beep rate increases. The tone reaches a maximum beep rate at 60° per second yaw rate. The tone sounds with the T/O trim button depressed and the T/O trim light on. The T/O trim beep rate correlates to approximately 45° per second yaw rate.

AUTOMATIC FLIGHT CONTROL SYSTEM (AFCS)

The AFCS provides roll, pitch, and yaw control augmentation, autopilot modes in roll and pitch axes, and terrain following in the pitch axis. Refer to TO 1F-15E-34-1-1 for terrain following description.

CONTROL AUGMENTATION SYSTEM (CAS)

Superimposed on the hydromechanical flight control system is a three channel, three axes control augmentation system (CAS). The CAS responds to electrical signals generated by forces applied to the control stick and to rudder pedal position. These signals modify the control surface deflections commanded by the hydromechanical flight control system to provide the desired flying qualities. The CAS also provides increased damping on all three axes. Since CAS inputs are applied directly to the actuator and the inputs are due to force and require no control stick or rudder motion, with the CAS on, limited aircraft control is retained with the loss of any or all mechanical linkages. The three channel design turns any axis off when a second like failure occurs. The CAS affects stabilator and rudder position only; the ailerons are not controlled by the CAS. A moderate yaw transient may occur and is normal when yaw CAS is disengaged, reengaged, or the landing gear is lowered.

CAS Caution Display

Three CAS caution displays (CAS YAW, CAS ROLL, and CAS PITCH), on the MPD/MPCD, come on any time their respective axis is disengaged by a failure in the CAS system or the switch is off. These cautions also light the master caution and the FLT CONTR caution on the caution panel. Any time the pitch or yaw CAS disengages, the roll CAS also disengages. A moderate yaw transient may occur and is normal when yaw CAS is disengaged or engaged. If the roll CAS is functioning normally, it can be re-engaged following the loss of pitch CAS. Roll CAS cannot be engaged without an operating yaw CAS. A LAT STK LMT caution indicates that roll commands must be limited to 1/2 lateral stick inputs.

NOTE

CAS YAW and LAT STICK LIMIT cautions may be displayed after a single engine shutdown. This is normal aircraft operation and a YAW CAS reset should be attempted.

CAS Switches

The following three positions are applicable to the roll, pitch, and yaw CAS switches located on the CAS control panel.

ON — Allows normal operation after engagement.

RESET — Engages disconnected axis (provided fault no longer exists). The switch is spring loaded from RESET to ON.

OFF — Disengages applicable axis.

TF Couple Switch

Selecting the TF COUPLE position couples the terrain following system to the autopilot. Selecting OFF deactivates automatic terrain following. Refer to TO 1F-15E-34-1-1 for expanded terrain following operations.

BIT Button

The BIT button is located on the CAS panel. Pressing and holding the BIT button permits initiation of the AFCS BIT when the AFCS pushbutton on the MPD is pressed, the aircraft has weight on wheels and the holding brake is ON. To initiate an AFCS BIT, the operator must press and release the pushbutton on the MPD/MPCD and verify AFCS IN TEST is displayed on the MPD/MPCD. Then release the CONSENT switch to allow BIT to run.

AUTOPILOT FUNCTIONS

The autopilot in the pitch axis provides attitude control, barometric altitude hold, radar altitude hold or radar altitude select and in the roll axis provides attitude hold, heading hold, tacan steering, navigation steering or ground track steering. Refer to TO 1F-15E-34-1-1 for terrain following description.

Upfront Control

The UFC is the primary autopilot mode selection and engagement controller. The basic autopilot mode is selected and engaged using the UFC but before any autopilot mode can be engaged, all three CAS axes, pitch, roll and yaw, must be on.

The UFC menus involved in autopilot engagement and display of system and mode status are menu 1 and the autopilot submenu. See figure 1-9. Menu 1 provides current autopilot status information such as the engagement mode, and whether it has been coupled with the existing steering mode. The autopilot submenu provides the means of coupling the current aircraft steer mode and selecting either the baro or radar altitude hold mode. When the autopilot is engaged the autopilot status (same as menu 1) is displayed centered on the top line. If A/P is not engaged, A/P is displayed centered on this line.

AUTOPILOT DISPLAYS

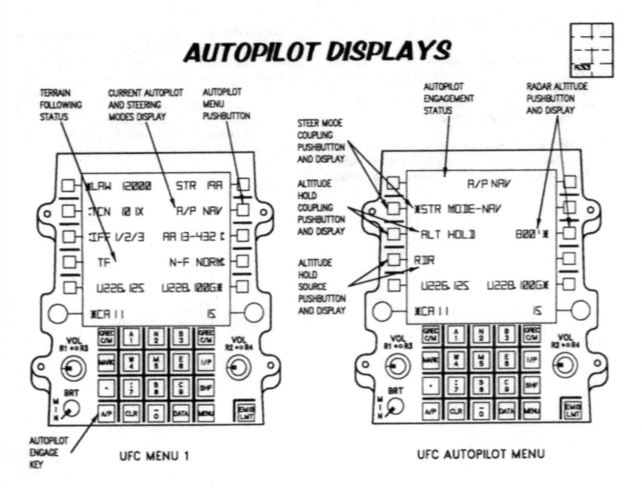

UFC MENU 1

UFC AUTOPILOT MENU

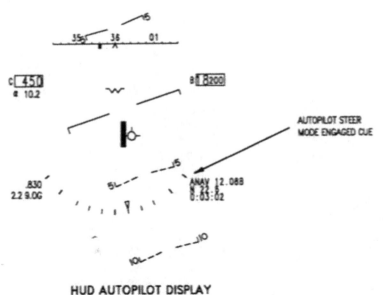

HUD AUTOPILOT DISPLAY

15E-1-(42-1)18-CATI

Figure 1-9

Autopilot Preselection

Autopilot modes of operation may be preselected on the autopilot submenu prior to, coupling of the basic autopilot. Any option with an asterisk (steer mode, altitude hold, radar altitude select) will be coupled when the UFC keyboard A/P button is pressed.

NOTE

Operating modes are remembered from the previous sortie. Before coupling the autopilot, review the autopliot submenu for preselections.

Autopilot Engagement-Basic A/P Mode

The basic autopilot is engaged by pressing the A/P key on the UFC keyboard. The autopilot automatically engages pitch attitude hold if pitch is within 0 $\pm 45°$ and heading hold if the bank angle is 0 $\pm 7°$. If the bank angle is greater than $\pm 7°$ and less than $\pm 60°$ roll, attitude hold is engaged until the bank angle is decreased to $\pm 7°$ and then automatically reverts to heading hold.

When the autopilot key is pressed, the UFC autopilot submenu replaces the current display to facilitate steer mode and/or altitude hold engagement selections unless TF is engaged. If automatic terrain following (ATF) is engaged, pressing the UFC A/P key does not change the current UFC format. It does provide the usual A/P engagement. If attitude hold is engaged it appears on menu 1 in the current autopilot mode display as A/P ATT. If heading hold is engaged it is displayed as A/P HDG.

Autopilot Disengagement

The autopilot modes are disengaged by pressing the paddle switch on the control stick, deselecting the mode or engaging a higher priority mode.

Autopilot Coupled With Steer Modes

The autopilot can be coupled with any one of three steer modes, navigation (NAV), ground track (GT), or tacan (TCN). Steer modes are selected from the EHSI display format (figure 1-30). The UFC autopilot submenu, line 2 will show the steer mode currently selected on the HSI and is used to couple the autopilot to the displayed steer mode. If ILST or ILSN is selected on the HSI, the coupling to the steer mode is inhibited since the autopilot cannot be coupled to fly an ILS approach. With the autopilot coupled, ILST and ILSN are removed from the HSI display.

NOTE

- If either ILS mode is selected on the HSI when the autopilot is coupled, the appropriate steer mode (TCN or NAV) is automatically selected and displayed on both the HSI and the UFC autopilot submenu. For example, if ILSN was selected, the NAV steer mode is automatically selected on the HSI (boxed) when autopilot is coupled.
- The TACAN steer mode no longer disengages automatically when flying through the zone of confusion (ZOC). In the ZOC, TACAN steering will parallel the desired course. Once out of the ZOC, TACAN steering will intercept and track the desired course.

Assuming that the basic A/P is already engaged, coupling of the selected steer mode is done from the autopilot submenu. Pressing the pushbutton next to the steer mode legend on the UFC displays an asterisk symbol next to the steer mode legend, couples the autopilot to the steer mode displayed, and displays an A/P symbol on the EHSI format. If NAV steer mode has been coupled, the autopilot status is displayed on menu 1 as A/P NAV, indicating that the autopilot is in the NAV steering mode. The two remaining steer modes, tacan and ground track, are selected and coupled with the autopilot in the same manner. In addition, the TACAN steer mode provides two display formats : PLAN view and course deviation indicator (CDI). When coupled to a steer mode, an 'A' is displayed on the HUD to the left of the steer mode (figure 1-9).

Altitude Hold

Altitude hold is selected and engaged from the autopilot submenu where it is displayed as ALT HOLD. One of two altitude sources is also displayed, either radar (RDR) or barometric (BARO). To change the altitude source, press the pushbutton next to the displayed source. Assuming the basic autopilot mode is engaged, the mode itself is selected by pressing the pushbutton next to ALT HOLD. An asterisk symbol appears next to ALT HOLD legend when selected.

BARO - With the BARO altitude source displayed on the autopilot submenu display, press the pushbutton next to the ALT HOLD legend to select the mode. ALT HOLD maintains baro altitude at selection.

When selected an asterisk symbol appears next to the mode. The mode can be engaged if the vertical velocity is less than 2000 ft/min and disengages at 2000 ft/min or greater. The current altitude is held but not displayed on the A/P submenu in baro altitude hold. (Note: with BARO selected, the radar altitude select line (PB 8) is blanked.)

WARNING

At low airspeeds (a function of gross weight and pressure altitude) when either the RDR or BARO altitude hold mode is being used, pitch authority becomes saturated and altitude hold will not be reliable. The system will not automatically trip off until the aircraft exceeds 2000 fpm vertical velocity.

Radar - With radar (RDR) selected as the altitude source, two options are selectable, radar altitude select and radar altitude hold. The primary difference between the two is that a specific altitude is selected via the keyboard for radar altitude select whereas radar altitude hold maintains the altitude at selection. Each is described in the following:

a. Radar altitude select. First enter the desired holding radar altitude using the UFC keyboard. The selected altitude can be any value between 1000 and 50,000 feet in increments of 10 feet. Once displayed on the scratchpad and confirmed as the desired altitude, the selection is transferred to the UFC display, opposite the ALT HOLD legend, by pressing the pushbutton next to the previously selected altitude PB 8). (Note that any previously selected altitude value is displayed immediately upon selection of the RDR altitude source.) Pressing the pushbutton next to the altitude digital readout a second time displays an asterisk to indicate the digital altitude value has been selected. The actual mode is now selected by pressing the pushbutton next to ALT HOLD. An asterisk next to it indicates the mode is selected. The engagement limits are the same as the disengage limits for Radar Altitude Hold. The aircraft will fly up or down to the selected altitude and automatically level off at that altitude. However, if you are climbing to a radar select altitude and then deselect that altitude, instead of reverting to altitude hold, the aircraft continues climbing to previously selected altitude. When flying up to a selected altitude, the system will try to maintain a 6000 fpm climb

schedule. Consequently during heavy gross weight operations, potential stall problems exist.

WARNING

With FCC Version 4.0 : If radar altitude select disengages because the aircraft descends below 950 feet radar altitude, the autopilot will default to radar altitude hold. The AUTOPILOT caution is displayed to alert the aircrew that the aircraft has transitioned from radar altitude select to radar altitude hold.

b. Radar altitude hold. This mode is selected to maintain the existing aircraft radar altitude. The engagement limit is defined as a radar altitude of 400 to 50,000 feet. Selection is accomplished by first noting that the radar altitude select (PB 8) displayed has no asterisk, then press the pushbutton next to ALT HOLD.

NOTE

Radar altitude hold or select will disengage if roll angle exceeds 55°.

The autopilot status on MENU 1 with altitude hold or altitude select engaged and NAV steering selected (on the EHSI) and asterisk (on autopilot submenu) is displayed as A/P NAV/ALT.

Radar altitude hold or select mode will automatically disengage if the aircraft vertical velocity exceeds the following limits:

GEAR UP

Altitude	VVI
<17,000 feet	8,000 fpm
17,000-20,000 feet	Varies linearly between 8,000 and 5,600 fpm
≥20,000 feet	5,600 fpm
GEAR DOWN	4,000 fpm

WARNING

The radar altimeter provides no forward looking capability. RDR ALT HOLD mode is not recommended for use over rolling/rugged terrain below 5,000 feet AGL.

Control Stick Steering

Control stick steering (CSS) during autopilot operation refers to manual control stick inputs in either pitch or roll without disengaging the autopilot. The stick force required for pitch CSS is one pound in attitude hold and 3½ pounds in altitude hold/select. Stick force for roll CSS varies between 1 to 3 pounds, dependent on the autopilot mode. In the ground track steering mode, if CSS is engaged, the bank angle must be reduced to less than ±7° to return to ground track. If the bank angle is greater than or equal to ±7° the autopilot will enter roll attitude hold until the bank angle is reduced. If an autopilot mode is disengaged during CSS the AUTO PLT caution will be displayed on the MPD/MPCD.

Autopilot Caution Displays

Caution displays relating to the autopilot system are the master caution light, the flight control caution light and the specific caution displayed on the appropriate MPD/MPCD in each cockpit. Cautions are triggered as a result of crew action or autopilot system initiation.

There are three ways the autopilot related cautions can be activated by crew action. First is disengagement of the autopilot using the flight control paddle switch; second is an unsuccessful autopilot engagement attempt; and third is to exceed the CSS forces in pitch or roll.

● The flight control stick paddle switch is the control used to disengage the autopilot from the flight control system in all non-terrain following operation. When pressed and disengagement occurs, the MASTER CAUTION, FLT CONTR (flight control) caution light and MPD/MPCD autopilot (AUTO PLT) caution are activated. To extinguish the caution lights, press the MASTER CAUTION light in the cockpit to reset the caution system.

● If the crew attempts to engage an autopilot mode and the attempt is unsuccessful, the MASTER CAUTION, FLT CONTR caution light and the MPD/MPCD autopilot caution are activated. Unsuccessful coupling also refers to the unsuccessful selection of a steer or altitude hold mode causing the same three caution cues to be activated. In either case all three visual indications will remain on indefinitely until reset by the cockpit MASTER CAUTION reset function.

● If the crew is using control stick steering during autopilot operation and disengages the autopilot by exceeding the control stick forces in either pitch or roll, the MASTER CAUTION, FLT CONTR caution and the MPD/MPCD cautions are activated.

Any autopilot disengagement not initiated by the crew produces a minimum of three caution indications, MASTER CAUTION, flight control caution and the MPD/MPCD AUTO PLT caution. In most cases, other related cautions will accompany this type of disengagement and will also be displayed.

The caution and warning system has been mechanized to provide caution indications to the crew of multiple autopilot related problems. The first autopilot related problem causes the MASTER CAUTION, flight control caution and the MPD/MPCD AUTO PLT caution to come on. After MASTER CAUTION reset, the crew is alerted to subsequent autopilot problems by the same system. The autopilot MPD/MPCD caution message is also repositioned to the top of the caution list.

CAS FUNCTIONAL FAILURE

CAS functional status is information available to the crew via the AFCS DETAIL BIT display. The data provided is intended as supplementary information as to the current operating mode of the flight control computer. The data may or may not be associated with an AFCS caution, but new information displayed will be accompanied by an AV BIT light. To see the functional failures displayed, first call up the BIT menu, second, press the DETAIL pushbutton, then third, press the AFCS pushbutton on the detailed BIT display. The definition and associated options are as listed below:

PCAS First Fail

One of the three channels of the flight control computer has detected a failure of an element (sensor, servo, switch, etc.) in the pitch axis of its channel. Although pitch CAS is in full normal operation, if a second channel detects a failure of the same element the pitch and roll axes will be shut down with a resulting degradation of pitch and roll handling qualities. Some of the first failures will automatically reset if the computer later determines normal operation, however, other failures are latched out until the PITCH RESET is cycled on the CAS control panel. Autopilot and Terrain Following remains functional.

CASI Servoloop

The CAS interconnect servo provides the harmonization between pitch CAS and the pitch mechanical controls. If a second like failure occurs in this interconnect, pitch and roll CAS will shut down with associated CAS PITCH and CAS ROLL cautions in addition to the CASI SERVOLOOP status. Attempts should first be made to reset roll CAS with the ROLL RESET switch, then pitch CAS with the PITCH RESET switch on the CAS control panel. If pitch CAS is not resettable and CASI SERVOLOOP status remains displayed, pitch CAS can be regained by positioning the pitch ratio switch to EMERGENCY prior to selecting pitch CAS reset.

NOTE

The combination of pitch CAS disengaged and Pitch Ratio switch in emergency degrades handling qualities and should be accomplished at a safe altitude, below 500 KCAS/1.0 M level flight condition. A small trim change may occur if pitch CAS is reset and subsequently disengaged.

RCAS First Fail

One of the three channels of the flight control computer has detected a failure of an element (sensor, servo, switch, etc.) in the roll axis of its channel. Although roll CAS is in full operation, if a second channel detects a failure of the same element the roll axes will shut down resulting in degraded roll characteristics. Some of the first failures will automatically reset if the computer later determines normal operation, however, other failures are latched out until the ROLL RESET is cycled on the CAS control panel.

ROLL Limit

A first failure has been detected in the AFCS schedule of roll authority vs airspeed. A second failure of the AFCS air data sensor will result in incorrect scheduling and an associated LAT STK LMT caution. At high airspeeds, above 550 KCAS/1.0 M, lateral stick inputs should be limited to one half of full authority.

AOA Fail

This status is displayed in association with a LAT STK LMT caution indicating the AFCS cannot determine the angle of attack. Roll CAS gain is set to zero which may result in degraded roll characteristics. Operations above 600 KCAS are permissible with lateral stick inputs limited to one-half full authority. Do not exceed one half lateral stick authority.

YCAS First Fail

One of the three channels of the flight control computer has detected a failure of an element (sensor, servo, switch, etc.) in the yaw axis of its channel. Although yaw CAS is in full operation, if a second channel detects a failure of the same element the roll and yaw axes will disengage resulting in lateral/direction stability degradation. Some of the first failures will automatically reset, however, other failures will be latched out until the YAW RESET is cycled on the CAS control panel.

Spin Recovery Failure

The AFCS provides spin recovery aid by disengaging CAS and selecting full mechanical roll authority if excessive yaw rate is detected. SPIN RECOVERY FAILURE in conjunction with a CAS YAW caution indicates yaw rate cannot be determined by the flight control computer and the spin recovery aid mode is inoperative. SPIN RECOVERY FAILURE status without an associated CAS YAW caution indicates full mechanical roll authority may be incorrectly selected. High AOA handling qualities and spin protection may be degraded. Avoid acrobatic maneuvers.

CAS ARI Off

The flight control system contains two harmonized ARI's, the mechanical ARI is scheduled as a function of stick position and the CAS ARI is scheduled as a function of roll rate and AOA. The mechanical ARI disengages at Mach 1.0 and the CAS ARI disengages at Mach 1.5. With the loss of the ability to determine Mach, roll rate, or AOA as a result of failures, the flight control computer disengages CAS ARI and displays CAS ARI OFF status. Although mechanical ARI is not affected by this, some additional aircrew coordination may be required during maneuvers above 30 units AOA.

RCP Stick Sensor

If the rear cockpit stick force sensor fails, pitch and/or roll CAS will disengage setting the CAS PITCH and/or CAS ROLL cautions with an associated RCP STICK status. CAS will be resettable, however, the rear cockpit stick force commands to the flight control computer will be inoperative. Stick inputs by the

WSO will result in sluggish performance and a reduction of loads (3.5g's maximum) capability. Only mild maneuvers should be attempted by the backseater.

CAS Rudder Pedal

If the rudder pedal position sensor fails, yaw CAS will disengage setting the CAS YAW caution with an associated CAS RUDDER PEDAL status. Yaw CAS will reset, however, the rudder pedal position sensor will be inoperative. Lateral directional stability will be normal for coordinated flight, but uncoordinated commands will tend to be washed out and should be avoided.

One Rudder CAS

If a rudder servo fails, the servo is disengaged and the CAS gain to the other servo is doubled. Yaw CAS will continue to work normally but total rudder power is reduced. Rolls must be limited to one half stick. No flight above the following limits:

Limits - 525 KCAS When >1.6 M
- With LANTIRN Pods
- 1.2 M <18,000 ft
- 600 KCAS, 18 - 34,000 ft
- 1.6 M Above 34,000 ft

Non-hydraulic BIT

NON-HYD is Displayed on the DETAIL BIT page as a result of AFCS initiated BIT detecting an incompatible state of the aircraft hydraulic pressure switches or the PRCA thermal switch. Some BIT tests requiring hydraulics will have been bypassed and therefore a full system test has not been accomplished. This status will remain displayed until a full system BIT can be initiated. Check the MPD/MPCD for cautions associated with the hydraulic systems. If all hydraulic systems are normal, proceed with the functional checkout of the Flight Control system.

BIT Code

Displayed as a result of any detected malfunction within the AFCS or associated flight control interface (for example BIT CODE 999A). BIT codes will cycle through all stored values and continuously repeat this process. In flight, BIT codes not associated with other functional failure information will not activate the AV BIT light. However, any stored code will activate the AV BIT light one minute after landing. BIT codes are intended as an aid to maintenance.

NOTE

Initiated BIT will clear all stored BIT codes. Pressing and holding the Emergency Disconnect Switch (EDS or paddle switch) and then pressing and holding the BIT consent switch also clears the stored BIT codes. To aid in aircraft maintenance, the AFCS BIT codes should be recorded before being cleared.

OVERLOAD WARNING SYSTEM (OWS)

An overload warning system (OWS) is provided. For the OWS to program properly, the external stores configuration must be correctly set in the PACS. A 900 Hz tone is heard in the headset to give warning that the maximum allowable g is being approached. The tone is first heard at 85% maximum allowable g or 1 g below the maximum allowable, whichever is lower, and is interrupted at a rate of 4 Hz to produce a beeping sound. At 92% the tone is interrupted at a rate of 10 Hz, until at 100% the voice warning "OVER G, OVER G" is heard. The "OVER G, OVER G" continues until the % of overload falls below 100%. If the overload condition is relieved in the middle of an "OVER G" transmission, the transmission will be completed before the voice warning is discontinued. Inflight, OWS operation may be verified by display of both current g and maximum allowable g on the HUD.

The OWS computes fuel changes at a maximum of forty (40) pounds per second. Whenever the OWS computed fuel is greater than the aircraft configuration can hold (e.g. tank jettison), the OWS will be inoperative until computations catch up with actual fuel quantity.

Component Malfunctions

Failure of systems which supply data to OWS can cause the OWS to malfunction. Since these systems are also of prime importance for flight, a failure would be apparent to the aircrew (for example, CAS dropoff, ADC BIT, fuel quantity malfunction, current G's unreasonable). If the aircrew detects a malfunction in one of these systems, the OWS should be considered inoperative and the flight manual non-OWS G limits should be observed, even though the HUD G window may still indicate that the OWS is operating.

Certain failures can result in a continuous "over-G" voice warning. Logic was therefore incorporated to shut down the OWS after 30 seconds of accumulated voice warning. Thus the aircrew should be aware that if the voice warning comes on for 30 seconds and then stops, it is not because the system has corrected itself. Checking the HUD in this situation will verify OWS shutdown, and the non-OWS G limits must be observed. The aircrew can verify that the OWS is operational by observing the following:

● Allowable G's are displayed on the HUD when airborne and current G's are of a reasonable value;

● The ARMT format on MPD/MPCD displays the actual configuration;

● The systems supplying information to the OWS are up (no ADC BIT failure, reasonable fuel quantity indications).

MPD/MPCD Display

When the aircraft is g loaded to 85% or more of the design limit, the overload conditions are stored in the CC memory and can be recalled as an information matrix on the MPD/MPCD. The overload conditions include normal acceleration in g's (ACC), the percent overload (OVL) and overload severity codes for selected components.

Figure 1-10 shows a typical OWS matrix. The matrix is displayed on the MPD/MPCD by selecting OWS from the menu display. The abbreviations used on the display are:

 a. ACC - Normal acceleration load factor. This is a two or three digit number with a decimal before the last digit understood (e.g., 92 is read as 9.2g).

 b. OVL - Percentage of overload expressed as a whole percentage. The percent overload is related to the component severity code as follows:

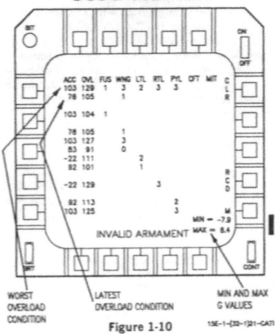

OVERLOAD WARNING SYSTEM SEVERITY CODE DISPLAY

WORST OVERLOAD CONDITION

LATEST OVERLOAD CONDITION

MIN AND MAX G VALUES

Figure 1-10

15E-1-(32-1)21-CA71

%OVL	SEVERITY CODE LEVEL
0% - 100%	0
101% - 110%	1
111% - 120%	2
121% - 130%	3
131% - 140%	4
141% and above	5

 c. FUS - Fuselage
 d. WNG - Wing
 e. LTL - Left tail boom
 f. RTL - Right tail boom
 g. PYL - Pylon
 h. CFT - Conformal fuel tanks
 i. MIT - Mass items
 j. CLR - Clear function for weight-on-wheels and to clear the OWS matrix from CC memory.
 k. RCD - Record function for the video tape recording set (VTRS).

The first line of the display shows the worst (highest) overload condition recorded during the flight. The second line is the latest overload condition encountered. Subsequent lines display overload percentages and severity codes for the listed components. This information is used to determine the required maintenance action. An overload value of exactly 100 will cause a 0 to be displayed, but a value of 100 plus .01 will cause the percent overload value to increase to 101 and cause a 1 to be displayed. All applicable inspections are based on severity codes and not percent overload, which is displayed for information only.

Stored entries are automatically removed from the CC during INS align if no entry exceeds 100%. Overloads over 100% latch indicator 72 on the avionics status panel (ASP) and can only be cleared by selecting CLEAR from the OWS display on the MPD/MPCD and having maintenance personnel reset the ASP in the nose wheelwell. The procedure to clear the matrix is contained in section II.

WARNING/CAUTION/ADVISORY LIGHTS

The red warning lights provide indications of system malfunctions that require immediate crew attention. Except for the gear handle and gear UNSAFE lights, the warning lights are prominently located at or near the top of the instrument panel in both cockpits. The left and right BURN THRU lights are only located in the front cockpit. The caution lights also provide indications of system malfunction which require less than immediate attention. There are two kinds of caution indications, the amber caution lights located on the caution lights panel in the front cockpit and on the warning/caution/advisory lights panel in the rear cockpit, and cautions which are displayed on the MPD's and MPCD's in both cockpits. Only two cautions, the EMER BST ON and the BST SYS MAL, appear as both yellow caution lights and MPD/MPCD cautions. The FLYUP ARM yellow caution light and the AUTO TF green advisory light appear only in the rear cockpit. MPD/MPCD cautions are initially displayed on the right MPD in the front cockpit and the right MPCD in the rear cockpit. Depending on the number of cautions displayed, they are presented in three columns written left to right as they occur. The most recent caution will appear at the top of the right column. See figure 1-11. If required, MPD/MPCD cautions can be moved from one display to another. In the front cockpit this is done by simultaneously pressing the MASTER CAUTION

light and using the castle switch on the stick to move the cautions, moving the castle switch toward the display where the cautions are desired. To move the cautions in the rear cockpit, press and hold the master caution and click the coolie switch on the appropriate hand controller toward the display where the caution is desired.

NOTE

When cautions are displayed on the left aft MPCD and the HUD switches to secondary mode, the cautions will be moved to the right aft MPCD. When the HUD is in secondary mode, moving the cautions to the left aft MPCD is inhibited. This prevents cautions from appearing on the WFOV HUD during secondary mode.

CAUTION LIGHTS

There are three yellow caution lights on the caution lights panel in the front cockpit and warning/caution/advisory lights panel in the rear cockpit which are classified as major category caution lights. These lights, ENGINE, FLT CONTR and HYD, provide a prompt that MPD/MPCD cautions from that particular category are being displayed. The MASTER CAUTION light comes on with any of the major category caution lights. The corresponding MPD/MPCD caution will remain on until the problem is corrected. The systems associated with each major category light caution are as follows:

ENGINE
ATDP	
FUEL HOT	INLET ICE
L BST PUMP	R BST PUMP
L INLET	R INLET
L BLEED AIR	R BLEED AIR
L ENG CONTR	R ENG CONTR
L OIL PRESS	R OIL PRESS

FLT CONT
AUTO PLT	CAS PITCH
RUDR LMTR	PITCH RATIO
CAS YAW	ROLL RATIO
CAS ROLL	LAT STK LMT

HYD
L PUMP	R PUMP
PC1A	PC1B
UTL A	UTL B
PC2A	PC2B

MPD/MPCD CAUTIONS

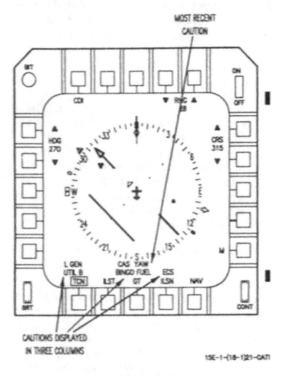

MOST RECENT
CAUTION

CAUTIONS DISPLAYED
IN THREE COLUMNS

15E-1-(18-1)21-CAT1

Figure 1-11

With double generator failure and the emergency generator operating, cautions will be displayed only on the MPCD in the front cockpit. These cautions can be removed by moving the front stick castle switch to the aft position. A second activation of the castle switch restores the cautions to the display. With a CC failure only, cautions are always displayed on any CRT that has the radar display format.

ADVISORY LIGHTS

The advisory lights, which are either green or white, indicate safe and normal conditions and impart information for routine purposes. Individual advisory lights are located throughout the cockpit and are described with their applicable equipment. A list of warning/caution/advisory lights, with causes of their coming on and corrective action to be taken is described in Section III. Intensity control of the lights is described in lighting, this section, MASTER CAUTION LIGHTS.

MASTER CAUTION LIGHTS

The MASTER CAUTION lights, on the upper instrument panel in both cockpits, come on simultaneously when any MPD/MPCD caution comes on. They also come on with all yellow caution lights except the following: PROGRAM, MINIMUM, CHAFF, FLARE, LOCK/SHOOT, AV BIT, LASER ARMED, EMIS LMT and FLY UP ARM. The MASTER CAUTION lights go out when the front cockpit MASTER CAUTION is pressed but, except for the AUTO PLT caution, the caution remains on until the malfunction is corrected. Although the MASTER CAUTION lights do not come on with the AV BIT caution, pressing either cockpit MASTER CAUTION light turns off the AV BIT. While it can be used to move MPD/MPCD cautions from one display to another as described above, the rear cockpit MASTER CAUTION cannot be used to turn off the MASTER CAUTION lights and re-set the master caution lights circuit.

AUDIO WARNING SYSTEM

The audio warning system is made up of both audio tones and voice warnings. The weapons lockon tone, TEWS caution and launch tones, ILS audio, and TACAN audio are volume controlled by the RICP for the cockpit and the ICSCP for the rear cockpit. The IFF mode 4 tone is generated by the IFF transponder in response to a valid mode 4 interrogation. The OWS tone is generated by the MPDP when the aircraft approaches design limit structural overload. When overload is exceeded, the tone is replaced with a voice warning. The unsafe landing warning tone is generated as a function of landing gear position, aircraft altitude, airspeed and rate-of-descent. The AOA stall warning tone is generated when the angle of attack exceeds 28.4 units.

The AFCS enables the departure warning tone when the yaw rate exceeds 30°/sec. The beep rate of the tone increases as the yaw rate increases, and the maximum beep rate is reached at a yaw rate of 60°/second. The LANTIRN system produces a bell tone to advise the aircrew that automatic terrain following has reverted to manual terrain following.

The voice warning system volume cannot be adjusted. The silence button on the ICSCP/RICP is used to silence any voice or tone warning for up to one minute.

The voice warning system activates the following warnings if conditions exist which cause the associated warning lights to come on:

- "AB BURN THRU LEFT"

- "AB BURN THRU RIGHT"

- "BINGO FUEL"

- "LOW ALTITUDE"

- "OBSTACLE AHEAD"

- "OVER-G"

- "TF FAILED"

- "WARNING, AMAD FIRE"

- "WARNING, FUEL LOW"

- "WARNING, ENGINE FIRE LEFT"

- "WARNING, ENGINE FIRE RIGHT"

- "WARNING, OVERTEMP LEFT"

- "WARNING, OVERTEMP RIGHT"

- "WARNING, TRANSFER PUMP"

Voice warnings for OBSTACLE AHEAD, OVER-G and TF FAILED, continue until the condition causing the voice warning system to activate is corrected. All other voice warnings repeat twice and do not repeat again unless the condition causing the warning is corrected and subsequently recurs.

Voice warning for the AMAD fire detection system and the FTIT indicators become effective with application of external power, or with JFS operation during first engine start. Voice warning for the engine fire detection system and fuel low level detection system becomes effective with application of external power, or with the emergency generator coming on the line during engine start.

BUILT - IN TEST (BIT) SYSTEM

The built-in test (BIT) system provides the crewmembers with displays of avionic system status. Most information is derived from BIT mechanizations in the avionics sets and from non-avionic BIT's implemented in computer software for other aircraft systems.

Three test methods are used; continuous, periodic and initiated. The continuous method constantly monitors particular signals for presence, value or logic. The periodic method automatically intersperses test signals and replies amongst operating signals in such a manner that they do not interfere with normal equipment operation. The initiated method must be initiated by the crewmember and causes an interruption of normal operation of the designated system for the duration of the test.

Equipment Status Displays

Equipment status displays (BIT, caution, and advisory) provide the aircrew with continuous status of the avionics equipment. The AV BIT caution lights are a cue to check equipment BIT status.

Failure to pass any BIT test causes the appropriate equipment indicator(s) on the avionics status panel in the nose wheelwell to latch, the front and rear cockpit AV BIT caution lights to come on, and if appropriate a system caution is displayed. Pressing the front cockpit MASTER CAUTION light turns off the AV BIT caution lights. BIT failures will be displayed by pressing the BIT button on the MENU display.

BIT DISPLAY

A MENU selectable BIT display (figure 1-12) contains the status of all BIT tested systems and is selected by pressing PB20 (BIT) on the main menu. The systems which may be BIT tested are displayed around the outer edge of the BIT display. To select a particular system for BIT, press the PB next to the desired system or combination of systems. The center of the BIT display is divided into two "windows". The upper "in-test" window displays the systems in which an initiated BIT is being performed. The lower "equipment failure" window displays the system(s) that are turned off, not installed or have failed BIT.

Initiated BIT

In addition to displaying the system BIT status the BIT display is used to command an initiated BIT. Those systems identified by the options on the display periphery have initiated BIT capability (figure 1-12). The basic BIT format is altered slightly depending on whether the aircraft is on the ground or airborne. AFCS, DSPL, ADC, EXCS and INS are displayed only when on the ground. AIU, RALT and LANT are removed when in armed TF. The BIT is initiated from either cockpit by pressing the button adjacent to the desired option. When a BIT is initiated the other options are removed and the STOP option is displayed. Pressing STOP button will terminate the BIT in process. If STOP is pressed while an LRU is performing BIT and the LRU remains locked in BIT for 5 seconds or longer, ESCAPE will replace the STOP legend. If ESCAPE is pressed, the BIT routines in the CC are reset so BIT can proceed on other systems. ESCAPE should only be used as a last resort to abort the initiated BIT after STOP has failed. System lockup may occur when ESCAPE is pressed.

BIT may be initiated one at a time or in certain combinations. In the case of AFCS and PACS, additional switchology is required. Selection of AUTO BIT, causes a simultaneous BIT of a majority of the avionic equipment. Refer to AUTO BIT.

NOTE

During ground operation, the DSPL legend on the BIT menu will not be displayed when either of the below conditions exist :

a. A top level armament display has been selected on any MPD/MPCD.

b. A nuclear display is selected which does not have the MENU legend displayed next to PB 11.

The above condition will exist if either a. or b. above was previously selected on any MPD/MPCD even though that MPD/MPCD is turned off. If a DSPL

BIT is required on the ground and DSPL legend is not displayed, turn on all MPD/MPCD. Deselect any top level armament or nuclear displays.

AUTO BIT

If the AUTO button is pressed, BIT are initiated in time sequence for systems turned on. Prerequisites for ground AUTO BIT are: the PACS, HUD, and other peripherals must be turned on and the radar timed in (if included). The sequence is initiated by pressing the pushbutton adjacent to AUTO and will take 3 1/2 to 4 minutes to run if radar is included or 1 minute if radar is OFF. The systems are displayed in the "in-test" window as they perform BIT and are removed when complete. The minimum time any equipment will be displayed is two seconds. If a failure is detected, the system is removed from the "in-test" window and is displayed in the "failure" window. When an LRU with an asterisk is displayed as no-go, DETAIL information may be available. If STOP is selected, all systems tests will be terminated, except the radar, ICSCP, and radar altimeter, which will continue to run. The following systems are tested during AUTO BIT:

AAI	IBS
ADC	ICS
ADF	IFF
AIM	M/4
AIU 1A	MPDP
AIU 1B	RALT
AIU 2	RDR
CMD	RMR
COMM	RWR
EMD	TCN
EWW	FWD UFC
EXCS	AFT UFC.

EXCS, ADC and MPDP are not tested during AUTO BIT when airborne. The radar altimeter is not tested during AUTO BIT when airborne if the TF radar is turned on (Armed TF/Fly-up).

BIT DISPLAY

(TYPICAL)

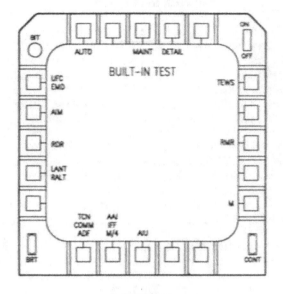

AIRBORNE

GROUND

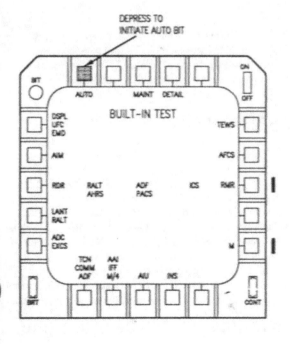

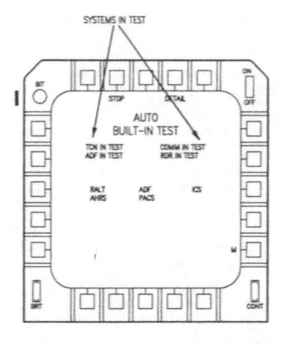

FUNCTIONAL FAILURES

Functional status information is provided on the DETAIL BIT display for the AFCS, TGT Pod, navigation FLIR and terrain following radar. This information is supplementary and may trigger the MASTER CAUTION light. When AFCS, TGT FLIR, NAV FLIR or TF RDR are displayed on any BIT format, check the DETAIL page for functional failure information. Refer to Section 3 for the meaning of AFCS functional failures. Refer to TO 1F-15E-34-1-1 for functional failure meanings for the LANTIRN system.

AFCS PREFLIGHT INITIATED BIT

For the AFCS, the BIT button on the CAS panel in the front cockpit must be pressed and held when BIT is initiated from the BIT display. This prevents inadvertent initiation of BIT on the AFCS for reasons of flight safety. AFCS BIT is terminated by pressing the paddle switch on the control stick or the STOP button on the BIT display. If AFCS BIT is interrupted, the message INCOMPLETE is displayed in the lower display window. Reinitiate AFCS BIT to clear the INCOMPLETE legend. Running a successful AFCS BIT will clear the INCOMPLETE. If the INS is powered, holding brake must be ON to perform AFCS initiated BIT.

CENTRAL COMPUTER (CC)

The central computer (CC) is a high speed, stored program, general purpose digital computer that performs mission oriented computation from data received from control panels and subsystems aboard the aircraft. The computations include A/A and A/G steering and weapon delivery, navigation, flight director, and control and display management. The CC provides the aircrew with steering and weapon delivery cues, target data, avionic system status, weapons configuration and flight data in the air-to-air attack, air-to-ground attack, visual identification (VI), and navigation (NAV) modes of operation. The CC computations are controlled by the operational flight program stored in the CC memory. Failure detection of the peripheral systems and CC internal operation is done by continual monitoring. Back up system substitution is also accomplished in the central computer. If the computer detects a power loss or failure there is a drastic change in the display formats. In the front cockpit, the left MPD displays the radar A/A format (with A/G format selectable), the MPCD displays ADI, the right MPD displays TEWS, and the HUD shows a backup format. In the rear cockpit, the left MPCD displays ADI, the left MPD has a radar display, the right MPD displays TEWS, and the right MPCD displays TSD.

CENTRAL COMPUTER INTERFACE

The central computer is interfaced with the radar, Programmable Armament Control System (PACS), AFCS, Air Data Computer (ADC), Attitude Heading Reference System (AHRS), Multipurpose Display System, Head Up Display (HUD), Signal Data Recorder (SDR), Radar Warning Receiver (RWR), Inertial Navigation Unit (INU), the Engine Diagnostic Unit (EDU), and the Avionics Status Panel. On F-15E 86-0183 THRU 87-0210 (BEFORE TO1F-15E-542), the CC also interfaces with the lead computing gyro (LCG). A CC reset is performed by pressing the CC reset button on the front cockpit sensor control panel. The CC reset should be initiated only if a CC problem is suspected.

MISSION NAVIGATOR (MN)

NOTE

If the CC is replaced, an INS precision velocity update (PVU) is required to correct for pointing errors. Refer to TO 1F-15E-34-1-1 for update procedures.

The CC maintains a MN routine separate from the INS. The MN integrates PVU corrected velocities for use in weapon delivery modes. It also provides relative target ranges in platform coordinates and allows position updates independent of the INS.

MULTIPLEX BUS (MUX BUS)

Coded messages are transmitted between the CC and remote terminals in both directions on the multiplex bus. The coded messages are in serial digital format. The CC (or MPDP in backup mode) establishes communications on the avionics 1553 mux bus by scheduling all messages. Messages are blocks of data that contain the total information to be transferred. The blocks of data in a message are called words. There are three types of words : command, status and data. The CC (or MPDP in backup mode) gives commands, inspects status and receives/sends data.

AVIONICS INTERFACE UNITS (AIU)

The avionics interface unit set consists of two avionics interface units, AIU no. 1 and AIU no. 2. The AIU set controls, processes, and routes interfacing signals between multiple aircraft systems. The table below lists the units and data that are lost if an AIU fails.

The AIU set communicates with the CC by way of the avionics 1553 mux bus. During backup mode, when the CC has failed, the AIU set will communicate with the multipurpose display processor (MPDP). Data which is transferred between the AIU set and the CC is listed below:

1. BIT data - aircraft systems and AIU set

2. Up-front display and control data

3. Aircraft systems discretes, mode, control, and status data

4. Cautions, warnings, and advisories

5. UHF and IFF initialization

6. Memory inspect data

System/Items Degraded/Function Lost Due To AIU Catastrophic Failure

Failed AIU	Item Degraded	Data Lost
AIU1(A)	UHF no. 1 radio	No Operation
AIU1(A)	All MPD/MPCD displayed cautions (except LOW ALT and LASER)	No longer displayed
AIU1(A)	TACAN	No operation
AIU1(A)	IFF/RICP (IFF functions)	No operation
AIU1(A)	ADF	No operation
AIU1(A)	UHF2 Cipher	No operation
AIU1(A)	KY-58	Function lost
AIU1(A)	EWWS	BIT function lost
AIU1(A)	PACS (missile caged and missile reject)	No operation
AIU1(B)	Left hand controller	All switch functions lost except for CMD dispenser switch
AIU1(B)	Fuel flow on MPD/MPCD	No data transfer (erroneous fuel flow data displayed)
AIU1(B)	ILS	No operation
AIU1(A) & (B)	Avionics BIT and ASP	No operation
AIU1(A) & (B)	Asymmetric thrust departure function	Function lost
AIU2	UHF 2 radio	No operation
AIU2	Right hand controller	Functions lost
AIU2	AAI	Function lost

System/Items Degraded/Function Lost Due To AIU Catastrophic Failure

Failed AIU	Item Degraded	Data Lost
AIU2	KIR	Function lost
AIU2	HF COMM (Not used)	No operation
AIU2	FWD/ REAR sensor control panel	No system control
AIU2	LANTIRN (NAV and Targeting)	All operation lost
AIU1(A) and AIU2	Radar altimeter (CARA)	No data transfer (Erroneous data display)
AIU1(A) and AIU2	Emission limit	No operation
AIU1(A) and AIU2	EMD (BIT data AIU1(A), BIT discretes - AIU2, serial data)	No operation
AIU1(A) and AIU2	ICSCP	No COMM transmit capability
AIU1(A) and AIU2	Control stick grip	All switch functions lost except weapon release and trigger
AIU1(A) and AIU2	UFC panel (both)	No operation
AIU1(A) or AIU2	TF function (Requires CARA data from both AIU1(A) and AIU2)	No operation
AIU1(A) and AIU2	LOW ALT warning	Indication lost
AIU1(B) and AIU2	FWD throttle	All switch functions lost
AIU1(B) and AIU2	FWD sensor control panel	No system control
AIU1(B) and AIU2	Master modes	No operation
AIU1(B) and AIU2	LASER ARMED warning	Indication lost

DATA TRANSFER MODULE SET (DTMS)

The Data Transfer Module Set (DTMS) consists of the main instrument panel Data Transfer Module Receptacle (DTMR) and the Data Transfer Module (DTM). Mission data is loaded, by the aircrew or operations personnel, on the ground and stored in the module. The module is carried to the aircraft, inserted into the DTM receptacle to initialize mission data (sequence points, TACAN data, weapons loading, A/A radar programming, radio programming and IFF programming). Refer to TO 1F-15E-34-1-1 for further details.

The DTM read function transfers mission data for sequence points, TACAN stations, list points, HUD titler, crew station display programming, radar display programming, communications, IFF modes and codes, PACS A/G programs (combat or training modes) and PACS weapon loaded data (combat or training modes).

The DTM write function receives mission data from the CC by way of the MPDP for HUD titler, A/A or A/G engagement, NAV (mark point), INS (alignment/terminal errors), OWS (warning data and peak matrix), caution advisories, engine monitor, avionics BIT monitor, terrain following data and AFCS data.

NOTE

The pilot needs to clear the CC buffer using the DTM display format after taxi. Refer to TO 1F-15E-34-1-1.

CONTROL STICK
(FRONT COCKPIT)

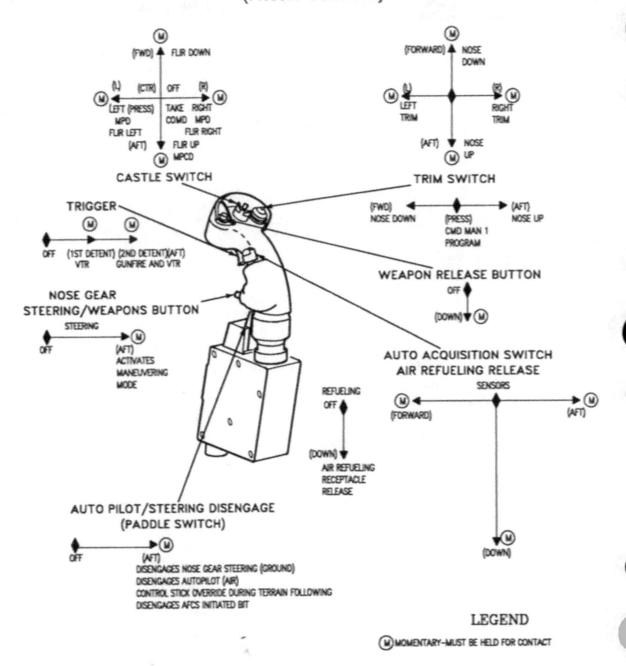

Figure 1-13 (Sheet 1 of 4)

15E-1-(4-1)06-CATI

FRONT COCKPIT CONTROLS

CONTROL STICK
(FRONT)

SWITCH	USE	SWITCH POSITION/ACTION				
WEAPON RELEASE BUTTON	WEAPON SYSTEM	PRESSED				
		WEAPON CONSENT/ RELEASE				
	VTRS	PRESSED				
		PROGRAMMED RE-CORDING ENABLE				
CASTLE	DISPLAY SCROLL	FOR-WARD	AFT	LEFT	RIGHT	PRESS
			MPCD	LEFT MPD	RIGHT MPD	
	DISPLAY TAKE COMMAND (PRESS AND RELEASE FIRST)	HUD	MPCD	LEFT MPD	RIGHT MPD	TAKE COMMAND ENABLE
	NAV FLIR (THROTTLE COOLIE DOWN SIMULTANEOUSLY	SNAP LOOK DOWN	SNAP LOOK UP	SNAP LOOK LEFT	SNAP LOOK RIGHT	
	CAUTION CONTROL (MASTER CAUTION LIGHT PRESSED SIMULTANEOUSLY		MPCD	LEFT MPD	RIGHT MPD	
TRIM		NOSE DOWN	NOSE UP	LEFT WING DOWN	RIGHT WING DOWN	CMD MANUAL 1 PROGRAM
GUN TRIGGER		FIRST DETENT	SECOND DETENT			RELEASE
		START CAMERA VIDEO	FIRE GUN			STOP FIRE GUN/ CAMERA

Figure 1-13 (Sheet 2)

CONTROL STICK (CONT)
(FRONT)

SWITCH	USE	SWITCH POSITION/ACTION			
		FOR-WARD	AFT	DOWN	RELEASE
AUTO ACQUISITION SWITCH	TARGETING FLIR (MANUAL)	NARROW /WIDE FOV	RETURN TO CUE	TRACK/ UNTRACK MN RESET 2	
	HRM	SMALLER WINDOW	1 LARGER WINDOW	MODE REJECT MN RESET 2	
	RBM	SMALLER WINDOW	LARGER WINDOW	MODE REJECT MN RESET 2	
	A/A RADAR	SS/BST-HIGH DATA RATE TWS/RAM	VERTICAL SCAN-NORMAL TWS	MODE REJECT	
	TSD	SMALLER CUE FOOT-PRINT	LARGER CUE FOOT-PRINT	RETURN TO P.P.MAP	
	AIR REFUELING			AIR REFUEL-ING PROBE DISEN-GAGE	
	A/G GUIDED WEAPON	CAGE/ UNCAGE		SLEW ENABLE	TRACK COMMAND
	A/G HUD		AUTO/ CDIP CDIP/ DIRECT		

Figure 1-13 (Sheet 3)

CONTROL STICK (CONT)
(FRONT)

SWITCH	USE	SWITCH POSITION/ACTION	
		PRESS AND RELEASE	PRESS AND HOLD
NOSEWHEEL STEERING BUTTON	WEIGHT ON WHEELS		MANEUVER MODE NOSE GEAR STEERING
	A/A WEAPONS	CAGE/UNCAGE	
	A/G GUIDED WEAPON	CAGE/UNCAGE	
		PRESS	PRESS AND HOLD
PADDLE SWITCH	AUTOMATIC FLIGHT CONTROL SYSTEM (AFCS)	DISENGAGE AUTOPILOT	TERRAIN FOLLOWING CONTROL STICK OVER-RIDE
	WEIGHT ON WHEELS	TERMINATES AFCS BIT	DISENGAGE NOSE GEAR STEERING

NOTE

1 ▸ PATTERN STEERING LINE ENABLE/DISABLE WHEN CURSOR FUNCTION IS TARGET

2 ▸ WHEN CURSOR FUNCTION IS MN UPDATE

Figure 1-13 (Sheet 4)

THROTTLE QUADRANT
(FRONT)

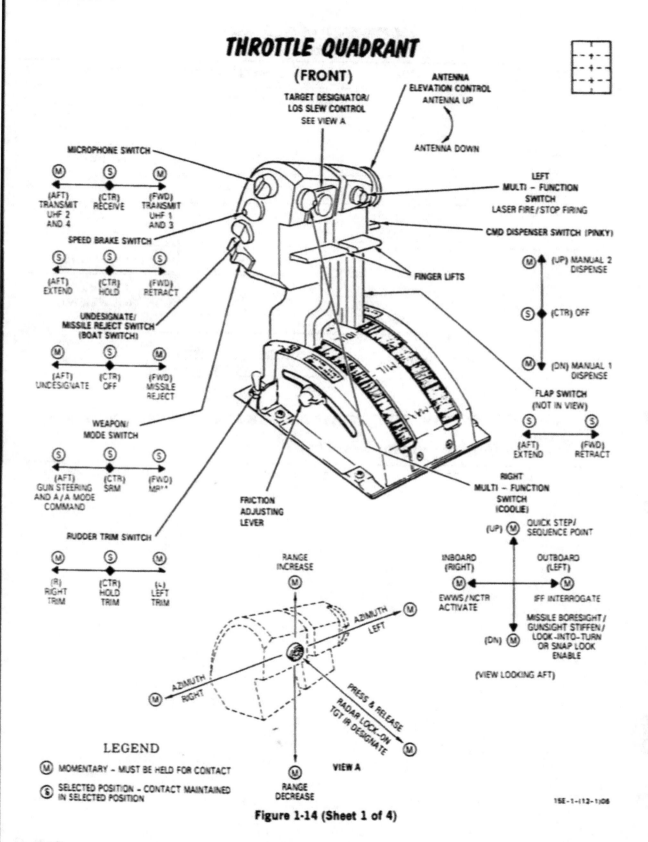

LEGEND

Ⓜ MOMENTARY – MUST BE HELD FOR CONTACT

Ⓢ SELECTED POSITION – CONTACT MAINTAINED IN SELECTED POSITION

15E-1-(12-1)06

Figure 1-14 (Sheet 1 of 4)

THROTTLE QUADRANT
(FRONT)

SWITCH	USE	SWITCH POSITION/ACTION		
COMMUNICATIONS	COMM	FORWARD	AFT	
		TRANSMIT ON RADIO 1 OR RADIO 3	TRANSMIT ON RADIO 2 OR RADIO 4	
BOAT		FORWARD	AFT	
	A/A RADAR	MISSILE REJECT	TARGET UNDESIGNATE	
	TARGETING FLIR		UNDESIGNATE	
	HRM/RBM/BCN SET		UNDESIGNATE TARGET/PSL	
	A/G GUIDED WEAPON	MISSILE REJECT	TARGET UNDESIGNATE	
SPEED BRAKE		FORWARD	CENTER	AFT
		RETRACT	HOLD	EXTEND
WEAPON MODE SELECT	WEAPON SYSTEM	FORWARD	CENTER	AFT
		MRM	SRM	GUN

Figure 1-14 (Sheet 2)

THROTTLE QUADRANT (CONT)
(FRONT)

SWITCH	USE	SWITCH POSITION/ACTION			
		UP	DOWN	IN-BOARD	OUT-BOARD
COOLIE	TARGETING FLIR	SE-QUENCE POINT SELECT			
	HRM/RBM BCN/SET PVU/TSD	SE-QUENCE POINT SELECT	MISSILE BS/ GUN-SIGHT STIFFEN/ LOOK INTO TURN ENABLE	EWWS/ NCTR ACTI-VATE	IFF INTER-ROGATE
	A/A RADAR	QUICK STEP			
	A/G GUIDED WEAPON		WEAPON BORE-SIGHT		
TDC		PRESS		RELEASE	
	TARGETING FLIR	LOS CONTROL ENABLE		DESIGNATION	
	HRM/RBM	CURSOR CONTROL ENABLE		DESIGNATION	
	A/A RADAR (ACQUISITION SYMBOL CONTROL)	RADAR SEARCH MODE -MINI RASTER		TARGET DESIGNATION	
	TSD	RANGE/BEARING LINE CONTROL		CUE COMMAND	
	A/G GUIDED WEAPON	LOS CONTROL			
	NAV/A/G HUD (HUD TD CIRCLE/ DIAMOND CONTROL)	LOS COMMAND ENABLE		DESIGNATION	
	NAV FLIR	ELECTRICAL BORESIGHT SLEW			

Figure 1-14 (Sheet 3)

THROTTLE QUADRANT (CONT)
(FRONT)

SWITCH	USE	SWITCH POSITION/ACTION	
LASER FIRE BUTTON		**PRESS AND RELEASE**	
	TARGETING FLIR	LASER FIRE/STOP FIRING	
	HRM/RBM	FREEZE/UNFREEZE	
	A/A RADAR		
	HUD	☐1 VELOCITY VECTOR CAGE/UNCAGE	
	TSD	TRACK/UNTRACK	
THUMBWHEEL	RADAR	**ROTATE**	
		ELEVATION RATE CONTROL	
PINKY	COUNTER MEASURES DISPENSER	**UP**	**DOWN**
		MANUAL NO. 2 (SEMIAUTOMATIC)	MANUAL NO.1
NOTE			
☐1 Must be 'In Command' of HUD and in NAV or INST Master Mode.			

Figure 1-14 (Sheet 4)

CONTROL STICK
(REAR COCKPIT)

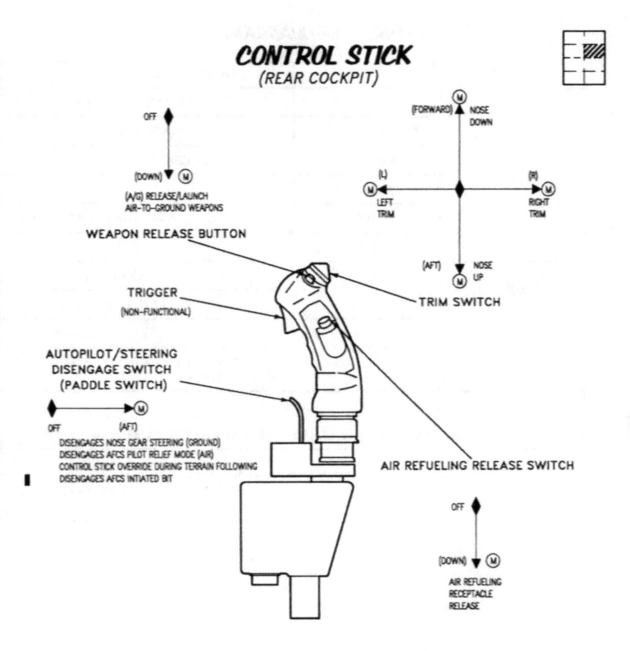

OFF

(DOWN)

(A/G) RELEASE/LAUNCH
AIR-TO-GROUND WEAPONS

(FORWARD) NOSE
DOWN

(L)
LEFT
TRIM

(R)
RIGHT
TRIM

(AFT) NOSE
UP

WEAPON RELEASE BUTTON

TRIGGER
(NON-FUNCTIONAL)

TRIM SWITCH

AUTOPILOT/STEERING
DISENGAGE SWITCH
(PADDLE SWITCH)

OFF   (AFT)

DISENGAGES NOSE GEAR STEERING (GROUND)
DISENGAGES AFCS PILOT RELIEF MODE (AIR)
CONTROL STICK OVERRIDE DURING TERRAIN FOLLOWING
DISENGAGES AFCS INITIATED BIT

AIR REFUELING RELEASE SWITCH

OFF

(DOWN)

AIR REFUELING
RECEPTACLE
RELEASE

15E-1-(4-5)03-CAT)

Figure 1-15 (Sheet 1 of 2)

REAR COCKPIT CONTROLS

CONTROL STICK
(REAR)

SWITCH	USE	SWITCH POSITION/ACTION			
		FWD	AFT	LEFT	RIGHT
TRIM	FLIGHT CONTROL TRIM	NOSE UP	NOSE DOWN	LEFT WING DOWN	RIGHT WING DOWN
WEAPON RELEASE BUTTON	WEAPON RELEASE	PRESSED			
	WEAPON SYSTEM	A/G WEAPON RELEASE IF IN A/G MASTER MODE			
	VTRS	PRESSED			
		PROGRAMMED RECORD ENABLE			
AIR REFUELING DISENGAGE		AIR REFUELING PROBE DISENGAGE			
PADDLE SWITCH	AUTOMATIC FLIGHT CONTROL SYSTEM (AFCS)	PRESS		PRESS AND HOLD	
		DISENGAGE AUTOPILOT			
	WEIGHT ON WHEELS	TERMINATES AFCS BIT		DISENGAGE NOSE GEAR STEERING	

Figure 1-15 (Sheet 2)

THROTTLE QUADRANT
(REAR)

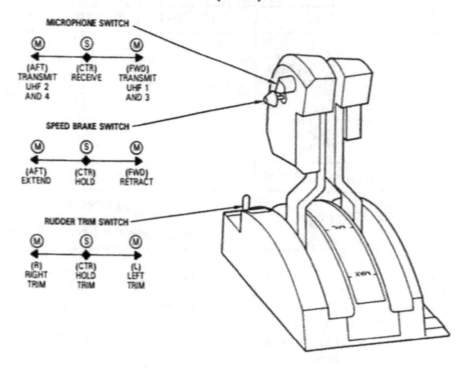

MICROPHONE SWITCH

(M)   (S)   (M)

(AFT)   (CTR)   (FWD)
TRANSMIT   RECEIVE   TRANSMIT
UHF 2   UHF 1
AND 4   AND 3

SPEED BRAKE SWITCH

(M)   (S)   (M)

(AFT)   (CTR)   (FWD)
EXTEND   HOLD   RETRACT

RUDDER TRIM SWITCH

(M)   (S)   (M)

(R)   (CTR)   (L)
RIGHT   HOLD   LEFT
TRIM   TRIM   TRIM

15E-1-(12-5)A

Figure 1-16 (Sheet 1 of 2)

THROTTLE QUADRANT
(REAR)

SWITCH	USE	SWITCH POSITION/ACTION		
COMMUNICA-TION	RADIOS	FORWARD		AFT
		TRANSMIT ON RADIO 1 OR RADIO 3		TRANSMIT ON RADIO 2 OR RADIO 4
SPEED BRAKE	SPEED BRAKE	FORWARD	CENTER (SPRING LOADED)	AFT
		RETRACT	SPEED BRAKE RESPONDS TO FRONT COCKPIT POSITION COMMAND	EXTEND
TRIM	RUDDER TRIM	RIGHT	CENTER	LEFT
		RIGHT TRIM	HOLD TRIM	LEFT TRIM

Figure 1-16 (Sheet 2)

HAND CONTROLLERS

The left and right hand controllers (figure 1-17) located on the forward inboard section of the left and right rear cockpit consoles, are used to provide sensor/display control.

HAND CONTROLLERS
(REAR COCKPIT)

LEFT CONTROLLER

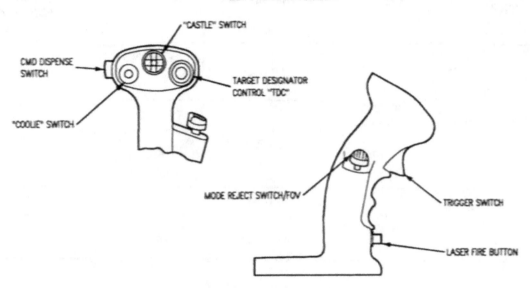

CMD DISPENSE SWITCH

"CASTLE" SWITCH

TARGET DESIGNATOR CONTROL "TDC"

"COOLIE" SWITCH

MODE REJECT SWITCH/FOV

TRIGGER SWITCH

LASER FIRE BUTTON

RIGHT CONTROLLER

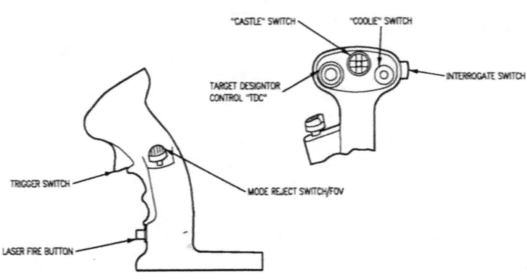

"CASTLE" SWITCH

"COOLIE" SWITCH

INTERROGATE SWITCH

TARGET DESIGNTOR CONTROL "TDC"

TRIGGER SWITCH

MODE REJECT SWITCH/FOV

LASER FIRE BUTTON

15E-1-(184-1)04-CAT1

Figure 1-17 (Sheet 1 of 4)

HAND CONTROLLERS
(REAR COCKPIT)

SWITCH	USE	SWITCH POSITION/ACTION				
		TRANSDUCER			PRESS AND RELEASE	
TDC	TARGET-ING FLIR	LOS CONTROL				
	HRM	CURSOR CONTROL			`1` EXPAND	
	RBM	CURSOR/`1` EL CONTROL				
	A/A RADAR	ACQUISITION SYMBOL/ `1` EL CONTROL				
	TSD	RANGE/BEARING LINE CONTROL				
	A/G GUIDED WEAPON	LOS CONTROL				
COOLIE	LEFT/ RIGHT CON-TROLLER	FORWARD	AFT	LEFT	RIGHT	
		SCROLL MPD	SCROLL MPCD	TAKE COMMAND LEFT DISPLAY/ `6` MOVE CAUTIONS	TAKE COMMAND RIGHT DISPLAY/ `6` MOVE CAUTIONS	
RIGHT CON-TROLLER INTERRO-GATE		FORWARD	AFT			
		IFF INTER ROGATE	EWWS AND NCTR ACTIVATE			
LEFT CON-TROLLER CMD DISPENSE		FORWARD	AFT			
		MANUAL 1	MANUAL 2 (SEMI-AUTOMATIC)			

Figure 1-17 (Sheet 2)

HAND CONTROLLERS (CONT)
(REAR COCKPIT)

SWITCH	USE	SWITCH POSITION/ACTION		
		FIRST DETENT	FIRST DETENT AND RELEASE	SECOND DETENT
TRIGGER	TARGETING FLIR		TRACK/UNTRACK	DESIGNATION CUE UPDATE
	HRM	EXPAND ENABLE/ PPI RANGE CHANGE ENABLE		DESIGNATION CUE UPDATE
	A/A RADAR	ELEVATION SLEW ENABLE		TARGET DESIGNATION
	RBM/BCN	ELEVATION SLEW ENABLE/PPI RANGE CHANGE ENABLE		DESIGNATION CUE UPDATE
	TSD		TRACK/UNTRACK	CUE COMMAND
	A/G GUIDED WEAPON	SLEW ENABLE	TRACK COMMAND	
MODE REJECT/ FOV		FORWARD	AFT	DOWN
	TARGET-ING FLIR (MANUAL)	NARROW/ WIDE FOV	RETURN TO CUE	UNDESIGNATE/ 5 MN RESET
	HRM/RBM	SMALLER WINDOW/RANGE 4	LARGER WINDOW/ RANGE 2 4	MODE REJECT/ 3 PSL/UN-DESIGNATE/ 5 MN RESET
	A/A RADAR	HIGH DATA RATE TWS/RAM	NORMAL TWS	MODE REJECT
	TSD	SMALLER CUE FOOTPRINT	LARGER CUE FOOTPRINT	RETURN TO P.P.
	A/G GUIDED WEAPON	NARROW/WIDE FOV	RETURN TO CUE	MISSILE REJECT

Figure 1-17 (Sheet 3)

HAND CONTROLLERS (CONT)
(REAR COCKPIT)

SWITCH	USE	SWITCH POSITION/ACTION				
LASER FIRE BUTTON	TARGETING FLIR	LASER FIRE/STOP FIRE				
	HRM/RBM	FREEZE/UNFREEZE				
	A/G GUIDED WEAPON	CAGE/UNCAGE				
		FORWARD	AFT	LEFT	RIGHT	PRESS
CASTLE	TARGET FLIR		TARGET	CUE	UPDATE	SEQUENCE POINT SELECT
	HRM/RBM	MAP	TARGET	CUE	UPDATE	SEQUENCE POINT SELECT
	BCN	MAP	TARGET			SEQUENCE POINT SELECT
	SET		TARGET	CUE	UPDATE	SEQUENCE POINT UPDATE
	TSD	RADAR CUE	FLIR CUE			SEQUENCE POINT SELECT
	A/A RADAR	MRM SEARCH MODE	SRM SEARCH MODE	TARGET UN-DESIG-NATE	MISSILE REJECT	QUICK STEP
	A/G GUIDED WEAPON	BORE-SIGHT				

NOTE

1	MUST ARM WITH TRIGGER 1/2 ACTION.
2	PATTERN STEERING LINE ENABLE/DISABLE WHEN CURSOR FUNCTION IS TARGET.
3	WHEN CURSOR FUNCTION IS TARGET.
4	CHANGES PPI RANGE WHEN TRIGGER SWITCH IS AT FIRST DETENT.
5	WHEN CURSOR ACTION IS UPDATE (MN).
6	WITH MC PRESSED.

Figure 1-17. (Sheet 4)

UPFRONT CONTROLS (UFC)

The upfront controls in the front and rear cockpit are the major interface units for control of avionics subsystems. The UFC consists of 10 functions buttons, six 20-character rows of display, four radio volume controls, two rotary switches, a 20 key data entry keyboard, a rotary brightness control knob, and an EMIS LMT pushbutton (figure 1-18). The UFC Built-in test (BIT) is implemented in three levels; basic self test, initiated BIT and continuous BIT. Basic self test is run each time the unit comes out of the off mode. Initiated BIT is run in response to the BIT initiate discrete input.

The third level of BIT is continuous as performed in normal operation. This method depends on the aircrew observation because of the large number of switches and display segments. Each level of BIT is desensitized such that a single glitch will not cause a no-go indication. The UFC provides control of the following systems:

a. Inertial Navigation System (INS) - data entry and display
b. Tacan
c. Auto pilot - attitude hold, altitude hold, radar preset altitude, and steer modes
d. Terrain Following (TF)
e. IFF/SIF
f. AAI
g. UHF Radios - including ADF and KY-58
h. ILS
i. NAV FLIR
j. JMC and JVC - (Future growth associated with JTIDS)
k. A/G stores delivery bias

Either of the two UFC's controls all systems and each is driven by its own processor (an AIU) with paths to the other AIU. This provides a redundancy when a UFC or processor failure occurs.

The UFC panel alphanumeric pushbutton keys as well as the other pushbuttons are read by the CC. Numbers 0-9 or letters A,N,B,W,M,E,S,C, - (dash), decimal point and colon are available.

0-9 Key	Enters number
SHF (shift) Key	Enables upper case functions on next key pressed

A/P Key	Selects autopilot format and couples autopilot
MARK Key	Mark and selects marked point for display
MENU Key	Selects menu format 1st Push - MENU 1 2nd Push - MENU 2 3rd Push - MENU 1
DATA Key	Selects data display format 1st Push - DATA 1 2nd Push - DATA 2 3rd Push - DATA 1
CLR (clear) Key	Three functions on successive pushes 1st Push - Removes last character entered 2nd Push - Clears all scratchpad 3rd Push - Clears display except radio data. Press one of the top 8 pushbuttons to recall the top 4 lines. All keyboard entries are active but data entry may be made for radios only. The scratchpad is enabled for display. If any of the top eight pushbuttons are pressed with data in the scratchpad the entry is invalid and the scratchpad flashes. If data is displayed, the CLR key blanks the scratchpad only. 4th Push - Clears all 6 rows of display. When all 6 rows are blanked; the scratchpad is not displayed and no data entry is permitted. MARK, A/P, DATA, MENU, I/P and EMIS LMIT are the only active keyboard keys.
I/P Key	Initiates IFF identification of Position (I/P)
Decimal Point (.) Key	Enters decimal point

GREC C/M Key	Left or Right key enables/disables guard receiver or changes between preset channel and manual frequency on appropriate radio
VOL R1,R2,R3,R4	Volume control for selected radio
EMIS LMT Key	Limits electronic emissions from the aircraft for passive operations. The low probability of intercept terrain following radar mode is automatically selected if TF radar is active, and other electronic emitters are switched to standby. The EMIS LMT light comes on when first selected. When pushbutton is pressed again the emission limit is deselected and most emitters return to their previous state of operation. However, tacan T/R must be reselected, TF must be reset and all IFF modes must be reselected or phasing re-enabled on the UFC.
BRT	Controls brightness of LCD displays
Left and Right Rotary/Depress Knobs	Pressing left knob selects between UHF 1 and JTIDS. Rotating the knobs selects radio channels 1 thru 20 and guard transmitter for appropriate radio. Pressing the right knob has no function at this date.

The UFC multifunction buttons are used as the options indicate except buttons 5 and 6 which are dedicated to radios/submenu displays. Buttons are numbered 1 thru 10 beginning at the top left. PB 1 thru 5 are top to bottom on the left. PB 6 thru 10 are top to bottom on the right.

UFC DISPLAYS

NOTE

When making an entry requiring a decimal point, the decimal point must be entered, except for manual UHF frequencies.

Since a large number of system functions have been integrated into the UFC several menus or display formats were developed. These displays are called data displays, menus, and submenus. There are 2 data displays, 2 menus and 19 submenus. Regardless of the data or submenu displayed, the radio communication information is always retained. The two data displays (DATA 1, DATA 2), menus (MENU 1, MENU 2), and the submenus pertaining to communications and radio navigation are described in the following paragraphs.

Data 1 Display

This displays current aircraft information. It is selected by pressing the DATA pushbutton on the UFC keyboard (Figure 1-18). On this format, pressing PB 1 shows LOS bearing and range to current steerpoint and ETE/ETA. The selection will initially power up to display steerpoint bearing and range. The PB may be pressed and released to toggle through the three selections. PB 2, 3 and 4 display calibrated, true and ground speeds respectively. Additionally, PB 3 and 4 control the display of true airspeed and groundspeed on the HUD and EADI formats (an asterisk is displayed on the UFC when the display is enabled). PB 7 displays either winds (from INS if in air data mode) or the CC clocktime (must be set each sortie by aircrew). The display will initially power-up to display time at PB 7. Radar (CARA) and baro-corrected altitudes are displayed by PB 8 and 9 respectively. In addition PB 8 controls the display of radar (CARA) altitude on the HUD and EADI formats (an asterisk is displayed on the UFC when display is enabled). PB 10 shows the current steerpoint. Steering can be changed by typing the new point in the scratchpad and entering it by pressing PB 10. Pressing PB 10 with a blank scratchpad calls up the point data submenu.

Data 2 Display

Pressing the DATA pushbutton a second time displays the data 2 display (figure 1-18). This display contains NAV data functions which provide the capability to determine what the remaining fuel will be at a selected sequence (steer or target) point, time enroute, and so forth. On the data 2 display, the sequence points are indicated by SP followed by the point number identifier; only steer and target points may be identified as sequence points (SP) on the data 2 display. Target 24, route alpha is the current line of

UFC DATA DISPLAYS

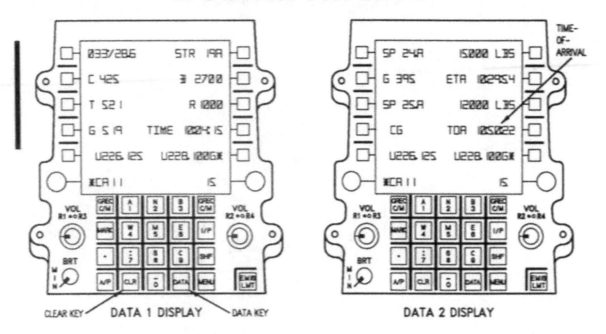

DATA 1 DISPLAY

DATA 2 DISPLAY

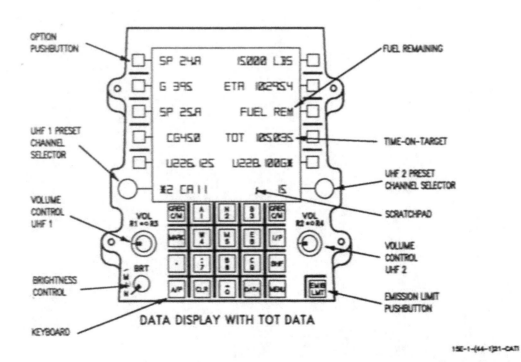

DATA DISPLAY WITH TOT DATA

15E-1-(44-1)21-CAT1

Figure 1-18

UFC MENU DISPLAYS

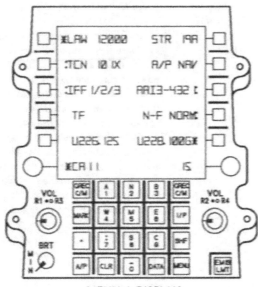

MENU 1 DISPLAY

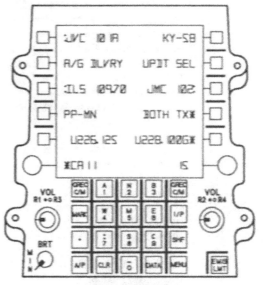

MENU 2 DISPLAY

15E-1-(41-1)21-CATI

Figure 1-19

sight point selected. As a result, the 15,000 pounds readout represents the amount of fuel remaining when the aircraft reaches the SP if the aircraft travels

at the current aircraft ground speed displayed, 395K, from the aircraft present position direct to SP24.A. Also shown is the calculated ETA to reach SP24.A. Pressing the pushbutton next to the ETA will provide the ETE. If range and bearing to SP24.A is desired, pressing the pushbutton next to the fuel remaining (15,000 lbs) will display the information.

Within the same format a second sequence point, SP25.A, is displayed automatically with data relating to it because it is the next point after the line-of-sight point with a time-on-target (TOT) assigned to it. The 12,000 lbs readout is estimated fuel remaining when

the aircraft gets to SP25.A. Pressing the pushbutton next to either time-of-arrival (TOA), fuel (12,000 lbs), or command ground (CG) speed will cause TOT to be displayed as shown on figure 1-18. This selection also displays the words FUEL REM in place of the fuel remaining, and CG speed to make the TOT is displayed next to CG. If no TOT has been stored for this point, OFF will appear next to TOT and CG. When CG is selected (asterisk) it will be displayed on the HUD just below AOA.

Menu 1 Display

Pressing the MENU pushbutton on the keyboard calls up the MENU 1 format (figure 1-19). The information displayed and controlled from menu 1 is described in the following paragraphs.

LAW The LAW (12000' AGL) with the asterisk displayed indicates the system has been enabled with the adjacent pushbutton and the low altitude voice warning and light will be activated if the aircraft first climbs above and then descends below the altitude (AGL) displayed. The LAW altitude is changed by keyboard entry into the scratchpad and pressing the pushbutton next to LAW (based on CARA).

TACAN The current tacan channel selected and operating is channel 101 mode X. The colon indicates power is on. Tacan channels are changed by keyboard entry of the new channel number into the scratchpad and pressing the pushbutton next to TCN. Turning the TACAN ON/OFF, changing between mode X or Y, and changing operating modes (A/A, TR or REC) is done from the TACAN submenu. Pressing with a clean scratchpad displays the TACAN submenu. Refer to TACAN system.

AAI Indicates the current air-to-air
3-4321 interrogation (AAI) mode and code (3-4321). Pressing with a blank scratchpad displays the AAI submenu. AAI modes and codes can be changed from this format using the procedure described under IFF, this section. Refer to TO 1F-15E-34-1-1 for detailed information.

N-F Indicates the current NORM
NORM mode/power status of the LANTIRN navigation FLIR. Pressing with a blank scratchpad displays the NAV FLIR submenu.

A/P NAV Indicates autopilot is engaged and current steer mode if any. In this case NAV steer mode. Pressing with a blank scratchpad displays the autopilot submenu.

IFF This IFF format indicates that
1/2/3 1/2/3 modes 1, 2, and 3 have been selected for operation. If only mode 3 had been selected, the 1 and 2 would not be displayed. If it is necessary to change mode 3's code, for example, first, press 3 to identify the mode to be changed, second, press SHF (shift) to select the upper case functions of the keyboard, third, select DASH (-), fourth, select the digital code, and fifth, enter the new code by pressing the pushbutton next to IFF. The entered mode and code is displayed for 5 seconds and is then replaced by only the enabled modes without codes. A colon indicates power is on. Modes are selected/deselected from the IFF submenu. IFF phasing selection and programming are also done from the IFF submenu. Refer to identification systems, this section, for more information.

TF Displays terrain following (TF) radar status (blank - OFF, N/R - not ready, STBY - standby) or correct TF submodes selected on TF display (NORM, Wx, ECCM, LPI or VLC). A colon is displayed if power is on. Refer to TO 1F-15E-34-1-1.

STR 19A Indicates that current steer (STR) point is number 19 route alpha (A). Steering to a new point is selected by typing the desired point in the scratchpad and pressing this pushbutton. Pressing this pushbutton with a blank scratchpad displays the point-data submenu.

Menu 2 Display

Menu 2 display (figure 1-19), is selected by a second pressing of the menu pushbutton. The information displayed is described in the following paragraphs.

JVC	JTIDS voice code (JVC) and
JMC	JTIDS mission code (JMC). For entry of JTIDS data. (Provisions only)
A/G DLVRY	Pressing this pushbutton displays the Air-to-Ground Delivery submenu
: ILS 109.70	Indicates current instrument landing system (ILS) localizer frequency selected, with the colon indicating it is being powered.
PP-MN	Pressing the pushbutton displays the PP keeping submenu (either INS, MN, TCN or A/D; current selection is mission navigator).
KY-58	Pressing this pushbutton displays a KY-58 submenu.
UPDT SEL	Pressing this pushbutton displays an update select submenu.

BOTH TX	Pressing the pushbutton displays an asterisk which permits transmission on both radio transmitters, either on the same or different frequencies provided neither radio is in a red mode (secure).

Submenus

Menu 1 and menu 2 provide access to submenus (figure 1-20) which contain selection of specific system functions. There are submenus for tacan, tacan programming, IFF, IFF programming, UHF 1, UHF 2, navigation FLIR, navigation FLIR boresight (from NAV FLIR), AAI, autopilot, point data latitude and longitude, UTM, UTM programming, point data range and bearing, direction and range offsets, present position keeping source, HUD titling, A/G delivery, update, and KY-58. Submenus can be selected when the scratchpad is blank by pressing the pushbutton next to the system of interest. For example, to select the IFF submenu, press the pushbutton next to IFF on the menu 1 display. Once displayed, system changes can be selected and made using keyboard entry. To return to either a menu or data display, press either the MENU or DATA pushbutton.

UFC MENU/SUBMENU MATRIX

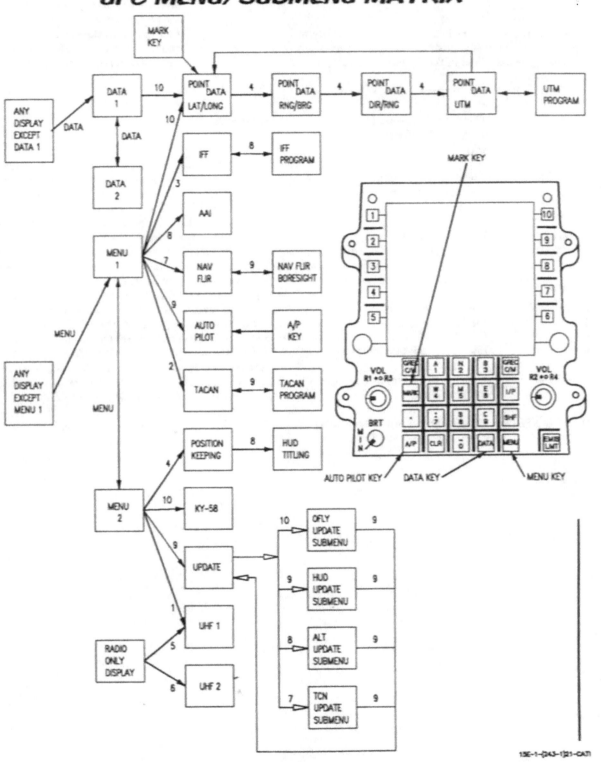

15E-1-(2)43-1(21-CA7)

Figure 1-20. (Sheet 1 of 2)

UFC MENU/SUBMENU MATRIX (Continued)

(CC INOP)

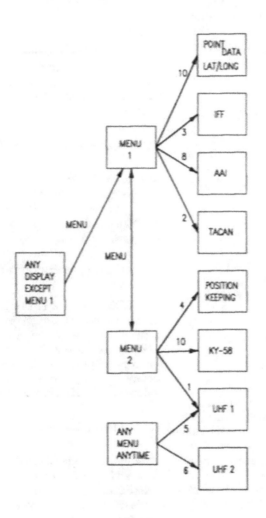

NOTES:
1. Numbers on the function lines represent multifunction
   switch actuations necessary to proceed to next menu/submenu.

Figure 1-20. (Sheet 2)

HEAD-UP DISPLAY (HUD)

The HUD control panel , (figure 1-21) is located on the main console. The holographic combiner displays projected raster (video) and stroke (symbols) imagery in a total field of view which measures 21° in elevation and 28 ° in azimuth. The HUD displays navigation, FLIR video, flight control and weapon delivery information.

HUD CONTROLS

Symbol Brightness (SYM BRT) Control

The SYM BRT control is a rotary knob. Clockwise rotation applies power to the HUD. This control adjusts brightness of the HUD stroke symbology only. Raster video imagery is not affected. A detented OFF position removes power from the HUD.

Symbol (SYM) Declutter Switch

The SYM switch is a three-position, toggle switch which removes and restores symbol information from the combiner display. REJ 1 and REJ 2 provide identical declutter functions. Selecting REJ 1 or REJ 2 for all master modes removes the Heading scale, Command Heading, Pitch Ladder, and Bank scale (provided TF radar is off). The NORM position restores all information.

DAY/AUTO/NIGHT Switch

The DAY, AUTO , NIGHT switch is a three-position, toggle switch which provides the pilot with a means to select appropriate raster and stroke imagery brightness levels for daytime or nighttime missions. The DAY position allows for the full range of the stroke symbology and raster video. The AUTO position provides automatic brightness adjustment of stroke symbology only based on ambient brightness data.

NOTE

The AUTO position does not provide adequate illumination at night.

The NIGHT position limits the brightness range of the stroke symbology and raster video to be compatible with night operations.

BIT Indicator

In normal operation, the BIT indicator is black. The BIT indicator is white when the HUD has failed. The BIT indicator resets when HUD power is cycled off and back on, or after a successful initiated BIT. If the fault condition still exists after either of the above, the BIT indicator will set white after approximately 60 seconds. When power is removed from the HUD, the BIT indicator holds at its last setting.

Test Button

When the momentary action pushbutton, located above the BIT indicator is pressed and held, an internally generated 18 X 28 FOV raster test pattern is displayed.

Video Brightness (VID BRT) Control

This rotary control fine adjusts the intensity of both the raster-generated video imagery and the stroke-generated symbology. This control ,usually left at the 12 o'clock position, is used to make the darkest shade of gray truly black.

Video Contrast (VID CONT) Control

The CONT control is a rotary, knob switch which adjusts the contrast level (shades of gray) of the raster generated video. Stroke generated symbology is not affected. When the CONT knob is ON, NAV FLIR imagery is processed for display on the HUD. A detented OFF position removes raster generated video from the HUD and restores NAV data in stroke.

Master Mode Switches

Four master mode switches are available : NAV, A/A, A/G and INST. When any of these switches are pressed, the light comes on to indicate that particular mode is selected. Only one master mode can be selected at a time.

SYSTEM POWER UP

Once aircraft electrical power is applied the HUD is turned on via the SYM BRT control and the raster via the VID CONT control.

HUD SYMBOLS

In this description, the following operational categories of HUD symbology are considered. Refer to figure 1-22.

HUD CONTROLS

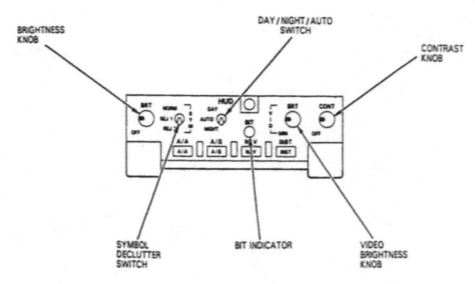

BRIGHTNESS KNOB

DAY / NIGHT / AUTO SWITCH

CONTRAST KNOB

SYMBOL DECLUTTER SWITCH

BIT INDICATOR

VIDEO BRIGHTNESS KNOB

15E-1-(245)04

Figure 1-21.

a. HUD nav, flight, and weapon delivery symbols that are common to most master modes (except A/G) and positioned depending on the weapon mode and sensor device selected.

b. HUD window displays, alphanumeric data with fixed locations.

Calibrated airspeed and barometric altitude data are displayed in digital format to remove graphics clutter and provide a direct readout of the data. Additionally, the crew can select true airspeed (T) or groundspeed (G) data and select radar (R) altitude for display. These selections are obtained through the UFC data 1 display.

Velocity Vector

The velocity vector displays the instantaneous aircraft flight path with respect to the earth. It is a small airplane symbol. The wings of the symbol always remain parallel to the wings of the aircraft. The vertical relationship between the waterline symbol (when displayed) and the velocity vector indicates

true AOA. Velocity vector azimuth displacement from HUD centerline indicates that drift (or a crab angle) is present. The vector symbol is limited to 8.5° radius of motion centered on the HUD. The velocity vector flashes if the data to the CC is degraded or the velocity vector is caged or limited.

The velocity vector may be caged by pressing the laser fire button on the throttle if in command of the HUD and in INST or NAV mode. Caging the velocity vector permits the velocity vector-referenced information (pitch ladder and steering information) to be retained near the center of the HUD when there are large yaw and/or crosswind angles.

Command Velocity

An analog command velocity wiper is displayed left of HUD window 1. The symbol rotates up and down from a horizontal position to indicate the difference between current aircraft speed and command velocity. The symbol rotation is limited from -80° to +80°, where 1° represents 1 knot of velocity. A positive angle signifies more velocity (forward throttle). The

HUD SYMBOLS

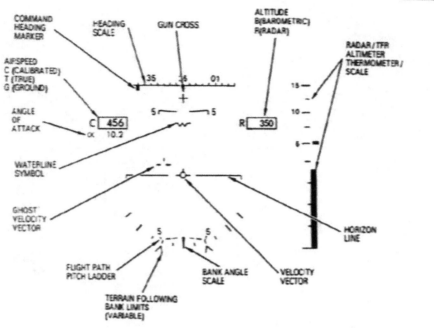

Figure 1-22

command velocity is based on groundspeed or true airspeed if selected on the UFC. Otherwise, command velocity is based on calibrated airspeed. If the command velocity source is invalid, this symbol is not displayed.

Ghost Velocity Vector

When the velocity vector is caged, a ghost velocity vector is displayed at the true velocity vector position. The symbol is presented during snap look and look into turn (NAV FLIR) operations. The pitch ladder and steering information are referenced to the caged position. The ghost velocity vector flashes when within 1.5° of the edge of the HUD.

Flight Path Pitch Ladder

The vertical flight path angle of the aircraft is indicated by the position of the flight path pitch ladder relative to the position of the velocity vector. The aircraft pitch attitude is indicated by the position of the aircraft waterline reference with respect to the pitch ladder about the stabilized wings of the velocity vector. The horizon line and the flight path pitch angle lines are displayed for each 5° between ±85°. Positive pitch lines are solid and negative pitch lines are dashed. The tabs at the end of each segment point toward the horizon. Each line has a number which maintains its orientation relative to the pitch ladder. The pitch lines themselves are angled (point) toward the horizon at an angle one-half the angle of pitch that the line represents. For example, the 40° positive pitch line angles 20° toward the horizon. The 90° dive point is indicated by a circle with an X enclosed. The 90° climb point is indicated by a circle.

The flight path pitch ladder is normally displayed in a position referenced to the velocity vector to provide flight path information. When the velocity vector becomes HUD-limited, the flight ladder does not transition back to the aircraft waterline symbol. The pitch ladder will always be referenced to the valid velocity vector while maintaining the artificial horizon on the horizon. If the velocity vector is not displayed, the pitch ladder is referenced to the aircraft waterline in azimuth and displays best available pitch referenced to the horizon. This transition may take up to two seconds.

The horizon bar is longer than other lines in the pitch scale and has tabs at each end that point toward the ground.

Heading Scale

The heading scale moves horizontally against a fixed caret index indicating aircraft magnetic heading from 0° through 360°. The two digit display is expressed in degrees x 10; e.g., 10° is displayed 01 and 250° is displayed 25.

The command heading marker (when displayed) moves against the scale and if the marker is limited, a digital readout of command heading is displayed at the end of the scale.

Bank Angle Scale

In terrain following operations with NAV or A/G master mode, a bank angle scale with tic marks 0°, 10°, 20°, 30°, 45°, and 60° is displayed at the bottom of the HUD. The 0° and 45° tic marks are double width. The 30° and 60° tic marks are double length. Terrain following bank angle limit carets are displayed against the scale. These limits are variable, however, which is indicated by positionable TF limit caret markers.

Waterline Symbol

An aircraft waterline position is indicated on the HUD by the display of a flying W symbol. The pitch ladder provides aircraft pitch attitude information when it is compared with the waterline symbol. If the velocity vector is not displayed, the pitch ladder slides to its waterline-referenced position in azimuth.

Gun Cross

The gun cross is fixed 2° above waterline in the azimuth center of the HUD and appears when the master arm switch is in ARM. The symbol indicates the projectile conversion point (without AOA or ballistic drop corrections) at the 2250-foot gun harmonization range. The symbol is also the position of the gun reticle pipper at zero mils depression (zero sight line). The gun cross is removed from the display by selecting the master arm switch SAFE position.

Reticle

The primary A/G reticle consists of a 50-mil circle, a 2-mil pipper (aim dot), and a range bar (analog bar) when radar A/G range is available. The reticle is displayed in all A/G attack modes when the CC and HUD are operable. The reticle is positioned in azimuth to one of several points, depending on the delivery mode selected.

    a. To the velocity vector (Auto mode).
    b. To the computed weapon impact point (CDIP mode).
    c. To the HUD depression angle set by the pilot (Direct and Manual modes via the UFC).
    d. To weapon boresight (when an EO guided weapon is selected).

Reticle Range Bar

When the CC receives valid laser and/or radar range data, the reticle range bar is displayed around the inside perimeter of the 50-mil reticle circle. The display priority is laser range and then radar range. The range bar, which rotates clockwise with increasing range, displays slant range from 0 to 23,000 feet. The range bar is limited to less than two revolutions around the perimeter of the reticle and contains an index to indicate the magnitude of the range displayed. The first revolution displays slant range from 0 to 12,000 feet and the second revolution displays slant range from 12,000 to 23,000 feet.

Break X

In the A/G master mode, a break X is displayed when the aircraft dive angle is greater than 3 degrees and the projected pullout altitude is below a specified level. The projected altitude is based on a 4.0-g pull attained in 2 seconds. If the TF radar is on, the BREAK X is based on 75% of the selected set clearance plane (SCP). If TF is not on, the pullout is based on the best available altitude. If radar altitude is available, the BREAK X is displayed if recovery is expected to occur below 200 feet. If baro altitude is used, the programmed altitude of the nearest sequence point is used to compute 400 ft ground clearance.

NOTE

In CDIP gun with pitch angles between -3° and -20°, 0 ft is used as minimum ground clearance altitude.

HUD WINDOWS

Figure 1-23 shows the location of the various windows. Windows 8, 9, and 12 are not fixed; they move dynamically as required. Windows 8 and 9 follow the location of the velocity vector. Window 12 follows the position of the range caret in the HUD radar range scale. When more than one item is commanded for display, the item highest in the list is displayed.

HUD Window 1

Aircraft calibrated airspeed is displayed. If the speed is invalid, OFF is displayed.

HUD Window 2

Aircraft AOA to the nearest tenth of a unit is displayed below the aircraft calibrated airspeed readout at all times.

HUD Window 2A

Aircraft true airspeed or groundspeed is displayed, preceded by T or G as selected on the Up-Front Control (UFC). If the selected airspeed source is invalid, the letter identifier and OFF is displayed.

HUD Window 3

This window displays the terrain following left turn obstacle (OBST) caution. The right turn caution is displayed in opposing window 15.

HUD Window 4

This window displays "IN CMD" legend when pilot has command of the HUD.

HUD Window 5

Emergency Cue

The emergency cue (legend "E" is displayed when the radar is in emergency mode.

Gun Rounds

The gun rounds display is a function of the number of rounds set on the weapon load display minus any rounds fired.

Missile Count

The type of missile loaded on the aircraft is identified by the PACS. With MRM selected, the display consists of M (MRM selected), the count of MRM's available for launch (STBY or RDY), and the type in priority for launch (A for AIM-120A; F or M for the AIM-7).

With SRM selected, the display is S (SRM selected), the total count of SRM's available for launch (in a STBY or RDY status), and the type in priority for launch: J for AIM-9P/P-1; P for AIM-9P-2/P-3; and L or M for those missiles respectively.

The off missile cue is displayed if the attack develops to a point where another on-board missile is in-envelope for a shot at the target. Refer to HUD AIM-7, AIM-9 and AIM-120A Symbols. Refer to TO 1F-15E-34-1-1.

HUD Window 6

Aircraft Mach number is displayed in all modes when the landing gear is up.

HUD Window 7

Target Mach

The target Mach number is displayed only in the visual ident (VI) mode.

Current G/Allowable G

The HUD displays both current and maximum allowable g. Allowable g is displayed for existing flight conditions, aircraft configuration, gross weight, and changes automatically as these factors change. Current g is displayed on the left and maximum allowable g on the right. The g data is not displayed with the landing gear down unless the CC is inoperative. In CC NOGO, only current g is displayed.

Overload Warning System (OWS) Inoperative

The OWOFF cue is displayed when the OWS system fails, or when airborne with an invalid armament condition.

Invalid Armament (INVARM) Cue

This cue is displayed only with Weight on Wheels (WOW) when the PACS senses an unidentifiable store on the aircraft, or if the aircrew programs a store mode that is not in the PACS inventory.

HUD FORMAT

WINDOWS – ALL MASTER MODES

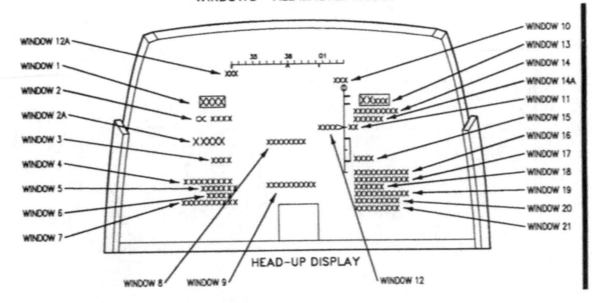

HEAD-UP DISPLAY

LEGEND

1. TRUE AIR OR GROUND SPEED IS SELECTED ON THE UP-FRONT CONTROL. X = G OR T DEPENDING ON SELECTED SPEED.

2. DISPLAYED IN ALL MASTER MODES/GEAR UP OR DOWN.

3. XXX CAN BE ANY OF THE EIGHT MISSILE CUES.

4. NOT DISPLAYED WITH GEAR DOWN.

5. ONLY WITH WEIGHT-ON-WHEELS AND INVALID WEAPONS ID IN PACS.

6. NOT DISPLAYED WITH GEAR DOWN UNLESS IN CC NO-GO. IN CC NO-GO, ONLY CURRENT G IS DISPLAYED.

7. VALID INS OR AFCS ON BB-1667 AND UP, GEAR UP WITH OWS OFF.

8. DISPLAYED IF RADAR NOT IN VI TRACK AND ONE OF THE BELOW CONDITIONS EXIST
   A. CADU, INS AND AFCS NOT VALID; INVALID ARMAMENT; WEIGHT-OFF-WHEELS.
   B. VALID ARMAMENT; OWS INVALID; WEIGHT-ON-WHEELS.
   C. VALID ARMAMENT; WEIGHT-OFF-WHEELS; LDG GEAR HANDLE UP; OWS INVALID AND CADU, INS AND AFCS NOT VALID.

9. DISPLAYED WHEN COMMAND HEADING CUE IS OUTSIDE OF HEADING SCALE LIMITS.

10. RADAR ALTITUDE DISPLAY IS SELECTED ON UP-FRONT CONTROL.

11. VERTICAL VELOCITY DISPLAYED IN NAV/INST MASTER MODE WITH GEAR DOWN ONLY WITH PRIORITY OVER RADAR CUES.

12. THE FOLLOWING COMBINATIONS ARE POSSIBLE:
    NAV DEGD.
    IFA, IFA X.X, IFA OK, SH NO TAXI, SH HOLD, SH XX.X, SH OK, GC NO TAXI, GC PP REQ, GC HOLD, GC XX.X, GC OK.
    OK=ALIGNMENT FINISHED, PP REQ=A PRESENT POSITION ENTRY IS REQUIRED. NO TAXI=AIRCRAFT SHOULD NOT BE TAXIED, HOLD = ALIGNMENT IS ON HOLD. XX.X=ALIGNMENT QUALITY.

13. DESTINATION CODE: BASE 1 THRU 99.01C; MARK 1 THRU 10

14. A/G MASTER MODE WITH NO TARGET DESIGNATED, XXX=NAV OCTCN (DEFAULT), NAV MASTER MODE: XXX=NAV, TCN OR GT.

15. FOR AIM-7WH, ZZZ=HDH OR DCY; FOR ANY MRM, ZZZ=SML, MED OR LRG DEPENDS ON TARGET TYPE SELECTION ON ARMT FORMAT. OFF MISSILE CUE HAS PRIORITY OVER TARGET TYPE CUE.

16. AIRSPEED MAY FLASH.

17. R CAN BE DISPLAYED W/SNIFF OR TSNIFF

18. DISPLAY TRNG IN HUD WINDOW 21 IN ALL MASTER MODES WHEN PACS IS IN TRAINING MODE.

19. HEIGHTH ABOVE TARGET (HAT) SENSOR CURRENTLY IN USE FOR A/G DELIVERY. "X" INDICATES EXTRAPOLATING RANGE.

15E-1-(D44-1)21-CATI

Figure 1-23. (Sheet 1 of 7)

HUD FORMATS (Continued)

SYMBOLS – ALL MASTER MODES

Symbol	Description	A/A MRM	SRM	GUN	VIS-IDENT	NAV/INST NAV	TACAN	ILS-NAV	ILS-TCN	GND TRK	A/G CDIP	CDIP/GUN	AUTO	AUTO LADD	GUIDED	DIRECT	MANUAL	ALL MODES CC NO-GO	SYM REJ 1	SYM REJ 2	SEE NOTES
1 2 3 4 5 6 7 8 9 10 11	WINDOW 1																				
1045	CALIBRATED AIRSPEED	X	X	X	X	X	X	X	X	X	X	X	X	X	X	X	X				
OFF	SPEED INVALID	X	X	X	X	X	X	X	X	X	X	X	X	X	X	X	X	X			
1 2 3 4 5 6 7 8 9 10 11	WINDOW 2																				
α 20.1	ANGLE-OF-ATTACK	X	X	X	X	X	X	X	X	X	X	X	X	X	X	X	X				②
1 2 3 4 5 6 7 8 9 10 11	WINDOW 2A																				
G 1045	GROUND SPEED	X	X	X	X	X	X	X	X	X	X	X	X	X	X	X	X				
T 1045	TRUE AIRSPEED	X	X	X	X	X	X	X	X	X	X	X	X	X	X	X	X				①
X OFF	SPEED INVALID	X	X	X	X	X	X	X	X	X	X	X	X	X	X	X	X				
1 2 3 4 5 6 7 8 9 10 11	WINDOW 3																				
O B S T	WARNING (TF LEFT TURN)	X	X	X	X	X	X	X	X	X	X	X	X	X	X	X	X	X			
1 2 3 4 5 6 7 8 9 10 11	WINDOW 4																				
I N C M D	IN COMMAND					X	X	X	X	X											
1 2 3 4 5 6 7 8 9 10 11	WINDOW 5																				
E	RADAR EMERGENCY MODE CUE	X	X	X	X	X	X	X	X	X	X	X	X	X	X	X	X	X			
7 0 0	ROUNDS REMAINING			X	X							X									
M 4 A	AIM-120A (AIM-120 COUNT)	X			X																
M 4 F	AIM-7F (AIM-7 COUNT)	X			X																
M 4 M	AIM-7M (AIM-7 COUNT)	X			X																
M 4 H	AIM-7MH (AIM-7 COUNT)	X			X																
S 4 J	AIM-9J (AIM-9 COUNT)		X		X																
S 4 P	AIM-9P (AIM-9 COUNT)		X		X																
S 4 L	AIM-9L (AIM-9 COUNT)		X		X																
S 4 M	AIM-9M (AIM-9 COUNT)		X		X																
X X X	OFF-MISSILE CUE	X	X	X	X																③
Z Z Z	TARGET TYPE CUE	X																			⑮
1 2 3 4 5 6 7 8 9 10 11	WINDOW 6																				
0 . 9 0 0	MACH	X	X	X	X	X	X	X	X	X	X	X	X	X	X	X	X				④
1 2 3 4 5 6 7 8 9 10 11	WINDOW 7																				
I N V A R M	INVALID WEAPON	X	X	X	X	X	X	X	X	X	X	X	X	X	X	X	X				⑤
T M 1 . 5	TARGET MACH				X																
-4 . 5 9 . 0 G	CURRENT G, MAX ALLOWABLE G	X	X	X	X	X	X	X	X	X	X	X	X	X	X	X	X	X			⑥
-4 . 5 G 0 W O F F	OWS OFF	X	X	X		X	X	X	X	X	X	X	X	X	X	X	X				⑦
0 W O F F	OWS OFF	X	X	X	X	X	X	X	X	X	X	X	X	X	X	X	X				⑧

15E-1-(2)44-2)21-CA71

Figure 1-23. (Sheet 2)

HUD FORMATS (Continued)

SYMBOLS – ALL MASTER MODES

Symbol	Description	MRM	SRM	GUN	VIS-IDENT	NAV	TACAN	ILS-NAV	ILS-TCN	GND TRK	CDIP	CDIP/GUN	AUTO	AUTO LADD	GUIDED	DIRECT	MANUAL	CC NO-GO	SYM REJ 1	SYM REJ 2	SEE NOTES
1 2 3 4 5 6 7 8 9 10 11	WINDOW 8																				
FLY UP	TF WARNINGS	X	X	X	X	X	X	X	X	X	X	X	X	X	X	X	X	X			
TF FAIL		X	X	X	X	X	X	X	X	X	X	X	X	X	X	X	X	X			
OBSTACLE		X	X	X	X	X	X	X	X	X	X	X	X	X	X	X	X	X			
G LIMIT		X	X	X	X	X	X	X	X	X	X	X	X	X	X	X	X	X			
TF LOW		X	X	X	X	X	X	X	X	X	X	X	X	X	X	X	X	X			
1 2 3 4 5 6 7 8 9 10 11	WINDOW 9																				
ROLL	TF CAUTIONS AND	X	X	X	X	X	X	X	X	X	X	X	X	X	X	X	X	X			
TURN RATE	N–F INFO	X	X	X	X	X	X	X	X	X	X	X	X	X	X	X	X	X			
TURN ACCEL	DIVE ANGLE	X	X	X	X	X	X	X	X	X	X	X	X	X	X	X	X	X			
DIV ANGLE		X	X	X	X	X	X	X	X	X	X	X	X	X	X	X	X	X			
UNARMED		X	X	X	X	X	X	X	X	X	X	X	X	X	X	X	X	X			
INS LIMIT		X	X	X	X	X	X	X	X	X	X	X	X	X	X	X	X	X			⑯
AIRSPEED		X	X	X	X	X	X	X	X	X	X	X	X	X	X	X	X	X			
NO TERRAIN		X	X	X	X	X	X	X	X	X	X	X	X	X	X	X	X	X			
ECCM		X	X	X	X	X	X	X	X	X	X	X	X	X	X	X	X	X			
N–F BRST		X	X	X	X	X	X	X	X	X	X	X	X	X	X	X	X	X			
N–F LOS		X	X	X	X	X	X	X	X	X	X	X	X	X	X	X	X	X			
1 2 3 4 5 6 7 8 9 10 11	WINDOW 10																				
1 6 0	RADAR RANGE SCALE	X	X	X	X																
1 2 3 4 5 6 7 8 9 10 11	WINDOW 11																				
8 0	HALF RADAR RANGE SCALE	X	X	X	X																
1 2 3 4 5 6 7 8 9 10 11	WINDOW 12																				
1 1 5 0	RANGE RATE, +–KTS	X	X	X	X																
1 2 3 4 5 6 7 8 9 10 11	WINDOW 12A																				
2 7 0	LIMITED COMMAND HEADING	X	X	X	X	X	X	X	X	X	X	X	X	X	X	X	X				⑨
1 2 3 4 5 6 7 8 9 10 11	WINDOW 13																				
4 6 3 5 0 / O F F	BARO ALTITUDE / INVALID	X	X	X	X	X	X	X	X	X	X	X	X	X	X	X	X				
1 2 3 4 5 6 7 8 9 10 11	WINDOW 14																				
V V 2 5 4 0 0	VERTICAL VELOCITY					X	X	X	X	X								X	X		⑪
V V O F F	VERTICAL VELOCITY OFF					X	X	X	X	X								X	X		
S N I F F	RADAR SPECIAL MODE	X	X	X	X	X	X	X	X	X	X	X	X	X	X	X	X	X			
T S N I F F	RADAR SPECIAL MODE	X	X	X	X	X	X	X	X	X	X	X	X	X	X	X	X	X			⑰
R	REJECT SENT TO RADAR	X	X	X	X	X	X	X	X	X	X	X	X	X	X	X	X	X			
F L O O D	RADAR SPECIAL MODE	X	X	X	X															X	
1 2 3 4 5 6 7 8 9 10 11	WINDOW 14A																				
R 1 5 0 0 0	RADAR ALTITUDE	X	X	X	X	X	X	X	X	X	X	X	X	X	X	X	X	X	X		⑩
R O F F	INVALID	X	X	X	X	X	X	X	X	X	X	X	X	X	X	X	X	X	X		
1 2 3 4 5 6 7 8 9 10 11	WINDOW 15																				
O B S T	WARNING (TF RIGHT TURN)	X	X	X	X	X	X	X	X	X	X	X	X	X	X	X	X	X			

Figure 1-23 (Sheet 3)

HUD FORMATS (Continued)

SYMBOLS – ALL MASTER MODES

		A/A				NAV/INST					A/G							ALL MODES			SEE NOTES
		MRM	SRM	GUN	VIS-IDENT	NAV	TACAN	ILS-NAV	ILS-TCN	GND TRK	CDIP	CDIP/GUN	AUTO	AUTO LADD	GUIDED	DIRECT	MANUAL	CC NO-GO	SYM REJ 1	SYM REJ 2	
1 2 3 4 5 6 7 8 9 10 11	WINDOW 16																				⑫
G C O K	GYRO COMPASS ALIGN MODE	X	X	X	X	X	X	X	X	X	X	X	X	X	X	X					
I F A P P R E Q	IN-FLIGHT ALIGN MODE	X	X	X	X	X	X	X	X	X	X	X	X	X	X	X					
S H N O T A X I	STORED HEADING ALIGN MODE	X	X	X	X	X	X	X	X	X	X	X	X	X	X	X					
H O L D		X	X	X	X	X	X	X	X	X	X	X	X	X	X	X					
X X . X		X	X	X	X	X	X	X	X	X	X	X	X	X	X	X					
N A V D E G D	DEGRADED NAV MODE	X	X	X	X	X	X	X	X	X	X	X	X	X	X	X					
A X X - X	PDT ALTITUDE	X	X	X	X																
1 2 3 4 5 6 7 8 9 10 11	WINDOW 17																				
J A M	RADER JAM CODE	X	X	X	X																
H O J	RADER HOJ CODE	X	X	X	X																
A O J	RADER AOJ CODE	X	X	X	X																
M E M	TRACK MEMORY	X	X	X	X																
N O Z O N E	NO ZONE	X	X																		
B A D T R K	BAD TRACK	X																			
T G T 9 9 .	PREPLANNED TARGET										X		X	X	X						
T G T	NON-PLANNED TARGET										X		X	X	X	X					
N A V 9 9 . 0 7 C	NAV STEER MODE					X					X	X	X	X	X	X	X	X	X		
T C N 1 0 3 X	TACAN STEER MODE						X				X	X	X	X	X	X	X	X	X		
I L S N 9 9 . 0 7 C	ILS-NAV STEER MODE							X										X			
I L S T 1 1 2 . 5	ILS-TACAN STEER MODE								X									X			⑬
G T 9 9 . 0 7 C	GROUND TRACK STEER MODE									X											
A X X X 9 9 . 0 7 C	AUTO PILOT SELECTED					X	X			X	X	X	X	X	X	X	X				⑭
1 2 3 4 5 6 7 8 9 10 11	WINDOW 18																				
R 1 5 0 . 1	RADER RANGE	X	X	X	X																
G 1 9 . 6	A/G RANGE										X	X	X	X	X						
N 9 8 0 . 7	NAV RANGE					X		X			X	X	X	X	X	X	X	X			
T 2 0 6 . 3	TACAN RANGE	X	X	X	X		X		X		X	X	X	X	X			X			
1 2 3 4 5 6 7 8 9 10 11	WINDOW 19																				
3 5 S E C	MRM TIME-TO-GO	X	X	X	X																
L O S T	MRM LOSTNGE	X	X	X	X																
1 : 1 5 T B U R S T	TIME-TO-BURST (NUCLEAR)										X	X	X	X	X	X	X				
1 : 1 5 T I M P C T	TIME-TO-IMPACT										X	X	X	X	X	X	X				
1 0 : 1 5 T P U L L	TIME-TO-PULL												X	X							
1 0 : 1 5 T R E L	TIME-TO-RELEASE										X	X	X	X							
1 0 : 1 5 T T G T	TIME-TO-TARGET										X	X	X	X	X						
0 1 : 3 0 : 1 5	NAV, TCN TIME-TO-GO					X	X	X	X												
1 2 3 4 5 6 7 8 9 10 11	WINDOW 20																				
C S E T 2 7 0	COURSE SET (ILS/TACAN)						X	X	X												
M K R	ILS MARKER BEACON							X	X										X		
U N C	UNCAGE (SRM)		X																		

15E-1-(3)44-4(21-CA7I

Figure 1-23. (Sheet 4)

HUD FORMATS (Continued)
SYMBOLS – ALL MASTER MODES

1 2 3 4 5 6 7 8 9 10 11	WINDOW 20	MRM	SRM	GUN	VIS-IDENT	NAV	TACAN	ILS-NAV	ILS-TCN	GND TRK	CDIP	CDIP/GUN	AUTO	AUTO LADD	GUIDED	DIRECT	MANUAL	CC NO-GO	SYM REJ 1	SYM REJ 2	SEE NOTES
1 7 L	LEFT ASPECT ANGLE	X	X	X	X																
0 1 R	RIGHT ASPECT ANGLE	X	X	X	X																
T	TAIL ASPECT ANGLE	X	X	X	X																
H	HEAD ASPECT ANGLE	X	X	X	X																
C D I P	CDIP DELIVERY MODE										X										
G U N	CDIP GUN MODE											X									
A U T O	AUTO DELIVERY MODE												X								
L A D D	AUTO LADD DELIVERY MODE													X							
G U I D E D	GUIDED DELIVERY MODE														X						
D I R E C T	DIRECT DELIVERY MODE															X					
M A N U A L	MANUAL DELIVERY MODE																X				(19)
L A S	LASER HAT SENSOR										X	X	X	X	X	X	X				
L A S X	EXTRAPOLATE										X	X	X	X	X	X	X				
A G R	RADAR HAT SENSOR (A/G RANGING)										X	X	X	X	X	X	X				
A G R X	EXTRAPOLATE										X	X	X	X	X	X	X				
R A L T	CARA HAT SENSOR										X	X	X	X	X	X	X				
R A L T X	EXTRAPOLATE										X	X	X	X	X	X	X				
B A R O	SYSTEM ALTITUDE HAT SENSOR										X	X	X	X	X	X	X				
1 2 3 4 5 6 7 8 9 10 11	WINDOW 21																				(18)
T R N G	PACS TRAINING MODE	X	X	X	X	X	X	X	X	X	X	X	X	X	X	X	X	X			

Figure 1-23. (Sheet 5)

15E-1-(2)44-5)21-CATI

HUD FORMATS (Continued)

SYMBOLS – ALL MASTER MODES

HUD SYMBOLOGY	MRM	SRM	GUN	VIS-IDENT	NAV	TACAN	ILS-NAV	ILS-TCN	GND TRK	CDIP	CDIP/GUN	AUTO	AUTO LADD	GUIDED	DIRECT	MANUAL	CC NO-GO	SYM REJ 1	SYM REJ 2
	A/A				NAV/INST					A/G							ALL MODES		
SHOOT CUE	X	X																	
PITCH STEERING [1]	X	X	X	X	X	X	X	X	X	X	X	X	X	X	X	X	X		
BANK STEERING					X	X	X	X	X			X					X		
AIRCRAFT WATERLINE SYMBOL [2]	X	X		X	X	X	X	X	X								X		
VELOCITY VECTOR [3]	X	X	X	X	X	X	X	X	X	X	X	X	X	X	X	X	X	X	X
GHOST VELOCITY VECTOR [4]	X	X	X	X	X	X	X	X	X	X	X	X	X	X	X	X	X	X	X
HEADING SCALE	X	X	X	X	X	X	X	X	X	X	X	X	X	X	X	X	X	X	X
PITCH LADDER	X	X	X	X	X	X	X	X	X	X	X	X	X	X	X	X	X	X	X
RANGE SCALE	X	X	X	X															
GUN CROSS	X	X	X	X	X	X	X	X	X	X	X	X	X	X	X	X	X		
R MIN, R MAX 1	X	X																	
R MAX 2 , RTR	X																		
ASE CIRCLE	X	X		X															
RETICLE RANGE BAR		X	X	X						X	X	X	X	X	X	X			
DYNAMIC SEEKER RANGE	X																		
A/A GUN RETICLE			X																
LAG LINE			X																
BULLET TIME-OF-FLIGHT			X																
STEERING DOT	X	X		X															
A/A TGT DESIGNATOR BOX	X	X	X	X															
BREAK X	X	X		X						X	X	X	X	X	X	X			
FOV/REF CIRCLE	X	X															X		
AIM-9L/M SEEKER POSITION		X												X					
VERT SCAN LINE	X	X	X	X															
SUPER SEARCH CIRCLE	X	X	X	X															
4 DEG BORESIGHT REF CIRCLE	X	X	X	X															
DISPLAYED IMPACT LINE										X									
PULL-UP CUE										X		X	X	X	X				
AZIMUTH STEERING LINE												X	X	X					
RELEASE CUE												X	X						

HUD FORMATS (Continued)
SYMBOLS – ALL MASTER MODES

HUD SYMBOLOGY	MASTER MODES																ALL MODES		
	A/A				NAV/INST					A/G									
	MRM	SRM	GUN	VIS-IDENT	NAV	TACAN	ILS-NAV	ILS-TCN	GND TRK	CDIP	CDIP/GUN	AUTO	AUTO LADD	GUIDED	DIRECT	MANUAL	CC NO-GO	SYM REJ 1	SYM REJ 2
COMMAND HEADING CUE	X	X	X	X	X	X	X	X	X	X	X	X	X	X	X	X	X	X	X
A/G TGT DESIGNATOR DIAMOND										X		X	X	X	X				
BANK SCALE AND POINTER					X	X	X	X	X			X	X			X	X	X	X
A/G GUN RETICLE										X	X	X	X	X	X	X			
NAV LOS DESIGNATOR					X	X	X	X	X	X	X	X	X	X					
RADAR ALTIMETER SCALE ⟨5⟩					X	X	X	X	X	X	X	X	X	X	X	X	X		
ELEVATION STEERING LINE												X	X						
LASER CUE	X	X	X	X	X	X	X	X	X	X	X	X	X	X	X	X			
TCN/ILS HUD CDI						X	X	X											
ILS GLIDESLOPE							X	X											
GBU-15 RANGE DATA														X					
ANGLE OF ATTACK	X	X	X	X	X	X	X	X	X	X	X	X	X	X	X	X			
COMMAND VELOCITY	X	X	X	X	X	X	X	X	X	X	X	X	X	X	X	X			

NOTES

⟨1⟩ WITH LANDING GEAR UP AND OWS OFF.

⟨2⟩ WOW WITH OWS OFF.

⟨3⟩ A/A OR A/G MASTER MODE – TF PITCH STEERING ONLY WHEN TF IS SELECTED.
NAV/INST MASTER MODE – TF PITCH STEERING IF TF SELECTED, ILS PITCH STEERING WHEN ILSN OR ILST IS SELECTED.

⟨4⟩ – AIRCRAFT SYMBOL WILL BE DISPLAYED IN A/A GUN MODE IF
(A) SYMBOL REJECT IS NOT SELECTED AND
(B) VELOCITY VECTOR IS HUD LIMITED.

⟨5⟩ – REJECT IN A/A MASTER MODE ONLY.

15E-1-(2)44-7)21-CA7I

Figure 1-23. (Sheet 7)

In such a case, OWS processing is disabled. If in flight, an invalid armament cue causes the OWOFF cue to be displayed.

HUD Window 8

Several different warnings concerning the Terrain Following (TF) system may be displayed.

HUD Window 9

Several cautions and information cues concerning the TF and Nav FLIR (NF) systems can be displayed.

HUD Window 10

The selected radar range scale is displayed when the radar is in a track mode.

HUD Window 11

One-half the selected range scale (displayed in window 10) is displayed in window 11.

HUD Window 12

The opening or closing range rate (Vc) in knots between the aircraft and A/A target is displayed when the radar is in track.

HUD Window 12A

If the command heading bug is limited (outside the displayed 30° scale), a digital readout of the command heading is displayed at the appropriate side of the scale.

HUD Window 13

The aircraft barometric altitude is displayed. The thousands and ten thousands digits are larger than the hundreds, tens, and units digits, except below 1000 feet, when all the digits are the large size.

If the barometric altitude is invalid, OFF is displayed.

HUD Window 14

ADC vertical velocity in feet per minute to the nearest 100 feet per minute is displayed in the NAV/INST master modes when the gear is down. Descents are indicated by negative signs preceding the numerical readout.

If the vertical velocity data is invalid, VV OFF is displayed.

When in A/G or A/A master mode, or in NAV/INST master mode with the gear handle up, SNIFF, TSNIFF or FLOOD is displayed when radar is in SNIFF mode or training SNIFF or FLOOD mode respectively. An R displayed at the far right of window 14 indicates mode rejects are being sent to the radar

HUD Window 14A

The aircraft radar altitude is displayed preceded by the letter "R" (if selected on the UFC, if not selected this window will be blanked). If the radar altitude is not valid, OFF preceded by "R" is displayed

HUD Window 15

This window displays the terrain following right turn OBST caution.

HUD Window 16

INS alignment cues are displayed as required. Refer to applicable paragraphs in this section. Also displays primary designated target (PDT) altitude.

HUD Window 17

Radar Jam Codes

The jam codes, when displayed, override all other window 17 displays. Refer to TO 1F-15E-34-1-1-1.

Track Memory (MEM)

Refer to A/A Radar Displays, TO 1F-15E-34-1-1.

No Zone

Refer to A/A Radar Displays and to AIM-7 Missile, TO 1F-15E-34-1-1-1.

Bad Track (BAD TRK)

This cue is displayed when the radar track quality is judged to be poor based on an inconsistent number of target updates (hits). Since the cue is not range dependent, it is designed to give an earlier indication of a degrading track than the MEM cue.

NAV Steer Displays

These cues are applicable to A/G target selection and to the NAV/INST master mode. Refer to applicable paragraphs in this section.

HUD Window 18

Range Displays

Window 18 always displays range data. A prefix letter identifies the display as R (radar), T (tacan), N (Nav), or G (A/G) designated range. Ranges are displayed with a resolution of 0.1 NM to a maximum of 999.9 NM. The maximum radar range displayed is 160 NM.

HUD Window 19

MRM Time To Go (Tgo)

The MRM prelaunch Tgo cue is steady and appears in radar track when target range is between Rmax 1 and Rmin. The value is the predicted MRM Time of Flight and is continuously updated as range and angle conditions change. The postlaunch Tgo, a function of target position and velocity data, provides an accurate display of the required illumination period. The indications are as follows:

Target does not maneuver.	Flashing Tgo counts down in real time.
Target maneuvers, staying in range.	Flashing Tgo countdown adjusted for target maneuvers.
Lost missile, target has maneuvered to or beyond missile limit	LOST is displayed for 15 seconds.
Flood Launch	Flashing Tgo counts down in real time.

Nav/Tacan Time To Go (Tgo)

In the NAV/INST master mode, the Tgo displays pertain to the NAV/TCN range displays shown in window 18.

A/G Attack Mode (Tgo)

The A/G Tgo values pertain to the A/G range data of window 18, and the A/G weapon delivery modes displayed in window 20.

HUD Window 20

ILS Cues

Various cues are displayed for the Instrument Landing System (ILS) in the NAV/ INST master modes. Refer to applicable paragraphs in this section.

CSET cue

In NAV/INST master modes, the "CSET xxx" will flash for 10 seconds when entering TCN, ILST or ILSN steer modes. The flashing of the cue is independent of the previously selected mode. Also, the cue will not flash or appear on the NAV/INST HUD when the course select value is changed on the HSI.

Uncage (UNC)

UNC is displayed when the NGS button is pressed an odd number of times to permit SRM seeker uncage (IR lockon). An even number of button depressions removes UNC from the HUD, breaks IR lockon, and returns the SRM seeker to the missile boresight or to the (AIM-9L/M) radar antenna Line of Sight (LOS).

Target Aspect Angle

Target aspect angle is displayed for the designated A/A target.

A/G Delivery Mode

A cue denoting the selected A/G weapon delivery mode is displayed for each delivery mode. In addition, a cue denoting the sensor currently in use to calculate the height above target (HAT) is displayed.

HUD Window 21

This window displays TRNG cue when PACS is in a training mode.

HUD MRM MODE

See HUD AIM-7 or AIM-120A Mode Symbols, refer to TO 1F-15E-34-1-1.

HUD SRM MODE

See HUD AIM-9 Mode Symbols, refer to TO 1F-15E-34-1-1.

HUD GUN MODE

See HUD GUN Mode Symbols, refer to TO 1F-15E-34-1-1.

HUD BACK-UP MODE

When the CC has failed and the MPDP has taken control of the mux bus and the displays, the HUD is in back-up mode. In back-up mode the HUD display format always appears in the gear-up position even if the gear is down. INS provides pitch and bank data and radar provides altitude data. The HUD format will only be displayed on the HUD (no repeater display).

MULTIPURPOSE DISPLAY PROCESSOR (MPDP)

The MPDP is a multiple processor symbol generator that simultaneously drives eight displays. The eight displays include four MPD, three MPCD, and the HUD. The MPDP generates and overlays symbology (graphic symbols and alphanumerics) onto the MPD and MPCD by raster and/or stroke methods. A separate display channel drives each display individually. Display output data generated by the MPDP may consist of either stroke written symbology (only), monochrome and color rasters, or hybrid with monochromatic raster symbology.

The primary functions of the MPDP include :

1. Produce stroke symbology and background video information for displays on:
   (a) Three MPCD
   (b) Four MPD
   (c) HUD
   (d) Video tape recorder (VTR)
2. Convert analog voltage signals from the overload warning system (ows) into digital values for transmission to the central computer (CC).
3. Data communications for the data transfer module (DTM).
4. Backup bus controller (CC no-go condition exists) for avionics 1553 mux bus.
5. Bus controller for JTIDS 1553 mux bus (not used).
6. BIT controller for HUD, MPCD, and MPD.
7. Primary display (HUD, MPD, and MPCD) controller when CC no-go exists.
8. Process discrete data from;
   a. Radar
   b. Radar warning receiver (RWR)
   c. Electronic warfare warning set (EWWS)
   d. Fuel quantity and acceleration data (for OWS function)
   e. LANTIRN NAV and targeting pods (video)
   f. Remote map reader (video)

g. Weapon stations (video)
9. Sends discrete data to;
   a. BIT discretes to AIU no. 1 and avionics status panel (ASP)
   b. Overload warning system (OWS)
   c. NAV targeting pod (weapon video)

The MPDP produces symbology for the HUD, MPD, and MPCD. It also does video processing for the MPD and MPCD. It initiates and controls data transfer with the HUD, MPD, and MPCD and communicates with the CC using the displays 1553 mux bus.

The central computer, in normal mode, is the primary display controller for the multipurpose display system. The MPDP general processor (GP) section becomes the primary display controller during backup mode (CC no-go exists).

The MPDP transfers serial data to and from the DTM. When transfer is complete the MPDP communicates the DTM data to the CC through the displays 1553 mux bus. The DTM is preprogrammed with flight operational data for a specific flight or mission. The DTM also has the ability to receive and store flight data from the MPDP.

The MPDP converts all displays to composite video for the VTR. This video can be any display format or a split screen format (a pair of display formats recorded side by side).

The MPDP provides control of the avionics 1553 mux bus when the CC is not operational. The MPDP receives a CC no-go from the CC and automatically takes command of the avionics 1553 mux bus. During this backup mode condition, the MPDP communicates with eight systems.

1. Inertial navigation set
2. Remote map reader
3. Radar system
4. Left and right engines
5. Flight control computer
6. Radar warning receiver system
7. LANTIRN system
8. Avionics interface unit set

The MPDP also provides normal communications with the MPD, MPCD, and HUD.

MULTI-PURPOSE DISPLAY/MULTI-PURPOSE COLOR DISPLAY (MPD/MPCD)

There are 4 multi-purpose displays (MPD) and 3 multi-purpose color displays (MPCD) in the aircraft. There are two MPD's in each cockpit, and 1 MPCD in the front cockpit and 2 MPCD's in the rear cockpit. The MPD's display system data, sensor video and weapon information in monochromatic format. The MPD's have 20 peripheral pushbuttons by which the crew can control weapons systems, sensors and data to be displayed. Legends are positioned adjacent to each pushbutton to advise the crew of the modes and options selectable for operation of the onboard radar, FLIR, navigation, and weapon systems. The exact content of data in the display formats is software programmable. The MPCD's display monochromatic or multicolor presentation of sensor and weapon video overlaid with symbology, advisory readouts and navigation data. Color coding of display data aids in quick interpretation of complex formats such as HSI and ADL. Color presentation of navigational maps also contributes to easy and accurate assessment of the tactical situation. The MPCDs also have 20 peripheral pushbuttons which provide control in the same manner as the MPD. Each MPD/MPCD has a power switch, a brightness switch, a contrast switch and a BIT indicator. Refer to figure 1-24.

Pushbuttons

There are twenty pushbuttons on each MPD/MPCD numbered 1 thru 20 counterclockwise from the upper button on the left side of the display to the left button on the top of the display.

Power Switch

A two position rocker switch provides electrical power to the MPD/MPCD's. When powering up the aircraft, the aircrew must turn on the MPD and MPCD's. However, if the aircrew experiences a brief power interrupt inflight, the MPD/MPCD displays will automatically come up without reselecting the power rocker switch.

Brightness Switch

A two-position, spring-loaded-to-center rocker switch provides a non-linear adjustment of stroke written symbol luminance or brightness. On the MPD the switch controls black level. On the MPCD this switch controls brightness and raster contrast. Backlighted arrow symbols on this rocker switch indicate an increase or decrease in CRT display brightness.

Contrast Switch.

A two-position, spring-loaded-to-center rocker switch provides adjustment of raster contrast, also called shade of gray. On the MPD's the switch adjusts both raster contrast and stroke brightness.

BIT Indicator

A magnetically controlled BIT ball rolls over to indicate white when MPD/MPCD has failed. In normal operation, the BIT ball is seen as black. When power is removed from the MPD/MPCD, the BIT ball will hold at its last setting. The BIT ball will reset automatically when the failure is corrected.

POWER UP OPERATION

Once electrical power is available, the individual MPD/MPCD must be turned on with the power switch. The display format that was being presented at aircraft shutdown will be initialized on each MPD/MPCD as shown on the MPD in figure 1-24. The letter M or M2 is displayed adjacent to the pushbutton in the lower right hand corner of each display unit. It is used to call up the menu 1 or menu 2 display. When power is turned on, the MPD/MPCD's will come up at a 50% default brightness level and will be fully active. Default brightness level is a function of the DAY/NIGHT switch setting on the interior lights control panel. Pressing the pushbutton adjacent to the M results in the menu display shown on the MPD in figure 1-24.

MENU DISPLAY

The menu displays can be selected by pressing the lower right hand pushbutton on any display. This pushbutton will always be labeled M or M2 From the menu display (figure 1-24) the individual system formats are selected by pressing the appropriate pushbutton adjacent to the system legend. Any format can be presented on any display unit except the air-to-ground radar format which is not selectable (legend not displayed) on a color display unit. Pressing the lower right hand pushbutton will alternate between the two menu displays. The menu 1 display has 18 separate display selections to choose from and one that permits display programming. Use of the various displays are described in other parts of this manual where the affected system(s) is covered.

MPD

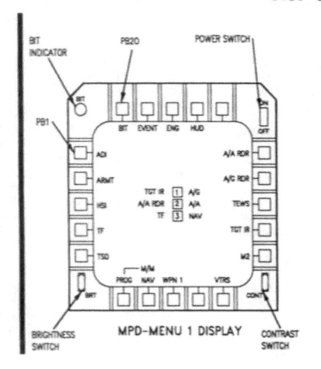
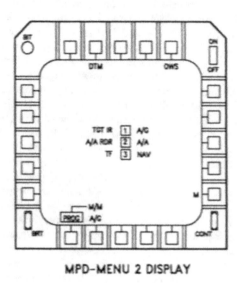

MPD—MENU 1 DISPLAY

MPD—MENU 2 DISPLAY

15E-1-(37-1)21-CA7)

Figure 1-24

NOTE

A/G radar not available on MPCD. WPN 1 and WPN 2 only available when video weapon loaded.

The menu display options are as follows:

MENU 1
PROG M/M	Program (Master Mode)
NAV	NAV master mode
WPN 1	Weapon 1
WPN 2	Weapon 2
VTRS	Video Tape Recording System
M2	Menu 2
TGT IR	LANTIRN Targeting FLIR
TEWS	Tactical Electronic Warfare System
A/G RDR	Air-to-Ground Radar
A/A RDR	Air-to-Air Radar
HUD	Head Up Display
ENG	Engine Parameters

EVENT	Event
BIT	Built-In-Test
ADI	Attitude Director Indicator
ARMT	Armament
HSI	Horizontal Situation Display
TF	Terrain Following
TSD	Tactical Situation Display

MENU 2
PROG M/M	Program master mode
A/G	Air-to-Ground (Master mode)
M	Menu 1
OWS	Overload Warning System
DTM	Data Transfer Module

Display Sequence Programming

To simplify operation, each MPD/MPCD can be programmed to provide hands-on access for up to three display formats. The pilot and/or WSO can then address a specific display with a switch integrated into the stick grip for the pilot, and a similar switch integrated into each hand controller for the WSO. To program the displays, first select the menu display, then press the PROG pushbutton. A box appears around PROG. Refer to figure 1-25. Then select the display formats in the order desired. When selected, the boxed sequence number is displayed in the center of the screen with the format name to the left. When master modes are assigned to a format, the master mode abbreviation is displayed to the right of the sequence number. The program numbers are assigned in the order the pushbuttons are pressed. For example, A/A RDR was selected first, A/G RDR second, and HSI third. With this accomplished, the display formats can now be displayed in the order selected through the HOTAS controls. To exit the program mode, press the pushbutton adjacent to program or scroll to one of the programmed displays. The box around PROG will be removed. To reprogram a particular display, reselect program, deselect the undesired display format, and select the one desired. Also, it is not necessary to program all seven head down displays. To sequence or scroll through the displays in the cockpit, toggle the castle toward the desired display Refer to figure 1-26. Each time the switch is toggled toward a display, it will scroll to the next programmed display format. The first aft movement of the front cockpit castle switch will present the ADI on the front cockpit MPCD. Quick access to the front cockpit ADI may not be possible with PACS nuclear display. Refer to TO 1F-15E-25-1. The rear cockpit four way coolie switch on the left hand controller controls the left MPD/MPCD, the right hand controller coolie switch controls the right MPD/MPCD. Moving the switch in a forward (or upward) direction will scroll through the display program on the inboard MPD. Moving it aft (or downward) scrolls through the display program on the outboard MPCD. Operation is the same for the left display or the right display. Program display rotation is summarized in figure 1-26. Note that the forward cockpit operation is independent from the rear and vice versa.

MASTER MODE PROGRAMMING

To simplify operation and reduce crew workload, a method of programming the displays as a function of master mode has been implemented. By selecting a master mode, as shown in figure 1-27, air-to-air (A/A), air-to-ground (A/G), navigation (NAV), and instrument (INST), a specific set of display formats can be displayed. Three of these master modes are programmable by the crewmembers while the fourth, INST, is preprogrammed and cannot be changed by the crewmembers.

Programming the displays as a function of master mode is shown in figure 1-27. Note that a display format cannot be programmed to a master mode until

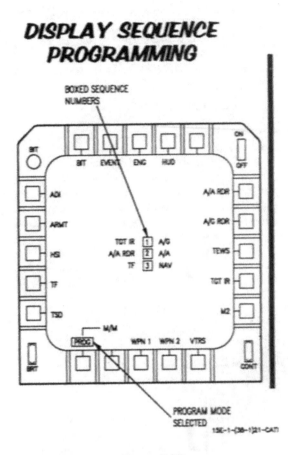

DISPLAY SEQUENCE PROGRAMMING

Figure 1-25

that display format has been assigned a display sequence number. To program the displays, first select program (PROG) on the menu display. Then select the master mode to be programmed, A/A, A/G or NAV. This is accomplished by alternate depressions of the display pushbutton under the legend M/M on the MPD/MPCD. Finally, press the pushbutton adjacent to the system display format desired. The master mode now appears next to the selected display format. The display formats on the top and bottom rows of the menu format can be programmed to one master mode. Those on the left and right sides can be programmed to three master modes. Also note that each master mode can be assigned to only one display format at a time. Each MPD/MPCD can be programmed using this procedure.

Instrument Master Mode

The preprogrammed set of display formats associated with the instrument master mode provides a one-step procedure to rapidly call up the A/A radar (left

MPD), attitude director indicator (ADI) (MPCD), and the horizontal situation indicator (HSI) (right MPD) in the cockpit. In the rear cockpit, the left MPCD displays HSI format, the right MPCD displays ADI format and the MPD's continue to display previous selection.

TAKE COMMAND OPERATION

A method of take command of operation without the need to have a separate take-command control panel in either cockpit is provided. Command can be taken from but cannot be given to the other cockpit. The cockpit can have command of one display but the rear cockpit can have command of two displays (one on each side). The following display formats have take command capability.

TSD	Tactical Situation Display
A/A	Air-to-Air Radar
A/G	Air-to-Ground Radar
TGT IR	Targeting FLIR
WPN 1	Weapon 1
WPN 2	Weapon 2
HUD	Head Up display (Cockpit only)
ARMT	Armament Display (Nuclear weapons only)

Take command is initiated in the front cockpit by means of the stick grip castle switch and is accomplished by first pressing the switch and releasing it. Then move the switch, within two seconds, in the direction of the HUD or MPD/MPCD which displays the format the crewmember desires to command. Vertical bars are presented at the bottom of the display format on the MPD/MPCD to indicate take command has been accomplished. Command of the HUD is indicated by the cue "IN CMD" displayed in window 4. Take command is initiated in the rear cockpit from the left and right hand controllers by the four way coolie switches. Moving the switch on the left hand controller to the left takes command of the format on the left hand MPCD and to the right takes command of the format on the left hand MPD. Moving the switch on the right hand controller to the left takes command of the right MPD and to the right takes command of the right MPCD. To minimize the need for the crew to converse about who's in command of a given system, visual cues are provided within the display format. In figure 1-28, a typical radar search display is shown. The display format on the left shows a solid cursor plus command lines between the display options. This indicates to the crewmember with this display format in his cockpit

that he has command of the radar. The display on the right has a dashed cursor and no lines between options indicating that the crewmember doesn't have command of the radar. If a crewmember is attempting to take command of a system the other crewmember is active on (for example, moving the acquisition symbol), a SYSTEM IN USE message will be presented on the display he is attempting to command. See figure 1-28. If command of the display is indeed required, a second command request within 5 seconds will be honored. Command of a display format remains until that format is commanded on another display or that display is used to take command of another format. When scrolling off of a commanded display format, command of that display format is retained. The hands on throttle and stick (HOTAS) controls of that format are non-functional while it is out of view. Control function and command are provided when the display format is recalled.

NOTE

Command cannot be taken for A/G radar if in radar A/A priority mode or the aircraft is within 15 seconds time to release.

INSTRUMENTS

Refer to foldout section for front and rear cockpit instrument panel illustrations For information about instruments that are an integral part of a system, refer to applicable paragraphs in this section.

VERTICAL VELOCITY INDICATOR (VVI)

The vertical velocity indicator is driven by electrical signals from the air data computer. A window on the instrument will display an OFF flag if electrical power is lost or the display is not valid. The indicator is in both cockpits.

STANDBY ATTITUDE INDICATOR

The standby attitude indicator is a self-contained electrically driven gyro-horizon type instrument. The OFF flag appears if there is a power loss to the indicator or the gyro is caged. The gyro is caged by pulling the knob. Do not turn the knob to lock the gyro in the caged position. The gyro cages to 0° pitch and roll regardless of airplane attitude. The caged position is approximately 4° nose up from the normal ground attitude and the gyro will precess 4° nose down after uncaging. Power should be applied to the instrument for at least 1 minute before caging. The indicator displays roll through 360°. Pitch display is limited by mechanical stops at 90° climb and 78° dive. As the aircraft climbs or dives, the pitch attitude changes smoothly until the stop is reached when the gyro tumbles 180° in roll. The indicator is in both cockpits.

PROGRAMMED DISPLAY ROTATION

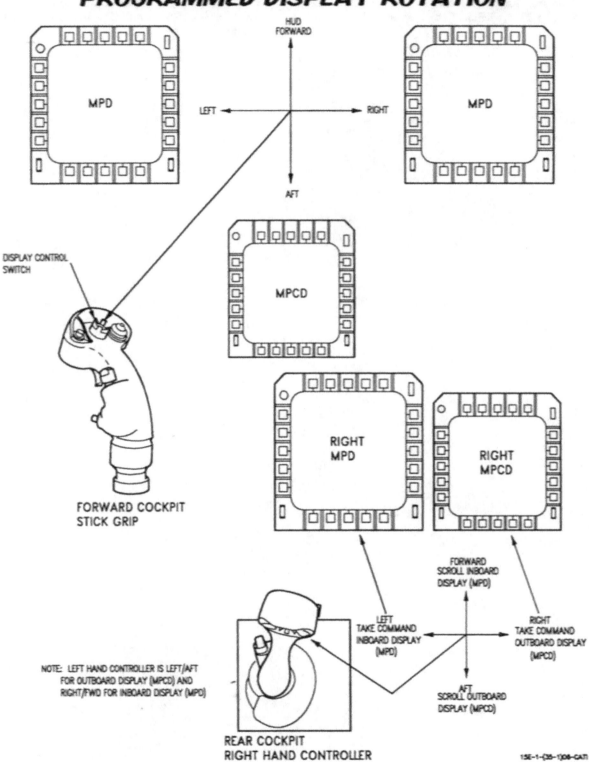

Figure 1-26

MASTER MODE PROGRAMMING

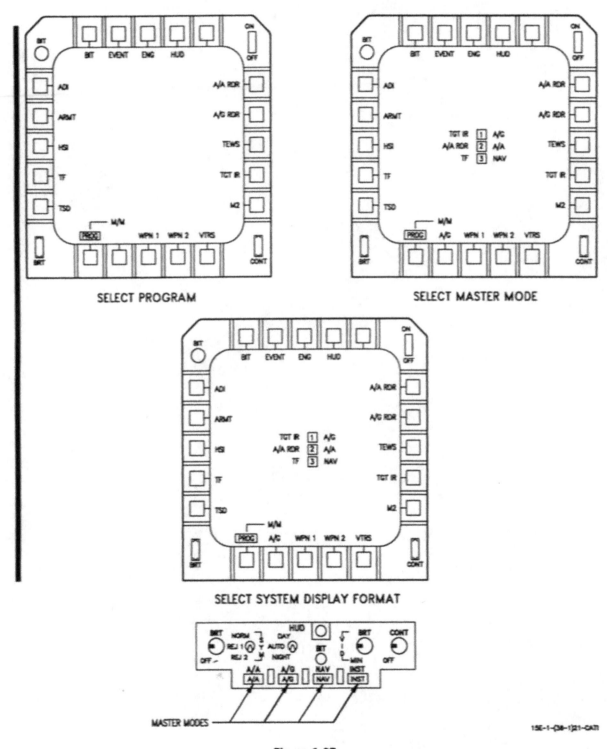

SELECT PROGRAM

SELECT MASTER MODE

SELECT SYSTEM DISPLAY FORMAT

MASTER MODES

Figure 1-27

TAKE COMMAND FORMATS

NOTES:
1. TAKE COMMAND CONTROL INDICATED BY SOLID CURSOR OR FOOTPRINT AND LINES DIVIDING OPTIONS ACROSS BOTTOM OF DISPLAY.

2. ABSENCE OF LINES BETWEEN OPTIONS AND A DASHED CURSOR OR FOOTPRINT INDICATES CREWMEMBER DOES NOT HAVE COMMAND OF DISPLAY.

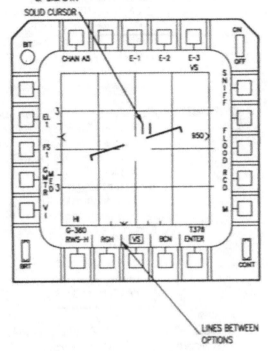

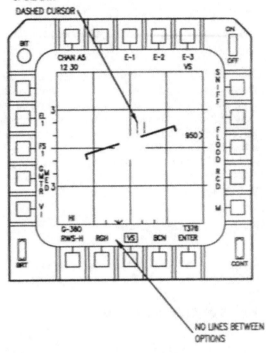

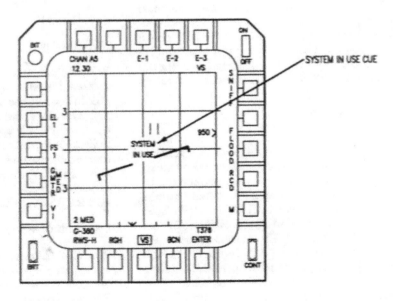

Figure 1-28

15E-1-(39-1)06-CATI

1-87

STANDBY AIRSPEED INDICATOR

The standby airspeed indicator operates directly from pitot-static pressures. It has a fixed scale of 60 to 850 knots and a rotation pointer. The indicator is in both cockpits.

STANDBY ALTIMETER

The standby altimeter operates directly from a static pressure source. The altimeter is in both cockpits. The barometric pressure in inches of mercury is set on both altimeters ; however the baro altitude displayed on the HUD, ADI and UFC is based on the cockpit altimeter baro setting only. On some aircraft, the thousand digit moves progressively with the pointer rotation, rather than when the pointer transits the 9 to 0 range only.

STANDBY MAGNETIC COMPASS

A conventional aircraft magnetic compass is mounted on the canopy arch in the front cockpit only.

ANGLE-OF-ATTACK (AOA) INDICATOR

The AOA indicator, in the front cockpit only, is driven by electrical signals from the probe and displays indicated AOA in units from 0 to 45. A T-shaped index mark is set at approximate optimum landing approach AOA (20 to 22 units). A window on the face of the instrument displays an OFF flag if electrical power is lost, there is invalid data from the ADC or a failure within the indicator. A triangular index mark is positioned full scale and is inoperative.

RADAR ALTIMETER

The radar altimeter indicates clearance over land and water from 0 to 50,000 feet. Radar altitude is utilized by the AFCS, LANTIRN navigation pod and the CC for terrain following (TF) and low altitude warning (LAW). Radar altitude is displayed on the TF display and is selectively displayed on the HUD, EADI and UFC. A radar altitude scale (thermometer) is also displayed on the HUD and EADI during TF. Refer to TO 1F-15E-34-1-1 for a detailed operational description of TF. The radar altimeter is controlled by the radar altimeter switch on the sensor control panel (SCP).

Radar Altimeter Switch

The RDR ALT switch on the sensor panel on the left console in the front cockpit has three positions:

OFF   Radar altimeter is deactivated. If LAW is enabled, the LAW warnings are activated. If TF is enabled, TF FAIL warning is activated.

ON   Radar altimeter is activated.

OVERRIDE   Radar altimeter is deactivated. If LAW is enabled, the LAW warnings are activated. If auto TF or manual TF with automatic flyup is coupled, TF FAIL warning is activated. If manual TF is engaged with manual flyup, a signal is sent to the terrain following system that radar altitude is not available.

WARNING

RDR ALT OVERRIDE is selectable for emergency situations only during manual terrain following with FLYUP ENABLE off. To ensure the greatest protection against low altitude conditions, the OVERRIDE position should not be used.

HUD Display

With the radar altimeter turned on, radar altitude is displayed in window 14A of the HUD provided radar altitude is selected on the UFC data 1 format. The display includes radar altitude rounded to the nearest ten feet. An "R" appears to the left of the readout indicating the altitude is radar. Should the altitude source become invalid, OFF is displayed in place of radar altitude . During CC failure, radar altitude is displayed on the HUD and EADI since barometric altitude is not available.

Low Altitude Warning

When LAW is enabled on the UFC menu 1, audio and visual warnings are activated when the aircraft descends below the selected LAW altitude on menu 1. The warnings are removed when either the aircraft climbs 20 feet above the selected LAW altitude, the

LAW function is disabled on the UFC menu 1, or the LAW altitude is changed to below the present radar altitude. If LAW is enabled and the radar altimeter fails, the LAW warnings are activated. If LAW is enabled, radar altitude is less than 5000 feet, aircraft attitude is less than 50° of roll and less than 20° of pitch, and the radar altimeter breaks track, the LAW warnings will be activated. The warnings are removed for these cases when either the fail condition corrects itself or the LAW function is disabled on the UFC menu 1.

Low Altitude Voice Warning

The 'LOW ALTITUDE' voice warning repeats twice when the aircraft descends below the selected LAW altitude and resets when the LAW condition is removed. This voice warning is a function of LAW only. It is not utilized by the terrain following system.

Low Altitude Warning Light

A red low altitude warning light, labeled LOW ALT, is located on the upper instrument panel in both cockpits. The LOW ALT light comes on when a LAW condition is encountered and remains on until the LAW condition is removed. This warning light is also used by the terrain following system to indicate a set clearance warning.

Up-Front Control

The UFC is used to set the LAW altitude, to enable the LAW function, and to select radar (CARA) altitude for display on the HUD and ADI. Baro altitude is always displaed boxed in the upper right corner of the HUD and ADI and also at PB 9 on UFC Data 1. The present LAW altitude, in feet, is displayed at PB 1 on UFC menu 1. To set a different LAW altitude, the desired LAW altitude is entered in the UFC scratchpad using the UFC keyboard. After verifying the correct altitude in the scratchpad, the upper left pushbutton adjacent to the LAW readout is pressed to change the LAW altitude to that in the scratchpad. The LAW function is enabled if an asterisk appears on the upper left adjacent to the LAW readout. Alternately pressing the upper left pushbutton with the scratchpad blank enables and disables the LAW function. Selecting "B" (asterisk) on UFC Data 1 displays radar (CARA) altitude on the HUD and ADI in addition to baro. When selected, an "R" with the CARA readout will be displayed below the baro altitude on the HUD and ADI.

Terrain Following

Radar altitude is used by the terrain following system to monitor proximity to the selected set clearance. When TF is enabled and either the LANTIRN NAV Pod or the AFCS detects the radar altitude approaching or below 75% of the TF set clearance, a SET CLEARANCE warning is activated. A manual or automatic flyup is initiated and the red LOW ALT warning light comes on. No voice warning is activated for the set clearance warning condition. If the radar altimeter fails, is turned off or breaks track during TF, the TF fail warnings will be activated and an automatic or manual flyup is initiated. The RDR ALT OVERRIDE switch position is available for emergency use only during manual TF with FLYUP ENABLE off. This switch position powers off the radar altimeter and sends a signal to the AFCS that radar altitude is not available. The AFCS during RDR ALT OVERRIDE does not perform its low altitude monitoring logic. For maximum protection from TF low altitude conditions, the OVERRIDE position should not be used. Refer to TO 1F-15E-34-1-1 for a detailed description of terrain following.

ATTITUDE DIRECTOR INDICATOR (ADI)

The ADI (figure 1-29) can be displayed on any MPD/MPCD and consists of the items indicated. The attitude sphere displays pitch and bank. The pitch markings on the sphere are in graduations of 5°, the bank markings begin at 10° increments up to 30°, then 45° and 60°. Signals are received from the INS or AHRS system. The primary attitude source is the INS. The pitch and bank steering bars are driven by signals from the CC. The bank steering bar provides command steering information to intercept tacan radials and navigation computer destinations. The ADI displays vertical velocity under the altitude window if gear is down. It is displayed as descending (−) or ascending (+). Angle of attack is displayed under the airspeed window when the landing gear is down. Command velocity (CV) is displayed if valid and landing gear is up, under the airspeed window. The units of CV are KCAS unless TAS or GS are selected on UFC Data 1. For example, if PB 4 (on Data 1) is selected (asterisk) then CV is in units of GS. The CV reference point is displayed next to the CV. It is displayed as a function of entering data into the upfront control for time-over-target purposes. When ILST or ILSN steer modes are selected on the HSI, ILS data is also displayed on the ADI (Figure 1-30).

ADI Invalid Displays

The major indication of attitude display problems is an X written across the attitude sphere. The word OFF written by the attitude source indicates the INS/AHRS is invalid. If the turn rate and/or inclinometer information is invalid the word OFF is written adjacent to the data. If the heading source is invalid OFF is written in the middle of the heading scale. If airspeed information is invalid the word OFF is displayed in the airspeed window. If vertical velocity is invalid OFF is written adjacent to it. If the selected source of altitude information is invalid OFF is written in the altitude window.

HORIZONTAL SITUATION INDICATOR (HSI)

The HSI can be displayed on any MPD/MPCD when selected from the MPD/MPCD main menu. When the MPCD is used, the data is color coded as follows :

1. TACAN data is green

2. INS data is blue

3. Heading data is orange

4. All other information is white.

The HSI (figure 1-29) provides a horizontal or plan view of the aircraft with respect to the navigation situation. The aircraft symbol in the center of the HSI is the airplane superimposed on the compass rose. The compass card rotates so that the aircraft heading is always under the top of the lubber line. Command heading and course selection function, plus the steering modes of TCN (PLAN or CDI), GT, ILST, ILSN and NAV are provided by using the display pushbutton. A selection for disabling/enabling automatic destination sequencing is available on the HSI format. The legend "AUTO SEQ" is displayed below PB 18 and is boxed when auto-sequencing is enabled. The selection is automatically enabled when power to the CC is cycled and the aircraft is on the ground. Data associated with ILS operation is also displayed, but only when ILSN/ILST is selected. Additional symbols which are displayed on the HSI are:

RANGE SCALE	There are five range scales (10, 20, 40, 80 and 160 nautical miles). The range represents the distance from the aircraft symbol to the perimeter of the compass rose. The navigation steer point and/or selected tacan station is presented so that their position with respect with current heading can be seen and easily interpreted.
TACAN AND INS NAV DATA	Two data blocks provide bearing, distance, and estimated time enroute (ETE) information about the selected tacan or NAV sequence point selected. The display also includes the tacan channel mode X or Y, or sequence point number.
HEADING MARKER	The marker is moved around by command heading selections made by the operator in all modes except NAV and GT. In NAV the marker is positioned to the command heading to fly for the steer point selected. In GT the marker is positioned to the command heading to fly to maintain a constant ground track.
BEARING POINTERS	Two bearing pointers are displayed, one for INS nav bearing and one for tacan station bearing. The two pointers are shaped and color coded when displayed on the color CRT.
ADF BEARING	A small lollypop symbol indicates the bearing of the transmitted signal. No symbol indicates ADF function is not selected. Selection of ADF is made on the UFC.

NAVIGATION/STEERING MODES

There are five steering modes listed at the bottom of the HSI display. They are TCN, ILST, GT, ILSN, and NAV, and are selected by pressing the desired mode pushbutton. The mode selected becomes boxed.

If the auto pilot has been coupled, the two ILS steer modes are removed from the display and auto-pilot

(A/P) is written on the display. A coupled ILS is not selectable.

TACAN Steering Mode

The display format with TCN selected is shown in Figure 1-30, sheets 1 and 1A. There are two display options available with TCN selected : course deviation indicator (CDI) or PLAN. The current selection is shown at PB 20 and pressing PB 20 will alternate between the two options.

ADI/HSI DISPLAYS

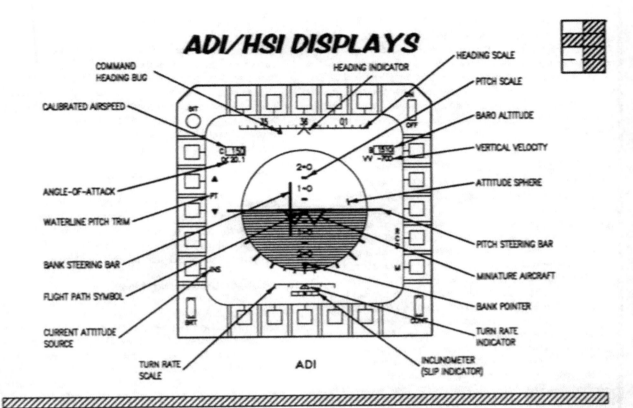

ADI

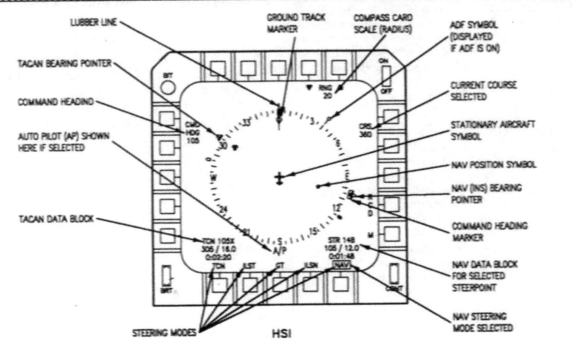

HSI

Figure 1-29

1-91

With CDI selected (sheet 1), a white set course pointer and course deviation indicator are drawn on the display. The set course pointer is drawn through the center of the aircraft symbol according to the course value shown between PB 14 and PB 15. The TO/FROM indicator is drawn adjacent to the aircraft symbol, and the course deviation indicator is drawn on the course deviation scale with full deflection being 10° of displacement.

With PLAN selected (sheet 1A), a green set course arrow is drawn through the center of the TACAN station symbol according to the course value shown between PB 14 and PB 15. There is no TO/FROM indicator and no course deviation indicator. If the selected range scale is too small to show the TACAN position, the TACAN position symbol and the set course arrow are removed. All other features of the HSI display format are the same for either CDI or PLAN. The course set pushbuttons (PB 14 decrement, PB 15 increment) are used to select the desired inbound or outbound radial to fly. The course can also be set by entering the value in the UFC scratchpad and transferring it to the HSI by pressing either PB 14 or PB 15. Since the TACAN channels and modes are selected with the UFC, additional information is provided on the HSI display format to indicate TACAN status. When the TACAN system is off, OFF is written in large red letters in the TACAN data block and above the TCN steer mode cue, and all TACAN indications such as the station position symbol, set course arrow, set course pointer, CDI, bearing pointer and TO/FROM indicator are removed.

ILST/ILSN Steering Modes

Selecting ILST or ILSN mode displays the format shown in figure 1-30, sheets 2 and 3. The CDI displays localizer deviation and the tacan TO-FROM indicator is removed. The course point indicates the selected inbound course to the localizer. The course set pushbutton (or UFC scratchpad) can be used to change the inbound course. The heading set pushbutton or UFC scratchpad can be used to move the heading marker.

GROUND TRACK Steering Mode

Selecting GT mode presents the HSI format shown on figure 1-30, sheet 4. The desired ground track is selected using the course set pushbutton or UFC scratchpad. The course pointer and CDI (course deviation indicator) will not be displayed.

NAVIGATION Steering Mode

Selecting NAV mode displays the bearing and heading to fly to get the steer point selected. As shown on figure 1-30, sheet 5, the heading marker moves to indicate the heading to fly. Command heading is also printed in the command heading window on the left side of the display. Course window displays ground track. Bearing, distance, and time-to-arrive are displayed in the lower right hand data block.

NOTE

When selecting the NAV STEER mode, with AUTO TF engaged, the aircraft may begin an immediate turn.

STEERING DISPLAY

(TACAN MODE / CDI)
GEAR DOWN

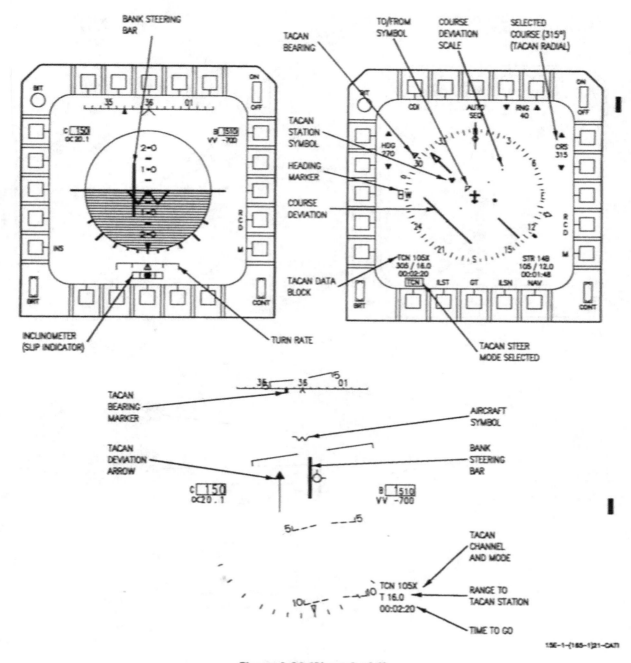

Figure 1-30 (Sheet 1 of 6)

STEERING DISPLAY

(TACAN MODE / PLAN VIEW)
GEAR DOWN

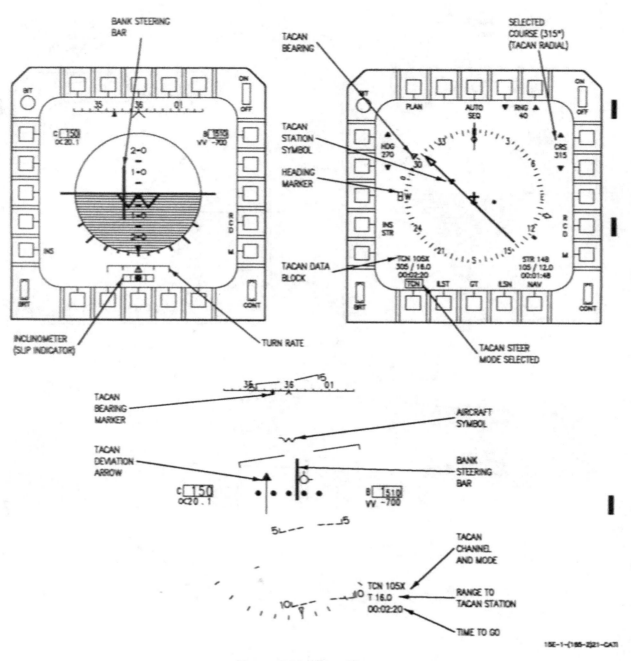

Figure 1-30 (Sheet 2)

15E-1-(195-2)21-CAT1

WARNING	

Control surfaces move during initiated BIT with hydraulic power applied. To prevent personnel injury or equipment damage, keep personnel and equipment clear of control surfaces.

NOTE

For valid BIT reporting, do not operate switches or controls. Do not rest feet on rudder pedals or hands on control stick. Pitch ratio and roll ratio switches should be in AUTO position for valid BIT reporting.

1. Set holding brake (if INS ON).

2. Select MENU/BIT on MPD/MPCD, then press and hold the BIT button on the CAS panel, then press and release the AFCS button on the MPD/MPCD.

3. When AFCS IN TEST is displayed on the MPD/MPCD, release the BIT button on the CAS panel.

   a. AFCS remains in BIT until BIT is completed, paddle switch is pressed STOP button on BIT display is pressed, or holding brake is released.

4. Upon exiting BIT, AFCS IN TEST is removed from MPD/MPCD.

   a. INCOMPLETE will be displayed in BIT display "failure" window if BIT is exited by any means other than completion.

PITOT-STATIC SYSTEM

The pitot-static system (figure 1-32) employs multiple pitot and static sources for redundancy and to provide each inlet controller with conditions peculiar to its inlet during asymmetric conditions. There is an airstream pitot-static mast on each side of the forward fuselage and a pitot mast and flush static port in each inlet duct.

PITOT HEAT SWITCH

The pitot heat switch is on the front cockpit ECS panel on the right console. Two circuit breakers are available to the pilot.

ON	Provides electrical power to the heating elements of all four pitot-static probes.
OFF	Pitot heat off.

AIR DATA COMPUTER

The air data computer (ADC) is a digital computer which receives inputs from the pitot-static system, the AOA probes, the left total temperature probe, the standby altimeter setting knob, the nose landing gear door switch, and the flap switch. The ADC corrects these inputs for sensor error as required, computes various parameters from this data and furnishes required parameters to aircraft equipment and cockpit displays (refer to figure 1-23). The ADC performs validity checks on critical data received by the using equipment or display and actuates appropriate cautions or warnings if the data is invalid. Operation of the ADC is entirely automatic and no controls are available to the pilot.

ANGLE-OF-ATTACK (AOA) PROBES

The AOA probes, on each side of the forward fuselage, measure local AOA and furnish this data to the ADC, the respective engine inlet controller, the AFCS, and the cockpit AOA indicator. Heaters to prevent ice formation are automatically energized when airborne. No controls are available to the pilot. The probes remain hot for some time after flight and contact should be avoided.

TOTAL TEMPERATURE PROBE

Total temperature probes, on the left and right forward fuselage, furnish temperature information to their respective engine air inlet controllers. The left probe furnishes temperature information to the air data computer.

TOT TEMP HI CAUTION

The TOT TEMP HI caution comes on when the sensed duct temperature is high enough to cause critical engine inlet heating. Such temperatures are the result of ram rise at high Mach number.

SIGNAL DATA RECORDER

The signal data recorder records various aircraft and flight parameters for later analysis. It is installed only on some aircraft.

PITOT-STATIC SYSTEM

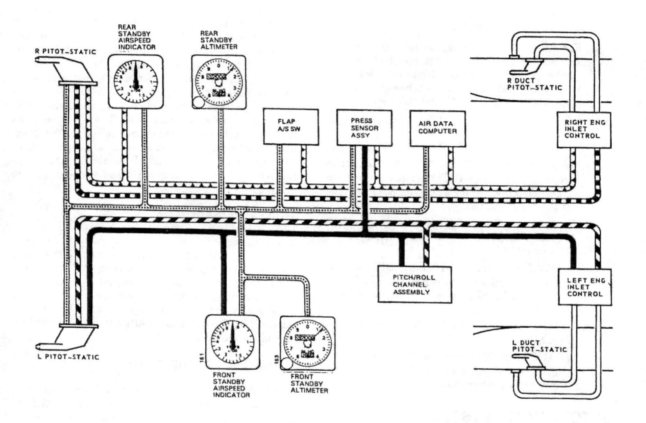

L &…… L & R STATIC 2   L STATIC 1

R PITOT   L PITOT

R STATIC 1   DUCT PITOT & STATIC

15E-1-(80)03

Figure 1-32

AIR DATA COMPUTER

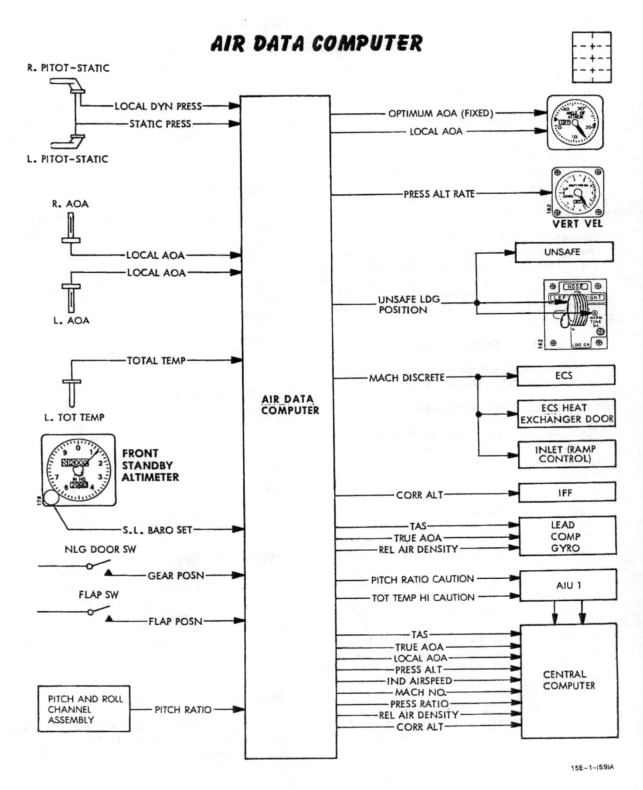

Figure 1-33

15E-1-(59)A

INSTRUMENTS

Refer to foldout section for front and rear cockpit instrument panel illustrations For information about instruments that are an integral part of a system, refer to applicable paragraphs in this section.

STANDBY AIRSPEED INDICATOR

The standby airspeed indicator operates directly from pitot-static pressures. It has a fixed scale of 60 to 850 knots and a rotation pointer. The indicator is in both cockpits.

STANDBY ALTIMETER

The standby altimeter operates directly from a static pressure source. The altimeter is in both cockpits. The barometric pressure in inches of mercury is set on the front cockpit altimeter only. On some aircraft, the thousand digit moves progressively with the pointer rotation, rather than when the pointer transits the 9 to 0 range only.

STANDBY MAGNETIC COMPASS

A conventional aircraft magnetic compass is mounted on the canopy arch in the front cockpit only.

VERTICAL VELOCITY INDICATOR

The vertical velocity indicator is driven by electrical signals from the air data computer. A window on the instrument will display an OFF flag if electrical power is lost or the display is not valid. The indicator is in both cockpits.

STANDBY ATTITUDE INDICATOR

The standby attitude indicator is a self-contained electrically driven gyro-horizon type instrument. The OFF flag appears if there is a power loss to the indicator or the gyro is caged. The gyro is caged by pulling the knob. Do not turn the knob to lock the gyro in the caged position. The gyro cages to 0° pitch and roll regardless of airplane attitude. The caged position is approximately 4° nose up from the normal ground attitude and the gyro will precess 4° nose down after uncaging. Power should be applied to the instrument for at least 1 minute before caging. The indicator displays roll through 360°. Pitch display is limited by mechanical stops at 90° climb and 78° dive. As the aircraft climbs or dives, the pitch attitude changes smoothly until the stop is reached when the gyro tumbles 180° in roll. The indicator is in both cockpits.

ANGLE-OF-ATTACK (AOA) INDICATOR

The AOA indicator, in the front cockpit only, is driven by electrical signals from the probe and displays indicated AOA in units from 0 to 45. A T-shaped index mark is set at approximate optimum landing approach AOA (20 to 22 units). A window on the face of the instrument displays an OFF flag if electrical power is lost, there is invalid data from the ADC or a failure within the indicator. A triangular index mark is positioned full scale and is inoperative.

RADAR ALTIMETER

The radar altimeter indicates clearance over land and water from 0 to 50,000 feet. Audio and visual warnings are activated when the aircraft approaches or descends below 75 % of the selected terrain clearance. Radar altitude generated by the radar altimeter is utilized by the AFCS, LANTIRN navigation and targeting pods and the CC. Radar altitude is also selectively displayed on the HUD, UFC, TSD, and the EADI display (TF ON). The system is controlled by the radar altimeter switch and the UFC. Refer to TO 1F-15E-34-1-1 for detailed and operational description.

Radar Altimeter Switch

The RDR ALT switch on the sensor panel on the left console in the front cockpit has three positions:

OFF	Radar altimeter is deactivated.
ON	Low altitude warning is deactivated. Radar altimeter is activated. Low altitude warning is activated if enabled on UFC.
OVERRIDE	Radar altimeter is deactivated and a signal is sent to the terrain following system that radar altitude is unavailable. Override function can be selected during manual TF but not automatic TF. Low altitude warning is deactivated.

HUD Display

With the radar altimeter turned on, radar altitude is displayed in window 12 of the HUD provided radar altitude is selected on the upfront control. The display, in feet, is boxed with an R or B to the left of the box, indicating the altitude is radar or barometric. Should the altitude source become invalid, an OFF will appear in the box.

Low Altitude Warning Light

A low altitude warning light, labeled LOW ALT, is on the upper instrument panel in both cockpits. The lights come on if the aircraft first climbs above a radar altitude, in feet, set by the upfront control unit and then descends below the set value. The LOW ALT lights remain on until the aircraft climbs above the set value, the radar altimeter is turned off, the altitude value set in the upfront control is changed, or the LAW function is disabled on the upfront control. Light is also used during terrain following to indicate low altitude condition.

Low Altitude Voice Warning

Whenever the LOW ALT light comes on, a voice warning which states "Low Altitude" is heard in the headsets in both cockpits. The voice warning repeats twice and resets when conditions change to cause the LOW ALT light to go out.

Upfront Control

The upfront control is utilized to set the low altitude warning light altitude, and the type altitude (radar/baro) for display on the HUD during normal operation and on the front cockpit MPCD during backup mode (ADI display) operation. Radar altitude can also be displayed on the upfront control by selecting the data 1 display and then checking for an R or B next to the altitude adjacent to the upper left button. If an R is displayed, the altitude displayed is radar altitude. If a B is displayed, the altitude displayed is barometric. To change the low altitude warning altitude, select the menu 1 display on the UFC, type in the new altitude on the keyboard for display on the scratchpad, then press the upper left button adjacent to the LAW readout. To change the status of the LAW function, press the upper left button after ensuring the scratchpad is clear. An asterisk to the left of LAW indicates function is enabled.

ATTITUDE DIRECTOR INDICATOR (ADI)

The ADI (figure 1-34) can be displayed on any MPD/MPCD and consists of the items indicated. The attitude sphere displays pitch and bank. The pitch markings on the sphere are in graduations of 5°, the bank markings begin at 10° increments up to 30°, then 45° and 60°. Signals are received from the INS

or AHRS system. The attitude source is selected by pressing the INS/AHRS pushbutton on the ADI display. The pitch and bank steering bars are driven by signals from the CC. The bank steering bar provides command steering information to intercept tacan radials and navigation computer destinations. The ADI displays vertical velocity under the altitude window if gear is down. It is displayed as descending (−) or ascending (+). Angle of attack is displayed under the airspeed window when the landing gear is down. Command velocity is displayed if valid and landing gear is up, under the airspeed window in the same units as the speed window. The CV reference point is displayed next to the CV. It is displayed as a function of entering data into the upfront control for time-over-target purposes.

ADI Invalid Displays

The major indication of attitude display problems is an X written across the attitude sphere. The word OFF written by the attitude source indicates the INS/AHRS is invalid. If the turn rate and/or inclinometer information is invalid the word OFF is written adjacent to the data. If the heading source is invalid OFF is written in the middle of the heading scale. If airspeed information is invalid the word OFF is displayed in the airspeed window. If vertical velocity is invalid OFF is written adjacent to it. If the selected source of altitude information is invalid OFF is written in the altitude window.

HORIZONTAL SITUATION INDICATOR (HSI)

The HSI can be displayed on any MPD/MPCD when selected from the MPD/MPCD main menu. When the MPCD is used, the data is color coded as follows :

1. TACAN data is green
2. INS data is cyan (light blue)
3. Heading data is orange
4. All other information is white.

The HSI (figure 1-34) provides a horizontal or plan view of the aircraft with respect to the navigation situation. The aircraft symbol in the center of the HSI is the airplane superimposed on the compass rose. The compass card rotates so that the aircraft heading is always under the top of the lubber line. Command heading and course selection function, plus the steering modes of TCN, GT, ILST, ILSN and NAV are provided by using the display pushbutton. Data associated with ILS operation is also displayed, but only when it is selected. Additional symbols which are displayed on the HSI are:

RANGE SCALE
There are five range scales (10, 20, 40, 80 and 160 nautical miles). The range represents the distance from the aircraft symbol to the perimeter of the compass rose. The navigation steer point and/or selected tacan station is presented so that their position with respect with current heading can be seen and easily interpreted.

TACAN AND INS NAV DATA
Two data blocks provide bearing, distance, and estimated time enroute (ETE) information about the selected tacan or NAV sequence point selected. The display also includes the tacan channel mode X or Y, or sequence point number.

HEADING MARKER
The marker is moved around by command heading selections made by the operator in all modes except NAV and GT. In NAV the marker is positioned to the command heading to fly for the steer point selected. In GT the marker is positioned to the command heading to fly to maintain a constant ground track.

BEARING POINTERS
Two bearing pointers are displayed, one for INS nav bearing and one for tacan station bearing. The two pointers are shaped and color coded when displayed on the color CRT.

ADF BEARING
A small lollypop symbol indicates the bearing of the transmitted signal. No symbol indicates ADF function is not selected. Selection of ADF is made on the UFC.

NAVIGATION/STEERING MODES

There are five steering modes listed at the bottom of the HSI display. They are TCN, ILST, GT, ILSN, and NAV, and are selected by pressing the desired mode pushbutton. The mode selected becomes boxed.

If the auto pilot has been coupled, the two ILS steer modes are removed from the display and auto-pilot (A/P) is written on the display. A coupled ILS is not selectable.

TACAN STEERING MODE

The display format with TCN (tacan) selected is shown in figure 1-35. The information displayed is described in the following. The course pointer is indicating the selected course is 315°. The TO-FROM symbol, a course deviation indicator (CDI) (full scale deflection is 10 degrees), and a course deviation scale are also present. The course set pushbuttons, increase, decrease, are used to select the desired inbound or outbound radial to fly. This can also be entered in UFC scratch pad and transferred to the HSI by pressing either the increment or decrement pushbutton. Since tacan channels and modes are selected with the up-front-control, some additional information is provided within the display format to provide Tacan status. There are obvious cues to advise the crew that the system is off, such as the course pointer and CDI being removed. In addition, the bearing pointer, and to-from indications are also removed. To ensure there is no doubt about TACAN status, OFF appears where station bearing, distance, and ETE are normally written, and also above TCN steer mode cue.

ILST OR ILSN STEERING MODES

When ILST or ILSN mode is selected, the CDI displays localizer deviation and the tacan TO-FROM indicator is removed. The course point indicates the selected inbound course to the localizer. The course set pushbutton (or UFC scratchpad) can be used to change the inbound course. The heading set pushbutton or UFC scratchpad can be used to move the heading marker.

GROUND TRACK STEERING MODE

Selecting this mode presents the HSI format shown on figure 1-35. The desired ground track is selected using the course set pushbutton or UFC scratchpad. The course pointer and CDI (course deviation indicator) will not be displayed.

NAVIGATION STEERING MODE

Selecting NAV mode displays the bearing and heading to fly to get the steer point selected. As shown on figure 1-35, the heading marker moves to indicate the heading to fly. Command heading is also printed in

ADI/HSI DISPLAYS

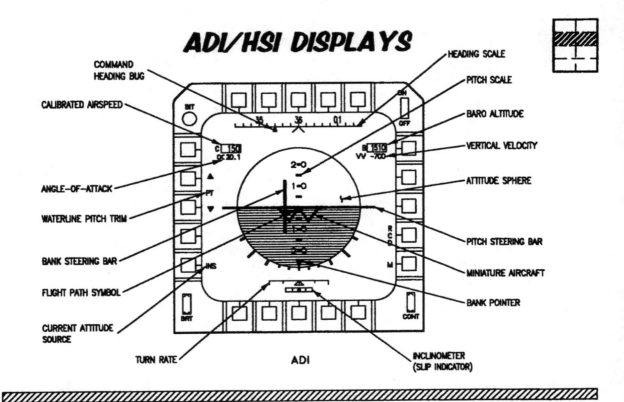

ADI

Labels (clockwise from top left):
- COMMAND HEADING BUG
- CALIBRATED AIRSPEED
- ANGLE-OF-ATTACK
- WATERLINE PITCH TRIM
- BANK STEERING BAR
- FLIGHT PATH SYMBOL
- CURRENT ATTITUDE SOURCE
- TURN RATE
- HEADING SCALE
- PITCH SCALE
- BARO ALTITUDE
- VERTICAL VELOCITY
- ATTITUDE SPHERE
- PITCH STEERING BAR
- MINIATURE AIRCRAFT
- BANK POINTER
- INCLINOMETER (SLIP INDICATOR)

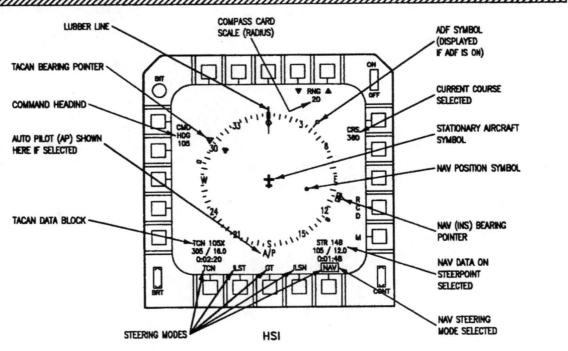

HSI

Labels (clockwise from top left):
- LUBBER LINE
- TACAN BEARING POINTER
- COMMAND HEADIND
- AUTO PILOT (AP) SHOWN HERE IF SELECTED
- TACAN DATA BLOCK
- STEERING MODES
- COMPASS CARD SCALE (RADIUS)
- ADF SYMBOL (DISPLAYED IF ADF IS ON)
- CURRENT COURSE SELECTED
- STATIONARY AIRCRAFT SYMBOL
- NAV POSITION SYMBOL
- NAV (INS) BEARING POINTER
- NAV DATA ON STEERPOINT SELECTED
- NAV STEERING MODE SELECTED

Figure 1-34

15E-1-(48-1)02-CATI

the command heading window on the left side of the display. Course window displays ground track. Bearing, distance, and time-to-arrive are displayed in the lower right hand data block.

NAVIGATION HEAD-UP DISPLAYS (HUD)

The HUD displays the following aircraft parameters in all modes: magnetic heading, airspeed, altitude, velocity vector, pitch scale, aircraft symbol, and (in air-to-air modes) aircraft Mach. The aircraft load factor to the nearest tenth of a g is displayed in all modes and this reading is limited to 9 g. The HUD displays both current and maximum allowable g for existing flight conditions, aircraft configuration, and gross weight. Current g is displayed on the left and maximum allowable g is displayed on the right. The maximum allowable display changes automatically as flight conditions and gross weight changes. If the overload warning system fails, the g display reverts to displaying only the current g and OW OFF will appear on the display next to the current g. The aircraft is also equipped with a provision to cage the velocity vector symbol in the A/G and NAV master mode. When the NAV master mode is initially selected, the velocity vector is positioned at the correct position. Flashing of the velocity vector indicates that the symbols actual position is out of the HUD field of view. Pressing and releasing the LASER/FIRE button on the throttle, with command of the HUD, centers the velocity vector and pitch scale in azimuth. A subsequent depression again frees the symbols in drift. The aircraft symbol is displayed when not in A/G master mode. In all navigation steering modes the heading, bank scale, velocity vector (in A/A mode), and pitch scales symbology can be removed by placing the HUD symbol switch on the HUD control panel to the reject 1 position. In addition to the flight parameters, the HUD displays navigational data if the avionics system is in the NAV mode. The NAV mode is selected by positioning the weapon select switch on the throttles to any position other than gun and pressing the NAV master mode pushbutton in the front cockpit. In NAV (navigation) mode, in addition to the flight parameters, the HUD displays bank steering to the destination selected, time-to-go and range to destination, steering mode selected, and nav destination selected. In TCN (tacan) mode, the HUD displays are the same as in NAV mode except that the bank steering displayed is to the selected tacan radial, the time-to-go and range displayed is to the tacan station, and destination is not displayed. In ILS/NAV and ILS/TCN (instrument landing set) modes, in addition to the flight

parameters, the HUD displays the following: bank and pitch steering bars for approach and landing on runway destination, time-to-go and range to destination (in ILS/NAV) or tacan station (in ILS/TCN), the steering mode selected, and the glideslope deviation scale and pointer for glide slope steering. Time-to-go is displayed to the nearest second with a maximum reading of 99. Also when the steering mode selected is either the ILS/NAV or ILS/TCN and the aircraft passes over the outer marker or middle marker beacon, MKR will be displayed on the HUD. Range to the nearest tenth of a nautical mile is displayed on the HUD for any mode selected on the steering mode panel. In all modes, angle-of-attack data in cockpit units is displayed on the HUD. When gear is down, all the HUD window symbols (the bank scale, course deviation indicator (ILS), ILS glideslope) on the HUD display are lowered to reduce pilot look angles from the velocity vector to the displays.

Airspeed and altitude parameters are displayed in digital formats. The crewmembers have the option of selecting either calibrated (C) or true (T) airspeed, or groundspeed (G) for display. Either C, T, or G is displayed next to the digital display. The altitude can also be referenced to either radar altimeter (R) or barometric (B). These selections are made from the UFC data 1 menu and are displayed in digital format. A bank scale is at the bottom of the HUD display and is graduated into 10° segments up to 30° then 15° segments up to 60°. If the command heading is beyond the 30° scale displayed, a digital readout of the heading appears at the end of the scale.

During terrain following mode, radar altitude is displayed as a thermometer scale with the selected terrain clearance displayed as an accented tic mark on the right side of the scale. A rectangular box symbol provides pitch command steering information referenced to the velocity vector and is displayed when manual TF is selected. TF warning cues are displayed above the velocity vector when a problem arises. TF caution cues are displayed below the velocity vector. If auto TF is selected the command signal is changed to a pitch command bar.

UFC NAVIGATION DISPLAYS

Navigation displays consisting of sequence point coordinates, elevation, range and bearing, offset data, and INS update data are contained on several submenus and are accessed from the menu and data displays on the upfront control. These submenus are used to verify data loaded into the aircraft via the DTM, provide steering and timing data for route

STEERING DISPLAYS

(ILS NAV MODE)
GEAR DOWN

LOCALIZER DEVIATION INDICATOR

LOCALIZER DEVIATION (SCALE)

BANK STEERING BAR (LOCALIZER)

GLIDESLOPE INDICATOR

GLIDESLOPE DEVIATION (SCALE)

FLIGHT PATH SYMBOL (BOWTIE)

TURN RATE

SLIP INDICATOR

HEADING INDICATOR

PITCH STEERING BAR (GLIDESLOPE)

MARKER BEACON

CDI

COMMAND HEADING

COURSE POINTER

ILS INBOUND COURSE SELECTED HERE

ILS NAV MODE SELECTED

NAV BEARING POINTER

TCN 105X
305 / 16.0
00:02:20

STR 148
105 / 12.0
00:01:48

HDG 270

CRS 315

RNG 40

COMMAND HEADING

LOCALIZER DEVIATION

GLIDESLOPE INDICATOR

GLIDESLOPE DEVIATION SCALE

CDI

BANK STEERING BAR (ILS LOCALIZER)

PITCH STEERING BAR (ILS GLIDESLOPE)

VERTICAL VELOCITY

ILSN DATA BLOCK

MARKER BEACON CUE

ILSN
N 12.6
00:03:02
MKR

Figure 1-35 (Sheet 1 of 5)

15E-1-(185-1)04-CAT1

STEERING DISPLAYS
(ILS TACAN MODE)
GEAR UP

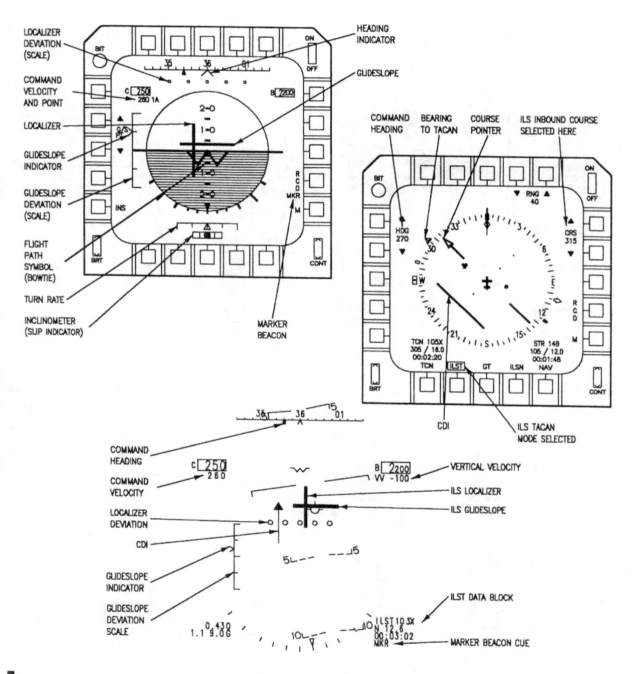

Figure 1-35.(Sheet 2)

15E-1-(185-2)04-CATI

STEERING DISPLAY

(NAV MODE)
GEAR UP

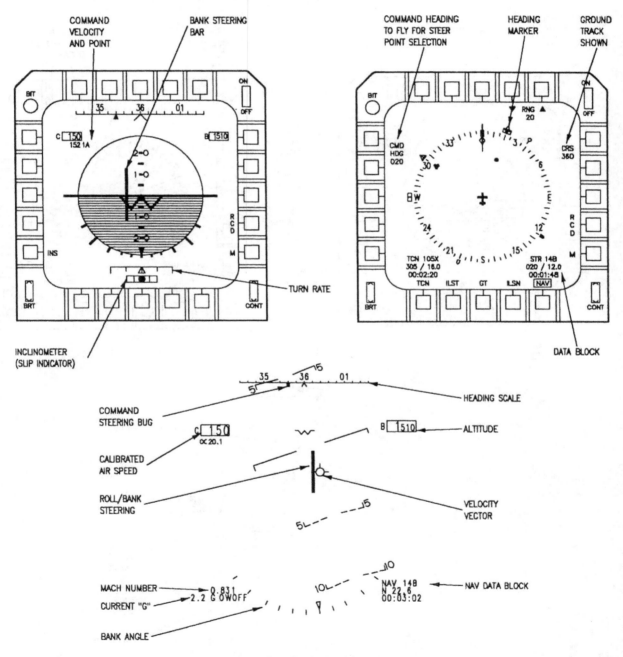

Figure 1-35.(Sheet 3)

15E-1-(188-3)04-CATI

STEERING DISPLAY

(TACAN MODE)
GEAR DOWN

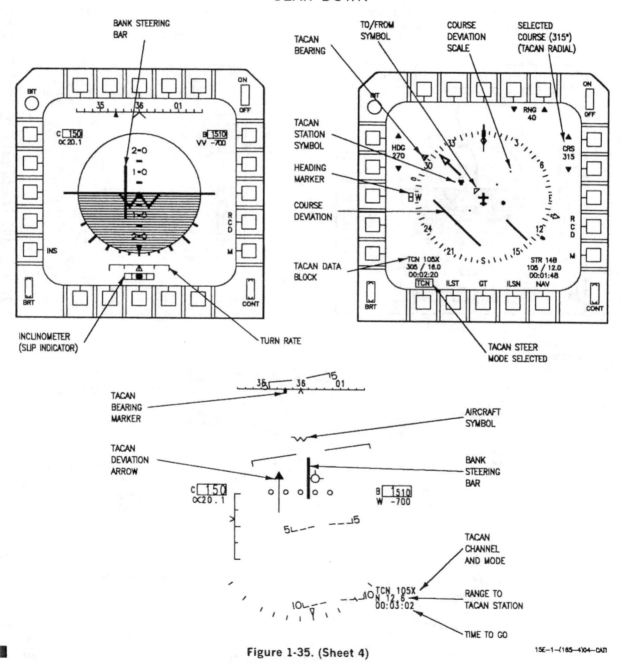

Figure 1-35. (Sheet 4)

15E-1-(165-4)04-CAT

STEERING DISPLAYS
(GROUND TRACK MODE)
GEAR UP

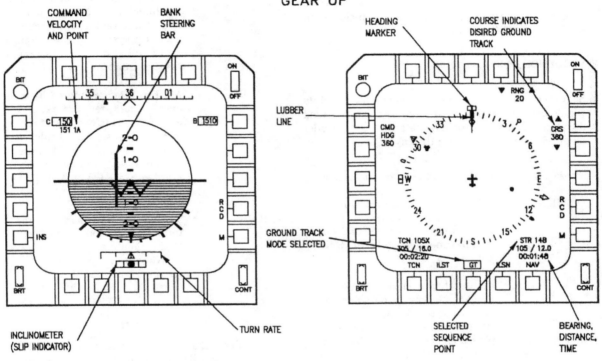

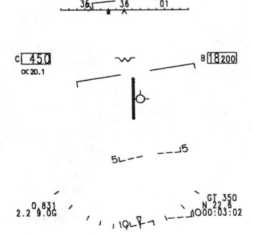

Figure 1-35. (Sheet 5)

15E-1-(165-5)04-CAT1

navigation and target attack, and to enter or change data for navigation and target attack. Route navigation and steering are described in TO 1F-15E-34-1-1.

In order to enter or change a specific item on the UFC, the appropriate submenu must be accessed. Procedures to enter or change data is included in section II, UFC Procedures.

SEQUENCE POINTS

Sequence points are a set of geographical points which can be overflown or used for sensor cuing during a mission. All points are stored as latitude/longitude and converted for display as lat/long.

These points are divided into the following categories.

LIST DTM loaded points which are used to generate steer, aim, target, and target offset points. The system can store a total of 99 list points.

STEER Points which comprise the basic route to be flown. Combined steer and target points cannot exceed 100 (all routes, A, B, and C). Displayed as the point number and route letter (17A).

AIM Always associated with a steer point, up to seven aim points per steer point. Displayed as the steer point number plus a decimal, tenth, and route letter (17.1A). The system can store up to 100 combined aim and offset points in all three routes.

TARGET Displayed as a point number followed by a decimal and route letter (18.B). Combined target and steer points cannot exceed 100. Target data also displayed in direction/range north and east of offset or range/bearing from offset point.

OFFSET Always associated with a target point, displayed as the target number, decimal, hundredths, and route letter (18.01B). The system can store up to seven offsets per target, maximum of 100 combined offset and aim points in all three routes. Point data also displayed in direction/range north and east of target or range/bearing from target.

MARK Mark points are entered by an overfly mark, radar mark, or an automatic overfly mark at weapon release; data displayed includes time of day. They are displayed as the mark sequence number preceded by M (M2) up to 10.

BASE The base point is normally the unit home station, is displayed as B and should agree with the PP coordinates during INS alignment.

NOTE

When changing sequence point numbers, the route letter does not need to be entered if the new point is in the same route (A, B, or C) as the old point.

Data 1 Display

The data 1 display (figure 1-36) contains current aircraft information. From this display, either the pilot or WSO can change: aircraft altitude source (radar or barometric); wind direction and speed (if PP source is ADC or INS failed); display of true, calibrated, or ground speed on other displays; TOD; and current steer point ETE/ETA; or the current steer point itself. On the data 1 display, all navigation points are preceded by STR. The specific type of point is determined by the use of a decimal and/or digits after the decimal as shown previously.

Point Data Submenus

The point data latitude/longitude submenu is accessed by pressing the button adjacent to the current steer point number (figure 1-36). Sequence point

DATA 1 DISPLAY/SUBMENUS

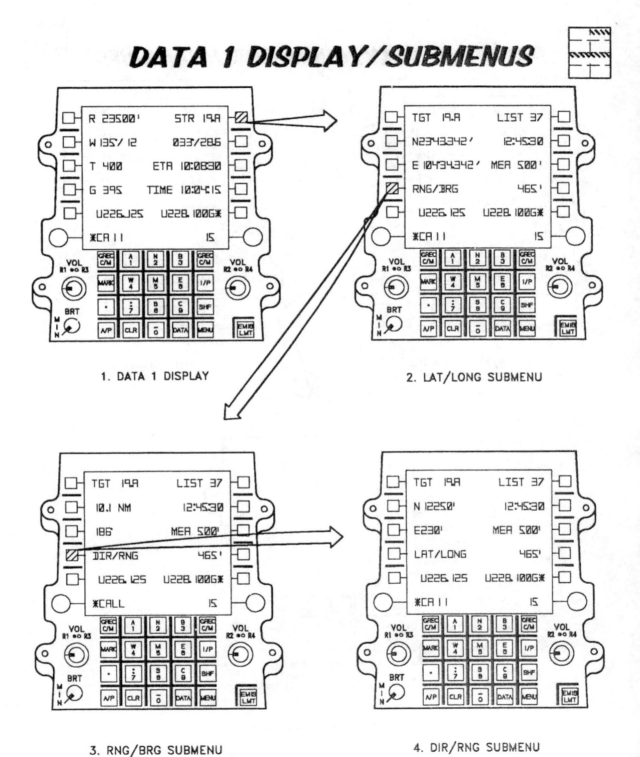

1. DATA 1 DISPLAY

2. LAT/LONG SUBMENU

3. RNG/BRG SUBMENU

4. DIR/RNG SUBMENU

Figure 1-36 (Sheet 1 of 3)

15E-1-(27-1)04-CAT1

DATA 1 DISPLAY/SUBMENUS (CONTINUED)

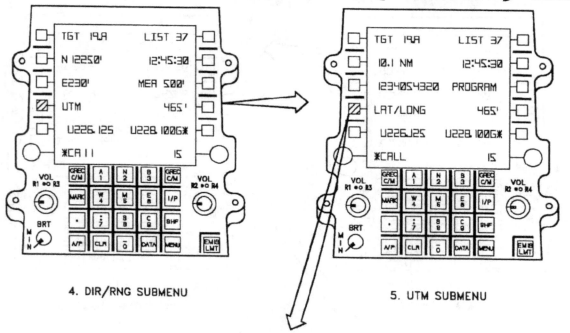

4. DIR/RNG SUBMENU

5. UTM SUBMENU

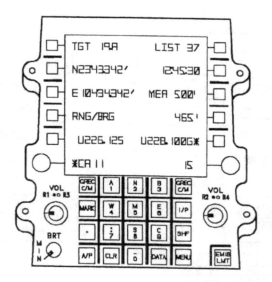

6. LAT/LONG SUBMENU

Figure 1-36 (Sheet 2)

DATA 1 DISPLAY/SUBMENUS (CONTINUED)

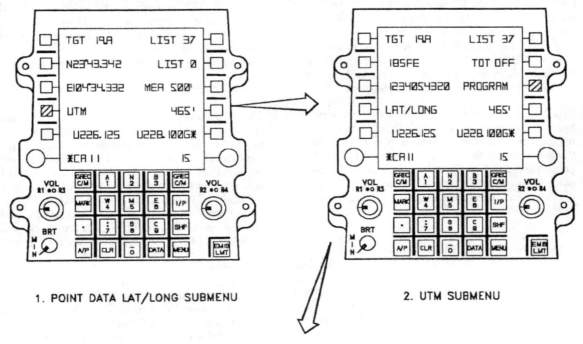

1. POINT DATA LAT/LONG SUBMENU

2. UTM SUBMENU

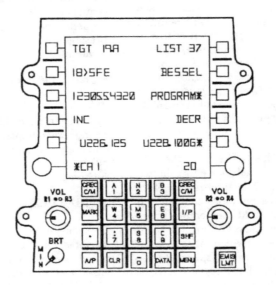

3. UTM PROGRAMMING SUBMENU

Figure 1-36. (Sheet 3)

15E-1-(27-3)04-CAT1

type, lat/long, elevation, and minimum enroute altitude (MEA) and time-on-target (TOT) may be changed.

The RNG/BRG submenu is available from the lat/long submenu only if there are offsets stored for a target or target offset point. Press RNG/BRG to enter the range/bearing submenu. On this display, the following items may be changed: current range to the point in NM and tenths of a NM, magnetic bearing to the point, ETA to the point (not available for aim, mark, or offset points), and point elevation.

Pressing the button next to DIR/RNG on the range/bearing submenu selects the direction/range submenu. The DIR/RNG submenu is available only if there are offsets stored for a target or target offset point. Direction N, S, E, or W and range in feet to the point shown may be changed. To return to the data 1 display at any time from the submenus, press the data button once.

To convert to UTM geographical coordinates from lat/long coordinates, the crewmember presses the button adjacent to UTM. This calls up the point data UTM submenu, figure 1-36. 18SFE represents the UTM grid zone and 10,000 meter squared block; the x and y coordinates are 1234054320. The number 1234054320 represents 12,340 meters in the eastern direction, and 54,320 meters in the northern direction. If data to the nearest meter is not available, the aircrew is not required to enter all five digits for each of the east and north coordinates. All that's required is to enter an even number of digits; the first half of the entry is defined as the east coordinate, and the second half is the north coordinate. For example, if the aircrew enters 123456, then east = 12,300 meters and north = 45,600 meters offset from the corner of the grid zone. A quick means is provided to return the lat/long coordinates; simply press the button adjacent to LAT/LONG.

The UTM PROGRAMMING, figure 1-36 (sheet 3), submenu allows the aircrew to select a new spheroid or to change the UTM 10,000 meter squared block identifier. The UTM programming submenu is selected from the point data UTM submenu by pressing the button adjacent to PROGRAM. For the UTM coordinate system, the globe is divided into a number of large oval-shaped sections called spheroids. To select a new spheriod, press the button adjacent to the term BESSEL. Successive depressions rotate through the seven spheriod options: Bessel, WGS, International (INTL), Clarke 66, Clarke 80, Everest, and Australian National (AUST NAT). To change the

10,000 meter squared block, first, press the button adjacent to 18>S F E until the caret is pointing at the letter which you wish to change. Next, press and hold either the increment (INC) or decrement (DECR) button until the desired letter of the alphabet is displayed. This procedure is repeated until the three desired characters are displayed. Note that the letters I and O are not used. Programming is exited by pressing the pushbutton adjacent to PROGRAM. Display will return to the UTM Program Submenu.

DATA 2 DISPLAY

The data 2 display (figure 1-37) provides time, ground speed, and fuel information pertaining to two selected points in the selected navigation route sequence. Pressing the button next to 15000 LBS (fuel remaining at SP 24.A) cycles range and bearing direct from A/C position to line-of-sight SP 24.A, and back to fuel remaining . Pressing the button next to ETA (estimated time of arrival at SP 24.A) cycles to ETE (estimated time enroute) to 24.A and back to ETA. The 12000 LBS shows the fuel remaining at SP 25.A if the route is flown at the command ground speed (CG) direct to the line-of-sight point (24.A) then following the route to the look ahead (end) point 25.A. TOA is the time of arrival at SP 25.A at the CG. Pressing either CG, fuel or TOA changes the display as shown in display 2. If there is no TOT stored for SP 25.A, OFF is displayed next to CG and TOT. A TOT may be entered on this display. The line-of-sight sequence point (SP 24.A) and the look ahead sequence point (SP 25.A) can be incremented by pressing the adjacent button or changed using the scratchpad.

MENU 1 DISPLAY

The menu 1 display (figure 1-38) is a basic avionic system status display. However it can be used to change steer points, to access the point data submenu, to access the tacan, NAV FLIR, AAI, IFF, and A/P submenus, or change the TF set clearance or LAW altitude.

MENU 2 DISPLAY

The menu 2 display (figure 1-39) contains control features for the secure speech system and the ILS which are explained under those system descriptions elsewhere in section I. It also allows access to the DIRECT/MANUAL bombing mode HUD reticle setting, present position source submenu, update submenu, and the HUD titling submenu (Refer to Video Tape Recorder System, this section).

DATA 2 DISPLAY

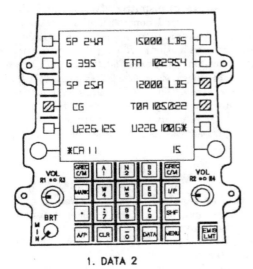

1. DATA 2

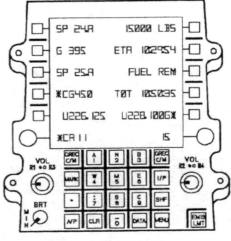

2. COMMAND GS

Figure 1-37

HUD Reticle Mil Setting

The HUD reticle is depressable only in direct or manual mode. Depression angle in mils is set by entering the desired setting in the scratchpad and pressing the HUD RET button.

Present Position Source Submenu

To select the PP source submenu, press the button next to PP-INS; the display appears as shown in figure 1-39. Either pilot or WSO may select the desired PP source and change the aircraft present position latitude and longitude.

Entering a new latitude and longitude to the INS should not be done without the INS, CC and UFC turned-on and evaluation of the INS stored PP at turn-on. When a new PP is entered the new values should be accurate to 600 feet (0.1 arc minute). Present position entered during alignment should be the actual location of the aircraft. PP corrections made after the aircraft has moved should be done by update after transition to NAV. The cockpit UFC will automatically initialize to the PP source submenu

when going from INS OFF to GC align, if the cockpit UFC is not on a submenu.

Update Submenu

Pressing the button adjacent to UPDATE selects the update submenu as shown in figure 1-39, display 3. This display allows the aircrew to update the INS position using data from the HUD, tacan, or by direct overfly freeze of a point. Prior to any attempted update, verify that the point to be updated is displayed next to UPDATE. If not, enter the point via the scratchpad. The point entered will become the current steer point.

To perform a HUD update, the desired update point must be identified using the HUD designation procedures in TO 1F-15E-34-1-1 after pressing HUD on the UFC. Once the point is designated, the CC calculates range errors between the stored latitude/longitude of the update point and the HUD designated location of the point; the errors are displayed in N/S and E/W feet on the display. (INV, for invalid, is displayed if a present position source is not available.) To accept the displayed errors, press ENTER and the INS position is updated. If the update is not desired,

MENU 1 DISPLAY

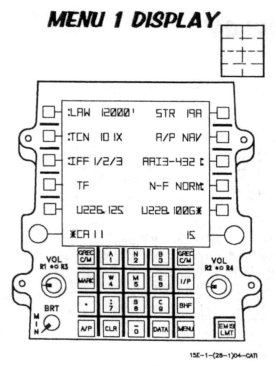

15E-1-(2B-1)04-CATI

Figure 1-38

the aircrew may perform another update or exit the update submenu.

To perform a tacan update the aircrew must first select the desired tacan channel and X or Y system on the UFC, then press the button next to the tacan channel. The CC calculates the directional range errors between the stored latitude/longitude of the tacan station and the range/bearing of the station to the current aircraft position. (INV is displayed if a PP source is not available or the tacan coordinates have not been stored.) The aircrew may then ENTER the update, perform another update, or exit the update submenu.

An overfly freeze update is accomplished by flying directly over the displayed steer point and pressing the OFLY FRZ button. The CC calculates the directional range errors between the stored coordinates and the aircraft present position and displays the N/S and E/W errors. The aircrew may ENTER the update, perform another update, or exit the update submenu.

UHF COMMUNICATIONS SYSTEM

The UHF communications system provides an air-to-air and air-to-ground communications, automatic direction finding (ADF), and monitoring of guard (emergency frequency). The system consists of two separate receiver-transmitters (UHF 1 and UHF 2) with their associated controls and indicators. Both radios have provisions for a speech unit (KY-58) for secure communications. Both receiver-transmitters transmit on manually selected frequencies or on 20 preset frequencies within the 225.000 to 399.975 MHz frequency range. The UHF radios can operate in Have Quick mode (anti-jam). The radios can be operated from ground power without cooling air; however, transmissions should be minimized.

NOTE

- If an annoying noise is received by one crewman whose UHF receiver is tuned to a low UHF frequency (230 to 260 MHz) while the second crewman is transmitting at a high UHF frequency on the other radio, the noise can be eliminated by placing the UHF 1 antenna selector switch to UPPER.

- If PACS is off only a tone will be transmitted on UHF 1 if an attempt to transmit is made.

UHF CONTROLS AND INDICATORS

The UHF 1 and UHF 2 radios are operated by controls on the intercommunications set control panel, the remote intercommunications control panel, the microphone switch on the throttles, the foot operated switches on the rear cockpit floor, and the upfront control.

INTERCOMMUNICATIONS SET CONTROL PANEL

The intercommunications set control panel is on the left console in the rear cockpit. Controls on the panel associated with the UHF radios are the voice warning silence pushbutton, the tone selector switch and the intercom function selector switch.

REMOTE INTERCOMMUNICATIONS CONTROL PANEL

The remote intercommunications control panel is on the left console in the front cockpit. Controls associated with the UHF radios are the voice warning

MENU 2 DISPLAY/SUBMENUS

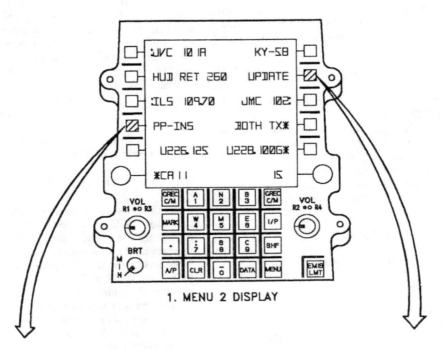

1. MENU 2 DISPLAY

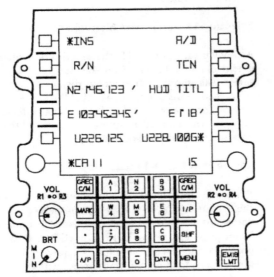

2. PP SOURCE SUBMENU

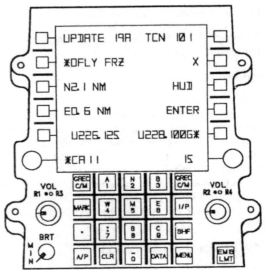

3. UPDATE SUBMENU

Figure 1-39

15E-1-(2B-1)04-CAT1

silence pushbutton, the UHF antenna selector switch, the VHF antenna selector switch, the tone selector switch, and the intercom function selector switch.

Voice Warning Silence Pushbutton

Pressing this pushbutton silences the voice warnings and the aural tones in progress for one minute. If still present after one minute, the warnings will be heard again.

UHF Antenna Selector Switch

The UHF antenna selector switch has positions of UPPER, LOWER and AUTO. Placing the switch to UPPER selects the upper antenna for UHF 1 radio and putting the switch to LOWER selects the lower antenna for UHF 1 radio. Placing the switch to AUTO (automatic) causes the UHF 1 radio to automatically select the antenna with the best signal. The UHF 2 radio always transmits and receives on the lower antenna.

VHF Antenna Selector Switch

This switch is presently inoperative.

Tone Selector Switch

The tone selector switch has positions of UHF 1 and UHF 2. The crewmember can transmit tone on the UHF 1 or UHF 2 by selecting either position.

Intercom Function Selector Switch

This switch is described in the Intercom System paragraphs, this section.

MICROPHONE SWITCH

A three-position microphone switch is on the inboard throttle control handle in each cockpit for UHF transmission. It is spring-loaded to the center, receive position. Pushing the switch forward enables transmission on radios 1 and 3. Pushing the switch aft enables transmission on radios 2 and 4. There are two foot-operated, push to transmit pushbuttons on the rear cockpit floor. The left pushbutton controls transmissions on UHF 1, the right pushbutton controls transmission on UHF 2.

OPERATION OF UHF RADIOS

When aircraft power is activated the radios selections on UHF 1 and UHF 2 radios from the previous flight are displayed on the UFC. The asterisk symbol displayed next to the preset channel number or the

manual frequency indicates the radio is turned on, UHF 1 channel 11 with cipher (C) and anti-jam (A) functions are selected, and UHF 2 manual frequency (228.100) had been previously selected (see figure 1-40). To confirm the operating status of UHF 1 press the pushbutton next to the UHF 1 digital readout to call up the UHF 1 submenu. When selected this submenu will appear as shown in figure 1-31. Absence of a colon, adjacent to U1, or asterisk in row 5 or 6 indicates the radio is off. Pressing the pushbutton next to U1 applies power to the system and the colon and asterisk symbol are displayed. The volume control for UHF 1 is on the left side of the UFC and labeled R1. R3 is reserved for JTIDS. The volume control for UHF 2 is on the right side. R4 is provided as a spare. Pressing the channel selector knob cycles between radios UHF 1 and 3 or UHF 2 and 4.

Selection Of Guard

After the selected radio is powered, press and release the shift (SHF) pushbutton key. Next, press the guard receiver (GREC) pushbutton key. The letter G appears next to the manual frequency readout (figure 1-41) indicating that the guard receiver is now active with that UHF radio. The process is repeated to deselect the guard receiver. To transmit on guard the preset channel selected must be rotated until the letter G appears adjacent to the channel selector. The guard transmit/receive function is available with either UHF radio.

Selecting The Displayed Manual Frequencies

As shown on figure 1-41, the asterisk indicates that preset channel 11 has been selected for UHF 1. To select the manual frequency displayed (226.125), press the GREC and C/M pushbutton key. C/M stands for channel and manual. The asterisk will move to the manual frequency indicating that it is now selected for transmit/receive on UHF 1.

Keying In A Manual Frequency

Press the desired numeric pushbutton keys so that the frequency is displayed in the scratchpad. The decimal if not entered is accomplished automatically. Then press either the UHF 1 or UHF 2 pushbutton opposite the current manual frequency being displayed. The two manual frequencies will swap display locations as shown in figure 1-40, so that if necessary, it is easy to return to the original manual frequency. To accomplish this, press the display pushbutton a second time.

UHF OPERATION DISPLAYS

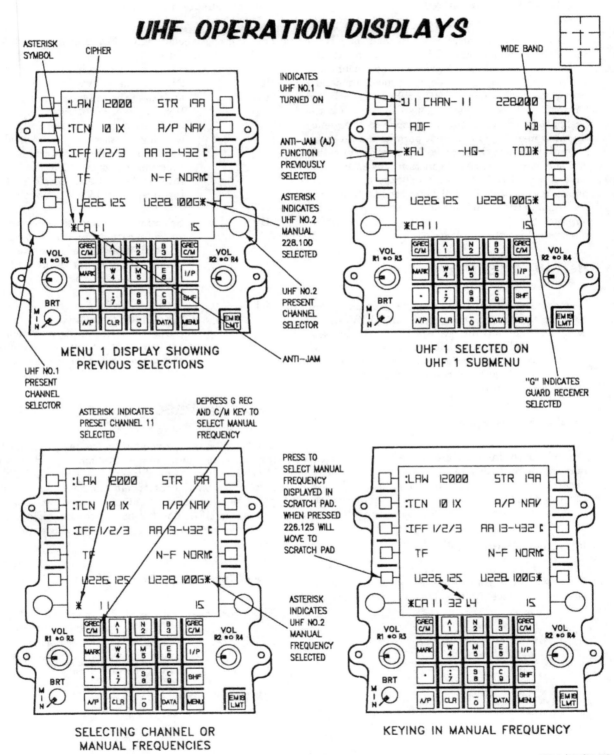

Figure 1-40

UHF 1 AND UHF 2 SUBMENUS

A separate submenu display is provided for UHF 1 and UHF 2. Selection of UHF 1 submenu (figure 1-41) is accomplished by pressing the pushbutton adjacent to the displayed frequency shown in menu 1 with a blank scratchpad. UHF 2 submenu is selected for display in a similar manner by pressing the pushbutton adjacent to the displayed frequency shown in menu 1. This format permits the programming of the preset channels (1-20), selection of cipher and anti-jam modes, ADF function plus selection of have quick (HQ) functions. To change channel 11's preset frequency of 228.000, key in the new frequency, confirm it in the scratchpad and press the pushbutton opposite the old frequency readout. The new frequency will now be displayed.

INTERCOM SYSTEM

The intercom system (ICS) provides communication between the two crewmembers, and between the crewmembers and the ground crew. An external receptacle and volume control are installed on the aircraft exterior for the ground crew. The exterior volume control knob controls intercom volume to the ground crew headset.

INTERCOM CONTROLS

Controls for the intercom are on the remote intercommunications control panel in front cockpit and the intercommunications set control panel in the rear cockpit. These controls are the ICS volume control knob and the intercom function selector switch.

ICS Volume Control Knob

The ICS volume control knob adjusts the intercom audio volume level for the crewmembers headset.

Intercom Function Selector Switch

This switch, labeled MIC, has positions of RAD ORIDE, ON and OFF.

RAD ORIDE	Selecting radio override will attenuate the radio communications in favor of intercom communication; however, the voice warning messages are not overridden, and the following warning tones are not overridden: yaw rate, angle of attack, unsafe landing, over G, and TEWS launch.
ON	Selecting ON provides direct communication from the cockpit in which it is selected with the other cockpit and/or the ground crew.
OFF	Selecting OFF turns off the microphone for intercom purposes; however, the crewmember can still transmit on the radio and normal side tone is provided.

SECURE SPEECH SYSTEM (KY-58)

The KY-58 is used for ciphering (coding) or deciphering (decoding) audio routed through the UHF 1 and UHF 2 receiver-transmitters. The controls for the system are on the intercommunications set control panel, the remote intercommunications control panel, and on the UFC. The KY-58 control, located on both the above control panels, is the cipher text selector switch.

Cipher Text Selector Switch

This switch has positions of ONLY and NORM.

ONLY	The radio can receive only the ciphered text and not clear text radio communications.
NORM	Permits reception of both cipher text and clear text radio communications.

UHF SUBMENUS

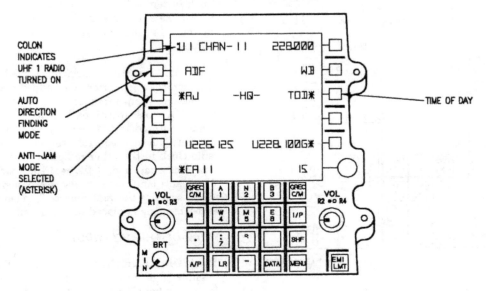

COLON
INDICATES
UHF 1 RADIO
TURNED ON

AUTO
DIRECTION
FINDING
MODE

ANTI—JAM
MODE
SELECTED
(ASTERISK)

TIME OF DAY

UHF 1 SUBMENU

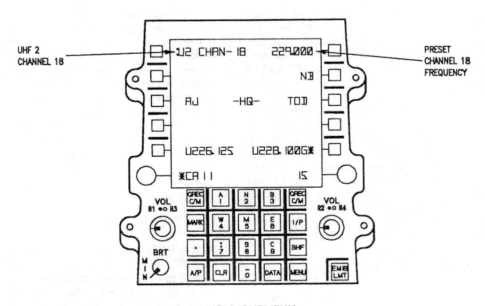

UHF 2
CHANNEL 18

PRESET
CHANNEL 18
FREQUENCY

UHF 2 SUBMENU

Figure 1-41

15E-1-(50-1)-CAT1

KY-58 SUBMENU DISPLAY

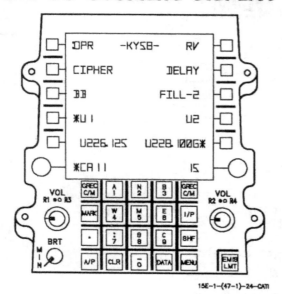

15E-1-(47-1)-24-CATI

Figure 1-42

UPFRONT CONTROL (KY-58)

To select the KY-58 submenu (figure 1-42), press the KY-58 pushbutton on the menu 2 display when nothing is displayed in the scratchpad. To activate the KY-58 system, press the pushbutton adjacent to OPR or RV. A colon appears to indicate the system is activated. At this time the other mode is automatically deselected. If it is desired to select a different fill variable number (1 to 6), enter the number on the keyboard and press the fill pushbutton. With RV selected the new variable number is provided to the KY-58 system. If CIPHER is displayed on the UFC, press the pushbutton and PLAIN is displayed. If CIPHER is selected, then BB (baseband) cannot be selected, DP (diphase) is automatically selected. Only one radio (UHF 1 or UHF 2) can be enabled at one time. The enabled radio will have an asterisk displayed next to its symbol (U1 or U2). If it is desired to enable DELAY mode, press the pushbutton adjacent to DELAY. It is enabled if OPR or RV is selected.

HAVE QUICK SYSTEM

The Have Quick radio uses a frequency hopping method to change the channel or frequency selected many times a second. To operate in the anti-jam

modes, all radios in a particular net must have the same word-of-day (WOD), time-of-day (TOD), net number, and the same frequencies stored in allocated preset channel locations. Description of the Have Quick system is based on training net operation. For training nets, channel 20 is used to store WOD and channels 14 thru 20 are used to store the preset frequencies.

The radios contain a clock, memory circuits, and a real time code generator. This added circuitry allows the radio to change frequencies many times a second. The WOD sets up the pattern for hopping the frequencies stored in the memory. A TOD signal from the anti-jam net control station synchronizes the radio clock to the other radios in the net. The clock times the operation of the real time code generator. When anti-jam modes are selected, signals are sent which activate the real time code generator and the anti-jam mode is placed in operation.

WORD-OF-THE-DAY (WOD)

The WOD is normally entered prior to flight, but it is possible to enter it in flight. The WOD defines the frequency hopping pattern for the day for the radio.

TIME-OF-DAY (TOD)

The TOD entry is normally performed before flight, but can be done in flight after the radio is turned on. TOD synchronizes the Have Quick radio to the net control station and the other radios in the net. After the radio is turned on it accepts the first TOD signal it receives on any channel or frequency in use. To ensure that the radio is operating in the correct net, request a TOD from the net control station, or request a TOD from another station in the net which has previously received TOD from the net control station. The TOD is heard in the headset as a short burst of varying tones followed by a steady tone. The steady tone lasts as long as the station keeps the sending transmitter in the tone setting. If anti-jam communication is attempted with an invalid TOD the received signal is not readable and it is necessary to request another TOD transmission.

HAVE QUICK II

A HAVE QUICK II radio operates in the basic HAVE QUICK mode. It also provides the additional capabilities of multiple word-of-day (MWOD) and all associated frequencies can be loaded at one time. When in the HAVE QUICK II mode, the MWODs and frequencies are stored in radio memory. Channels 00 thru 15 are not required for WOD and preset frequency storage. Channel 00 is used for setting the radio to the proper mode. Channels 15 thru 19 are free for use during normal operation.

MULTIPLE-WORD-OF-DAY (MWOD)

All WOD's which make a MWOD have their own unique date code attached to them which corresponds to the day of the month the WOD is to be used. A date code can be any number between 301.000 thru 331.000. The first day of the month equals 301.00 and the last day equals 331.000. If the radio is turned off, no WOD's or frequencies are lost. They are permanently stored in the radio until they are intentionally erased or changed. However, it must be identified to the radio which one of the up to six WOD's is to be used. With the exception of channel 20, which is required to initialize MWOD function, all preset channels are available for use. The radio also has the capability to automatically changeover from one day's WOD to the next with no action required by the pilot.

WORD-OF-THE-DAY (WOD)

WOD's are normally entered before flight but can also be entered during flight. They can be loaded into either or both UHF radios. Since multiple WOD's can be entered, a date code associated with each new WOD, is used to specify the day of the month. The date is required to uniquely identify the appropriate WOD when reinitializing at midnight. Once the WOD information has been entered, today's date must be entered to set the radio's clock so it can select the correct WOD for use.

TIME-OF-DAY (TOD)

The TOD starts the HAVE QUICK radio's clock and synchronizes all radios on the same net, allowing communication in anti-jam mode. When the radio is initially powered up, it accepts the first TOD signal it receives on any frequency or channel in use. You can get the TOD from a remote signal generator or from another aircraft. When the TOD is received from another aircraft, only those receiving it at the same time will be able to communicate in the anti-jam mode, as they will be out of sync with other HAVE QUICK users. When received, the TOD is heard as a short burst of varying tones followed by a steady tone.

IDENTIFICATION SYSTEM

IFF TRANSPONDER SET

The IFF (identification friend or foe) transponder set provides automatic identifications of the airplane in which it is installed when challenged by surface or airborne interrogator sets, and provides momentary identification of position (I/P) upon request. The modes provided are mode 1, mode 2, mode 3/A, mode 4, and mode C. Modes 1, 2, and 3/A are selective identification feature (SIF) modes. Mode 4 is used for highest confidence identification (crypto), and mode C is used for altitude reporting. The codes for modes 1 and 3/A can be set in the cockpit. Mode 2 is set using the control box in door 3R. Mode 4 is keyed in door 3R by maintenance personnel using the KIK. Mode 2 cannot be changed in flight. Mode 4 can be changed between 4A and 4B in flight or can be zeroized.

TRANSPONDER CONTROLS

Controls for the IFF are located on the remote intercom control panel in the front cockpit and the UFC. The controls consist of the mode 4 selector switch, the mode 4 reply switch, the master switch, the IFF antenna selector switch, and the mode 4 crypto switch.

Mode 4 Selector Switch

The mode 4 selector switch is a lever-lock switch with positions of B, A and OUT.

B	Enables mode 4/B reply.
A	Enables mode 4/A reply.
OUT	Disables all mode 4 replies.

Mode 4 Reply Switch

LIGHT	When the mode 4 system replies to valid interrogation being transmitted above a minimum threshold rate, the REPLY light illuminates.
AUDIO	Allows audio tone when valid

REC   interrogations are received. The light operation works as described in LIGHT above.

OFF   Disables the mode 4 AUDIO REC and LIGHT functions.

Master Switch

LOW   System operates with reduced sensitivity. Mode reception is reduced; however, mode 4 response to a valid interrogation is normal.

NORM   System operates at full sensitivity.

EMERG   Selects normal sensitivity emergency IFF operation. Allows the system to respond to interrogations in modes 1, 2, 3A, C and 4.

Mode 4 Crypto Switch

The crypto switch is a lever-lock switch with positions of HOLD, NORM and ZERO.

HOLD   In this position, mode 4 crypto codes are stored when power is removed from the aircraft.

NORM   Permits normal operation of the crypto codes with power on the aircraft.

ZERO   Sets the code settings back to zero. Seat ejection also zeroes the codes.

IFF Antenna Selector Switch

The antenna selector switch is on the left console next to the ICCP.

UPPER   Selects upper antenna

LOWER   Selects lower antenna

BOTH   Provides automatic antenna selection

IFF MODE 4 CAUTION

NOTE

On this aircraft an IFF mode 4 reply fault is indicated by an IFF MODE 4 caution appearing on the MPD/MPCD and the MASTER CAUTION light coming on.

The IFF MODE 4 caution on the MPD/MPCD can be caused to appear by failure to respond to a valid interrogation, zeroized code, or internal component failure.

NOTE

The logic in the mode 4 system is such that while the reply LIGHT is on (plus a small time delay after it goes out), the operation of the IFF MODE 4 caution is inhibited. Therefore, in a high density interrogation environment, it may be desirable to place the MODE 4 LIGHT/AUDIO RECEIVE SWITCH to LIGHT or AUDIO REC to minimize the effects of spurious signals or system overloads mixed in with valid responses.

IDENTIFICATION OF POSITION (IP)

Pressing the I/P pushbutton on the UFC enables the IFF system to transmit momentary identification of position when interrogated on modes 1, 2, and 3. The response is continued for a period of 15 to 30 second duration after the pushbutton is released.

IFF EMERGENCY OPERATION

Upon ejection from the cockpit, the IFF emergency mode automatically becomes active if mode 1, 2, 3A, or C is enabled.

IFF SUBMENU

The IFF submenu is selected and displayed from the UFC menu 1 format. Pressing the pushbutton next to IFF with nothing in the scratchpad calls up the IFF submenu (figure 1-43). From this display the various functions, modes, codes, and programming of the IFF can be done. For example, mode C is enabled or disabled from this submenu. From this display mode 1 code can be selected and deselected. Also the IFF can be programmed to operate at specific modes and codes as a function of the time. This is referred to as phasing (PH). Phasing permits the selection of up to 13 mission segments for automatic change of IFF operation based on TOD information and is expected to be based on authentication procedures for a given theatre of operation. Phasing will be programmed by the DTM. Note that the IFF operation here refers to all IFF modes and codes including mode C. The programming option, when selected, permits changing of the phasing program.

To enable or disable an IFF mode, press the mode pushbutton next to the displayed mode. If the mode was previously enabled it will become disabled, if it was previously disabled it will become enabled. An asterisk appears next to all enabled modes. To change the codes for mode 1, type the code on the keyboard and enter by pressing the mode 1 pushbutton. Seven and three are the largest values for the first and second digits of the code. To change the codes for mode 3, type the codes on the keyboard and enter by pressing the mode 3 pushbutton. Seven is the largest value for any code digit. Trailing zeros are not required.

To enter the phase programming mode, press the PROGRAM pushbutton. An asterisk appears next to the PROGRAM display. The UFC displays a one (1) for the phase and the prestored associated data (modes/codes and time). To select a different phase number for monitoring or programming, press the phase (PH) pushbutton and the number will increment by one each time it is pressed and released. The prestored phase numbers are incremented in sequential order. The UFC will display the new phase number and its associated data (modes/codes and time).

To remove the indicated phase from the phases, type a zero (0) phase number on the keyboard and enter by pressing the PH pushbutton. The current phase number remains displayed but the modes 1, 2, 3 and C and time are blanked. PROGRAM and IFF remain displayed. To enable or disable a mode for the displayed phase, press the mode pushbutton next to the displayed mode (mode 1, 2, 3, C). If the mode was previously enabled it will become disabled, if it was previously disabled it will become enabled. An asterisk appears next to all enabled modes. The enable modes are stored in memory for the displayed phase.

To exit the programming mode, press the PROGRAM pushbutton. The display will revert to the IFF submenu. Phasing is enabled by pressing the PH pushbutton.

IFF INTERROGATOR SET

The interrogator control panel contains the controls for providing air-to-air (AAI) target identification. Refer to TO 1F-15E-34-1-1 for description of the AAI system.

INTERFERENCE BLANKER SYSTEM (IBS)

The interference blanker system prevents or reduces electromagnetic interference between TEWS and other aircraft systems which utilize radio frequency (rf) transmitters and receivers.

INERTIAL NAVIGATION SYSTEM (INS)

The INS is a self-contained, fully automatic ring laser gyro (RLG) system which supplies the primary attitude reference for the aircraft and provides continuous present position (PP) monitoring. In addition, the INS provides aircraft attitude, heading, velocity, and acceleration information to the LANTIRN, radar, AFCS and CC.

NOTE

The PP enetered should be the actual aircraft location. Further corrections after the aircraft has moved should be done by update after transition to NAV.

INERTIAL SENSOR ASSEMBLY (ISA)

The primary component of the INS is the ISA, which contains three complete RLG's, (roll, pitch, and yaw), three accelerometers, a high voltage power supply, and a calibration memory/temperature multiplexer. The sensors provide output signals of angular rates and linear accelerations with respect to an orthogonal set of axes.

Ring Laser Gyro

The RLG is a key element of the INS. It is a rate-integrating gyro which does not use a spinning mass like a conventional gyroscope. The RLG detects and measures angular rotation by measuring the

IFF SUBMENU

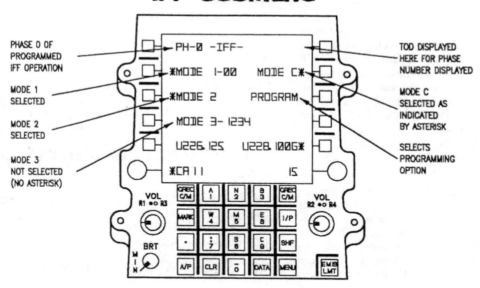

PHASE O OF
PROGRAMMED
IFF OPERATION

MODE 1
SELECTED

MODE 2
SELECTED

MODE 3
NOT SELECTED
(NO ASTERISK)

PH-0 -IFF-

MODE 1-00   MODE C

*MODE 2   PROGRAM

MODE 3- 1234

U226.125   U228.100G*

*CA 11   15

TOD DISPLAYED
HERE FOR PHASE
NUMBER DISPLAYED

MODE C
SELECTED AS
INDICATED
BY ASTERISK

SELECTS
PROGRAMMING
OPTION

15E-1-(40-1)-25-CAT1

Figure 1-43

effective frequency difference between two con-trarotating (one clockwise, one counterclockwise) laser beams in a ceramic block. As the two laser beams travel simultaneously around the cavity, mirrors reflect each beam around the enclosed path. When the gyro is at rest, the two beams have the same frequency because the optical path is the same in both directions. However, when the gyro is subjected to an angular turning rate about an axis perpendicular to the plane of the two beams, one beam sees a greater path length and the other beam sees a shorter length. The two resonant frequencies effectively change to adjust to the longer or shorter optical path; the effective frequency differential is directly propor-tional to the angular turning rate.

INERTIAL NAVIGATION DIGITAL COMPUTER

The inertial computer contains all circuits necessary for gyro and accelerometer signal processing and for computing North/South, East/West, and vertical velocities and accelerations; X, Y and Z velocities and accelerations; body rates; body angle and linear accel-erations; and pitch, roll, magnetic heading and true heading. It also contains the necessary circuits for calculation of wander angle, inertial altitude, latitude,

and longitude and computes platform correction sig-nals for gyro compass and stored heading alignments. A Kalman filter is implemented to model errors in velocity, position, and calibration to provide enhanced alignment and inflight performance. The computer also performs BIT functions and provides computer mode control.

INS Performance Monitor

The INS performance monitor (stored at shutdown) maintains a history of recent alignment and naviga-tion data. Navigation data is stored in two configura-tions: pure inertial (no updates) and aided inertial (updates included). Data is stored on the basis of a complete flight defined by:
    a. Nose gear up limit switch closed for takeoff.
    b. Ground speed less than 80 knots for landing.
    c. INS mode transition from align to NAV.

Data storage includes, but is not limited to: type and time of alignment; flight data for last 12 flights; time in NAV; initial latitude and longitude; final latitude and longitude; and inertial cumulative error.

To have complete performance monitor data, an on-ground visual overfly update at the end of flight is required prior to INS shutdown.

The INS also has continuous/periodic BITs, initiated BIT, and power-up tests to monitor system performance.

INS MODE KNOB

The INS mode knob is located on the sensor control panel (SCP, figure 1-44) and controls the following functions:

OFF   Removes power from the INS.

STORE Selects the stored heading (SH) alignment mode and uses gyrocompass alignment parameters which were stored at the time of the last system shut-off for rapid INS alignment. PP source submenu is called up on the pilot's UFC when SH is selected. The aircraft must not have been moved since the last shutdown. SH alignment is complete approximately 40 seconds after turn-on and should achieve approximately GC align accuracy. The accuracy is directly affected by the INS accuracy of the previous flight and error rate at the time of the last system shutdown. Alignment complete is indicated by SH OK in HUD window 16 and on the air-to-ground (A/G) radar precision velocity update (PVU) display.

If STORE is selected and the INS has determined that stored heading alignment is not available (GC had not been performed; or groundspeed of previous flight >3 knots or error rate of previous flight was >1 nm/hr) the INS will automatically switch to GC align mode.

GC   Selects the gyrocompass (GC) mode which is the most accurate mode of INS alignment. PP source submenu is called up on pilot's UFC when GC selected. Full GC alignment requires approximately 4 minutes. Alignment complete is indicated by GC OK in HUD window 16 and on the PVU display.

NAV   This is the primary navigation mode. The INS solves the navigation problem by sensing aircraft accelerations, applying appropriate corrections and determining aircraft velocity and position. Steering to destination is computed in the CC based on inertially derived present position. The knob must be pulled up before it can be rotated out of NAV.

If the mode switch is positioned directly from OFF to NAV, the INS will perform a GC alignment and after align complete is reached the INS will automatically transition to the NAV mode.

GYROCOMPASS AND STORED HEADING ALIGNMENT AND NAV

There are several displays on the HUD and PVU display during INS alignment that indicate system align status. The display will reflect the INS operation. This may differ from the switch selection on the sensor control panel. See figure 1-44.

GC PP REQ SH PP REQ	Present position update required. Displayed for GC or SH alignment if last shutdown position differs from the INS stored base location by more than 2 NM. When displayed the pilot or WSO must insert new PP on UFC PP source submenu. INS alignment is continuing using the stored base location while PP REQ is displayed.

NOTE

The PP can be entered more than once during an alignment cycle, the PP should reference the aircraft base location. Once the aircraft leaves the base location, changes should be done by update in the NAV mode. If a new PP is entered during a GC alignment, the INS may restart a full GC alignment (restart the 4 minute sequence) at the time the PP is entered depending on the time in the alignment cycle that the entry is made. If a new PP is entered during a SH alignment or align HOLD, the INS will automatically switch to GC alignment mode and restart the alignment.

GC NO TAXI SH NO TAXI	NO TAXI is displayed for approximately 60 seconds after GC or STORE is selected until INS attitude is valid (figure 1-45). During this time the aircraft should not be moved. Movement during this time will require the INS to be turned off (2 seconds minimum), back on and then restart alignment.

NOTE

NAV may be selected at any time after NO TAXI is removed, but degraded accuracy should be expected if NAV is selected before GC or SH OK is displayed.

GC XX.X SH XX.X IFA XX.X	INS alignment quality is indicated by a numerical countdown from 15.9 in GC, SH or IFA. This display indicates the accuracy of alignment. It does not indicate the expected accuracy at the end of flight. A full GC should result in an indication of approximately 1.0 ; a complete SH should result in an indication of SH OK. SH quality is directly affected by previous alignment accuracy.
GC HOLD	Displayed if INS senses motion while GC or SH alignment is in progress. This indicates that the INS is retaining the existing alignment quality until the aircraft motion stops and the holding brake is engaged or until the aircraft takes off. If the holding brake is engaged and the INS detects no motion, the system will resume a GC alignment and GC XX.X will be displayed as above.

NOTE

● If new PP is entered when INS is in a HOLD mode the INS will switch to GC alignment and restart the alignment.

● If the aircraft takes off with GC HOLD displayed, the GC HOLD is removed with nose gear up and the INS automatically enters the NAV mode; degraded accuracy should be expected.

● If the aircraft is stopped but the holding brake is not engaged, the INS will not reenter the GC mode; degraded accuracy should be expected.

SENSOR CONTROL PANEL

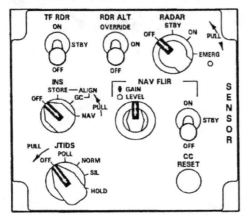

15E-1-(24-1)-CATI-19

Figure 1-44

GC OK SH OK IFA OK	Indicates which align mode was done and that the INS alignment is complete; displayed until NAV selected or takeoff.

The GC indicates the INS is in the gyrocompass align mode; the SH indicates the INS is in the stored heading align mode; and IFA indicates the INS is in the inflight align mode. IFA mode requires position and/or velocity updates. IFA also requires initialization of data by the CC at the start of IFA selection. OK, PP REQ, NO TAXI, HOLD, and XX.X (align quality) are displayed in one HUD window based on the following priorities order: 1-OK, 2-PP REQ, 3-NO TAXI, 4-HOLD, 5-XX.X. During alignment when the INS mode knob is positioned to GC or SH, the present position submenu is automatically called up on the pilot's UFC.

The present position stored in the INS and being used for alignment will be displayed. If the PP is correct no action is required. If the PP is not correct the pilot should enter the correct PP. The new entered PP should be accurate to 600 feet (0.1 arc minute). Depending on the time in the GC alignment that the new PP is entered, the alignment may start over. If a new PP is entered from SH, the INS will automatically switch to the GC alignment mode.

NAV DEGD	Displayed on the HUD indicates the INS is in a degraded NAV mode caused by transition to NAV via mode switch, early exit of IFA, or INS automatic transition without alignment being completed. Aided alignment (position and velocity updates) can be performed during NAV to improve NAV accuracy.

NOTE

If an IFA is being performed the IFA and associated display will replace NAV DEGD if displayed.

INS UPDATES

Updates to the INS should be done during IFA alignment or done to improve the accuracy of the INS when it has drifted off when NAV DEGD is indicated. Updates should be done only with source data that is correct and more accurate than the INS. Updating the INS with bad data will induce more error and INS may not be able to recover.

When the INS updates are performed the INS uses a Kalman filter using inputs from the CC. The INS compares the data received such as the source of update, error, the variance of the error and the correlation of the error. The INS determines if the error is reasonable in reference to recent INS operation and previous updates. Based on CC inputs, the INS will accept a smaller or larger portion of an update based on the quality of the update and the update source.

ATTITUDE HEADING REFERENCE SET (AHRS)

The attitude heading reference set supplies aircraft magnetic heading to various avionic systems. The AHRS is also the standby system which provides attitude (roll and pitch) information if the primary (INS) system fails. AHRS attitude is displayed when AHRS is selected on the ADI.

AHRS INTERFACE

The INS provides roll and pitch data to the radar set. The AHRS is informed by the INS of INS attitude validity. If INS attitude is invalid, the AHRS sends

GYROCOMPASS ALIGNMENT DISPLAYS

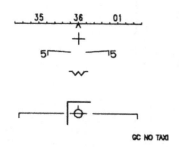

HUD DISPLAY

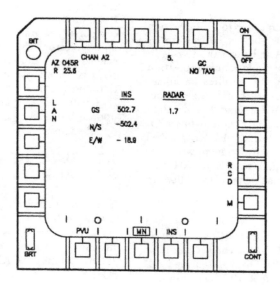

A/G PVU RADAR DISPLAY

Figure 1-45

15E-1-(187-1)02-CAT1

attitude information to the radar set. The AHRS provides the CC with magnetic heading at all times and informs the computer when the AHRS is in the slaved mode of operation. The AHRS supplies magnetic heading to the HSI to position the compass card when AHRS is selected.

COMPASS CONTROL PANEL

The compass control panel, on the right console, provides the necessary controls to operate the gyromagnetic compass system. These controls are the sync indicator meter, push to sync knob, fast erect pushbutton, hemisphere switch, latitude control knob, and the mode selector knob.

Sync Indicator Meter

The sync indicator meter indicates the direction (plus or minus) between the AHRS directional gyro and the magnetic azimuth detector, in the slaved mode.

Push To Sync Knob

The push to sync knob is a combination push to sync and push to turn (set heading) knob. When the knob is pressed and the mode selector knob is in SLAVED, the AHRS provides fast synchronization of the gyro stabilized magnetic heading output to the magnetic azimuth detector. When the mode selector knob is in DG and AHRS is selected on the ADI, pressing and rotating the push to sync knob will slew the AHRS heading output through 360° of rotation (on the compass card) while the heading on the HUD remains steady.

Fast Erect Pushbutton

Depressing the fast erect pushbutton causes the AHRS pitch and roll erection loops to revert to the fast erection rate. If the aircraft is in unaccelerated flight and there is an obvious disagreement between the attitude indicator and the visually verified attitude of the aircraft, go to straight-and-level unaccelerated flight and momentarily press the fast erect pushbutton to re-erect the gyro for correct attitude sensing. During the fast erect condition the AHRS will indicate invalid BIT outputs, and level, unaccelerated flight must be maintained until a correct attitude is obtained.

Hemisphere Switch

The hemisphere switch selects the northern (N) or southern (S) hemisphere for operation of AHRS.

Latitude Control Knob

The latitude control knob manually inserts present position latitude, in DG and slaved mode, so that the AHRS can determine the correction needed for gyro drift due to the earths rotation.

Mode Selector Knob

The mode selector knob is a three-position rotary knob with positions of COMP, DG, and SLAVED. The SLAVED mode is normally used. In the SLAVED mode, directional gyro sensed heading is continuously corrected to the heading sensed by the magnetic azimuth detector and the result is transmitted to other aircraft systems. The COMP mode is usually selected only when there is a gyro malfunction. In the COMP mode, the reading sensed by the magnetic azimuth detector is transmitted to other aircraft systems. The DG mode is used in latitudes higher than 70° or where the earth magnetic field is appreciably distorted. In the DG mode, the directional gyro heading is transmitted to other aircraft systems. When the DG mode is initially selected, the aircraft magnetic heading must be set into the system with the PUSH TO SYNC knob. The system then uses this reference for subsequent heading indications. In the SLAVED and DG modes, apparent drift compensation is inserted with the hemisphere (N-S) switch and the latitude control knob. When in either of these modes, ensure that the hemisphere and latitude settings correspond with the actual latitude.

COMP	Heading sensed from the magnetic azimuth detector.
DG	Heading sensed from the directional gyro.
SLAVED	Heading sensed from the directional gyro continuously corrected by the magnetic azimuth detector.

TACAN (TACTICAL AIR NAVIGATION) SYSTEM

The tacan system functions to give precise air-to-ground bearing and distance information at ranges up to approximately 300 miles (depending on aircraft altitude) from an associated ground or shipboard transmitting station. It determines the identity of the transmitting station and indicates the dependability of the transmitted signal. Tacan information except in A/A mode is presented on the HSI, the ADI, and the HUD. In A/A mode, both distance and bearing are received if cooperating aircraft (such as refueling tanker aircraft) have bearing transmission capability.

When operating in conjunction with aircraft having air-to-air capability, the A/A mode provides line of sight distance between two aircraft operating their tacan sets 63 channels apart. Up to five aircraft can determine line of sight distance from a sixth lead aircraft in the A/A mode, provided their tacan sets are set 63 channels apart from the lead aircraft. The limit of operation is four times the distance between the lead aircraft and the nearest aircraft. The lead aircraft will indicate distance from one of the other five, but it cannot readily determine which one. Before operating in the A/A mode, the frequencies used by each aircraft must be coordinated.

TACAN CONTROLS

The controls for tacan operation are on the intercommunications set control panel, the remote intercommunications control panel, and the UFC. The tacan volume control on the ICSCP/RICP adjusts the volume level of the tacan station identification audio tone. Operation of the tacan system is done using the upfront control.

Tacan Submenu

The tacan submenu is selected and displayed from menu 1. When displayed, all the tacan functions are presented as shown in figure 1-36. For example, tacan channel 101 is shown as the current channel selected and the system is being powered as indicated by the colon symbol adjacent to TCN. The asterisk symbol indicates the system currently has the transmit/receive (T-R) mode selected.

To change the tacan channel number, type the new number on the keyboard and check it in the scratchpad, then enter it by pressing the pushbutton next to TCN display. To select a tacan mode (A/A, T-R, REC), press the pushbutton next to the respective display. An asterisk appears next to the selected mode. To change the channel mode from Y to X or X to Y, press the pushbutton next to the X or Y currently being displayed. Return to menu 1 is accomplished by pressing the MENU key. As noted in the figure, tacan has a program sub-menu that permits indexing of 12 tacan stations for navigation updating and present position keeping purposes.

Tacan Channel Programming

The UFC provides for storing 12 tacan stations for navigation update purposes, using latitude, longitude, altitude and magnetic variation. This submenu, as shown in figure 1-46, is selected by pressing the pushbutton adjacent to PROGRAM on the tacan submenu. In most cases these stations will be programmed into the data transfer module. To select a different tacan channel number for the displayed index number, enter the channel number on the keyboard and enter it by pressing the pushbutton next to the TCN display. To select a different index number (stored number for the station), increment the number by one by pressing the pushbutton next to the INDEX display. This provides the new index number and associated data in memory for display on the UFC. To change the latitude of the tacan station, first press the SHF (shift) key on the UFC and then N or S. Type in the latitude value, including leading zeroes. Then enter the latitude by pressing the latitude pushbutton (below the INDEX pushbutton). A new longitude is entered the same way except the SHF key must be pressed and then either the W or E key is pressed.

NOTE

When programming channel and index numbers, index numbers should be changed before the channel numbers. Failure to use this sequence could result in an incorrect channel number being entered into an index number.

To change the magnetic variation (MV), press the SHF key then the E or W key. Type in the M/V value and leading zeroes. Enter new M/V by pressing the pushbutton second from the bottom on the right side of the UFC.

To change the altitude of the tacan station, type the altitude value on the keyboard and enter by pressing the pushbutton just above the M/V pushbutton. This new altitude is stored in memory for the tacan station. To change the channel mode from Y to X or X to Y, press the pushbutton next to the X or Y currently being displayed.

INSTRUMENT LANDING SYSTEM

The instrument landing system (ILS) provides the capability for the aircraft to make a precision landing approach and descent. The localizer function provides lateral guidance information to position the

TACAN SUBMENU DISPLAYS

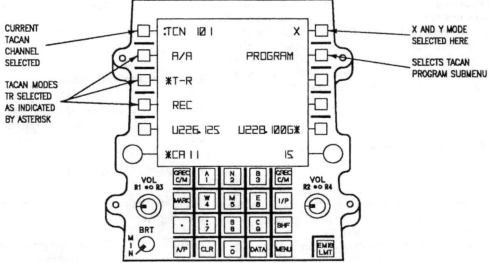

CURRENT
TACAN
CHANNEL
SELECTED

TACAN MODES
TR SELECTED
AS INDICATED
BY ASTERISK

X AND Y MODE
SELECTED HERE

SELECTS TACAN
PROGRAM SUBMENU

TACAN SUBMENU DISPLAY

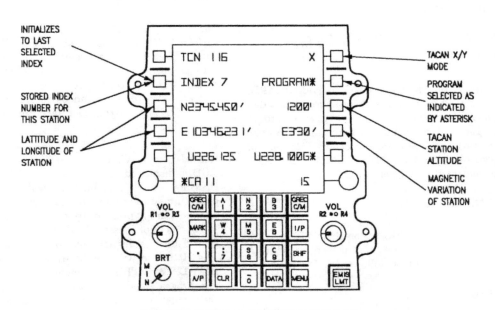

INITIALIZES
TO LAST
SELECTED
INDEX

STORED INDEX
NUMBER FOR
THIS STATION

LATTITUDE AND
LONGITUDE OF
STATION

TACAN X/Y
MODE

PROGRAM
SELECTED AS
INDICATED
BY ASTERISK

TACAN
STATION
ALTITUDE

MAGNETIC
VARIATION
OF STATION

TACAN PROGRAM SUBMENU DISPLAY

Figure 1-46

15E—1—(45—1)03—CAT1

1-131

aircraft on the runway center line during approach. The localizer frequency range is 108.10 to 111.95 MHz. The localizer frequency is entered and selected on the menu 2 display on the UFC (see figure 1-29). The localizer identification tone can be heard in the headset during ILS operation. The glideslope function provides vertical guidance information to position the aircraft on the glideslope angle during the final approach. Glideslope steering symbols are displayed on the HUD and ADI. When the ILSN or ILST steering mode is selected from the HSI, ILSN or ILST appears on the HUD (see figure 1-47).

NOTE

ILST and ILSN are not available when TF is on.

When the aircraft captures the glideslope center, the pitch steering bar appears on the HUD to join with the bank steering bar, and the pitch steering bar appears on the ADI. A MKR also flashes on the HUD and on the ADI when flying over marker beacon. ILS guidance information is displayed on the HUD and ADI (figure 1-47).

ILS Volume Control Knob

The ILS volume control knob on the Intercom Control Panel adjusts the volume level of the localizer and station identification audio.

VIDEO TAPE RECORDER SET (VTRS)

The VTRS is installed to record individual MPD, MPCD, and HUD displays. There are two video taping options available, non-programmed recording and programmed recording. In both cases the crew interface with the VTRS includes the VTRS control panel, one or more of the MPD/MPCD's, the HUD, and the control stick trigger switch.

VTRS CONTROL PANEL

The controls for the VTRS are on the VTRS control panel on the right console of the front cockpit. A description of the controls follows:

Record Switch

This switch has positions of enable and unthread.

ENABLE	Enables the VTRS to record. Also, the INS must be turned on.
UNTHREAD	If the INS is on, selecting unthread unthreads the video tape. The VTRS automatically unthreads when the INS is turned off.

Minutes Remaining Counter

This indicates minutes of video tape remaining. The counter is reset by pressing and turning the reset knob.

VTRS ADVISORY LIGHTS

These consist of the RCD (record) and EOT (end of tape) lights.

RCD	Illuminates green when recording is in progress.
EOT	Illuminates white to indicate end of tape or no tape in recorder.

NON-PROGRAMMED RECORDING

For non-programmed recording ensure that RECORD ENABLE is selected on the VTRS control panel. Then either crewmember presses the MPD/MPCD pushbutton next to the RCD cue on the display. This initiates recording of the display of interest. Two displays can be recorded at the same time using non-programmed recording, but there are exceptions.

Record Cue - When recording is not commanded, RCD is displayed adjacent to the MPD pushbutton. Pressing this pushbutton will initiate non-programmed recording of that display. The same pushbutton is pressed to stop recording. For the HUD, the pilot presses the flight stick trigger into the first detent to initiate non-programmed recording. The RCD cue will not be displayed on the PACS, BIT, DTM, VTRS, and menu displays. To initiate non-programmed recording of these display formats, they must be called up on a display which has recording already in progress. The non-programmed RCD cue is available on the following display formats:

ILS DISPLAYS
GEAR DOWN

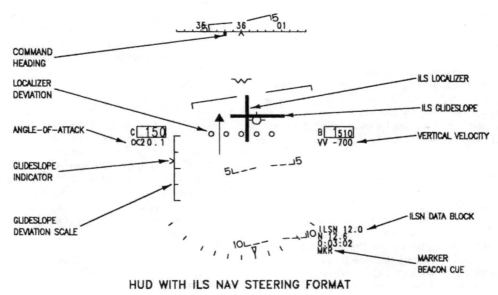

COMMAND HEADING

LOCALIZER DEVIATION

ILS LOCALIZER

ILS GLIDESLOPE

ANGLE-OF-ATTACK

VERTICAL VELOCITY

GLIDESLOPE INDICATOR

GLIDESLOPE DEVIATION SCALE

ILSN DATA BLOCK

MARKER BEACON CUE

HUD WITH ILS NAV STEERING FORMAT

LOCALIZER INDICATOR

LOCALIZER DEVIATION (SCALE)

LOCALIZER STEERING BAR

GLIDESLOPE STEERING BAR

GLIDESLOPE DEVIATION

MARKER BEACON

TURN RATE

INCLINOMETER (SLIP INDICATOR)

ADI WITH ILS FORMAT

Figure 1-47

15E-1-(34-1)03-CAT1

A/A RADAR	TGT IR
A/G RADAR	WPN1
ADI	WPN2
HSI	OWS
TF	ENGINE
TSD	HUD REPEATER
TEWS	

Non-Programmed Recording in Progress Cue - The central computer (CC) clock time is displayed adjacent to the record pushbutton whenever non-programmed recording is in progress for that display. The PACS, BIT, DTM, VTRS, and display formats do not display this cue. Nevertheless, these five display formats will be recorded if they are called up on an MPD or MPCD with recording in progress.

PROGRAMMED RECORDING

If the crewmembers know in advance which cockpit display(s) they wish to record, they can program the VTRS through a VTRS display menu to record particular display(s) before the fact. This is called programmed recording. Because programmed recording occurs automatically, the workload of the crewmembers is reduced. Another advantage of programmed recording is that after the program is entered, the recording procedure can be controlled with Hands-On Throttle and Stick (HOTAS) functions. The aircrew procedures for programmed recording are described in the following paragraphs.

VTRS Selection - Pressing the MPD or MPCD pushbutton adjacent to M calls up the menu display shown in figure 1-48.

Pressing the VTRS pushbutton selects the VTRS display shown in figure 1-38. The VTRS display will indicate those selections which were selected the previous time this display was called up. For example, if the aft cockpit right-hand MPCD was previously selected and the VTRS was set in the Standby (STBY) mode, the resultant display would look like figure 1-48.

Record Options and Priorities - The crewmember can select or deselect any two of the eight available record options by pressing the pushbutton adjacent to the desired option. Also note that the options are separated for front cockpit and aft cockpit. A boxed priority number 1 appears adjacent to the first record option selection, and a boxed priority number 2 appears adjacent to the second record option selection, as shown in figure 1-48. This procedure is referred to as programmed recording. No recording will actually occur at this point because OFF has been selected as the VTRS Option. To deselect a record option, the crew member simply presses the adjacent pushbutton, and the boxed priority number is removed. If the number 1 priority record option is deselected, the number 2 priority record option will automatically be reassigned number 1 priority, and the boxed priority number will change accordingly. If two record options have already been selected, any attempt to select a third record option will be ignored by the system.

Split-Screen Video - As with the F-15 C/D VTRS, the F-15E VTRS has the capability to record split-screen video for the majority of display format pairs. For split-screen video to occur, the displays must be synchronized, i.e., the displays must be refreshed at the same rate. Some of the display formats are ineligible for split-screen video due to incompatible synchronization rates. If any two of the following formats are selected, only the first one selected will be recorded:

TSD	TGT FLIR
WPN 1	TF E^2
WPN 2	NAV FLIR (on HUD or HUD Repeater)

The end result of a split-screen video recording is a display with 50% horizontal video compression, and full-size vertical video. That is, both displays are regular height, but their width is compressed by one-half.

VTRS Options - The three VTRS Options are displayed on the bottom of the VTRS Display. They are OFF, STBY, and RUN. Each VTRS option can be selected by pressing the corresponding pushbutton. In addition, the central computer will automatically select the OFF VTRS option, as shown in figure 1-38 whenever no record options have been selected. If a crewmember attempts to select either STBY or RUN without first selecting a record option, then a cue is displayed in the center of the VTRS display. When no record options have been selected, OFF is the only available VTRS option. The cue is automatically removed after the crewmember selects a record option. The STBY OPTION enables the AUTO function, if selected. With STBY selected, recording of programmed displays occurs when the weapon release (pickle button) is pressed. In the A/A master mode, the displays will be recorded for missile time-of-flight(TOF) plus 5 seconds. In the A/G master mode,

PROGRAMMED RECORDING DISPLAYS

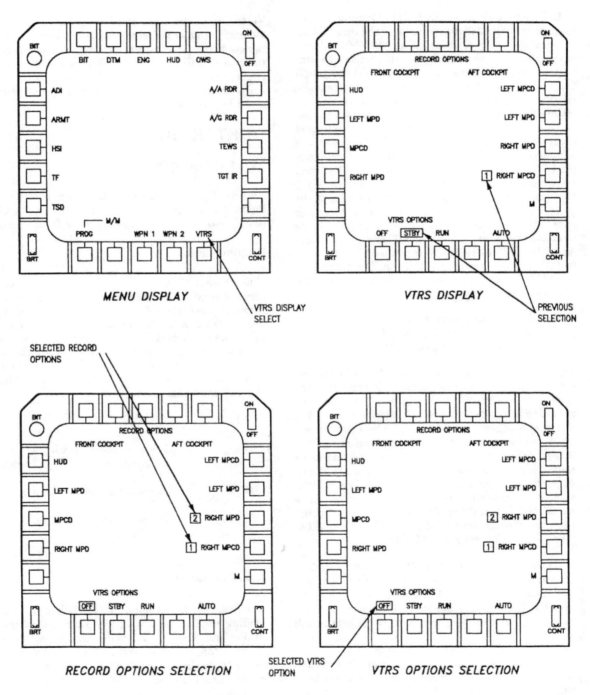

MENU DISPLAY

VTRS DISPLAY

VTRS DISPLAY
SELECT

PREVIOUS
SELECTION

SELECTED RECORD
OPTIONS

RECORD OPTIONS SELECTION

SELECTED VTRS
OPTION

VTRS OPTIONS SELECTION

Figure 1-48

15E-1-(40-1)-CAT1

they will be recorded from weapon consent through weapon release plus 10 seconds. The RUN option initiates recording of the programmed display(s), without the need to use the trigger switch.

Auto Function - The VTRS AUTO function may be selected or deselected independent of the three VTRS Options previously discussed. The AUTO function is boxed when selected. By pressing the adjacent push-button, the box is removed and the AUTO function is deselected. When the AUTO function is selected by a crewmember, the VTRS will automatically record the HUD whenever predetermined conditions exist. That is, the AUTO function will interrupt recording of programmed or non-programmed displays, and will automatically record the HUD. When the predetermined conditions no longer exist, the VTRS will revert to recording the previously selected display(s). One predetermined condition is the selection of the gun (using the throttle weapon mode switch) together with a radar-detected target within 10nm of the the aircraft. The other predetermined conditions involve AIR-TO-AIR missile launch commanded by the control stick weapon release pushbutton. The duration of the AUTO recording equals the missile time of flight plus 5 seconds.

HUD Recording in Progress Cue - The central computer clock time cue is displayed in the lower left corner of the HUD to indicate recording in progress.

Programmed Recording in Progress Cue - In general, the central computer clock time is displayed on the right side of the MPD/MPCD when programmed recording is in progress. Also, an asterisk is displayed above and below the clock time. The asterisks are displayed to distinguish programmed recording from non-programmed recording. For the programmable armament control set (PACS), BIT, and DTM displays, the clock time cue will not be displayed. However, if programmed recording is in progress on a particular MPD and one of these displays is called up, then the recorder will record the PACS, BIT or DTM format on the programmed MPD(s).

Weapon Consent Cue - A small tick mark placed on the left edge of the recording. Identical in appearance to the weapon release tick mark but separated positionally. The weapon consent cue is present while the pickle button is pressed or the trigger is held in full action.

Weapon Release Cue - A small tick mark is displayed on the left edge of the recording to mark the time of weapon release. The duration of this cue is one

second. The purpose of the weapon release cue is is to help the crewmember search his video tape recordings after flight, freezing the playback machine at the time of weapon release.

Voice Communications and Aural Tones - In order to aid correlation of inflight occurrences with post flight review of the video tape recording, voice communications to and from the crewmembers are recorded on the audio track of the VTRS. Likewise, aural tones voice warnings, weapon consent and weapon release tones are recorded.

LIGHTING EQUIPMENT

EXTERIOR LIGHTING

Exterior lights are controlled from either the exterior lights control panel or the miscellaneous control panel, both on the left console in the front cockpit.

Position Lights

The position lights include a green light on the forward edge of the right wing tip, a red light on the forward edge of the left wing tip, and a white light just below the tip of the left vertical tail fin. The position lights are controlled by a knob on the exterior lights control panel labeled POSITION. With the anti-collision lights on, the position lights automatically go to steady full brilliance, regardless of the position of the position lights knob.

OFF	Lights are off.
1 - 5	Guide numbers for varying brightness from off to full bright.
BRT	Lights are at full brightness.
FLASH	The lights will flash at full brightness.

Anti-Collision Lights

There are three red anti-collision lights; one on the leading edge of each wing just outboard of the air intake and another just below the tip of the right vertical tail fin. The anti-collision lights are controlled by a single toggle switch on the exterior lights control panel labeled ANTI-COLLISION. The switch positions are OFF and ON.

Formation Lights

Six green electroluminescent formation lights are provided. Two lights are on the wingtips behind the position lights, two lights are on the side of the forward fuselage just forward of the cockpit, and two lights are on the aft fuselage just aft of wing trailing edge. The formation lights are controlled by a single knob on the exterior lights control panel labeled FORMATION.

OFF	Lights are off.
1-5	Guide numbers for varying brightness from off to full bright.
BRT	The lights are at full brightness.

Vertical Tail Flood Lights

Two vertical tail flood lights are installed on the right and left aft fuselage to illuminate the vertical tails during night join-ups and formation flying. They are controlled by a single switch on the exterior lights control panel.

OFF	Lights are off.
DIM	Lights are on in a dimmed condition.
BRT	Lights are at full brightness.

Landing and Taxi Lights

The landing and taxi lights are on the nose gear strut. They are controlled by a toggle switch on the miscellaneous control panel. The lights are off, regardless of switch position, when the landing gear handle is in the up position.

OFF	Lights are off.
LDG LIGHT	If the landing gear handle is down, the landing light is turned on.
TAXI	If the landing gear handle is down, the taxi light is turned on.

INTERIOR LIGHTING

Except for the utility floodlights, and UFC display lighting, all the controls for interior lights are on the interior lights control panel on the right console in each cockpit.

Upfront Control Display Lighting

The UFC Liquid Crystal Display (LCD) consists of six display rows. A brightness control (BRT) provides a full range of adjustment for night utilization. Backlighting is not required because the LCD is a reflective type display.

A simple and quick method of clearing the LCD is as follows:

To Blank	Press
Scratchpad	CLR key twice
Top 4 Rows	CLR key with blank scratchpad
All 6 Rows	CLR key twice

To Recall	Press
Bottom 2 Rows	Either of bottom two display pushbuttons
Top 4 Rows (when bottom 2 rows are displayed)	Any of the top eight display pushbuttons with a blank scratchpad
All 6 Rows	Any of the top eight pushbuttons

Instrument Lighting

Integral lighting is provided for all instruments and panels on the front cockpit instrument panel including the MPDs, MPCD, UFC, circuit breaker panels and the HUD. Integral lighting is also provided to the radio call, emergency hook and emergency vent panels. Instrument lighting is provided to the front cockpit standby compass whenever the STBY COMP switch is ON. Rear cockpit integral instrument lighting is provided for all instruments and panels on the rear instrument panel including the MPDs and MPCDs. Integral lighting is also provided to the UFC, the command selector valve panel, the emergency hook panel and the radio call panel. The lights are controlled by the instrument panel lights knob in either cockpit, labeled INST PNL, which provides variable lighting between positions OFF and BRT.

Console Lighting

The console lights are controlled by the CONSOLE knob in either cockpit which provide variable lighting between positions OFF and BRT.

Storm/Flood Lighting

Four storm/flood lights are provided in the front cockpit and two in the rear cockpit for secondary lighting. The front cockpit has a light above each console and two above the main instrument panel. The rear cockpit has one light above each console. The lights in each cockpit are controlled by the storm/flood lights knob labeled STORM FLOOD, which provides variable lighting between OFF and BRT. In either cockpit, if the warning/caution/advisory lights are in the dimmed condition, moving the storm/flood lights knob to full BRT causes the warning/caution/advisory lights to revert to full intensity, regardless of the position of the WARNING CAUTION control knob.

Utility Flood Lights

A portable utility flood light is provided in each cockpit and is normally stowed on a bracket above the right console. An alligator clip attached to the light may be used to fasten the light to various locations in the cockpit at the crewmember's discretion. The utility light in the front cockpit is the only cockpit light designed to illuminate the cockpit which operates from JFS generator power.

Standby Compass Light

Lighting for the front cockpit standby compass is controlled by the STBY COMP switch and the INST PNL knob. With the STBY COMP switch ON, variable lighting is provided between positions OFF and BRT of the INST PNL knob. In the rear cockpit, although a STBY COMP switch is provided, there is no standby compass installed.

Chart Lights

A chart light is provided in the front cockpit on the canopy bow and in the rear cockpit above the right console. The lights, which illuminate maps and other documents on the crewmember's knee board, are mounted by adjustable positioning joints. The lights are controlled by the CHART LT knob in either cockpit, which provides variable lighting between positions OFF and BRT.

Display Lighting Switch

A DISPLAY switch is provided in each cockpit which controls the maximum illumination level for the MPD/MPCD displays. The positions are DAY and NIGHT.

Warning/Caution Lights Control Knob

A control is provided in each cockpit on the interior lights control panel to switch the warning/caution/advisory lights from bright intensity to the low intensity range, and then to vary the brightness within the low intensity range. The control is labeled WARNING CAUTION. The control only works provided the flight instrument lights knob is not in OFF, the storm/flood lights knob is not in full BRT, and the warning/caution lights control knob has been momentarily placed to the RESET position. Once in the low intensity range, the warning/caution/advisory lights can be brought back to bright intensity by turning the flight instrument lights knob to OFF, turning the storm/flood lights knob to full BRT, or removing and re-applying power to the aircraft. The master caution light is also dimmed when the warning caution lights knob is placed to RESET, but intensity cannot be varied.

Lights Test Switch

A lights test switch, labeled LT TEST, is provided to test the warning/caution/advisory lights.

OFF	The switch is spring loaded off.
ON	Serviceable warning/ caution/ advisory lights will illuminate (except T.O. TRIM).

OXYGEN SYSTEM

NORMAL OXYGEN SUPPLY

The normal system pressure is 70 psi with a usable pressure range of 55 to 90 psi. When the system is not operating (pilot not using system oxygen) the allowable pressure range is 55 to 120 psi. The pressure should remain within these limits until the converter is depleted.

Oxygen Low Caution

The OXY LOW caution is displayed when oxygen quantity is below 4 liters. The caution also comes on with the oxygen quantity test button in either cockpit pressed when the oxygen quantity gage pointer drops below 4 liters.

EMERGENCY OXYGEN SUPPLY

A 10 minute supply of oxygen is furnished by a gaseous oxygen storage bottle on the left rear of each ejection seat. The supply is activated automatically on ejection, or is activated manually by pulling the emergency oxygen green ring just forward of the bottle on the left seat arm rest.

OXYGEN REGULATOR

The oxygen regulator, on the front and rear cockpit right consoles, automatically controls the pressure and flow rate of normal oxygen based on demand and cockpit altitude.

Supply Lever

A two-position lever on the right corner of each regulator panel, controls the flow of oxygen from the regulator.

ON	The proper mix of cockpit air and oxygen is supplied to the mask.
OFF	Breathing is not possible with the mask on.

Diluter Lever

A two-position diluter lever, in the center of each regulator, controls the mixture of air and oxygen.

100%	Pure oxygen is delivered.
NORMAL	The scheduled mixture of air and oxygen is delivered.

Emergency Lever

A three-position emergency lever is on the lower left corner of each regulator panel.

EMERGENCY	Continuous positive pressure oxygen is delivered to the mask.

NORMAL	Normal operation is provided.
TEST MASK	Positive oxygen pressure is supplied.

Oxygen Flow Indicator

The oxygen flow indicator on each regulator panel alternately shows white for flow and black for no-flow with each breath under normal conditions. Continuous black indicates no air/oxygen is being furnished and continous white indicates a leak in the system.

Oxygen Pressure Gage

The oxygen pressure gage on each regulator panel indicates oxygen delivery to the regulator. The normal indication is approximately 70 psi.

OXYGEN QUANTITY GAGE

The oxygen quantity gage, is on the front and rear cockpit ECS panel.

OXYGEN QUANTITY GAGE TEST BUTTON

The oxygen quantity gage test button, on the front and rear cockpit ECS panel, tests the operation of the gage and the OXY LOW caution. Depressing the test button causes the gage needle to rotate from the present quantity indication to 0. As the needle passes below 4 liters the OXY LOW caution should come on. Upon release of the test button, the gage needle should rotate from 0 to an indication of the present quantity. The OXY LOW caution should go out as the needle passes above 4 liters.

OXYGEN HOSE STOWAGE FITTING

An oxygen hose stowage fitting is provided in the front and rear cockpit above and outboard of the right console. The oxygen hose should be stowed in this fitting at all times when not in use to prevent hose contamination and damage to the console by a flailing hose.

ENVIRONMENTAL CONTROL SYSTEM

The environmental control system (ECS) provides conditioned air and pressurization, for the cockpit and avionics, windshield anti-fog and anti-ice, anti-G, canopy seal, and fuel pressurization. The ECS uses engine bleed air from both engines for normal operation. Cooling for the avionics, with the air source knob OFF or the cockpit temperature switch OFF, automatically switches to ram air. Ram air cooling is automatically supplied to the avionics whenever compressor inlet duct pressure drops. See foldout section for the ECS schematic.

ECS vents and louvers are located on the center instrument panel and along the canopy rails in both cockpits.

AIR SOURCE KNOB

The air source knob, on the air conditioning control panel on the right console, selects the engine bleed air source for the ECS system.

BOTH	Supplies bleed air from both engines.
L ENG	Shuts off bleed air from the right engine.
R ENG	Shuts off bleed air from the left engine.
OFF	Shuts off bleed air from both engines.

CAUTION

Selection of OFF on the air source knob or cabin temperature control switch will switch avionics from normal cooling to ram air cooling. Overheat damage to the avionics may occur. Monitor the ECS caution on the MPD/MPCD.

AIR FLOW SELECTOR SWITCH

The air flow selector switch allows three cockpit flow selections.

MAX	Maximum air flow
NORM	Normal air flow
MIN	Minimum air flow

Flow selection is at the discretion of the pilot. The change in flow from MIN to MAX is not always perceptible to the pilot.

BLEED AIR CAUTIONS

The L and/or R BLEED AIR MPD/MPCD caution comes on when a bleed air leak is detected between the engine and the primary heat exchanger.

COCKPIT PRESSURIZATION

Control of the pressure schedule by the cockpit pressure regulator is automatic. Refer to figure 1-49 for the cockpit pressure schedule.

COCKPIT PRESSURE ALTIMETER

The pressure altitude of the cockpit is indicated on a 0-50,000 foot pressure altimeter on the right main instrument panel.

COCKPIT TEMPERATURE CONTROL

Cockpit temperature is controlled by the cabin temperature control knob and switch on the air conditioning control panel.

COCKPIT PRESSURE SCHEDULE

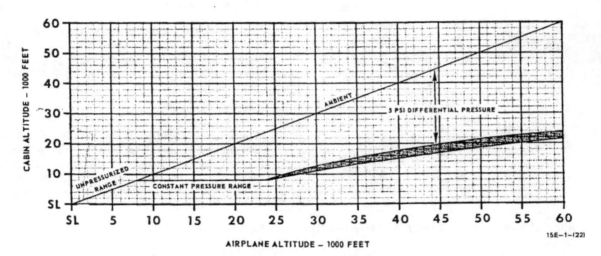

Figure 1-49

AUTO   Cockpit temperature is automatically maintained at the temperature selected on the control knob.

MANUAL   Cockpit temperature may be manually changed with the control knob but is not automatically maintained.

OFF   a. Turns off ECS air to the cockpit, avionics, and windshield anti-fog.

               b. Avionics cooling automatically switches to ram air.

               c. The canopy seal, fuel pressurization, radar waveguide, anti-g and windshield anti-ice continue to operate.

AVIONICS PRESSURIZATION AND TEMPERATURE

The pressurization and temperature control of the avionics system is automatic.

ECS CAUTION

The ECS caution warns of overtemperature or low air flow of the avionics cooling air. With the ECS operating normally, the ECS caution may come on during low speed flight, particularly at high power settings, or during idle descents. When the ECS caution comes on during single engine operation on the ground, selected avionics equipment will automatically be turned off.

DISPLAY FLOW LOW CAUTION

The DISPLAY FLOW LOW caution warns of inadequate cooling air flow to the cockpit displays. Caution lights are located in both the forward and aft cockpits. In the forward cockpit, the DSPL FLO LO light is located on the right subpanel. In the aft cockpit, the DISPLAY FLOW LOW light can be found above the right MPD.

A differential pressure switch monitors the difference between cabin pressure and display cooling line pressure. If the differential pressure drops below a required value, the cockpit display cooling flow is assumed low and the caution will illuminate. The caution light will remain on until adequate differential pressure is restored.

EMERGENCY VENT CONTROL

The emergency vent handle on the right main instrument sub panel, when turned 45° CCW electrically dumps cabin pressure. Extension of the handle shuts off ECS air to the cockpit, diverts all ECS cooling air to the avionics and allows ram air to enter the cockpit.

The amount of cockpit ram air flow is controlled by how far the handle is extended. At full travel the handle is locked. If the handle is pushed in and rotated clockwise (CW), normal ECS operation is restored.

WINDSHIELD ANTI-FOG

Windshield anti-fog air is supplied when cockpit air conditioning is operating. The anti-fog air temperature may be regulated by the pilot with the anti-fog switch. If the emergency vent handle is turned 45° CCW and pulled, windshield anti-fog hot air is automatically selected.

Anti-Fog Switch

The anti-fog switch allows the pilot to select a range of temperatures for anti-fog air. The switch is electrically held in the HOT or COLD position and automatically resets to NORMAL when electrical power is lost.

NORMAL   Anti-fog air is supplied at normal temperature.

HOT   Anti-fog air is hotter than normal.

COLD   Anti-fog air temperature is controlled by the cockpit temperature control knob and may be varied from colder than normal to hotter than normal.

The position of this switch is at the pilot's discretion for his own comfort. If the switch is in the COLD position and a condition where windshield fogging is anticipated, select HOT.

ANTI-G SYSTEM

The anti-g system is automatic and delivers cooled bleed air to the anti-g suit. The airflow into the suits is proportional to the g force experienced. A manual inflation button in the valve allows each pilot to inflate his suit for checking the system. The system incorporates an automatic pressure relief valve.

ANTI-ICING SYSTEMS

ENGINE ANTI-ICE SWITCH

The engine anti-ice system is comprised of the inlet ice detector and the engine anti-ice valve. The engine anti-ice valve and the inlet ice detector are functionally unrelated. The detector only senses engine inlet ice build up and turns on the INLET ICE caution. The engine heat switch, on the front cockpit ECS panel, controls the engine anti-ice airflow to the engine nose cone and stationary inlet guide vanes and electrically heats the inlet pressure probe. The DEEC will automatically shut off the engines anti-ice when the altitude is above 30,000 feet or the engine inlet temperature is above 15°C (60°F) regardless of switch position.

ON   Activates the engine anti-ice system.

OFF   Deactivates the engine anti-ice system.

TEST   Checks detector operation, and turns on the INLET ICE caution.

INLET ICE CAUTION

The INLET ICE caution indicates an icing condition in the left engine inlet duct. The INLET ICE caution remains on as long as the icing condition exists and will not be extinguished by activating the engine anti-ice system.

WINDSHIELD ANTI-ICE SWITCH

The windshield anti-ice switch on the ECS panel controls hot airflow from the primary heat exchanger to the windshield exterior anti-ice nozzle.

> **CAUTION**
>
> Use of the windshield anti-ice system under non-icing conditions may damage the windshield.

ON   Activates the windshield anti-ice system

OFF   Deactivates the windshield anti-ice system.

WINDSHIELD HOT CAUTION LIGHT

The WINDSHLD HOT caution light comes on when windshield anti-ice air temperature is excessive. It does not detect the temperature of the windshield and may not warn of impending windshield damage.

STORES JETTISON SYSTEMS

Emergency jettison is provided by the emergency jettison button. Selective jettison is provided by the select jettison knob/button in conjunction with the MPD/MPCD. When the landing gear handle is down, the selective jettison controls are deenergized. The gear handle safety interlock can be bypassed by the armament safety switch.

Regardless of master arm switch position, when either the emergency jettison or select jettison (in COMBAT, A/A or A/G position only) button is pressed, all arming solenoids are automatically deenergized before jettison and all stores are jettisoned unarmed.

Emergency Jettison Button

The emergency jettison button is located on the center of the front instrument panel to the left of the MPCD. This button, when pressed, will simultaneously jettison all pylons with cartridges installed and all AIM-7 missiles. Although the button is spring-loaded to the normal position, a means is provided to determine that the button is not stuck in the jettison position. In the normal position only the color black on the inside lip of the button guard can be seen above the button. If the button is stuck in the jettison position, yellow color can be seen in the switch guard below the black color.

> **CAUTION**
>
> Emergency jettison button is hot when electrical power is on the aircraft.

Select Jettison Knob/Button

When pressed, the select jettison button (figure 1-50) jettisons stores depending on the knob positions described below:

OFF	Removes power from the selective jettison button.
COMBAT	Selective jettison button first press initiates combat jettison program 1. Second press initiates combat jettison program 2. See figure 1-50.
A/A	Selects air-to-air selective jettison. Refer to figure 1-51.
A/G	Selects air-to-ground selective jettison. Refer to figure 1-52.
ALTN REL	Used for nuclear weapons release.
MAN RET	Refer to TO 1F-15E-34-1-1.
MAN FF	Refer to TO 1F-15E-34-1-1.

Programming Combat Jettison

Combat jettison is a two-push capability. With COMBAT selected on the SELECT JETT knob, the first push will jettison whatever is assigned to the CBT 1 program and the second will jettison whatever is assigned to the CBT 2 program.

Programming combat jettison is accomplished by selecting the ARMT display on the MPD/MPCD, then selecting the CBT JETT display (figure 1-40). The SELECT JETT knob may be in either OFF or COMBAT. Select the CBT 1 program by pressing the 1 button. Then select the station from the top five buttons followed by STORE, RACK or PYLON from the left of the MPD/MPCD (STORE is automatically boxed when the display is selected). Press the ENTER button to complete programming for CBT 1. Repeat these steps for CBT 2, with 2 selected on the display. If the SELECT JETT knob is in COMBAT, CBT 1 and CBT 2 will be boxed on the display.

Armament Safety Switch

The armament safety switch, on the left console outboard of the anti-g valve, allows the gear handle safety interlock to be bypassed for armament circuit checkout.

SAFE	Normal circuitry is used.
OVERRIDE	The switch is solenoid held until electrical power is removed, the landing gear handle is placed UP, or the switch is manually placed to SAFE.

BOARDING STEPS

A boarding steps position indicator on the left canted bulkhead will display UP when the steps are retracted and DOWN when the steps are extended.

CANOPY SYSTEM

The cockpit area is enclosed by a clamshell type canopy. Refer to foldout section for ejection seat illustration. The main components of the canopy system are a hydraulic actuator which provides manual and powered operation of the canopy, a locking mechanism, and a pyrotechnic canopy remover for emergency jettison. Latches on the canopy frame and along the lower edge of the canopy engage fittings on the cockpit sill structure to lock the canopy to the fuselage. An inflatable seal, installed around the edge of the canopy frame, retains cockpit pressure when the canopy is locked.

NORMAL CANOPY SYSTEM

For normal canopy operation, an internal canopy control handle (figure 1-43) is provided on the right side of the cockpit under the canopy sill in both cockpits. For operation of the canopy from outside the aircraft, an external canopy control handle is located on the left side of the aircraft below the canopy. The external canopy control handle duplicates operation of the internal canopy control handle. An accumulator provides hydraulic power for powered operation of the canopy (2-1/2 to 3 cycles) when utility hydraulic pressure is not on the aircraft. A hand pump is installed in the nose wheelwell to operate the canopy with hydraulic pressure off the aircraft and accumulator hydraulic pressure depleted. The canopy can be operated without accumulator pressure by moving the external canopy control handle or one of the internal canopy handles to the UP or DN position, as desired, and then operating the hand pump in the nose wheelwell. For ground egress with accumulator hydraulic pressure depleted, the canopy can be opened by placing the internal canopy control handle to UP and then pushing up on the canopy. A

PROGRAMMING COMBAT JETTISON

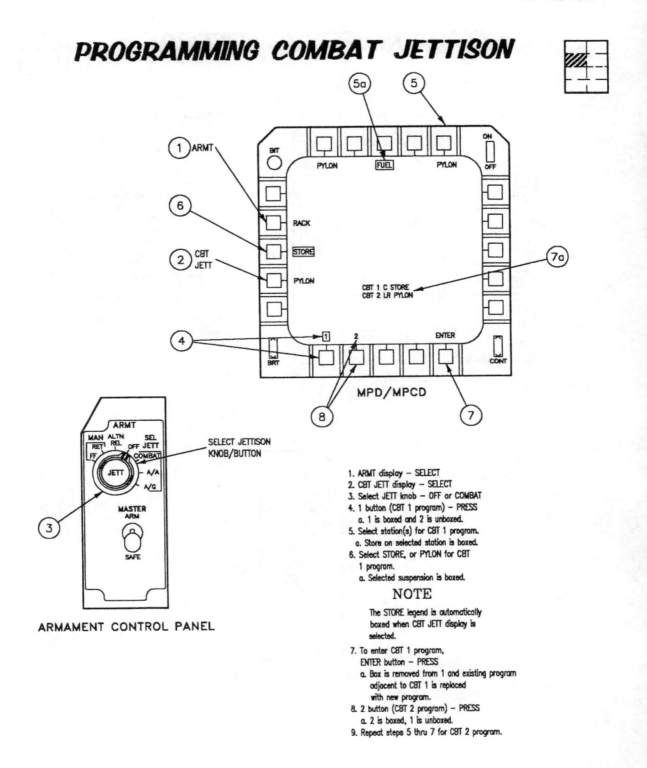

ARMAMENT CONTROL PANEL

MPD/MPCD

1. ARMT display – SELECT
2. CBT JETT display – SELECT
3. Select JETT knob – OFF or COMBAT
4. 1 button (CBT 1 program) – PRESS
   a. 1 is boxed and 2 is unboxed.
5. Select station(s) for CBT 1 program.
   a. Store on selected station is boxed.
6. Select STORE, or PYLON for CBT
   1 program.
   a. Selected suspension is boxed.

NOTE

The STORE legend is automatically boxed when CBT JETT display is selected.

7. To enter CBT 1 program,
   ENTER button – PRESS
   a. Box is removed from 1 and existing program adjacent to CBT 1 is replaced with new program.
8. 2 button (CBT 2 program) – PRESS
   a. 2 is boxed, 1 is unboxed.
9. Repeat steps 5 thru 7 for CBT 2 program.

Figure 1-50

A/A SELECTIVE JETTISON

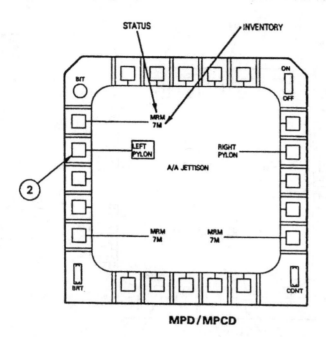

STATUS

INVENTORY

MRM
7M

LEFT
PYLON

RIGHT
PYLON

A/A JETTISON

MRM
7M

MRM
7M

BRT

BRT

ON

OFF

CONT

MPD/MPCD

1. Select JETT knob – A/A
   a. A/A JETTISON cue appears on display.
   b. MRM status can be displayed as: MRM, STBY, RDY, HUNG or FAIL.
   c. When no weapon is on a station, the inventory and line segment is omitted.
2. Select weapon to be jettisoned.
   a. Selected MRM or PYLON is boxed. Select buttons are mutually exclusive (only one can be selected at a time).
   b. If an SRM is hung, the pylon of the last hung AIM-9 is automatically boxed when A/A JETTISON is displayed.
3. Select JETT button – PRESS
   a. MRM status, line segment, and MRM or PYLON is removed;
   b. HUNG status appears if jettison is not successful.
4. Repeat steps 2 and 3 for each weapon.
5. Select JETT knob – AS DESIRED

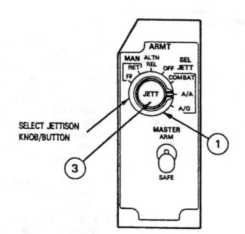

SELECT JETTISON
KNOB/BUTTON

ARMAMENT CONTROL PANEL

15E-1-(30-1)-CATI

Figure 1-51

PROGRAMMED RECORDING DISPLAYS

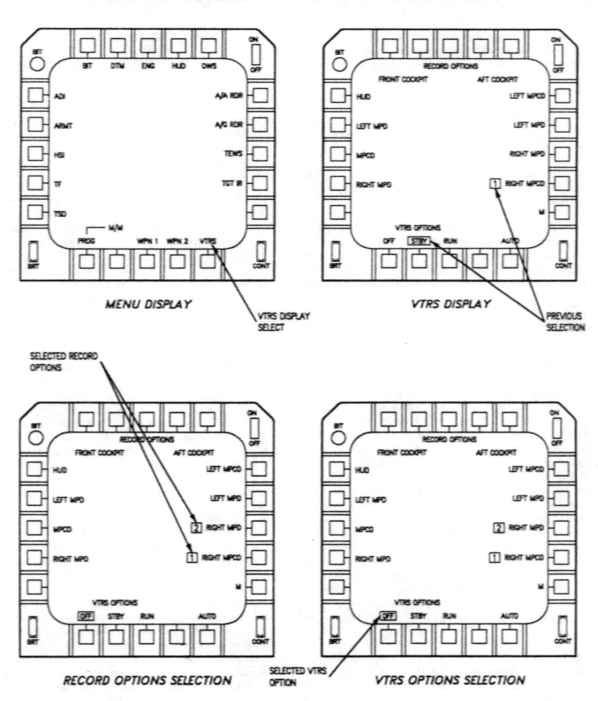

MENU DISPLAY

VTRS DISPLAY

RECORD OPTIONS SELECTION

VTRS OPTIONS SELECTION

15E-1-(40-1)-CATI

Figure 1-51

PROGRAMMED RECORDING

If the crewmembers know in advance which cockpit display(s) they wish to record, they can program the VTRS through a VTRS display menu to record particular display(s) before the fact. This is called programmed recording. Because programmed recording occurs automatically, the workload of the crewmembers is reduced. Another advantage of programmed recording is that after the program is entered, the recording procedure can be controlled with Hands-On Throttle and Stick (HOTAS) functions. The aircrew procedures for programmed recording are described in the following paragraphs.

VTRS Selection - Pressing the MPD or MPCD pushbutton adjacent to M calls up the menu display shown in figure 1-51.

Pressing the VTRS pushbutton selects the VTRS display shown in figure 1-51. The VTRS display will indicate those selections which were selected the previous time this display was called up. For example, if the aft cockpit right-hand MPCD was previously selected and the VTRS was set in the Standby (STBY) mode, the resultant display would look like figure 1-51.

Record Options and Priorities - The crewmember can select or deselect any two of the eight available record options by pressing the pushbutton adjacent to the desired option. Also note that the options are separated for front cockpit and aft cockpit. A boxed priority number 1 appears adjacent to the first record option selection, and a boxed priority number 2 appears adjacent to the second record option selection, as shown in figure 1-51. This procedure is referred to as programmed recording. No recording will actually occur at this point because OFF has been selected as the VTRS Option. To deselect a record option, the crew member simply presses the adjacent pushbutton, and the boxed priority number is removed. If the number 1 priority record option is deselected, the number 2 priority record option will automatically be reassigned number 1 priority, and the boxed priority number will change accordingly. If two record options have already been selected, any attempt to select a third record option will be ignored by the system.

Split-Screen Video - VTRS has the capability to record split-screen video for the majority of display format pairs. For split-screen video to occur, the displays must be synchronized, i.e., the displays must be refreshed at the same rate. Some of the display

formats are ineligible for split-screen video due to incompatible synchronization rates. If any two of the following formats are selected, only the first one selected will be recorded:

TSD	TGT FLIR
WPN 1	TF E^2
WPN 2	NAV FLIR (on HUD or HUD Repeater)

The end result of a split-screen video recording is a display with 50% horizontal video compression, and full-size vertical video. That is, both displays are regular height, but their width is compressed by one-half.

VTRS Options - The three VTRS Options are displayed on the bottom of the VTRS Display. They are OFF, STBY, and RUN. Each VTRS option can be selected by pressing the corresponding pushbutton. In addition, the central computer will automatically select the OFF VTRS option, as shown in figure 1-51 whenever no record options have been selected. If a crewmember attempts to select either STBY or RUN without first selecting a record option, then a cue is displayed in the center of the VTRS display. When no record options have been selected, OFF is the only available VTRS option. The cue is automatically removed after the crewmember selects a record option. The STBY OPTION enables the AUTO function, if selected. With STBY selected, recording of programmed displays occurs when the weapon release (pickle button) is pressed. In the A/A master mode, the displays will be recorded for missile time-of-flight(TOF) plus 5 seconds. In the A/G master mode, they will be recorded from weapon consent through weapon release plus 10 seconds. The RUN option initiates recording of the programmed display(s).

Auto Function - The VTRS AUTO function may be selected or deselected independent of the three VTRS Options previously discussed. The AUTO function is boxed when selected. By pressing the adjacent pushbutton, the box is removed and the AUTO function is deselected. When the AUTO function is selected by a crewmember, the VTRS will automatically record the HUD whenever predetermined conditions exist. That is, the AUTO function will interrupt recording of programmed or non-programmed displays, and will automatically record the HUD. When the predetermined conditions no longer exist, the VTRS will revert to recording the previously selected display(s). One predetermined condition is the selection of the gun (using the throttle weapon mode switch) together with a radar-detected target within 10nm of the aircraft. The other predetermined conditions involve AIR-TO-AIR missile launch commanded by the control stick weapon release pushbutton. The duration of the AUTO recording equals the missile time of flight plus 5 seconds.

HUD Recording in Progress Cue - The central computer clock time cue is displayed in the lower left corner of the HUD to indicate recording in progress.

Programmed Recording in Progress Cue - In general, the central computer clock time is displayed on the right side of the MPD/MPCD when programmed recording is in progress. Also, an asterisk is displayed above and below the clock time. The asterisks are displayed to distinguish programmed recording from non-programmed recording. For the programmable armament control set (PACS), BIT, MENU, VTRS and DTM displays, the clock time cue will not be displayed. However, if programmed recording is in progress on a particular MPD and one of these displays is called up, then the recorder will record the PACS, BIT or DTM format on the programmed MPD(s).

Weapon Consent Cue - A small tick mark placed on the left edge of the recording. Identical in appearance to the weapon release tick mark but separated positionally. The weapon consent cue is present while the pickle button is pressed or the trigger is held in full action.

Weapon Release Cue - A small tick mark is displayed on the left edge of the recording to mark the time of weapon release. The duration of this cue is one second. The purpose of the weapon release cue is to help the crewmember search his video tape recordings after flight, freezing the playback machine at the time of weapon release.

Voice Communications and Aural Tones - In order to aid correlation of inflight occurrences with post flight review of the video tape recording, voice communications to and from the crewmembers are recorded on the audio track of the VTRS. Likewise, aural tones voice warnings, weapon consent and weapon release tones are recorded.

LIGHTING EQUIPMENT

EXTERIOR LIGHTING

Exterior lights are controlled from either the exterior lights control panel or the miscellaneous control panel, both on the left console in the front cockpit.

Position Lights

The position lights include a green light on the forward edge of the right wing tip, a red light on the forward edge of the left wing tip, and a white light just below the tip of the left vertical tail fin. The position lights are controlled by a knob on the exterior lights control panel labeled POSITION. With the anti-collision lights on, the position lights automatically go to steady full brilliance, regardless of the position of the position lights knob.

OFF	Lights are off.
1 - 5	Guide numbers for varying brightness from off to full bright.
BRT	Lights are at full brightness.
FLASH	The lights will flash at full brightness.

Anti-Collision Lights

There are three red anti-collision lights; one on the leading edge of each wing just outboard of the air intake and another just below the tip of the right vertical tail fin. The anti-collision lights are controlled by a single toggle switch on the exterior lights control panel labeled ANTI-COLLISION. The switch positions are OFF and ON.

Formation Lights

Six green electroluminescent formation lights are provided. Two lights are on the wingtips behind the position lights, two lights are on the side of the forward fuselage just forward of the cockpit, and two lights are on the aft fuselage just aft of wing trailing edge. The formation lights are controlled by a single knob on the exterior lights control panel labeled FORMATION.

OFF	Lights are off.
1-5	Guide numbers for varying brightness from off to full bright.
BRT	The lights are at full brightness.

Vertical Tail Flood Lights

Two vertical tail flood lights are installed on the right and left aft fuselage to illuminate the vertical tails during night join-ups and formation flying. They are controlled by a single switch on the exterior lights control panel.

OFF	Lights are off.
DIM	Lights are on in a dimmed condition.
BRT	Lights are at full brightness.

Landing and Taxi Lights

The landing and taxi lights are on the nose gear strut. They are controlled by a toggle switch on the miscellaneous control panel. The lights are off, regardless of switch position, when the landing gear handle is in the up position.

OFF	Lights are off.
LDG LIGHT	If the landing gear handle is down, the landing light is turned on.
TAXI LIGHT	If the landing gear handle is down, the taxi light is turned on.

INTERIOR LIGHTING

Except for the utility floodlights, and UFC display lighting, all the controls for interior lights are on the interior lights control panel on the right console in each cockpit.

Upfront Control Display Lighting

The UFC Liquid Crystal Display (LCD) consists of six display rows. A brightness control (BRT) provides a full range of adjustment for night utilization. Backlighting is not required because the LCD is a reflective type display.

Instrument Lighting

Integral lighting is provided for all instruments and panels on the front cockpit instrument panel including the MPDs, MPCD, UFC, circuit breaker panels and the HUD. Integral lighting is also provided to the radio call, emergency hook and emergency vent panels. Instrument lighting is provided to the front cockpit standby compass whenever the STBY COMP switch is ON. Rear cockpit integral instrument lighting is provided for all instruments and panels on the rear instrument panel including the MPDs and MPCDs. Integral lighting is also provided to the UFC, the command selector valve panel, the emergency hook panel and the radio call panel. The lights are controlled by the instrument panel lights knob in either cockpit, labeled INST PNL, which provides variable lighting between positions OFF and BRT.

Console Lighting

The console lights are controlled by the CONSOLE knob in either cockpit which provide variable lighting between positions OFF and BRT.

Storm/Flood Lighting

Four storm/flood lights are provided in the front cockpit and two in the rear cockpit for secondary lighting. The front cockpit has a light above each console and two above the main instrument panel. The rear cockpit has one light above each console. The lights in each cockpit are controlled by the storm/flood lights knob labeled STORM FLOOD, which provides variable lighting between OFF and BRT. In either cockpit, if the warning/caution/advisory lights are in the dimmed condition, moving the storm/flood lights knob to full BRT causes the warning/caution/advisory lights to revert to full intensity, regardless of the position of the WARNING CAUTION control knob.

Utility Flood Lights

A portable utility flood light is provided in each cockpit and is normally stowed on a bracket above the right console. An alligator clip attached to the light may be used to fasten the light to various locations in the cockpit at the crewmember's discretion. The utility light in the front cockpit is the only cockpit light designed to illuminate the cockpit which operates from JFS generator power.

Standby Compass Light

Lighting for the front cockpit standby compass is controlled by the STBY COMP switch and the INST PNL knob. With the STBY COMP switch ON, variable lighting is provided between positions OFF and BRT of the INST PNL knob. In the rear cockpit, although a STBY COMP switch is provided, there is no standby compass installed.

Chart Lights

A chart light is provided in the front cockpit on the canopy bow and in the rear cockpit above the right console. The lights, which illuminate maps and other documents on the crewmember's knee board, are mounted by adjustable positioning joints. The lights are controlled by the CHART LT knob in either cockpit, which provides variable lighting between positions OFF and BRT.

Display Lighting Switch

A DISPLAY switch is provided in each cockpit which controls the maximum illumination level for the MPD/MPCD displays. The positions are DAY and NIGHT.

Warning/Caution Lights Control Knob

A control is provided in each cockpit on the Interior Lights Control Panel to independently switch the warning/caution/advisory lights from bright intensity (day mode) to the low intensity range (night mode), and then to vary the brightness within the low intensity night mode. The control is labeled WARNING CAUTION, and is variable between the OFF position and BRT (bright), with a momentary RESET position at the maximum clockwise position. Variable lighting is provided for the night mode whenever the instrument panel lights (INST PNL) knob is not OFF, the STORM FLOOD lights knob is not full BRT, and the WARNING CAUTION knob is set to RESET and then varied between OFF and BRT. The dimmed night lights revert back to the bright day mode when main aircraft power is interrupted, INST PNL lights are turned OFF, or the STORM FLOOD lights are full BRT. The MASTER CAUTION light is also dimmed in the night mode, but intensity cannot be varied.

In the day mode, this control also permits the pilot to vary the intensity of the LOCK/SHOOT lights on the canopy bow. In this mode and in a high ambient light environment, the pilot should be aware that the LOCK/SHOOT lights can be set too dim to be seen. Also, when the pilot selects the low intensity night mode, the LOCK/SHOOT lights are disabled.

Lights Test Switch

A lights test switch, labeled LT TEST, is provided to test the warning/caution/advisory lights. If in the low intensity night mode, the lights will test at the dimmed setting, as controlled by the WARNING

CAUTION control knob.

OFF   Removes power from lights test circuit

ON   Serviceable warning/ caution/ advisory lights (including rear cockpit LEFT/RIGHT ENGINE FIRE lights) will come on (except T.O. TRIM).

OXYGEN SYSTEM (F-15E 86-0183 THRU 90-0232 BEFORE TO 1F-15E-561)

NORMAL OXYGEN SUPPLY

The normal system pressure is 70 psi with a usable pressure range of 55 to 90 psi. When the system is not operating (aircrew not using system oxygen) the allowable pressure range is 55 to 120 psi. The pressure should remain within these limits until the converter is depleted.

OXYGEN LOW Caution

The OXY LOW caution is displayed when oxygen quantity is below 4 liters. The caution also comes on when the oxygen quantity test button in either cockpit pressed when the oxygen quantity gage pointer drops below 4 liters.

EMERGENCY OXYGEN SUPPLY

A 10 minute supply of oxygen is furnished by a gaseous oxygen storage bottle on the left rear of each ejection seat. The supply is activated automatically on ejection, or is activated manually by pulling the emergency oxygen green ring just forward of the bottle on the left seat arm rest.

OXYGEN REGULATOR

The oxygen regulator, on the front and rear cockpit right consoles, automatically controls the pressure and flow rate of normal oxygen based on demand and cockpit altitude.

Supply Lever

A two-position lever on the right corner of each regulator panel, controls the flow of oxygen from the regulator.

ON   The proper mix of cockpit air and oxygen is supplied to the mask.

OFF   Breathing is not possible with the mask on.

Diluter Lever

A two-position diluter lever, in the center of each regulator, controls the mixture of air and oxygen.

100%   Pure oxygen is delivered.

NORMAL   The scheduled mixture of air and oxygen is delivered.

Emergency Lever

A three-position emergency lever is on the lower left corner of each regulator panel.

EMER-   Continuous positive pressure oxy-
GENCY   gen is delivered to the mask.

NORMAL   Normal operation is provided.

TEST   Positive oxygen pressure is sup-
MASK   plied.

Oxygen Flow Indicator

The oxygen flow indicator on each regulator panel alternately shows white for flow and black for no-flow with each breath under normal conditions. Continuous black indicates no air/oxygen is being furnished and continuous white indicates a leak in the system.

Oxygen Pressure Gage

The oxygen pressure gage on each regulator panel indicates oxygen delivery to the regulator. The normal indication is approximately 70 psi.

OXYGEN QUANTITY GAGE

The oxygen quantity gage, is on the front and rear cockpit ECS panel.

Oxygen Quantity Gage Test Button

The oxygen quantity gage test button, on the front and rear cockpit ECS panel, tests the operation of the gage and the OXY LOW caution. Depressing the test button causes the gage needle to rotate from the present quantity indication to 0. As the needle passes below 4 liters the OXY LOW caution should come on. Upon release of the test button, the gage needle should rotate from 0 to an indication of the present quantity. The OXY LOW caution should go out as the needle passes above 4 liters.

OXYGEN HOSE STOWAGE FITTING

An oxygen hose stowage fitting is provided in the front and rear cockpit above and outboard of the right console. The oxygen hose should be stowed in this fitting at all times when not in use to prevent hose contamination and damage to the console by a flailing hose.

MOLECULAR SIEVE OXYGEN GENERATING SYSTEM (MSOGS) (F-15E 90-0233 AND UP AND F-15E 86-0183 THRU 90-0232 AFTER TO 1F-15E-561)

The MSOGS provides a continuously available supply of breathing gas for the aircrew. MSOGS consists of a concentrator with an integral, self-charging backup oxygen supply (BOS), and panel mounted oxygen breathing regulator for each crew member.

The MSOGS uses conditioned aircraft engine bleed air extracted from the ECS from dual sources and electrical power from the aircraft essential bus to provide a continuous supply of oxygen enriched breathing gas. If a total ECS air-conditioning failure/shutdown occurs, ram air would cool the engine bleed air from the secondary source before it goes to the concentrator. This secondary source provides preconditioned air to MSOGS as long as engine bleed air is available from either engine. Inlet air from either source is cycled through the beds by an electrically driven valve. Nitrogen is removed and dumped overboard while the remaining output of oxygen rich breathing gas is supplied to the aircrew.

BIT

Power-up BIT

Power-up BIT is a self-test of the monitor/controller to assure it is capable of performing the monitoring functions, and is performed each time the unit is turned on.

The Power-up BIT lasts approximately three minutes. When the Power-up BIT is successfully completed, the OXY BIT light in both cockpits will come on. The light may be reset by pressing the OXY BIT button/light in the cockpit. If Power-up BIT fails, the OXYGEN caution light will come on.

Manual BIT

Manual BIT is a check of the concentrator 3-way valve operation, BOS pressure and the caution circuitry. When the OXY BIT button/light in the forward cockpit is pressed and held the MASTER CAUTION and OXYGEN lights come on and BOS gas will be supplied to the regulator. The pressure gauge on the regulator front plate will indicate the BOS gas pressure available.

Monitoring BIT

Monitoring BIT will continuously monitor the oxygen concentration, and periodically monitor other parameters to assure proper system operation.

The monitoring BIT will shut the inlet air valve if the outlet pressure is greater than 70 psig, and if the product gas O_2 concentration is less than 34% O_2 at sea level. The minimum O_2 concentration threshold increases as altitude increases. A failure detected by the Monitoring BIT will automatically light the OXYGEN caution light and automatically switch the system to BOS mode.

MSOGS CONCENTRATOR

The MSOGS concentrator contains dual beds of molecular sieve materials. Pressurized air from either source is cycled through the beds by an electrically driven valve. Nitrogen is removed and dumped overboard while the remaining output of oxygen rich breathing gas is supplied to the aircrew.

WARNING

The MSOGS is not specifically designed to filter out all traces of all possible contaminates that can be introduced into the ECS. Contaminates can only be introduced through the ECS by other aircraft system failures or flight in a chemical/biological environment. The MSOGS was not designed to be a chemical/biological defense system.

Backup Oxygen System (BOS)

When fully charged, the BOS provides at least 16 man-minutes (8 minutes per crew member) of oxygen enriched breathing gas for use in case of concentrator failure, pre-conditioner bleed duct rupture or total loss of aircraft electrical power. The BOS is mechanically charged whenever MSOGS is producing at least 93% oxygen content gas and the concentrator inlet pressure is 60 psig or greater. When the BOS is filled to its maximum pressure (450 psig) a pressure booster is automatically shut off. If charged, the BOS is the breathing gas source if the oxygen system is used on the ground prior to engine start. A manual BIT can be performed periodically during flight to monitor BOS pressure.

Monitor/Controller

The monitor/controller measures the oxygen concentration of the concentrator product gas, activates a caution signal, BIT indicators, controls BOS fill operation, 3-way valve operation and performs power-up, monitoring and initiated BIT. The monitor/controller checks for two types of failures: critical and non-critical.

Critical failures are:

    a. Low product gas oxygen concentration..
    b. Low concentrator outlet pressure
    c. RAM or checksum faults
    d. Concentrator outlet, BOS and Cabin pressure transducer faults
    e. Accuracy check fault

When a critical failure is detected, the monitor/controller will automatically activate the OXYGEN caution light, switch to BOS breathing gas, and trip the concentrator BIT and remote BIT indicators on the Avionics Status Panel.

Non-critical failures are:

a. Pressure reducer fault
b. Inlet air pressure or inlet filter outlet pressure transducer fault
c. BOS fault
d. Inlet filter failure
e. Inlet valve fails to open

When a non critical failure is detected, the monitor/controller will automatically trip either the concentrator BIT indicator or the filter BIT indicator, plus the remote BIT indicator on the Avionics Status Panel. The caution light will not come on for a non-critical failure.

BREATHING REGULATOR

The MSOGS regulator is a panel mounted, diluter-demand, g-compensated oxygen regulator similar to the standard CRU-73/A. Modifications have been made to provide positive pressure breathing as a function of g-forces (PBG). This function is activated via a pressure signal from an external anti-g valve.

Supply/Mode Control Lever

A three position lever located on the right side of the regulator panel, controls the flow of breathing gas to the crew member.

OFF	The inlet valve is closed and the crew member receives no gas.
ON	The regulator supplies manual breathing pressure and positive pressure breathing as a function of altitude (PPB).
PBG	The regulator provides positive-pressure breathing as a function of G_Z as well as altitude.

WARNING

Injury may result if PBG is selected without compatible life support equipment.

CAUTION

Do not lift the regulator toggle switch when switching regulator from OFF to ON or ON to OFF. Damage to the regulator will result. The switch lever is locked out of the PBG position to avoid inadvertent actuation.

Diluter Lever

A two position lever, located in the center of the regulator panel, controls the mixture of MSOGS gas and air.

100%	100% MSOGS gas is delivered.
NORMAL	MSOGS gas and cabin air are mixed as a function of altitude

Emergency Lever

A three position lever located on the lower left of the regulator panel.

EMERGENCY	Continuous positive pressure is delivered to the mask as well as positive pressure breathing as a function of altitude and G_z (with supply lever ON/PBG).
NORMAL	Normal operation is provided.
TEST MASK	Spring loaded, momentary position that must be held to provide positive pressure to test mask seal.

Flow Indicator

The flow indicator on each regulator panel alternately show white for flow and black for no-flow with each breath under normal conditions. Continuous black indicates no air/MSOGS gas flow is being furnished and continuous white indicates a leak in the system.

ENVIRONMENTAL CONTROL SYSTEM (ECS)

The environmental control system (ECS) provides conditioned air and pressurization, for the cockpit and avionics, windshield anti-fog and anti-ice, anti-G, canopy seal, and fuel pressurization. The ECS uses engine bleed air from both engines for normal operation. Cooling for the avionics, with the air source knob OFF or the cockpit temperature switch OFF, automatically switches to ram air. Ram air cooling is automatically supplied to the avionics whenever compressor inlet duct pressure drops. See foldout section for the ECS schematic.

ECS vents and louvers are located on the center instrument panel and along the canopy rails in both cockpits.

AIR SOURCE KNOB

The air source knob, on the air conditioning control panel on the right console, selects the engine bleed air source for the ECS system.

BOTH	Supplies bleed air from both engines.
L ENG	Shuts off bleed air from the right engine.
R ENG	Shuts off bleed air from the left engine.
OFF	Shuts off bleed air from both engines.

CAUTION

Selection of OFF on the air source knob or cabin temperature control switch will switch avionics from normal cooling to ram air cooling. Overheat damage to the avionics may occur. Monitor the ECS caution on the MPD/MPCD.

AIR FLOW SELECTOR SWITCH

The air flow selector switch allows three cockpit flow selections.

MAX	Maximum air flow
NORM	Normal air flow
MIN	Minimum air flow

Flow selection is at the discretion of the aircrew. The change in flow from MIN to MAX is not always perceptible to the aircrew.

BLEED AIR CAUTIONS

The L and/or R BLEED AIR caution is displayed on the MPD/MPCD when a bleed air leak is detected between the engine and the primary heat exchanger.

COCKPIT PRESSURIZATION

Control of the pressure schedule by the cockpit pressure regulator is automatic. Refer to figure 1-52 for the cockpit pressure schedule.

COCKPIT PRESSURE ALTIMETER

The pressure altitude of the cockpit is indicated on a 0-50,000 foot pressure altimeter on the right main instrument panel.

COCKPIT TEMPERATURE CONTROL

Cockpit temperature is controlled by the cockpit temperature control knob and switch on the air conditioning control panel.

AUTO	Cockpit temperature is automatically maintained at the temperature selected on the control knob.
MANUAL	Cockpit temperature may be manually changed with the control knob but is not automatically maintained.
OFF	a. Turns off ECS air to the cockpit, avionics, and windshield anti-fog.
	b. Avionics cooling automatically switches to ram air.
	c. The canopy seal, fuel pressurization, radar waveguide, anti-g and windshield anti-ice continue to operate.

AVIONICS PRESSURIZATION AND TEMPERATURE

The pressurization and temperature control of the avionics system is automatic.

ECS CAUTION

The ECS caution warns of overtemperature or low air flow of the avionics cooling air. With the ECS operating normally, the ECS caution may come on during low speed flight, particularly at high power settings, or during idle descents. When the ECS caution comes on during single engine operation on the ground, selected avionics equipment will automatically be turned off.

COCKPIT PRESSURE SCHEDULE

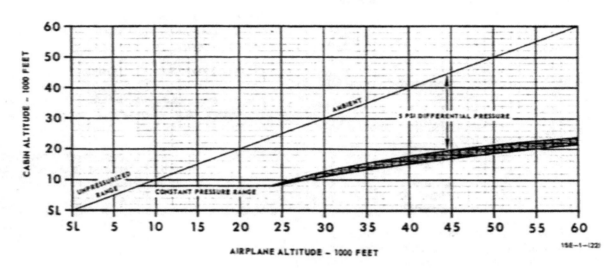

AIRPLANE ALTITUDE – 1000 FEET

15E-1-(22)

Figure 1-52

DISPLAY FLOW LOW CAUTION

The DISPLAY FLOW LOW caution warns of inadequate cooling air flow to the cockpit displays. Caution lights are located in both the forward and aft cockpits. In the forward cockpit, the DSPL FLO LO light is located on the right subpanel. In the aft cockpit, the DISPLAY FLOW LOW light can be found above the right MPD.

A differential pressure switch monitors the difference between cabin pressure and display cooling line pressure. If the differential pressure drops below a required value, the cockpit display cooling flow is assumed low and the caution will illuminate. The caution light will remain on until adequate differential pressure is restored.

EMERGENCY VENT CONTROL

The emergency vent handle on the right main instrument sub panel, when turned 45° CCW electrically dumps cabin pressure. Extension of the handle shuts

off ECS air to the cockpit, diverts all ECS cooling air to the avionics and allows ram air to enter the cockpit.

The amount of cockpit ram air flow is controlled by how far the handle is extended. At full travel the handle is locked. If the handle is pushed in and rotated clockwise (CW), normal ECS operation is restored.

ANTI-G SYSTEM

The anti-g system is automatic and delivers cooled bleed air to the anti-g suit. The airflow into the suits is proportional to the g force experienced. A manual inflation button in the valve allows the aircrew to inflate the suit for checking the system. The system incorporates an automatic pressure relief valve.

WINDSHIELD ANTI-FOG

Windshield anti-fog air is supplied when cockpit air conditioning is operating. The anti-fog air temperature may be regulated by the pilot with the anti-fog advisory lights switch. If the emergency vent handle is turned 45° CCW and pulled, windshield anti-fog hot air is automatically selected.

Anti-Fog Switch

The anti-fog switch allows the pilot to select a range of temperatures for anti-fog air. The switch is electrically held in the HOT or COLD position and automatically resets to NORMAL when electrical power is lost.

NORMAL	Anti-fog air is supplied at normal temperature.
HOT	Anti-fog air is hotter than normal.
COLD	Anti-fog air temperature is controlled by the cockpit temperature control knob and may be varied from colder than normal to hotter than normal.

The position of this switch is at the pilot's discretion for his own comfort. If the switch is in the COLD position and a condition where windshield fogging is anticipated, select HOT.

WINDSHIELD ANTI-ICE SWITCH

The windshield anti-ice switch on the ECS panel controls hot airflow from the primary heat exchanger to the windshield exterior anti-ice nozzle.

ON	Activates the windshield anti-ice system
OFF	Deactivates the windshield anti-ice system.

CAUTION

Use of the windshield anti-ice system under non-icing conditions may damage the windshield.

WINDSHIELD HOT Caution Light

The WINDSHLD HOT caution light comes on when windshield anti-ice air temperature is excessive. It does not detect the temperature of the windshield and may not warn of impending windshield damage.

MSOGS (F-15E 90-0233 AND UP AND F-15E 86-0183 THRU 90-0232 AFTER TO 1F-15E-561)

The MSOGS primary air source is from the high pressure water separator and the secondary air source is from the anti-fog valve inlet line. A source control valve and temperature sensor automatically selects the primary or secondary source based on available pressure and temperature.

The primary source air temperature during normal operation, through the majority of the flight envelope, ranges between -20°F and +130°F. However, during normal operation in the upper left corner of the flight envelope (high altitude/low speed) the primary source air temperature could drop in the -20°F to -50°F range. Therefore, the concentrator inlet air temperature will be automatically controlled by selecting the secondary air source as required to limit the minimum inlet air temperature.

BOARDING STEPS

A boarding steps position indicator on the left canted bulkhead will display UP when the steps are retracted and DOWN when the steps are extended. The retractable boarding steps are released by pressing one of two release buttons. One release button is located inside the top kick-in step and another release button is located on the retractable step door. Pressing either button allows the steps to free fall to the down position. See figure 2-2.

CANOPY SYSTEM

The cockpit area is enclosed by a clamshell type canopy and an impact resistant windshield. Refer to foldout section for ejection seat illustration. The main components of the canopy system are a hydraulic actuator which provides manual and powered operation of the canopy, a locking mechanism, and a pyrotechnic canopy remover for emergency jettison. Latches on the canopy frame and along the lower edge of the canopy engage fittings on the cockpit sill structure to lock the canopy to the fuselage. An inflatable seal, installed around the edge of the canopy frame, retains cockpit pressure when the canopy is locked.

NORMAL CANOPY SYSTEM

For normal canopy operation, an internal canopy control handle (figure 1-53) is provided on the right side of the cockpit under the canopy sill in both cockpits. For operation of the canopy from outside the aircraft, an external canopy control handle is located on the left side of the aircraft below the canopy. The external canopy control handle duplicates operation of the internal canopy control handle. An accumulator provides hydraulic power for powered operation of the canopy (2-1/2 to 3 cycles) when utility hydraulic pressure is not on the aircraft. Accumulator may not fully close the canopy if the ambient temperature is outside the 30°F thru 110°F range. A hand pump is installed in the nose wheelwell to operate the canopy with hydraulic pressure off the aircraft and accumulator hydraulic pressure depleted. The canopy can be operated without accumulator pressure by moving the external canopy control handle or one of the internal canopy handles to the UP or DN position, as desired, and then operating the hand pump in the nose wheelwell. For ground egress with accumulator hydraulic pressure depleted, the canopy can be opened by placing the internal canopy control handle to UP and then pushing up on the canopy. A nitrogen charge in the canopy actuator aids in opening the canopy manually. The internal and external canopy control handles are used to lock the canopy mechanically by placing the handle to LOCKED from the DN position, once the canopy is fully closed.

Internal Canopy Control Handle

The canopy control handle has four positions: LOCKED, DN, HOLD and UP. The front and rear handles are interconnected and follow each other in position when one handle is moved.

LOCKED	Causes a hydraulic block, therefore it is necessary to have the canopy against the windscreen before placing the handle in LOCKED. Placing the handle to the LOCKED position mechanically locks the canopy.
UP	Raises canopy to maximum open position. If selected from the LOCKED position, the canopy will first unlock, then move 1.5 inches aft before rising.
DN	Lowers canopy full down, then forward against the windscreen.
HOLD	Creates a hydraulic lock and stops the canopy at any point in the open or close cycle. This position may be used when the canopy is to be left open for an extended period.

External Canopy Control Handle

The external canopy control handle (figure 1-53) is normally stowed flush with the fuselage on the left side of the aircraft below the canopy. When the handle retaining pushbutton is pushed, the handle springs outboard approximately 2 inches from the fuselage. After rotating the handle full aft to the UP position, canopy will move slightly aft and start opening. To stop the canopy at any point in its opening travel rotate the handle slightly forward from the full aft position to the HOLD position. To close the canopy rotate the handle forward to the DOWN position. The LOCKED position mechanically locks the canopy and produces a hydraulic block in the canopy system. The handle is stowed flush with the fuselage by manually pushing inboard until the retaining latch is engaged.

CANOPY CONTROL HANDLES

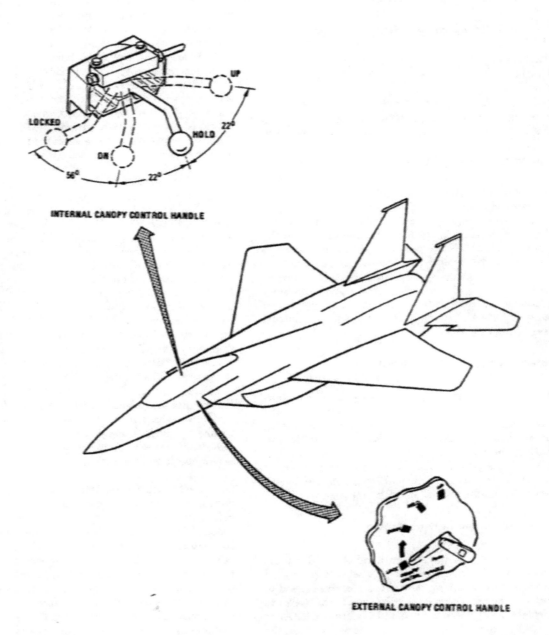

INTERNAL CANOPY CONTROL HANDLE

EXTERNAL CANOPY CONTROL HANDLE

15E-1-(54)

Figure 1-53

CANOPY UNLOCKED Warning Lights

The CANOPY UNLOCKED warning light on the upper right of the instrument panel in each cockpit comes on whenever the canopy is unlocked or the canopy actuated initiator lanyard is disconnected.

Canopy Actuated Initiator Firing Indicator

The canopy actuated initiator firing indicator is located on the bulkhead in back of the seat in the front cockpit. The indicator is a gray cylinder-like housing containing an orange spiral spring which extends when the canopy actuated initiator is fired. Refer to foldout section for ejection seat illustration.

EMERGENCY CANOPY SYSTEM

For canopy jettison, a pyrotechnic canopy remover operates independently of the normal canopy system. The canopy remover, behind the front seat, is designed to safely jettison the canopy only from the closed and LOCKED position. When the ejection control handle, or either an internal or external canopy jettison handle is pulled, the remover mechanically unlocks and jettisons the canopy. Improperly placed or unsecured items near the canopy remover may actuate the canopy jettison bellcrank causing loss of the canopy.

Internal Canopy Jettison Handle

A black and yellow striped canopy jettison handle is located under the left canopy sill just aft of the instrument panel in both cockpits. Depressing an unlock button on the inboard side of the handle, and pulling the handle aft fires the canopy jettison system. The handle, once pulled to the fired position, is locked in the fired position where it remains locked until the handle and initiator are replaced.

External Canopy Jettison Handle

The external canopy jettison handle is a T-handle located within an access door just below and forward of the external canopy control handle, and is used to jettison the canopy from outside the aircraft (refer to airplane entry/aircrew extraction, section III). After pushing a release button to open the access door, the handle and its lanyard is played out 8 feet from the aircraft and then pulled. This fires the external canopy jettison system.

EJECTION SEAT SYSTEM

An ejection seat is installed in each cockpit and a sequencing system is provided which allows for selection of various single or dual ejection options. See command selector valve below. Once ejection is initiated, whether dual or single, each ejection seat is a fully automatic catapult rocket system. Three ejection modes are automatically selected. Refer to figure 1-54. Mode 1 is a low speed mode during which the parachute is deployed almost immediately after the seat departs the aircraft; Mode 2 is a high speed mode during which a drogue chute is first deployed to slow the seat, followed by the deployment of the parachute; Mode 3 is a high altitude mode in which the sequence of events is the same as mode 2 except that man-seat separation and deployment of the parachute is delayed until a safe altitude is reached. Controls are provided to adjust seat height and lock shoulder harness. Refer to foldout section for ejection seat illustration. After TO 1F-15E-552, the ejection seat is equipped with primary and redundant ejection systems and a canopy breaker. The primary and redundant systems are isolated and independent of each other. Both ejection systems are initiated simultaneously when an ejection control handle is pulled. However, a built-in delay in the redundant system allows the primary system to work before the redundant system starts. The time delay prevents any interference of primary and redundant system ejection sequencing. Also, if the primary system fails prior to canopy jettison, the redundant system will jettison the canopy and eject the seat. If both the primary and redundant system fail to jettison the canopy, the redundant system will still fire the seat catapults and with the addition of the seat mounted canopy breaker, provide through the canopy ejection. The redundant system will eject the seat regardless of canopy position (open, closed or in-between).

On aircraft with SEAWARS installed, an automatic backup method is incorporated to release the parachute canopy when landing in sea water. SEAWARS consist of two releases mounted outboard of the Koch connectors on the parachute risers. Each release contains an electronics package (sensor), battery, cartridge, and canopy release fitting. Immersion in sea water activates the sensors which mechanically release the parachute risers from the aircrew's restraint harness. With SEAWARS installed, the normal procedures for connecting and releasing the Koch fitting are the same.

Command Selector Valve

A command selector valve is provided in the rear cockpit to select the desired ejection sequence to be initiated from the rear cockpit, or provide for single ejection for solo flight. Positioning is accomplished by

pulling full aft then turning to the desired position. To release from aft initiate, pull then turn clockwise. Solo position requires use of a collar. Refer to foldout section for ejection seat system performance. After TO 1F-15E-552, the redundant system by-passes the command selector valve. However a built-in delay allows the primary system to work before the redundant system starts.

NORM (vertical)	Single rear seat ejection when initiated from the rear cockpit. Dual ejection (rear seat first) when initiated from the front cockpit.
AFT INITIA-TION (horizontal)	Dual ejection (rear seat first) when initiated from either seat. After TO 1F-15E-552 if a failure occurs in the primary system the front seat will not eject unless the forward crewmember initiates his own ejection.
SOLO (45° CCW)	Single ejection from front cockpit only. Ejection from the front seat is immediate. Ejection from the rear seat is impossible. After TO 1F-15E-552 the aft seat will eject after the forward crewmember has ejected however, if a failure occurs in the front seat primary system, the aft seat will be ejected by the redundant system first followed by ejection of the forward crewmember.

After TO 1F-15E-552 there are potential failure modes which will result in ejection of the forward crewmember first, by the primary mode, followed by ejection of the aft crewmember, by the redundant system. This situation is not optimum since injury to the rear seat occupant can occur; but it does provide for a means of escape that was not previously available.

Seat Adjust Switch

The seat adjust switch is in each cockpit on the left side of the cockpit above the console. The switch has the three positions of UP and DN and is spring-loaded to the center off position. Maximum vertical seat travel is 5 inches. The seat adjustment actuator does not cut off power to the electric motor at either limit of travel. Release the seat adjust switch when the seat reaches an upper or lower limit to prevent damage to the actuator motor.

Ejection Control Handles

There are two ejection control handles, one mounted on each forward upper side of the seat. The controls are interconnected so that actuation of either control initiates ejection. The ejection control pull force is approximately 45 pounds.

Ejection Controls Safety Lever

The ejection controls safety lever is located immediately aft of the left ejection control handle. With the safety lever rotated up and forward both ejection control handles are mechanically locked, and a yellow and black checkerboard placard is displayed to the seat occupant reading EJECTION CONTROLS LOCKED. With the safety lever rotated aft and down, the ejection control handles are unlocked and a black and white placard is displayed reading EJECTION CONTROLS ARMED.

Shoulder Harness Inertia Reel

Shoulder harness restraint is provided by a dual strap shoulder harness inertia reel mounted in the seat below the headrest pads. Automatic locking of the inertia reel occurs when the reel senses excessive rate of strap payout. Manual locking and unlocking of the reel is controlled by the shoulder harness lock/unlock handle.

Shoulder Harness Lock/Unlock Handle

The inertia reel control handle on the left arm rest of the seat is spring tensioned and has two positions.

LOCKED	The inertia reel prevents the reel straps from being extended, and ratchets any slack in the straps back into the reel. This prevents the crewmember from leaning forward without first unlocking the reel.

UNLOCKED   The reel allows the crewmember to lean forward. The inertia portion of the reel will automatically lock the reel when it senses excessive rate of strap pay out. Once the reel has locked automatically, the locked condition must be released by cycling the control lever to locked and back to unlocked.

Restraint Release System

The crewmember is held in the ejection seat by a lap belt and the shoulder harness straps. In addition, two survival kit retaining straps connect the torso harness to the survival kit stored under the rigid seat pan. These straps are not intended for crewmember restraint. During ejection, the lap belt, inertia reel straps and seat pan release are automatically released by the recovery sequencer prior to seat-man separation.

Restraint Emergency Release Handle (Before TO 1F-15 582)

The restraint emergency release handle, on the right armrest aft of the ejection control handle, can be used as a backup system to the seat automatic seat-man separation function. Pulling the restraint emergency release handle causes release of the lap belt, the inertia reel straps, the seat pan, and the recovery parachute pilot chute from its compartment. Thus, should automatic man-seat separation not occur after ejection, pulling the handle releases all harness restraints except the parachute risers and the survival kit, and also deploys the recovery parachute. The handle is actuated by depressing the trigger on the inside of the handle grip, and then pulling vertically until the handle goes full travel.

WARNING

In aircraft prior to incorporation of TO 1F-15E-582, if the restraint emergency release handle is pulled with the seat still in the aircraft, safe ejection is impossible.

Emergency Manual Chute Handle (After TO 1F-15-582)

The emergency manual chute handle is on the right arm rest aft of the ejection control handle. With the seat in the launch rails, the handle is locked and cannot be pulled out of its stowed position. Once the seat is clear of the launch rails the handle can be used to ballistically deploy the recovery parachute and to release the harness restraints. The handle must be pulled full travel (approximately 6 inches) to ensure that the harness restraints release.

Battery Window

A battery window, a small circular hole on the right side of the seat forward of the seat rail, gives indication of the status of the seat sequencing system battery. If the battery is activated, a red plunger will puncture the white window.

Survival Kit

The survival kit consists of a fabric case which houses a life raft, rucksack, and an auxiliary container. The life raft and rucksack are attached to the survival kit case by a dropline. The auxiliary container, which is for storage of items to be retained with the crewman, is secured inside the survival kit. An AN/URT-33C radio beacon is installed in the kit. The survival kit stows in the seat bucket beneath the rigid seat pan. The pan pivots for withdrawal of the kit during seat-man separation. The kit is attached to the crewmember's harness by attachment fittings on the kit retaining straps. A survival kit auto/manual deployment selector, located on the inside of the forward right thigh support of the kit, permits the crewmember to select either manual or automatic deployment of the kit. With the ejection seat in the aircraft, the survival kit connectors are disconnected when the restraint emergency release handle is actuated.

ACES II EJECTION SEQUENCES

MODE 1 OPERATION 150 KNOTS

(E) FULL INFLATION
T = 1.80

(D) SEAT–MAN RELEASE ACTUATED
T = 0.45

(F)

(C) PARACHUTE FIRED
T = 0.20

CATAPULT
INITIATION
T = 0.0 SEC

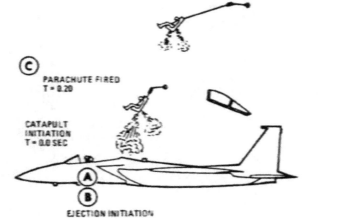

EJECTION INITIATION

(A) EJECTION CONTROL HANDLE PULLED TO ACTUATE
SEAT–MOUNTED GAS INITIATOR AND:
- POWERED INERTIA REEL RETRACTS SHOULDER STRAPS
- CANOPY REMOVER FIRES.
- CANOPY JETTISONS AND PULLS LANYARD TO FIRE
  CANOPY ACTUATED INITIATOR.
- IFF SWITCH ACTUATED.

NOTE

IN A DUAL EJECTION; THERE IS A
0.4 SECOND DELAY BETWEEN REAR
AND FRONT SEAT CATAPULT INITIATION

(B) ROCKET CATAPULT FIRES. SEAT MOVES UP RAILS AND:
- RECOVERY SEQUENCER POWER SUPPLY ENERGIZED.
- COMMUNICATIONS AND SHIPS OXYGEN LINES DIS-
  CONNECT.
- EMERGENCY OXYGEN IS TRIPPED.
- RECOVERY SEQUENCER SWITCH
  TRIPPED BY STRIKER PLATE.
- STAPAC PITCH CONTROL SYSTEM INITIATED.

(C) PARACHUTE DEPLOYMENT MORTAR FIRES
AS SEAT CLEARS AIRCRAFT.

(D) RECOVERY SEQUENCER INITIATES HARNESS
RELEASE ACTUATOR AND:
A. LAP BELT AND SHOULDER HARNESS STRAPS
   RELEASE FROM SEAT STRUCTURE.
B. PILOT IS SEPARATED FROM SEAT.
C. RADIO BEACON INITIATED (IF AUTO SELECTED).

(E) PARACHUTE FULLY INFLATED

(F) SURVIVAL KIT DEPLOYED (PROVIDED AUTO
SELECTED ON DEPLOYMENT SELECTOR

15E-1-(53-11A

Figure 1-54 (Sheet 1 of 2)

EJECTION SEQUENCES
MODE 2 OPERATION 600 KNOTS

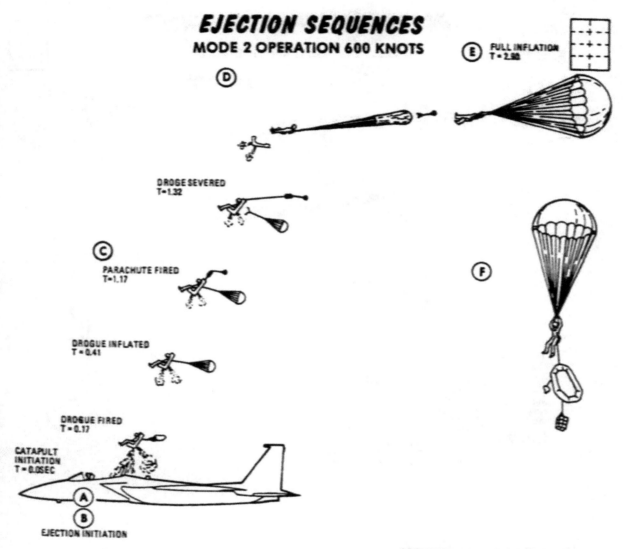

D

E FULL INFLATION
T = 2.90

DROGE SEVERED
T = 1.32

C

PARACHUTE FIRED
T = 1.17

F

DROGUE INFLATED
T = 0.41

DROGUE FIRED
T = 0.17

CATAPULT
INITIATION
T = 0.0SEC

A

B

EJECTION INITIATION

NOTE

- TIMES INDICATED ARE AFTER CATAPULT FIRING. TO DETERMINE TOTAL TIME, A TIME FACTOR FOR THE PERIOD BETWEEN EJECTION HANDLE INITIATION AND CATAPULT FIRING MUST BE ADDED TO THE FIGURES SHOWN. THIS TIME INTERVAL REPRESENTS ESSENTIALLY THE TIME IT TAKES TO REMOVE THE CANOPY AFTER THE EJECTION HANDLE IS PULLED, AND IS APPROXIMATELY 0.3 SECONDS AT ZERO AIRSPEED AND BECOMES SLIGHTLY LESS AS AIRSPEED INCREASES. THERE IS AN ADDITIONAL DELAY OF 0.4 SECONDS BETWEEN REAR AND FRONT SEAT FIRING FOR DUAL EJECTION.

- IN MODE 3, WHICH IS DESIGNED FOR HIGH ALTITUDE CONDITIONS, THE DROGUE IS DEPLOYED AS IN MODE 2, BUT MAN–SEAT SEPARATION AND DEPLOYMENT OF THE PARACHUTE ARE DELAYED UNTIL THE PROPER ALTITUDE IS ENCOUNTERED.

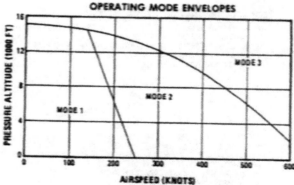

OPERATING MODE ENVELOPES

MODE 3

MODE 2

MODE 1

PRESSURE ALTITUDE (1000 FT)

AIRSPEED (KNOTS)

15E-1-(153-2)A

Figure 1-54 (Sheet 2)

A (Forward)	The kit automatically deploys after man-seat separation.
M (Aft)	To deploy the kit after man-seat separation the survival kit release handle on the right rear of the kit must be pulled.

AN/URT-33C Radio Beacon Selector Switch

Access to the radio beacon auto/manual selector is gained through a cutout in the front of the seat pan. The selector is a rocker switch. When the left arm (as viewed by the seat occupant) is pressed, MAN is selected. When the right arm is pressed, AUTO is selected.

MAN	Radio beacon will not activate at man-seat separation.
AUTO	Radio beacon activates at man-seat separation.

STORES JETTISON SYSTEMS

Emergency jettison is provided by the emergency jettison button. Selective jettison is provided by the select jettison knob/button in conjunction with the MPD/MPCD. When the landing gear handle is down, the selective jettison controls are deenergized. The gear handle safety interlock can be bypassed by the armament safety switch.

Regardless of master arm switch position, when either the emergency jettison or select jettison (in COMBAT, A/A or A/G position only) button is pressed, all arming solenoids are automatically deenergized before jettison and all stores are jettisoned unarmed.

Emergency Jettison Button

The emergency jettison button is located on the center of the front instrument panel to the left of the MPCD. This button, when pressed, will simultaneously jettison all carted pylons (stations 2, 5, and 8) and all carted stores (CFT stations 1 thru 6) and all AIM-7 missiles. Although the button is spring-loaded to the normal position, a means is provided to determine that the button is not stuck in the jettison position. In the normal position only the color black on the inside lip of the button guard can be seen

above the button. If the button is stuck in the jettison position, yellow color can be seen in the switch guard below the black color.

CAUTION

Emergency jettison button is hot when electrical power is on the aircraft.

Select Jettison Knob/Button

When pressed, the select jettison button (figure 1-55) jettisons stores depending on the knob positions described below:

OFF	Removes power from the selective jettison button.
COMBAT	Selective jettison button first press initiates combat jettison program 1. Second press initiates combat jettison program 2. See figure 1-55.
A/A	Selects air-to-air selective jettison. Refer to figure 1-56.
A/G	Selects air-to-ground selective jettison. Refer to figure 1-57.
ALTN REL	Used for nuclear weapons release.
MAN RET	Refer to TO 1F-15E-34-1-1.
MAN FF	Refer to TO 1F-15E-34-1-1.

Programming Combat Jettison

Combat jettison is a two-push capability. With COMBAT selected on the SELECT JETT knob, the first push will jettison whatever is assigned to the CBT 1 program and the second will jettison whatever is assigned to the CBT 2 program.

Programming combat jettison is accomplished by selecting the ARMT display on the MPD/MPCD, then selecting the CBT JETT display (figure 1-55). The SELECT JETT knob may be in either OFF or COMBAT. Select the CBT 1 program by pressing the 1 button. Then select the station from the top five buttons followed by STORE, RACK or PYLON from the left of the MPD/MPCD (STORE is automatically boxed when the display is selected). Press the

ENTER button to complete programming for CBT 1. Repeat these steps for CBT 2, with 2 selected on the display. If the SELECT JETT knob is in COMBAT, CBT 1 and CBT 2 will be boxed on the display.

NOTE

Selection of the combat jettison display reinitializes the two-push sequence and resets the first push jettison to the CBT 1 program, even if previously used during the mission.

Armament Safety Switch

The armament safety switch, on the left console outboard of the anti-g valve, allows the gear handle safety interlock to be bypassed for armament circuit checkout.

SAFE — Normal circuitry is used.

OVERRIDE — The switch is solenoid held until electrical power is removed, the landing gear handle is placed UP, or the switch is manually placed to SAFE.

PROGRAMMABLE ARMAMENT CONTROL SET (PACS)

Refer to TO 1F-15E-34-1-1 for description and operation of the PACS.

TACTICAL ELECTRONIC WARFARE SYSTEM (TEWS)

Refer to TO 1F-15E-34-1-1-1 for description of the TEWS.

INTERFERENCE BLANKER SYSTEM (IBS)

The interference blanker system prevents or reduces electromagnetic interference between TEWS and other aircraft systems which utilize radio frequency (rf) transmitters and receivers.

RADAR SYSTEM

Refer to TO 1F-15E-34-1-1 for description and operation of the Radar System.

LANTIRN NAVIGATION POD (NAV Pod)

Refer to TO 1F-15E-34-1-1 for description and operation of the LANTIRN navigation pod.

LANTIRN TARGETING POD (TGT Pod)

Refer to TO 1F-15E-34-1-1 for description and operation of the LANTIRN targeting pod.

WEAPON SYSTEMS

Refer to TO 1F-15E-34-1-1 for a detailed and operational description of the following systems.

Aircraft Weapons Capabilities
AAI System
Stores Jettison System
Weapon Employment
Suspension Equipment
Combat Weapons
Training Weapons

PROGRAMMING COMBAT JETTISON

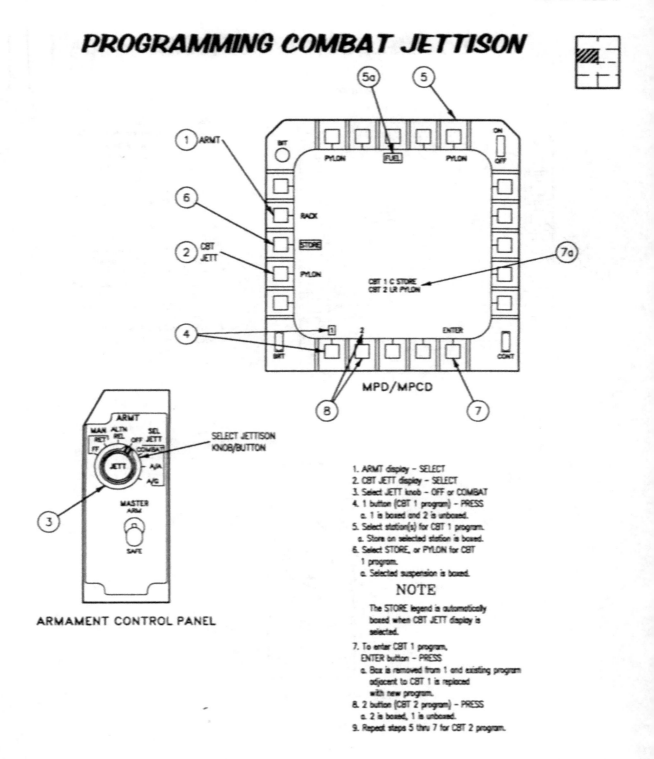

ARMAMENT CONTROL PANEL

MPD/MPCD

1. ARMT display – SELECT
2. CBT JETT display – SELECT
3. Select JETT knob – OFF or COMBAT
4. 1 button (CBT 1 program) – PRESS
   a. 1 is boxed and 2 is unboxed.
5. Select station(s) for CBT 1 program.
   a. Store on selected station is boxed.
6. Select STORE, or PYLON for CBT
   1 program.
   a. Selected suspension is boxed.

NOTE

The STORE legend is automatically
boxed when CBT JETT display is
selected.

7. To enter CBT 1 program,
   ENTER button – PRESS
   a. Box is removed from 1 and existing program
   adjacent to CBT 1 is replaced
   with new program.
8. 2 button (CBT 2 program) – PRESS
   a. 2 is boxed, 1 is unboxed.
9. Repeat steps 5 thru 7 for CBT 2 program.

15E-1-(29-1)03-CAT1

Figure 1-55

A/A SELECTIVE JETTISON

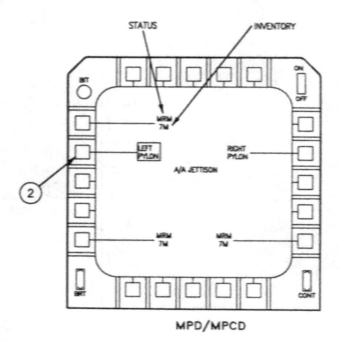

MPD/MPCD

1. Select JETT knob – A/A
   a. A/A JETTISON cue appears on display.
   b. MRM status can be displayed as: MRM, STBY, RDY, HUNG or FAIL.
   c. When no weapon is on a station, the inventory and line segment is omitted.
2. Select weapon to be jettisoned.
   a. Selected MRM or PYLON is boxed. Select buttons are mutually exclusive (only one can be selected at a time).
   b. If an SRM is hung, the pylon of the last hung AIM-9 is automatically boxed when A/A JETTISON is displayed.
3. Select JETT button – PRESS
   a. MRM status, line segment, and MRM or PYLON is removed;
   b. HUNG status appears if jettison is not successful.
4. Repeat steps 2 and 3 for each weapon.
5. Select JETT knob – AS DESIRED

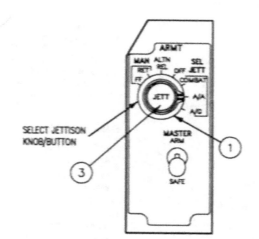

ARMAMENT CONTROL PANEL

15E-1-(30-1)-0A71

Figure 1-56

A/G SELECTIVE JETTISON

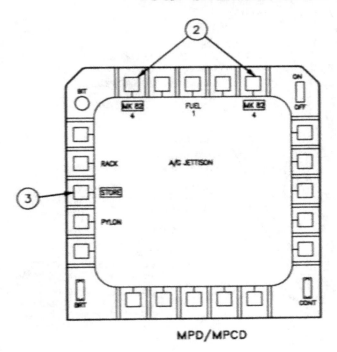

MPD/MPCD

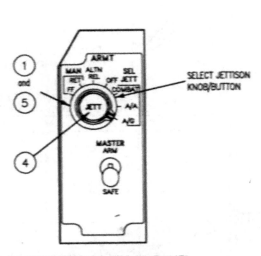

ARMANENT CONTROL PANEL

1. Select JETT knob – A/G
   a. A/G JETTISON cue appears on display.

NOTE

STORE is displayed if store is onboard.
PYLON is selected if no stores are onboard.

2. Select aircraft station(s)
   a. Weapon on selected station(s) is boxed.

NOTE

If the MPCD display systems fails, aircraft
stations can be selected using the under-
lighted MPCD pushbuttons.

3. Select STORE or PYLON.
   a. Selected suspension is boxed.

4. JETT button – PRESS
   a. CC sends jettison signals to selected
      station(s).

   b. Weapon inventory and quantity legend
      change as items are jettisoned.

NOTES

● NOSE ARM and TAIL ARM signals are
  removed during jettison.

● CFT stations are jettisoned first, followed
  by the adjacent wing station after a 65
  msec delay.

5. Select JETT knob – A/A, COMBAT or OFF
   a. A/A display appears.

STORE   PYLON

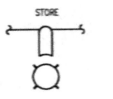   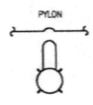

Figure 1-57

SERVICING DIAGRAM

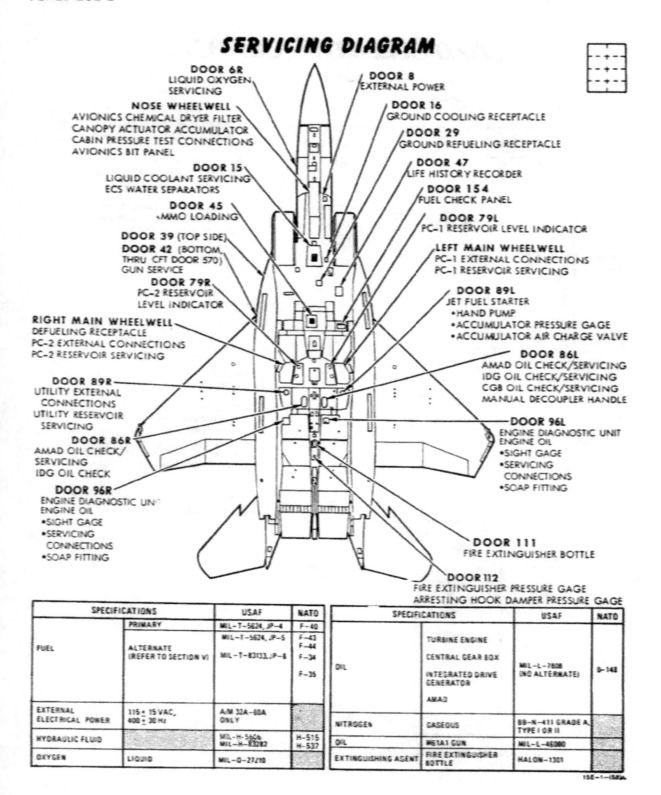

DOOR 6R
LIQUID OXYGEN SERVICING

NOSE WHEELWELL
AVIONICS CHEMICAL DRYER FILTER
CANOPY ACTUATOR ACCUMULATOR
CABIN PRESSURE TEST CONNECTIONS
AVIONICS BIT PANEL

DOOR 15
LIQUID COOLANT SERVICING
ECS WATER SEPARATORS

DOOR 45
MMO LOADING

DOOR 39 (TOP SIDE)
DOOR 42 (BOTTOM, THRU CFT DOOR 570)
GUN SERVICE

DOOR 79R
PC-2 RESERVOIR
LEVEL INDICATOR

RIGHT MAIN WHEELWELL
DEFUELING RECEPTACLE
PC-2 EXTERNAL CONNECTIONS
PC-2 RESERVOIR SERVICING

DOOR 89R
UTILITY EXTERNAL
CONNECTIONS
UTILITY RESERVOIR
SERVICING

DOOR 86R
AMAD OIL CHECK/
SERVICING
IDG OIL CHECK

DOOR 96R
ENGINE DIAGNOSTIC UNIT
ENGINE OIL
•SIGHT GAGE
•SERVICING
CONNECTIONS
•SOAP FITTING

DOOR 8
EXTERNAL POWER

DOOR 16
GROUND COOLING RECEPTACLE

DOOR 29
GROUND REFUELING RECEPTACLE

DOOR 47
LIFE HISTORY RECORDER

DOOR 154
FUEL CHECK PANEL

DOOR 79L
PC-1 RESERVOIR LEVEL INDICATOR

LEFT MAIN WHEELWELL
PC-1 EXTERNAL CONNECTIONS
PC-1 RESERVOIR SERVICING

DOOR 89L
JET FUEL STARTER
•HAND PUMP
•ACCUMULATOR PRESSURE GAGE
•ACCUMULATOR AIR CHARGE VALVE

DOOR 86L
AMAD OIL CHECK/SERVICING
IDG OIL CHECK/SERVICING
CGB OIL CHECK/SERVICING
MANUAL DECOUPLER HANDLE

DOOR 96L
ENGINE DIAGNOSTIC UNIT
ENGINE OIL
•SIGHT GAGE
•SERVICING
CONNECTIONS
•SOAP FITTING

DOOR 111
FIRE EXTINGUISHER BOTTLE

DOOR 112
FIRE EXTINGUISHER PRESSURE GAGE
ARRESTING HOOK DAMPER PRESSURE GAGE

SPECIFICATIONS		USAF	NATO
FUEL	PRIMARY	MIL-T-5624, JP-4	F-40
	ALTERNATE (REFER TO SECTION V)	MIL-T-5624, JP-5	F-43 F-44
		MIL-T-83133, JP-8	F-34
			F-35
EXTERNAL ELECTRICAL POWER	115 ± 15 VAC, 400 ± 30 Hz	A/M 32A-60A ONLY	
HYDRAULIC FLUID		MIL-H-5606 MIL-H-83282	H-515 H-537
OXYGEN	LIQUID	MIL-O-27210	

SPECIFICATIONS		USAF	NATO
OIL	TURBINE ENGINE CENTRAL GEAR BOX INTEGRATED DRIVE GENERATOR AMAD	MIL-L-7808 (NO ALTERNATE)	O-148
NITROGEN	GASEOUS	BB-N-411 GRADE A, TYPE I OR II	
OIL	M61A1 GUN	MIL-L-46000	
EXTINGUISHING AGENT	FIRE EXTINGUISHER BOTTLE	HALON-1301	

15E-1-1589A

Figure 1-58

SECTION II

NORMAL PROCEDURES

TABLE OF CONTENTS

Preparation For Flight 2-1
Preflight Check 2-1
Before Entering Front Cockpit 2-4
Front Cockpit Interior Check 2-4
Starting Engines 2-6
Before Taxiing (Front Cockpit) 2-8
Before Entering Rear Cockpit 2-12
Rear Cockpit Interior Check 2-12
Before Taxiing (Rear Cockpit) 2-12B
Taxiing 2-12C
Before Takeoff 2-12C
Takeoff 2-13
Climb Techniques 2-13
Inflight 2-15
Instrument Flight Procedure 2-15
Missed Approach/Go Around 2-16
Descent Check/Before Landing 2-16
Landing Technique 2-16
After Landing 2-17
Hot Refueling 2-18
Engine Shutdown 2-18
Aircrew Egress (BOTH)
(After TO 1F-15E-602) 2-18A
Combat Jettison Programming (BOTH) 2-18A
OWS Matrix Display (BOTH) 2-19
UFC Procedures 2-19
INS Procedures 2-22
Update Procedures 2-24
External Power Start 2-26
Scramble 2-27
Quick Turn (BOTH) 2-28

PREPARATION FOR FLIGHT

TAKEOFF AND LANDING DATA CARD

If the takeoff distance exceeds one-half the available runway, the takeoff and landing data card in the Aircrew's Checklist should be completed.

WEIGHT AND BALANCE

For maximum gross weight limitations, refer to section V, Operating Limitations. For weight and balance information refer to the individual aircraft's DD Form 365-4 (FORM F), section V, Operating Limitations and the handbook of Weight and Balance Data, TO 1-1B-40.

NOTE

Some aircrew procedures are separated into front cockpit and rear cockpit. Other procedures are combined and are coded for applicable crewmember action. Items coded (BOTH) are applicable to both the pilot and weapon system officer. Items coded (WSO) are applicable to the weapon system officer. Items not coded are applicable to the pilot only.

PREFLIGHT CHECK

1. Check Form 781 for aircraft status and release.

NOTE

If aircraft forms indicate replacement of the radar power supply (610), radar antenna (031), INU or the CC, a precision velocity update (PVU) is required to reduce pointing errors. Refer to TO 1F-15E-34-1-1.

2. Takeoff and landing data - COMPUTE (if required)

EXTERIOR INSPECTION

1. Check general condition. Refer to figure 2-1. Check aircraft exterior for abnormalities which could affect flight (e.g., cracks or leaks). Check all sensors (AOA, pitot/static, inlet ice, total temperature). The ground intercom compartment door will be open. The hydraulic and JFS accumulator circular access panels (4) may be open for after start servicing. Check all other doors and panels closed and fastened. Check intakes clear of foreign objects. Check all external/internal inlet

ramps in up position. Check tires for condition and inflation. Check gear struts for extension. Check landing gear pins (3), arresting hook pin, and canopy strut removed.

COCKPIT ENTRY

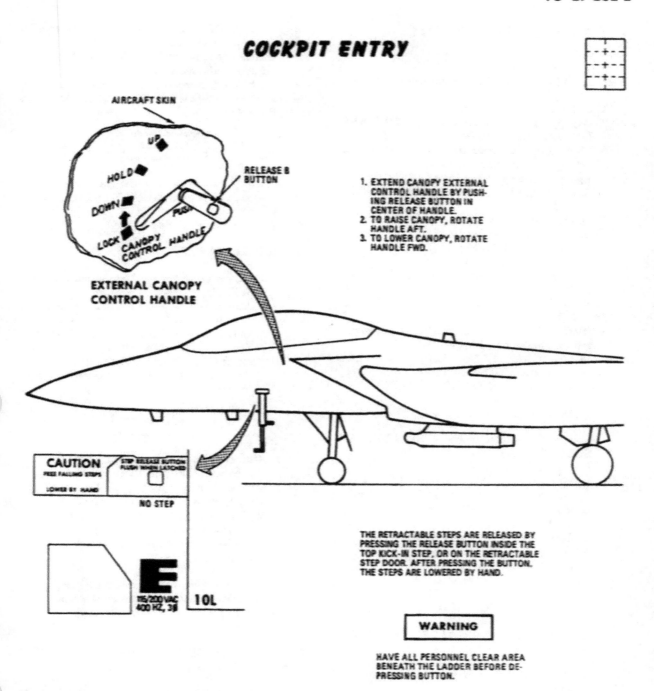

EXTERNAL CANOPY CONTROL HANDLE

1. EXTEND CANOPY EXTERNAL CONTROL HANDLE BY PUSHING RELEASE BUTTON IN CENTER OF HANDLE.
2. TO RAISE CANOPY, ROTATE HANDLE AFT.
3. TO LOWER CANOPY, ROTATE HANDLE FWD.

THE RETRACTABLE STEPS ARE RELEASED BY PRESSING THE RELEASE BUTTON INSIDE THE TOP KICK-IN STEP, OR ON THE RETRACTABLE STEP DOOR. AFTER PRESSING THE BUTTON, THE STEPS ARE LOWERED BY HAND.

WARNING

HAVE ALL PERSONNEL CLEAR AREA BENEATH THE LADDER BEFORE DEPRESSING BUTTON.

15E-1-(52)A

Figure 2-2

BEFORE ENTERING FRONT COCKPIT

Refer to foldout section for ejection seat illustration.

1. External electrical power - OFF
2. Canopy initiator indicator - NOT FIRED AND LANYARD ATTACHED TO INITATOR
   If indicator has been fired, the gray cap and orange spring will be exposed.
3. Ejection controls safety lever - LOCKED
4. Seat hose quick disconnect coupling - CHECK SECURE
5. Safety pins - REMOVED
   a. Canopy jettison handle pin
   b. Ejection seat safety pins (2)
   c. Canopy actuated initiator pin
6. Auto/manual seat kit deployment selector - AUTO
7. Radio beacon auto/manual selector - AS DESIRED
8. (Before TO 1F-15E-582) Restraint emergency release handle - FULLY DOWN
   (After TO 1F-15E-582) Emergency manual chute handle- FULLY DOWN
9. Battery window - NO RED SHOWING

For Solo Flight -

1. Command selector valve - SECURED IN SOLO POSITION
2. Rear cockpit - SECURED
   a. Ejection controls safety lever - LOCKED
   b. Solo flight tie down strap - INSTALLED
   c. Map case cover - SECURED
   d. TGT FLIR - OFF
   e. Emergency landing gear handle - IN
   f. Emergency brake/steering handle - IN
   g. Circuit breakers - IN
   h. Arresting hook switch - UP
   i. Oxygen supply lever - OFF
   j. TEWS - AS REQUIRED
   k. CMD - AS REQUIRED
   l. RMR - CHECK INSTALLED OR INSERT
   m. Oxygen hose - SECURED TO STOWAGE FITTING
   n. Utility light - SECURED TO STOWAGE FITTING

FRONT COCKPIT INTERIOR CHECK

A thorough cockpit interior preflight shall be accomplished before each flight. The design features of the aircraft greatly simplify this task. Switch positions designated AS DESIRED allow pilot preference in switch/control positioning. AS REQUIRED indicates those switches that will differ with mission requirements. If no specific requirement exists, pilot preference may be used. Normally, those avionics switches designated AS DESIRED or AS REQUIRED should be OFF for start.

CAUTION

Do not place any item on the glare shield, as scratching the windshield is probable.

1. Interior check - COMPLETE

(Before TO1F-15E-602)

   a. Harness and personal equipment leads - FASTEN
      Attach parachute risers to harness buckles. Attach survival kit and ensure straps are snug within the limits of personal comfort. Secure and firmly adjust lap belt. Connect oxygen, G suit and communication leads. Check operation of shoulder harness locking mechanism.

WARNING

● After connecting the parachute risers to the harness, lift the locking lever on each koch fitting and verify the actuating lever is full up and snug against the inner part of the locking lever. If the actuating lever will not seat properly, disconnect the release and use a different harness.

● Failure to adjust the survival kit straps to achieve a snug fit between the crewmember and kit may result in injury during ejection.

(After TO 1F-15E-602, when Aircrew Eye/Respiratory Protection is worn)

   a. Blower strap assembly - REMOVE AND STOW
   b. Sit in seat
   c. Blower electrical power - CONNECT
   d. Blower assembly - INSTALL
   e. Emergency oxygen - CONNECT
   f. Oxygen regulator - ON

All data on pages 2-4A and 2-4B deleted.

g. Blower hose - REMOVE FROM AQD (Armored Quick Disconnect)
h. Oxygen hose - CONNECT TO AQD
i. Blower hose - CONNECT TO VENTILA-TION INLET
j. Crossover valve - ROTATE TO VERTICAL
k. Survival kit - CONNECT
   Ensure straps are secure within the limits of personal comfort.

WARNING

● Failure to adjust the survival kit straps to achieve a snug fit between the crewmember and the kit may result in injury during ejection.
● Survival kit straps must be connected under hoses to prevent restriction of air flow.

l. Lap belt - CONNECT
   Ensure lap belt is secure and firmly adjusted.

WARNING

Lap belt must be connected under hoses to prevent restriction of airflow.

m. Shoulder harness - FASTEN

WARNING

After connecting the parachute risers to the harness, lift the locking lever on each koch fitting and verify the actuating lever is full up and snug against the inner part of the locking lever. If the actuating lever will not seat properly, disconnect the release and use a different harness.

n. Anti-g suit - CONNECT
o. Intercommunication unit - DISCONNECT AND STOW
p. Aircraft communication cord - CONNECT

Left Console -

a. Ground power panel - ALL SWITCHES AUTO
b. Armament safety switch - SAFE

c. Emergency air refueling switch guard - DOWN
d. Integrated communications controls - AS DESIRED
   (1) Volume knobs - AS DESIRED
   (2) Crypto switch - NORM
   (3) MIC switch - ON
   (4) UHF antenna switch - AUTO
   (5) Tone switch - AS DESIRED
   (6) Cipher text switch - AS REQUIRED
   (7) Mode 4 selector switch - AS REQUIRED
   (8) Mode 4 reply switch - AS DESIRED
   (9) IFF master switch - AS REQUIRED
e. EWWS enable switch - OFF, GUARD DOWN
f. IFF antenna switch - BOTH
g. Sensor control panel - OFF
h. Exterior lights panel - AS REQUIRED
i. Flyup enable switch - OFF, GUARD DOWN
j. NCTR enable switch - AS REQUIRED
k. V-MAX switch - COVER CLOSED AND SAFETY WIRED
l. Flap switch - UP
m. Friction lever - AS DESIRED
n. Throttles - OFF
o. Fuel control panel - SET
   (1) Fuel dump switch - NORM
   (2) Wing switch - AS REQUIRED
   (3) Center switch - AS REQUIRED
   (4) Conformal tank switch - STOP TRANS
   (5) Slipway switch - CLOSE
   (6) Conformal tank emergency transfer switch - NORM
   (7) External transfer switch - WING/CTR (AS DESIRED with CFTs)
p. Nuclear consent switch - COVER CLOSED
q. CAS switches - ON
r. TP COUPLE switch - OFF
s. Miscellaneous control panel - SET
   (1) Anti-skid switch - NORM
   (2) Inlet ramp switches - AUTO
   (3) Roll ratio switch - AUTO
   (4) Landing/taxi light switch - OFF
t. Canopy jettison handle - FORWARD
u. Emergency landing gear handle - IN
v. Arresting hook switch - UP

Instrument Panel -

a. Landing gear handle - DOWN
b. Pitch ratio switch - AUTO
c. Master arm switch - SAFE
d. Select jettison knob - OFF, BUTTON NOT PRESSED

e. Fire lights - NOT PRESSED

f. Fire test/extinguisher switch - OFF

g. HUD control panel - AS REQUIRED

h. Emergency jettison button - NOT PRESSED

i. Emergency brake/steer handle - IN

j. DTM - INSERTED

k. Circuit breakers - IN

l. JFS handle - IN

m. Holding brake switch - OFF

Right Console -

a. Emergency vent handle - IN AND VERTICAL

b. (F-15E 86-0183 THRU 90-0232 Before TO 1F-15E-561)

Oxygen system - CHECK AND SET

Pressure - 55 to 120 psi

Regulator - CHECK

(1) Oxygen supply lever - FULLY ON

It is possible for the oxygen supply lever to stop at an intermediate position between OFF and ON. Assure the lever is all the way ON.

(2) Emergency lever - NORMAL

(3) MASK - ON

Breath normally for 3 cycles and check flow indicator operation. Hold breath, all flow should stop and the indicator should show no flow (black). A white indicator indicates a leak which must be corrected before flight.

Indicator - CHECK

(4) Diluter lever - 100%

(5) Emergency lever - EMERGENCY

(6) Oxygen flow - CHECK (Return Diluter and Emergency levers to NORM)

Connections - CHECK

Emergency Oxygen - CHECKED

(7) Pressure - CHECK

(8) Actuating ring - STOWED and CHECKED

c. Anti-ice switches - SET

(1) (F-15E 86-0183 THRU 90-0232) Anti-ice switches - OFF

(2) (F-15E 90-0233 AND UP)
Engine anti-ice switches - ON
Pitot and windshield anti-ice switches - OFF

d. Engine control panel - SET

(1) Generator switches - ON

(2) Emergency generator switch - AUTO

(3) ENG CONTR switches - ON

(4) JFS starter switch - ON

(5) Engine master switches - ON

(6) EXT PWR switch - AS REQUIRED

e. Air conditioning control panel - SET

(1) Temperature control switch - AUTO

(2) Air source knob - NORM

(3) Air flow selector switch - BOTH

f. Interior lights controls - AS DESIRED

g. Compass control panel - AS REQUIRED

(1) Latitude - SET

(2) Hemisphere - SET

h. Video tape record switch - UNTHREAD

After Front Cockpit Check Is Complete -

VERIFY:

VERIFY items are those items which, if not correctly positioned, could cause a safety hazard and/or system damage.

1. Emergency air refueling switch - NORM (GUARD DOWN)

2. Throttles - OFF

3. Formation lights - OFF

4. Emergency landing gear handle - IN

5. Arresting hook switch - UP

6. Landing gear handle - DOWN

7. Master arm switch - SAFE

8. Emergency jettison button - NOT PRESSED

9. Emergency brake/steer handle - IN

10. Emergency vent handle - IN AND VERTICAL

11. Engine control switches - ON

12. Anti-ice switches - SET

a. (F-15E 86-0183 THRU 90-0232)
All anti-ice switches - OFF

b. (F-15E 90-0233 AND UP)
Engine anti-ice switches - ON
Pitot and windshield anti-ice switches - OFF

13. Avionics - OFF (RADAR, HUD, INS, TF RADAR, NAV FLIR)

STARTING ENGINES

Normal engine start procedure does not use external power. With the JFS running, power is available to operate the AMAD fire warning system, the intercom system between the aircrew and the ground, and the cockpit utility light. Engine rpm and FTIT indications on the EMD are inoperative until the emergency generator comes on line at 15-17% rpm during engine start. The rest of the engine instruments are inoperative until a main generator comes on at 56-58% rpm during first engine start.

On F-15E 90-0233 AND UP, the ENGINE category light will come on and remain lit until the second engine starts and no engine faults exist. With external electrical power or during the second engine start, the ENGINE category light will be on until the IDEEC is powered up by the engine alternator at about 10% rpm. It will come on again momentarily, between 15-29% rpm, indicating that the IDEEC is automatically performing a self test. If the engine is started with the ENG CONTR switch in OFF, the ENGINE category stays on throughout the start cycle, indicating the engine is in SEC mode. During engine starts, the engine anti-ice switch will be placed in the ON position for all starts, to provide additional starting stall margin. Test cell data has shown a hot start may occur on warm engine restarts if the engine is started without anti-ice flow. The engine anti-ice switch should be set as required for ambient conditions.

Because a JFS accumulator was discharged to start the JFS, the JFS LOW caution will come on when power is available to display the caution. It will go out when accumulators are recharged by a running engine.

When the fingerlift is raised, the JFS will engage and accelerate the engine. JFS engagement is indicated by an audible decrease in JFS whine when the JFS clutch engages. JFS whine decrease is followed immediately by an increase to a higher pitch than before engagement. Engine rotation is apparent within approximately 5 seconds. If electrical power is not available, rotation can be felt and heard. If electrical power is available, rpm increase can be seen on the EMD. The JFS will continue to smoothly accelerate engine rotation without hesitation until light-off occurs or steady-state windmill (23-30%) is reached. A normal start is indicated by rpm acceleration occuring before initial FTIT movement.

Monitor engine indications on the EMD and compare against the operating limitations listed in section V. After first engine start, the JFS automatically decouples from that engine and is ready for the second engine start. After second engine start, the JFS shuts down automatically.

The following procedure is applicable to either engine. The right engine is normally started first to permit checking utility hydraulic pressure with only the right pump operating.

JFS START

1. Engine master switches - CHECK ON

2. JFS switch - CHECK ON
3. JFS handle - PULL AND RELEASE

NOTE

If JFS does not start, starter switch should be set OFF. Wait 30 seconds after cycling switch before trying second start so JFS can decelerate, and start sequence relay deenergize. Failure to wait 30 seconds may result in a JFS no start.

4. Starter READY light - ON (within 10 sec; 15 sec if temperature below −18°C/0°F)
5. Fire extinguisher switch - TEST. Observe the AMAD fire warning light on and voice warning activated.

ENGINE START

CAUTION

To prevent possible failure of the CGB shear section and to prevent the DEEC from going into the secondary mode, do not cycle the ENG CONTROL switches until 1 minute after engine start.

NOTE

(F-15E 90-0233 AND UP) Make sure Engine anti-ice switch is ON

1. Finger lift - RAISE AND RELEASE
   This engages the JFS to the engine.
2. EMD RPM display - OBSERVE INDICATING
3. Fire extinguisher switch - TEST
   Check all fire lights on and voice warnings activated.
4. Throttle - IDLE (18% RPM)
5. Engine instruments - CHECK
   Engine limits are contained in section V.

CAUTION

Abort the start if no oil pressure occurs within one minute.

6. JFS deceleration - CONFIRM
7. Warnings and caution lights - TEST (Check AB BURN THRU warning lights)

8. UHF #2 - ON

9. EMER BST ON caution - OBSERVE ON
   The EMER BST ON caution comes on after first generator comes on line to indicate both emergency generator and emergency boost pump are operating properly. Thirty seconds after the main generator comes on the line, the BST SYS MAL caution also comes on as the emergency generator cuts off. This indicates that the emergency fuel boost pump is now operating off an abnormal power source. When the second main generator comes on the line, both EMER BST ON and BST SYS MAL cautions go out.

NOTE

If automatic avionics shutdown occurs due to low ECS cooling airflow only UHF #2 will be available, All major caution lights will be inoperable. In addition, the right engine ramp may move to the full up position. Start other engine as soon as possible to obtain sufficient ECS airflow. If two engine operation is not possible, single engine operation at 71 - 73% rpm will provide sufficient ECS airflow.

10. Total fuel quantity - CHECK

11. Hydraulic caution light - CHECK

12. Other engine - START

NOTE

At idle rpm the left engine fuel flows displayed on the EMD and MPD/MPCD may oscillate between 200 and 1600 pph, may momentarily drop to zero, and may differ between EMD and MPD/MPCD displays. The fuel flow displays should all stabilize when the left engine rpm is increased above idle.

13. Engine instruments - CHECK

14. JFS - CONFIRM OFF; JFS SWITCH ON

15. ECS - CHECK
    Ensure ECS caution off and airflow present.

16. Inlet ramp switches - CHECK AUTO (Observe ramps down)

17. Engine anti-ice switch - AS REQUIRED

WARNING

If access to door 10L or 10R is required by maintenance personnel, both engines must be shut down to prevent possible inlet ramp activation which could cause ramp/door collision with resulting personnel injury.

BEFORE TAXIING (FRONT COCKPIT)

1. Canopy - CLOSE IF DESIRED (WAIT 10 SEC BEFORE LOCKING)

WARNING

After TO 1F-15E-552 the ejection seat will fire with the canopy in any position from full closed to full open. However to reduce the possibility of injury, the canopy should be closed prior to ejecting.

2. MPDs/MPCDs - ON

3. HUD - ON

4. DTM - TRANSFER AS REQUIRED

5. Brakes - CHECK

6. Holding Brake - ON

7. Sensor control panel - SET
   a. NAV FLIR power switch - STBY
   b. Radar power switch - STBY
   c. Radar altimeter power switch - ON
   d. TF radar power switch - STBY
   e. INS - ALIGN (see INS alignment procedures)
      INS may be switched to NAV after OK (approximately 4 minutes for GC, 30 seconds for SH)

8. Flight Controls - CHECK (CAS OFF)
   a. AFCS BIT - NOT IN TEST
   b. CAS PITCH, CAS ROLL, CAS YAW - OFF
   c. Antiskid - CHECK NORM
   d. Pitch Trim Compensator - CHECK (If desired)
      (1) Stick full forward and hold —Verify stabilator trailing edge travels down rapidly with stick application until full stick is reached, then more slowly as the

pitch trim compensator runs to full travel. Observe stabilator inboard leading edge tips just visible above wing trailing edge.

(2) Stick full aft and hold —Verify stabilator trailing edge travels up rapidly with stick application until full aft stick is reached, then move more slowly as the pitch trim compensator runs to full travel.

e. Stick full aft and left - Observe stabilator trailing edge up (left further up than right) rudder left, left aileron up, right aileron down.

NOTE

Observe that the rudders travel smoothly and follow stick movement during each leg.

f. Stick full left and full forward - Observe right stabilator leading edge moves into view and rudders move right (ailerons should not move)

g. Stick full forward and full right - Observe left aileron moves down and right aileron moves up, rudders move left, and left stabilator leading edge in view.

h. Stick full right and full aft - Observe stabilator trailing edge moves to full up (right higher than left) and rudder moves right (ailerons should not move).

i. Rudder - Check. Hold stick neutral and paddle switch pressed. Move rudder pedals left and right and observe 1/2 rudder travel (15°).

NOTE

During flight control check, stabilator chatter may be noted. This is characterized by airframe vibrations during the flight control stick movement. Vibrations are normal if they stop within 3 to 4 seconds after flight control movement has stopped.

9. Trim - CHECK AND SET
   a. Trim pitch, roll, and yaw off neutral
   b. T/O TRIM button - PUSH
      Lateral stick and rudders should drive to center and longitudinal stick to takeoff

position. The departure warning tone should beep.
   c. T/O trim light - ON
   d. T/O trim button - RELEASE
10. AFCS preflight BIT - INITIATE

WARNING

AFCS BIT will cycle the controls and the control surfaces. Flight and ground crew must stay clear of the flight control system while AFCS BIT is IN TEST. Ground crew should observe stabilators during first 30 seconds of PBIT. If any motion is detected, suspect a bad stabilator actuator valve.

NOTE

- Flight crew must stay clear of rudder pedals and stick. Do not cycle the speed brake or flaps while AFCS BIT is IN TEST. Interference will cause incorrect BIT results.

- Any BIT code occurring during a Preflight BIT run is considered acceptable for flight provided this code does not reappear on a subsequent BIT run. All BIT codes even if they clear on subsequent BIT runs should be reported for tracking purposes.

a. Select MENU/BIT on MPD/MPCD, press and hold BIT button on CAS panel then press and release AFCS button on MPD/MPCD. When AFCS IN TEST is displayed on MPD/MPCD, release BIT button on CAS panel.
b. AFCS remains IN TEST until complete, holding brake is released, paddle switch is pressed, or STOP button is pressed.
c. AFCS BIT requires approximately 3 minutes to complete. If INCOMPLETE is displayed on MPD/MPCD, wait at least 15 seconds and reinitiate BIT.
d. Steps 11 thru 20 may be performed during AFCS BIT.

11. Engine control switches - CHECK
    a. (F15E-86-0183 THRU 90-0232)(1 minute after engine start) -OFF - CHECK DEEC - THEN ON

Check DEEC reverts to secondary mode (nozzles close) and L and R CONTR cautions are displayed.

b. (F-15E-90-0233 AND UP) Engine control transfer - CHECK
(1) ENG CONTR switch - ON
(2) ENG CONTR caution - OFF
(3) Nozzle position - 90 TO 100%
(4) RPM - 65 TO 75%
(5) ENG CONTR switch - OFF
(6) ENG CONTR caution and ENGINE category light - ON
(7) Nozzle position - LESS THAN 5% Confirm nozzle operation with ground crew
(8) ENG CONTR switch - ON
(9) ENG CONTR caution and ENGINE categroy light - OFF
(10) Nozzle position - 90 TO 100% confirm nozzle operation with ground crew

c. (F-15E 90-0233 AND UP) ATDP test - INITIATE
(1) Press and release ATDP TEST - CHECK TEST LEGEND BOXED
(2) Left engine control - OFF
Check both DEEC revert to secondary mode (nozzles close). L and R ENG CONTR cautions are displayed. MASTER CAUTION and ENGINE category lights on.
(3) Left engine control - ON
(4) Press and release ATDP TEST - CHECK LEGEND BOX REMOVED, L AND R ENG CONTR CAUTIONS NO LONGER DISPLAYED.
(5) Repeat steps a thru d for right engine control switch.

12. Avionics - AS REQUIRED (AAI, IFF, ILS/TACAN)
13. Slipway door - CHECK (if AAR is planned)
14. Oxygen - CHECK
a. (F-15E 86-0183 THRU 90-0232 Before TO 1F-15E-561) Oxygen - CHECK
(1) Quantity - CHECK
(2) Oxygen test - OBSERVE OXY LOW caution AT 4 LITERS
b. (F-15E 90-0233 AND UP and F-15E 86-0183 THRU 90-0232 After TO 1F-15E-561) Oxygen system - CHECK AND SET
(1) Regulator - CHECK
(a) Oxygen supply lever - ON (PBG if required)
It is possible for the oxygen supply lever to stop at an intermediate position between OFF and ON. Make sure the lever is all the way ON.

WARNING

Injury may result if PBG is selected without compatible life support equipment.

CAUTION

Do not lift the regulator toggle switch when switching regulator from OFF to ON or ON to OFF. Damage to the regulator will result. The switch lever is locked out of the PBG position to avoid inadvertent actuation.

(b) Emergency lever - NORMAL
(c) MASK - ON
Breathe normally for 3 cycles and check flow indicator operation. Hold breath, all flow should stop and the indicator should show no flow (black). A white indicator indicates a leak which must be corrected before flight.
(2) Pressure - 10 to 60 psi (Green Band)
(3) Indicator - CHECK
(a) Diluter lever - 100%
(b) Emergency lever - EMERGENCY
(c) Oxygen flow - CHECK (Return Diluter and Emergency levers to NORM)
(4) Connections - CHECK
(5) Emergency Oxygen - CHECKED
(a) Pressure - CHECK
(b) Actuating ring - STOWED and CHECKED
(6) OXY BIT Light - CHECK ON (Reset if desired)

15. Fuel quantity gage - CHECK
a. Tank quantity - CHECK
b. BIT - CHECK
c. BINGO bug - SET
d. CFT switch - NORM (WITH CFT)
16. Bleed air - CHECK
17. PACS - PROGRAM AS REQUIRED

All data on pages 2-10A and 2-10B deleted.

CAUTION

For the OWS to program properly and prevent possible aircraft over-G the external store configuration, including external tanks, must be set in the PACS.

18. OWS severity codes - CHECK CLEARED
19. MPD/MPCD - PROGRAM AS DESIRED
20. Master Modes - PROGRAM (if desired)

Once AFCS preflight BIT complete:

21. Radar STBY BIT - INITIATE
    a. GND indication - CONFIRM
    b. Previous matrix - CHECK
22. Radar power switch - ON
23. Auto BIT - INITIATE (AS REQUIRED). When MPD/MPCD have test pattern displayed, ensure the indicated total fuel reading is within 800 pounds of the fuel gauge. Failure of this check indicates an unreliable OWS.

When RADAR IN TEST appears on BIT page:

24. Radar Track Test and Operate BIT - INITIATE
25. Flight Controls - CHECK (CAS ON)
    a. Select MENU/BIT/DETAIL/AFCS on the MPD/MPCD and verify no BIT codes/failures.
    b. Select yaw, roll, pitch to ON/RESET on the CAS panel.

NOTE

Six seconds of programmed rudder oscillation may be noticed after each ground engagement of Yaw CAS. This is normal AFCS operation.

    c. Verify CAS PITCH, CAS ROLL, CAS YAW cautions - OUT
    d. Pitch ratio switch - EMERG (Observe 0.3 to 0.5 PITCH RATIO)
    e. (BOTH) Stick full forward and hard against forward stop (zero lateral input).
    f. Observe root of both stabilator leading edges visible .
    g. Stick to neutral and pitch ratio switch - AUTO (OBSERVE 0.9 TO 1.0 PITCH RATIO).
    h. Stick full aft and against aft stop. Observe stabilators trailing edge in view.

    i. Stick full aft and left - Observe stabilator trailing edge up (left further up than right) rudder left, left aileron up, right aileron down.

NOTE

Observe that the rudders travel smoothly and follow stick movement during each leg.

    j. Stick full left and slowly full forward - Observe right stabilator leading edge moves into view and rudders move right (ailerons should not move)
    k. Stick full forward and full right - Observe left aileron moves down and right aileron moves up, rudders move left, and left stabilator leading edge in view.
    l. Stick full right and slowly full aft - Observe stabilator trailing edge moves to full up (right higher than left) and rudder moves right (ailerons should not move).
    m. Rudder - Check. Hold stick neutral and paddle switch pressed. Move rudder pedals left and right and observe full rudder travel (30°).
    n. With stick and rudder pedals neutral, verify the flight control surfaces are at takeoff trim position.
    o. Verify AFCS contains no BIT codes or functional failures. If CAS will not stay on - ABORT.
26. Flaps - DOWN
27. Speed brake - CYCLE
28. JFS LOW caution - OUT
29. INS mode knob - NAV (when aligned)
30. MPD individual display maintenance BIT - CHECK

MENU 1

BIT

MAINT

DSPL

THIS DISPLAY

Display will have test pattern and total fuel reading. Ensure fuel indication is within 800 pounds of gauge. Failure of this check indicates an unreliable OWS.

STOP

will terminate this BIT.

NOTE

Refer to TO 1F-15E-34-1-1 for A/G systems checks for LANTIRN nav pods

31. AAI BIT - INITIATE
    AAI system does not time-out before being checked during AUTO BIT. Therefore a system specific BIT is recommended to ensure proper operation.
32. Avionics/BIT - CHECK BIT FOR CODES
33. Cautions/Warnings - CHECK OFF
34. Standby attitude indicator - CAGED THEN UNCAGED
35. Anti-g suit - CHECK
36. Altimeter - SET AND CHECK
    a. HUD and Altimeter should agree within ±60 feet.

NOTE

If the altimeter is not within tolerance, the aircraft may be flown provided that the altimeter checks within ±75 feet of field elevation. The ±75 feet of field elevation is an operational restriction and does not necessarily reflect instrument tolerances.

37. AVTRS/VTR - PROGRAM/ENABLE
38. Radar - PROGRAM/VERIFY WEAPON MODES (MRM/SRM)
39. UFC - SELECT AND PROGRAM AS REQUIRED
40. (F-15E 90-0233 AND UP and F-15E 86-0183 THRU 90-0232 After TO 1F-15E-561) OXY BIT light - CHECK

BEFORE ENTERING REAR COCKPIT

Refer to foldout section for ejection seat illustration.

1. Canopy initiator indicator - NOT FIRED AND LANYARD ATTACHED TO INITATOR
   If indicator has been fired, the gray cap and orange spring will be exposed.
2. Ejection controls safety lever - LOCKED
3. Seat hose quick disconnect coupling - CHECK SECURE
4. Safety pins - REMOVED
   a. Canopy jettison handle pin
   b. Ejection seat safety pins (2)

c. Canopy actuated initiator pin
5. Auto/manual seat kit deployment selector - AUTO
6. Radio beacon auto/manual selector - AS DESIRED
7. (Before TO 1F-15E-582) Restraint emergency release handle - FULLY DOWN
   (After TO 1F-15E-582) Emergency manual chute handle - FULLY DOWN
8. Battery window - NO RED SHOWING

REAR COCKPIT INTERIOR CHECK

A thorough cockpit interior preflight shall be accomplished before each flight. The design features of the aircraft greatly simplify this task. Switch positions designated AS DESIRED allow pilot preference in switch/control positioning. AS REQUIRED indicates those switches that will differ with mission requirements. If no specific requirement exists, pilot preference may be used. Normally, those avionics switches designated AS DESIRED or AS REQUIRED should be OFF for start.

1. Interior check - COMPLETE

(Before TO 1F-15E-602)

a. Harness and personal equipment leads - FASTEN
   Attach parachute risers to harness buckles. Attach survival kit and ensure straps are snug within the limits of personal comfort. Connect oxygen, G suit, and communication leads. Check operation of shoulder harness locking mechanism.

WARNING

- After connecting the parachute risers to the harness, lift the locking lever on each koch fitting and verify the actuating lever is full up and snug against the inner part of the locking lever. If the actuating lever will not seat, disconnect the release and use a different harness.

- Failure to adjust the survival kit straps to achieve a snug fit between the crew member and kit may result in injury during ejection.

(After TO 1F-15E-602, when Aircrew Eye/Respiratory Protection is worn)

    a. Blower strap assembly - REMOVE AND STOW

    b. Sit in seat

    c. Blower electrical power - CONNECT

    d. Blower assembly - INSTALL

    e. Emergency oxygen - CONNECT

    f. Oxygen regulator - ON

    g. Blower hose - REMOVE FROM AQD (Armored Quick Disconnect)

    h. Oxygen hose - CONNECT TO AQD

    i. Blower hose - CONNECT TO VENTILATION INLET

    j. Crossover valve - ROTATE TO VERTICAL

    k. Survival kit - CONNECT
       Ensure straps are secure within the limits of personal comfort.

WARNING

● Failure to adjust the survival kit straps to achieve a snug fit between the crewmember and the kit may result in injury during ejection.
● Survival kit straps must be connected under hoses to prevent restriction of air flow.

    l. Lap belt - CONNECT
       Ensure lap belt is secure and firmly adjusted.

WARNING

Lap belt must be connected under hoses to prevent restriction of airflow.

    m. Shoulder harness - FASTEN

WARNING

After connecting the parachute risers to the harness, lift the locking lever on each koch fitting and verify the actuating lever is full up and snug against the inner part of the locking lever. If the actuating lever will not seat properly, disconnect the release and use a different harness.

    n. Anti-g suit - CONNECT
    o. Intercommunication unit - DISCONNECT AND STOW
    p. Aircraft communication cord - CONNECT

Left Console -

    a. Intercomm set control panel - SET
       (1) Volume knobs - AS DESIRED
       (2) Crypto switch - NORM
       (3) MIC switch - ON
       (4) Cipher text switch - AS REQUIRED
       (5) Tone switch - OFF
    b. EW control panel - SET AS REQUIRED
    c. Sensor control panel - SET
       (1) TGT FLIR power switch - OFF
       (2) LASER switch - SAFE
    d. Nuclear consent switch - SAFE (COVER CLOSED)
    e. Canopy jettison handle - FORWARD

Instrument panel -

    a. Emergency landing gear handle - IN
    b. Arresting hook switch - UP
    c. Emergency brake/steer handle - IN

Right Console -

    a. Command selector valve - NORM (VERTICAL)
    b. (F-15E 86-0183 THRU 90-0232 Before TO 1F-15E-561)
       Oxygen system - CHECK AND SET
       Pressure - 55 to 120 psi
       Regulator - CHECK
       (1) Oxygen supply lever - FULLY ON
          It is possible for the oxygen supply lever to stop in an intermediate position between OFF and ON. Insure the lever is all the way ON.
       (2) Emergency lever - NORMAL
       (3) Mask - ON
          Breath normally for 3 cycles and check

flow indicator operation. Hold breath, all flow should stop and the indicator should show no flow (black). A white indicator indicates a leak which must be corrected before flight.

Indicator - CHECK

(4) Diluter lever - 100%

(5) Emergency lever - EMERGENCY

(6) Oxygen flow - CHECK

Connections - CHECK

Emergency oxygen - CHECK

(7) Pressure - CHECK

(8) Actuating ring - STOWED AND CHECKED

b. TEWS control panel - SET

(1) ICS switch - OFF

(2) RWR switch - OFF

(3) EWWS switch - OFF

c. Countermeasures dispenser control panel - SET

(1) Mode switch - OFF

(2) Flare switch - NORM (COVER DOWN)

d. RMR - CHECK CASSETTE INSTAL-LED/INSERT

e. Circuit breakers - IN

f. Interior lights controls - AS DESIRED

BEFORE TAXIING (REAR COCKPIT)

1. Warning and caution lights - TEST

2. MPD's/MPCD's - ON

3. INS - CONFIRM ALIGN (see INS alignment procedure)

4. DTM - TRANSFER (AS REQUIRED)

5. Avionics - AS REQUIRED (AAI, ILS, UHF, TACAN, TEWS, CMD)

6. Sensor control panel - SET

a. TGT FLIR - STBY

b. LASER switch - SAFE

7. Avionics systems - CHECK/PROGRAM, INSERT/VERIFY UFC MISSION DATA, INITIATE BIT AS REQUIRED

8. Radar - PROGRAM/VERIFY WEAPON MODES (MRM, SRM)

9. PACS - PROGRAM AS REQUIRED

| CAUTION |

For the OWS to program properly, the external store configuration, including external tanks, must be programmed in the PACS.

10. Oxygen - CHECK

a. (F-15E 86-0183 THRU 90-0232 Before TO 1F-15E-561) Oxygen test - CHECK CAU-TION MESSAGE AND MASTER CAU-TION

b. (F-15E 90-0233 AND UP And 86-0183 THRU 90-0232 After TO 1F-15E-561) Oxygen system - CHECK AND SET

(1) Regulator - CHECK

(a) Oxygen supply lever - ON (PBG if required)

It is possible for the oxygen supply lever to stop at an intermediate position between OFF and ON. Make sure the lever is all the way ON.

| WARNING |

Injury may result if PBG is selected without compatible life support equipment.

| CAUTION |

Do not lift the regulator toggle switch when switching regulator from OFF to ON or ON to OFF. Damage to the regulator will result. The switch lever is locked out of the PBG position to avoid inadvertent actuation.

(b) Emergency lever - NORMAL

(c) MASK - ON

Breathe normally for 3 cycles and check flow indicator operation. Hold breath, all flow should stop and the indicator should show no flow (black). A white indicator indicates a leak which must be corrected before flight.

(2) Pressure - 10 to 60 psi (Green Band)

(3) Indicator - CHECK

(a) Diluter lever - 100%

        (b) Emergency lever - EMERGENCY
        (c) Oxygen flow - CHECK (Return Diluter and Emergency levers to NORM)
    (4) Connections - CHECK
    (5) Emergency Oxygen - CHECKED
        (a) Pressure - CHECK
        (b) Actuating ring - STOWED and CHECKED
11. Anti-g suit - CHECK OPERATION
12. Standby attitude indicator - CAGE THEN UNCAGE
13. Altimeter - SET AND CHECK
    a. Altimeter should agree with HUD altimeter within ±60 feet.

NOTE

If the altimeter is not within tolerance, the aircraft may be flown provided that the altimeter checks within ±75 feet of field elevation. The ±75 feet of field elevation is an operational restriction and does not necessarily reflect instrument tolerances.

TAXIING

As the throttles are moved out of idle, confirm that the holding brake switch goes OFF and that the holding brake is released. As aircraft starts to roll, apply brakes to check operation. When clear, actuate nose gear steering in both directions to ensure proper operation. During taxi, check all flight instruments. At high gross weights, make all turns at minimum practicable speed and maximum practicable radius. At low gross weight, taxi speed requires continual attention due to excess thrust at IDLE.

Nose gear damage can result during turns at high gross weight when using asymmetric thrust and/or asymmetric braking. At heavy gross weights, avoid abrupt nose gear steering inputs. Make turns at minimum practical speed and maximum practical radius, and avoid operations on rough and uneven taxiways or runways; failure to do so may result in tire damage.

1. Holding brake - OFF

2. Brakes - CHECK
3. Nose gear steering - CHECK
4. Flight instruments - CHECK

If taxiing is required before INS alignment is complete and the aircraft is stationary again before takeoff, place the holding brake ON to continue the alignment.

To prevent a skid and possible tire failure, the aircraft must be completely stopped before placing the holding brake ON.

BEFORE TAKEOFF

1. (BOTH) Harness - CHECK
   Ensure all buckles, straps, and fittings secure and properly adjusted.
2. (BOTH) Ejection control safety lever - ARMED
3. (WSO) Command select valve - AS BRIEFED
4. (BOTH) Flight controls - CHECK FREE
5. (BOTH) Flaps - CHECK DOWN
6. T/O trim - CHECK
   If the aircraft is manually trimmed nose down from takeoff trim, nosewheel lift-off speed may be increased.
7. (BOTH) Canopy - CLOSE, WAIT 10 SEC, THEN LOCK
   The canopy may bounce slightly as it lowers on canopy sill.

CAUTION

Ensure canopy has completed movement and wait 10 seconds before moving handle to LOCKED position. If there is a heavy load when attempting to place the handle in LOCKED, recycle the handle to DN and again perform locking procedure. Ensure canopy unlock light is on with handle in DN and goes out with handle in LOCKED. Ensure the handle is full forward.

8. (BOTH) IFF - ON,
9. Radar - ON
10. (WSO) TGT Pod - STBY
11. Pitot heat/anti-ice - ON AS REQUIRED
12. (BOTH) Warnings, cautions, BIT lights, and circuit breakers - CHECK
13. Holding brake - OFF

TAKEOFF

Advance engines to 80% (some aircraft creep may occur) and check instruments. When ready for take-off, release brakes and advance throttles to MIL or MAX as desired. Monitor engine instruments for proper operation, assuring that nozzles remain below 80% at MIL.

WITH CFT

Move the stick to approximately one-half aft stick at the rotation speed specified in figure A3-10 (with PW-220 engine) or B3-10 (with PW-229 engine) and rotate to a 10 to 12° pitch attitude. Applying aft stick at a lower speed may result in nose wheel bouncing. With CFTs, the aircraft has increased pitch response. Excessive aft stick can lead to high pitch rate. Retract gear and flaps when airborne.

TAKEOFF WITHOUT CFT

For normal takeoffs, move the stick to approximately one-half aft stick at about 130 knots and rotate to approximately 10° pitch attitude. For maximum performance takeoffs (minimum ground roll), move the stick full aft at a speed below the nose wheel lift-off speed in figure A3-11 (with PW-220 engine) or B3-11 (with PW-229 engine) and rotate to 12° pitch attitude. Nose wheel lift-off speed and takeoff speed is increased for heavy gross weights and/or forward center of gravity. Additional aft stick will compensate for these effects, but rotation rates could be unacceptably high, leading to over-rotation. Retract gear and flaps when airborne.

AFTERBURNER OPERATION

During normal afterburner operation, observe exhaust nozzles open progressively with each afterburner segment; thrust and fuel flow increase proportionately. As throttles are advanced from minimum to maximum afterburner, the increase in thrust is fairly smooth and continuous.

CLIMB TECHNIQUES

MIL Power - For drag index of 40 of less, climb at 350 KCAS to 0.88 Mach, then maintain Mach to cruise altitude. For indexes between 40 and 100, use 330 KCAS/0.83 Mach. Greater than 100, use 310 KCAS/0.74 Mach.

MAX Power - For drag index of 60 or less, climb at 350 knots to 0.95 Mach. If Mach increases above 0.95 at 40° pitch attitude, hold 40° and allow the Mach to increase. (Mach will rise only slightly before returning to 0.95.) For drag index greater than 60, climb at 350 KCAS to 0.92 Mach, then maintain 0.92 Mach.

TAXI TURNING RADIUS

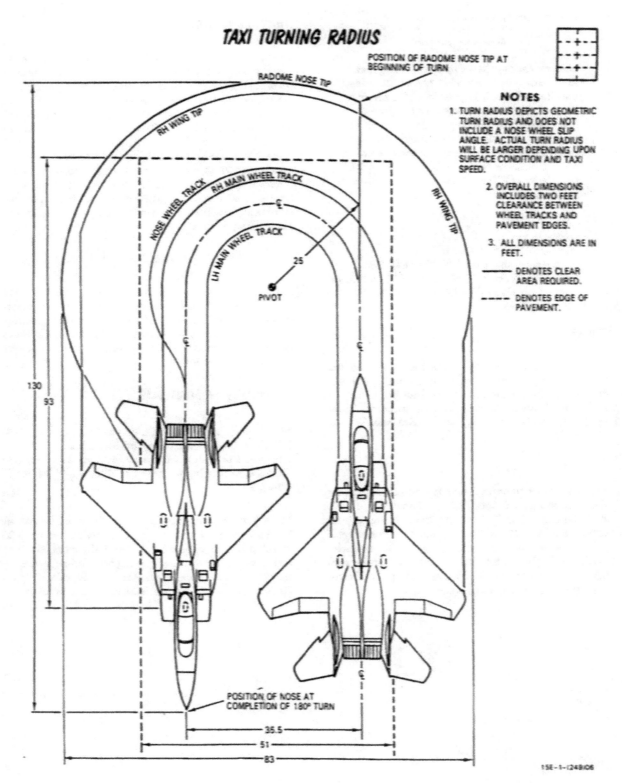

POSITION OF RADOME NOSE TIP AT BEGINNING OF TURN

RADOME NOSE TIP

RH WING TIP

NOSE WHEEL TRACK

RH MAIN WHEEL TRACK

RH WING TIP

LH MAIN WHEEL TRACK

25

PIVOT

130

93

POSITION OF NOSE AT COMPLETION OF 180° TURN

35.5

51

83

NOTES

1. TURN RADIUS DEPICTS GEOMETRIC TURN RADIUS AND DOES NOT INCLUDE A NOSE WHEEL SLIP ANGLE. ACTUAL TURN RADIUS WILL BE LARGER DEPENDING UPON SURFACE CONDITION AND TAXI SPEED.

2. OVERALL DIMENSIONS INCLUDES TWO FEET CLEARANCE BETWEEN WHEEL TRACKS AND PAVEMENT EDGES.

3. ALL DIMENSIONS ARE IN FEET.

————— DENOTES CLEAR AREA REQUIRED.

- - - - - DENOTES EDGE OF PAVEMENT.

15E-1-(249)06

Figure 2-3

INFLIGHT

NOTE

Refer to TO 1F-15E-34-1-1 for A/G Inflight and Terrain Following checks.

Continually monitor aircraft systems operation throughout the flight. Periodically check attitude of ADI vs standby AI. Frequently check engine instruments (EMD), cabin pressure, oxygen system operation, fuel quantity (internal vs. total), and fuel transfer.

Optimum cruise and maximum endurance should be found in the performance data section and is attained by flying the correct Mach number for configuration and altitude. If the performance charts are not available and accuracy is not a significant factor, 12 units AOA may be used for optimum cruise and 14.5 units AOA may be used for maximum endurance.

FUEL MONITORING

With three external tanks installed, fuel transfer should be checked by selecting stop transfer on external wing tanks and observing fuel transfer from the centerline tank. When centerline transfer is confirmed the external wing tank switch should be returned to normal. To prevent fuel pump damage/failure, the CFT transfer switch must be placed in the STOP TRANS position when all CFT fuel has been transferred.

After all external fuel tanks (wing, centerline, and CFT) are empty and the internal wing tanks start feeding, a check should be made to ensure that a differential of 750 pounds is not being exceeded between tank 1 and each internal wing tank. The transfer rate should be periodically monitored until tank 1 and the internal wing tanks are empty.

During low altitude/high speed flight, fuel consumption can be as high as 150,000 PPH (2500 pounds per minute) and may exceed fuel transfer capability. This will cause premature reduction of feed tank fuel level. Maneuvering and acceleration can cause fuel gage errors resulting in a fuel state over 1000 pounds less than gage indication. To avoid dangerously low fuel states as a result of these factors, maintain situation awareness, make more frequent fuel checks, and closely monitor feed tank fuel quantity.

With external tanks installed, an asymmetric external fuel imbalance may occur. Compare the internal fuel pointer with the total counter for indications of trapped external fuel. During sustained cruise power an external wing tank may not transfer fuel until after the other external wing tank is empty. The aircraft may be safely flown below 30 units AOA with an asymmetric load as great as one full external wing tank.

INSTRUMENT FLIGHT PROCEDURES

GENERAL

The HUD is the primary indicator for instrument flight.

RECOMMENDED AIRSPEEDS

The holding, penetration, and downwind airspeed for instrument approach may vary from those recommended. At normal approach gross weight, acceleration and high residual thrust characteristics of turbofan engines, combined with low aerodynamic drag, make precise speed control difficult. The recommended technique during instrument approach is to select a power setting which allows the aircraft to stabilize at the approximate recommended airspeed.

Holding

The recommended holding airspeed is 250 knots.

Penetration

Normally, after power is set (approximately 72%), lower nose to approximately 10° and allow airspeed to increase slowly to 300 knots. The speed brake can be used if a higher descent rate is required. Approaching final approach fix, slow to 200-250 knots and lower gear and flaps.

INSTRUMENT APPROACHES

In the pattern, select a power setting that will maintain 200 to 250 knots. Approaching final, lower gear and flaps, and slow the aircraft. Maintain on-speed AOA on final. The speed brake can be used to control descent and airspeed. On GCA final, the velocity vector can be used to indicate glideslope. If a 2 1/2° glideslope is used, holding 2 1/2° flight path angle with the velocity vector provides a good basis from which corrections, if required, can be made.

On an ILS approach, use of the bank steering bar in the ILS mode is not recommended until approximately aligned with the final approach heading. Bank steering information on the HUD and ADI automatically switches from 30° maximum bank angle to the final approach mode of 15° maximum bank angle when the glideslope is intercepted. If the glideslope is intercepted with a considerable difference between aircraft heading and final approach course, a 15° bank angle may not be sufficient to align the aircraft on final approach. When an ILS mode is selected, CSET flashes on the HUD for 5 seconds to remind the pilot to set the final approach course. Interception of the center of the glideslope and automatic shift to approach mode is indicated by the appearance of glideslope indications on the HUD and ADI. Glideslope and localizer information is displayed on the ADI.

WARNING

HUD ILS command guidance is mechanized for a 3° glideslope. If other than a 3° glideslope is being flown, the generated glideslope commands will place the aircraft approximately 1/2 dot off the glide path. Therefore, during any ILS approach, crosscheck generated steering commands with raw glideslope data.

Use the best available range information. ILST normally provides the most accurate range information if the tacan station is suitably located. ILSN mode provides range to the coordinates entered for the STEER TO destination.

On final approach, steer the velocity vector to the flight director cross. Velocity vector position on the pitch scale may be used to reduce the effect of an overly sensitive flight director cross (out of HUD limit). A flashing (caged) velocity vector may be used but it will not indicate the actual azimuth of the flight path.

MISSED APPROACH/GO AROUND

Advance power as required and retract speed brake. Retract gear and flaps when climb is established.

DESCENT CHECK/BEFORE LANDING

Descents from high altitude may cause windshield fogging. The hot position should be selected before descent if fogging is anticipated.

1. Master arm switch - SAFE
2. CMD mode switch - OFF
3. (BOTH) Altimeters - SET AND CHECK
4. TGT FLIR switch - STBY/OFF
5. Landing light - ON
6. TF radar power switch - as required
7. Holding brake - OFF

WARNING

Landing with holding brake on (engaged) will cause loss of control when struts compress and throttle is placed in IDLE.

LANDING TECHNIQUE

The aircraft can accommodate several different landing techniques, however, the procedures described are recommended.

NORMAL LANDING

Approaching the break, set power to maintain altitude and airspeed (300 knots minimum). The speed brake may be used as required. On downwind, below 250 knots, lower gear and flaps.

During base turn, reduce speed to arrive on final at on-speed AOA (20-22 units). If faster than on-speed, the aircraft will float for considerable distance. If slower than on-speed, minor buffet may be noticed.

At the flare point, smoothly retard the throttles to IDLE and reduce rate of descent. Ground effect will cushion the aircraft, and touchdown may be difficult to recognize. Raising the nose too high in the flare will cause ballooning, and possibly a hard landing and tail/engine ground contact. For high gross weights, fly on-speed AOA, but delay reducing power until well into the flare (refer to section VI). After touchdown, maintain directional control with rudder and raise the nose to approximately 13° pitch attitude to achieve aerodynamic braking. With CFT's the aircraft has increased pitch response. Aerobraking is highly effective at airspeeds above 90 knots and significantly reduces the possibility of hot brakes, excessive tire wear, and blown tires. Therefore, aerobraking should be accomplished first followed by normal braking.

> **CAUTION**
>
> Limit pitch attitude to 15° to avoid dragging the tail. The aircraft symbol (W on the HUD) will flash at 13°.

At 80-90 knots fly the nose to the runway and apply brakes as required (at high gross weight, or forward CG, the nose will begin to fall at proportionally higher airspeeds, refer to section VI). Due to high idle thrust, the aircraft may not decelerate after the nose wheel is on the ground unless braking is used.

> **WARNING**
>
> With low gross weight (less than 2000 lbs of fuel), use caution in turns and avoid excessive speed. Weight-off-wheels switch may break contact and cause loss of brakes.

CROSSWIND LANDING

Landing is not recommended if the 90° crosswind component exceeds 30 knots. Fly a normal pattern adjusted to avoid excessively steep or shallow base turns. On final, establish a wings-level crab to counteract drift and maintain the flight path straight down the runway. It may be necessary to adjust power or delay throttle reduction in the flare to avoid abrupt sink rates or counteract the effects of turbulence. In gusty or turbulent conditions, use normal on-speed AOA; however, AOA deviations are more critical. Hold the crab through touchdown. After touchdown, maintain ground track with rudder. Use aileron into the wind to maintain a wings-level attitude. After touchdown, if the crosswind component exceeds 25 knots, do not increase pitch attitude to greater than 10°. If directional control becomes difficult, lower the nose and brake in a three-point attitude. See Wind Components Chart, figure A1-11.

> **NOTE**
>
> When landing with an asymmetric load, it is desirable to place the heavy wing into the wind.

MINIMUM RUN LANDING

When stopping distance is critical, fly final at 23 units AOA, and use a flatter approach angle (1 ½° - 2°). Precise control of the touchdown point can be achieved using the velocity vector. If runway is dry and gross weight is 45,000 pounds or less, lower nose after touchdown and commence maximum anti-skid braking. Maximum anti-skid braking is achieved by applying maximum pedal pressure. If gross weight is greater than 45,000 pounds, use aerobraking technique. See section VII for slippery runway techniques.

NO FLAP LANDING

No flap landings require no special technique. Approach speed is slightly faster at on-speed AOA and the aircraft is more sensitive in pitch. Allow for higher pitch attitude and slower deceleration on final.

AFTER LANDING

1. (BOTH) Ejection controls safety lever - LOCKED
2. Command Selector valve - NORMAL
3. Speed brake - IN
4. Flaps - UP
5. (BOTH) IFF modes - DESELECT
6. Mode 4 crypto switch - HOLD MOMENTARILY AND RETURN TO NORM
7. Radar power knob - STBY
8. TF radar - OFF
9. Trim - T/O
10. Landing/taxi light - AS REQUIRED
11. Formation lights - OFF
12. Pitot heat and windshield switches - OFF
13. Anti-ice switches - OFF
14. Mode 4 selector switch - OUT
15. INS - UPDATE (if position known)

SINGLE-ENGINE TAXI

1. (BOTH) Avionics - OFF (AAI, ILS, TACAN, SENSORS, HUD, TEWS, RADAR)
2. MPDs/MPCDs - OFF
   The right display in each cockpit should be left on to monitor cautions.
3. UHF #2 - VERIFY ON

4. Either throttle - OFF

5. Corresponding engine master switch - OFF
   Placing the engine master switch OFF resets the automatic avionics shutdown system.

NOTE

Automatic avionics shutdown may occur due to low ECS cooling airflow at idle RPM. Single engine RPM at 71 - 73% should provide sufficient airflow.

HOT REFUELING

Stop short of the refueling area for tanks/stores safety check. If suspected hot brake or other unsafe condition exists, do not enter refueling area. Consider all available methods of escape should a fire or other emergency occur. Taxiing clear, ground egress, and static ejection are some of the options available. Follow ground crew directions into the refueling area, and establish communications with the ground crew. If you suspect a malfunction stop refueling. Do not transmit on UHF except in an emergency. After refueling complete and when cleared by ground crew, taxi clear of the area. Do not use high power in congested areas.

Before Refueling -

1. (BOTH) After landing checklist - COMPLETE

2. Holding brake - ON

3. (BOTH) Avionics - OFF (AAI, ILS, TACAN, MPD's/MPCD's, SENSORS, HUD, TEWS, RADAR)

4. Anti-collision lights - OFF

5. Slipway switch - OPEN

NOTE

Either engine may be shut down for hot refueling. In actual combat situations, both engines may be left running.

6. Either throttle - OFF

7. Inoperative engine master switch - OFF

8. UHF#2 - VERIFY ON

NOTE

Automatic avionics shutdown may occur during refueling due to low ECS cooling airflow. The most notable indication will be blanking of the right displays. Single engine rpm at 71 - 73% should provide sufficient airflow for avionics cooling. Make sure UHF #2 continues to operate if auto shutdown occurs. The inoperative engine ramp may extend full up with automatic avionics shutdown.

9. (BOTH) Canopy - CLOSED
   Hot refueling with the canopy closed provides maximum protection in the event of a fire.

10. (BOTH) Fuel quantity - NOTE

11. RPM - SET AT 71-73%

During Refueling -

12. (BOTH) Keep hands visible to refueling supervisor. Be prepared to shut down engine and evacuate aircraft or taxi clear of area as directed by ground crew if an emergency occurs.

After Refueling -

13. (BOTH) Fuel quantity indicator - CHECK AND NOTE TOTAL QUANTITY

14. Slipway switch - CLOSED

15. External lights - AS REQUIRED

16. Avionics - AS REQUIRED

ENGINE SHUTDOWN

1. Slipway switch - OPEN (if required)

2. OWS matrix - CHECK

3. INS - UPDATE (perform and accept overfly update to known PP can be done anytime after landing)

4. Video recorder - UNTHREAD

5. (BOTH) LANTIRN pods - OFF

6. INS - OFF (obtain mission data)

7. (BOTH) Avionics - OFF (AAI, ILS, TACAN, SENSORS, HUD, TEWS, RADAR)
   Turn avionics OFF, including systems controlled on the UFC, before shutting down engines to prevent false BIT warnings on the status panel.

8. Throttles - OFF
   a. (F-15E 86-0183 THRU 90-0232) Throttle(s) - OFF AFTER 15 SECONDS
   b. (F-15E 90-0233 AND UP) Throttles - OFF 15 SECONDS AFTER INS OFF, IDLE 5 MIN (Can include taxi at idle power).

Wait 15 seconds after INS shutoff to allow the VTR to unthread. Before the emergency generator drops off the line, ensure that the L and R GEN OUT caution lights and the landing gear indicator lights come on. Illumination of these lights indicates that the generator failure circuit is functioning and the emergency generator is supplying both AC and DC essential power.

AIRCREW EGRESS (BOTH) (After TO 1F-15E-602)

When Aircrew Eye/Respiratory Protection is worn -

1. Ejection controls safety lever - LOCKED
2. Shoulder harness - RELEASE
3. Lapbelt - REL;EASE
4. Survival kit - RELEASE
5. Anti-g suit - DISCONNECT
6. Crossover valve - ROTATE TO HORIZONTAL
7. Blower hose - DISCONNECT
8. Oxygen hose - DISCONNECT
9. Blower hose - CONNECT TO AQD
10. Oxygen regulator- OFF
11. Emergency oxygen hose - DISCONNECT
12. Aircraft communications cord - DISCONNECT
13. Intercommunication unit - CONNECT
14. Blower - REMOVE FROM BRACKET
15. Blower electrical connector - DISCONNECT
16. Blower strap assembly - RECONNECT
17. Exit aircraft

COMBAT JETTISON PROGRAMMING (BOTH)

1. ARMT display - SELECT
2. CBT JETT display - SELECT
3. Select JETT knob - OFF or COMBAT
4. 1 button (CBT 1 program) - PRESS
   a. 1 is boxed and 2 is unboxed.
5. Select station(s) for CBT 1 program.
   a. Store on selected station is boxed.
6. Select RACK, STORE or PYLON for CBT 1 program.

a. Selected suspension is boxed.

NOTE

The STORE legend is boxed when CBT JETT display is selected.

7. To enter CBT 1 program, ENTER button - PRESS
   a. Box is removed from 1 and existing program adjacent to CBT 1 is replaced with new program.
8. 2 button (CBT 2 program) - PRESS
   a. 2 is boxed, 1 is unboxed.
9. Repeat steps 5 thru 7 for CBT 2 program.

OWS MATRIX DISPLAY (BOTH)

To display the OWS matrix -

1. From MENU 2, OWS menu - SELECT

To clear the OWS matrix -

2. CLEAR pushbutton - PRESS (CLEAR boxed) Ensure maintenance personnel toggle OWS reset switch on the ASP and reset ASP 72.

WARNING

To prevent injury, do not clear maintenance personnel to enter the nose wheelwell unless one engine is shut down.

3. Matrix cleared - CHECK (CLEAR unboxed and ASP 72 black)

UFC PROCEDURES

DATA FORMATS

Numerous different types of data may be entered on the UFC for navigation. In most cases, data is entered by first selecting the appropriate menu display, data display, or submenu; typing the data into the scratch pad; and pressing the UFC button adjacent to the data to be changed or entered.

SEQUENCE Points

Sequence point types include steer, target, aim, offset, mark, and base and are entered in basically the same manner. However, the aircrew must pay attention to the use of the decimal point, tenths and hundredths digits, and route letter identifiers.

a. For steer point 18A, type 18, shift (SHF), A, press sequence point button.
b. For target point 17.B, type 17, decimal, SHF, B, press sequence point button.
c. For aim point 18.1A, type 18, decimal, 1, SHF, A, press sequence point button.
d. For offset point 17.01B, type 17, decimal, 01, SHF, B, press sequence point button.
e. For base point, type B, press sequence point button.

When changing navigation point numbers, the route letter identifier needs to be entered only if it is different from the current display letter. Entering a zero for a point, when in Point Data submenu, removes that point from the mission route unless it is your current steer to point.

Latitude/Longitude

To enter a point latitude and longitude, type the hemisphere, degrees, minutes, and thousandths of minutes. When the hemisphere key (N, S, E, or W) is pressed, the degree symbol, minutes symbol, decimal, and entered letter are displayed on the scratchpad. Leading zeros must be included if the latitude degrees are less than two digits or the longitude degrees are less than three digits.

a. For 38°45.6 north latitude, type SHF, N, 38456, press latitude button.
b. For 90°22.1 east longitude, type SHF, E, 090221, press longitude button.

UTM Spheroid, Grid, and Coordinates

UTM coordinates are changed/entered on the UTM or program submenu; the spheroid grid are changed on the UTM program submenu. Grid numbers can be changed on the UTM submenu.

a. For UTM coordinates 6897064356, type 6897064356, press UTM coordinate button.
b. To change the UTM spheroid, press the button adjacent to the current spheriod to cycle through until the desired spheroid is displayed.
c. To change the UTM grid number to 18, type 18, press grid number button.
d. To change the UTM grid letter, press the button adjacent to the grid identifier until the letter to be changed is preceded by an asterisk, then press the INCR or DECR button to obtain the desired letter.

Point Elevation

Navigation point elevation is entered in feet above or below (−)MSL.

    a. For 1250 feet MSL, type 1250, press elevation button.

Point MEA

The MEA for any point along the route may be entered from 400 to 30,000 feet.

    a. For 1000 feet, type 1000, press MEA button.

Range/Bearing

Type offset range in NM and tenths.

    a. For 10.1 NM, type 10, decimal, 1, press range button.

Type offset bearing in degrees true.

    a. For 35° true bearing, type 035, press bearing button.

Direction/Range

Type offset direction/range in cardinal direction and feet.

    a. For 15,250 feet north, type SHF, N, 15250, press N/S button.

Time

Current time or route times are entered in hours, minutes, and seconds.

    a. To enter 16 hours, 35 minutes, 15 seconds, type 163515, press time button.

Magnetic Variation (if INS invalid)

Magnetic variation is entered in degrees and minutes east or west. The degree symbol appears in the scratchpad when E or W is pressed.

    a. To enter a mag var of W3°30', type SHF, W, 0033, press mag var button.

Wind Direction and Speed

Wind direction (bearing) is entered in degrees true and speed in knots on the Data 1 Format.

    a. For wind 185° true and 45 knots, type 185, SHF, dash, 045, press wind button.

DATA ENTRY/DISPLAY (BOTH)

Mission data must be entered from the appropriate display on the UFC; some data can be entered/changed on more than one display. As data is typed on the UFC keyboard it appears in the scratchpad. When the appropriate button is pressed to enter the data, the new data is displayed next to the button and the scratchpad is blank.

Present Position

Present position entry is required during INS alignment if HUD window 16 displays PP REQ. Present position also should be entered if the pilot determines that the PP display on the UFC after INS turn-on is incorrect. When a new PP is entered the PP should be known to an accuracy of 600 ft (0.1 arc minute). When entered the PP becomes the base point.

1. Menu 2 display - SELECT
2. PP INS source submenu - SELECT
3. Type present latitude
4. Latitude button - PRESS
5. Type present longitude
6. Longitude button - PRESS

Magnetic Variation (Mag Var)

Magnetic variation is not required as an input to the INS for its alignment or navigation operation. INS provides mag var from a stored mag var table based on the latitude and longitude of the aircraft. Mag var accuracy is dependent on aircraft location. During normal operation the CC uses mag var from the INS. If the INS has failed, the CC will use the last known good mag var. If the INS has failed and/or air data is selected, then mag var can be entered via the UFC for use by the CC.

1. Menu 2 display - SELECT
2. PP INS source submenu - SELECT
3. Type present position mag var
4. Mag var button - PRESS

Sequence Point Number

1. Data 1/Menu 1 display - SELECT
2. Type new mission point number and letter
3. Mission point button - PRESS

Sequence Point Lat/Long

1. Data 1/Menu 1 display - SELECT
2. Point data submenu - SELECT
3. Coordinate button - PRESS UNTIL LAT/LONG SUBMENU APPEARS
4. Type point latitude
5. Latitude button - PRESS
6. Type point longitude
7. Longitude button - PRESS

Sequence Point Elevation

1. Data 1/Menu 1 display - SELECT
2. Point data submenu - SELECT
3. Type mission point elevation
4. Mission point elevation button - PRESS

Sequence Point MEA

1. Data 1/Menu 1 display - SELECT
2. Point data submenu - SELECT
3. Type mission point MEA
4. Mission point MEA button - PRESS

Sequence Point UTM's

1. Data 1/Menu 1 display - SELECT
2. Point data submenu - SELECT
3. Coordinate button - PRESS UNTIL UTM DISPLAY APPEARS

To change UTM coordinates:

4. Type point UTM coordinates
5. UTM coordinate button - PRESS

To change UTM spheroid:

4. Program button - PRESS
5. Spheroid button - PRESS UNTIL DESIRED SPHEROID APPEARS

To change UTM grid number:

4. Type new UTM grid number
5. Grid identifier button - PRESS

To change UTM grid letter:

4. Program button - PRESS
5. Grid identifier button - PRESS UNTIL CARET PRECEDES LETTER TO BE CHANGED
6. INCR or DECR button - PRESS TO DISPLAY DESIRED LETTER

7. Repeat steps 5 and 6 for other grid letters to be changed.

Offset Data

1. Data 1/Menu 1 display - SELECT
2. Point data submenu - SELECT
3. Coordinate button - PRESS UNTIL RNG/BRG IS DISPLAYED
4. RNG/BRG button - PRESS

To change offset range/bearing data:

5. Type range from offset point to target
6. Range button - PRESS
7. Type bearing from offset point to target
8. Bearing button - PRESS

To change direction/range data:

5. DIR/RNG button - PRESS
6. Type N/S distance from offset point to target.
7. N/S button - PRESS
8. Type E/W distance from offset point to target
9. E/W button - PRESS

Tacan Data

Twelve tacan stations may be stored in addition to the mission points. The data is used for tacan navigation or updates.

1. Menu 1 display - SELECT
2. Tacan submenu - SELECT
3. Program button - PRESS
   Program submenu appears with the selected tacan channel number, its index number, and coordinates.
4. Press index button to increment 1 thru 12 to the desired index number or type and enter the INDEX number.
5. Type desired tacan channel number.
6. TCN button - PRESS
7. Type tacan station latitude
8. Latitude button - PRESS
9. Type tacan station longitude
10. Longitude button - PRESS
11. Type tacan station mag var
12. Mag var button - PRESS
13. Type tacan station elevation
14. Elevation button - PRESS
15. Press mode button to select either X or Y channel system
16. Repeat steps 4 thru 15 for each of 12 programmed tacan stations

NOTE

When programming channel and index numbers, index numbers should be changed before the channel numbers. Failure to use this sequence could result in an incorrect channel number being entered into an index number.

HUD Titling

HUD titling data is entered for identification of the video tape recorder and signal data recorder outputs.

HUD titling is performed in the following manner.

1. Menu 2 display - SELECT
2. PP source submenu - SELECT
3. HUD TITL submenu - SELECT
4. Type month and date
   a. To enter the date of June 30, type 06, SHF, dash,30.
5. Month-day button - PRESS
6. Type year
   a. To enter the year 1989, type 89.
7. Year button - PRESS
8. Type mission number
   a. To enter the mission number 5, type 05.
9. MSN button - PRESS
10. Type aircraft tail number
    a. To enter aircraft tail number 86-0183, type 86, SHF, dash, 0183.
11. A/C button - PRESS
12. Type wing number
    a. To type wing number 131, type 0131.
13. WNG button - PRESS
14. Type local use data
    a. Local 1 and 2 (LOC-1, LOC-2) are four-digit numbers for local use (gun number or squadron). Type digits.
15. LOC-1 or LOC-2 button - PRESS

INS PROCEDURES

INS ALIGNMENTS (BOTH)

During the selected ground alignment mode, present position should be entered only when the aircraft is not moving and with the holding brake applied.

During INS alignment, displays called out as appearing in HUD window 16 also appear on the radar A/G PVU display if selected on an MPD/MPCD. INS mode knob position is selected by the pilot; all other alignment steps may be accomplished by either crewmember.

Normal GC Alignment (Switch OFF to GC)

1. (P)INS mode knob - GC
   After approximately 7 seconds, HUD displays GC PP REQ or GC NO TAXI. If the pilot's UFC is not displaying a submenu, the PP submenu is automatically selected on the UFC for the pilot evaluation of the PP being used for INS alignment. If the PP is acceptable no input is required. If PP REQ is displayed a new PP must be entered. GC PP REQ remains until a new PP is entered or transitions to NAV. INS attitude stabilization requires approximately 30 seconds and is accomplished while either PP REQ or NO TAXI is displayed.

NOTE

The PP entered should be the aircraft location and both latitude and longitude must be re-entered (even if only one required corrections). Position corrections after the aircraft has moved should be done by update after transition to NAV but may result in poor performance. Therefore, it is vitally important that PP is entered correctly when aligning.

2. Present position - INPUT NEW PP IF REQUIRED
3. GC NO TAXI - displayed for 60 seconds on HUD window 16.
4. HUD window 16 - GC 15.9 (After approximately 30 seconds dependent on other priority displays.)
   The display of GC 15.9 in place of NO TAXI indicates that attitude has stabilized. Alignment quality number (15.9) decrease indicates alignment accuracy improvement. The aircraft may be taxied and flown at this time, however, degraded accuracy should be expected.

NOTE

Taxiing is allowed with GC selected. GC HOLD is displayed while the aircraft is in motion. To continue the alignment, the holding brake must be turned ON after the aircraft is stopped and the INS detects no aircraft motion; GC HOLD will be replaced with GC XX.X (alignment quality).

5. HUD window 16 - GC OK (After approximately 4 minutes)
   Display of GC OK indicates GC alignment complete.

6. (P)INS mode knob - NAV

SH Alignment

1. (P)INS mode knob - STORE
   After approximately 7 seconds, HUD displays SH PP REQ or SH NO TAXI. The PP submenu is automatically selected on the pilot's UFC (if not in submenu) for the pilot's evaluation of the PP being used for INS alignment. If PP REQ is displayed or if the pilot determines the INS PP is incorrect, the present position must be entered and the INS will not display SH but will display GC and will enter a full GC alignment. INS attitude stabilization requires approximately 30 seconds and is accomplished while either PP REQ or NO TAXI is displayed.

2. HUD window 16 - SH NO TAXI

NOTE

If the aircraft is moved with STORE selected, GC HOLD is displayed while the aircraft is in motion. The INS will discard the SH alignment and continue a GC alignment if the aircraft is stopped and the holding brake turned ON and the INS detects no aircraft motion; GC HOLD will be replaced with GC XX.X (alignment quality).

3. HUD window 16 - SH OK
   SH OK should be displayed in approximately 30 seconds because the SH alignment time of 30 seconds is run concurrent with the attitude stabilization time of 30 seconds. SH OK indicates SH alignment complete.

4. (P)INS mode knob - NAV
   The INS mode switch should be switched to NAV prior to movement of the aircraft.

Direct Transition GC Alignment (OFF to NAV)

1. (P)INS mode knob - NAV
   After approximately 7 seconds, HUD displays GC PP REQ or GC NO TAXI. The PP submenu is automatically selected on the pilot's UFC (if not in a submenu) for the pilot evaluation of the PP being used for INS alignment. If the PP is acceptable no input is required. If PP REQ is displayed a new PP must be entered. GC PP REQ remains until a new PP is entered or transitions to NAV. INS attitude stabilization requires approximately 30 seconds and is accomplished while either PP REQ or NO TAXI is displayed.

NOTE

The PP entered should be the aircraft location. Further corrections after the aircraft has moved should be done by update after transition to NAV.

2. Present position - INPUT NEW PP IF REQUIRED

3. GC NO TAXI - displayed for 60 seconds on HUD window 16.

4. HUD window 16 - GC 15.9 (After approximately 40 seconds dependent on other priority displays.)
   The display of GC 15.9 in place of NO TAXI indicates that attitude has stabilized. Alignment quality number (15.9) decrease indicates alignment accuracy improvement. The aircraft may be taxied and flown at this time, however, degraded accuracy should be expected.

NOTE

Taxiing is allowed with GC selected. GC HOLD is displayed while the aircraft is in motion. To continue the alignment, the holding brake must be turned ON after the aircraft is stopped and the INS detects no aircraft motion; GC HOLD will be replaced with GC alignment quality.

5. HUD window 16 - Blank (After approximately 4 minutes)
   Indicates GC OK and transition to NAV.

PERFORMANCE MONITOR DATA

To insure complete INS performance monitor data is stored, an on-ground visual overfly update must be performed at the end of flight. The update may be performed at any location on the ground. The update PP should be known to an accuracy of 600 feet (0.1 arc minute). At the aircraft shutdown location, the INS should be turned off with the mode switch. The performance monitor data can be reviewed for the current flight by turning the INS off, and after 10 seconds turning the INS back on. The data can be displayed on the MPD as follows:

Push PB 11 for master menu
Push PB 20 for BIT menu
Push PB 18 for maintenance menu
Push PB 9 for INS 1st flight data
Push PB 13 for each of the second through twelfth flight

Data displayed for the most recent flight is as follows:

Initial latitude and longitude
Type of ground alignment; time in align and IFA if appropriate
Final aided latitude and longitude
Time in Nav
Final unaided latitude
Final unaided longitude
Groundspeed
RER (Radial Error Rate)
*CEP (Circular Error Probable)
*Number of flights in CEP calculation (max of 12)
In spec or maintenance, check recommendation.

Data which may be displayed for second through twelfth last flight is as follows:

Type of ground alignment and time in align
Groundspeed
RER
*CEP (Same for all flights stored)
*Number of flights in CEP calculation (max of 12).
* - Same for all flights stored.

UPDATE PROCEDURES (BOTH)

INS and/or mission navigator (MN) present position may be updated by comparison with tacan data (TCN update), visual position (OFLY or HUD updates), radar ground target position (RBM or HRM update) or target pod line of sight data (LANTIRN update). Also a provision for altitude only updates is included.

Following an update procedure, the distance from the INS or MN present position to the tacan, HUD, overfly, radar, or target pod derived position is shown on the update format. If the distances are ≤ 3000 feet, they are shown in feet N/S and E/W. If greater than 3000 feet, the distances are shown in nautical miles to the nearest tenth. The difference data can be either accepted or rejected.

System altitude updates can be accomplished with the overfly, altitude-only or target pod formats. Altitude error data is always displayed in feet. System altitude is also updated if the INS or MN present position (PP) is updated with these formats.

With all update formats, if INS PP is updated, then so is MN PP and system altitude, if applicable. INS-PP keeping must be used for an INS update. If MN PP-keeping is selected, INS update errors will be invalid (INV).

1. UFC Menu 2 display - SELECT
2. UPDT SEL (PB 7) - SELECT
3. Select desired update mode
   a. OFLY (PB 10)
   b. HUD (PB 9)
   c. ALT (PB 8)
   d. TCN (PB 7)

Tacan Update

4. TCN (PB 7) - SELECT
5. Ensure desired tacan channel number and system (X or Y) is selected.
6. Toggle PB 10 to desired source for update (INS or MN)
7. To accept the update, ENTER button - PRESS

8. To reject the update, exit the update submenu or perform another update.

Overfly Freeze Update

An INS overfly freeze update done on the ground after landing is done to store complete performance data. The update can be done anytime/place where present position is known.

4. OFLY (PB 10) - SELECT
5. When directly over the point to be updated (selected at PB 1), FREEZE button - PRESS
6. Toggle PB 10 to desired source for update (INS or MN or ALT)
7. To accept the update, ENTER button - PRESS
8. To reject the update, exit the update submenu or perform another update.

HUD Update (P)

4. HUD (PB 9) - SELECT
5. NAV (or INST) master mode - SELECT
6. Take command of HUD
7. Press and hold the TDC to slew line-of-sight symbol over visual update point (update point selected at PB 1).
8. Toggle PB 10 to desired source for update (INS or MN)
9. To accept the update, ENTER button - PRESS
10. To reject the update, exit the update submenu or perform another update

Altitude Update

An altitude-only update can be performed using two methods - overflying a steer-to point with a known elevation or overflying a known surface elevation (lake, ocean or plain). If the surface (SURF) format is to be used, PB 1 is toggled to display "SURF" and then the surface elevation is entered at PB 2. CC provided system altitude is displayed at PB 3 for both formats.

4. ALT (PB 8) - SELECT

Steer-to Format

5. When directly over the point to be updated (selected at PB 1), FREEZE button - PRESS
6. To accept the update, ENTER button - PRESS
7. To reject the update, exit the update submenu or perform another update.

SURF Format

5. Toggle PB 1- SURF displayed
6. Enter surface elevation at PB 2 via UFC scratchpad
7. When over surface, FREEZE button - PRESS
8. To accept the update, ENTER button - PRESS
9. To reject the update, exit the update submenu or perform another update

LANTIRN Update

Refer to TO 1F-15E-34-1-1 for a detailed description of the LANTIRN system.

1. Take command of FLIR display on MPD/MPCD
2. PB 17 -VERIFY CORRECT SEQUENCE POINT NUMBER DISPLAY
3. Cursor UPDT function - SELECT
4. MN, INS or ALT update (PB 16) - SELECT
5. Slew cursor over update point, position errors and command track displayed
6. Fire Laser
7. Accept by full action TDC(pilot) or Trigger (WSO)

Real Beam Map (RBM) Update

Refer to TO 1F-15E-34-1-1 for a detailed description of the RBM mode.

1. Take command of RBM display
2. PB 17 - VERIFY CORRECT SEQUENCE POINT NUMBER
3. Cursor UPDT function - SELECT
4. Mission Navigator or INS update - SELECT
5. Slew cursor over update point, position errors displayed
6. Accept or deselect update

High Resolution Map (HRM) Update

Refer to TO 1F-15E-34-1-1 for a detailed description of the HRM mode.

1. Take command of HRM display
2. PB 17 - VERIFY CORRECT SEQUENCE POINT NUMBER
3. Cursor UPDT function - SELECT
4. Mission Navigator or INS update - SELECT
5. Slew cursor over update point, position errors displayed
6. Accept or deselect update

PVU Update

Refer to TO 1F-15E-34-1-1 for a detailed description of the PVU mode.

NOTE

If the INU, CC or radar antenna has been replaced or the CC program has been reloaded, an INS PVU is required to correct for pointing errors. This should be done as early in the flight as practical.

1. Take command of radar A/G display
2. PVU function - SELECT

MN update

3. Wait for errors to appear and stabilize
4. Accept update by full action TDC(pilot) or Trigger(WSO)

NOTE

MN PVU update is zeroed out after 5 minutes.

INS update

3. INS (PB 8) - SELECT
4. INS PVU - INITIATE, FULL ACTION TDC (PILOT) OR TRIGGER (WSO)
5. Wait for errors to appear
6. Initiate update by full action TDC (pilot) or Trigger (WSO)
7. Perform gentle climbs, dives, accelerations, decelerations and turns at less than 45° bank.
8. To exit and update, MN - SELECT

EXTERNAL POWER START
(Following cockpit interior check)

If external power is to be used more than 2 minutes before starting engines, ensure the number 1 ground power switch is in A ON, CC and PACS switches are OFF, and all other ground power switches are in AUTO. If cooling air is available, avionics may be on as desired.

1. External power switch - RESET

NOTE

If finger lifts are raised with electrical power on the aircraft and engine master switches ON, an engine will engage without command as the JFS starts.

2. Holding brake - ON
3. (BOTH) MPD's/MPCD's/HUD - ON (if cooling air available)
4. Fire extinguisher switch - TEST
5. (BOTH) Warning and caution lights - TEST

JFS START

1. Engine master switches - CHECK ON
2. JFS switch - CHECK ON
3. JFS handle - PULL AND RELEASE

WARNING

If the JFS does not start, the starter switch should be placed OFF. Wait 30 seconds after cycling the switch to allow the start sequence relay to disengage and the JFS to decelerate before trying a second start. Failure to wait 30 seconds may result in a JFS no start.

4. JFS READY light - ON (within 10 seconds)

ENGINE START

1. Right throttle finger lift - RAISE AND RELEASE
2. Right throttle - IDLE (18% N2)
3. (BOTH) Engine instruments - CHECK
4. JFS deceleration - CONFIRM
5. External power - DISCONNECT
6. EMER BST ON and BST SYS MAL cautions - OBSERVE ON

The EMER BST ON caution does not come on with external power applied. When external power is disconnected the EMER BST ON caution and BST SYS MAL caution come on immediately. This condition is normal and both lights will go out after the second main generator comes on the line. To check the emergency generator/emergency boost pump system, cycle the emergency generator switch to MAN and then back to AUTO. The BST SYS MAL caution goes off and the EMER BST ON caution remains on while the switch is in MAN.

7. Left engine - START (steps 1 thru 3)
8. JFS - CONFIRM OFF; JFS SWITCH ON
9. ECS - CHECK Ensure ECS caution is off and airflow is present.
10. Inlet ramp switches - CHECK AUTO
11. Engine anti-ice switch - AS REQUIRED
12. Engine control switches - CYCLE (engine and ENG CONTR cautions OFF)

Confirm nozzle operation with the ground crew

BEFORE TAXI

1. Continue with normal procedures.

SCRAMBLE

AIRCRAFT SETUP

NOTE

All aircraft maintenance, loading of fuel, weapons and stores should be done prior to performing the INS GC alignment to get the best STOR alignment results.

1. (BOTH) Complete the Before Flight procedures through Before Taxiing.
2. When the INS has aligned in GC (GC OK), INS mode knob - OFF. If the aircraft is not moved the INS is ready for a stored heading alignment.
3. (BOTH) Do Engine Shutdown procedure.

NOTE

Leave UHF radio and individual displays on.

4. (BOTH) Ejection controls safety lever - LOCKED
5. Avionics switches - ON (EXCEPT RADAR and INS)
6. Pitot Heat - ON
7. Do not move the aircraft.

If these actions have not been accomplished, use normal prodecures.

JFS/ENGINE START

1. Use normal procedures.

BEFORE TAXIING

1. (BOTH) Multi purpose display switches - ON
2. INS mode knob - STORE

Best INS performance is obtained by selecting NAV immediately after SH OK is displayed. However if PP is not correct or 'GC PP REQ' is displayed on HUD, a full GC alignment is required.

3. Present position - CHECK
4. For GC alignment, enter PP and perform full GC alignment (approximately 4 minutes)
5. (BOTH) Communications and navigation equipment - CHECK
6. Radar - ON
7. (BOTH) Altimeters - SET AND CHECK
8. CAS - RESET
9. For SH alignment, INS mode selector knob - NAV (SH OK)
10. (BOTH) Flight controls - CHECK FREE
11. (BOTH) Flaps - CHECK DOWN
12. (BOTH) IFF - AS REQUIRED
13. T/O trim - CHECK
    If the aircraft is manually trimmed nose down from takeoff trim, nosewheel lift-off speed may be increased.
14. (BOTH) Standby attitude indicator - UNCAGE
15. (BOTH) Canopy - CLOSE, WAIT 10 SEC, THEN LOCK
    The canopy may bounce slightly as it lowers on canopy sill.

CAUTION

Ensure canopy has completed movement and wait 10 seconds before moving handle to LOCKED position. If there is heavy load when attempting to place the handle in LOCKED, recycle handle to DN and again perform locking procedure. Ensure canopy unlock light is on with handle DN and goes out with handle LOCKED. Ensure the handle is full forward.

16. (BOTH) Warnings, cautions, BIT lights, and circuit breakers - CHECK
17. (BOTH) Personal equipment and harness - CHECK
18. (BOTH) Weapons - CHECK

19. If NAV not selected in step 9, INS mode selector knob - NAV (GC OK in approximately 4 minutes)

BEFORE TAKEOFF

1. (BOTH) Ejection controls safety lever - ARMED

QUICK TURN (BOTH)

1. After landing checks - COMPLETE
2. Communication with groundcrew - ESTABLISH (if required)

3. Engine shutdown - COMPLETE (if required)

4. Aircraft setup - COMPLETE (if required)

5. Consider cumulative brake heating effect.

WARNING

After an abort or full stop taxi back landing, consider the cumulative heating effect on the brakes in the event the second takeoff results in an abort.

SECTION III

EMERGENCY PROCEDURES AND ABNORMAL OPERATION

TABLE OF CONTENTS

STARTING
AMAD Fire During Start 3-2A
JFS READY Light Does Not Come On 3-2A
JFS Fails to Engage or Abnormal
    Engagement/Disengagement 3-2A
Emergency Generator Not On
    Line On Start 3-3
Abnormal Engine Start 3-3
GROUND OPERATION
ECS MALFUNCTIONS 3-4
Display FLOW LOW Caution 3-5
INS Problems 3-5
Brake Overheat 3-5
Loss Of Brakes 3-5
Loss of Directional Control 3-6
Cabin Pressurization Malfunction 3-6
Ground Egress 3-7
TAKEOFF
Abort 3-7
External Stores Jettison 3-7
Engine Failure On Takeoff 3-8
Asymmetric Thrust Departure
    Prevention System 3-8
Afterburner Failure 3-8
Engine Fire On Takeoff 3-9
Pitch Ratio Failure 3-9
Tire Failure During Takeoff 3-9
Landing Gear Fails To Retract 3-9
INFLIGHT
Out-Of-Control Recovery 3-9
Ejection 3-10
Engine Stall/Stagnation 3-11
Single Engine Operation 3-12
Double Engine Stall/Stagnation/Failure 3-12
Restart (-220 engines) 3-13
Restart (-229 engines) 3-14
JFS Assisted Restart 3-15
Air Inlet System Malfunction 3-17
Engine Control Malfunction (-220 engines) ...3-17
Engine Control Malfunction (-229 engines) ...3-17
Nozzle Failure 3-18
Engine Fire Inflight 3-18

Afterburner Burn Thru 3-19
AMAD Fire Inflight 3-19
Smoke, Fumes, Or Fire In Cockpit 3-19
Canopy Unlocked Inflight/Loss
    of Canopy 3-20
Extreme Cockpit Temperature 3-20
Bleed Air Caution 3-20
ECS Caution 3-20
Asymmetric Thrust Departure
    Prevention (ATDP) System Caution 3-20A
Oxygen Caution 3-20A
Display Flow Low Caution 3-20B
Oil System Malfunction 3-20B
EMER BST ON And/Or BST SYS
    MAL Caution 3-20B
Fuel Boost Pumps Inoperative 3-20B
Fuel Transfer System Malfunction 3-20C
Uncommanded Fuel Venting 3-22
Inflight Fuel Leak 3-22
Generator Failure 3-23
Double Generator Failure 3-23
AMAD Failure 3-24
Runaway Trim 3-24
Flight Control System Malfunction 3-24
LAT STK LMT Caution 3-25
Speed Brake Failure 3-26
Boarding Steps Extended 3-26
ADC Failure 3-26
INS Failure 3-26
Heading Error 3-27
Central Computer Failure 3-28
Avionics Interface Unit Failure 3-29
Lantirn Overtemperature Condition 3-29
Multipurpose Display
    Processor (MPDP) Failure 3-30
LANDING
Controllability Check 3-30
Single-Engine Operation 3-30
Flap Malfunctions 3-31
Blown Tires 3-31
Anti-Skid Malfunction 3-31
Hydraulic Failure 3-32
Landing Gear Unsafe 3-32
Landing Gear Emergency Extension 3-34

Landing with Abnormal Gear
    Configuration 3-35
Approach-End Arrestment...................................3-35

Departure-End Arrestment.....................................3-35

This section covers the operation of the aircraft during emergency/abnormal conditions. It includes a discussion of problem indications and corrective actions as well as procedural steps when applicable. Adherence to these guidelines will insure maximum safety for the aircrew and/or aircraft. The situations covered are representative of the most probable malfunctions. However, multiple emergencies, weather or other factors, may require modification of the recommended procedures. Accomplish only those steps required to correct or manage the problem. When dealing with emergency/abnormal conditions, it is essential that you determine the most correct course of action using sound judgment, common sense and a full understanding of the applicable system(s). When practical, advise other concerned agencies (i.e., flight lead, tower, etc.) of the problem and intended course of action. The following rules are basic to all emergency/abnormal conditions. You should thoroughly understand and apply them.

1. MAINTAIN AIRCRAFT CONTROL
2. ANALYZE THE SITUATION AND TAKE THE PROPER ACTION
3. LAND AS SOON AS PRACTICABLE

During any inflight emergency, when structural damage or any other failure is known or suspected that may adversely affect aircraft handling characteristics, perform a Controllability Check.

Retain the canopy during all emergencies that could result in crash or fire such as crash landing, aborted takeoff, or arresting gear engagement. The protection the canopy affords you during such emergencies far outweighs the isolated risk of entrapment due to canopy malfunction or overturn. During ground egress, consider normal canopy opening procedures first to preclude the possibility of a static seat ejection.

STARTING

AMAD FIRE DURING START

AMAD fire may be recognized by illumination of the AMAD fire light, voice warning "Warning, AMAD Fire," or by ground crew notification. Extinguisher actuation will discharge the fire extinguisher into the AMAD compartment and automatically shut down the JFS. If this action does not suffice, ground fire extinguishers may be required. If fire light is on (steady light):

1. AMAD light - PUSH
2. Fire extinguisher - DISCHARGE
3. Throttles - OFF

JFS READY LIGHT DOES NOT COME ON

If the JFS ready light does not come on within 10 seconds, and -

    a. The JFS sounds normal.
    b. The AMAD fire light tests normally, then the JFS light is inoperative, and the start may be continued (The JFS READY light is required to monitor inflight JFS air start).

If the above cues are not present or JFS did not start on the first accumulator:

    a. JFS switch - CYCLE

    b. Have ground crew check JFS system.

If no abnormality is found and 30 seconds has elapsed, another JFS start may be attempted.

JFS FAILS TO ENGAGE OR ABNORMAL ENGAGEMENT/DISENGAGEMENT

Failure to engage is indicated by no decrease in JFS whine after the fingerlift is raised. This may be caused by the throttle not being full off, dirty switch contacts, master switch not on, an electrical malfunction, or low CGB servicing. If the normal starting sequence has been interrupted (one engine shut down for some reason), it may be necessary to cycle the engine master switch to reset the control circuits. Once the JFS has engaged (JFS whine decreased), any abnormal sound or other indication requires immediate JFS shutdown. These can include no JFS whine increase, no engine rotation, rpm hangup, or JFS disengagement. If the JFS fails to decelerate after either engine start, shut down the JFS and both engines. This may indicate AMAD lubrication pump failure.

If JFS fails to engage -

1. Throttle - ENSURE FULL OFF

2. Engine master switch - CYCLE
3. Fingerlift - RAISE AND RELEASE

If still no engagement -

4. Engine master switch - OFF
5. Do not attempt another start

If engagement/disengagement is abnormal -

1. Throttle - OFF
2. Engine master switch - OFF
3. JFS switch - OFF
4. Do not attempt another start

EMERGENCY GENERATOR NOT ON LINE ON START

On internal power starts, the emergency generator should come on line within 30 seconds after raising fingerlift for first engine start. This is indicated by an increasing rpm indication on the engine monitor display. The emergency generator does not power the emergency boost pump during first engine start; therefore, the EMER BST ON caution will not illuminate until the first main generator comes on line. The emergency generator should remain on the line for 30 seconds after the first main generator is on line. There is a remote possibility of the emergency generator dropping off line prematurely. If this occurs before a main generator comes on line, the rpm and FTIT indications go blank. Regard a BST SYS MAL caution less than 30 seconds after the first main generator comes on line as an indication that the emergency generator has dropped off line prematurely.

If emergency generator not on line 30 seconds after raising fingerlift -

1. Emergency generator switch - CYCLE THRU ISOLATE

If emergency generator still does not come on line -

2. Engine master switches - OFF
3. JFS - OFF
4. Abort

If emergency generator prematurely drops off line -

1. Throttle(s) - OFF

2. Engine master switch(es) - OFF
   Have maintenance investigate malfunction

ABNORMAL ENGINE START

ENGINE FAILS TO START

If no indication of light - off 30 seconds (-220 engines) or 20 seconds (-229 engines) after throttle advanced to IDLE -

1. Throttle - OFF

If another start attempt desired -

2. Engine - WINDMILL FOR 10 SECONDS
3. Throttle - IDLE

If another start attempt not desired -

2. Engine master switch - OFF
3. JFS - OFF
4. Complete engine shutdown procedure

ENGINE FAILS TO ACCELERATE NORMALLY

If both rpm and FTIT appear to stop increasing during the start sequence -

1. Throttle - OFF
2. Engine master switch - OFF
3. JFS switch - OFF
4. Complete engine shutdown procedure

AUTO-ACCELERATION ABOVE IDLE

If auto-acceleration occurs, place the throttle OFF, press the ENG FIRE PUSH light and place the engine master switch OFF.

HOT START

If one of the following conditions occur during engine start, the starting FTIT limit of 680°C may be exceeded:
- Rpm acceleration simultaneous with or after initial FTIT movement.
- FTIT above 500°C with rpm below 40%
- FTIT rises rapidly thru 580°C
- Rpm stops increasing then decreases while FTIT is stable or increases.

If starting FTIT is exceeded, allowing the engine to windmill after shutdown will assist cooling.

1. Throttle - OFF

If FTIT starting limit not exceeded -

   2. Engine - WINDMILL (10 seconds after FTIT indicates 200°C).
     The JFS can be engaged when rpm is below 30%.
   3. Air source knob - SELECT ENGINE TO BE STARTED
   4. Throttle - IDLE
   5. Air source knob - BOTH (idle rpm)

If FTIT exceeded starting limit -

   2. Engine - WINDMILL (if practical)
   3. Engine master switch - OFF

   4. JFS switch - OFF
   5. Complete engine shutdown procedure

ENGINE FIRE DURING START

   1. Fire warning light - PUSH

If warning light remains on -

   2. Throttle - OFF
   3. Fire extinguisher - DISCHARGE
   4. JFS switch - OFF

GROUND OPERATION

ECS MALFUNCTIONS

DUAL ENGINE OPERATION (ECS CAUTION ON)

An ECS caution during engine ground operation is an abnormal condition. Make sure that the cockpit temperature control switch is in the AUTO position and that the air source knob is at BOTH. If the caution remains on, the ECS is not operating properly and avionics may suffer heat damage. Shutting down either engine will provide automatic avionics shutdown to protect the avionics equipment from overheat. In the event the automatic avionics shutdown does not occur, turning off all avionics except UHF will protect this equipment.

   1. Temperature Control Switch - AUTO
   2. Air Source Knob - BOTH

If the ECS caution remains on after 2 minutes -

   3. Either throttle - OFF

Automatic avionics shutdown will occur at this time -

   4. Abort Mission

If automatic avionics shutdown does not occur -

   5. Avionics (except UHF) - OFF
   6. Remaining engine - SHUTDOWN (as soon as practical)

SINGLE ENGINE OPERATION (AUTOMATIC AVIONICS SHUTDOWN)

During single engine operation inadequate avionics cooling airflow is possible. When inadequate cooling is detected, an immediate automatic avionics shutdown occurs. The only indication of this condition will be blank displays.

Automatic avionics shutdown disables the following avionics:
- HUD
- RMR
- MPDP
- RADAR
- ADC
- JTIDS (when available)
- EWWS
- AIU #1
- AFCS Flight Control Computer
- ILS
- CC
- IBS
- PACS
- RWR Low Band Receiver/Processor
- RWR Power Supply
- AHRS
- Left and Right Air Inlet Controller
- VTRS
- UHF #1
- MPDs
- MPCDs

The MASTER CAUTION light and major category light are shutdown as a result of the automatic avionics shutdown of AIU #1.

Advancing the throttle to increase single engine rpm to 73% should provide adequate airflow to avionics and normal avionics operation will resume in two minutes. If normal operation does not resume, it may be necessary to start the second engine.

1. Single engine rpm - INCREASE (to 73%)

If avionics remain shutdown after two minutes -

2. Abort mission

DISPLAY FLOW LOW CAUTION

During dual engine operation, a Display Flow Low caution is an abnormal condition and indicates low cooling air flow to the cockpit displays. Turning off all non-essential displays will help protect them from heat damage.

During single engine operation, a slight increase in rpm above idle (to 73%) may be required to extinguish the light with ECS operating normally

1. Non-essential displays - OFF
2. Abort Mission

INS PROBLEMS

EXCESSIVE GROUNDSPEED/POSITION ERROR

If groundspeed and present position/update errors are excessive prior to take-off, another alignment may be attempted. Generally, groundspeed error of 6 knots or more, and/or positional error of 2 miles or more, are considered excessive for normal operations. Lesser errors may be considered excessive for certain missions. The INS should be off for at least 5 seconds prior to another alignment. Allow the INS to remain in the GC mode as long as possible. If possible, monitor the ground speed and present position for at least one minute to assess accuracy.

BRAKE OVERHEAT

Brake overheat occurs whenever the kinetic energy absorbed by either the right or left wheel brake exceeds 23 million foot pounds. Depending on the severity of the stop, brake energies in excess of this

limit can result in tire deflation and fire. Tire deflation due to wheel thermal fuse plug activation generally occurs within 20 minutes of initial brake application. Fires are usually fueled by wheel and brake contaminates and easily extinguished; however, if extreme overheat occurs (brake energies in excess of 48 million foot pounds), hydraulic fluid fires are a possibility due to the deterioration of seals within the brake assembly. Brake overheat should be considered: when brakes are applied at speeds in excess of 100 knots, when brakes are dragging during taxi, or when successive stops from airspeeds in excess of normal taxi speeds are made within one hour of each other. Refer to Section V, figure 5-3, for brake energy determination. If brake overheat is suspected:

1. Notify tower that brake overheat exists.
2. Taxi aircraft to closest safe location
   Use brakes only as needed to stop or turn.
3. Turn aircraft into the wind.
4. Wheels - CHOCKED
5. Brakes - RELEASE
6. Shutdown engines after firefighting equipment arrives.

WARNING

Fuel draining overboard after engine shutdown can contact a hot wheel and cause a fire. Engine shutdown before arrival of firefighting equipment should be avoided when hot brakes exist.

7. If necessary to egress aircraft, move away from aircraft along nose line.

WARNING

When hot brakes exist, stay clear of an area extending at least 300 feet in a 45° cone around the axle on both sides of the wheel until brakes have cooled or until thermal release plugs have deflated the tires.

LOSS OF BRAKES

Loss of normal brakes may be caused by a defective anti-skid system, faulty brakes, improper strut servicing (causing loss of WOW signal) or UTL A hydraulic pressure loss. Malfunction of the anti-skid system may not illuminate the anti-skid light, however, failures may be recognized by no apparent braking action. In any case, it is important to remember when assessing the status of brakes, that very little deceleration will be sensed by the pilot at speeds above 100 knots regardless of whether the anti-skid system has failed. Therefore, aerodynamic braking should be accomplished first during the landing roll, followed by braking action as required. If loss of brakes is determined, turn the anti-skid switch to PULSER at high speed or OFF at taxi speed. If braking is not restored, pulling the emergency brake/steering handle provides an alternate power source for brakes/steering and bypasses the anti-skid/pulser system. Sufficient accumulator pressure is available to safely stop the aircraft. Repeated brake applications deplete the system faster than a smooth steady application. If UTL B is operating, the JFS accumulator will remain charged. If the JFS LOW caution is on, the emergency brake system is not reliable for taxi since accumulator pressure can no longer be monitored. Do not pull the emergency brake/steering handle in flight as the nosewheel will follow rudder commands, and touchdown protection is lost. If UTL A is available normal operation can be restored by pushing in the emergency brake/steering handle and releasing the paddle switch. When brake failure occurs during landing roll, consider lowering the tail hook before attempting to restore braking. While taxiing, if stopping distance is critical, use the emergency brake/steering handle first.

If loss of brakes occurs -

1. Brakes - RELEASE
2. Anti-skid switch - OFF OR PULSER (as required)
3. Brakes - REAPPLY
   Place the anti-skid switch to OFF at taxi speed.

If braking is not restored -

4. Brakes - RELEASE
   Completely remove both feet from brake pedals.
5. Emergency brake/steering handle - PULL
   Pulling the emergency brake above 70 knots increases the possibility of blown tires.
6. Paddle switch - HOLD PRESSED
   Holding the paddle switch pressed will ensure that the nose gear steering shifts to the JFS accumulator pressure.

7. Brakes - REAPPLY
   To avoid blowing tires, light brake pedal pressure should be applied initially to develop a feel for effective braking.

LOSS OF DIRECTIONAL CONTROL

Directional control problems with the nose gear on the ground may be caused by a blown tire, nose gear shimmy, defective nose gear steering, defective anti-skid, overextended strut, or a faulty brake. For a known blown tire or brake loss refer to the appropriate emergency procedure. If the cause of the directional control problem cannot be determined, time spent in fault isolation may worsen the situation. In this case, a single procedure (pulling the emergency brake/steering handle) is recommended. Use of this procedure, provides an alternate source for powered braking/steering and disables the anti-skid and pulser system(s), thereby accommodating all of the various failure modes which may have caused the directional control problem.

1. Brakes - RELEASE
2. Emergency brake/steer handle - PULL
   Because the anti-skid has been removed, be prepared for a possible wheel lockup and a subsequent blown tire(s).
3. Paddle switch - HOLD PRESSED
   This ensures that the nose gear steering will shift to JFS hydraulic accumulator pressure.

If departing a prepared surface -

4. Throttles - OFF (conditions permitting)

CABIN PRESSURIZATION MALFUNCTION

Cabin pressurization malfunctions may be detected by discomfort in the ears and can be verified by the cabin pressure altimeter. On the ground, if the cabin pressure altimeter does not agree with the actual field elevation perform the following before opening the canopy:

1. Emergency vent handle - TURN

{CAUTION}

If the cockpit pressure altitude is lower than actual field elevation, the canopy may separate from the aircraft if the canopy is opened before cockpit pressure is dumped.

GROUND EGRESS

| WARNING |

Crew members must coordinate the type of escape to be used before initiating ground egress or ejection.

If time is extremely critical, consider ground ejection. The emergency evacuation procedures are identical to normal egress. Exercise care to avoid catching personal equipment on the canopy rail hooks. If canopy jettison is required, remain in the seat to minimize possibility of injury as the canopy departs. The boarding ladder may be extended by foot pressure on a button inside the upper foot well. Although other egress means are available, depending on the urgency

and critical nature of the situation, egress via the boarding ladder is the safest method. The fastest egress is made by hanging from the canopy rail and dropping. Egress by this method may result in injury.

1. Ejection controls safety lever - LOCKED
2. Shoulder harness - RELEASE
3. Lap belt - RELEASE
4. Survival kit straps - RELEASE
5. G-suit - DISCONNECT

After TO 1F-15E-602, if Aircrew Eye/Respiratory Protection is worn -

6. AQD - REMOVE
7. Canopy - OPEN

NOTE

The canopy may not depart the aircraft if it is jettisoned with the canopy unlocked.

If manual canopy operation is required -

8. Canopy control handle - UP
9. Canopy - PUSH

TAKEOFF

ABORT

The decision to abort or continue takeoff depends on many factors, most of which relate to a specific takeoff situation. Considerations should include, but are not limited to, the following:

a. Runway factors: Runway remaining, surface condition (wet, dry, etc.), type and/or number of arresting gear available, obstructions alongside or at the departure end, wind direction and velocity, weather and visibility.

b. Aircraft factors: Weight, stores aboard, nature of the emergency, velocity at decision point, and importance of getting airborne.

c. Stopping factors: Maximum braking (see Minimum Run Landing, section II), speed brake, hook, jettisoning stores, engine shutdown.

Consider aborting after airborne where sufficient runway is available. Normally, with the short takeoff distances of the aircraft, abort is not a problem, but early decision will provide the most favorable circumstances.

1. Throttles - IDLE
2. Brakes - APPLY
   If aborting with a blown main tire or if a main tire blows during abort, place the antiskid switch to PULSER and use braking on the good tire.
3. Hook - AS REQUIRED

If hot brakes are suspected -

4. Use Brake Overheat procedure.

EXTERNAL STORES JETTISON

Two means exist to jettison external stores: the emergency jettison button on the center of the front instrument panel and the select jettison knob/button on the armament control panel in the front cockpit.

WARNING

- The emergency jettison button jettisons pylons on stations 2, 5, and 8 and all CFT stores (air-to-air and air-to-ground). When airborne, the possibility exists of wing station missile/store/pylon collision with CFT mounted stores and subsequent missile/store/pylon collision with the aircraft. Ground jettisoning may result in the store/pylon striking the ground before the pylon aft pivots release. Under these conditions, the wing mounted pylon stores will probably rotate horizontally, and will strike the landing gear if the rotation is in that direction. The centerline pylon will almost certainly strike the landing gear.

- Air-to-ground stores on CFT stations must be jettisoned before air-to-ground stores on wing stations to ensure safe separation.

CAUTION

If centerline or inboard release is required with the landing gear down, damage may occur to the aircraft.

Do not use emergency jettison on the ground, or with AIM-7 missiles aboard, except as a last resort or in extreme emergency. For complete selective jettison procedures, refer to stores jettison systems, section I, and combat jettison programming, section II.

ENGINE FAILURE ON TAKEOFF

Depending on the type of failure and aircraft conditions, MIL power may be sufficient to sustain flight. The aircraft accelerates better at a reduced AOA. If afterburner is required, use only that necessary to maintain safe flight.

If decision is made to continue takeoff, input one-half aft stick at the rotation speed for continued takeoff found in figure A3-10 (-220 engines with CFTs) or figure A3-11 (-220 engines without CFTs) or figure

B3-10 (-229 engines with CFTs) or figure B3-11 (-229 engines without CFTs) and rotate to a 10° pitch attitude. Delaying rotation in this way results in increased single engine rate of climb at takeoff. With CFTs, figures A3-12 thru A3-16 (-220 engines) or figures B3-12 thru B3-16 (-229 engines) should also be checked to determine if adequate single engine rate of climb is available at this takeoff speed. If available runway permits, the takeoff speed may be increased somewhat by delaying rotation until either runway limitations or tire limit speeds dictate rotation. This will result in correspondingly increased ground roll distance.

If takeoff is continued -

1. Throttle(s) - AS REQUIRED
2. Climb to a safe altitude and investigate

ASYMMETRIC THRUST DEPARTURE PREVENTION SYSTEM (ATDPS) FAILURE (F-15E 90-0233 AND UP) (-229 engines)

When the ATDP caution is ON, loss of augmentor or transfers to secondary mode on one engine can result in a sudden loss of thrust on both engines. Refer to Engine Control Malfunction.

AFTERBURNER FAILURE

The engine has an automatic afterburner recycle capability using the light-off detector. If the afterburner does not light satisfactorily or a blowout occurs, the DEEC will automatically resequence the afterburner ignition system a maximum of three times in approximately 12 seconds providing the throttle remains above MIL. If the afterburner does not light during these attempts, the throttle must be retarded to MIL or below before further attempting to light the afterburner.

If the ENG CONTR caution is on, afterburner operation may be prevented or may be limited to only the first and second segment. If the DEEC has transferred to secondary mode, afterburner operation is prevented and approximately 80 to 85% of MIL thrust is available. Cycling the engine control switch may return the engine to normal operation. The engine control switch may be cycled ON-OFF-ON at MIL or below. If the ENG CONTR caution goes off, the engine will operate normally. However, if there is

All data on pages 3-8A and 3-8B deleted.

a malfunction in the afterburner control, the ENG CONTR caution may come on again when afterburner is reselected. Refer to Engine Control Malfunction, page 3-13.

ENGINE FIRE ON TAKEOFF

If you decide to abort -

1. Fire warning light - PUSH

If warning light remains on -

2. Throttle - OFF
3. Fire extinguisher - DISCHARGE

If you decide to continue -

1. Climb to safe altitude and follow Engine Fire Inflight procedures

PITCH RATIO FAILURE

If takeoff is made with the CAS ON, it is unlikely that pitch ratio failure will cause any control difficulty, and takeoff may be continued. The PITCH RATIO caution may be the only noticeable indication of failure. However, if the failure occurs with CAS OFF, longitudinal stick forces may be considerably higher than normal, and late nosewheel liftoff will likely result. In this case, aborting the takeoff is preferred if

conditions permit. If takeoff is continued with CAS OFF, maneuver conservatively since the ARI is inoperative.

TIRE FAILURE DURING TAKEOFF

Tire failure is very difficult to recognize and may not be noticed in the cockpit. If a failure is suspected, or confirmed, and:

If takeoff is discontinued -

1. Abort
2. Anti-skid - PULSER

If takeoff is continued -

1. Gear - DO NOT RETRACT
2. Follow Blown Tires procedure

LANDING GEAR FAILS TO RETRACT

If the warning light in the landing gear handle stays on after the handle is placed up or comes on in flight, the gear or gear doors are not correctly sequenced. Reduce airspeed below 250 knots, check landing gear circuit breaker in, and lower the gear. If the gear comes down normally, attempt another retraction. If the light is still illuminated, lower the gear, reduce weight, and land.

INFLIGHT

OUT-OF-CONTROL RECOVERY

The aircraft is out of control when it does not properly respond to aircrew flight control inputs. An example of this is attempting to perform a slow speed, nose high reversal in one direction and the aircraft will not roll in that direction. An out-of-control situation will progress to a departure if the situation is not corrected by smoothly neutralizing controls to reduce AOA or yaw rate. A departure is characterized by an uncommanded flight path change such as a nose slice, roll away from a lateral input, or excessive yaw rates. The departure warning tone may sound indicating high yaw rate and is the best indication of an impending spin. If a continuous warning tone is heard and the controls are not neutral, it is imperative that the controls be neutralized immediately in a smooth

manner. This action should recover the aircraft from all departures.

Abrupt neutralization of longitudinal controls while out-of-control or in a departure, where high yaw rates are present, may aggravate the situation and induce a spin. Releasing all rudder and stick pressure (hands off) once the controls are at or near neutral will result in neutral controls if trimmed near 1g.

If the controls are not neutralized at the first indication of departure or when the departure warning tone begins, a spin may develop. Spins are typified by a high yaw rate accompanied by a high rate departure warning tone. The turn needle will be steady and fully deflected in the direction of spin. For recovery from a positive g spin, maintain neutral longitudinal stick and apply full lateral stick with the yaw the same direction as the turn needle. Rudder is not needed but, if used, must be against the yaw, opposite the direction of the turn needle. Neutralize all controls when the aircraft recovers from the spin and allow large residual motion to subside. Spin recovery is indicated by departure warning tone stopping, sustained nose low attitude, increasing airspeed, and AOA decreasing from greater than 45 units.

An auto-roll is a rudder roll caused by rudder deflections with neutral cockpit controls. The aircraft may slowly self-recover; however, for a rapid recovery from a positive g auto-roll, apply full rudder against the roll. Do not use aileron to stop the roll as this input may induce a spin. If unsure of the roll direction, use the ADI to determining roll direction. Do not use the turn needle as it oscillates during rolls. The departure warning tone may not sound. Neutral controls will recover the aircraft from all negative g conditions including spins and auto-rolls; however, rudder with the roll will produce a faster recovery from a negative g auto-roll.

Do not move the throttles unless in afterburner. If in afterburner, reduce power to MIL.

1. Controls - SMOOTHLY NEUTRALIZE AND RELEASE

Abrupt neutralization of longitudinal control during a departure where high roll and yaw rates are present may temporarily aggravate the out-of-control situation and induce a spin. If controls are neutralized at the first indication of departure (large uncommanded roll or yaw), the aircraft will recover quickly. Opposite rudder may be used to counter roll rates; however, lateral stick inputs should be avoided.

If aircraft is not recovering, an auto roll is possible -

2. Rudder - OPPOSITE ROLL

WARNING

Aileron against the roll can induce a spin.

If aircraft is still not recovering, an upright spin is most probable -

3. Longitudinal stick - CENTERED
4. Lateral Stick - FULL IN DIRECTION OF YAW (turn needle)
5. Aircraft recovers (tone ceases) - CONTROLS NEUTRAL

WARNING

If the departure warning tone malfunctions (i.e., yaw rate gyro failure) and stops prior to 30 degrees per second, neutralizing controls may result in yaw acceleration and a redeveloped spin. Use other indications of spin recovery in conjunction with the departure warning tone.

If recovery is not apparent by 10,000 feet AGL -

6. Eject

EJECTION

Ejection can be accomplished at ground level between zero and 600 knots airspeed with wings level and no sink rate. Appreciable forces are exerted on the body when ejection is performed at airspeeds above 450 knots. Above 600 knots, ejection is extremely hazardous due to excessive wind blast forces. The seat will not fire unless the canopy has separated. Ground ejection cannot be accomplished unless the canopy is down and locked or has been jettisoned previously. After TO 1F-15E-552 the seat, whether in flight or on the ground, will fire regardless of canopy position (full open to full closed) and will fire through the canopy if the canopy fails to separate. Basic procedures are shown in figure 3-7. Minimum ejection altitudes for various flight conditions and attitudes are shown in the ejection seat performance charts in the foldout section.

● Time and circumstances permitting, the pilot will make the decision to eject.

● Time and circumstances permitting, the pilot will alert the WSO to prepare for ejection and then direct individual ejections or initiate ejection for both crewmembers, as briefed.

● WSO initiated ejection of the pilot shall be limited to emergency/combat situations when so directed by the pilot or when the pilot is incapacitated. The pilot should consider the experience level of the WSO, the degree of training/proficiency, and meticulously brief on ejection signals (ICS and visual) and the exact circumstances under which the WSO will eject the crew.

- The above procedure in no way precludes either occupant from initiating ejection at any time he determines that circumstances warrant such action.

WARNING

- If dual ejection is initiated without alerting the other crewmember, incapacitation on ejection may occur due to improper body position.
- If fire/smoke is the cause for ejection, a dual ejection should be made. Individual ejection by the WSO could incapacitate the pilot from intense heat and fire caused by windblast and draft effects of a jettisoned canopy.

1. Ejection handle(s) - PULL (make every attempt to pull both handles)

ENGINE STALL/STAGNATION

Engine stalls are the result of a disruption of airflow across one or more fan/compressor blades. Although many conditions affect compressor airflow (i.e., aircraft maneuvering, ice, DEEC, afterburner backpressure, etc.) most will not exceed the designed stall margin of the engine. On F-15E 90-0233 AND UP (-229 engines), the IDEEC includes logic to detect and automatically recover most engine stalls without pilot action.

The fan bypass duct provides a convenient passage for pressure disturbances created in the afterburner section to travel directly forward to the fan/compressor. If the engine nozzle does not position properly when operating the afterburner, pressure pulses can be transmitted forward to the fan/compressor causing the blade to exceed the stall limit. Hence, most stalls will be associated with use of the afterburner. High altitude/slow flight and maneuvering all increase the sensitivity to stall because they increase airflow disturbances to the face of the engine. On F-15E 90-0233 AND UP (-229 engines, cycling the control mode switch (PRI to SEC or SEC to PRI),particularly during throttle transients or high altitude/idle power operation, may cause stalls.

If the fan/compressor stall does not self-clear, the disturbed airflow will propagate through the compressor, resulting in a stagnation. Unstable burning then occurs in the combustion chamber causing

higher than normal temperatures and rpm decreasing to sub-idle (less than 60%). To clear this condition, the engine must be shutdown and restarted. Stalls normally produce an audible pop, bang, or thud, but may occur without audible warning. Engine instruments may not indicate anything unusual, but rpm rollback, increased FTIT and nozzle opening may be noted for more severe stalls at MIL and above. Generally, the stall will be self-clearing; however, quickly retarding the throttle to MIL (IDLE if non-afterburner stall) will aid recovery. If a stagnation develops, it will be characterized by rising FTIT and decreasing rpm with no change in throttle position. FTIT may exceed 1000°C (-220 engines) or 1070°C (-229 engines) or stabilize at some lower level. FTIT above 1000°C (-220 engines) or 1070°C (-229 engines) will result in engine damage. To prevent catastrophic engine damage, immediate corrective action should be taken. It is possible that a stagnated engine may also display a fire plume trailing the aircraft if the throttle is not placed to OFF. This plume may persist until the throttle is placed to OFF and the stagnation cleared. A GEN OUT caution and EMER BST ON caution may be the first indication of engine stagnation. With a single engine stagnation and no other anomaly, the GEN OUT and EMER BST ON should be the only cautions on before engine shutdown. If altitude permits, immediately lower the nose to maintain 350 knots. Post stagnation engine operation is keyed to FTIT. If 1000°C (-220 engines) or 1107°C (-229 engines)was not exceeded, normal engine operating limits apply. If 1000° was exceeded, the engine may be started to provide redundant hydraulic and electric power, but should be left at IDLE unless additional thrust is required to ensure safe recovery. After a stagnation has cleared, engine parameters at MIL will initially be lower until the DEEC can retrim.

SINGLE ENGINE STALL/STAGNATION (-220 engines)

1. Throttle - CHOP TO IDLE (MIL if in AB)
    If afterburner stall does not clear at MIL, chop the throttle to IDLE.

If FTIT continues to rise -

2. Throttle - OFF
3. Perform restart

If FTIT exceeded 1000° -

4. Throttle - LEAVE AT IDLE (if practical)

SINGLE ENGINE STALL/STAGNATION
(-229 engines)

  1. Throttle - CHOP TO IDLE (MIL if in AB)
    If afterburner stall does not clear at MIL, chop the throttle to IDLE.

If RPM is less than 60% with no response to throttle movement, or if FTIT continues to rise -

  2. Throttle - OFF
  3. Perform restart

If engine overtemp warning activated (1107°C) -

  4. Throttle - SET AT 80% RPM OR LESS (if practical)

SINGLE ENGINE OPERATION

If the engine will not start, best cruise may be approximated by a climb at 250 knots until rate of climb stops. Accelerate to 0.6 Mach(-220 engines) or 0.7 Mach (-229 engines) in MIL. Cruise climb as fuel weight decreases.

DOUBLE ENGINE STALL/STAGNATION/FAILURE

Three conditions can cause double engine flameout: all boost pumps inoperative, empty feed tanks or mechanical failure of both engines. If both main boost pumps and the emergency boost pump are not operating, restart is possible only within a severely restricted flight envelope. If altitude permits, immediately lower the nose to maintain 350 knots. Check rpm and FTIT to determine whether the engines are flamed out or stagnated. If the flameouts were caused by temporary fuel starvation, they may restart. If the engines are stagnated, they must be shut down and restarted. Shut down the right engine first unless FTIT exceeds 1000°C (-220 engines) or engine overtemp warning activated (-229 engines). If this occurs, shut down the engine with the lower FTIT.

During a double engine out situation, regardless of airspeed, altitude or cause, attempt a spooldown restart; however, the primary task is to maintain enough hydraulic power for aircraft control while getting at least one engine producing normal power. A single engine at about 18% or both engines at 12%, will provide enough hydraulic power for flight control and emergency generator operation. An airspeed of 350 knots will normally maintain 12% rpm or greater.

At low speed, a momentary steep dive may be required to rapidly attain 350 knots; however, a shallow dive (10° or less) will maintain 350 knots and 12% rpm. Once steady state rpm is established, excessive airspeed/dive angle reduces time available for restart. If sufficient rpm is not maintained to fully power the emergency generator system, the emergency generator output may degrade to powering only the ISOLATE functions. In this case, RPM and FTIT will still be available. If this occurs, increase airspeed to increase engine rpm and cycle the emergency generator switch to ISOLATE and back to MAN to restore full emergency generator power. The JFS, when engaged, will provide sufficient hydraulic power for flight control and emergency generator operation permitting a minimum rate of descent glide at 210 knots.

During a double engine stagnation, allow one engine to remain in stagnation while commencing a restart on the other engine. Prolonged overtemperature increases damage and reduces the probability of successful restart of that engine; therefore, shut down the second engine and commence a restart as soon as a restart is indicated on the first engine.

Eject before losing flight control. Imminent loss of control is indicated by loss of the emergency generator and/or control transients as the first PC system drops to 0.

DOUBLE ENGINE STALL/STAGNATION
(-220 engines)

  1. Both throttles - CHOP TO IDLE (MIL if in AB)
    If afterburner stall does not clear at MIL, chop throttle(s) to IDLE.

If FTIT on both engines continues to rise -

  2. Throttle (right engine) - OFF WHILE ESTABLISHING 350 KNOTS
    If FTIT exceeds 1000°C , shut down engine with lower FTIT.
  3. Perform Restart procedure
    If optimum restart parameters are not met by the time rpm decreases through 30%, place the throttle to midrange regardless of FTIT, airspeed or altitude.
  4. At rpm increase on engine being started or if restart unsuccessful, shut down other engine
  5. Other engine - RESTART

If above restart attempts fail -

    6. JFS assisted restart - PERFORM (if conditions permit)

DOUBLE ENGINE STALL/STAGNATION (-229 engines)

    1. Both throttles - CHOP TO IDLE (MIL if in AB)
        If afterburner stall does not clear at MIL, chop throttle(s) to IDLE.

If RPM on both engines is less than 60% with no response to throttle movement, or FTIT on both engines continues to rise -

    2. Throttle (right engine) - OFF WHILE ESTABLISHING 350 KNOTS
        If FTIT exceeds 1107°C , shut down engine with lower FTIT.
    3. Perform Restart procedure
        If optimum restart parameters are not met by the time rpm decreases through 30%, place the throttle to midrange regardless of FTIT, airspeed or altitude.
    4. At rpm increase on engine being started or if restart unsuccessful, shut down other engine
    5. Other engine - RESTART

If above restart attempts fail -

    6. JFS assisted restart - PERFORM (if conditions permit)

RESTART (-220 engines)

Ignition and fuel are continuously supplied when the throttles are at IDLE or above. If an engine does flameout and auto start does not occur, it is unlikely that a start can be accomplished as cycling the throttles through OFF does not recycle either ignition circuits or fuel flow. Therefore, restarts are generally required only because an engine has been shut down for some reason. Restarts may be made with rpm as low as 12% (fuel flow and/or ignition may not be available below approximately 12%); however, for optimum restart capability, place the throttle in midrange when the following conditions are met: a. RPM between 30% and 50%. b. FTIT below 800°C.

Normally the fastest restart is accomplished by placing the throttle to midrange as rpm unwinds (spooldown restart) rather than waiting for rpm to stabilize (windmill restart), or attempting a JFS assisted

restart. Advancing the throttle at a minimum 30% when rpm is decreasing should allow time for a relight before rpm drops to 12%. There is a high probability of hot starts, hung starts or no lights below 250 knots (primary mode) or 275 knots (secondary mode). If airspeed is insufficient and rpm drops below 12%, airspeeds up to 450 knots may be required to regain 12%.

> **CAUTION**
>
> If the engine rpm is allowed to drop to 0%, it may thermally seize. If this occurs, the engine will not rotate even with high airspeeds or engagement of the JFS. If a restart is planned, maintain engine rpm above 0%.

If the rpm drops below 12%, the DEEC may transfer to and lock up in SEC. A normal SEC mode windmill restart can be made; however, engine control switch cycling (i.e. ON-OFF-ON) will not restore the primary ENG CONTR mode.

Restart indications are practically the same as during ground start. Initially, both rpm and FTIT increase. FTIT may reverse several times, but rpm should continue to increase.

Restart at or near minimum recommended airspeeds above 35,000 feet may be characterized by very slow rpm and FTIT increases and/or fluctuations during engine acceleration to idle. Up to two minutes may be required to achieve a successful restart. During this period there will be no response to throttle movement above idle and the DEEC will inhibit pilot inputs until a stabilized flight idle has been established. If fluctuations occur, the restart can normally be completed without re-initiation by accelerating or decelerating toward 300 knots and/or decreasing altitude.

An unsuccessful restart is indicated by a steady decrease in rpm trend (rpm begins to decrease), or by FTIT increasing through 800°C with rpm hung or decreasing. If either of these conditions occur and a start with the ENG CONTR switch ON is unsuccessful, consider a secondary mode (SEC) start (ENG CONTR switch OFF). If the control system senses a condition which could prevent safe operation in the primary mode, an automatic transfer to SEC will occur and a SEC start will result regardless of the ENG CONTR switch position. The start procedure for either a primary or secondary start is the same; however, a higher airspeed is required for SEC start.

Momentary fluctuations of RPM and FTIT may be observed in SEC mode (typically for less than 10 seconds) during the engine acceleration to idle. Restart time for a SEC start will range from about 30 seconds at sea level to as much as 60 seconds above 30,000 feet.

RESTART (-229 engines)

Ignition and fuel are continuously supplied when the throttles are at IDLE or above. If an engine does flameout and auto start does not occur, it is unlikely that a start can be accomplished as cycling the throttles through OFF does not recycle either ignition circuits or fuel flow. Therefore, restarts are generally required only because an engine has been shut down for some reason. Restarts may be made with rpm as low as 12% (fuel flow and/or ignition may not be available below approximately 12%); however, for optimum restart capability, place the throttle in mid-range when the following conditions are met:

1. RPM between 30% and 50%.
2. FTIT below 800°C.

Normally the fastest restart is accomplished by placing the throttle to midrange as rpm unwinds (spool-down restart) rather than waiting for rpm to stabilize (windmill restart), or attempting a JFS assisted restart. Advancing the throttle at a minimum 30% when rpm is decreasing should allow time for a relight before rpm drops to 12%. There is a high probability of hot starts, hung starts or no lights below 275 knots and at or above 30,000 feet. If airspeed is insufficient and rpm drops below 12%, airspeeds up to 450 knots may be required to regain 12%.

> **CAUTION**
>
> If the engine rpm is allowed to drop to 0%, it may thermally seize. If this occurs, the engine will not rotate even with high airspeeds or engagement of the JFS. If a restart is planned, maintain engine rpm above 0%.

During restart, there will be no response to throttle movement above IDLE and the IDEEC will inhibit pilot inputs until a stabilized flight idle has been established.

Stabilizing or increasing rpm is normally the first indication of light-off during restart. The fuel manifold drain port on the pressurizing and dump valve is capped, resulting in normal light-off time of 5 seconds or less after advancing throttle to mid-range. However, RPM and FTIT turn around are slow, making light-off subtle and difficult to detect. This condition should not be confused with a hung start. For PRI restarts below 30,000 feet .MSL, if light-off is not indicated in 20 seconds, place the throttle to OFF and attempt a restart in SEC.

IDEEC overtemperature protection logic attempts to limit FTIT during start to 870°C, which may result in decreasing, hung or slowly increasing RPM. If a hung start occurs below 30,000 feet MSL (stabilized FTIT 870°C or less, RPM hung and definitely stabilized below 60%), increase airspeed to a maximum of 400 knots/0.9 Mach. If the hung start persists, attempt a restart in SEC.

Above 30,000 feet MSL, the restart should be initiated by moving the throttle to mid-range at 50% RPM regardless of FTIT or airspeed to increase the probability of light-off. If unable to move the throttle to mid-range at 50%, do so at as high an RPM as possible and always by 30%. Obtain 400 knots/0.9 Mach by diving or using the good engine to minimize RPM spooldown rate, and quickly decrease altitude to less than 30,000 feet MSL. If light-off indications are not noted within 20 seconds after advancing the throttle, or if FTIT exceeds 870°C (hot start), move the throttle to OFF and reinitiate a PRI restart. If a hung start occurs (RPM stable with FTIT stable at 870°C or less), keep the throttle at mid-range until below 30,000 feet MSL, then reinitiate a PRI restart.

If the control system senses a condition which could prevent safe operation in the primary mode, an automatic transfer to SEC mode will occur and a SEC start may result regardless of the ENG CONTR switch position. The start procedure for either a primary or secondary start is the same; however, a higher airspeed is required for SEC start.

Windmill restarts at 25,000 feet MSL and above with alternate fuels may result in no lights. If light-off indications are not noted within 20 seconds, move the throttle to OFF, descend and hold airspeed to maintain 12% RPM, and reinitiate the restart when below 25,000 feet MSL.

During a SEC start, 60 to 70 seconds are required for light-off and acceleration to mid-range from the time the throttle is advanced from OFF. If a SEC spooldown restart is initiated below 20,000 feet with RPM in the 40 to 50% range, as much as 30 seconds may be required to see positive RPM response. Do not confuse this slow response with a no-light. Higher altitude/lower RPM (30-40%) SEC spooldown restarts will show normal positive RPM indications within 20 seconds. Restarts initiated at higher RPM in general will typically accelerate slowly in the 40-50% RPM range.

JFS ASSISTED RESTART

JFS airstart capability has been incorporated for assistance in engine restarting. This capability is intended for use when encountering engine stall/stagnations after all other restart options have been attempted or rejected as being impractical. The probability of a successful JFS airstart and engine engagement will be enhanced if the aircraft is within the envelope depicted in figure 3-1. Additionally, the centerline pylon should be jettisoned if at all possible. If the centerline pylon will not jettison, it may be necessary to descend to lower altitudes to achieve a JFS airstart. In all cases, proper consideration to the safe ejection envelope should be made prior to attempting the JFS airstart procedure. During restart attempts, ensure that at least one engine is rotating (even in stagnation) at or above 18% rpm to provide sufficient hydraulic power for the emergency generator and flight controls.

> **WARNING**
>
> When doing a JFS assisted restart, the engine display format on the MPD/MPCD may freeze if power is lost to the DEEC/IDEEC. The EMD will continue to correctly display engine parameters and should be used in this case.

If a JFS assisted restart is desired:

1. Throttle - OFF

2. Centerline pylon - JETTISON (if required)
   If both engines are below minimum rpm for generators (approximately 56%) or both main generators are inoperative, the centerline pylon can only be jettisoned by pressing the emergency jettison button.

3. JFS switch - CHECK ON

After at least one engine is below 40% rpm -

4. JFS handle - PULL AND RELEASE
   Use single accumulator for inflight JFS starts. If both accumulators are discharged simultaneously the JFS may accelerate too rapidly and fail to start.

> **WARNING**
>
> If the JFS does not start, the starter switch should be placed OFF. Wait 30 seconds after cycling the switch to allow the start sequence relay to disengage and the JFS to decelerate before trying a second start. Failure to wait 30 seconds may result in a JFS no start.

5. JFS ready light - CHECK ON (within 10 seconds)

INFLIGHT JFS STARTING ENVELOPE

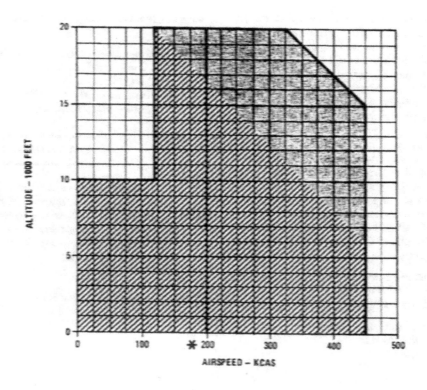

LEGEND

CLEAN CENTERLINE ONLY.

CLEAN CENTERLINE OR CENTERLINE PLYON INSTALLED (WITH OR WITHOUT STORES).

* DUE TO POSSIBLE MAIN ENGINE HOT START, JFS ASSISTED ENGINE START NOT RECOMMENDED BELOW 200 KNOTS.

Figure 3-1

15E–1–(7)

After engine is below 30% rpm -

```
CAUTION
```

To preclude a possible CGB shear section failure, do not move the engine control switch until the engine achieves idle.

6. Finger lift - RAISE AND RELEASE
   Attempts to engage the JFS above 30% rpm may shear the CGB shaft. Once the JFS is engaged, sufficient hydraulic pressure to the flight controls should be available to permit a controlled minimum rate of descent glide (approximately 210 knots).
7. Throttle - MID RANGE (after engine reaches steady state motoring speed of 26 to 29% rpm)

```
CAUTION
```

When shutting down an engine with the JFS running, release the finger lift before reaching the cutoff position to prevent immediate JFS reengagement and possible CGB shear section failure.

8. Other engine - START (if applicable)
9. JFS - CONFIRM OFF

AIR INLET SYSTEM MALFUNCTION

INLET LIGHT ON

An illuminated caution light indicates either an AIC failure, ramp position error or a diffuser ramp that did not lock or unlock at the appropriate Mach number. Airspeed should be reduced below Mach +1.0 and if above Mach 0.95 accelerations are limited to +4.0 g to -1.0 g.

1. Inlet ramp switch - EMERG
2. Throttle - MIL (if above Mach 1.0)
3. Limit aircraft accels to +4.0g to -1.0g (if above .95 Mach)
4. Reduce and maintain airspeed below Mach 1.0.

ROLL RATIO and RUDR LMTR CAUTION ON -

If the engine rpm does not decrease as the throttle is moved to idle, and ROLL RATIO (and possibly RUDR LMTR) caution is displayed, an AIC malfunction has probably occurred resulting in a false high Mach signal to the engine.

1. Determine if engine rpm respond to throttle movement

If rpm does not respond to throttle movement -

2. Engine control switch - OFF
3. Refer to Engine Control Malfunction procedures

If rpm does respond to throttle movement -

2. Refer to Engine Control Malfunction procedures

ENGINE CONTROL MALFUNCTION (-220 engines)

The ENG CONTR caution will come on as a result of a failure of the Mach number signal, failure of an electrical signal used for afterburner control, or if the DEEC has transferred from the primary to the secondary mode due to DEEC failure detection. If the ENG CONTR caution is on and the nozzle is less than 5%, it should be assumed that the engine control is in the secondary mode. When engine control is in the secondary mode, the nozzle is closed, afterburner operation is prevented, and only about 80% of normal MIL thrust is available. Cycling the ENG CONTR switch may return the engine to normal operation.

If supersonic -

1. Throttles - MIL
2. Slow to subsonic

If subsonic -

1. Throttle - 80%-85% RPM
2. ENG CONTR switch - CYCLE ON-OFF-ON
   Successful transfer from primary to secondary control can be accomplished throughout the flight envelope except at MAX power above 40,000 feet and less than 300 knots.

If engine operation abnormal -

3. Engine control switch - OFF
   Gear down idle thrust will be greater than normal.

ENGINE CONTROL MALFUNCTION (-229 engines)

The ENG CONTR caution will come on as a result of a failure of an electrical signal used for after burner control, or if the IDEEC has transferred from the primary to the secondary mode due to IDEEC failure detection. If the ENG CONTR caution and corresponding INLET caution are ON, a Mach number failure is most likely the cause. If the ENG CONTR caution is ON, the corresponding INLET caution is OFF and the corresponding nozzle position is greater than 5%, a fault inhibiting partial or full afterburner is probable. If the ENG CONTR caution is ON, the L and R INLET cautions are OFF and the nozzle position is less than 5%, the engine is probably in secondary mode. When engine control is in secondary mode, the nozzle is closed, afterburner operation is prevented, only 70-80% of normal MIL thrust is available, and both ground idle and approach idle thrust are disabled which will increase taxi speed. Cycling the ENG CONTR switch may return the engine to normal operation.

If supersonic -

1. Throttles - MIL
2. Slow to subsonic

If above 30,000 feet -

1. Throttle - MINIMIZE MOVEMENT
2. Descend below 30,000 feet

If subsonic and below 30,000 feet-

1. Throttle - 80%-85% RPM
2. ENG CONTR switch - CYCLE ON-OFF-ON

NOTE

Cycling the ENG CONTR switch from OFF to ON above 30,000 feet may cause an engine stall.

If engine operation abnormal or ENGINE category light and ENG CONTR caution message still on -

3. ENG CONTR switch - OFF
4. Land as soon as practical. Gear down idle thrust will be greater than normal.

After landing -

5. Shutdown the engine to reduce taxi speed (if required).

NOZZLE FAILURE

The cockpit nozzle indication is nozzle control unit commands, not actual nozzle position. It is possible for the nozzle to fail open or closed and still have normal cockpit indications. Engine stall when selecting afterburner may be an indication of a nozzle failed closed. A loss of thrust and lower than normal FTIT at MIL may be an indication of a nozzle failed open. If nozzle malfunction is indicated, leave the ENG CONTR switch ON. Do not use MIL or afterburner unless required to maintain flight. Gear down idle thrust will be greater than normal with the nozzle full closed.

ENGINE FIRE INFLIGHT

If a fire light comes on, or a voice warning "Warning, Engine Fire, Left (or Right)" is heard, or indications of an engine/aft fuselage fire are observed, perform this procedure. A fire in the afterburner section or in the vicinity of the nozzle will not cause a FIRE light to come on, the L (R) BURN THRU light will come on and the "AB Burn Thru, Left (Right)" voice warning will be heard. If an afterburner/nozzle burn through occurs, reducing the throttle to IDLE should extinguish the fire within 30 seconds. If the initial throttle reduction causes the light to go out or fire indications to cease and the fire detection system tests good, restrict thrust on the affected engine. If a fire light is accompanied by other indications of a fire (e.g., smoke, control difficulties, bleed air light, hydraulic or electrical anomalies), complete the procedure. With indications of explosion or catastrophic failure, do not delay completing engine shutdown steps. This may terminate fuel to the fire before it becomes self sustaining. Once the light has been pushed and the fuel shut off, do not depress the light again unless engine restart is necessary. If the fire extinguisher is used successfully, do not consider restarting the engine unless absolutely necessary.

1. Throttle - IDLE

If warning light goes off or fire out -

2. Fire warning system - TEST
3. Monitor other fire indications closely

If warning light remains on or fire persists -

2. Fire warning light - PUSH
3. Throttle - OFF
4. Fire extinguisher - DISCHARGE

If fire persists -

5. Eject

AFTERBURNER BURN THRU

If a fire occurs in the afterburner section, the left or right afterburner burn through lights will come on and the voice warning will be heard.

    1. Throttles - RETARD TO MIL OR BELOW

AMAD FIRE INFLIGHT

The most likely cause of an AMAD fire light in flight is the generators. If indications of a fire (AMAD Fire Light and "Warning, AMAD Fire" voice warning) exist, check electrical indications as well. Turning off a generator may remedy the situation.

    1. Throttles - REDUCE

If fire warning light goes out -

    2. Fire warning system - TEST
    3. Monitor other fire indications closely
    4. Discontinue mission

If fire warning light remains on -

    2. AMAD light - PUSH
    3. Fire extinguisher - DISCHARGE

If fire warning light still remains on -

    4. Emergency generator switch - MANUAL
       The EMER BST ON caution should come on and the BST SYS MAL caution should remain off. If the BST SYS MAL caution is on when both generator switches are turned OFF, double engine flameout may occur due to lack of boost pump pressure.
    5. Affected generator switch - OFF

If unable to determine which generator is affected -

    6. Both generator switches - OFF (one at a time to isolate source)

If fire persists -

    7. Eject

SMOKE, FUMES, OR FIRE IN COCKPIT

Consider all unidentified odors in the cockpit as toxic. Do not confuse condensation from the air conditioning system with smoke. The most probable source of visible smoke or fumes in the cockpit is from the engine or residual oil in the ECS ducts which can enter the cockpit through the ECS system via the center pedestal air outlet and/or cabin defog outlets. This smoke is blue grey in color, has a characteristic pungent odor, and may cause the eyes to sting. This odor may be noticed during engine run-up (if accomplished), during takeoff roll and, occasionally, during supersonic flight. Another possible source of smoke or fumes is an electrical malfunction or overheat in equipment located in the cockpit. In the event of electrical short or overload condition, this equipment may generate electrical smoke (usually white or grey in color) but should not cause an open fire since cockpit equipment uses very little electrical current. Cockpit electrical wiring insulation may smolder and create smoke, but will not erupt into a seriously damaging fire. There are no fuel or hydraulic lines passing through or near the cockpit area, hence, the possibility of cockpit fire is remote. Both main generators may be turned off after emergency boost system operation is confirmed.

If smoke or fumes detected -

    1. Oxygen regulator - 100% AND EMERGENCY
       Placing the diluter lever to 100% and the emergency lever to EMERGENCY will provide pure oxygen under positive pressure. This will prevent smoke and fumes from entering the mask even if the mask leaks.

WARNING

The emergency oxygen supply (bailout bottle) does not supply sufficient oxygen flow for normal breathing unless the oxygen supply hose is disconnected from the CRU-60/P. This action would permit smoke and fumes to enter the mask.

If required -

    2. Emergency vent handle - TURN AND PULL (below 25,000 feet)

If electrical smoke confirmed -

    3. Non-essential electrical equipment - OFF
    4. Land as soon as practical

If cockpit visibility restricted -

    5. Canopy - JETTISON

WARNING

If the cockpit is the source of the smoke or fumes, canopy jettison may cause an eruption of flames around the pilot.

If electrical fire/smoke persists -

6. Emergency generator switch - MAN

The EMER BST ON caution should come on and the BST SYS MAL caution should remain off.

If the BST SYS MAL caution is on when both generator switches are turned OFF, double engine flameout may occur due to lack of boost pump pressure.

7. Both main generator switches - OFF

If electrical fire still persists -

8. Emergency generator switch - ISOLATE

NOTE

In ISOLATE mode, rear cockpit power and intercom are lost. WSO should be advised prior to initiating ISOLATE mode.

If fire is intolerable -

9. Eject.

CANOPY UNLOCKED INFLIGHT/LOSS OF CANOPY

CANOPY UNLOCKED

The CANOPY UNLOCKED caution indicates that either the canopy locking mechanism has moved to the unlocked position or the canopy actuated initiator lanyard has become disconnected. The following procedures are recommended:

1. Slow to below 250 knots
2. Emergency vent handle - TURN (below 25,000 feet)
3. Canopy control handle - FULL FORWARD

CANOPY LOST

Air-to-ground communication may be possible up to about 400 knots, but airspeed should be reduced as much as practical and precautions taken to remain within the cockpit confines to prevent injury from the slipstream. Severe problems may be encountered by the WSO. Rapidly slowing below 200 knots and reducing altitude enables intercockpit communication and reduces the wind effects on the WSO. The WSO can attain the lowest slipstream profile by lowering the seat full down, grasping the lower instrument panel with the left hand and leaning full forward while using the right hand for helmet/mask retention. If necessary, select COLD MIC to prevent noise interference with pilot's radio.

1. Slow to lowest practical airspeed (200 knots maximum)
2. Descend to lowest practical altitude
3. Land as soon as practical

EXTREME COCKPIT TEMPERATURE

If temperature control cannot be maintained in AUTO, switch to MANUAL and adjust temperature control. If this fails and temperature becomes excessive, pull the emergency vent handle. Observe caution at altitude and consider descent. If temperature hot and altitude low, consider a climb to cooler air and/or deceleration to slower speed.

BLEED AIR CAUTION

Bleed air malfunctions have the potential for developing into serious situations. Depending on the location of the hot air leak, various indications can result, causing pilot confusion and misinterpretation. Therefore, prompt action is required by the pilot.

If left or right bleed air caution comes on -

1. Air source knob - OPPOSITE SOURCE

If caution remains on -

2. Throttle - IDLE

If both cautions come on -

1. Air source knob - OFF (below 25,000 feet)

ECS CAUTION

An ECS caution indicates low airflow or overtemperature of the avionics cooling air. In either case, avionics damage due to heat is the primary concern. Very low or high engine rpm can degrade ECS operation; therefore, maintain moderate airspeeds and rpm if the ECS caution is on. Shut down the radar first as it is very heat sensitive and reduces the cooling air available for other systems. Turn off non-essential avionics for their own protection. Avionics that cannot be turned off (AHRS, xfmr rectifiers, IFF, AIC, ADC, signal data recorder, etc.) will continue to be heat damaged. Turning the emergency vent handle dumps cockpit pressurization. Pulling the handle diverts ECS cockpit air to the avionics and allows ram flow to enter the cockpit as a function of handle extension. Turning the cockpit temperature control switch OFF will switch avionics cooling to ram air. The ECS caution will continue to monitor avionics cooling air flow and temperature. Optimum ram air cooling is obtained at 400 knots and 15,000 feet.

ECS turbine bearing disintegration and failure generally causes a high pitched whine that increases in pitch as engine rpm rises (starting about 80%). It can be accompanied by vibration in the floor area, an ECS light, and/or smoke and fumes. The only way to shut the ECS turbine down is by placing the cabin temperature control switch or air source knob to OFF.

NOTE

When landing with an illuminated ECS light, an automatic avionics shutdown may occur upon touchdown or during landing rollout. If so, the HUD and cockpit displays will blank, UHF 1 will be inoperative. Aerobrake using backup visual references.

1. Maintain 250-450 knots (75-85% rpm)

If caution remains on -

2. Non-essential avionics - OFF
3. Emergency vent handle - TURN AND PULL (below 25,000 feet)

If caution still remains on -

4. Cabin temperature control switch - OFF

ASYMMETRIC THRUST DEPARTURE PREVENTION (ATDP) SYSTEM CAUTION (F-15E 90-233 AND UP)

When ATDP caution is ON, the aircraft is unprotected from asymmetric thrust induced yaw departures and may also be susceptible to dual secondary mode transfers. When operating in afterburner at high dynamic pressures, the yaw moment can be large enough to cause permanent structural aircraft damage or even aircraft loss.

The caution indicates either system operating mode is other than commanded or air data is invalid. With the caution present, the aircraft flight envelope is restricted based on airframe configuration.

WARNING

When configured without CFT, do not fly above 650 KCAS when Mach is greater than 1.3 and altitude is less than 35,000 feet. When configured with CFT, do not fly above 525 KCAS when Mach is greater than 1.35 and altitude is less than 35,000 feet or above 600 KCAS when Mach is between 1.25 and 1.35 and altitude is less than 35,000 feet.

Refer to Engine Control Malfunctions.

OXYGEN CAUTION (F-15E 90-0233 AND UP; ALSO F-15E 86-0183 THRU 90-232 AFTER TO 1F-15E-561)

A Molecular Sieve Oxygen Generating System (MSOGS) OXYGEN caution indicates a low Positive Pressure Oxygen (PPO$_2$) concentration, a low concentrator outlet pressure or incorrect internal BIT answers. The Backup Oxygen System (BOS) will be automatically engaged when the generator light comes on.

If OXYGEN caution comes on -

1. Oxygen pressure gage - CHECK (greater than 60 psig)
   A pressure reading greater than the normal MSOGS operating range (up to 450 psi) indicates the system has automatically selected the BOS as the source of breathing gas.

If BOS is not available or when BOS pressure falls below 50 psi -

2. Descend below 10,000 feet MSL.

DISPLAY FLOW LOW CAUTION

A DISPLAY FLOW LOW caution indicates low cooling air flow to the cockpit displays. The cockpit displays include the UFCs, HUD, RMR, MPDs, and MPCDs. The primary concern in this case is damage to the displays due to overheat. Turning Internal Countermeasures Set off will increase cooling supply pressure to the cockpit displays. Non-essential displays should be turned off for their own protection. The RMR and MPCDs are the most heat sensitive displays and have no overheat protective circuitry and therefore should be turned off as soon possible. The MPDs have overheat protection which will cycle the units off and on during periods of extreme overheat. The HUD is the most reliable display and has limited overheat protection circuitry which will turn itself off upon impending heat damage. The HUD will remain off until turned on again by the pilot. If cabin airflow is normal, it can be assumed that some cooling air flow is available to the displays. As a minimum, the HUD, UFCs, and the aft cockpit R/H MPD should remain on. This will provide the pilot with flight information and allow the Weapons Systems Operator to monitor fault indications. Also, turning the emergency vent handle below 25,000 feet will lower cabin pressure, and therefore increase display cooling flow.

SINGLE ENGINE OPERATION

During single engine low or high rpm operation, ECS performance will be degraded and a DISPLAY FLOW LOW caution may come on with the ECS operating normally. Display cooling is marginal but is adequate for short term operations. Optimum cooling is achieved by operating at 80-82% rpm below 40,000 feet.

1. Internal Countermeasues Set - OFF (as soon as practical)

If caution remains on -

2. Non-essential displays - OFF
3. Emergency vent handle - TURN (below 25,000 feet)

If in single engine operation -

4. Maintain 80-82% rpm below 40,000 feet

OIL SYSTEM MALFUNCTION

Engine oil system malfunctions include over or under pressure, and excessive fluctuations. If the oil pressure stays below 8 psi but above 0 psi and appreciable time at altitude is expected, consider engine shutdown. If oil pressure stays at 0 psi or above 100 psi and the other engine is operating normally, the engine should be shut down without delay to limit damage. If the engine is left running and vibration or other indications of possible engine seizure occur, shut down the engine and make a single-engine landing.

If oil pressure is out of normal range -

1. Throttle - IDLE

If oil pressure below 8 psi or pegged at 100 psi -

1. Throttle - OFF (conditions permitting)

EMER BST ON AND/OR BST SYS MAL CAUTION

The EMER BST ON and BST SYS MAL cautions provide indication of the status of both the emergency fuel boost pump system and the emergency generator system. A single caution or combination of cautions require the following aircrew actions:

EMER BST ON	BST SYS MAL	AIRCREW ACTION
ON	OFF	Refer to generator failure or boost pump failure as applicable.
OFF	ON	Follow applicable boost pump failure procedure.
ON	ON	Do not turn main generators OFF or place emergency generator switch to ISOLATE as this may fail the emergency boost pump.

FUEL BOOST PUMPS INOPERATIVE

There are various combinations of indications to warn of a single or multiple fuel boost pump failure. A single boost pump failure is indicated by a L or R

BST PUMP caution on or a BST SYS MAL caution on or a BST SYS MAL caution on without an EMER BST ON caution. A multiple failure is indicated by two or more of the above cautions on. Total electrical failure including the emergency generator causes total boost pump failure without the usual cautions. With total boost pump failure, fuel is available to the engine by gravity feed only and fuel vaporization with resulting flameout of one or both engines is probable. Flameout is most likely to occur during the first 30 seconds of gravity feed operation and is more probable above 15,000 feet and/or at low power settings.

Fuel vaporization is caused by a combination of loss of boost pump pressure, and high altitude (low ambient pressure) or high fuel temperature. Fuel temperature is increased by electrical, AMAD, and hydraulic systems heat being transferred to the fuel in the heat exchangers. The probability of fuel vaporization can be decreased by reducing fuel temperature and descending to a lower altitude. Increased fuel flow is the most effective method of reducing fuel temperature. Reducing electrical load aids in reducing fuel temperature, but this effect is delayed. The primary consideration is to ensure that at least one engine continues to operate.

SINGLE OR DOUBLE (ANY TWO) FUEL BOOST PUMP FAILURE

With only one boost pump operating, prudence dictates that the aircraft be operated at the lowest practical altitude below 30,000 feet and at a higher (but not afterburner) power setting.

1. Land as soon as practical

BOTH MAIN FUEL BOOST PUMPS AND EMERGENCY BOOST PUMP INOPERATIVE (TOTAL BOOST PUMP FAILURE)

1. Descend to minimum practical altitude using maximum practical power on at least one engine (not afterburner).

   If the situation permits, maintain high power settings for at least 3 minutes to cool the fuel, and descend with both throttles at military power. As the descent becomes more restricted by weather, airspeed, etc., maintain one throttle at military while retarding the other as necessary toward IDLE. If the retarded engine operates at IDLE and additional power reduction is required, you can then retard the advanced throttle as required. Use of the speed brake should be considered.

2. Reduce electrical load to the minimum practical

3. Maintain split throttles until established in traffic pattern

   Maintain one engine at as high a power setting as possible until the throttle must be retarded to permit landing.

FUEL TRANSFER SYSTEM MALFUNCTION

The primary indication of a fuel transfer system malfunction is the fuel gage. Other indications include premature FUEL LOW caution, BINGO caution, wing low tendency and appropriate voice warnings.

INTERNAL TANK(S) FAIL TO TRANSFER

If tank 1 transfer pump has failed a differential greater than approximately 750 pounds between tank 1 and the internal wing tanks will be observed. If this occurs, the fuel in tank 1 should be considered trapped and as the wing tanks empty aircraft CG will shift forward, ending up near the design limit of the aircraft. If feed tank fuel quantity begins to drop with fuel remaining in either internal wing tank , a wing tank transfer pump has probably failed. If any or all transfer pumps fail, the fuel in the affected tanks will gravity transfer to the feed tanks when tanks with operating transfer pumps are empty and the fuel level (height) in the feed tanks drops below the level of fuel in the affected tank(s). Gravity transfer may be confirmed by observing the simultaneous decrease of fuel quantities in the affected tank(s) and feed tanks. Gravity transfer may not occur until after FUEL LOW caution comes on and very low feed tank quantities are reached (300 to 400 pounds in each tank). Gravity transfer will not completely refill the feed tanks, and may not keep up with feed tank usage, depending on total fuel quantity and pitch attitude. At fuel flow rates above 3,500 pounds per hour per engine, gravity transfer will not keep up with engine demand from the feed tanks. If transfer pump failure is suspected:

1. Throttles - RETARD (less than 3,500 pph/ engine)

For tank 1 transfer failure -

2. Slipway switch - CHECK CLOSED

If slipway switch closed-

    3. Stay below 30 units AOA.

4. Maintain approximately 250 knots for cruise and plan for a minimum fuel descent.
5. Land as soon as practical.

EXTERNAL TANK FAILS TO TRANSFER

With wing tanks installed, if the external fuel tanks fail to transfer completely or if STOP TRANS is selected due to an emergency and any external tank, including the centerline, is partially full, the aircraft may exceed the aft CG limit as internal fuel decreases due to fuel moving aft in the external tanks. Cycling the external tank switch or slipway door, may restore transfer. If the landing gear is cycled under these conditions, it may fail to retract due to WOW switch malfunction. Ensure fuel on board will allow flight to a suitable landing base with the gear down if transfer is not restored. If not, it may be necessary to jettison the tanks for controllability or range considerations. Landing with up to a full tank on one side will normally present no problem, but perform a Controllability Check when practical. With pitch CAS inoperative, the CG shift due to movement of trapped fuel in external tanks can degrade aircraft handling characteristics.

1. External transfer switch - WING/CTR
2. External tank fuel control switches - CYCLE
3. Landing gear circuit breaker - IN
4. Slipway switch - CYCLE
5. Throttle(s) - MIL

If external tank still fails to transfer or STOP TRANS is selected -

6. Maintain minimum 250 knots
7. Use minimum pitch angles for maneuvering
8. Jettison external tanks if required

If partially full external tanks are retained -

9. Maintain 18 units AOA on final.

CFT FAILS TO TRANSFER

CFT fuel transfer failure is indicated by voice warning, "WARNING, TRANSFER PUMP", the FUEL PUMP caution and can be verified by reference to the fuel quantity indicator. There is no provision for transfer of CFT fuel if both transfer pumps on one side fail. If both pumps on one side fail, it may be desirable to stop CFT transfer to maintain balance. If only one CFT pump fails, it may be difficult at low fuel flows, using the fuel quantity gage, to determine which side has failed. To confirm if a CFT pump has

failed, the MPD caution can be deleted by momentarily placing the CFT switch to STOP TRANS. If the caution is not removed from the MPD, the failed pump is not in the CFT. Refer to Internal Tank(s) Fail To Transfer procedure.

If both main generators fail, all CFT transfer pumps automatically shut off. If fuel is not critical, do not transfer CFT fuel. If fuel is critical, CFT fuel can be transferred using the CFT emergency transfer switch. The landing gear handle must be up to prevent fuel from transferring to the other CFT. Wait until internal fuel decreases about 1000 pounds then select L or R. When internal tanks are full, place the switch to NORM. Wait until internal fuel again decreases about 1000 pounds, then select L or R as required to maintain fuel balance. Repeat until the CFT's are empty.

If both generators fail and fuel critical -

1. Landing gear handle - UP

After internal fuel decreases about 1000 pounds -

2. Conformal tank emergency transfer switch - L or R

When internal tanks full -

3. Conformal tank emergency transfer switch - NORM
4. Repeat steps 1 thru 3 for opposite CFT

EMERGENCY FUEL TRANSFER/DUMP (EXTERNAL TANKS), GEAR DOWN

Fuel in external tanks cannot be transferred and/or dumped unless the landing gear handle is up or the fuel low level system is activated. If it is necessary to transfer or dump fuel with the gear down, the following procedure will permit external fuel transfer/dump without raising the landing gear.

1. Emergency landing gear handle - PULL
2. Landing gear handle - UP
3. Fuel gauge - MONITOR
4. Fuel dump switch - DUMP (if required)
5. Landing gear handle - DOWN (when dumping completed)

If UTL A pressure zero, or after TO 1F-15E 517-

6. Emergency landing gear handle - RESET

UNCOMMANDED FUEL VENTING

Fuel flowing unintentionally from the dump mast(s) in flight is, in all probability, due to abnormal venting caused by fuel transfer system and/or fuel pressurization/vent system failures (the probability of a spontaneous dump system failure is extremely low). If fuel dump is selected with abnormal venting, the internal fuel tanks could overpressurize and rupture. Cycling the fuel dump switch may also increase the fuel loss rate. Therefore, the fuel dump switch should not be cycled in an attempt to correct uncommanded fuel venting (cycling the switch is acceptable if normal fuel dumping does not stop when the switch is moved from DUMP to NORM). Feed tank fuel cannot be dumped or vented. Turning the air source knob to OFF may reduce the fuel loss rate if fuel pressurization malfunctions are contributing to the venting flow.

CAUTION

If fuel dump is selected during abnormal venting, the internal fuel tanks could over-pressurize and rupture.

---

1. Fuel dump switch - NORM
2. External tank/conformal tank fuel control switches - STOP TRANSFER
   If any external tank is partially full, the aircraft may exceed the aft CG limit at light internal fuel weights due to fuel moving aft in the external tanks. In this case, it may be necessary to jettison the external tanks.
3. Slipway switch - OPEN
4. Air source knob - OFF (below 25,000 feet)
   Expect a possible ECS light once the air source knob is turned off.

If fuel venting continues and flight to an emergency landing site requires more than feed tank fuel -

5. Emergency generator switch - MAN
   The EMER BST ON caution should come on and the BST SYS MAL caution should remain off.
6. Main generator switches - OFF
   If the BST SYS MAL caution is on when both generator switches are turned OFF, double engine flameout may occur due to lack of boost pump pressure.

7. Fuel gage - MONITOR FEED TANK
   Feed tanks may be refilled by turning on a main generator thus activating transfer pumps, or by allowing fuel to gravity feed from internal wing tanks.

When feed tank fuel is sufficient for flight to an emergency landing site -

8. Main generator switches - ON

INFLIGHT FUEL LEAK

Prompt action is required to isolate the source of the leak to minimize fuel loss and fire hazard. If the leak can be associated with one engine bay, feed tank, or side of the aircraft, then the fire warning light for the engine on that side should be pressed to close the airframe fuel shutoff valve. Placing the throttle OFF will not isolate leaks upstream of the engine fuel control. If the leak is upstream of the airframe fuel shutoff valve, fuel loss may be reduced by stopping all fuel transfer and shutting off the fuel boost pumps. The transfer and boost pumps can be shut off by turning both main generators OFF. This will reduce but will probably not stop the leak. Monitor feed tank fuel quantity and turn the main generators ON as required to prevent feed tank depletion. Failure of some fuel system components can cause loss of all fuel in a few minutes. Consider increasing airspeed (without afterburner) to maximize range by using fuel which would otherwise be lost.

WARNING

Afterburner may ignite leaking fuel.

NOTE

Checking the fuel flow gages may help to determine associated engine bay.

If leak can be associated with one engine bay -

1. Fire warning light - PRESS
2. Throttle - OFF

If source of leak cannot be determined -

1. Either fire warning light - PRESS
2. Throttle - OFF

If leak continues -

3. Fire warning light - RESET
4. Engine - RESTART
5. Other engine fire warning light - PUSH
6. Other engine throttle - OFF

If leak continues and flight to emergency landing site not assured -

7. External tank/conformal tank fuel control switches - STOP TRANSFER
8. Fire warning light - RESET
9. Engine - RESTART
10. Emergency generator switch - MAN (EMER BST ON caution on and BST SYS MAL caution off)
11. Both main generator switches - OFF
12. Fuel gage - MONITOR FEED TANKS
13. Main generator switches - ON AS REQUIRED FOR FUEL TRANSFER AND FOR LANDING
14. External tank switches - ON AS REQUIRED

After landing -

15. Shutdown engines using fire warning lights, engine master switches, and throttles.

GENERATOR FAILURE

A generator failure is indicated by a L GEN OUT or R GEN OUT caution. The emergency generator will come on and power the emergency boost pump and the EMER BST ON caution will come on. If the BST SYS MAL caution comes on, the emergency generator has probably failed. Normal flight electrical loads (except TEWS pods) can be handled by one generator. Check hydraulic warning lights and gages for indication of AMAD failure. Check engine instruments for indication of stall/stagnation or flameout.

1. Generator switch - CYCLE

If generator still failed -

2. Generator switch - OFF

DOUBLE GENERATOR FAILURE

If both generators fail, the emergency generator will automatically power the essential buses providing the emergency generator is not in ISOLATE. The HYDRAULIC caution and the landing gear warning light will come on and the landing gear warning tone will sound. Operation of the landing gear warning light/tone is due to loss of the ADC. The gear should operate normally. Hydraulic system operation can be verified only by proper operation of hydraulic powered systems. Refer to Emergency Power Distribution Chart (figure 3-5) for equipment that will be operative/inoperative when the emergency generator is on line. If either generator can be reset, the electrical system will revert to normal operation.

The following indicators/instruments will fail immediately and, except for the fuel flow, oil pressure, exhaust nozzle indications which go blank, will tend to remain at the last valid reading:

Vertical velocity indicator
AOA indicator
Exhaust nozzle position indications
Oil pressure indications
Fuel flow indications
Oxygen quantity indicators
PC1 hydraulic pressure indicator
PC2 hydraulic pressure indicator
Utility hydraulic pressure indicator

The only display powered by the emergency generator is the front MPCD which will display ADI format and cautions. With double generator failure and the emergency generator operating, cautions are displayed only on the MPCD in the cockpit. These cautions can be removed by pressing the castle switch on the cockpit control stick to any position. A second activation of the castle switch restores the cautions to the display. If double generator failure occurs at night, all instrument and console lights will fail and the flood lights (utility and storm) must be used for cockpit illumination. Partial failure of the left main generator may also result in failure of the instrument and console lights; power can be restored in this case by turning the left generator switch off.

NOTE

On aircraft before 89-0072, if a dual generator failure occurs, the front cockpit MPCD may not receive enough power to operate and consequently the ADI display will be lost. If this occurs, utilize the standby flight instruments which will still be operational.

1. EMER BST ON caution - CHECK ON
   If the EMER BST ON caution is not on, cycle the emergency generator switch to ISOLATE and back to MAN. If the emergency

generator does not power the emergency/ essential buses, engine rpm and FTIT indications will go blank. Operation of the engines can be confirmed by advancing the throttle and noting thrust response.

NOTE

In ISOLATE mode, rear cockpit power and intercom are lost. WSO should be advised prior to initiating ISOLATE mode.

2. Main generator switches - CYCLE

If main generators still failed and emergency generator is inoperative -

3. Follow Both Main Fuel Boost Pumps and Emergency Boost Pump Inoperative (Total Boost Pump Failure) procedure.
    All internal transfer pumps will be inoperative and fuel will gravity transfer to the feed tanks.

WARNING

With both main generators inoperative the nozzles will stay full closed with the landing gear down and idle thrust will be substantially higher than normal.

NOTE

Feed tank fuel cannot be monitored. Flameout due to fuel starvation may occur with prolonged use of high power settings. With total electrical failure, the standby attitude indicator will display an OFF flag but is reliable for 9 minutes after loss of electrical power.

AMAD FAILURE

AMAD failure is indicated by the simultaneous loss of the PC system, the utility pump, and the generator on the same side. If this occurs:

1. Throttle - IDLE
2. Refer to Electrical and Hydraulic Failures.

If double AMAD failure occurs -

1. Eject
    If double AMAD failure occurs, total hydraulic and electrical power are lost and aircraft control is impossible.

RUNAWAY TRIM

Sufficient control is available to land the aircraft from a runaway trim in any direction. Unless other flight control malfunctions are evident, leave pitch and roll ratio switches in AUTO. If a runaway trim condition cannot be controlled with the normal trim controls, use of the takeoff trim button may be effective in returning the trim to a near neutral position. Pulling the AFCS ESS AC circuit breaker removes power from the trim actuators while leaving the rest of the flight control system operational (upper AFCS ESS AC circuit breaker is for pitch trim, and the lower AFCS ESS AC circuit breaker is for both roll and yaw trim).

FLIGHT CONTROL SYSTEM MALFUNCTION

The CAS is a highly reliable, three channel fail-operate/fail-safe system which continuously self-checks its operation. If the system senses two channels, of the same CAS axis failure, it will drop itself off line. If a flight control system anomaly is apparent, but adequate aircraft control can be maintained, do not disengage CAS as it may be responsible for maintaining controlled flight. If it were to be disengaged, not only would aircraft control be jeopardized, but it may not be possible to reengage. If the CAS fails and cannot be reset, handling qualities are satisfactory for most mission tasks. If pitch CAS fails while supersonic above 600 knots, pilot induced oscillations (PIO) may occur. If the malfunction involves both the CAS and the mechanical system, handling qualities may be severely degraded. Perform a Controllability Check, if practical, before landing. If the malfunction is in pitch or roll ratio, evaluate handling qualities at approach speed with the applicable ratio switch in both AUTO and EMERG. Handling qualities may be considerably different at approach speeds than at higher speeds. If selecting EMERG does not noticeably improve controllability, land with the switch in AUTO. If landing with pitch ratio EMERG and pitch CAS OFF, fly a flat 18 unit AOA approach.

Failure of the PRCA - ARI interconnect cable can cause out of control roll oscillations especially at high gross weights. Such a failure results in more rudder movements than desired with lateral stick movement. Failure of the interconnect cable would be indicated by the rudders deflecting in the same direction as the stick, regardless of the fore/aft position of the stick. Inflight failure will cause roll oscillations at high gross weights and noticeable yaw excursions at low fuel states. This malfunction can be corrected by disengaging the ARI (roll ratio switch - Emergency).

NOTE

Placing either ratio switch to EMERG will fail the aileron-rudder interconnect (ARI), and will remove pitch and/or roll compensations provided by the ratio changer. Selection of the emergency pitch system will also disable pitch trim compensation. Handling qualities are adequate for recovery.

PITCH SYSTEM MALFUNCTION

1. Slow to below 250 knots

If pitch ratio below 0.4 or if aircraft still difficult to control -

2. Pitch ratio switch - EMERG
3. Pitch ratio indicator - OBSERVE 0.3 to 0.5

If pitch ratio EMERG and pitch CAS OFF -

4. Fly a flat 18 unit AOA approach

WARNING

With CFT's installed, if pitch CAS drop off occurs with the pitch ratio in emergency or pitch CAS is off line and the pitch ratio switch is placed to emergency, a 3g or greater nose-up transient will occur.

NOTE

The reduced stabilator authority, with pitch ratio in EMERG, will prevent normal aerodynamic braking after landing. The limited aerodynamic braking may necessitate lowering the nose and applying wheel brakes early.

ROLL SYSTEM MALFUNCTION

1. Roll ratio switch - EMERG

WARNING

● Destructive structural loads caused by excessive pitch and yaw excursions can occur during supersonic loaded rolls when the roll ratio light is on at Mach 1.5 or above with the roll ratio switch in AUTO. Until the roll ratio switch is placed in EMERG, avoid high lateral roll rates above Mach 1.5 at negative or high positive g.

RUDDER SYSTEM MALFUNCTIONS

Two different rudder control system malfunctions are possible; failure/jamming of the rudder control cables or failure of a rudder actuator. If the rudder control cable is broken or jammed, flight control inputs which cause rudder movement will probably result in irreversible deflection of one or both rudders. Rudder trim will appear to correct the problem if rudder deflection is small; however, subsequent rudder inputs will aggravate the out-of-trim condition. Failure of a rudder actuator may cause the corresponding rudder to drive to a fully deflected position and remain there. This condition may be visually confirmed through use of mirrors, chase, etc. In either of these failures, the aircraft is controllable as long as the CAS remains on.

WARNING

If a rudder malfunction is apparent, do not turn the CAS off as this may cause loss of aircraft control.

If CAS disengages, a single fully deflected rudder may be counteracted with rudder and aileron; however, depending on the degree of dual rudder deflection, sufficient control may not be available to counteract the effects of a broken/jammed rudder cable. Avoid all unnecessary turns to prevent increasing the amount of irreversible deflection. Avoid unnecessary g loading since aircraft control will be reduced as AOA increases. Consider use of asymmetrical thrust to aid in reducing yaw effects. If possible turn in direction of failed rudder.

LAT STK LMT CAUTION

A LAT STK LMT caution on the MPD/MPCD may be an indication that the AOA is invalid, static or pitot pressure is invalid, or left or right rudder CAS servo is inoperative. In this case, more than 1/2 lateral stick may cause departure or structural failure.

1. Do not exceed 1/2 lateral stick until BIT display check

2. Check AFCS DETAIL BIT display on MPD/MPCD

3. Refer to AFCS Functional Status Summary.

NOTE

LAT STICK LIMIT and CAS YAW cautions may be displayed after a single engine shutdown. This is normal aircraft operation and the pilot should attempt a YAW CAS reset.

SPEED BRAKE FAILURE

If either a hydraulic or electric failure occurs, the speed brake will be closed by air pressure. If the speed brake will not retract, pulling the SPD BK circuit breaker will remove electric and hydraulic power, and allow air load closure.

1. Speed brake circuit breaker - PULL

BOARDING STEPS EXTENDED

Malfunction of the lock-up mechanism can allow the boarding steps to extend in flight. Normally there is no indication, except that the position indicator will indicate DOWN. At high speed, some buffet may be present. The boarding steps have extended in flight at speeds as high as Mach 2 with no adverse effect. However, if the steps fail structurally, pieces will probably enter the left engine inlet. For this reason, if the steps extend, reduce airspeed as soon as practical.

ADC FAILURE

Operation of the Air Data Computer is entirely automatic, and no control over the system is available to the pilot.

The primary indications of ADC failure are failure/freezing (with associated OFF indications) of the vertical velocity, warning light in the landing gear handle, and when airborne, landing gear warning tone. Due to the various systems interface, any or all of the following systems may malfunction or be unreliable if the ADC fails. These are: ECS, Inlets, Pitch Ratio, Altitude Hold, Total Temp, IFF Mode-C, LCG, Navigation/Attack Steering, and HUD (except pitch ladder and heading scale).On F-15E 90-0233 AND UP, the ATDP caution is another possible indication of ADC failure. Also, the ATDPS is on additional system that could malfunction or be unreliable if the ADC fails.

NOTE

Loss of ADC information to the inlet controller may cause internal ramp component fluctuation with associated vibration and utility hydraulic fluctuation with no visible ramp movement.

Pilot action during ADC system malfunction should be based on timely recovery using the standby instruments for flight. Indications of subsequent loss or partial recovery of any of the above secondary systems may be experienced as a result of the aircraft transiting various flight regimes. Cross-check the primary and secondary ADI instruments. If a large discrepancy exists, check AFCS detail BIT functional status.

INS FAILURE

If the INS fails, the ATTITUDE caution is displayed. If the INS is the selected data source, OFF is displayed next to INS and an X is displayed on the ADI attitude ball. Master caution and the AV BIT caution will also come one. Select the attitude source that is still valid and monitor the standby attitude indicator.

AIR DATA (A/D) MODE

The A/D mode is a backup to the primary INS mode. If the INS fails, the CC automatically switches to the A/D navigation mode. The CC uses true airspeed, wind velocity, and magnetic heading to derive aircraft position and compute steering to destination. INS computation of inertially derived aircraft velocity and position is not disturbed by selection of the A/D mode. Wind and magnetic variation may be entered in the UFC. The A/G radar PVU display may be selected and PVU updates entered to update the INS. The most accurate PP update methods are radar high resolution map (HRM), and LANTIRN and OVERFLY updates.

The A/D mode may be manually selected from the PP source submenu on the UFC if large errors appear in the INS present position, wind, and ground speed.

INS INFLIGHT ALIGNMENT (IFA)

This INS mode takes 20 minutes and requires continuous PVU updates and three position updates to reach specification level accuracies. Prior to doing the IFA operation, the aircraft should be flown straight and level for 1 to 2 minutes, then upgrade the AHRS by doing a fast erect and sync operation.

If the INS attitude fails, PP errors will also normally increase. The INS may be realigned to reset the attitude and to regain PP accuracy.

Both attitude and PP accuracy are improved as the length of an inflight alignment increases. The aircraft does not need to be flown straight and level during an IFA; some maneuvering in fact helps the system analyze the problems and increase alignment accuracy. Aircraft maneuvers should be limited to ±45° of pitch and ±60° of bank.

The INS mode knob must be turned OFF, then directly to NAV. The INS enters a standby mode until IFA is selected on the radar A/G PVU display; the INS enters the IFA mode and receives AHRS attitude, heading, best available true airspeed, and MN position. In the PVU mode, the radar automatically accomplishes periodic updates and displays the errors on the MPD/MPCD, along with IFA alignment quality (starting at 15.9). The displayed errors are accepted and updates sent to the INS by (WSO) pressing the appropriate hand controller trigger to the second detent and releasing or (pilot) pressing and releasing the TDC on the throttle. Along with the PVU updates, HRM map, RBM map, and LANTIRN position updates increase IFA accuracy.

NOTE

During IFA, if position update is done using the radar antenna (RBM or HRM), the radar is taken out of the PVU mode and the IFA display is also removed. The IFA does continue and NAV DEGRADED is displayed if updates are continued. Eventually the NAV DEGRADED is removed (approximately 20 minutes).

PRECONDITION THE AHRS

1. Maintain straight and level unaccelerated flight.
2. AHRS control panel sync knob - PUSH
3. AHRS control panel fast erect button - PUSH
4. Wait approximately 30 seconds before performing alignment.

ALIGNMENT

1. INS mode knob - OFF FOR 5 SECONDS, THEN NAV

2. IFA mode - SELECT

   The INS is in a standby mode until the IFA mode is selected on the A/G radar PVU display. The CC then sends the best available navigation data to the INS for initialization.

3. HUD window 16 - IFA 15.9

   Once the INS is in the IFA mode and accepting PVU updates, the INS alignment quality begins to count down. The aircraft maneuvers should be limited to ±45° of pitch and ±60° of bank during the IFA. The INS requires three position updates during the 20 minutes preferably two high accuracy updates (LANTIRN/OVERFLY).

4. PVU error data - ACCEPT (Perform some maneuvers while doing steps 4 and 5, heading changes, gentle S turns, climb/dive, level accelerations.

5. Position update - 3 to 5 high accuracy updates during 20 minutes.

6. HUD window 16 - IFA OK

   It will take approximately 20 minutes to accomplish a full IFA alignment. Accuracy is increased by other INS updates (HRM, RBM, and LANTIRN) during the IFA. The aircrew may stop the IFA at any time after IFA 15.9.

7. IFA mode - DESELECT

   The aircrew may stop the IFA at any time the accuracy is considered sufficient for mission requirements. The INS remains in the IFA mode until deselected on the A/G radar PVU display. If the IFA is not allowed to continue until reaching IFA OK, the INS will indicate NAV DEGD.

HEADING ERROR

Magnetic heading is available on the HUD, ADI, HSI, TSD and standby compass (front cockpit only). The magnetic heading normally comes from the INS unless INS data is invalid; the data is then supplied by the AHRS. If the selected heading source is invalid, OFF replaces the heading display on the ADI; select the other heading source. If both INS and AHRS heading data are invalid, OFF replaces the heading display on the ADI and the lubber line is removed from the HSI.

1. Other heading source - SELECT
2. Sync button - PUSH

3. AHRS mode selector knob - COMP or DG

   If the AHRS platform has not failed, DG may be used. If this mode is inoperative, the COMP position allows direct readout of the magnetic azimuth detector, and the HSI behaves similar to the standby compass (good only in straight and level flight). In either COMP or DG, the CC does not use any AHRS inputs.

4. Magnetic variation - ENTER

   The HUD should now have correct magnetic heading displayed.

If AHRS DG mode is used -

1. Select AHRS on ADI
2. EHSI heading - SET TO HUD HEADING

   Push and rotate the AHRS sync knob to set HSI heading. Insure that latitude and hemisphere settings are correct.

CENTRAL COMPUTER FAILURE

If a central computer failure occurs or is suspected, attempt to reset the CC. The MPDP becomes backup bus controller.

WARNING

In the event of a CC failure, the ADTPS will not provide protection against departure, regardless of ADC status. Additionally, status of connection between engines is unknown with a CC or AIU failure. In this case, an augmentor failure or transfer to SEC mode may cause a sudden loss of thrust on both engines.

AVAILABLE FUNCTIONS WITH CC FAILURE

COMM,IFF AAI, EWWS	Normal
TACAN/ILS	Normal (ADI format)
TEWS	Degraded
A/A RADAR	Search, TWS-ND, STT, Vert scan, Designated TWS
A/G RADAR	RBM
Basic aircraft performance	ADI format
CAUTIONS	Fully displayed for supported systems. With CC failure only, cautions are always displayed on any MPD/MPCD that has the radar display format.
NAV	TSD display format PP lat/long (UFC) Two steer points maintained Update of INS (overfly only)
TF	Manual TF with selectable set clearance TF displays supported
NAV FLIR	Video provided to HUD status on UFC
Weapon employment	AIM-9, Boresight AIM-7, Flood AIM-120, None GUN, Fixed cross

DISPLAY FORMAT CHANGES WITH CC FAILURE

The display formats that are available with CC failure have some of the information from the standard formats, and in some cases the formats are supplemented with additional information. The changes in the backup formats are described in the following paragraphs.

Backup ADI Display Format

Since the HSI format cannot be displayed, some of its selections, such as steer modes and course select, are included in the backup ADI format. Display items not available are angle-of-attack, pitch trim adjust, command heading marker, attitude source display, on demand record, master menu select, calibrated/true airspeed, barometric altitude, and commanded speeds. Display items added to the backup ADI format are steer mode selections, steer point data block, tacan data block, and course select options.

The backup ADI format displays ILS data similar to the normal format but calibrated airspeed and baro altitude are not displayed with CC failure. However, ground speed and radar altitude are both available. If ILST is selected, the ILS data is unchanged. The ADI receives localizer and glideslope raw data to move the pitch/bank steering bars.

Backup HUD Display Format

With a CC failure the following information is available on the HUD:

Magnetic heading	Pitch ladder
Groundspeed	Bank scale
Radar altitude	Gun cross

Vertical velocity	Waterline symbol
Velocity vector	Pitch/bank steer bars
MRM reference circle	Selected steer mode
Current G loading	Steer point range

When ILST or ILSN steer modes are selected ILS localizer and glideslope raw data is displayed on the HUD. If ILST steer mode is selected, the tacan channel is also displayed. No AOA information is displayed, but localizer deviation is displayed normally.

Backup TSD Display Format

On the backup TSD display format two selectable parameters remain: map scale selection and INS position update. The aircraft present position symbol remains, but no cursor or target related functions remain. The remaining update function is for overfly only.

UFC Display Format

With a CC failure, all radio/comm, tacan, ILS, KY-58, AAI, and IFF functions remain operable. Menu 1 information concerning steer point, TF, and NAV FLIR status is available. Data is also available on the point data submenu, menu 2 present position source, plus current aircraft latitude/longitude and current magnetic variation.

AVIONICS INTERFACE UNIT FAILURE

1. MPDP/AIU-1 switch (GND PWR panel) - CYCLE

The following systems/data are affected if AIU 1 fails -

UHF 1 radio	Inoperative
Left hand controller	Inoperative
Cautions (except LOW ALT, LASER ARMED)	Not displayed
Fuel flow on MPD/MPCD	No data
Avionics BIT and ASP	Inoperative
ILS	No data/operation
TACAN	No data/operation

UHF 1 radio	Inoperative
IFF	Inoperative
ADF	No data
EWWS	Inoperative
KY-58	Inoperative
Seat ejection auto beacon	Inoperative
Voice Warning	No engine overtemp LT/RT
F-15E 90-0233 AND UP, ATDP	Inoperative

The following systems/data are affected if AIU 2 fails -

UHF 2 radio	Inoperative
Right hand controller (aft)	Inoperative
AAI	Inoperative
KIR	Inoperative
HF communication	Inoperative
Aft sensor control panel	No system control
TGTFLIR gain/level	defaults to AUTO
LANTIRN (nav and targeting)	Presence not sensed by OWS
Voice Warning	No engine overtemp LT/RT

The following systems/data are affected if AIU 1 and AIU 2 fail -

Radar altimeter (CARA)	No data
Intercom set control panel	No comm control
Fwd throttle and stick	No HOTAS functions
Fwd sensor control panel	No system control
Upfront controls (both)	Inoperative
Master modes	Selection fixed
LOW ALT and LASER ARMED warning	Indication lost
Voice Warning	Inoperative

LANTIRN OVERTEMPERATURE CONDITION

If the navigation pod or target pod develops an overheat condition, a NAV POD HOT or TGT POD HOT caution will be displayed on the MPD or MPCD in both cockpits. The caution display causes the master caution light in the cockpit to come on.

1. TGT FLIR or NAV FLIR and TF RDR power switch(es) - OFF

MULTIPURPOSE DISPLAY PROCESSOR (MPDP) FAILURE

If one of the four power supplies in the MPDP fail the following functions are lost -

Power Supply A Failure
 FWD MPCD
 Right Aft MPD
 Displays 1553 Bus A (Fwd MPCD, Fwd left MPD, Aft left MPCD, Aft right MPD)
 GP I/O (backup mode capability)
 1553 avionics bus
 SGP Bus A (Fwd MPCD, Fwd left MPD, Aft left MPCD, Aft right MPD; In backup mode - lose Fwd MPCD, Aft MPD)
 JTIDS 1553
 Radar

Power Supply B Failure
 Aft right MPCD
 Fwd right MPD
 EWWS, OWS, RWR
 1553 displays Bus B (HUD, Fwd right MPD, aft left MPD, aft right MPCD)
 SGP Bus B (HUD, Fwd right MPD, aft left MPD, aft right MPCD)

Power Supply C Failure
 Aft left MPCD
 HUD backup mode

 1553 displays Bus B (HUD, Fwd right MPD, aft left MPD, aft right MPCD)
 Radar
 Fwd left MPD

Power Supply D Failure
 1553 displays Bus A (Fwd MPCD, Fwd left MPD, aft left MPCD, Aft right MPD)
 VTR
 Aft left MPD
 HUD (primary)
 TEST PATTERN (initiated BIT)

NOTE

In the event of a power supply C or D failure, removing power from the CC will result in a six display backup mode of operation.

If a total MPDP failure occurs all systems which require an MPD/MPCD or HUD to be displayed (i.e. radar, INS, PACS) are lost. The EMDs and the standby instruments are still functional.

NOTE

If several front and rear cockpit displays go blank or display STANDBY, a recycle of power to MPDP should return the system to normal operation.

LANDING

CONTROLLABILITY CHECK

If handling characteristics for recovery are suspect, perform a controllability check. If recovery is possible, plan to fly the final approach at the AOA determined in the controllability check and delay reducing power until well into the flare.

1. Attain a safe altitude.
2. Reduce gross weight to minimum practicable.
3. Establish landing configuration.
    Use of flaps is not recommended if structural damage to the wing is suspected.
4. Slow aircraft to no less than on-speed AOA (20-22 units)
    Slow only to that AOA/speed which allows acceptable handling characteristics.

If recovery is possible -

5. Maintain landing configuration and fly straight-in approach no slower than AOA found in step 4.
6. Delay reducing power until well into the flare

SINGLE-ENGINE OPERATION

Single-engine operation provides adequate power for flight. Since loss of electric and hydraulic redundancy is the major concern, make every attempt, consistent with safety and prudence, to have the ailing engine running, even at idle. Otherwise, normal procedures should be followed, making appropriate allowance for reduced thrust. Reduce gross weight as practicable; plan ahead to avoid situations requiring high thrust levels. A windmilling engine can cause repeated flight control transients, reduced control sensitivity, momentary split flaps and CAS disengagements as the hydraulic switchover valves operate. Audible noises may be heard as switchover valves operate. After PC pressure has decreased to near zero, the transients will cease and the CAS may be reset and flap operation will be normal. Monitor hydraulic pressure as windmill rpm sufficient to cause transients may occur with the tachometer indicating 0%. To prevent repeated switchover valve cycling, avoid stabilized flight where engine windmilling conditions produce hydraulic pressure fluctuations between 800-2000 psi.

If landing single engine with an ECS caution, automatic avionics shutdown will occur upon touchdown. UHF 1 will be inoperative, along with the HUD and the MPDs/MPCDs. Aerobrake using backup visual references. If the ECS caution is not illuminated and power is below 73%, expect automatic avionics shutdown during landing rollout.

FLAP MALFUNCTIONS

If a split-flap situation occurs and the flaps cannot be retracted, fly a wider than normal pattern using normal AOA and airspeeds. Sufficient control will be available either CAS-ON or CAS-OFF under most configurations, but a controllability check should be performed if doubt exists. With CAS-ON, only a slight rolling tendency will be noticed. CAS-OFF, the tendency is more pronounced, but not severe. UTL A and PC1 B, or a UTL B and PC2 B failure will cause a split flap if the flaps are extended.

BLOWN TIRES

Selecting PULSER prevents continuous loss of brake pressure due to skid sensing on the blown tire and allows braking on the good tire. If both main tires are blown, be prepared to counter any skid with timely nose gear steering inputs in the direction of the skid. The skid potential increases as speed decreases due to loss of vertical tails and rudders effectiveness. Overcorrection, no input at all, or initial inputs away from the skid may result in loss of directional control. Maneuvering mode of nose gear steering may be needed for adequate control.

At high speed, lateral stick can be used to maintain a wings level attitude and relieve some of the load on the blown tire. The anti-skid switch should be placed from PULSER to OFF when slowed to taxi speed.

Stop straight ahead if possible and shut down as soon as fire equipment is available. Do not taxi unless an emergency situation exists.

When landing with a known blown main tire, an approach-end arrestment should be considered to avoid the possible braking/directional control problems discussed above. Landing on the runway centerline is recommended regardless of arrestment options. The anti-skid switch should be placed to PULSER before landing. Maneuver conservatively since ARI is disengaged with gear down and PULSER selected.

If a main tire blows on landing rollout, consider a midfield or departure-end arrestment.

If the nose tire is blown, the possibility of engine FOD due to rubber being thrown from the nose wheel exists. Hold the nosewheel off as long as practicable (below 70 knots), and insure engines are at IDLE when nosewheel touchdown occurs.

LANDING WITH KNOWN BLOWN MAIN TIRE

1. Anti-skid switch - PULSER (before landing)
2. Consider approach-end arrestment.

BLOWN MAIN TIRE DURING LANDING ROLLOUT

1. Hook - AS REQUIRED
2. Anti-skid switch - PULSER
3. Use braking on good tire as required.

ANTI-SKID MALFUNCTION

An ANTI-SKID caution, either in flight or on the ground, should be interpreted as a potential loss of the normal braking system. Therefore, continued operation should be with the anti-skid switch OFF or PULSER (as required). The pulser brake system will activate automatically when the ANTI-SKID caution comes on. If the system does not automatically activate, it can be selected by placing the anti-skid switch to PULSER. When the system is activated, the ARI is disengaged with the gear handle down. Pulser operation can be confirmed by applying brake pedal and feeling the oscillatory brake pressure relief. Limit use of the pulser system to slowing the aircraft from landing speed down to taxi speed. Turn the anti-skid switch OFF when slowed to a comfortable taxi speed. The intensity of brake pressure relief appears to increase as speed decreases even though the pulser brake cycle rate is constant. If runway length is insufficient for aerobraking followed by non-anti-skid wheel braking, plan an approach-end arrestment. If the ANTI-SKID caution comes on inflight or on the ground:

1. Anti-skid switch - PULSER

During pulser operation, pedal pressure over that required for safe deceleration may cause excessive tire wear.

For taxi -

2. Anti-skid switch - OFF

Aircraft creeps and cannot be completely stopped with pulser brakes.

HYDRAULIC FAILURE

Refer to hydraulic flow diagram (figure 3-2) and BIT panel for systems affected.

A failure of a single hydraulic system is not considered a critical item because of dual systems and reservoir level sensing (RLS) incorporated in the hydraulic system design. Although not considered critical, proper treatment of the situation is warranted, as with any emergency, due to the possibility of subsequent failures which may compound the problem. With UTL A failure, if conditions warrant, an approach-end arrestment is recommended. For multiple hydraulic failures, the pilot must refer to the Hydraulic Flow Diagram, this section, to determine systems affected and corrective action required.

UTL A FAILURE

A UTL A failure is the only single hydraulic failure which requires aircrew action.

1. Landing gear - EXTEND (use Landing Gear Emergency Extension procedure)
2. If conditions warrant, an approach-end arrestment is recommended.
3. Emergency brake/steer handle - PULL AFTER NOSEWHEEL IS ON THE GROUND (pulling the emergency brake handle above 70 knots increases the possibility of blown tires).

UTL A AND PC2 A FAILURE

A UTL A and PC2 A failure reduces aircraft control appreciably. The pitch ratio and roll ratio CAUTIONS will be visible.

1. Slow to subsonic.

2. Conduct controllability check.
3. Landing gear - EXTEND (use Landing Gear Emergency Extension procedures)
4. If conditions warrant, an approach-end arrestment is recommended.
5. Emergency brake/steer handle - PULL AFTER NOSEWHEEL IS ON THE GROUND (pulling the emergency brake handle above 70 knots increases the possibility of blown tires).

TOTAL UTILITY SYSTEM FAILURE

A UTL B caution light and a decreasing utility system hydraulic pressure will be the primary early indication of a total system failure. When UTL A subsequently fails, pitch ratio may fluctuate when the CSBPC switches to back-up hydraulic power (PC2 A). If this fluctuation produces undesirable flight effects, place the pitch ratio switch to emergency. A PC1B or PC2B caution followed by a UTL A caution is also an indication of a possible total utility system failure. In either case if there is a possibility of a total utility system failure, consideration should be given to lowering the landing gear normally before UTL A fails completely. Engines should be shut down as soon as possible after landing consistent with arrestment procedures to limit damage to cavitated utility hydraulic pumps.

1. Land as soon as possible.
2. Landing gear - EXTEND (if necessary use Landing Gear Emergency Extension procedure).
3. Consider an approach-end arrestment.
4. Emergency brake/steer handle PULL AFTER NOSEWHEEL IS ON THE GROUND (pulling the emergency brake handle above 70 knots increases the possibility of blown tires).

LANDING GEAR UNSAFE

If one or both main gear indicate unsafe, but all gear are visually confirmed to have extended and appear to be locked, leave the gear handle down and, if conditions warrant, an approach-end arrestment is recommended. If the nose gear indicates unsafe, but is visually confirmed to have extended and appears to be locked, leave the gear handle down and make a normal landing. In either case, the anti-skid should be OFF/PULSER. Yawing the aircraft or pulling g loading may assist in obtaining a locked indication.

HYDRAULIC FLOW DIAGRAM

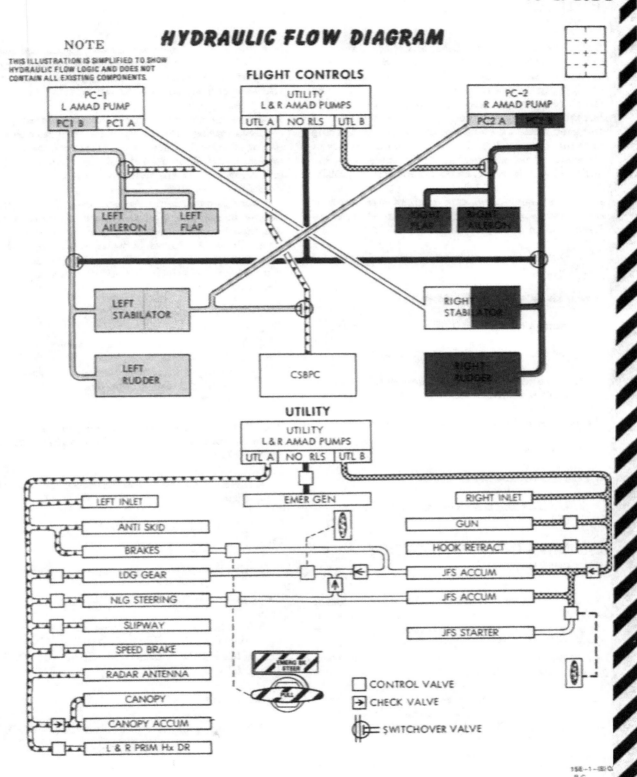

Figure 3-2

If all three gear extend without any of the three gear down indicators (green lights) on and the gear is visually confirmed down, a circuit breaker(s) is probably popped. In this situation, test the lights. If any of the three lights test good, anti-skid is not available but there will be no warning light. If the lights do not test good, anti-skid should be available (but warning of failure may not be). Because of the uncertainty of the status of the anti-skid system in these cases, the anti-skid switch should be placed to OFF/PULSER.

If you are unable to visually confirm gear status or one or more gear have failed to extend, refer to Landing Gear Emergency Extension.

1. Obtain visual confirmation of gear status (if practical)

If gear visually confirmed down -

2. Anti-skid - OFF/PULSER

If one or both main gear indicate unsafe -

3. If conditions warrant, an approach-end arrestment is recommended.

If nose gear indicates unsafe -

3. Make normal landing

If gear not visually confirmed down -

2. Use Landing Gear Emergency Extension procedure

LANDING GEAR EMERGENCY EXTENSION

Failure of the gear to extend may be caused by loss of UTL A hydraulic pressure, mechanical or electrical failure of a system component, or physical jamming of the gear. Pulling the emergency landing gear handle (far enough out to lock) bypasses the normal electrical and hydraulic controls and ports JFS accumulator pressure to open the gear doors and unlock the landing gear. The landing gear, aided by air loads, then free falls to down and locked. Providing no component or UTL A failure exists, resetting the

emergency landing gear handle with the normal handle DOWN will restore pressure to the extend side of the gear actuator, close the landing gear doors and allow the JFS accumulator to recharge.

If failure to extend is due to a mechanical jam, repeated cycling with the normal system may be the only method to dislodge the object causing the jam. If normal hydraulic and electrical power are available and completion of the following steps does not successfully extend all landing gear, restore normal system operation by pushing the emergency landing gear handle in and ensuring the circuit breaker is in. Attempt to extend the landing gear normally several times. Pause 10 seconds between each movement of the control handle and pull g during the extension cycle. If this fails, refer to Landing With Abnormal Gear Configuration.

1. Airspeed - BELOW 250 KNOTS
2. Landing gear handle - DOWN
3. Emergency landing gear handle - PULL UNTIL LOCKED

    Yawing the aircraft and slowing to below 200 knots may aid in obtaining gear down indications.

With UTL A pressure available and gear fails to extend or cannot be confirmed down (BEFORE TO 1F-15E-517) -

4. Refer to Landing Gear Emergency - Landing, Figure 3-4.

AFTER TO 1F-15E-517 or with UTL A pressure zero -

4. Emergency landing gear handle - RESET

If any gear fails to extend -

5. Landing gear control circuit breaker - PULL, WAIT AT LEAST 30 SECONDS
6. EMERGENCY LANDING GEAR HANDLE - PULL

If gear extend -

7. Landing gear control circuit breaker - RESET

If gear still fails to extend or cannot be visually confirmed down -

    8. Refer to Landing Gear Emergency - Landing, figure 3-4.

If any gear retracts -

    5. Emergency landing gear handle - PULL (DO NOT RESET)

LANDING WITH ABNORMAL GEAR CONFIGURATION

Before attempting to land with an abnormal gear configuration, consider arresting gear limitations, crosswinds, and other weather factors, runway and overrun condition. If conditions are not favorable - eject. If conditions favor landing, refer to the specific gear configurations shown in Figure 3-4, Landing Gear Emergency - Landing.

When landing with an abnormal gear configuration, fly 18 units AOA with a flat approach, plan on landing on runway centerline and attempt to land 800 to 1,200 feet prior to the cable (if an arrested landing is desired) or in the normal touchdown zone if arrestment is not planned. If an arrestment is planned, enough fuel should be reserved to allow for at least one missed arrestment, go-around and another attempt.

A concern when landing with abnormal gear configurations is that the damaged gear, external stores, or a stabilator will catch the arresting cable causing loss of directional control and collateral damage to the aircraft. For this reason, approach end arrestment is not recommended when the main landing gear wheel and brake stack are both missing or the main gear is partially broken off (stub strut). When landing with a damaged or missing main landing gear wheel and tire, but an intact brake stack, an approach end arrestment is recommended. The brake stack will pass over the cable and allow a successful approach end arrestment. The aileron should be used to keep the wings level and reduce the weight on the abnormal gear. Refer to Landing Gear Emergency - Landing Chart.

If landing with one main gear up, be prepared to counter wing dip on landing with aileron. Some power may be necessary to hold the non-gear wing up. Attempt to engage the arresting gear in a wings level altitude. If the arrestment is unsuccessful, a go-around should be initiated if fuel and conditions

permit. If a go-around is not possible, the anti-skid switch must be placed to PULSER to restore braking on the extended main gear. This braking, in conjunction with nose gear steering, may assist in maintaining directional control. If landing with missing landing gear wheel (stub strut), refer to Landing Gear Emergency - Landing chart.

APPROACH END ARRESTMENT

Anticipate a missed engagement. Consider the type of emergency, availability of backup arresting gear, runway condition and length, weather, fuel state, and any other pertinent factors in determining the proper action in event of a missed engagement. With all gear down, touch down at least 800 feet from the arresting gear to allow enough time to lower the nosewheel to the runway before engagement.

CAUTION

    Above 35,000 pounds, an arrestment with the nosewheel in the air may result in nose gear failure and extensive aircraft damage.

Throttles must be at idle before engagement. After engagement, control arresting gear rollback using power and light braking and await the arresting gear chief's instruction. Refer to figure 3-3 for engagement limitations.

    1. Reduce landing weight.
    2. Hook - DOWN
    3. Inertia reel - LOCKED
    4. Lower nose immediately after touchdown.
    5. Throttles - IDLE
    6. Engage arresting gear in the center with brakes off.

        Engagements up to 1/4 cable length off-center produce only minor yawing motions which are easily controlled with nosewheel steering.

DEPARTURE END ARRESTMENT

If there is any doubt about your ability to stop the aircraft on the remaining runway, lower the tail hook. Stopping short of the arresting gear will only require raising the hook, but rolling over arresting gear when it is needed may cause serious damage and/or injury. Engage as close to center as possible, without brakes, and aligned with the runway. Place the hook down at

LANDING GEAR EMERGENCY - LANDING
BEFORE LANDING CONSIDERATIONS -

1. JETTISON ARMAMENT (CONSIDER RETAINING RACKS)
2. DUMP OR BURN EXCESS FUEL
3. RETAIN EMPTY DROP TANKS (DEPRESSURIZE - OPEN SLIPWAY)
   IF FUEL LOW LIGHT ON, PLACING THE AIR SOURCE KNOB
   OFF IS THE ONLY MEANS TO DEPRESSURIZE THE TANKS

4. FLAPS - DOWN
5. FLY 18 UNITS AOA WITH FLAT APPROACH
6. FOR PLANNED ARRESTMENT, LAND 800 - 1200 FEET PRIOR TO CABLE
7. LAND ON RUNWAY CENTERLINE

LANDING NOT RECOMMENDED

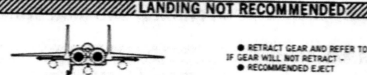

- RETRACT GEAR AND REFER TO ALL GEAR UP
IF GEAR WILL NOT RETRACT -
- RECOMMENDED EJECT

ONE MAIN - NO NOSE

ARRESTMENT NOT RECOMMENDED

- 170 KNOTS TOUCHDOWN SPEED

ALL GEAR UP

- LOWER, REMOVE, OR LAND PAST CABLE
- ANTI-SKID OFF
- LAND ON SIDE OF RUNWAY TOWARD GOOD GEAR
- HOLD WINGS LEVEL AS LONG AS POSSIBLE
- USE NOSEWHEEL STEERING AND GOOD BRAKE
  TO MAINTAIN TRACK

STUB MAIN GEAR

- DO NOT SHUT DOWN ENGINES UNTIL STOPPED
- TRY TO HAVE CABLES REMOVED BEFORE LANDING

BOTH MAIN - NO NOSE/STUB NOSE

APPROACH END ARRESTMENT RECOMMENDED

- JETTISON « TANK
- BE PREPARED TO COUNTER WING DIP
- SAVE FUEL FOR REATTEMPT IF MISSED
IF ARRESTMENT NOT PRACTICAL -
- DO NOT SHUT DOWN ENGINES UNTIL STOPPED

NO MAIN - NOSE DOWN

- ANTI-SKID - OFF/PULSER
- SAVE FUEL FOR REATTEMPT, IF MISSED
- BE PREPARED TO COUNTER WING DIP
IF ARRESTMENT NOT PRACTICAL -
- RETRACT GEAR AND REFER TO ALL GEAR UP
IF GEAR WILL NOT RETRACT (ARRESTMENT NOT POSSIBLE) -
- REFER TO STUB MAIN GEAR

ONE MAIN - NOSE DOWN

- ANTI-SKID - OFF/PULSER
- SAVE FUEL FOR REATTEMPT, IF MISSED
- BE PREPARED TO COUNTER WING DIP
IF ARRESTMENT NOT PRACTICAL -
- LAND ON SIDE OF RUNWAY TOWARD GOOD GEAR
- HOLD WINGS LEVEL AS LONG AS POSSIBLE
- USE NOSEWHEEL STEERING AND GOOD BRAKE
  TO MAINTAIN TRACK

NO MAIN WHEEL - BRAKE STACK INTACT

15E-1-(10)03

Figure 3-4

least 2000 feet before the arresting gear, and reduce speed as much as possible. After engagement, use brakes and/or power to reduce arresting gear recoil and await the arresting gear chief's instruction.

1. Hook - DOWN

2. Engage arresting gear squarely with brakes off, throttles idle, and in a three-point attitude. Engagements up to 1/4 cable length off-center produce only minor yawing motions which are easily controlled with nosewheel steering.

ARRESTMENT GEAR DATA

MAXIMUM ENGAGEMENT GROUNDSPEEDS

SYSTEM	AIRCRAFT GROSS WEIGHT - POUNDS			
	BELOW 50,000	50,000 TO 60,000	60,000 TO 68,000	68,000 TO 81,000
BAK-9	135 KNOTS	130 KNOTS	120 KNOTS	113 KNOTS
BAK-12/BAK-14	145 KNOTS	145 KNOTS	140 KNOTS	138 KNOTS
BAK-12/BAK-14 Dual or extended runout	160 KNOTS	160 KNOTS	140 KNOTS	138 KNOTS
BAK-13	150 KNOTS	145KNOTS	143 KNOTS	142 KNOTS

NOTES

- USE STANDARD BAK-12 LIMITATIONS UNLESS YOU POSITIVELY DETERMINE THAT BAK-12 DUAL OR EXTENDED RUNOUT IS INSTALLED
- AVOID HARD BRAKING AND/OR ABRUPT STEERING INPUTS DURING ARRESTMENT
- MAXIMUM ENGAGEMENT SPEEDS ARE VALID ONLY WITH IDLE THRUST, AIRCRAFT IN A THREE POINT ATTITUDE, AND ENGAGEMENT ON CENTER
- FOR ARRESTMENT WITH GEAR OTHER THAN THOSE LISTED, ENGAGE AT THE LOWEST POSSIBLE WEIGHT AND SPEED
- ENGAGEMENTS MAY BE MADE AT SPEEDS SLIGHTLY HIGHER THAN THOSE SHOWN BUT THERE IS THEN A POSSIBILITY OF HOOK FAILURE OR STRUCTURAL DAMAGE
- A BAK-14 SYSTEM CAN REQUIRE UP TO 7 1/2 SECONDS FROM ACTIVATION TO FULLY UP AND LOCKED, CONTROLLER REACTION TIME WILL INCREASE THIS TIME

Table 3-1

EMERGENCY POWER DISTRIBUTION
EMERGENCY GENERATOR OPERATING
SWITCH IN AUTO OR MAN

L GEN OUT		R GEN OUT

INOPERATIVE EQUIPMENT

ENGINE-
- AB BURN THRU DETECTION
- CFT AFT TRANSFER PUMPS
- ENGINE ANTI-ICE
- ENGINE OIL PRESSURE INDICATIONS
- FUEL FLOW INDICATORS
- FUEL TRANSFER PUMPS
- ICE DETECTOR
- L&R BOOST PUMPS
- L&R DUCT TEMP PROBE HEATERS
- L&R ENG INLET CONTROLLERS
- L&R TOTAL TEMP PROBE HEATERS
- NOZZLE POSITION INDICATIONS
- F-15E 90-233 AND UP, ASYMMETRIC THRUST DEPARTURE PREVENTION SYSTEM

FLIGHT INSTRUMENTS-
- ANGLE OF ATTACK INDICATOR
- VERTICAL VELOCITY INDICATORS

NAVIGATION EQUIPMENT-
- ADF
- ATTITUDE HEADING REFERENCE SYSTEM
- IFF INTERROGATOR
- ILS
- KY-58
- STANDBY COMPASS LIGHT
- TACAN
- UHF R/T NO.2

OTHER-
- AIR DATA COMPUTER
- AIU NO.2
- ANTI-COLLISION LIGHTS
- CENTRAL COMPUTER
- CONSOLE LIGHTS
- FORMATION LIGHTS
- HUD
- INSTRUMENT LIGHTS
- IRE (IFF REPLY EVALUATOR)
- JETTISON (USING A/G SELECT AND SELECT JETTISON CONTROLS)
- KIR (INTERROGATOR COMPUTER)
- KIT (TRANSPONDER COMPUTER)
- LANTIRN POD
- LANDING & TAXI LIGHTS
- MPCD (REAR)
- MPD'S (ALL)
- OVERLOAD WARNING
- OXYGEN GAGE
- PC-1 HYD PRESS INDICATOR
- PC-2 HYD PRESS INDICATOR
- PITCH RATIO INDICATOR
- POSITION LIGHTS
- RADAR
- RADAR ALTIMETER
- RMR
- SEAT ADJUST
- TEW (RWR, EWWS, ICS)
- TIS
- UTILITY HYD PRESS IND
- UTILITY FLOOD LIGHT (REAR CKPT)
- VERTICAL TAIL LIGHTS
- VTRS
- WPN NORM RELEASE/LAUNCH
- WINDSHIELD ANTI-ICE SYSTEM

Figure 3-5. (Sheet 1 of 3)

EMERGENCY POWER DISTRIBUTION
EMERGENCY GENERATOR OPERATING
SWITCH IN AUTO OR MAN

| L GEN OUT | | R GEN OUT |

OPERATIVE EQUIPMENT

ENGINE-
AMAD FIRE DETECTION SYS
AMAD FIRE EXTINGUISHER SYS
BLEED AIR LEAK DETECTOR
EMER FUEL BOOST PUMP
[1] ENG AND A/B IGNITION
ENG FIRE EXTINGUISHER SYSTEM
ENG FIRE DETECTION
  SYSTEM
ENG RPM INDICATION
PTIT INDICATION
FUEL DUMP (EXT TANKS ONLY)
FUEL LOW AND BINGO LIGHTS
[1] FUEL PRESS AND VENT
FUEL QUANTITY INDICATORS
L & R ENG FUEL SHUTOFF VALVES
SELECTED CFT CENTER
  TRANSFER PUMP

FLIGHT INSTRUMENTS
[1] STANDBY AIRSPEED
[1] STANDBY ALTIMETER
STANDBY ATTITUDE INDICATOR

NAVIGATION EQUIPMENT-
INTERCOM
[2] IFF TRANSPONDER
INS
UHF R/T NO.1

OTHER-
AERIAL REFUELING
AERIAL REFUELING FLOOD LIGHTS
AFCS/CAS
AIU NO.1
AN/ALE-45 CMD
ANTENNA SELECT
ANTI-SKID
ARRESTING HOOK
CHART LIGHTS
EMERGENCY JETTISON POWER
  (EMERG JETT BUTTON)
ENVIRONMENTAL CONTROL SYSTEM
FLAPS
ICSCP/RICP
LANDING GEAR
LANDING GEAR POSITION INDICATORS
MASTER CAUTION RESET
MPCD-FRONT (EADI FORMAT ONLY)
MPDP
NOSEWHEEL STEERING
PITCH RATIO
PULSER BRAKE SYSTEM
SPEEDBRAKE
STORM/FLOOD LIGHTS
TRIM (AIL/RUD/STAB)
UP-FRONT CONTROLS
UTILITY FLOOD LIGHT (FRONT CKPT)
VOICE WARNING SYSTEM
WARNING/CAUTION/ADVISORY
  LIGHTS
WARNING/CAUTION/ADVISORY
  LIGHTS TEST

Figure 3-5 (Sheet 2)

EMERGENCY POWER DISTRIBUTION
EMERGENCY GENERATOR OPERATING
SWITCH IN ISOLATE
OPERATIVE EQUIPMENT

AERIAL REFUELING (DEGRADED
   OPERATION)
ARRESTING HOOK
EMER BST ON CAUTION LIGHT
EMER FUEL BOOST PUMP
[1] EMERGENCY NOSEWHEEL STEERING

[1] ENG AND A/B IGNITION
   ENG RPM AND FTIT INDICATIONS
[1] FUEL PRESS AND VENT
[1] STANDBY AIRSPEED
[1] STANDBY ALTIMETER

NOTE

[1] ALTHOUGH OPERATIVE, ITEMS ARE NOT POWERED BY
THE EMERGENCY GENERATOR
[2] WHEN ANY MODES ARE SELECTED, THE IFF
TRANSPONDER WILL SQUAWK EMERGENCY (ONLY WITH
WEIGHT OFF WHEELS)

Figure 3-5. (Sheet 3)

AIRPLANE ENTRY / AIRCREW EXTRACTION

> ### WARNING
>
> IF LEFT ENGINE IS RUNNING, APPROACH AIRPLANE
> ONLY IF SECURED BY AN ADEQUATE RESTRAINING LINE.

NORMAL ENTRY

1. PUSH HANDLE RELEASE BUTTON ON NORMAL CONTROL HANDLE,
   ALLOWING THE HANDLE TO SPRING OUT
2. ROTATE THE HANDLE FULLY AFT. THE CANOPY WILL UNLOCK
   AND OPEN.

MANUAL ENTRY

1. ENSURE NORMAL CONTROL HANDLE IS OUT AND ROTATED FULL
   AFT.
2. LIFT CANOPY AND INSTALL SAFETY STRUT.

> ### CAUTION
>
> DAMAGE TO CANOPY SHEAR BOLT WILL
> RESULT IF CANOPY IS LIFTED TOO HIGH

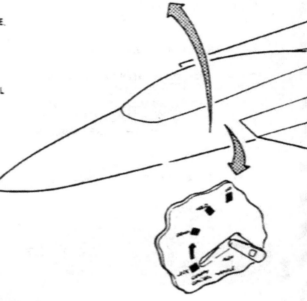

EMERGENCY ENTRY

1. PRESS BUTTON TO OPEN DOOR 9, AND REMOVE T–HANDLE.
2. TO JETTISON CANOPY, PULL T–HANDLE TO FULL LENGTH
   APPROXIMATELY 8 FEET) AND YANK HARD.

EXTRACTION - EJECTION SEAT

> ### WARNING
>
> DO NOT ACTUATE EITHER EJECTION
> SEAT FIRING HANDLE. ROTATE THE
> EJECTION CONTROLS SAFETY LEVER
> FORWARD AND UP AGAINST THE LEFT
> EJECTION FIRING HANDLE TO
> SAFETY THE SEAT.

1. EJECTION CONTROLS SAFETY LEVER FORWARD TO LOCKED POSITION.

2. RELEASE LAP BELT.

3. RELEASE LEFT AND RIGHT SURVIVAL KIT BUCKLES.

4. RELEASE LEFT AND RIGHT PARACHUTE HARNESS STRAPS.

5. OPEN FACE MASK, IF REQUIRED.

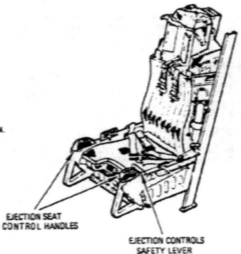

EJECTION SEAT
CONTROL HANDLES

EJECTION CONTROLS
SAFETY LEVER

15E - 1 - 16

Figure 3-6

EJECTION PROCEDURES

IMMEDIATE EJECTION

- ALERT REAR CREWMEMBER
- IF AT LOW ALTITUDE; ATTEMPT TO TRADE AIRSPEED FOR ALTITUDE AND TO EJECT WINGS LEVEL WITH ZERO SINK RATE
- ASSUME PROPER EJECTION POSITION

CONTROLLED EJECTION

IF TIME AND CONDITIONS PERMIT (BEFORE ASSUMING THE PROPER EJECTION POSITION):

- ATTEMPT TO ACHIEVE OPTIMUM EJECTION PARAMETERS
  - 5,000 – 10,000 FEET (AGL), 150-250 KNOTS
  - EJECT NO LOWER THAN 2,000 FEET (AGL)
  - TIGHTEN LAP BELT, HELMET CHIN STRAP AND OXYGEN MASK
  - LOWER HELMET VISOR
  - STOW LOOSE EQUIPMENT
  - COMMAND SELECTOR VALVE – AFT INITIATE
  - THROTTLES – IDLE, SPEEDBRAKE – (AS REQUIRED)

1. EJECTION CONTROL HANDLES – PULL
GRASP THE EJECTION HANDLES AND PULL SO THAT THE HANDLES WILL ROTATE UP AND TOWARD THE BACK OF THE SEAT. ALTHOUGH ACTUATION OF EITHER HANDLE IS SUFFICIENT TO INITIATE EJECTION, BOTH HANDLES SHOULD BE GRASPED, IF POSSIBLE, TO PREVENT ARM FLAILING. CONTINUE HOLDING THE HANDLES UNTIL MAN–SEAT SEPARATION. BE PREPARED TO RELEASE THE HANDLES AT MAN–SEAT SEPARATION SINCE THE HANDLES WILL NOT DETACH FROM THE SEAT.

WARNING

- MINIMUM ALTITUDES ARE DEPENDENT UPON DIVE ANGLE, AIRSPEED, AND BANK ANGLE. RECOMMENDED MINIMUMS ARE 10,000 FEET (AGL) IF OUT OF CONTROL, AND 2000 FEET (AGL) IN CONTROLLED FLIGHT.

- BEFORE TO 1F-15E-552,
IF THE COMMAND SELECTOR VALVE IS IN SOLO, THE REAR SEAT WILL NOT EJECT, NOR CAN THE REAR SEAT EJECT ONCE THE FRONT SEAT HAS BEEN EJECTED. FAILURE TO INSTALL THE SOLO FLIGHT COLLAR WILL CAUSE A 0.4 SECOND DELAY IN FRONT SEAT EJECTION.

- IF THE EMERGENCY OXYGEN GREEN RING IS PULLED WHILE STILL IN THE COCKPIT, THE AIRCRAFT OXYGEN HOSE MUST BE DISCONNECTED FROM THE CRU-60P CONNECTOR, OR THE EMERGENCY OXYGEN WILL VENT INTO THE AIRCRAFT SYSTEM.

CANOPY SEPARATION FAILURE
(BEFORE TO 1F-15E-552)

IF CANOPY DOES NOT JETTISON AFTER PULLING THE EJECTION CONTROL HANDLE, PULL THE HANDLE AGAIN SHARPLY. IF CANOPY STILL DOES NOT JETTISON, RE-MAIN IN POSITION FOR EJECTION AND PERFORM THE FOLLOWING WHILE KEEPING ARMS INBOARD IN READINESS TO REGRASP THE EJECTION CONTROL HANDLE

IF CANOPY FAILS TO SEPARATE

1. CANOPY JETTISON HANDLE – PRESS UNLOCK BUTTON AND PULL

IF CANOPY STILL FAILS TO SEPARATE

2. CANOPY CONTROL HANDLE – UP POSITION

IF CANOPY STILL FAILS TO SEPARATE

3. PULL CANOPY AFT AND THEN PUSH TO OPEN.

NOTE

REFER TO FOLDOUT SECTION FOR EJECTION SEAT PERFORMANCE CHARTS

WARNING

THE FOLLOWING PROCEDURES ARE PRESENTED AS A LAST RESORT ACTION FOR THE CREW TO DEPART THE AIRCRAFT AND NO IN-DEPTH STUDIES HAVE BEEN MADE TO CONFIRM WHETHER OR NOT THEY WILL BE SUCCESSFUL. CREW SAFETY MAY BE JEOPARDIZED USING THESE PROCEDURES; HOWEVER, THIS MAY BE PREFERABLE TO REMAINING WITH THE AIRCRAFT

EJECTION SEAT FAILURE
IF CANOPY SEPARATES AND EJECTION SEAT DOES NOT FIRE
(BEFORE TO 1F-15E-552)

1. MAINTAIN 200-250 KNOTS, IF POSSIBLE
2. SURVIVAL KIT STRAPS – RELEASE
3. APPLY FULL NOSE DOWN TRIM WHILE HOLDING THE AIRPLANE LEVEL
4. STICK – RELEASE

NOTE

PROCEED FROM STEP 4 TO STEP 5 AS QUICKLY AS POSSIBLE.

5. RESTRAINT EMERGENCY RELEASE – ACTUATE, WHILE PUSHING UP ON LEFT PITOT PROBE SUPPORT

15E-1-(15-1)1B

Figure 3-7 (Sheet 1 of 2)

DESCENT AND MANUAL
SURVIVAL EQUIPMENT DEPLOYMENT

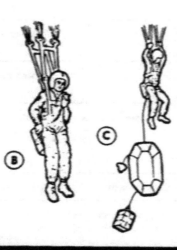

A IF EMERGENCY OXYGEN FAILS TO RELEASE AUTOMATICALLY UPON EJECTION PULL THE OXYGEN RELEASE RING ON REAR OF LEFT ARMREST.

B AFTER PARACHUTE DEPLOYMENT OPEN THE FACE MASK. IF SURVIVAL KIT DOES NOT DEPLOY AUTOMATICALLY, GRASP KIT HANDLE WITH RIGHT HAND AND PULL.

C LIFE RAFT INFLATION IS INITIATED BY GRAVITY WHEN THE DROP LINE IS FULLE EXTENDED AFTER KIT OPENING.

> **WARNING**
>
> IF THE SURVIVAL KIT IS DEPLOYED AFTER LANDING IN WATER, A SNATCH PULL ON THE DROP LINE (NEAR CO_2 BOTTLE) IS REQUIRED TO INFLATE THE LIFE RAFT.

MANUAL SEPARATION

IF BELOW 15,000 FEET (MSL) AND HARNESS RELEASE ACTUATOR FAILS TO OPERATE

> **WARNING**
>
> THE FOLLOWING PROCEDURES BYPASS THE HIGHLY RELIABLE AUTOMATIC SYSTEM AND SHOULD BE USED ONLY AS A LAST RESORT.

BEFORE TO 1F-15E-582

A PUSH UP ON LEFT PITOT SUPPORT AND SIMUTANEOUSLY PULL THE RESTRAINT EMERGENCY RELEASE HANDLE. AFTER HANDLE IS PULLED, PUSH ON BOTH PITOT SUPPORTS EVENLY.

> **WARNING**
>
> YOU WILL BE REQUIRED TO MANUALLY ASSIST SEAT / PERSONNEL PARACHUTE CONTAINER SEPARATION. PUSHING ON ONLY ON PITOT SUPPORT MAY CAUSE BINDING PREVENTING THE RECOVERY PARACHUTE FROM SEPARATING FROM SEAT. DO NOT GRASP THE PITOT SENSING INLET HOUSINGS. SEVERE ARM / HAND INJURY COULD OCCUR IF PARACHUTE MORTAR FIRES WHILE GRASPING THE INLET HOUSINGS.

> **NOTE**
>
> ONCE THE RESTRAINT EMERGENCY RELEASE HANDLE HAS BEEN ACTUATED, THE LAP BELT, INERTIA REEL, SEAT PAN, PERSONNEL PARACHUTE CONTAINER, AND PILOT CHUTE ARE RELEASED.

B JERK ON THE PARACUTE RISERS, OR USE ANY OTHER METHOD TO FORCE THE PERSONNEL PARACHUTE CONTAINER FROM THE SEAT.

> **WARNING**
>
> IF THE PILOT CHUTE DOES NOT SEPARATE THE PERSONNEL PARACHUTE CONTAINER FROM THE SEAT, THE CREW MEMBER MAY BE ATTACHED TO THE SEAT BY THE PARACHUTE RISERS.

AFTER TO 1F-15E-582

A WHEN CLEAR OF AIRCRAFT, PULL EMERGENCY MANUAL CHUTE HANDLE.

> **WARNING**
>
> THE EMERGENCY MANUAL CHUTE HANDLE MUST BE PULLED TO ITS FULL TRAVEL TO ASSURE RESTRAINT RELEASE.

B SHOULD CHUTE DEPLOY BUT AUTOMATIC SEAT SEPARATION FAIL TO OCCUR, CONTINUE PULLING THE EMERGENCY MANUAL CHUTE HANDLE AND MANUALLY OPEN THE LAP BELT.

15E-1-(15-2)18

Figure 3-7 (Sheet 2)

Warning/Caution/Advisories

DISPLAY	CAUSE	CORRECTIVE ACTION/REMARKS
RED WARNING LIGHTS		
AI	Air intercept threat	Information
AMAD FIRE	Fire condition	Refer to emergency procedure (Front cockpit only)*
L BURN THRU R BURN THRU	Abrupt temperature change in AB section	Retard throttles out of AB range (Front cockpit only)
CANOPY UNLOCKED	Canopy unlocked or canopy actuated initiator lanyard disconnected	GROUND: Relock canopy or connect lanyard AIR: Airspeed - 200 KNOTS Cockpit pressure - DUMP Canopy - LOCK
FIRE	Excessive temperature in indicated area	Refer to emergency procedures
Landing Gear Handle	Gear up and aircraft in landing regime, gear not in selected position, no control power, or ADC failed	Climb or Refer to emergency procedures*
LOW ALT (LOW ALTITUDE)	Aircraft has descended below 75% of set clearance plane value or AFCS system determines or predicts you will reach less than 75% of ground clearance if action not taken	Climb to proper altitude and check system for problems
LOW ALT	Aircraft has descended below LAW altitude selected in UFC menu 1	Climb above LAW altitude
OBST	Obstacle in flight path requiring more than 2g to clear	Climb or turn
SAM	Missile threat	Information
TF FAIL	Terrain following failed	Do not rely on terrain following indications
UNSAFE	Gear up and aircraft in landing regime, gear not in selected position, no control power, or ADC failed	Information (Rear cockpit only)
* ADDITIONAL INFORMATION AVAILABLE IN THIS SECTION		

Warning/Caution/Advisories (CONT)

DISPLAY	CAUSE	CORRECTIVE ACTION/REMARKS
YELLOW CAUTION LIGHTS (CAUTION LIGHT PANEL)		
AV BIT	Avionics BIT failure	Check BIT display on MPD/MPCD If FLT CONTR caution also on - Refer to LAT STK LMT caution*
BST SYS MAL	Emergency boost pump logic malfunction	Refer to emergency procedure*
CHAFF	Flashing: Dispensing chaff Steady: Chaff dispenser empty	Information
DISPL FLO LO	Inadequate cooling air flow to cockpit displays	Refer to emergency procedure*
EMER BST ON	Emergency boost pump supplying pressure	Check BST SYS MAL caution out/off
ENGINE	Engine systems failure	Check MPD/MPCD cautions
FLARE	Flashing: Dispensing flares Steady: Flare dispenser empty	Information
FLYUP ARM	Flyup enable switch ON	Information (Rear cockpit only)
FLT CONTR	Flight control system failure	Check MPD/MPCD cautions
FUEL LOW	Left feed tank below 540 pounds and/or Right feed tank below 960 pounds	Use minimum power – Check all tanks
L GEN	Left/right generator failure	Refer to emergency procedure*
R GEN		
HYD	Hydraulic systems failure	Check MPD/MPCD cautions
MINIMUM	Dispensable stores at predetermined level	Information
NUCLEAR	Nuclear armament malfunction	Check armament display
☐1☐ OXYGEN	Oxygen concentration is below acceptable limits	Refer to Emergency Procedues
NOTES		
*ADDITIONAL INFORMATION AVAILABLE IN THIS SECTION		
☐1☐ F-15E 90-0233 AND UP; ALSO F-15E 86-0183 THRU 90-232 AFTER TO 1F-15E-561		

Warning/Caution/Advisories (CONT)

DISPLAY	CAUSE	CORRECTIVE ACTION/REMARKS
YELLOW CAUTION LIGHTS (MISCELLANEOUS)		
EMIS LMT	EMIS LMT switch ON	Information
FLAPS	Flaps in transit	Information
LASER ARMED	Target pod laser armed	Information (Front cockpit only)
LOCK/SHOOT	Steady: Radar locked on Flashing: Shoot cue	Information (Canopy bow)
MASTER CAUTION	One or more cautions displayed	Check caution lights and MPD/MPCD
HUD WARNINGS (TF)		
FLYUP	Flyup initiated	Recover aircraft to safe altitude and determine cause of flyup
G-LIMIT	Flyup command greater than 2.1g	Climb to 0g command. Recover at safe altitude. Determine cause of failure.
OBSTACLE	Obstacle requiring more than 2.0g is in aircraft flight path	Climb or turn away from obstacle
TF FAIL	Terrain following failed	Recover aircraft to safe altitude. Determine cause of failure.
TF LOW	Below 75% of selected terrain clearance or predicted to descend below 75% of selected clearance	Climb and recover aircraft to safe altitude. Determine cause of descending below set clearance.
HUD CAUTIONS (TF)		
ROLL	Roll angle exceeding 45° in TF mode	Decrease roll angle below 45°
TURN RATE	TF mode turn rate exceeded	Reduce turn rate
TURN ACCEL	TF mode turn acceleration limit exceeded	Reduce turn acceleration
DIVE	Dive angle ≥ 15°	Reduce dive angle to < 15°
UNARMED	Malfunctions preclude auto flyup	Determine cause of flyup fault
INS LIMIT	Drift, pitch or vector angle exceeded	Reduce exceeded limit
AIRSPEED	Airspeed too slow to accomplish flyup maneuver or exceeding TF radar limit	Adjust speed accordingly
NO TERRAIN	TF radar cannot determine terrain altitude	Information. Continue following TF commands.

Warning/Caution/Advisories (CONT)

DISPLAY	CAUSE	CORRECTIVE ACTION/REMARKS
HUD CAUTIONS (cont)		
ECCM	Jamming interfering with TF radar	Select TF Radar ECCM mode if appropriate
N-F LOS	NAV FLIR LOS out of tolerance	Use NAV FLIR only with extreme caution
N-F BRST	NAV FLIR in boresight mode	Forward TDC may be used to slew NAV FLIR video
MPD/MPCD CAUTIONS		
ANTI-SKID	Anti-skid inoperative or OFF	Refer to emergency procedure*
ATTITUDE	Unreliable attitude source	Check standby attitude indicator* Select operable mode
AUTO PLT	Auto pilot malfunction and /or mode disengagement	Information
BINGO FUEL	Fuel at preset amount	Information
CAUTION	Caution lights are no longer functional	Information, cautions are not being displayed
L BLEED AIR	Left/right bleed air leak or overtemperature	Refer to emergency procedure*
R BLEED AIR		
BST SYS MAL	Emergency boost pump logic malfunction	Refer to emergency procedure*
L BST PUMP	Left/right boost pump failure	Refer to emergency procedure*
R BST PUMP		
CAS PITCH	Control augmentation system inoperative or disengaged in mode shown	CAS pitch - RESET
CAS ROLL		CAS roll - RESET
CAS YAW		CAS yaw - RESET/CAS roll - RESET
ECS	Environmental control system flow low or high temperature	Refer to emergency procedure*
L ENG CONTR	Left/right DEEC failed, Mach number failure, engine overspeed, AB inhibited, or switch OFF	Refer to emergency procedure*
R ENG CONTR		
EMER BST ON	Emergency boost pump supplying pressure	Check BST SYS MAL caution off/out
FIRE SENSOR	Failed fire/temperatue sensor	Information

* ADDITIONAL INFORMATION AVAILABLE IN THIS SECTION

Warning/Caution/Advisories (CONT)

DISPLAY	CAUSE	CORRECTIVE ACTION/REMARKS
MPD/MPCD CAUTIONS (CONT)		
FUEL HOT	Engine fuel temperature	Throttles - ADVANCE AS FEASIBLE Ground: If light does not go out within five minutes - ABORT
HOOK	Hook unlocked	Slow and cycle hook
IFF MODE 4	Mode 4 OUT/zeroized or not responding	Check mode 4 not in OUT Check proper A or B code
INLET ICE	Ice buildup in left engine inlet	Anti-ice engine heat switch - ON
L INLET	Left/right engine inlet control failure	Refer to emergency procedure *
R INLET		
JFS LOW	JFS accumulator pressure low	JFS start/emergency gear/brakes/steering may be inoperative*
LAT STK LMT	AFCS failure	Do not exceed 1/2 lateral stick Refer to LAT STK LMT caution*
NAV POD HOT	Navigation pod overtemperature	Turn OFF NAV FLIR and TF RDR
L OIL PRESS	Left/right oil pressure low	Check oil pressure
R OIL PRESS		
OXY LOW	4 liters oxygen remaining	Below 1/2 liter - Descend below 10,000 feet MSL
PC1 A	Designated RLS valve has actuated to shut off subsystem	Refer to Hydraulic Flow Diagram for systems affected*
PC1 B		
PC2 A		
PC2 B		
PITCH RATIO	CSBPC failure, pitch ratio failure or EMERG selected	Pitch ratio switch - EMERG*
L PUMP	Left/right utility pump pressure low	Information
R PUMP		
ROLL RATIO	Roll ratio incorrect or EMERG selected	Roll ratio switch - EMERG*

*ADDITIONAL INFORMATION AVAILABLE IN THIS SECTION

Warning/Caution/Advisories (CONT)

DISPLAY	CAUSE	CORRECTIVE ACTION/REMARKS
MPD/MPCD CAUTIONS (CONT)		
RUDR LMTR	Rudder limiter not scheduling properly	No high speed large rudder input Verify rudder available before landing
TGT POD HOT	Target pod overtemperature	Turn OFF Pod
TOT TEMP HI	Critical inlet temperature (3 minute limit)	Reduce airspeed
UTL A	Designated RLS valve has actuated to shut off system	Refer to Hydraulic Flow Diagram for systems affected*
UTL B		If UTL A and PC 2 failure - Refer to emergenc procedure*
WNDSHLD HOT	Anti-ice air hot	Windshield anti-ice switch - OFF
XFER PUMP	Wing or CFT fuel transfer pump inoperative	Monitor wing and CFT fuel transfer*
GREEN ADVISORY LIGHTS		
AUTO TF	Auto terrain following selected	Information (Rear cockpit only)
FLAP	Flaps are down	Information
LEFT	Left main gear down and locked	Information
MASTER ARM	Master arm switch in ARM	Information (Rear cockpit only)
NOSE	Nose gear down and locked	Information
PROGRAM	Countermeasure dispenser in semi-auto mode and stored dispense program awaiting action	Information
RIGHT	Right main gear down and locked	Information
RCD	Recorder function commanded and record enabled	Information
READY (JFS)	JFS ready for engine engagement	Information
READY (AR)	Air refueling system ready	Information
T/O TRIM	Trim is takeoff position	Information
*ADDITIONAL INFORMATION AVAILABLE IN THIS SECTION		

Warning/Caution/Advisories (CONT)

DISPLAY	CAUSE	CORRECTIVE ACTION/REMARKS
MPD/MPCD CAUTIONS (CONT)		
FUEL HOT	Engine fuel temperature	Throttles - ADVANCE AS FEASIBLE Ground: If light does not go out within five minutes - ABORT
HOOK	Hook unlocked	Slow and cycle hook
IFF MODE 4	Mode 4 OUT/zeroized or not responding	Check mode 4 not in OUT Check proper A or B code
INLET ICE	Ice buildup in left engine inlet	Anti-ice engine heat switch - ON
L INLET	Left/right engine inlet control failure	Refer to emergency procedure *
R INLET		
JFS LOW	JFS accumulator pressure low	JFS start/emergency gear/brakes/steering may be inoperative*
LAT STK LMT	AFCS failure	Do not exceed 1/2 lateral stick Refer to LAT STK LMT caution*
NAV POD HOT	Navigation pod overtemperature	Turn OFF NAV FLIR and TF RDR
L OIL PRESS	Left/right oil pressure low	Check oil pressure
R OIL PRESS		
OXY LOW	4 liters oxygen remaining	Below 1/2 liter - Descend below 10,000 feet MSL
PC1 A	Designated RLS valve has actuated to shut off subsystem	Refer to Hydraulic Flow Diagram for systems affected*
PC1 B		
PC2 A		
PC2 B		
PITCH RATIO	CSBPC failure, pitch ratio failure or EMERG selected	Pitch ratio switch - EMERG*
L PUMP	Left/right utility pump pressure low	Information
R PUMP		
ROLL RATIO	Roll ratio incorrect or EMERG selected	Roll ratio switch - EMERG*

*ADDITIONAL INFORMATION AVAILABLE IN THIS SECTION

AFCS FUNCTIONAL STATUS SUMMARY

FUNCTIONAL STATUS	INDICATIONS	CREW ACTIONS	COMMENTS
PCAS FIRST FAIL	AV BIT LIGHT ON'	●RESET AV BIT ●CALL UP BIT PAGE ●SELECT PCAS RESET TO POSSIBLY CLEAR FIRST FAIL	FLIGHT CONTROL SYSTEM REMAINS FUNCTIONAL. IF IN TF, IT REMAINS FUNCTIONAL.
PCAS DISENGAGE	MASTER CAUTION ON FLIGHT CONTROL CATEGORY LIGHT ON CAS PITCH CAUTION MESSAGE ON CRT CAS ROLL CAUTION MESSAGE ON CRT PITCH HANDLING QUALITIES DEGRADED NO AUTO PILOT MODES FLYUP COMMANDED IF IN ARMED MANUAL OR ATF NO AUTOMATIC ROLL TO WINGS LEVEL	●RESET MASTER CAUTION ●ATTEMPT RESET OF ... —CAS ROLL —CAS PITCH IF RESET FAILS: —STAY BELOW 600 KCAS ●CALL UP BIT PAGE AND CHECK IF CASI-SERVOLOOP HAS FAILED —IF PCAS NO RESET, SELECT PITCH RATIO EMERG AND REFER TO CASI SERVOLOOP STATUS. ●RECOVER FROM FLYUP AND ASSESS PROBLEM	
RCAS FIRST FAIL	AV BIT LIGHT ON	●RESET AV BIT ●CALL UP BIT PAGE AND DETERMINE PROBLEM ●SELECT RCAS RESET TO POSSIBLY CLEAR FIRST FAIL	FLIGHT CONTROL SYSTEM REMAINS FULLY FUNCTIONAL.
RCAS DISENGAGE	MASTER CAUTION ON FLIGHT CONTROL CATEGORY LIGHT ON CAS ROLL CAUTION MESSAGE ON CRT AUTO PLT caution if autopilot previously engaged POSSIBLE DEGRADED ROLL RESPONSE NO AUTOPILOT MODES (EXCEPT ATF)	●RESET MASTER CAUTION ●ATTEMPT RESET OF RCAS IF RESET FAILS —STAY BELOW 600 KCAS	DEGRADED ROLL DAMPING AND ROLL RESPONSE. NO ROLL AUTOPILOT, NO ROLL RATE LIMITING, ONLY 1/2 DIFFERENTIAL STABILATOR AVAILABLE.

AFCS FUNCTIONAL STATUS SUMMARY (CONT)

FUNCTIONAL STATUS	INDICATIONS	CREW ACTIONS	COMMENTS
YCAS FIRST FAIL	AV BIT LIGHT ON	●RESET AV BIT ●CALL UP BIT PAGE ●SELECT YAW CAS RESET TO POSSIBLY CLEAR FIRST FAIL	FLIGHT CONTROL SYSTEM REMAINS FUNCTIONAL.
YCAS DISENGAGE	MASTER CAUTION ON FLIGHT CONTROL CATEGORY LIGHT ON CAS YAW AND ROLL MESSAGE ON CRT LATERAL/DIRECTIONAL STABILITY DEGRADED NO AUTO PILOT MODES (EXCEPT ATF)	●RESET MASTER CAUTION ●ATTEMPT RESET OF... —CAS YAW —CAS ROLL IF RESET FAILS —STAY BELOW 600 KCAS/ 1.7M (1.5M WITH CFTS AND LANTIRN) AND LAND AS SOON AS PRACTICAL	
SPIN RECOVERY	FIRST FAIL AV BIT LIGHT ON	●RESET AV BIT ●CALL UP BIT PAGE ●LIMIT LATERAL STICK INPUTS TO 1/2	IF SPIN RECOVERY IS LISTED BUT NOT CAS YAW, OR FULL MECHANICAL ROLL AUTHORITY INCORRECTLY SELECTED. SPIN RECOVERY AID MAY NOT BE AVAILABLE. HIGH ANGLE-OF-ATTACK HANDLING QUALITIES MAY BE DEGRADED. IF RESET FAILS AND BOTH SPIN RECOVERY AND CAS YAW ARE DISPLAYED, FULL MECHANICAL AUTHORITY IS NOT SELECTED IN SPIN.
SPIN RECOVERY WITH YAW CAS DISENGAGE	MASTER CAUTION ON CAS YAW CAUTION MESSAGE ON CRT	●RESET MASTER CAUTION ●ATTEMPT RESET OF CAS YAW ●CALL UP BIT PAGE ●IF IN A SPIN, PUT GEAR DOWN TO GET FULL AUTHORITY ●REDUCE MANEUVERS TO "YCAS DISENGAGE" LIMITS. ●LIMIT LATERAL STICK INPUTS TO 1/2 EXCEPT FOR SPIN RECOVERY.	
CAS ARI-(2ND FAIL)	AV BIT LIGHT ON	●RESET AV BIT ●CALL UP BIT PAGE ●REQUIRES COORDINATED FLIGHT CONTROL INPUTS.	POSSIBLE TO HAVE RELATED FAIL INDICATIONS, I.E., ● AOA FAIL ● ROLL LIMIT

AFCS FUNCTIONAL STATUS SUMMARY (CONT)

FUNCTIONAL STATUS	INDICATIONS	CREW ACTIONS	COMMENTS
ROLL LIMIT	AV BIT LIGHT ON	●RESET AV BIT ●CALL UP BIT PAGE ●IF >550 KCAS/1.0M, LIMIT TO 1/2 STICK INPUTS	LATERAL ROLL AUTHORITY MAY BE INCORRECT. PITCH RATIO MAY BE INCORRECT.
ROLL LIMIT WITH LATERAL STICK LIMIT CAUTION	MASTER CAUTION ON FLIGHT CONTROL CATEGORY LIGHT ON LATERAL STICK LIMIT MESSAGE ON CRT	●RESET MASTER CAUTION ●LIMIT LATERAL STICK INPUTS TO 1/2	
AOA FAIL	MASTER CAUTION ON FLIGHT CONTROL CATEGORY LIGHT ON LATERAL STICK LIMIT MESSAGE ON CRT SPEEDBRAKE RETRACTS (IF EXTENDED)	●RESET MASTER CAUTION ●LIMIT LATERAL STICK INPUTS TO 1/2	
CASI SERVOLOOP	AV BIT LIGHT ON MASTER CAUTION ON FLIGHT CONTROL CATEGORY LIGHT ON CAS PITCH CAUTION MESSAGE ON CRT CAS ROLL CAUTION MESSAGE ON CRT	●RESET MASTER CAUTION ●ATTEMPT RESET OF... —ROLL CAS —PITCH CAS ●IF PITCH CAS NO RESET, CALL UP BIT PAGE ●IF CASI SERVOLOOP DISPLAYED, SELECT PITCH RATIO EMERG ●SELECT PITCH RATIO EMERG WHEN STRAIGHT AND LEVEL BELOW 500 KCAS/1.0 M. EXPECT G TRANSIENT FROM -1/2 TO +1.0G/SEC ●THEN, ATTEMPT RESET OF PITCH CAS	CASI SERVOLOOP FAIL WILL SHOW UP WITH PITCH CAS FAIL, ROLL CAS FAIL.
R/C/P STICK	AV BIT LIGHT ON MASTER CAUTION ON FLIGHT CONTROL CATEGORY LIGHT ON CAS PITCH CAUTION MESSAGE ON CRT CAS ROLL CAUTION MESSAGE ON CRT	●RESET MASTER CAUTION ●RESET ROLL AND PITCH CAS ●CALL UP BIT PAGE AND DETERMINE FAILURE ●TURN CAS OFF TO IMPROVE RESPONSE, IF ONLY AFT STICK INPUTS ARE REQUIRED.	RCP STICK FORCE SENSOR HAS FAILED. RCP STICK INPUTS RESULTS IN REDUCED PERFORMANCE AND REDUCES RCP G CAPABILITY TO 3.5G MAXIMUM.

AFCS FUNCTIONAL STATUS SUMMARY (CONT)

FUNCTIONAL STATUS	INDICATIONS	CREW ACTIONS	COMMENTS
CAS RUDDER PEDAL	AV BIT LIGHT ON MASTER CAUTION ON FLIGHT CONTROL CATEGORY LIGHT ON CAS YAW CAUTION MESSAGE ON CRT	●RESET MASTER CAUTION ●ATTEMPT RESET OF YAW AND ROLL CAS ●CALL UP BIT PAGE AND DETERMINE FAILURE	RUDDER PEDAL POSITION SENSOR HAS FAILED. LARGER PEDAL INPUTS REQUIRED TO OVERCOME CAS FOR EQUIVALENT RESPONSE. NORMAL MECHANICAL PLUS DAMPENING IS AVAILABLE.

ONE RUDDER CAS	AV BIT LIGHT ON
	MASTER CAUTION ON
	FLIGHT CONTROL CATEGORY LIGHT ON
	LATERAL STICK LIMIT MESSAGE ON CRT
		●RESET MASTER CAUTION
		●CALL UP BIT PAGE AND DETERMINE FAILURE
		●LIMIT LATERAL STICK INPUTS TO 1/2
		●ATTEMPT YAW AND ROLL CAS RESET
		●OBSERVE THE FOLLOWING LIMITS: - 525 KCAS WHEN > 1.6M.
		   - WITH LANTIRN PODS.
		    ●1.2 M < 18,000 FT
		    ●600 KCAS, 18-34,000 FT,
		    ●1.6M ABOVE 34,000 FT
			RUDDER SERVO HAS FAILED. CAS GAIN IS DOUBLED TO REMAINING RUDDER. TOTAL RUDDER POWER REDUCED.

SECTION IV

CREW DUTIES

GENERAL AIRCREW RESPONSIBILITIES

The safe operation of the aircraft is the responsiblity of both aircrew members. The flight manual and checklist is based on a definite division of responsibilities between cockpits. Each aircrew member should have a thorough working knowledge of Aircraft Systems, Normal/Emergency Procedures, Operating Limitations, and Aircraft Flight Characteristics.

CREWMEMBER IN COMMAND OF AIRCRAFT

The primary responsibility of the crewmember in command of the aircraft is to ensure mission accomplishment within acceptable safety limits. Specific responsibilities are:
a.Conduct adequate integral aircrew briefings to ensure definite division of responsibility during flight.
b. Accomplish Normal/Emergency Procedures as outlined in this manual.
c. Operation of the aircraft within published operating and structural design limitations.
d. Ensure use of abbreviated checklist on all flights.

CREWMEMBER IN CONTROL OF AIRCRAFT

The crewmember actually in control of the aircraft is responsible for flying the aircraft and operating auxiliary equipment under his control in accordance with this manual. Those procedures requiring immediate response will be accomplished as required; however, aircrew member not in control of the aircraft will be required to read the procedure from the checklist when time and circumstances permit. The crewmember in control of the aircraft will call for checklist items when required during flight profile.

CREWMEMBER NOT IN CONTROL OF AIRCRAFT

The crewmember not in control of the aircraft shares overall responsibility for the safe accomplishment of the mission. In addition, he is responsible for operating auxiliary equipment under his control in accordance with this manual. Specifically, his responsibilities are:
a. Perform navigational duties as required.
b. Assist other aircrew member in monitoring flight progress.
c. Assist other aircrew member in monitoring aircraft systems and detecting system malfunctions.
d. Initiate required inflight checklist items when not called for by crewmember in control of aircraft.
e. Monitor instruments during all climbs and descents and advise the other crewmember of any deviations from established flight parameters.
f. Clear the flight area whenever possible.

SECTION V

OPERATING LIMITATIONS

TABLE OF CONTENTS

General 5-1
Crew Requirements...................................... 5-1
Instrument Markings................................... 5-1
Engine Limitations 5-1
Primary Fuel... 5-1
Alternate Fuel.. 5-1
Airspeed Limitations 5-6
Systems Restrictions.................................. 5-6
Prohibited Maneuvers 5-8
LANTIRN Restrictions 5-9
Gross Weight Limitations.......................... 5-9
Center of Gravity Limitations................... 5-9
Acceleration Limitations 5-10
External Stores Limitations 5-10

GENERAL

All aircraft/system limitations that must be observed during normal operation are covered herein. Some limitations that are characteristic only of a special phase of operation (emergency procedures, flight through turbulent air, etc.) are not covered here; however, they are contained along with the discussion of the operation in question.

NOTE

All references to airspeed quoted in knots refer to calibrated airspeed.

CREW REQUIREMENTS

The minimum crew for safe flight in F-15E aircraft is one.

INSTRUMENT MARKINGS

Instrument markings are shown in figure 5-1.

ENGINE LIMITATIONS

Refer to figure 5-2.

PRIMARY FUEL

The primary fuel is JP-4. F-40 is the NATO equivalent fuel. However, NATO F-40 may not contain corrosion inhibitor at some locations. Operation without corrosion inhibitor should be restricted to 10 consecutive hours.

ALTERNATE FUEL

The aircraft may be operated on JP-8, NATO F-34, NATO F-35, JP-5, NATO F-43, NATO F-44, or commercial JET A or JET A-1 and JET B. Except for freeze point and possible icing and corrosion inhibitor differences, JET B and JP-4 are equivalent and the same operating limitations apply.

NOTE

Alternate fuels are much more prone to leak than JP-4. Guidelines provided in TO 1-1-3 should be used to evaluate leaks when they occur.

Operating and throttle handling limitations for approved alternate fuels are the same as for primary fuels except: Ground starts with temperature below −20°C (−4°F) with alternate fuel may produce more smoke and require a longer time for engine light-off. Ground starts should not be attempted with fuel temperature below −40°C (−40°F). When using alternate fuels, hot starts may occur during spool-down airstarts at airspeeds less than 350 knots for altitudes above 30,000 feet. Alternate fuel airstarts may require longer engine light-off times.

Alternate fuels may be intermixed in any proportion with primary fuels during ground or air refueling operations. No change in operating limitations, retrim not required. Most alternate fuels are heavier, refer to Fuel Quantities in section I.

2750 – 3250 PSI – NORMAL, (NO DEMAND ON SYSTEM)

2000 – 2750 NORMAL WITH RAPID CONTROL
MOVEMENT

3250 – 3400 IF PRESSURE EXCEEDS 3250
STEADY STATE, AN ENTRY MUST
BE LOGGED ON FORM 781.

3400 MAXIMUM

HYDRAULIC PRESSURE

RGY
15E–1–(14)

Figure 5-1

ENGINE LIMITATIONS

GROUND

CONDITION	FTIT°C	RPM%	OIL PSI	REMARKS
START	680	-	-	NOTE 5
IDLE	-	-	15-80	NOTE 5
MILITARY/AB	960	94	30-80	NOTES 2, 5, 6, 8 AND 10
TRANSIENT	970	94	30-80	NOTES 2, 5, 8 AND 10
FLUCTUATION	±10	±1	±10	NOTES 2, 3, 4 AND 6

FLIGHT

CONDITION	FTIT°C	RPM%	OIL PSI	REMARKS
AIRSTART	800	-	-	
IDLE	-	-	15-80	
MILITARY/AB	970	96	30-80	NOTES 1, 2 AND 7
TRANSIENT	990	96	30-80	NOTES 2, AND 11
FLUCTUATION	±10	±1	±10	NOTES 2, 3, 4 AND 6

NOTES

1. Use of VMAX switch is prohibited
2. FTIT and RPM limitations include fluctuations
3. In phase fluctuation of more than one instrument, or short term cyclic fluctuations accompanied by thrust surges, indicate engine control problems
4. Nozzle fluctuations are limited to ±2% at military power and above. Fluctuations are not permitted below military power.
5. Any oil pressure from 0 to 100 (pegged) PSI is acceptable during start and initial operation for a period not exceeding 1 minute after reaching idle.
6. Oil pressure fluctuations of ±10PSI are acceptable if the average is within limits
7. At less than 0g, oil pressure may drop as low as 0PSI
8. For engine operation at military or above, oil pressure must increase 15PSI minimum above idle oil pressure
9. Engine nozzle position is limited to 30% open or less at military power
10. Maximum temperature limited to 30 seconds
11. Maximum temperature limited to 10 seconds.

Figure 5-2

AIRSPEED AND
AFTERBURNER OPERATING ENVELOPE
F100-PW-220 ENGINE

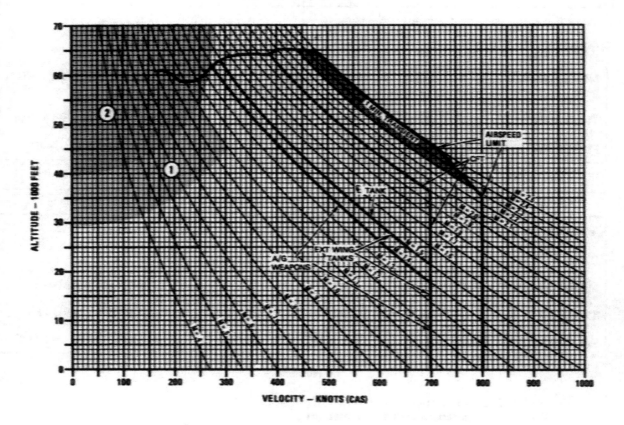

NOTES

THE DEEC AUTOMATICALLY LIMITS AFTERBURNER OPERATION TO ALLOW
UNRESTRICTED THROTTLE MOVEMENT THROUGHOUT THE FLIGHT ENVELOPE.

REGION 1 – DEEC LIMITS INITIATION OF AFTERBURNER SEGMENTS
TO I THRU IV. SEGMENT 5 BLOCKED.

REGION 2 – DEEC LIMITS AFTERBURNER SEGMENT TO SEGMENT 1 OR
BLOCKS SEGMENT SEQUENCING.

RY
15E-1-(106)21

Figure 5-3

SYSTEMS LIMITATIONS

	AIRSPEED	LOAD FACTOR
LANDING GEAR EXTENSION/RETRACTION (Minimize Sideslip)	300 KCAS (CLEAN OR MISSILES ONLY, WITH OR WITHOUT CFT'S)	1.25g
	250 KCAS (ANY CONFIGURATION)	2.0g
FLIGHT WITH GEAR EXTENDED	300 KCAS (CLEAN OR MISSILES ONLY, WITH OR WITHOUT CFT'S)	1.25g
	250 KCAS (ANY CONFIGURATION)	2.0g
FLAPS DOWN	250 KNOTS	0.0 to +4.0g Load factor
CANOPY OPEN (INCLUDING WIND)	60 Knots	
INLETS EMERGENCY POSITION	Above 0.95 MACH	-1.0 to +4.0g

SYSTEMS

JET FUEL STARTER

Maximum 10 seconds (15 seconds if temperature below 0° F) between JFS start initiation and READY light.

Starter engagement time shall not exceed 90 seconds except, if a hot start occurs, the time may be extended to 150 seconds.

Minimum 10 seconds between first engine at idle speed and engagement for second engine start. If the engine engagement time exceeds 90 seconds, wait 20 seconds before again engaging or shutting down the JFS.

FLIGHT CONTROLS

To insure the flight control hydraulic fluid is sufficiently warm before takeoff, observe the listed warm up times for the corresponding temperature range.

Temperature	Time (minutes)
+4°C (+40°F) AND UP	No restriction
-4°C (+25°F) to +3°C (39°F)	5
-18°C (0°F) to -5°C (+24°F)	8
-32°C (-26°F) to -19°C (-9°F)	10
-46°C (-50°F) to -33°C (-27°F)	12

Figure 5-4

Due to alternate fuel freeze points, fuel in external tanks may not transfer after sustained operation (5 minutes or longer) below 200 knots above 25,000 feet or 250 knots above 45,000 feet.

NATO F-34 and NATO F-44 may not contain corrosion inhibitor and NATO F-35, NATO F-43, JET A-1 and JET B may not contain icing or corrosion inhibitors. Restrict operation without icing inhibitor to one flight. Restrict operation without corrosion inhibitor to 10 consecutive hours.

Refer to TO 42B1-1-14 for additional fuel usage data.

AIRSPEED LIMITATIONS

Maximum airspeeds are shown in figure 5-3. Additional limitations may be imposed by external stores. Limiting airspeed for operation of various aircraft systems are shown in figure 5-4.

SYSTEMS RESTRICTIONS

JFS LIMITATIONS

JFS limitations are shown on figure 5-4.

BRAKES

The brakes are limited in the amount of energy they can absorb and dissipate in the form of heat without damage. A measure of the amount of heat absorbed by the brakes is the kinetic energy expended, measured in millions of foot-pounds. The amount of heat added to the brakes for each braking effort during a landing rollout or taxiing is cumulative and is a function of the speed of the aircraft and its gross weight at the time the brakes are applied. The heat generated in the brakes is transferred to the wheel and tire and (depending on the severity of the stop) can cause the tire pressure to rise to dangerous levels. Thermal fuse plugs within the wheel are designed to prevent wheel explosion by relieving pressure from the tire when the wheels attains a particular temperature.

Brake energy zones for flaps-speedbrake extended landings are provided in figure 5-5. Brake overheat occurs when the energy absorbed by an individual brake exceeds normal zone limits. In the caution zone fuse plug release is possible. In the danger zone, fuse plug release is expected, wheel/brake damage may occur, and brake fires are possible. In the extreme danger zone brake energies exceed all tested conditions and wheel/brake damage is certain. The brake energy limit chart should be used whenever a takeoff is aborted, for flaps-up landings, or when the pilot suspects that the combination of gross weight, IAS, and the number of stops and decelerations will result in brake energies in the caution or danger zones.

HOLDING BRAKE

To avoid brake damage, the holding brake should not be set when cumulative per brake energy exceeds 16.6 million foot pounds.

EXTERNAL FUEL TRANSFER

An adverse CG condition may develop if STOP/TRANSFER is selected while fuel remains in the external tanks. This condition develops as internal fuel continues to feed while fuel moves in the external tanks. With pitch CAS off, external fuel transfer should not be stopped except in an emergency.

NEGATIVE G FLIGHT

Negative g flight is limited to 10 seconds at all power settings.

BRAKE ENERGY LIMITS

CONDITIONS:
FLAPS 30°
SPEEDBRAKE EXTENDED
5000 FT ~ 90 DEG F

DATE: 15 AUGUST 1989
DATA BASIS: ESTIMATED

NOTES:

1. SUBTRACT 60 PERCENT OF THE HEADWIND COMPONENTS FROM THE INDICATED AIRSPEED. THE FULL TAILWIND COMPONENT MUST BE ADDED.

2. CHART ASSUMES BOTH LEFT AND RIGHT BRAKE ABSORB EQUAL ENERGY. ACTUAL DISTRIBUTION MAY VARY.

3. SUCCESSIVE STOPS OCURRING WITHIN ONE HOUR OF EACH OTHER SHALL BE CONSIDERED CUMULATIVE AND THE RESULTING BRAKE ENERGIES SHALL BE ADDED TOGETHER WHEN DETERMINING BRAKE OPERATING ZONE.

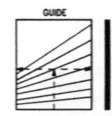

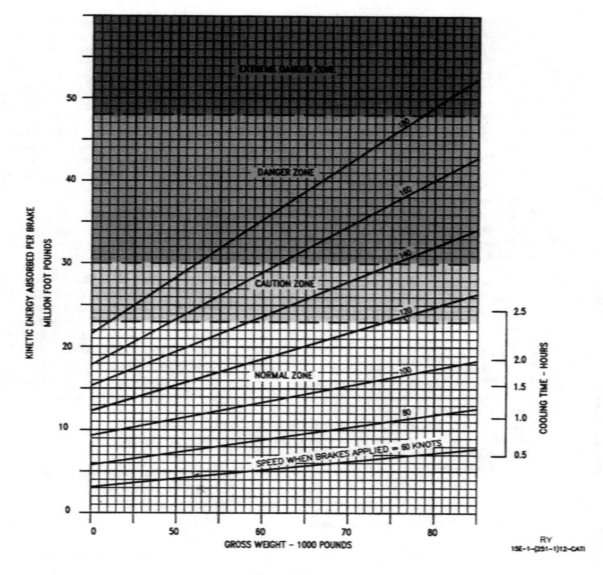

RY
15E-1-(251-1)12-CATI

Figure 5-5

PROHIBITED MANEUVERS

The following maneuvers are prohibited.

GENERAL

    a. Spins.

    b. Zero g flight, except transient.

    c. AOA over 30 units with any of the following:

        (1) Fuel asymmetry (wing & CFT) over 600 pounds.

        (2) Fuel asymmetry over 200 pounds when the asymmetric missile load is 3 or more. Fuel asymmetry is the summation of any combination of imbalance between the internal wing tanks and/or the conformal fuel tanks, when installed. For example, if the right CFT has 400 pounds more than the left CFT and the left internal wing tank has 200 pounds more than the right internal wing tank, the net fuel asymmetry is 200 pounds. Asymmetric missile load is the summation of any combination of missile loadings. For example, 4 missiles (any type) on one side and 1 missile on the other side result in an asymmetric missile load of 3 missiles. Fuel asymmetry shall not be used to balance missile asymmetry in determining compliance with this limitation.

        (3) Air-to-ground stores, whether carried on the CFT or the wing stations, wing mounted tanks or cargo pods. An exception is SUU-20B/A on stations 2 and/or 8 with no other stores (including LANTIRN pods) aboard, which are limited to 35 units AOA.

        (4) Gear down.

        (5) LANTIRN pods.

        (6) Inoperative tank 1 fuel transfer pump.

    d. With CFTs, no flight above 600 KCAS when Mach number greater than 1.8.

    e. With CFTs, above 600 KCAS when the Mach number is greater than 1.3, limit roll inputs to ½ lateral stick with slow stick inputs, maximum of 90° bank angle change, and +3g's maximum.

ROLLS

    a. Full lateral stick inputs in less than 1 second with LANTIRN pods.

    b. Full lateral stick rolls in excess of 360°.

    c. Full lateral stick rolls in excess of 180° initiated at less than +1.0g or greater than +3.0g.

    d. Rolls in excess of 360° under any of the following conditions:

        (1) Airspeed above 550 knots or Mach 1.4, whichever is less.

        (2) Any CAS axis disengaged.

    e. Rolls in excess of 180° initiated at other than +1.0g above 500 knots or Mach 1.4, whichever is less.

NOTE

For all aircraft configurations not specifically prohibited herein, with full CAS, mild to moderate rolls below 550 knots or Mach 1.4, whichever is less, are not limited by bank angle change or initial g provided that the OWS limit is not exceeded (voice warning activated) or without an operative OWS, the unsymmetrical acceleration limits shown in figure 5-7 are not exceeded. Longitudinal control coordination may be required to prevent g excursions outside these limits during the roll.

    f. Rolls in excess of 90° with gear down.

    g. Rolls at more than 20 units AOA, below Mach 1.0 with PITCH RATIO or ROLL RATIO light ON.

    h. Rolls with roll CAS on, above 475 knots below 12,000 feet, with abrupt lateral stick deflection. Such rolls shall be performed with smooth lateral stick deflections. Close formation flight in this speed/altitude region is not recommended.

    i. Rolls in excess of 90° with more than 1/2 lateral stick displacement at Mach number greater than 1.8 at altitudes above 40,000 feet.

WITHOUT OPERATIVE OWS

    a. With wing-mounted tanks, cargo pods, or air-to-ground stores:

        (1) Rolls over 360°

        (2) Rolls over 180° started at other than +1.0g.

        (3) Rolls at less than 0.0 g above 600 knots.

b. More than 1/2 lateral stick with full or partially full CFTs, full or partially full wing-mounted tanks, cargo pods, or air-to-ground stores or, above Mach 1.0, with empty wing-mounted tanks.

CAS OFF

a. Operation above 600 knots with any CAS axis OFF or inoperative.

LANTIRN RESTRICTIONS

● AUTO TF is prohibited.

● Minimum set clearance in mountainous terrain in IMC is 500 feet while terrain following.

NOTE

"Mountainous terrain" is defined as a vertical change that exceeds 900 feet per nautical mile, (which equates to a 15% slope change). This restriction only applies along the anticipated aircraft flight path. Terrain that exceeds a change of 13,000 feet per nautical mile will cause CARA dropout and a flyup.

● Terrain following is prohibited with a degraded INS attitude platform or TF attitude fail or after performing an in-flight alignment.

● Manual terrain following with flyup enabled (Armed Manual) is authorized. Aircrew must ensure the aircraft remains within system limits for flyup protection. Increase vigilance at heavy gross weights (above 68,000 pounds), especially if pitch CAS fails - pilot induced oscillations (PIO) are likely.

GROSS WEIGHT LIMITATIONS

The maximum allowable gross weight for flight/ground operations and landing is 81,000 pounds.

The maximum allowable landing sink rate versus gross weight is shown in figure 5-6.

CAUTION

At heavy gross weight, avoid abrupt nose gear steering inputs and make turns at minimum practical speed and maximum practical radius. Avoid operations on rough and uneven taxiways or runways. Failure to do so may result in tire damage.

CENTER OF GRAVITY LIMITATIONS

During ground operations below 76,000 pounds gross weight, the forward CG limit is 22% MAC (gear down). Add 0.5% MAC for each 2,000 pounds above 76,000 pounds gross weight.

Longitudinal center of gravity may be adversely affected by failure of internal transfer tanks to feed properly. With a malfunctioning tank 1 transfer system and the wing tanks feeding normally, the aircraft CG will shift forward until the wing tanks run dry and tank 1 starts to gravity feed. This forward CG condition will increase aircraft departure suceptibilty.

Without CFTs, the aircraft CG limit (gear up) is as follows:

a. With wing pylons - 29.0% MAC.
b. Without wing pylons - 29.9% MAC.

With CFTs, the aft CG limit (gear up) is as follows:

a. With air-to-air missiles or no stores on CFTs - 29.3% MAC
b. With air-to-air missiles or no stores on CFTs and with LANTIRN pods - 28.8% MAC
c. With air-to-ground stores on CFTs - 27.8% MAC
d. With air-to-ground stores on CFTs and with LANTIRN pods - 27.3%

ACCELERATION LIMITATIONS

With the Overload Warning System (OWS) operative, the maximum allowable acceleration is continuously displayed on the HUD. The OWS tones indicate proximity to the maximum allowable g (85% and 92% of design limit load) and the OWS voice warning indicates that the maximum allowable g is exceeded, see figure 5-7.

With the OWS inoperative, the maximum accelerations allowed for flight in smooth or moderately turbulent air are as shown in figure 5-7. Separate plots are provided for symmetrical maneuvers (maneuvers without any roll rate) and unsymmetrical maneuvers (maneuvers with an accompanying roll rate such as rolling pullouts, etc.).

Maximum acceleration may be reduced by limitations applicable to a specific store as shown on the External Stores Limitations chart.

EXTERNAL STORES LIMITATIONS

LANTIRN production Navigation pod carriage limits are shown in figure 5-8.

For airspeed, and Mach number limits, BAL refers to the limits shown in figure 5-3 for the specific aircraft configuration. For acceleration limits with OWS, BAL refers to the limit shown on the HUD and indicated by the voice warning. External store limits other than BAL are not programmed in the OWS. Where only a positive G limit is shown, the negative G limit is the OWS limit. For acceleration limits without OWS, BAL refers to the acceleration limits shown in Figure 5-7 for the specific aircraft configuration.

Only the external stores configuration shown in the External Stores Limitation chart (figure 5-9) may be loaded and carried. Additional stores will be added to the chart upon completion of flight testing of stores configurations.

CAUTION

● Flares should not be carried in the left outboard fuselage CMD station or in the outer row on the left inboard fuselage CMD station when the LANTIRN Targeting pod is installed.

NOTE

● Conformal fuel tanks must be installed when the LANTIRN pods are carried.

● Firing of the 20 MM gun is authorized. Inspect the AN/ALQ-135 ICS Control Oscillator boxes (in the gun bay) for external damage after each 10,000 rounds are fired.

ALLOWABLE LANDING
SINK RATE

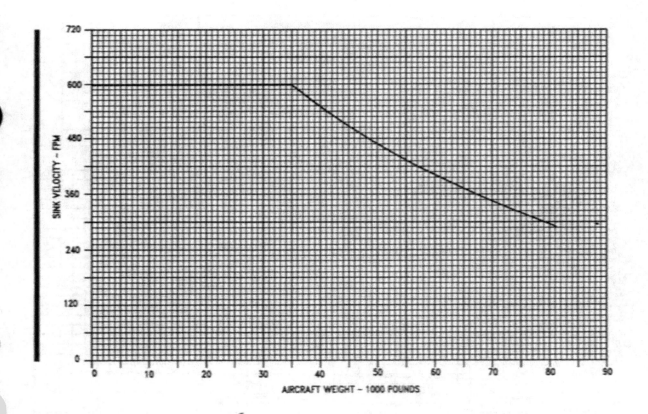

Figure 5-6

ACCELERATION LIMITATIONS
OVERLOAD WARNING SYSTEM INOPERATIVE
SYMMETRICAL MANEUVERING

NOTES

1. Negative Load Factor varies linearly from -3Gs at 750 KCAS to -1G at 800 KCAS.
2. Airspeed limits with CFTs and/or A/G Stores is 700 KCAS; with Tanks is 660 KCAS.
3. See External Store Limitations For Additional Acceleration Limits

CONFIGURATION	AIM-9	AIM-7	Wing Tanks or Wing A/G Stores/Pods	CFT	CFT AIM-7	CFT A/G Stores
A ⟨1	with or without	with or without	with M < 1.0 or without	without		
B	with or without	with or without	with M > 1.0	without		
C	with or without		with < 600 KCAS or without	with	with or without	
D	with or without		with > 600 KCAS	with	with or without	
E	with or without		with < 600 KCAS or without	with		with
F	with or without		with > 600 KCAS	with		with

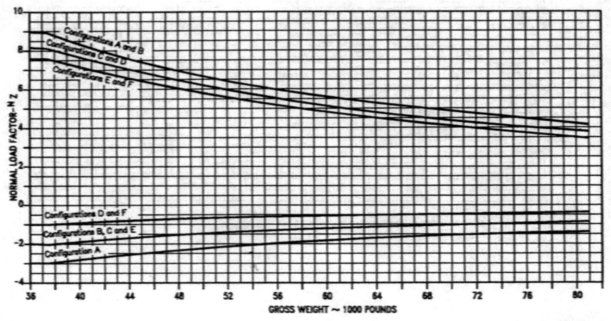

Figure 5-7 (Sheet 1 of 2)

15E-1-(170-1)21-CAT1

ACCELERATION LIMITATIONS
OVERLOAD WARNING SYSTEM INOPERATIVE
ASYMMETRICAL MANEUVERING

NOTE

1. Full stick with tanks Empty; 1/2 stick with tank fuel or Air-To-Ground stores.
2. Configuration has 1/2 stick capability.
3. Configuration has FULL stick capability; with wing tanks, 1/2 stick M > 1.0.
4. See External Store Limitations For Additional Acceleration Limits.

CONFIGURATION	AIM-9	AIM-7	Wing Tanks or Wing A/G Stores/Pods	CFT	CFT AIM-7	CFT A/G Stores
A 1	with or without	with or without	with M < 1.0 or without	without		
B 2	with or without	with or without	with M > 1.0	without		
C 2	with or without		with < 600 KCAS or without	with	with or without	
D 2	with or without		with > 600 KCAS	with	with or without	
E 3	with or without		with Empty < 600 KCAS or without	with Empty	with or without	
F 3	with or without		with Empty > 600 KCAS	with Empty	with or without	
G 2	with or without		with < 600 KCAS or without	with		with
H 2	with or without		with > 600 KCAS	with		with

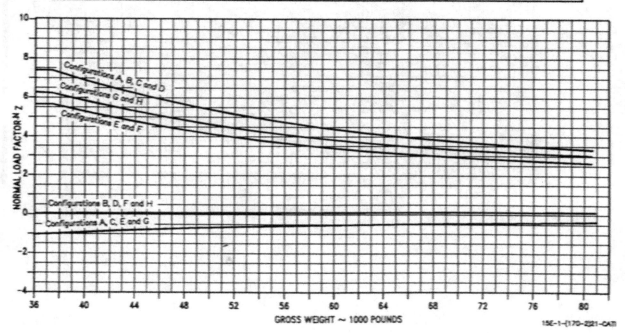

Figure 5-7 (Sheet 2)

LANTIRN POD CARRIAGE

TARGETING POD

NOTE

CFT'S MUST BE INSTALLED.

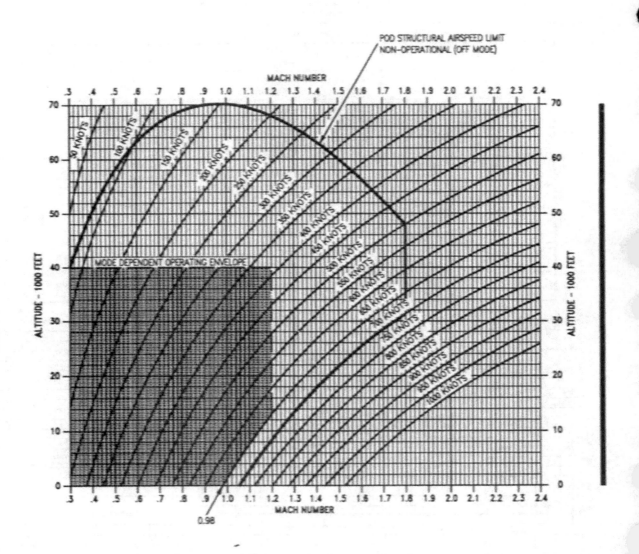

Figure 5-8 (Sheet 1 of 4)

LANTIRN POD CARRIAGE (Continued)

NAVIGATION POD

NOTE
CFT'S MUST BE INSTALLED.

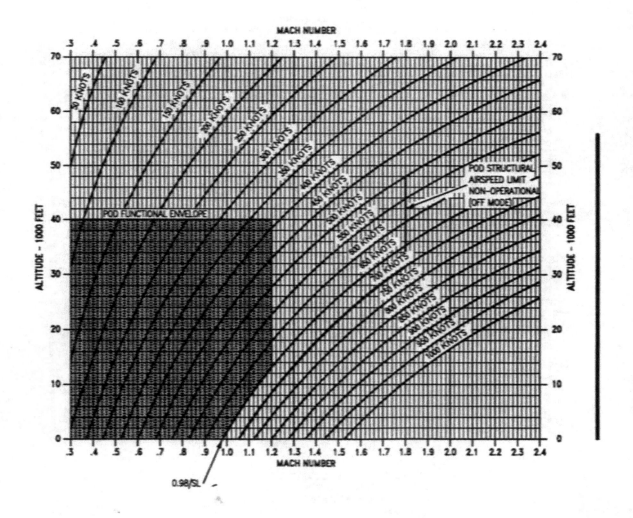

0.98/SL

15E-1-(168-2)21-CAT1

Figure 5-8 (Sheet 2)

LANTIRN POD CARRIAGE (Continued)

FLIGHT RESTRICTIONS WITH TWO LANTIRN PODS INSTALLED

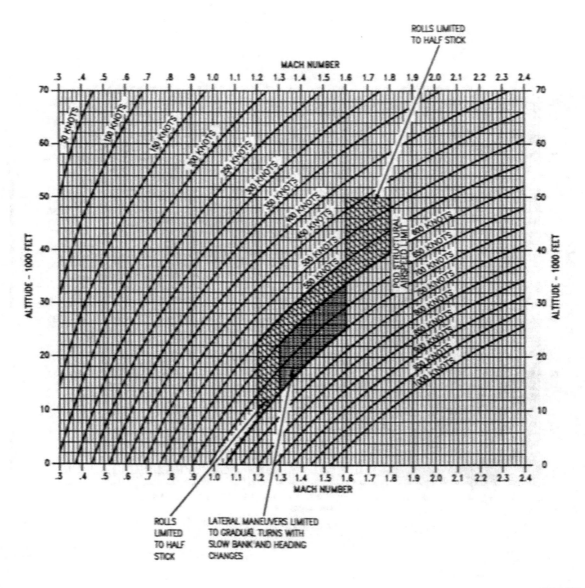

Figure 5-8 (Sheet 3)

LANTIRN POD CARRIAGE (Continued)

FLIGHT RESTRICTIONS WITH SINGLE LANTIRN POD INSTALLED

NOTE

● CFT'S MUST BE INSTALLED

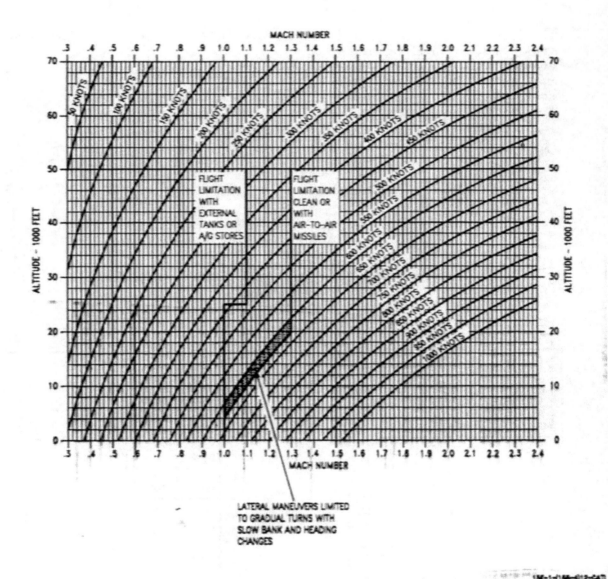

LATERAL MANEUVERS LIMITED
TO GRADUAL TURNS WITH
SLOW BANK AND HEADING
CHANGES

Figure 5-8 (Sheet 4)

EXTERNAL STORES LIMITATIONS
EXTERNAL STORES STATION IDENTIFICATION

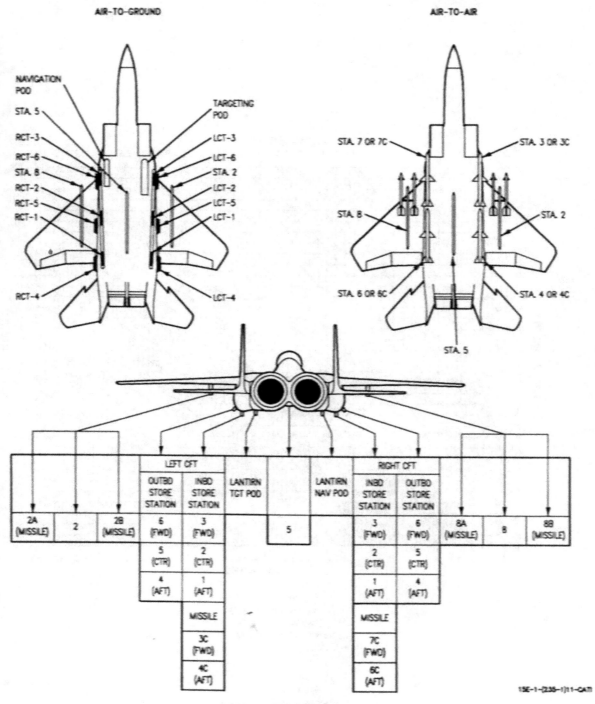

Figure 5-9 (Sheet 1 of 14)

15E-1-(235-1)11-CATI

EXTERNAL STORES LIMITATIONS

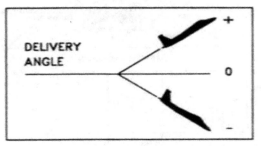

DELIVERY ANGLE

15E-1-(235-2)21-CATI

GENERAL

1. NORMAL F-15E RELEASE SEQUENCE:
   LCT-1/RCT-1
   STATION 5
   LCT-3/RCT-3
   LCT-4/RCT-4
   LCT-6/RCT-6
   LCT-5/RCT-5
   LCT-2/RCT-2
   STATION 2
   STATION 8

2. A FUEL TANK IS OPTIONAL ON STATION 5 WITH ALL STORE CONFIGURATIONS UNLESS OTHERWISE NOTED.

3. MIXED LOADS OF AIR-TO-AIR MISSILES, AIS PODS, AND CATMS ARE OPTIONAL ON STATIONS 2A, 2B, 8A, 8B WITH ALL STORE CONFIGURATIONS UNLESS OTHERWISE NOTED.

4. CFT MOUNTED AIR-TO-AIR MISSILES ARE OPTIONAL WITH ALL STORE CONFIGURATIONS UNLESS OTHERWISE NOTED.

5. LANTIRN PODS ARE OPTIONAL WITH ALL STORE CONFIGURATIONS UNLESS OTHERWISE NOTED.

6. MOST RESTRICTIVE LIMITS APPLY WHEN CARRYING MIXED LOADS.

7. CAPTIVE, INERT AND TRAINING STORE CONFIGURATIONS ARE AUTHORIZED UNLESS OTHERWISE NOTED.

8. CFT AIR-TO-GROUND STORES MUST BE RELEASED BEFORE WING AIR-TO-GROUND STORES.

9. MIXED LOADS OF DIFFERENT A/G STORES (I.E., MK-82 AND MK-84), DIFFERENT STORE TYPES (I.E. MK-82 AIR AND MK-82SE) AND DIFFERENT STORE MODELS (I.E. A/B AND C/B) ARE NOT AUTHORIZED UNLESS DEPICTED AS A SEPARATE STORE CONFIGURATION. THIS RESTRICTION APPLIES TO ALL AIRCRAFT STATIONS.

10. DOWNLOADS PER NORMAL F-15E RELEASE SEQUENCE ARE AUTHORIZED. MIRROR IMAGES ON ALL ASYMMETRIC DOWNLOADS ARE AUTHORIZED UNLESS OTHERWISE NOTED.

11. CFT AIR-TO-AIR OR AIR-TO-GROUND STORES STATION LOADING IS SHOWN BY LISTING AUTHORIZED STATION NUMBER IN L/R CFT COLUMNS. REFER TO SHEET 1 FOR CFT STORES STATION IDENTIFICATION.

12. SMOOTH STICK INPUTS AND NO ROLLING MANEUVERS ALLOWED FOR CARRIAGE ABOVE 600KCAS/1.2 MACH WITH ASYMMETRIC CFT CONFIGURATIONS.

13. JETTISON LIMITS ARE APPLICABLE ONLY FOR SELECTIVE JETTISON IN THE CFT RELEASE SEQUENCE. SELECTIVE JETTISON MODES WITH RIPPLE INTERVALS LESS THAN THE STORE MINIMUM INTERVAL ARE NOT AUTHORIZED.

14. MINIMUM RELEASE INTERVAL APPLIES ONLY TO BOMBS RELEASED FROM THE SAME A/G STATION. WHEN PERFORMING RIPPLE SINGLE RELEASES FROM MULTIPLE STATIONS, DIVIDE THE RELEASE INTERVAL BY NUMBER OF STATIONS SELECTED.

15. SIDESLIPS ARE RESTRICTED TO 9 DEGREES SUBSONICALLY WITH NO RESTRICTIONS SUPERSONICALLY. (THIS EQUATES TO GREATER THAN ½ RUDDER PEDAL DEFLECTION).

16. WITH CFT MOUNTED AIR-TO-GROUND STORES, LIMIT ASYMMETRIC MANEUVERS ABOVE 25 UNITS AOA TO +3G.

17. DO NOT ROLL THE AIRCRAFT UNTIL AT LEAST ONE SECOND AFTER WEAPON RELEASE.

Figure 5-9 (Sheet 2)

EXTERNAL STORES LIMITATIONS

FUEL TANKS
LANTIRN PODS

STORE	LINE NUMBER	SUSPENSION	STATION LOADING									MAXIMUM KCAS OR IMN OR WHICHEVER IS LESS		
			2	L CFT		LTP	5	LNP	R CFT		8	CARRIAGE	EMPLOYMENT	JETTISON
				OUT BD	INBD				INBD	OUT BD				
610 GALLON FUEL TANK	101	SUU-73/A				OPT	◯	OPT				660 1.5 ②	NA	625 1.25 ①
	102	SUU-59C/A BRU-47/A	◯							◯		660 1.5	NA	300 0.7
LANTIRN PODS	103	ADU-577/A				●						See Remarks	NA	NA
		ADU-576/A						●						

Figure 5-9 (Sheet 3)

EXTERNAL STORES LIMITATIONS

NA - NOT APPLICABLE
NE - NOT ESTABLISHED
BAL - BASIC AIRCRAFT LIMITS
LTP - LANTIRN TARGETING POD
LNP - LANTIRN NAVIGATION POD

WEIGHTS INCLUDE SUSPENSION EQUIPMENT

LINE NUMBER	ACCELERATION-G				DELIVERY ANGLE	STORES CONFIGURATION WEIGHT-LBS	REMARKS
	CARRIAGE		EMPLOYMENT	JETTISON			
	SYM	UNSYM					
101	BAL	BAL	NA	+0.8 to +1.2	NA	Empty - 636 Full - 4601	① With both LANTIRN pods. With one or no LANTIRN pods, jettison limits are 660KCAS/1.5M. ② Mach is limited to 1.0 below 25,000 ft MSL and 1.1 above 25,000 ft MSL for single LANTIRN pod carriage. ● AIM-7 employment not authorized with centerline tanks. ● Ejector pitch valve settings should be -1 (horizontal) fwd and -1 (horizontal) aft.
102						Empty - 1382 Full - 9312	● Centerline fuel tank, AIM-7s and MXU-648 pods are authorized. Most restrictive limits apply. No other stores are authorized. ● AIM-7 employment not authorized with wing tanks . ● Ejector pitch valve settings should be -1 (horizontal) fwd and -1 (horizontal) aft.
103	See Remarks			NA		(LTP) 621 (LNP) 520	● Conformal fuel tanks must be installed when LANTIRN pods are carried. ● LANTIRN pods are subject to carriage limits in Figure 5-8. ● LANTIRN adapters cannot be flown without pods attached. ● Auto or manual TF is prohibited when carrying AN/ASQ-T17 or AN/ASQ-T25 ACMI pods and GRDCUS pods unless the internal pod radar altimeter is disconnected. ● Use of LPI mode is prohibited. **WARNING** Do not fire the "Tactical" (not eye safe) LASER within 2000 feet of another aircraft. Reflected energy may cause eye damage. Never lase inhabited areas.

Figure 5-9 (Sheet 4)

EXTERNAL STORES LIMITATIONS

ACMI PODS
TRAVEL PODS
INSTRUMENTATION
PODS

STORE	LINE NUMBER	SUSPENSION	STATION LOADING									MAXIMUM KCAS OR IMN OR WHICHEVER IS LESS		
				L CFT					R CFT					
			2	OUT BD	INBD	LTP	5	LNP	INBD	OUT BD	8	CARRIAGE	EMPLOYMENT	JETTISON
AN/ASQ T-17, T-20, T-21, T-25 AIS PODS	104	SUU-59C/A BRU-47/A ADU-407/A LAU-114/A	⊶			OPT		OPT			✛	700 2.0	NA	600 0.98 ①
		SUU-59C/A BRU-47/A ADU-552/A LAU-128/A												
MXU-648 A/A-10, -30, -50 TRAVEL POD	105	SUU-59C/A BRU-47/A (Sta 2 & 8) SUU-73/A BRU-47/A (Centerline) BRU-47/A (LC2 & RC2)	●		2		●		2		●	550 0.95		NA
GRDCUS SHOOTER POD	106	SUU-59C/A BRU-47/A ADU-407/A LAU-114/A	⊶								✛	700 2.0		600 0.98 ②
G, E, J & X BAND HARD-BACK BEA-CON POD	107	SUU-59C/A BRU-47/A (Sta 2 & 8) SUU-73/A BRU-47/A (Centerline)	●				●				●	660 1.4		NA

Figure 5-9 (Sheet 5)

EXTERNAL STORES LIMITATIONS

NA - NOT APPLICABLE
NE - NOT ESTABLISHED
BAL - BASIC AIRCRAFT LIMITS
LTP - LANTIRN TARGETING POD
LNP - LANTIRN NAVIGATION POD

WEIGHTS INCLUDE SUSPENSION EQUIPMENT

| LINE NUMBER | ACCELERATION-G | | | | DELIVERY ANGLE | STORES CONFIGURATION WEIGHT-LBS | REMARKS |
| | CARRIAGE | | EMPLOYMENT | JETTISON | | | |
	SYM	UNSYM					
104	BAL	BAL	NA	+0.5 to +2.0 ①	NA	(T-17) 972 (T-20) 973 (T-21) 974 (T-25) 972 (T-17) 977 (T-20) 978 (T-21) 979 (T-25) 977	① Limit is for pylon jettison only and is prohibited with CFT stores aboard. ● Simultaneous operations of both the aircraft radar altimeter (CARA) and the T-17 or T-25 radar altimeter may result in radio frequency interference. ● AIS pods may be carried on stations 2A or 2B or 8A or 8B.
105	-1.0 to +5.0	0.0 to +3.0		NA		(Empty) CFT (-10 Pod) 130 (-30,-50 Pod) 98 Sta 2 or 8 (-10 Pod) 501 (-30,-50 Pod) 469 Sta 5 (-10 Pod) 446 (-30,-50 Pod) 414	● Travel pods may be carried in any combination on stations 2, 5, 8, LC2 or RC2. ● Maximum cargo weight 300 pounds per pod. ● Maximum roll rate 120°/sec (½ lateral stick). ● Do not cart BRU-47/A racks or pylons.
106	-2.0 to +9.0	-1.0 to +7.2		+0.5 to +2.0 ②		1185 (2x Pylons, 4x Launchers, 4x Adapters, 1x Pod)	② Limit is for pylon jettison only and is prohibited with CFT stores aboard. ● GRDCUS Pods may be carried on Station 2A, 2B, 8A or 8B. ● GRDCUS Pods may be carried with any certified configuration unless other wise noted. ● Simultaneous operation of both the aircraft radar altimeter (CARA) and the GRDCUS radar altimeter may result in radio frequency interference.
107	-2.0 to +9.0	-1.0 to +7.2		NA		(Sta 2 & 8) 444 (Centerline) 389	● The Hardback Beacon Pod must be configured with sway brace pads. ● No CFT mounted stores are allowed with a wing mounted beacon pod. ● Do not cart the BRU-47/A, Hardback Beacon Pods are non-jettisonable.

Figure 5-9 (Sheet 6)

EXTERNAL STORES LIMITATIONS

MISSILES

STORE	LINE NUMBER	SUSPENSION	STATION LOADING									MAXIMUM KCAS OR IMN OR WHICHEVER IS LESS		
			2	L CFT		LTP	5	LNP	R CFT		8	CARRIAGE	EMPLOYMENT	JETTISON
				OUT BD	INBD				INBD	OUT BD				
AGM-65 A/B/D. T-MISSILE	301	SUU-59C/A BRU-47/A LAU-117	▲			OPT		OPT			▲	660 1.1	500 0.8 ④	600 0.95
		SUU-59C/A BRU-47/A ADU-578/A LAU-88/A, A/A	✚								✚			300 0.7 ①
TGM-65 A/B/D	301 A	SUU-59C/A BRU-47/A LAU-117	▲								▲	660 1.4	NA	600 0.95
		SUU-59C/A BRU-47/A ADU-578/A LAU-88/A, A/A	✚								✚			300 0.7 ①
CATM-9 P/L/M (Captive Air Training Missile)	302	SUU-59C/A BRU-47/A ADU-407/A LAU-114/A	✚								✚	700 2.0	NA	600 0.98 ⑤
AIM-9P/L/M	303	SUU-59C/A BRU-47/A ADU-407/A LAU-114/A	✚								✚		700 2.0	
		SUU-59C/A BRU-47/A ADU-552/A LAU-128/A												
AIM-7F/M	304	LAU-106A/A			3C 4C			7C 6C				650 1.4	650 1.4 ⑥	600 0.98 ⑦

Figure 5-9 (Sheet 7)

EXTERNAL STORES LIMITATIONS

NA - NOT APPLICABLE
NE - NOT ESTABLISHED
BAL - BASIC AIRCRAFT LIMITS
LTP - LANTIRN TARGETING POD
LNP - LANTIRN NAVIGATION POD

LINE NUMBER	ACCELERATION-G				DELIVERY ANGLE	STORES CONFIGURATION WEIGHT-LBS	REMARKS
	CARRIAGE		EMPLOYMENT	JETTISON			
	SYM	UNSYM					
301	-0.5 to +6.0 ②	-0.5 to +4.8 ③	+0.9 to +1.1	+1.0 LEVEL ①	-15° to 0°	(AGM-65A/B) 1934 (AGM-65D) 1982	① (LAU-88) Jettison limit is for pylon jettison only.
						(AGM-65A/B) 4654 (AGM-65D) 4798	② Above 10,000 ft MSL, between Mach 0.6 and Mach 1.0, limit is 3.0g or 15 units AOA
							③ Above 10,000 ft MSL, between Mach 0.6 and Mach 1.0, limit is 2.4g or 15 units AOA
							④ AGM-65 employment (launch) authorized only from chin station of LAU-88/A when shoulder stations are empty and from LAU-117/A.
							● Dual launches are not authorized.
							● ADU-578/A required only when carrying AIM-9 series missiles.
301 A	-2.0 to +6.0 ②	-1.0 to +4.8 ③	NA	+0.8 +1.2 ①	NA	(TGM-65A/B) 1934 (TGM-65D) 1982	● Mixed loads of AGM-65, TGM-65 and T-Missile are authorized.
							● Any download of LAU-88, regardless of LAU-88 release sequence is authorized.
						(AGM-65A/B) 4654 (AGM-65D) 4798	● (LAU-117) pitch valve settings should be -1 (horizontal) fwd and -1 (horizontal) aft.
302	BAL	BAL	NA	+0.5 to +2.0 ⑤	NA	1678	⑤ Jettison limit is for pylon jettison only and is prohibited with CFT stores aboard
							● Mixed loads of AIM-9P, L and Ms are authorized
303			-0.5 to +7.33			(AIM-9P) 1758 (AIM-9L/M) 1838	● CATM-9P/L/M optional configurations: (1) Canards only (2) Wings/Rollerons only (3) With canards and wing minus rollerons (4) Without canards or wings
						(AIM-9P) 1886 (AIM-9L/M) 1966	
304	BAL	BAL	-0.5 to +7.2	+0.5 to +3.0	NA	2040	⑥ With a fuel tank or MXU-648 Travel Pod on station 5, or wing fuel tanks, employment is not authorized.
							⑦ With a fuel tank or MXU-648 Travel Pod on station 5, jettison limit is 300KCAS/0.7Mach.
							● CATM-7 carriage not authorized.
							● Mixed loads of AIM-7F and Ms are authorized.

Figure 5-9 (Sheet 8)

EXTERNAL STORES LIMITATIONS

GP BOMBS
LASER GUIDED
BOMBS

STORE	LINE NUMBER	SUSPENSION	STATION LOADING								MAXIMUM KCAS OR IMN OR WHICHEVER IS LESS		
			2	L CFT		LTP	5	LNP	R CFT		8	CARRIAGE	EMPLOYMENT	JETTISON
				OUT BD	INBD				INBD	OUT BD				
MK-82 LDGP MK-82 AIR (BSU-49/B fin)	501	BRU-46/A (OUTBD) BRU-47/A (INBD)		6 5 4	3 2 1	OPT		OPT	3 2 1	6 5 4		660 1.4	600 0.95	600 0.95
MK-82 Snakeye (MK-15 fin)													500 0.85 ①	600 0.95
MK-84 LDGP MK-84 AIR	502	BRU-47/A (CFT) SUU-59C/A BRU-47/A (Sta 2 & 8)			2				2			660 1.4	600 0.95	600 0.95
	503	BRU-47/A			3 1				3 1				(LDGP) 500 0.85 (AIR) 525 0.85	(LDGP) 500 0.85 (AIR) 525 0.85
	504	BRU-47/A			2				3 1			660 1.4	600 0.95	600 0.95
GBU-24/B,	505	BRU-47/A (CFT) SUU-59C/A BRU-47/A (Sta 2 & 8)			2				2			660 1.4	(LC2, RC2) 550 0.95 (Sta 2 & 8) 500 0.85	(LC2, RC2) 550 0.95 (Sta 2 & 8) 500 0.85
	506	BRU-47/A			2				2				600 0.95	600 0.95
GBU-10C/B D/B E/B	507	BRU-47/A (CFT) SUU-59C/A BRU-47/A (Sta 2 & 8)			2				2			660 1.2	600 0.95	600 0.95
	508	BRU-47/A			2				2					

Figure 5-9 (Sheet 9)

EXTERNAL STORES LIMITATIONS

NA - NOT APPLICABLE
NE - NOT ESTABLISHED
BAL - BASIC AIRCRAFT LIMITS
LTP - LANTIRN TARGETING POD
LNP - LANTIRN NAVIGATION POD

LINE NUMBER	ACCELERATION-G				DELIVERY ANGLE	STORES CONFIGURATION WEIGHT-LBS	REMARKS
	CARRIAGE		EMPLOYMENT	JETTISON			
	SYM	UNSYM					
501	-2.0 to +6.0	-1.0 to +4.8	+0.5 to +5.0	+0.8 to +1.2	-45° to +45° UN-RETARDED -20° to +20° RETARDED	(LDGP) 6060 (AIR) 6480	① High Drag configuration. In Low drag configuration employment limit is 600 KCAS/0.95M. ● MK-82 LDGP, MK-82 AIR and MK-82 Snakeye (LD) minimum ripple interval is 60 MSEC, MK-82 SE (HD) minimum ripple interval is 200 MSEC. ● Ejector pitch valve settings should be -1 (horizontal) fwd and -2 (diagonal) aft.
						6600	
502	-2.0 to +6.0	0.0 to +4.8	+0.5 to +6.0	+0.8 to +1.2	-45° to +45° UN-RETARDED -20° to +20° RETARDED	8622	● Ejector pitch valve settings should be -1 (horizontal) fwd and -3 (vertical) aft. ● Minimum ripple interval is 60 MSEC.
503						(LDGP) 7880 (AIR) 8040	
504	-2.0 to +6.0	0.0 to +4.8	+0.5 to +6.0	+0.8 to +1.2	-45° to +45° UN-RETARDED -20° to +20° RETARDED		● Mirror image carriage not authorized. ● Ejector pitch valve settings should be -1 (horizontal) fwd and -3 (vertical) aft. ● Minimum ripple interval is 60 MSEC.
505	-2.0 to +6.0	-1.0 to +4.8	+0.5 to +6.0	+0.8 to +1.2	-45° to +45°	9946	● Minimum ripple interval is 80 MSEC. ● (Line 504 configuration) Air to air missiles, CATMs, and AIS pods may not be carried on stations 2A, 2B, 8A and 8B. ● Ejector pitch valve settings should be -1 (horizontal) fwd and -3 (vertical) aft.
506						4630	
507	-1.0 to +5.0	0.0 to +3.0	+0.5 to +5.0	+0.8 to +1.2	-45° to +45°	9010	● Minimum ripple interval is 80 MSEC. ● (Line 506 configuration) Air to air missiles or CATMs may not be carried on stations 2A, 2B, 8A and 8B. ● AIS pods may be carried on stations 2A, 2B, 8A, or 8B. ● Ejector pitch valve settings for station 2 & 8 should be -1 (horizontal) fwd and -3 (vertical) aft, and for LC2 & RC2 should be -1 (horizontal) fwd and -2 (diagonal) aft.
508						4162	

Figure 5-9 (Sheet 10)

EXTERNAL STORES LIMITATIONS

CLUSTER BOMB UNITS/ DISPENSERS

STORE	LINE NUMBER	SUSPENSION	STATION LOADING										MAXIMUM KCAS OR IMN OR WHICHEVER IS LESS		
			2	L CFT		LTP	5	LNP	R CFT		8		CARRIAGE	EMPLOYMENT	JETTISON
				OUT BD	INBD				INBD	OUT BD					
SUU-20B/A with BDU-33B/B or BDU-33 D/B Practice Bomb	701	SUU-59C/A BRU-47/A	♟			OPT		OPT			♟		600 0.95	600 0.95	450 0.90 ①
SUU-20B/A with MK-106 Practice Bomb	702														
CBU-52, CBU-58, CBU-71	703	BRU-46/A (Outbd) BRU-47/A (Inbd)		6 5 4	3 2 1				3 2 1	6 5 4			600 1.2	600 0.95	600 0.95
CBU-87, CBU-89	704	BRU-46/A (Outbd) BRU-47/A (Inbd)		6 5 4	3 2 1				3 2 1	6 5 4			660 1.4	600 0.95	500 0.9
MK-20 Mod 3, Mod 4	705	BRU-46/A (Outbd) BRU-47/A (Inbd)		6 5 4	3 2 1				3 2 1	6 5 4			660 1.4	600 0.95	600 0.95

Figure 5-9(Sheet 11)

EXTERNAL STORES LIMITATIONS

NA - NOT APPLICABLE
NE - NOT ESTABLISHED
BAL - BASIC AIRCRAFT LIMITS
LTP - LANTIRN TARGETING POD
LNP - LANTIRN NAVIGATION POD

LINE NUMBER	ACCELERATION-G				DELIVERY ANGLE	STORES CONFIGURATION WEIGHT-LBS	REMARKS
	CARRIAGE		EMPLOYMENT	JETTISON			
	SYM	UNSYM					
701	-2.0 to +6.5	-1.0 to +4.8	+0.7 to +5.0	+0.8 to +2.0 ①	-45° to +45°	Empty 1294 Full 1570	① Do not cart BRU-47/A on stations 2 and/or 8. Jettisonable only with pylon attached. ● Mixed loads of BDU-33 and MK-106 practice bombs are permitted. ● Minimum ripple interval is 100 MSEC.
702					-20° to +45°	Empty 1294 Full 1354	
703	-2.0 to +6.0	-1.0 to +4.8	+0.5 to +6.0	+0.8 to +1.2	-45° to +45°	(CBU-52) 9420 (CBU-58, 71) 9720	● Minimum ripple interval is 90 MSEC. ● Ejector pitch valve settings are -1 (horizontal) fwd and -3 (vertical) aft
704	-2.0 to +6.0	-1.0 to +4.8	+0.5 to +6.0	+0.8 to +1.2	-45° to +45°	(CBU-87) 11,400 (CBU-89) 8472	● Minimum ripple interval is 80 MSEC. ● Ejector pitch valve settings should be -1 (horizontal) fwd and -3 (vertical) aft.
705	-2.0 to +6.0	-1.0 to +4.8	+0.5 to +6.0	+0.8 to +1.2	-45° to +45°	6880	● Minimum ripple interval is 100 MSEC ● Ejector pitch valve settings should be -1 (horizontal) fwd and -2 (diagonal) aft ● Use only modified 30 inch Kevlar lanyards for both fuzing arming and fin activation wires

Figure 5-9 (Sheet 12)

EXTERNAL STORES LIMITATIONS

MISCELLANEOUS

STORE	LINE NUMBER	SUSPENSION	STATION LOADING									MAXIMUM KCAS OR IMN OR WHICHEVER IS LESS		
			2	L CFT		LTP	5	LNP	R CFT		8	CARRIAGE	EMPLOYMENT	JETTISON
				OUT BD	INBD				INBD	OUT BD				
BLU-107	901	BRU-46/A (OUTBD) BRU-47/A (INBD)		6 5 4	3 2 1	OPT		OPT	3 2 1	6 5 4		600 1.2	600 0.95	600 0.95
BDU-38/B	902	BRU-47/A			2				2			660 1.4	600 0.95 ①	600 0.95 ①

Figure 5-9 (Sheet 13)

EXTERNAL STORES LIMITATIONS

NA - NOT APPLICABLE
NE - NOT ESTABLISHED
BAL - BASIC AIRCRAFT LIMITS
LTP - LANTIRN TARGETING POD
LNP - LANTIRN NAVIGATION POD

LINE NUMBER	ACCELERATION-G				DELIVERY ANGLE	STORES CONFIGURATION WEIGHT-LBS	REMARKS
	CARRIAGE		EMPLOYMENT	JETTISON			
	SYM	UNSYM					
901	-2.0 to +6.0	-1.0 to +4.8	+0.7 to +1.3	+0.8 to +1.2	-10° to +10°	5928	● Minimum ripple interval is 200 MSEC. ● Ejector pitch valve settings should be -1 (horizontal) fwd and -1 (horizontal) aft.
902	-2.0 to +6.0	-1.0 to +4.8	+0.5 to +6.0	+0.8 to +1.2	-10° to +40°	1432	① Minimum employment and jettison airspeeds are 250 KCAS/0.42 Mach to allow for chute deployment. ● Ejector pitch valve settings should be -2 (diagonal) fwd and -2 (diagonal) aft.

Figure 5-9 (Sheet 14)

SECTION VI

FLIGHT CHARACTERISTICS

TABLE OF CONTENTS

Handling Qualities 6-1
Stalls 6-3
Flight With Asymmetric Loads 6-4
Departures 6-6
Spin Characteristics 6-6A
Engine Operation During   Departure and Spin .. 6-8
Autorolls 6-8
Slow Speed Flight 6-9
Negative G Flight Characteristics 6-9
Low-Altitude High-Speed Flight 6-10

HANDLING QUALITIES

GENERAL

The hydro-mechanical and CAS systems operate together to produce handling qualities which do not vary significantly throughout the flight envelope. Section I describes in detail the various components of the flight control system. This section discusses some of the resultant handling qualities and describes how they change with various failures.

HANDLING CHARACTERISTICS

Pitch CAS ON, Pitch Ratio AUTO

Pitch response to stick input does not vary appreciably with airspeed, altitude, engine power, or configuration change. There is an approximate 1 to 1.5 g increase in stick dig in tendency as the aircraft decelerates through Mach 1, at high g loading. In high altitude, high Mach number flight, stick forces increase. Stick forces also increase at high angle of attack (AOA) to produce a natural "nose heaviness" near stall. At gross weight above approximately 50,000 pounds there is a noticeable longitudinal "deadband" in the control stick (fore and aft movement of the stick produces no aircraft response). This deadband is only present when the stick is moved rapidly during fine tracking tasks such as formation flying or air-to-ground gunnery. The deadband is most apparent when the stick is slightly forward of the trimmed position (at approximately 0.8g), and goes away at more positive or more negative g loadings. The dead band gets more pronounced as gross

weight increases. Because of the automatic trim feature, the stick force required to maintain a desired g does not change with airspeed or configuration change. The automatic trim does not trim off control forces; you select a desired stick force by use of the manual trim. For example, if you trim for hands-off, 1 g level flight, the aircraft will tend to remain in 1 g level flight, regardless of thrust, airspeed, or configuration changes. There is some delay in the automatic trim function. This is particularly noticeable when rolling out of a turn. The nose will tend to rise, requiring some forward stick force, even if the aircraft was not trimmed in the turn. In this case, do not retrim immediately, since most of the nose-up tendency will disappear in a very short time.

Pitch CAS OFF, Pitch Ratio AUTO

The aircraft feels less solid in pitch (less pitch damping) and precise maneuvers, such as tracking and air refueling are more difficult. Slow to approximately 250 knots to improve handling qualities for air refueling. The automatic trim is less effective, causing larger trim transients during airspeed or configuration changes, or when rolling out of turns. Supersonic, above 600 knots, and transonic between 0.8 and 1.0 Mach, pitch control is very sensitive and pilot induced oscillations (PIO) may occur, particularly at higher gross weights and with external fuel tanks. Close formation and air refueling may be very difficult. If this occurs, release the stick and reduce speed. Maximum stabilator available is slightly less at all speeds, resulting in higher stick forces at high g and less available g at full aft stick. At higher altitude, this reduction can be as much as 2 g. Below 10,000 feet, the reduction in available g is negligible. During takeoffs and landings, the nose feels heavier and some mild pitch oscillations may occur. Because of the reduced stabilator effectiveness, the nose cannot be raised as early during takeoff roll nor held up as long during landing.

Pitch CAS ON, Pitch Ratio EMERG

Very little degradation in handling qualities is noticeable. Maximum stabilator deflection is reduced at low speed. The greatest danger in this condition is the severely degraded handling qualities if pitch CAS drops off.

Pitch CAS OFF, Pitch Ratio EMERG

Stick forces are very high at low speed, and pitch control is very sensitive at high subsonic speed. Automatic trim is not available. Available AOA and g are severely reduced at both supersonic and low speed. During landing, stick forces are very high, pitch response is slow, and flare capability is greatly reduced. Recommended AOA is approximately 21 units at touchdown speed. Control is adequate for landing, but avoid high sink rate at slow speed. An approach at 18 units AOA or less provides sufficient flare capability for landing.

LATERAL-DIRECTIONAL CHARACTERISTICS

Yaw and Roll CAS ON, Roll Ratio AUTO

Roll response to stick input does not vary appreciably throughout the flight envelope. Full lateral stick produces a high roll rate through most of the flight envelope. Continuous full-stick rolls can result in aircraft pitch and yaw excursions, which can cause high structural loads and possible loss of control due to inertial coupling. This tendency is greatest with negative or high positive g loads and above 550 knots or Mach 1.4. Lateral stick forces are light, and initial roll acceleration is high, particularly during low altitude, high speed subsonic flight. At these conditions, there is a tendency to overcontrol. The ARI, supplemented by CAS, permits all rolling maneuvers to be made with lateral stick only. No coordinating rudder is necessary, even at high AOA. When the stick is near full aft, lateral stick causes large rudder deflection in the direction of lateral input. With forward stick (stick forward of trimmed position), the rudder deflection is opposite to lateral input. With gear down, full aileron is available at any stick position and coordinating rudder is maintained. The aircraft can be rolled using rudder; however, maximum roll rate can be achieved using only lateral stick at all AOA. At higher AOA, either rudder alone, lateral stick alone, or both together may be used to achieve the desired roll response.

Yaw and Roll CAS ON, Roll Ratio EMERG

Roll response will be slightly degraded at most flight conditions. Mechanical ARI is inoperative which results in some adverse yaw when rolling at high AOA. Lateral-directional control during landing will be slightly degraded, particularly in the presence of crosswind.

Yaw or Roll CAS OFF, Roll Ratio AUTO

Dutch roll (roll-yaw motion) damping is greatly reduced, particularly at approach speed. Roll can produce uncommanded yaw, especially at termination. Precise tracking is difficult. Initial roll acceleration is reduced, but maximum roll rate can be greater than with the CAS ON. The tendency to overcontrol in roll at high speed is reduced. The ARI is less effective. During landing, the airplane tends to wallow and some rudder may be necessary for coordinated flight.

Yaw or Roll CAS OFF, Roll Ratio EMERG

Roll rate is reduced at all speeds. Roll response is very sluggish, and stick forces are high, particularly at low speed. There is no ARI. Approach and landing in crosswind, turbulence, or with an asymmetric load is difficult.

External Stores

External stores (particularly the centerline tank only configuration) reduce aircraft stability. The centerline tank, by itself, reduces the lateral-directional stability while wing stores, with or without the centerline tank loaded, reduce the longitudinal stability. With the CAS on, there is little noticeable effect, particularly below 30 units AOA. With the CAS off, there is a noticeable increase in pitch sensitivity with external stores loaded. Store inertia will affect roll response. More time is required to attain or stop a given roll rate, particularly at high AOA.

The CFT's increase the pitch sensitivity of the aircraft. The LANTIRN pods decrease the lateral directional stability of the aircraft.

CG Affects

The aircraft CG will be maintained within limits during release of CFT stores if the normal release sequence is followed. Stores that fail to release (hung stores) from the aft CFT stations (L/RC-1, 4) may cause the aircraft CG to move behind the aft limit, especially at low fuel states (less than 5,000 lbs). All flight with CG out of limits should be done cautiously with maneuvers limited to those required to recover the aircraft. The CAS may mask the adverse effects of having the CG behind the aft limits. Flying qualities will degrade significantly with a failed pitch CAS. Following a pitch CAS failure, consideration should be given to improving the longitudinal stability by jettisoning wing tanks or wing-mounted A/G stores if aircraft pitch response is too sensitive for adequate control.

HEAVY GROSS WEIGHT

The aircraft exhibits no adverse handling qualities at maximum gross weight.

> **WARNING**
>
> The control system masks the weight effects to the point where the pilot can put the aircraft in a high AOA, high sink rate condition with little warning.

Control system masking of weight effects is particularly apparent during traffic patterns and landings. For this reason, a wide pattern or straight-in approach is recommended. Fly final approach at on speed AOA, but delay reducing power until well into the flare to prevent an excessive sink rate. Expect the nose to drop at a significantly higher airspeed during aerobraking.

> **NOTE**
>
> Heavyweight operations with three full external tanks, or external stores, are more susceptible to departure than operations with centerline tank only.

The CFT-equipped aircraft exhibits much the same flying qualities as the basic aircraft at comparable weights. The effect of the CFTs are minor over much of the flight envelope for most maneuvers. The most noticeable longitudinal effect is an increase in pitch response and maneuverability and pitch sensitivity over the basic aircraft at similar weights. During takeoff, less aft stick is needed for rotation, especially with three external tanks. Aerial refueling and formation flying are largely unaffected by CFTs. During maneuvering flight, CFTs increase the maximum AOA capability of the aircraft by about 4 CPU. During landing approaches; aircraft with CFTs lack the normal aircraft buffet onset cues at 20 to 21 CPU and have lower speed stability. It may be necessary to refer to the AOA indicators more often to prevent AOA overshoots during pattern and flare. With the pitch CAS off the aircraft exhibits satisfactory flying qualities for a backup mode. However, as with the basic aircraft, high gain tasks such as close formation or aerial refueling with three external tanks may be very difficult with a failed pitch CAS.

At subsonic Mach numbers the lateral-directional flying qualities of the aircraft are not significantly affected by CFTs. CFT-equipped aircraft retain the good departure resistance of the basic aircraft. Supersonically, however, the reduction in directional stability due to the CFTs results in larger, less comfortable yaw excursions during rolling maneuvers.

The aircraft exhibits good handling qualities with partially-full to full CFTs. At these higher weights the aircraft response to control inputs may be initially slowed by the higher inertias, although the control system will often mask this effect. Longitudinally, the higher inertias will also be partially offset by the increased pitch response caused by the aerodynamic effects of the CFT installation. Aircraft flying qualities during aerial refueling and formation flying are good, although higher power settings will be required for these maneuvers than with the basic aircraft.

STALLS

1 G STALLS

Light buffet begins at approximately 15 units AOA, increases in intensity to 23 units, then remains fairly constant. External stores decrease buffet onset AOA and increase the buffet level. Required aft stick force increases with increasing AOA (CAS On or Off). Some wing rock and yaw oscillation occurs above 30 units AOA. This is accentuated in the centerline tank configuration. With full aft stick, AOA stabilizes at 38 units or above with airspeed 100 knots or less (this varies with c.g. position, aft c.g. giving higher AOA). As AOA increases above 30 units, lateral stick becomes less effective in generating roll. The rudder is more effective than lateral stick for roll control approaching the stall. At stall (full aft stick) neither lateral stick nor rudder are very effective. The vertical velocity (cockpit gage) will probably be pegged going down. Recovery from a stall is immediate when the stick is moved forward. Lateral stick inputs should be removed before the stick is moved forward to recover from a stall or departures could be induced. Any sideslip present will induce a roll with forward stick motion.

ACCELERATED STALLS

Accelerated stall characteristics are heavy buffet with moderate yaw and roll oscillations averaging less than 10° of sideslip and 20° of bank. All buffet and yaw/roll activity diminishes rapidly with airspeed bleed-off. With external stores, buffet onset is earlier and buffet level is greater. Airspeed bleed-off tends to be more rapid.

NEGATIVE ANGLE-OF-ATTACK STALLS

In a level flight negative g stall, AOA is below zero units. The last few inches of forward stick travel does not increase AOA, and moving the stick back from the forward stop does not produce any response during the first few inches of stick motion. Positive aft stick force may be required to eliminate negative g and recover to normal flight. Negligible lateral or directional activity occurs at stall with no buffet. External stores have little effect.

LANDING CONFIGURATION STALLS

With gear and flaps down, stall characteristics are much the same as in the 1 g stall; however, buffet begins at about 23 units AOA. External stores decrease buffet onset AOA and increase buffet level. The roll and yaw motions, buffet, and indicated airspeed are similar to the 1 g stall. Any lateral control input above 35 units AOA can produce excessive adverse yaw rate (apparent flight control reversal), and a spin may rapidly develop.

FLIGHT WITH ASYMMETRIC LOADS

The aircraft will tend to turn into the heavy wing during takeoff roll. Since lateral stick away from the heavy wing is required to keep the wings level, any aft stick movement produces yaw away from the heavy wing (because of ARI action). Therefore, avoid abrupt pitch changes.

Although aerodynamic asymmetry has some drag effect, the primary source of degraded departure warning and resistance is weight asymmetry. The centerline tank only configuration further aggravates the condition due to the reduction of the lateral-directional stability. High AOA's, high subsonic Mach numbers, and higher altitudes tend to amplify the characteristics created by the asymmetry. However, the aircraft may be safely flown at 30 units AOA or below with an asymmetric load as great as one full external wing tank. Lateral asymmetries have a pronounced effect on roll performance above 30 units AOA in that little capability remains to roll into the heavy wing. If the critical AOA for a given asymmetric loading is exceeded, the aircraft will roll in the direction opposite the heavy wing. At higher AOA's, this roll rate can be quite rapid.

In addition to increased departure susceptibility, lateral asymmetry also degrades the recovery characteristics. As the asymmetry increases, the recovery is delayed. Control can be regained by reducing AOA and increasing speed.

Landing may be made with asymmetric loading if turns are shallow and a flat approach is flown. Fly final approach at on speed AOA but delay reducing power until well into the flare. Avoid a large or abrupt flare. With a large asymmetric load, avoid crosswinds over 15 knots. When in doubt, perform a controllability check before landing.

WEIGHT LIMITS

Lateral weight asymmetry is measured by summing the moments about the lateral center of gravity. Each moment is a product of the distance from the lateral c.g. in feet and the weight of the differential fuel or store in pounds. For example, a 650 pound internal wing fuel imbalance equals 5,000 foot-pounds (7.7 feet X 650 pounds). The airplane is very departure resistant below 5,000 foot-pounds of asymmetry. If you have two AIM-7's on one side and none on the other, you need only 200 pounds wing fuel difference to add up to 5,000 foot-pounds. Two AIM-7's and two AIM-9's on one side result in more than 7,000 foot-pounds asymmetry. The aircraft is spin resistant below 7,000 foot-pounds. Spin recovery has been demonstrated up to 10,000 foot-pounds of asymmetry. Figure 6-1 summarizes the preceding data. Figure 6-1A shows asymmetric contributions for various loads.

DEPARTURE/SPIN SUSCEPTIBILITY SUMMARY

Lateral Asymmetry (Foot-Pounds)	Departure (All Loadings)	Spin	
		Without centerline Tank	With centerline Tank Only
0 to 5,000	Resistant	Extremely resistant	Resistant
Greater than 5,000 (Less than 7,000)	Susceptible	Resistant	Resistant
7,000 to 10,000	Extremely Susceptible	Resistant	Susceptible

Notes: - This table applies to altitudes above approximately 20,000 feet.
- Departure resistance is increased considerably at lower altitudes.
- At 37 to 44 units AOA and 0.45 to 0.76 Mach number, departure resistance is decreased over that stated. The table presents the overall departure susceptibility, considering the low probability of remaining within this limited region of instability.

Figure 6-1

LATERAL ASSYMETRY CONTRIBUTIONS

Weapon/Store	Store Station	Weight (Pounds)	Buttline (Inches)	Lateral Asymmetry (Foot-Pounds)
Gun		264	65.5	1440
Wing Pylon	2 or 8	371	115.3	3570
LAU-128/A	2B or 8A 2A or 2B	82	105.5 125.0	720 850
AIM-9L	2B or 8A 2A or 8B	195	99.6 130.9	1620 2130
AIM-7F	3 or 7 4 or 6 -4 CFT Stations	510	58.5 55.4 70.7	2490 2350 3000
ACMI Pod	2B or 8A 2A or 8B	160	99.6 131.5	1330 1760
LANTIRN Navigation Pod		520	46.4	2010
Internal Wing Fuel			89.7	7.5 x Fuel Imbalance
External Wing Fuel			94.5	7.9 x Fuel Imbalance
-4 CFT Fuel			67.3	5.6 x Fuel Imbalance

Figure 6-1A

DEPARTURES

A departure from controlled flight is characterized by an uncommanded flight path change such as a nose slice, roll away from a lateral input, or excessive yaw rates, as in a spin whereas an out-of-control condition exists when the aircraft is not responding properly to pilot inputs. The initial presence of the yaw rate warning tone indicates a departed flight condition that, if not corrected immediately, may quickly transition to a spin. Record all departures and spins on AFTO 781. Include aircraft configuration, flight parameters, wing/CFT fuel, and any other significant information.

Departures should not be encountered below 30 units AOA at any altitude, airspeed, or loading. However, loss of directional stability and subsequent rolling departures may be encountered when attempting high sideslip maneuvers (cross controls) even with CAS ON. These departures are preceded by an apparent increase in the sideslip with a constant rudder pedal input. The aircraft is resistant to departure at lower altitudes. Above 30 units AOA, external stores or asymmetry increases the departure susceptibility. The centerline tank only configuration further increases departure susceptibility which, if combined with lateral asymmetry, markedly increases the likelihood of departure. Due to the increased drag with three external tanks installed, significantly more altitude is required to attain flying speed during recovery from post stall gyrations than is required with only air-to-air missiles installed or clean. Jettison of stores is not recommended due to the possibility of stores-to-aircraft collision.

The aircraft has a small flight regime where it is directionally unstable, and has increased susceptibility to departure and spin. This can occur in any configuration with any weight asymmetry if the yaw, angle of attack, and airspeed combine in just the right amounts. While this area of instability is not hard and fast, it generally occurs between 40-44 units AOA when there is sideslip. The pilot must be cautious not to use abrupt stick or rudder inputs at high AOA with sideslip. Smoothly neutralizing the controls at the first indication of departure (such as a roll away from lateral input, nose slice, or excessive yaw rate - i.e. departure warning tone) will normally recover the aircraft to controlled flight quickly. Even though the aircraft exhibits high directional stability, large lateral asymmetries can cause the aircraft to quickly enter a spin if not promptly recovered from a departure.

NOTE

While the region of decreased departure resistance actually occurs between 40-44 units AOA, lag in the AOA system during maneuvering flight can result in cockpit gauge readings of 37-44 units AOA when actual AOA is 40-44 units.

SYMMETRIC LOADS

In the region of directional instability even a symmetrically loaded aircraft will usually exhibit one or more classic signs of an impending stall, such as wing rock (it may only be one) or some yaw excursions. Departure may be characterized by a nose slice and a rolling departure. Departures with a centerline tank only configuration will be more abrupt and will exhibit higher yaw rates. Neutralizing the controls at departure, results in recovery, usually within one complete rotation in roll, with negligible altitude loss. It is possible to enter an autoroll during the recovery from a rolling departure. While the aircraft remains spin resistant, high yaw rates may be experienced before the aircraft settles into a low energy 1 g stall. It should be noted, that with a centerline tank only configuration loaded, introducing and holding full lateral stick at or near longitudinal center during the departure roll may cause spin entry in as little as three seconds. Vertical stall, tailslide, 1 g stall, or accelerated stall below 200 knots in the clean configuration show no tendency to spin if there is no lateral asymmetry.

CENTER OF GRAVITY

As longitudinal CG approaches the aircraft forward design limit of 22% MAC, full aft stick maximum angle of attack will be reduced. This reduced performance may cause the aircraft to stagnate in the region of 40-44 units AOA. This stagnation may be of sufficient time for yawing moments and sideslip angles to increase to the point of overcoming aircraft directional stability, resulting in departure from controlled flight. Monitor for tank 1 transfer malfunctions which may result in forward CG.

ASYMMETRIC LOADS

Departure susceptibility (Figure 6-1) is most affected by lateral c.g. position (internal wing fuel and/or stores, tanks, or missiles imbalance). Adequate lateral control and departure resistance exists up to 30 units AOA, with up to one full external wing fuel tank and one empty (36,200 foot-pounds of asymmetry). As

AOA is increased above 30 units AOA, more lateral stick is required to hold up the heavy wing. This results in increasing sideslip (nose away from the heavy wing) due to reduced directional stability, rudder deflection through the ARI, and the proverse yawing moment (yaw in the direction of lateral stick input) caused by the aileron/differential stabilator deflections. If AOA continues to increase, the rudder is no longer able to reduce the sideslip into the heavy wing; and the aircraft will depart with a yaw and roll acceleration away from the heavy wing. At 40 units AOA or above, the yaw and roll accelerations cannot be controlled by lateral stick. If full aft stick is maintained during or after a 1 g stall or abrupt pull-up, the aircraft will depart (with the yaw rate tone as the first warning) with a very pronounced roll away from the heavy wing and a descending spiral is likely. Therefore, controls should be smoothly neutralized immediately following the stall/departure. When the aircraft approaches the flight regime of directional instability, lateral weight asymmetries greater than 5,000 foot-pounds tend to provide enough sideslip to make departure inevitable; and again, departure will be without warning. In summary, the aircraft is considered susceptible to departure with lateral asymmetries above 5,000 foot-pounds and extremely susceptible with greater than 7,000 foot-pounds.

Out-of-control/departed flight conditions with asymmetric loads will usually take longer to recover due to the higher yaw rates involved. With 7,000 to 10,000 foot-pounds of asymmetry, recovery may be significantly delayed, with several peaks in AOA and yaw rate and 1-1/2 to 2 rolls during the departure. Abrupt entries into high AOA regions will result in a departure and loss of control without warning. During slow entry rate approaches to stall with asymmetric loads (especially greater than 5,000 foot-pounds), the ever

increasing amount of lateral stick or rudder to control heading and bank angle should serve as ample warning that loss of control is imminent. Controls must be neutralized immediately at departure to effect recovery. The most significant effect on recovery capability is the amount of time between departure and neutralized control. Longitudinally centered lateral stick against rotation in roll will result in a spin. Even though the aircraft exhibits a high directional stability, large lateral asymmetry can cause the aircraft to quickly enter a spin if not promptly recovered from a departure.

Asymmetric Thrust Departure Prevention System (ATDPS)

Asymmetric thrust at high dynamic pressure leads to a departure characterized by rapid uncommanded sideslip, which can exceed aircraft structural design limits. Protection against asymmetric thrust departures is provided by the ADTPS.

SPIN CHARACTERISTICS

SYMMETRIC LOADS

A laterally symmetric aircraft in the cruise configuration (i.e., gear and flaps up and speedbrake in) is extremely spin resistant with any combination of lateral-directional control inputs when aft stick is maintained. Full cross-controls at full aft stick over a wide range of speeds fails to achieve spins. The extreme spin resistance is a result of the basic high AOA stability and flight control system design. Full lateral control applied opposite to the direction of roll during an autoroll will result in a spin if the lateral stick input is prolonged. Following departure in a laterally symmetric aircraft, full lateral control inputs

with the stick near the neutral position may cause a spin in as little as 3 seconds. With the centerline tank only configuration, full lateral control deflections applied opposite to the rotation following a departure can result in spins in even less time.

ASYMMETRIC LOADS

With lateral asymmetries of 5,000 foot-pounds or less, except for centerline tank only loading, there is no significant increase in spin susceptibility. When aft stick is maintained with any combination of lateral control inputs, the aircraft will remain extremely spin resistant. However, with AOA above 30 units, spins are attainable in as little as three seconds with lateral control inputs (no rudder required) against the rotation at departure. With the centerline tank only configuration, the aircraft is still spin resistant while maintaining aft stick at departure with up to 5,000 foot-pounds of asymmetry. With 5,000 foot-pounds of asymmetry, the aircraft with the centerline tank only configuration is closer to being considered spin susceptible when full lateral inputs are applied with the stick near neutral following a departure. Only 1 to 2 seconds may be required to develop a spin. Overall, the aircraft with 5,000 foot-pounds or less asymmetry is considered extremely spin resistant without a centerline tank and resistant with the tank. With the exception of the centerline tank only configuration, the aircraft is still spin resistant with asymmetries to 10,000 foot-pounds. The decreased spin resistance for asymmetries greater than 5,000 foot-pounds is due to the increasing rolling moment caused by the increased asymmetry. As asymmetry increases, the susceptibility to spin increases and neutralizing the controls must not be delayed.

SPIN MODES

Three different erect spin modes may be entered. The two most common are a highly oscillatory mode with medium yaw rates and a smooth flat spin with high yaw rates. The third mode, encountered very infrequently, is characterized by low yaw rates (approximately 60°/second) and mild oscillations.

The highly oscillatory spin mode will exhibit average AOA in excess of cockpit gage range (70-80 units), with average yaw rates of 60° to 90° per second.

Oscillations of ±32 units AOA and ±20° per second yaw rate are typical. Neutralizing the controls during a highly oscillatory spin usually will result in a recovery in as little as 1 to 1-1/2 turns with an altitude loss of approximately 2,500 to 4,000 feet. However, with neutral controls, it may require as much as 3-1/2 turns and 7,000 feet to self-recover, or the spin could progress to a flat spin. Delaying recovery or inadvertently applying pro-spin controls may cause a flat spin. Applying aileron in the direction of the spin will recover the aircraft almost immediately and prevent flat spin entry in all cases. Application of aileron opposite the spin direction (i.e., pro-spin) will accelerate the yaw, and a flat spin can develop rapidly. Characteristics of the highly oscillatory spin are not significantly different for various symmetric loadings, altitudes, gross weights, c.g.'s or power settings.

The flat spin mode with symmetric loadings will exhibit average AOA in excess of cockpit gage range (70-90 units), with average yaw rates of 75° to 135° per second. Periods of high (i.e., 3 to 4 g) negative "eyeballs out" longitudinal g forces are experienced. These spins are uncomfortable and disorienting due to high yaw rates and g forces. The flat spin is often very steady with no oscillations apparent to the pilot; however, in some cases, mild oscillations may be present. When a flat spin has developed, recovery is no longer possible with neutral controls. Nearly full aileron/differential stabilator deflections in the spin direction are required for recovery. Rudder deflections in either direction have little effect on spin recovery. Recovery will not be immediately apparent and will require approximately two or four turns, with at least 3,000 to 6,000 feet of altitude loss (approximately 10 to 20 seconds) to stop the rotation. Full aileron deflection, which is required for satisfactory recovery, is made available by the spin recovery mode of the flight control system. This mode allows the pilot to use full aileron deflection regardless of fore and aft stick position, 5 seconds after yaw rate exceeds 41.5° per second. Normal aileron control is restored when yaw rate is reduced to less than 30° per second. Full aileron deflection is available with the stick at longitudinal neutral regardless of yaw rate. Yaw rate reduction (i.e., recovery) is smooth and quite slow, and may not be apparent for some time. With application of aileron opposite the spin direction (i.e., pro-spin), the yaw rate will accelerate and "eyeballs out" g force may reach 4 to 5 g. With the aileron again applied in the direction of the spin (anti-spin), recovery will be even slower due to increased yaw rate. For asymmetric loadings (i.e., 5,000-7,000 foot-pounds), turns to recover from the smooth spin will increase by 1 to 1-1/2 turns, with an additional altitude loss of 1,000 to 2,000 feet when compared to symmetric loadings.

In the low rate spin mode the aircraft AOA will be in excess of the cockpit gage range (this condition also exists for higher rate modes), but the average value of 60 to 65 units is lower than that of the other erect spin modes. Oscillations of ±12 units in AOA are typical. Average yaw rate will be between 45 and 60 degrees/second, usually with oscillations of ±10 degrees/second. As a result, the departure tone beep rate may not be constant during this spin mode (figure 6-2). Delaying recovery controls or inadvertently applying pro-spin controls can cause the aircraft to progress into higher rate spin mode. Applying full lateral stick in the direction of the spin will normally recover the aircraft quickly. Occasionally, the amplitude of the spin oscillations will reduce and the low-rate spin will become very smooth. Should this occur, aircraft recovery will be slowed. If the aircraft is in the low rate spin mode, and is not recovering with full anti-spin controls (especially with yaw rate gyro failure) landing gear may be lowered. This results in a control system change which insures full anti-spin aileron deflection is available with full lateral stick regardless of longitudinal stick position. Flaps should not be extended during spins as they may increase the number of turns for recovery.

INVERTED SPINS

The inverted spin can be caused by full lateral stick or full rudder deflection at the full forward stick position (i.e., inverted stall). The spin direction is in the direction of rudder deflection. The inverted spin is generally stabilized at −55 to −60 units AOA, with 40° to 45° per second yaw rate. No buffet or roll/yaw oscillations exist. After neutralizing the controls, the aircraft will recover from the spin in approximately 1-1/2 turns, with 4,000 feet altitude loss.

ENGINE OPERATION DURING DEPARTURE AND SPIN

Engine stagnation requiring shutdown and restart is possible in an out-of-control maneuver. Dual engine stagnation has occurred during extremely violent, forced departure. Engine stagnation has also occurred

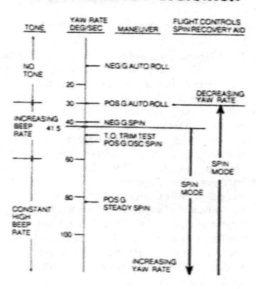

DEPARTURE TONE OPERATION

Figure 6-2

when very slow airspeed/high AOA has resulted in AB blowout and engine stall. No engine anomaly has occurred during stall, vertical stall or tailslide at MIL or IDLE throttle setting.

AUTOROLLS

An autoroll is a sustained combination of rolling and yawing motion. The rolling and yawing motion is sustained by a residual rudder surface deflection and inertial coupling which may continue after controls are neutralized. An autoroll differs from a spin in that it is primarily a rolling maneuver with a small yaw rate and AOA of 20 to 25 units.

Typical autoroll entry conditions are : 200 to 300 knots, 20 to 30 units AOA, rolling with rudder alone and then easing the stick forward. It can be terminated by applying rudder against the roll. A negative g autoroll can be terminated by neutralizing the controls. The wing is not stalled during an autoroll.

POSITIVE G AUTOROLLS

During a positive g autoroll, roll and yaw will be in the same direction. The turn needle will fluctuate from side to side and cannot be used to determine direction. The roll direction should be obvious; however, if in doubt, use the ADI. The departure warning may or may not sound since the yaw rate will be slightly above or below 30°/sec, the point at which beeping begins (Figure 6-2). Neutralizing the controls and rudder application opposite the rolling motion will terminate the maneuver. The more rudder applied, the faster the recovery. When the roll stops, a negative g pitch over will occur. The severity of the negative g pitch over is a function of the rate of recovery and is worse if pitch CAS is off. An abrupt application of rudder may cause negative g pitch over of up to two negative g. To minimize negative g pitch over and aid in pilot orientation, slowly apply rudder to the deflection required to stop the roll. Aileron against the roll in an autoroll is a pro spin input which can induce a spin.

NEGATIVE G AUTOROLLS

During negative g autorolls, yaw and roll will be in opposite directions. Negative g autorolls are normally entered at negative g and sustained by maintaining forward stick. A negative g autoroll normally exhibits slow roll and yaw rates, and the departure warning tone will not sound. Neutralizing the controls is sufficient to terminate the maneuver. Neutral controls and rudder application with the rolling motion will speed the recovery. If the stick was sufficiently forward during entry, considerable aft stick may be required to reduce the negative g during both the maneuver and recovery. Negative g autorolls can be extremely disorienting because of negative g's.

SLOW SPEED FLIGHT

The aircraft exhibits no unusual slow speed flight characteristics. For a symmetrically loaded airplane (i.e., no weight asymmetry), the handling qualities remain acceptable up to the point where there is sufficient airflow over the controls and wings to provide control power or lift. In many cases at very slow speed, full aft stick and/or a pegged vertical velocity may be the only sign(s) of a low energy 1 g stalled condition.

For an asymmetrically loaded aircraft (i.e., weight asymmetry), maintain a minimum of 300 knots, except during low speed tactical maneuvers, maximum range descents, holding, instrument approaches and landing. This minimum airspeed provides reasonable handling qualities and adequate maneuver margins for terrain and collision avoidance.

NEGATIVE G FLIGHT CHARACTERISTICS

Aircraft response to roll and yaw control inputs at negative load factors can be extremely disorienting. Abrupt rudder or cross controls can result in pilot induced out-of-control situations.

During negative g maneuvers, pitch rates increase rapidly with decreasing load factor including negative g. Large aileron inputs cause the aircraft to roll out from under you with the disorienting and uncomfortable effect of being thrown up around the side mirror.

Rudder response varies with AOA and under negative g, can produce adverse effects. At positive g, left rudder produces left wing down roll. However, as positive g is reduces, rudder input produces more and more yaw induced sideslip and has less effect on generating roll. As angle of attack becomes negative (between 0 and -0.5g) rudder input produces all sideslip and no roll. Large rudder inputs will result in extreme sideslip angle and the aircraft will be flying sideways, resulting in high cockpit lateral g's. At load factors more negative than about -0.5g, rudder will cause a roll in the opposite direction and will be accompanied by high pitch rate and pitch angle changes. This condition is extremely disorienting due to the combined effect of negative and lateral g and severe pitch and roll oscillations. Avoid abrupt manual rudder inputs at negative load factors. If this situation is encountered, neutralizing or releasing the controls will recover the aircraft.

The combined effect of aileron and manual rudder input at negative g can be even more dramatic. With forward stick, ailerons easily overcome any opposite direction rolling movement. If cross controls are applied, inertial coupling can produce extremely rapid and disorienting oscillatory rolls (in the direction of the aileron input) in excess of 200°/second. Cross control rolls should be avoided. If this situation is encountered, neutralizing or releasing the controls will recover the aircraft.

Asymmetry has little effect on recovery from negative AOA out-of-control rolls. Oscillations in all axes and roll rates are accentuated; however, neutral controls will still recover the aircraft almost immediately.

LOW - ALTITUDE HIGH SPEED FLIGHT

The aircraft is susceptible to gusts during low-altitude, high-speed flight due to low wing loading/high lift wing characteristics. In areas of very heavy turbulence, such as found in mountainous desert terrain, flight above about 0.8 Mach may induce abrupt vertical motions. Minor lateral/directional motion will also occur. None of these disturbances significantly alter the aircraft flight path. Flight with external stores increases the wing loading and reduces the effects of gusts on the aircraft.

SECTION VII

ADVERSE WEATHER OPERATION

TABLE OF CONTENTS

Turbulence and Thunderstorms 7-1
Snow, Ice, Rain and Slush 7-2
Cold Weather Operation 7-4
Hot Weather/Desert Operation...................7-5

This section provides for operation in adverse weather. Section II of this manual provides normal instrument flight procedures. These procedures differ from, or are in addition to, those contained in section II.

TURBULENCE AND THUNDERSTORMS

Avoid areas of icing, turbulence, hail, or thunderstorms, when possible, due to the increased danger of engine stagnation. If these areas cannot be avoided, turn on the engine anti-icing system before weather penetration. Monitor FTIT gages continuously during weather penetration. Increasing FTIT is an indication of engine icing. The INLET ICE caution warns of icing conditions in the engine inlet. When possible, anticipate icing and turn on the anti-icing system to warm the engine inlet guide vanes.

PENETRATION

Thunderstorm penetration has not been flight tested. The aircraft structure is capable, subsonic, of withstanding the accelerations and gust loadings associated with the largest thunderstorms. The aircraft is stable and comparatively easy to control in severe turbulence if speed is not high. Severe damage may be caused by hail and lightning. Hail damage to the speed brake is increased significantly if the speed brake is extended.

PENETRATION AIRSPEED

Optimum thunderstorm penetration speed is 300 knots or best cruise, whichever is lower. Optimum thunderstorm penetration speed is a compromise between pilot comfort, controllability, structural stress, and engine inlet air distortion. At high speed, aircrew discomfort and structural stress are greater. At slow speed, controllability is reduced and inlet airflow distortion due to turbulence may cause compressor stall and/or engine stagnation.

THUNDERSTORM PENETRATION

Place the windshield anti-ice switch ON at the first sign of ice or before entering known icing conditions. Establish recommended penetration speed. Perform or check the following:

1. Throttle - ADJUST TO MAINTAIN DESIRED PENETRATION SPEED
2. Pitot heat switch - ON
3. Engine anti-ice switch - ON
4. Windshield anti-ice switch - ON
5. Lower seat.

If night penetration -

6. Storm flood switch - BRT
7. Instrument lights - BRT
8. Console lights - BRT
9. Anti-collision lights - OFF

IN THE STORM

Maintain a normal instrument scan with added emphasis on the attitude indicator (EADI) and power setting. Attempt to maintain attitude and accept altitude, AOA, and airspeed fluctuations. Ice or hail may damage the pitot tubes or AOA probe.

SNOW, ICE, RAIN AND SLUSH

TAXIING

Painted areas on runways, taxiways, and ramps are significantly slipperier than nonpainted areas. When painted areas are wet, braking may be negligible. Painted areas may serve as condensation surfaces and it is possible to have wet, frosty, or icy conditions on these areas when the overall weather is dry. With snow or ice, the approach end of the runway is usually slipperier than other areas due to melting and refreezing. There is sufficient braking effectiveness to overcome residual thrust at the very slow taxi speed required on slippery surfaces. Use care to avoid imprudent taxi speed since the braking required to quickly reduce taxi speed may cause skidding. Use of the groundspeed indicator to properly manage taxi speed is recommended. Avoid hard turns on snow or ice-covered taxiways. Expect the nose to overshoot the desired position and skid sideways when using the maneuvering nosewheel steering mode. If the nosewheel skids, straighten the nosewheel and again initiate the turn. The windshield anti-ice switch may be used momentarily to clear ice or moisture from the windshield. Inlet lip and engine face icing can occur when the ambient temperature is between 10°C (50°F) and −20°C (−4°F) and the dew point is within 0° to 3°C (5°F) of ambient temperature. If a half inch or more ice build-up is observed on the leading edge of the inlet variable ramp, mission abort should be considered. Ice ingestion from the lip or engine face even with engine anti-ice ON, can cause engine FOD and slight loss of power. Inlet lip and engine face ice build-up during taxi can be minimized during icing conditions by observing the following: Before engine start, insure the ground surface directly below and just forward of the inlet face is clear of snow, slush and water whenever the ambient temperature is below 10°C (50°F). After engine start, turn on engine anti-ice if either visible moisture is present or the dew point is within 3°C (5°F) of ambient temperature with the ambient temperature between 10°C (50°F) and −20°C (−4°F). While taxiing, avoid stopping where inlets are above areas covered by snow, slush or water. Prior to takeoff, minimize engine operation above IDLE power with ambient temperature between 2°C (36°F) and 10°C (50°F). In this temperature range and at IDLE power, water droplets in the airstream will remain above freezing. Above IDLE power, the temperature decrease thru the inlet duct is such that water will freeze on impact causing ice formation. After landing, single engine taxi during icing conditions is recommended to prevent exposure of both engines, to possible ice FOD. If taxiing single-engine with power below 73%, expect automatic avionics shutdown. Do not turn the engine anti-ice switch OFF until engine shutdown.

TAKEOFF

Do not attempt takeoff with ice or snow on the aircraft.

INFLIGHT

There is always a possibility of engine and/or airframe icing in instrument conditions. Icing is most likely when takeoff is made into low clouds with temperature near freezing. Flight operations are normally above serious icing levels and the aircraft's high performance will usually enable you to move out of dangerous areas quickly. When icing is encountered, take immediate action to avoid further accumulation. Flight through ice and/or rain requires no special technique; however, engine and windshield anti-ice systems do require attention. Turn on the engine anti-ice when icing is anticipated. Do not wait until the INLET ICE caution comes on since this indicates that ice has already formed in the inlets. The L and/or R INLET caution may come on in icing conditions below 1.33 Mach due to ice blockage of the duct static port. When icing conditions no longer exist, turning the engine anti-ice off reduces FTIT and increases engine life. Momentary application of windshield anti-ice may be used to clear precipitation from the windshield during the approach.

> **NOTE**
>
> Icing of the AOA probes may cause pitch and roll CAS to disengage. The speed brake may also retract due to erroneous AOA information.

LANDING

When stopping distance is critical, fly final approach as slow as possible up to 23 units AOA. Precise control of airspeed and touchdown point is critical. Use of speed brake may assist in airspeed control and decreased landing roll. The velocity vector, airspeed, and AOA on the HUD can be used as aids. On a wet runway, anticipate hydroplaning. If the runway is slippery, raising the flaps will allow aerobraking to lower speeds, thereby reducing the braking required to slow to taxi speed. Landing roll can also be reduced by shutting down one engine after touchdown when committed to stop. During single-engine operations at idle, expect automatic avionics shutdown. Aerobrake until full aft stick is achieved. Hold full aft stick until the nose drops. With a crosswind, do not jeopardize directional control by attempting to aerodynamic brake to very low airspeeds. If conditions prevent a normal aerodynamic braking attitude, consider lowering the nose and commencing maximum anti-skid braking. Maximum wheel braking is obtained with the brake pedals fully depressed; therefore, use as much pedal force as possible (not just enough to get anti-skid cycling) without jeopardizing your ability to maintain directional control. Failure to hold the pedals fully depressed may extend the landing roll.

HYDROPLANING

Operation on wet or flooded runways may produce three conditions under which tire traction may be reduced to an insignificant value.

DYNAMIC HYDROPLANING

As the tire velocity is increased, the hydrodynamic pressure acting on the leading portion of the tire footprint will increase to a value sufficient to support the vertical load acting on the tire. The speed at which this occurs is called total hydroplaning speed. Any increase in ground speed above this critical value lifts the tire completely off the runway, leaving the tire supported by the fluid alone. Since the fluid cushion is incapable of sustaining any appreciable shear forces, braking and side force coefficients drop to near zero. The total hydroplaning speed is equal to nine times the square root of tire pressure. The tables below indicate the hydroplaning speeds for typical tire pressures:

MLG TIRE PRESSURE (PSI)	TOTAL HYDRO-PLANING SPEED (KTS)	NLG TIRE PRESSURE (PSI)	TOTAL HYDRO-PLANING SPEED (KTS)
210	130	205	128
230	136	230	136
260	145	275	149
300	155		
325	162		
355	169		

VISCOUS HYDROPLANING

Viscous hydroplaning occurs due to the inability of the tire to penetrate the very thin film found under damp runway conditions. This condition is aggravated when more viscous fluid such as oil, fuel, rubber deposits and/or dust are present. The condition is improved on a coarse textured runway. Viscous hydroplaning occurs at medium to high speeds with rolling or skidding tires. The speed at which it occurs is not dependent on tire pressure.

REVERTED RUBBER HYDROPLANING

Occurs after a locked-wheel skid has started on a wet runway. Enough heat may be produced to turn the trapped water to steam. The steam will heat the rubber sufficiently to revert it to its natural state and will seal the tire grooves. The tire then rides on a cushion of steam which greatly reduces the friction coefficient and may continue to do so to very low speeds.

AFTER LANDING

Ensure windshield anti-ice switch is OFF. Single engine taxi is recommended on slippery surfaces. Expect automatic avionics shutdown during single-engine taxi below 73% rpm. Use extra care when turning from runway to taxiway as transition from a relatively dry to a slippery surface can cause rotational skids. A rotational skid is insidious and will likely result in a ground loop if it starts. Slow nearly to a stop before attempting a turn under these conditions.

COLD WEATHER OPERATION

BEFORE ENTERING COCKPIT

The entire aircraft must be free of snow, ice, and frost. These are a major flight hazard and result in a loss of lift and increased stall speed. They must be removed before flight. Do not chip or scrape away ice as damage to aircraft may result.

1. Shock struts, pitot tube, fuel vents, and actuating cylinders are free of ice or dirt.
2. Fuel drain cocks free of ice.
3. All exterior covers removed.
4. JFS accumulators - 2900 PSI MINIMUM - 4000 PSI (MIL-H-83282 hydraulic fluid below −29°C (−20°F))

INTERIOR CHECK

In temperatures below 0°C (32°F), difficulty may be experienced when connecting the oxygen mask hose to the T-connector. Apply a small amount of heat to the T-connector to alleviate this problem. If the oxygen mask is not fastened, keep it well clear of the face to prevent freezing of the valves.

STARTING JFS

With the hydraulic system serviced with MIL-H-5606 hydraulic fluid, normal JFS starts may be made if the temperature is above −35°C (−31°F). Between −35°C (−31°F) and −40°C (−40°F), use double bottle starts. Below −40°C (−40°F), preheating is required.

With the hydraulic system serviced with MIL-H-83282 hydraulic fluid, normal JFS starts may be made if the temperature is above −29°C (−20°F). Between −29°C (−20°F) and −40°C (−40°F), use double bottle starts. Below −40°C (−40°F), preheating is required.

STARTING ENGINES

At temperatures below −18°C (0°F), allow the JFS to run for 1 minute prior to engaging an engine. If ambient temperature is below −30°C (−22°F), insure that gear pins are in until aircraft hydraulic and electrical power are available.

BEFORE TAXIING

NOTE

Warm up of fluids can be speeded up by cycling the controls.

Operate all flight controls and the speedbrake through several cycles. Turn on the windshield anti-ice, if required. Cycle the ENG CONTR at least twice to prevent sluggish nozzle movement which may cause compresser stall at afterburner initiation. At temperatures below −40°C (−40°F), avionics may require up to 30 minutes warm-up before operating normally. Turn on engine anti-ice if visible moisture present and ambient temperature is between +10°C (+50°F) and −20°C (−4°F). Do not wait until the INLET ICE caution comes on. Use of engine anti-ice is not time limited and does not degrade engine thrust significantly. Expect idle rpm to be around 55%. Idle oil pressure may be below 15 psi. This is acceptable for taxi.

TAXIING

Avoid taxiing in deep or rutted snow since frozen brakes will likely result. Increase space between aircraft while taxiing at sub-freezing temperatures to insure safe stopping distance and to prevent icing of aircraft surfaces by melted snow and ice blown by the jet blast of preceding aircraft. The high idle thrust can produce high taxi speeds. Control taxi speeds to avoid high-speed stops or turns on slippery taxiways.

TAKEOFF

Below −20°C (−4°F), MIL rpm may be as low as 87% and FTIT may be as low as 810°C.

AFTER LANDING

Single engine taxi is recommended for easier control of taxi speed. Expect automatic avionics shutdown at single-engine operation below 73% rpm. Idle thrust is high, and remains essentially constant as temperature decreases. When wearing bulky arctic survival clothing and winter flying gloves, rapid egress from the cockpit by disconnecting the torso harness will be impeded due to the inability to see the connectors and degraded sense of touch.

BEFORE LEAVING AIRCRAFT

Leave canopy open, weather permitting, to permit circulation. This decreases windshield and canopy frosting. Check that protective covers are installed.

Engine intake duct covers should not be installed until two hours after engine shutdown to prevent condensation from puddling and freezing, preventing subsequent engine rotation.

HOT WEATHER/DESERT OPERATION

Do not operate the engine in a sand storm or dust storm, if avoidable. Park aircraft crosswind and shut down engine to prevent sand or dirt from damaging engine.

APPENDIX A

PERFORMANCE DATA
WITH F100-PW-220 ENGINES

PART 1	INTRODUCTION	A1-1
PART 2	ENGINE DATA	A2-1
PART 3	TAKEOFF	A3-1
PART 4	CLIMB	A4-1
PART 5	RANGE	A5-1
PART 6	ENDURANCE	A6-1
PART 7	DESCENT	A7-1
PART 8	APPROACH AND LANDING	A8-1
PART 9	COMBAT PERFORMANCE	A9-1

PART 1

INTRODUCTION

TABLE OF CONTENTS

Charts

Station Loading A1-4
F-15E Gross Weights (Lbs) and
  CG Location (%MAC) A1-8
Standard Atmosphere Table A1-10
Stall Speeds A1-11
Airspeed Conversion A1-15
Airspeed Position Error Correction A1-17
Altimeter Position Error Correction A1-18
Wind Components A1-19

NOTE

All performance data are based on JP-4 fuel and are also applicable for JP-8 fuel.

DRAG INDEX SYSTEM

Most of the charts use the drag index system to effectively present the many combinations of weight/drag effects on performance. The Airplane Loading chart (figure A1-1) contains the drag number and weight of each externally carried store. The weight and drag number for external store suspension equipment are listed separately. The drag index for a specific configuration may be found by multiplying the number of stores carried by its drag number, and adding the drag number of the applicable suspension equipment. The total drag index may then be used to enter the planning data charts. The F-15E Gross Weights and CG Location (%MAC) chart (figure A1-2) contains the weight and % CG for certain "typical" load configurations. Charts applicable for all loads and configuration are labeled ALL DRAG INDEXES. Charts labeled INDIVIDUAL DRAG INDEXES contain data for a range of drag numbers; i.e., individual curves/columns for a specific drag number. Supersonic data is not compatible to the drag index system; therefore, each chart is labeled for a specific configuration.

STALL SPEEDS CHARTS

The Stall Speeds charts (figures A1-4 thru A1-7) present stall speeds for various combinations of gross weight, bank angle, power setting and altitude. The data is based on having the gear and flaps down (figures A1-4, A1-5) or gear and flaps up (figures A1-6, A1-7).

USE

Enter the appropriate chart with the applicable gross weight and proceed horizontally to the right to intersect the applicable bank angle. From this intersection, descend vertically and intersect the applicable altitude curve. Then project horizontally left to read the stall speed.

Sample Problem

Configuration: Flaps Down, Gear Down, Maximum Thrust

A. Gross weight	40,000 Lb
B. Bank angle	15°
C. Altitude	10,000 Ft
D. Stall speed	107 Kt

AIRSPEED CONVERSION

The Airspeed Conversion charts, (figures A1-8 and A1-9) provide a means of converting calibrated airspeed to true Mach number and true airspeed.

INDICATED AIRSPEED

Indicated airspeed (IAS) is the uncorrected airspeed read directly from the indicator.

CALIBRATED AIRSPEED

Calibrated airspeed (CAS) is indicated airspeed corrected for static source error.

EQUIVALENT AIRSPEED

Equivalent airspeed (EAS) is calibrated airspeed corrected for compressibility. There is no provision made for reading equivalent airspeed.

SAMPLE STALL SPEEDS

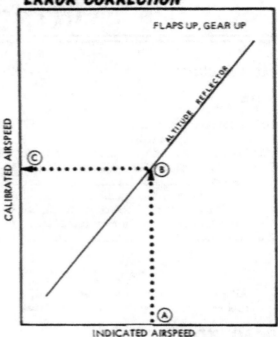

SAMPLE AIRSPEED POSITION ERROR CORRECTION

15E-1-(63)

15E-1-(64)

TRUE AIRSPEED

True airspeed (TAS) is equivalent airspeed corrected for density altitude. Refer to the Airspeed Conversion charts (figures A1-8 and A1-9).

AIRSPEED POSITION ERROR CORRECTION CHART

Under normal conditions, the air data computer compensates for the static source position error. If an air data computer malfunction occurs, the primary airspeed/Mach indicator becomes inoperative and airspeed is read from the standby indicator. The indicated airspeed read on this indicator may be corrected to calibrated airspeed by utilizing the Airspeed Position Error Correction chart (figure A1-10).

USE

Enter the appropriate chart with the indicated airspeed read from the standby indicator. In the flaps down, gear down configuration at 10,000 feet and below read the calibrated airspeed from the tabulated chart. In the flaps up, gear up configuration, enter the chart with the indicated airspeed and project vertically up to the appropriate altitude reflector curve. From this point, project horizontally left to read the calibrated airspeed.

Sample Problem

Configuration: Flaps Up, Gear Up

A. Indicated airspeed	300 Kt
B. Altitude reflector line	40,000 Ft
C. Calibrated airspeed	312 Kt

Configuration: Flaps Down, Gear Down (10,000 Ft and below)

A. Indicated airspeed	200 Kt
B. Gross weight	40,000 Lb
C. Calibrated airspeed	198.5 Kt

ALTIMETER POSITION ERROR CORRECTION CHART

Under normal conditions, the ADC compensates for the static source position error. If an ADC malfunction occurs, the primary altitude indicator becomes inoperative and altitude is read from the standby indicator. The indicated altitude read on this indicator may be corrected to calibrated altitude by utilizing the Altimeter Position Error Correction chart (figure A1-11).

USE

Enter the appropriate chart with indicated airspeed. In the flaps retracted, gear up configuration project horizontally right to the assigned altitude reflector. From this point, project vertically up to the reflector line. From this point, project horizontally left to read the △H altitude correction. In the full flaps, gear down configuration project vertically up to the appropriate gross weight curve. From this point project horizontally left to read the △H altitude correction. In either case apply the △H altitude correction to the altimeter and fly indicated altitude.

Sample Problem

Configuration: Flaps up, Gear Up

A. Indicated airspeed	400 Kt
B. Assigned altitude	55,000 Ft
C. Reflector line	
D. △H correction	+375 Ft
E. Indicated altitude necessary to maintain assigned altitude (B+D)	55,375 Ft

Configuration: Flaps Down, Gear Down

A. Indicated airspeed	155 Kt
B. Gross weight	40,000 Lb
C. △H correction	+60 Ft

WIND COMPONENTS CHART

A standard Wind Components chart (figure A1-12) is included. It is used primarily for breaking a forecast wind down into crosswind and headwind components for takeoff computations. It may, however, be used whenever wind component information is desired. It is not to be used as a ground controllability chart.

SAMPLE ALTIMETER POSITION ERROR CORRECTION

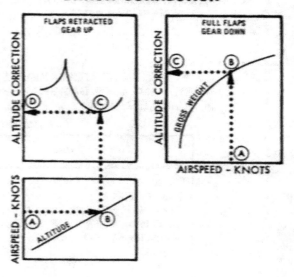

15E-1-1651

USE

Determine the effective wind velocity by adding one-half the gust velocity (incremental wind factor) to the steady state velocity; e.g., reported wind 050/30 G40, effective wind is 050/35. Reduce the reported wind direction to a relative bearing by determining the wind direction and runway heading. Enter the chart with the relative bearing. Move along the relative bearing to intercept the effective wind speed arc. From this point, descend vertically down to read the crosswind component. From the intersection of bearing and wind speed, project horizontally left to read headwind component.

Sample Problem

Reported wind 050/35, runway heading 030.

A. Relative bearing	20°
B. Intersect windspeed arc	35 Kt
C. Crosswind component	12 Kt
D. Headwind component	33 Kt

STATION LOADING

OPERATING WEIGHT (Basic airplane weight plus crew)

F-15E .... 32,500 pounds

BASIC TAKEOFF WEIGHT (Operating weight plus full internal fuel and ammunition)

F-15E .... 46,000 pounds

NOTE

FOR PRECISE AIRPLANE BASIC WEIGHT, REFER TO WEIGHT AND BALANCE DATA HANDBOOK, TO 1-1B-40, FOR THE PARTICULAR AIRPLANE

CONFIGURATION DRAG

ITEM	WEIGHT (POUNDS)	DRAG NUMBER
F-15E	-	0
Two -4 CFTs	E 4,206	20.1
(F-15E Production Model)	F 13,667	
LANTIRN Navigation Pod (AN/AAQ-13) and Adapter (ADU-576/A)	520	9.5
LANTIRN Targeting Pod (AN/AAQ-14) and Adapter (ADU-577/A)	621	7.4

ITEM	WEIGHT PER ITEM (POUNDS)	DRAG NUMBER WITHOUT CFT		DRAG NUMBER WITH CFT			
		CENTER-LINE STATION	OTHER STATIONS	CENTER-LINE STATION	WING STATIONS	CFT STATIONS WITHOUT BOMBS/TANKS ON WING STATIONS	CFT STATIONS WITH BOMBS/TANKS ON WING STATIONS
Air-to-Air Missiles							
AIM-7F, -7M	510	-	1.8	-	-	2.3	2.3
AIM-9L, 9M	195	-	2.1	-	2.1	-	-
AIM-9P/P-1	170	-	2.1	-	2.1	-	-
AIM-9P-2/P-3	180	-	2.1	-	2.1	-	-
AIM-120A	338	-	1.3	-	2.3	1.7	1.7
CATM-9L/M-1	195	-	2.1	-	2.1	-	-
Air-to-Ground Missiles							
AGM-65A, B	481	-	3.7	-	3.7	-	-
AGM-65D	485	-	3.7	-	3.7	-	-
AGM-65G	687	-	3.7	-	3.7	-	-
AGM-130A,B	2962	-	TBD	-	TBD	-	-

Figure A1-1 (Sheet 1 of 4)

STATION LOADING (CONT)

ITEM	WEIGHT PER ITEM (POUNDS)	DRAG NUMBER WITHOUT CFT		DRAG NUMBER WITH CFT			
		CENTER-LINE STATION	OTHER STATIONS	CENTER-LINE STATION	WING STATIONS	CFT STATIONS WITHOUT BOMBS/ TANKS ON WING STATIONS	CFT STATIONS WITH BOMBS/ TANKS ON WING STATIONS
Pylons, Launchers and Adapters							
SUU-73/A Center-line Pylon with BRU-47/A	316	3.3	-	3.3	-	-	-
SUU-59C/A Wing Pylon with BRU-47/A	371	-	3.3	-	3.3	-	-
LAU-128/A Launcher and AIM-9/AIM-120 Adapter (ADU-552/A)	111	-	1.1	-	1.1	-	-
LAU-88A/A Launcher (Triple Rail) and AGM-65 Adapter (ADU-578/A)	573	-	9.6	-	9.6	-	-
LAU-117/A Launcher (Single Rail) for AGM-65	135	-	1.4	-	1.4	-	-
LAU-114/A Launcher and AIM-9 Adapter (ADU-407/A)	79	-	1.2	-	1.2	-	-
General Purpose Weapons							
MK-82 LDGP	505	-	-	-	-	0.8	0.9
MK-82 SE	550	-	-	-	-	1.4	1.5
MK-82 AIR (With BSU-49 Fin)	540	-	-	-	-	1.1	1.2
MK-84 LDGP	1970	3.0	2.1	3.0	2.3	2.8	3.0
MK-84 AIR (With BSU-50 Fin)	2010	5.4	3.9	5.4	4.2	5.1	5.6

Figure A1-1 (Sheet 2)

STATION LOADING (CONT)

ITEM	WEIGHT PER ITEM (POUNDS)	DRAG NUMBER WITHOUT CFT		DRAG NUMBER WITH CFT			
		CENTER-LINE STATION	OTHER STATIONS	CENTER-LINE STATION	WING STATIONS	CFT STATIONS WITHOUT BOMBS/ TANKS ON WING STATIONS	CFT STATIONS WITH BOMBS/ TANKS ON WING STATIONS
Guided Weapons							
GBU-10A/B	2053	10.5	7.5	10.5	7.5	9.8	10.7
GBU-10C/B, D/B	2081	10.5	7.5	10.5	7.5	9.8	10.7
GBU-12B/B, C/B	610	-	-	-	-	3.9	4.3
GBU-15(V)-4/B	2502	-	5.6	-	5.6	-	-
GBU-24/B	2323	7.8	5.6	7.8	5.6	5.6	6.2
Dispensers/Rockets							
CBU-52B/B	785	-	-	-	-	4.6	5.0
CBU-58/B	810	-	-	-	-	4.6	5.0
CBU-71/B	810	-	-	-	-	4.6	5.0
CBU-87/B (TMD)	950	-	-	-	-	2.9	3.2
CBU-89/B (TMD)	706	-	-	-	-	2.9	3.2
MK-20 Rockeye	486	-	-	-	-	1.5	1.6
TMU-28/B Spray Tank	E 567 F 1935	-	4.9	-	4.9	-	-
Special Weapons							
B61	716	2.5	1.8	2.5	1.8	1.8	2.0
Miscellaneous Stores							
610 Gallon Fuel Tank	E 320 F 4285	12.2	5.5	12.2	6.0	-	-
610 Gallon Fuel Tank (With Bombs on Inboard CFT Station)	E 320 F 4285	-	-	12.2	8.2	-	-
610 Gallon Fuel Tank (With Bombs on Out-board CFT Station)	E 320 F 4285	-	-	12.2	12.3	-	-
SUU-20B/A Practice Dispenser (Empty)	276	5.0	3.6	5.0	3.9	3.9	3.9
MK-106 PB (Incl)	F 306	4.2	3.0	4.2	3.3	3.3	3.3
BDU-33 PB (Incl)	F 414	4.2	3.0	4.2	3.3	3.3	3.3
BDU-48 PB (Incl)	F 336	4.2	3.0	4.2	3.3	3.3	3.3
BDU-38 (B61 Training Shape)	716	2.6	1.8	2.5	1.8	1.8	2.0

E - Empty   F - Full   PB - Practice Bomb

Figure A1-1 (Sheet 3)

STATION LOADING (CONT)

ITEM	WEIGHT PER ITEM (POUNDS)	DRAG NUMBER WITHOUT CFT		DRAG NUMBER WITH CFT			
		CENTER-LINE STATION	OTHER STATIONS	CENTER-LINE STATION	WING STATIONS	CFT STATIONS WITHOUT BOMBS/ TANKS ON WING STATIONS	CFT STATIONS WITH BOMBS/ TANKS ON WING STATIONS
AN/AXQ-14 Data Link Pod (for GBU-15)	450	3.3	-	3.3	-	-	-
P-4A/AX AIS Pod	160	-	2.1	-	2.1	-	-
AN/ASQ-T17 AIS Pod	122	-	2.1	-	2.1	-	-
AN/ASQ-T20 AIS Pod	123	-	2.1	-	2.1	-	-
AN/ASQ-T21 AIS Pod	124	-	2.1	-	2.1	-	-
AN/ASQ-T25 AIS Pod	122	-	2.1	-	2.1	-	-
BLU-107 Durandal	494	-	-	-	-	1.2	1.4
MXU-648A/A-50 Cargo Pod	E 98 F 398	3.6	3.6	3.6	3.6	-	-
Ammunition							
(512 Live Rounds)	289	-	-	-	-	-	-
(Spent Cartridges)	136	-	-	-	-	-	-

E - Empty   F- Full

Figure A1-1 (Sheet 4)

F-15E GROSS WEIGHTS (LBS) AND CG LOCATION (%MAC)

STORE	#	FULL FUEL		CFT EMPTY		3200 LBS REMAINING		COMMENTS
		WEIGHT	CG	WEIGHT	CG	WEIGHT	CG	
MK-82 SE	12	69100	27.1	59600	25.8	49700	27.7	
	8	66900	26.8	57400	25.4	47500	27.3	
	4	64700	26.1	55200	24.6	45300	26.4	
MK-82 AIR	12	69000	27.0	59500	25.7	49600	27.6	
	8	66800	26.7	57300	25.3	47400	27.2	
	4	64600	26.1	55200	24.5	45300	26.3	
MK-82 LDGP	12	68500	26.8	59100	25.5	49200	27.3	
	8	66500	26.6	57100	25.1	47200	27.0	
	4	64500	26.0	55000	24.5	45100	26.3	
MK-84 AIR	4	70500	25.9	61100	24.5	51200	26.1	STA 2, 8, LC/RC 2
	2	66500	26.1	57000	24.6	47100	26.4	LC/RC 2
MK-84 LDGP	4	70400	25.8	60900	24.4	51000	26.0	STA 2, 8, LC/RC 2
	2	66400	26.1	57000	24.5	47100	26.3	LC/RC 2
GBU-10C/B	4	70000	26.0	60600	24.6	50700	26.2	STA 2, 8, LC/RC 2 NO AIM-9
	2	66600	26.1	57200	24.6	47300	26.4	LC/RC 2
GBU-10G/B	4	70200	25.5	60800	23.9	50900	25.5	STA 2, 8, LC/RC 2 NO AIM-9
	2	66800	25.8	57300	24.3	47400	26.0	LC/RC 2
GBU-24/B	4	71000	26.1	61500	24.7	51600	26.3	STA 2, 8, LC/RC 2 NO AIM-9
	2	67100	26.2	57700	24.7	47800	26.5	LC/RC 2
GBU-24A/B	4	71100	25.5	61700	23.9	51800	25.5	STA 2, 8, LC/RC 2 NO AIM-9
	2	67200	25.8	57700	24.3	47800	26.0	LC/RC 2
GBU-12	8	67400	26.6	57900	25.2	48000	27.1	
	4	64900	26.3	55500	24.8	45600	26.7	
CBU-52 CBU-58 CBU-71	12	72200	27.3	62700	26.1	52800	28.0	
	8	69000	27.0	59500	26.7	49600	27.6	
	4	65700	26.2	56300	24.7	46400	26.6	

Figure A1-2 (Sheet 1 of 2)

F-15E GROSS WEIGHTS (LBS) AND CG LOCATION (%MAC) (CONT)

STORE	#	FULL FUEL		CFT EMPTY		3200 LBS REMAINING		COMMENTS
		WEIGHT	CG	WEIGHT	CG	WEIGHT	CG	
CBU-87	12	73900	27.8	64400	26.7	54500	28.5	
	8	70100	27.3	60600	26.1	50700	28.1	
	4	66300	26.4	56800	24.9	46900	26.8	
CBU-89	12	71000	27.3	61500	26.0	51600	28.0	
	8	68100	27.0	58700	25.6	48800	27.5	
	4	65300	26.2	55800	24.7	45900	26.5	
MK-20	12	68300	26.9	58900	25.5	49000	27.4	
	8	66400	26.6	56900	25.1	47000	27.1	
	4	64400	26.0	55000	24.5	45100	26.3	

NOTE

1. CENTER OF GRAVITY DATA BASED ON F-15E 88-1688.

2. BASIC AIRCRAFT CONFIGURATION IS: FULL OF FUEL (INTERNAL AND CFT), 2 x LANTIRN PODS, 4 x AIM-9L, NO GUN AMMO AND LIGHTWEIGHT CREW (170 LBS).

3. CG LOCATIONS ARE FOR GEAR UP. ADD 0.3% MAC FOR GEAR DOWN ABOVE 70,000 POUNDS. BELOW 70,000 POUNDS ADD 0.4% TO MAC.

4. CENTER OF GRAVITY TRACK IS FAIRLY LINEAR BETWEEN POINTS SHOWN.

5. AS FUEL IS BURNED FROM 3200 LBS REMAINING TO 2700 LBS REMAINING, CG MOVES AFT 0.6% MAC. FROM 2700 LBS TO BINGO, CG REMAINS CONSTANT.

6. ADD 0.6% MAC FOR EACH LANTIRN POD REMOVED AND SUBTRACT 621 LBS IF TARGETING POD REMOVED AND 520 LBS IF NAV POD REMOVED.

7. ADD 0.05% MAC AND SUBTRACT 195 LBS FOR EACH AIM-9 REMOVED.

8. WITH CENTERLINE TANK, SUBTRACT 0.5% MAC AND ADD 4600 LBS. AFTER CENTERLINE TANK FUEL IS BURNED, CG TRACK IS AS DESCRIBED ABOVE.

9. ABOVE DATA ASSUMES NORMAL DOWNLOADING OF STORES FROM BOTH CFT'S SIMULTANEOUSLY. IF CONFIGURATION HAS MORE THAN 1 STORE PER CFT, AND IF ONE CFT IS FULLY DOWNLOADED BEFORE THE OTHER, THE ABOVE DATA DOES NOT APPLY.

10. SUBTRACT 0.2% MAC AND ADD 289 LBS IF FULL LOAD OF GUN AMMO IS CARRIED.

11. SUBTRACT 0.3% MAC AND ADD 90 LBS IF HEAVYWEIGHT CREW (215).

12. SUBTRACT 600 LBS IF NO ICS (C.G. IS UNCHANGED).

Figure A1-2 (Sheet 2)

STANDARD ATMOSPHERE TABLE

W = 0.076475 LB/CU FT = 0.0023769 SLUGS/CU FT
1 IN. OF HG = 70.732 LB/SQ FT = 0.4912 LB/SQ IN.
a_0 = 1116.5 FT/SEC = 661.5 KNOTS

STANDARD SEA LEVEL AIR:
T = 59°F (15°C)
P = 29.921 IN. OF HG

U.S. STANDARD ATMOSPHERE, 1966

ALTITUDE FEET	DENSITY RATIO $\rho/\rho_0 = \sigma$	$1/\sqrt{\sigma}$	AIR TEMPERATURE		SPEED OF SOUND RATIO a/a_0	PRESSURE	
			DEG. F	DEG. C		IN. OF HG	RATIO $P/P_0 = \delta$
-2,000	1.0598	0.9714	66.132	18.962	1.0068	32.15	1.0745
-1,000	1.0296	0.9855	62.566	16.981	1.0034	31.02	1.0368
0	1.0000	1.0000	59.000	15.000	1.0000	29.92	1.0000
1,000	0.9711	1.0148	55.434	13.019	0.9966	28.86	0.9644
2,000	0.9428	1.0299	51.868	11.038	0.9931	27.82	0.9298
3,000	0.9151	1.0454	48.302	9.057	0.9896	26.82	0.8962
4,000	0.8881	1.0611	44.735	7.075	0.9862	25.84	0.8637
5,000	0.8617	1.0773	41.169	5.094	0.9827	24.90	0.8320
6,000	0.8359	1.0938	37.603	3.113	0.9792	23.98	0.8014
7,000	0.8106	1.1107	34.037	1.132	0.9756	23.09	0.7716
8,000	0.7860	1.1279	30.471	-0.849	0.9721	22.22	0.7428
9,000	0.7620	1.1456	26.905	-2.831	0.9686	21.39	0.7148
10,000	0.7385	1.1637	23.338	-4.812	0.9650	20.58	0.6877
11,000	0.7156	1.1822	19.772	-6.793	0.9614	19.79	0.6614
12,000	0.6932	1.2011	16.206	-8.774	0.9579	19.03	0.6360
13,000	0.6713	1.2205	12.640	-10.756	0.9543	18.29	0.6113
14,000	0.6500	1.2403	9.074	-12.737	0.9507	17.58	0.5875
15,000	0.6292	1.2606	5.508	-14.718	0.9470	16.89	0.5643
16,000	0.6090	1.2815	1.941	-16.699	0.9434	16.22	0.5420
17,000	0.5892	1.3028	-1.625	-18.681	0.9397	15.57	0.5203
18,000	0.5699	1.3246	-5.191	-20.662	0.9361	14.94	0.4994
19,000	0.5511	1.3470	-8.757	-22.643	0.9324	14.34	0.4791
20,000	0.5328	1.3700	-12.323	-24.624	0.9287	13.75	0.4593
21,000	0.5150	1.3935	-15.889	-26.605	0.9250	13.18	0.4406
22,000	0.4976	1.4176	-19.456	-28.587	0.9213	12.64	0.4223
23,000	0.4807	1.4424	-23.022	-30.568	0.9175	12.11	0.4046
24,000	0.4642	1.4678	-26.588	-32.549	0.9138	11.60	0.3876
25,000	0.4481	1.4938	-30.156	-34.530	0.9100	11.10	0.3711
26,000	0.4325	1.5206	-33.720	-36.511	0.9062	10.63	0.3552
27,000	0.4173	1.5480	-37.286	-38.492	0.9024	10.17	0.3398
28,000	0.4025	1.5762	-40.852	-40.473	0.8986	9.725	0.3250
29,000	0.3881	1.6052	-44.419	-42.455	0.8948	9.297	0.3107
30,000	0.3741	1.6349	-47.985	-44.436	0.8909	8.885	0.2970
31,000	0.3605	1.6654	-51.551	-46.417	0.8871	8.488	0.2837
32,000	0.3473	1.6968	-55.117	-48.398	0.8832	8.106	0.2709
33,000	0.3345	1.7291	-58.683	-50.379	0.8793	7.737	0.2586
34,000	0.3220	1.7623	-62.249	-52.361	0.8754	7.382	0.2467
35,000	0.3099	1.7964	-65.816	-54.342	0.8714	7.041	0.2353
36,000	0.2981	1.8315	-69.382	-56.323	0.8675	6.712	0.2243
37,000	0.2844	1.8753	-69.700	-56.500	0.8671	6.397	0.2138
38,000	0.2710	1.9209	-69.700	-56.500	0.8671	6.097	0.2038
39,000	0.2583	1.9677	-69.700	-56.500	0.8671	5.811	0.1942
40,000	0.2462	2.0155	-69.700	-56.400	0.8671	5.538	0.1851
41,000	0.2346	2.0645	-69.700	-56.500	0.8671	5.278	0.1764
42,000	0.2236	2.1148	-69.700	-56.500	0.8671	5.030	0.1681
43,000	0.2131	2.1662	-69.700	-56.500	0.8671	4.794	0.1602
44,000	0.2031	2.2189	-69.700	-56.500	0.8671	4.569	0.1527
45,000	0.1936	2.2728	-69.700	-56.500	0.8671	4.355	0.1455
46,000	0.1845	2.3281	-69.700	-56.500	0.8671	4.151	0.1387
47,000	0.1758	2.3848	-69.700	-56.500	0.8671	3.956	0.1322
48,000	0.1676	2.4428	-69.700	-56.500	0.8671	3.770	0.1260
49,000	0.1597	2.5022	-69.700	-56.500	0.8671	3.593	0.1201
50,000	0.1522	2.5630	-69.700	-56.500	0.8671	3.425	0.1145
51,000	0.1451	2.6254	-69.700	-56.500	0.8671	3.264	0.1091
52,000	0.1383	2.6892	-69.700	-56.500	0.8671	3.111	0.1040
53,000	0.1318	2.7546	-69.700	-56.500	0.8671	2.965	0.09909
54,000	0.1256	2.8216	-69.700	-56.500	0.8671	2.826	0.09444
55,000	0.1197	2.8903	-69.700	-56.500	0.8671	2.693	0.09001
56,000	0.1141	2.9606	-69.700	-56.500	0.8671	2.567	0.08578
57,000	0.1087	3.0326	-69.700	-56.500	0.8671	2.446	0.08176
58,000	0.1036	3.1063	-69.700	-56.500	0.8671	2.331	0.07792
59,000	0.09877	3.1819	-69.700	-56.500	0.8671	2.222	0.07426
60,000	0.09414	3.2593	-69.700	-56.500	0.8671	2.118	0.07078
61,000	0.08972	3.3386	-69.700	-56.500	0.8671	2.018	0.06746
62,000	0.08551	3.4198	-69.700	-56.500	0.8671	1.924	0.06429
63,000	0.08150	3.5029	-69.700	-56.500	0.8671	1.833	0.06127
64,000	0.07767	3.5881	-69.700	-56.500	0.8671	1.747	0.05840
65,000	0.07403	3.6754	-69.700	-56.500	0.8671	1.665	0.05566

15E-1-(66)

Figure A1-3

STALL SPEEDS
MILITARY THRUST

AIRPLANE CONFIGURATION
GEAR AND FLAPS DOWN
ALL DRAG INDEXES

REMARKS
ENGINE(S): (2) F100-PW-220
U.S. STANDARD DAY, 1966

GUIDE

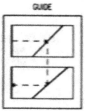

DATE:15 JUNE 1988
DATA BASIS: ESTIMATED

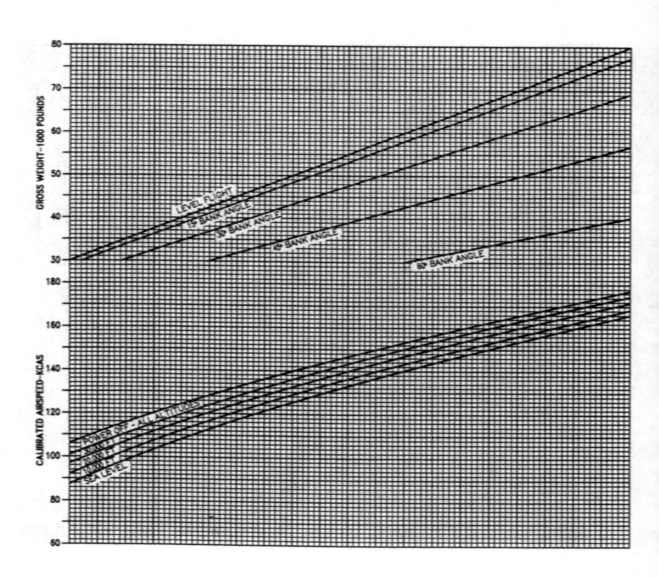

Figure A1-4

STALL SPEEDS
MAXIMUM THRUST

AIRPLANE CONFIGURATION
GEAR AND FLAPS DOWN
ALL DRAG INDEXES

REMARKS
ENGINE(S): (2) F100-PW-220
U.S. STANDARD DAY, 1966

GUIDE

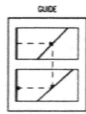

DATE: 15 JUNE 1988
DATA BASIS: ESTIMATED

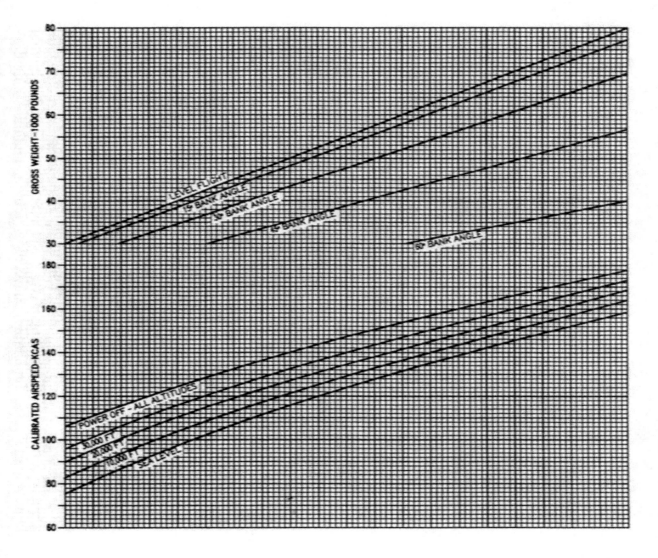

15E-1-(177-1)03-CAT1

Figure A1-5

STALL SPEEDS
MILITARY THRUST

AIRPLANE CONFIGURATION
GEAR AND FLAPS UP
ALL DRAG INDEXES

REMARKS
ENGINE(S): (2) F100-PW-220
U.S. STANDARD DAY, 1966

GUIDE

DATE:15 JUNE 1988
DATA BASIS: ESTIMATED

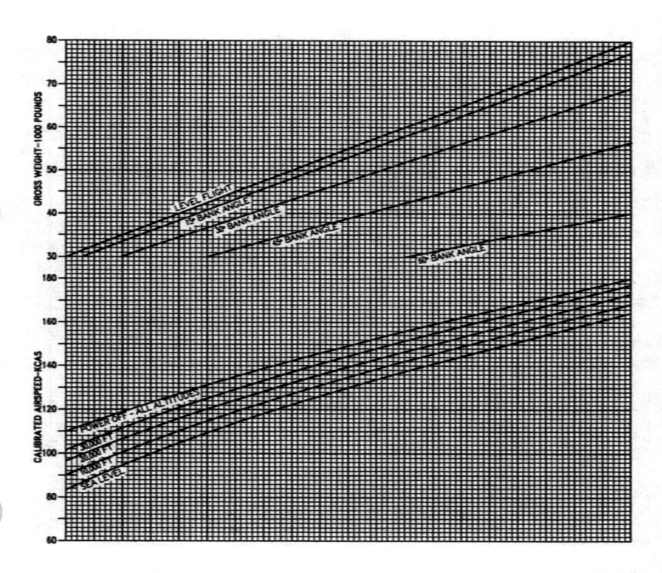

15E-1-(88-1)03-CATI

Figure A1-6

STALL SPEEDS
MAXIMUM THRUST

AIRPLANE CONFIGURATION
GEAR AND FLAPS UP
ALL DRAG INDEXES

REMARKS
ENGINE(S): (2) F100-PW-220
U.S. STANDARD DAY, 1968

GUIDE

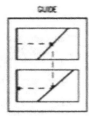

DATE: 15 JUNE 1988
DATA BASIS: ESTIMATED

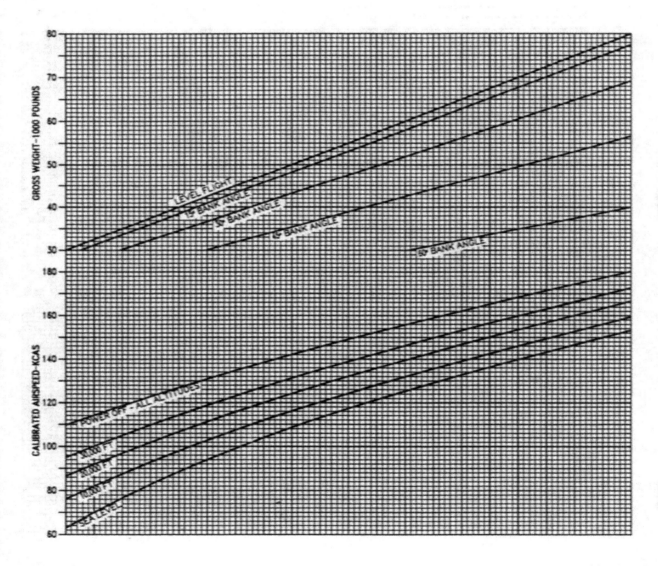

15E-1-(178-1)03-CAT1

Figure A1-7

AIRSPEED CONVERSION
LOW MACH

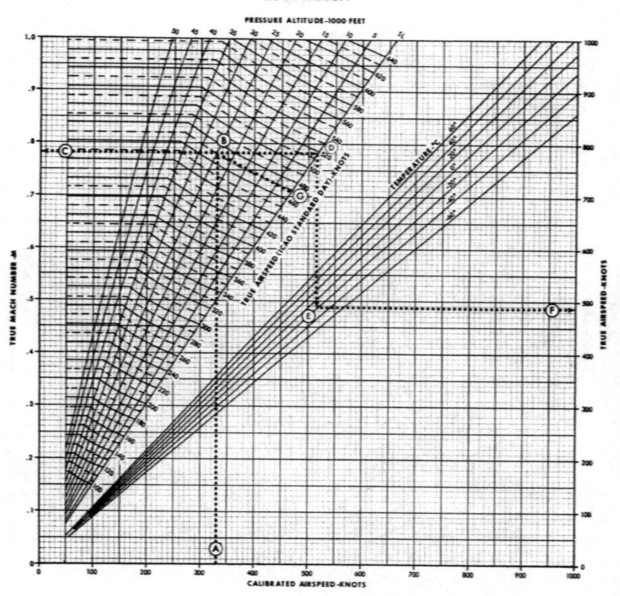

EXAMPLE
A = CAS = 330 KNOTS
B = ALTITUDE = 25,000 FEET
C = MACH = .782
D = SEA LEVEL LINE
E = TEMPERATURE = -20°C
F = TAS = 486 KNOTS
G = TAS (STANDARD DAY) = 472 KNOTS

15E-1-(89)

Figure A1-8

AIRSPEED CONVERSION

HIGH MACH

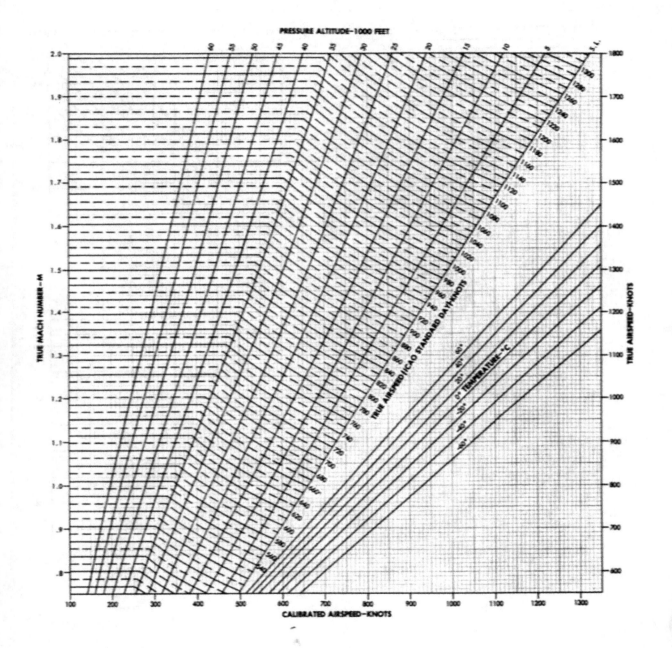

Figure A1-9

AIRSPEED POSITION ERROR CORRECTION
1G FLIGHT

AIRPLANE CONFIGURATION
FLAPS AND GEAR AS NOTED

REMARKS
ENGINE(S): (2) F100-PW-220
U.S. STANDARD DAY, 1966

GUIDE

DATE: 1 AUGUST 1986
DATA BASIS: ESTIMATED

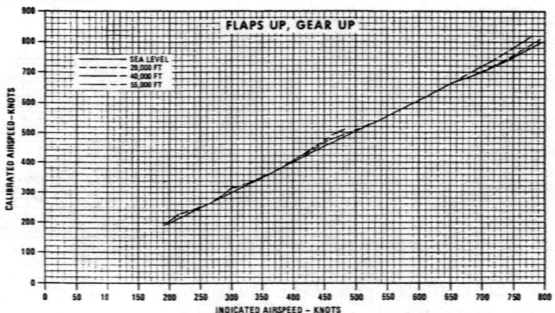

FLAPS DOWN, GEAR DOWN
10,000 FT AND BELOW

INDICATED	CALIBRATED AIRSPEED-KTS		
AIRSPEED—KTS	GW 30,000	GW 40,000	GW 50,000
140	137	—	—
160	158	157	—
180	178.5	178	177
200	198.5	198.5	198
220	219	218.5	218.5
240	239	239	239

15E-1-(71)

Figure A1-10

A1-17

ALTIMETER POSITION ERROR CORRECTION
STANDBY ALTIMETER ONLY

AIRPLANE CONFIGURATION
ALL DRAG INDEXES
FLAPS AND GEAR AS NOTED

REMARKS
ENGINE(S): (2) F100–PW–220
U.S. STANDARD DAY, 1966

NOTE
ASSIGNED ALTITUDE + ΔH = INDICATED
ALTITUDE. FLY INDICATED ALTITUDE.

DATE: 1 AUGUST 1986
DATA BASIS: ESTIMATED

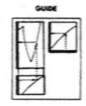

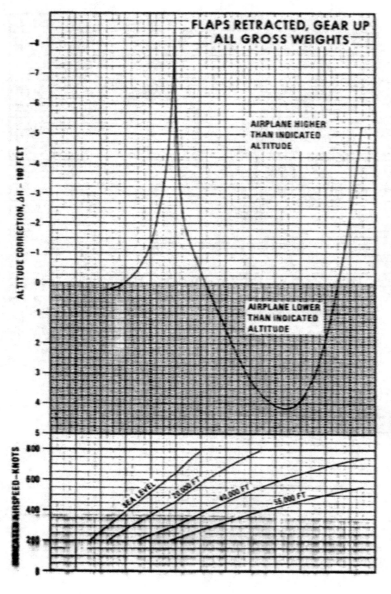

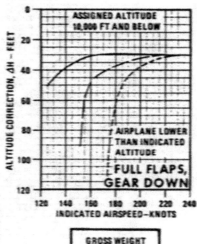

158–1–(72)

Figure A1-11

WIND COMPONENTS

- DETERMINE THE EFFECTIVE WIND VELOCITY BY ADDING ONE-HALF THE GUST VELOCITY (INCREMENTAL WIND FACTOR) TO THE STEADY STATE VELOCITY: E.G. REPORTED WIND 050/30 G40, EFFECTIVE WIND IS 050/35.

- CROSSWIND LIMITS FOR RCR VALUES, 12-16 AND 16-23 MAY BE OBTAINED BY INTERPOLATING BETWEEN THE LIMITS SHOWN.

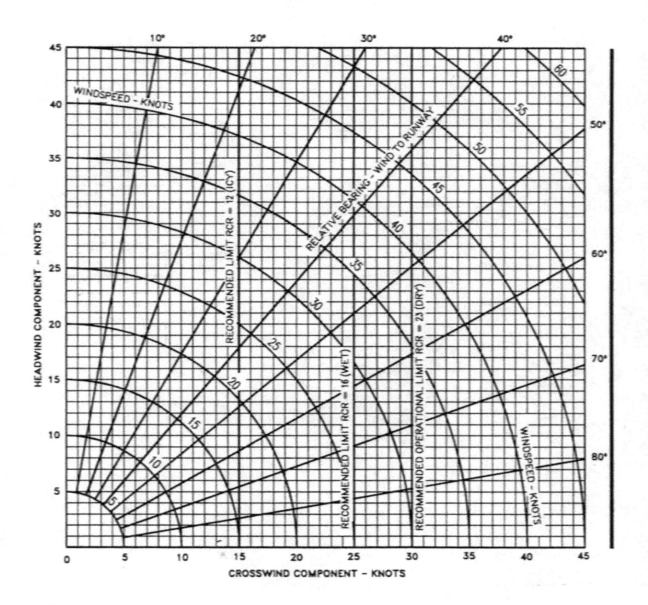

Figure A1-12

PART 2

ENGINE DATA

This part not applicable.

PART 3

TAKEOFF

TABLE OF CONTENTS

Charts

Density Ratio A3-8
Minimum Go Speeds-With CFT........................... A3-9
Maximum Abort Speed-With CFT A3-10
Takeoff Distance-With CFT................................ A3-12
Minimum Go Speeds-Without CFT.................... A3-14
Maximum Abort Speed-Without CFT............... A3-15
Takeoff Distance-Without CFT A3-17
Rotation Speed/Nosewheel Liftoff Speed/
Takeoff Speed-With CFT A3-19
Nosewheel Liftoff Speed/Takeoff Speed
-Without CFT A3-21
Single Engine Rate of Climb A3-23

DENSITY RATIO CHART

This chart (figures A3-1) provides a means of obtaining a single factor (density ratio) that may be used to represent a combination of temperature and pressure altitude. Density ratio must be determined before the Minimum Go Speed and Maximum Abort Speed charts can be utilized.

USE

Enter the chart with existing temperature, and project vertically to intersect the applicable pressure altitude curve. From this point, project horizontally to the left scale to read density ratio.

Sample Problem

A. Temperature	60°F
B. Pressure Altitude	2000 Ft
C. Density ratio	0.93

SAMPLE DENSITY RATIO

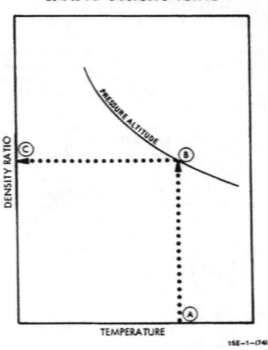

15E-1-074I

MINIMUM GO SPEED CHART

These charts (figures A3-2, A3-6) provide the means of determining the minimum speed at which the aircraft can experience an engine failure and still take off under existing conditions of temperature, pressure altitude, gross weight, and the runway length remaining. Separate plots are provided for maximum and military thrust conditions, and for aircraft with and without CFT's installed. The data is based on an engine failure occurring at the minimum go speed and allows for a 3-second decision period with one engine operating at its initial thrust setting. In the case of a military thrust takeoff, an additional 3-second period is allowed for advancing the operating engine throttle to maximum thrust.

WARNING

If an engine is lost above the maximum abort speed but below the minimum go speed, the pilot can neither abort nor take off safely on the runway length remaining without considering such factors as reducing gross weight or engaging the overrun end arrestment cable. Refer to Engine Failure During Takeoff, section III.

USE

Enter the applicable plot with the prevailing density ratio, and project horizontally to the available runway length grid line. Parallel the nearest guideline up or down to intersect the baseline. From this point descend vertically to intersect the applicable takeoff gross weight curve, then horizontally to read minimum go speed. If this projected line lies entirely to the right of the gross weight curve single engine failure can be tolerated at any speed between zero and the highest speed shown with the ground roll being within the available runway length. If the above projected line lies entirely to the left of the gross weight curve, single engine failure takeoff cannot be accomplished with the available runway length. With CFTs, the recommended rotation speeds are given in figure 3-10. Without CFTs, with an engine failure before nose rotation at high gross weights,˜, the ground roll will be shortened if aft stick is relaxed until 10 to 15 knots below takeoff speed. This situation will be obvious to the pilot.

SAMPLE MINIMUM GO SPEED

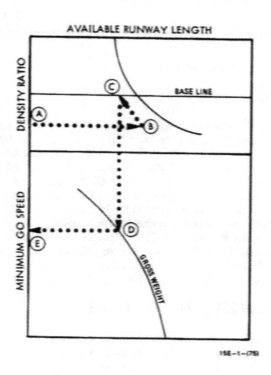

15E–1–(75)

Sample Problem

Maximum Thrust Takeoff With CFT (with fuel tanks or A/G stores on wing pylons)

A. Density ratio	0.90
B. Available runway length	9000 Ft
C. Parallel guideline to base-line	
D. Takeoff gross weight	75,000 Lb
E. Minimum go speed	172 KCAS

NOTE

This problem assumes maximum thrust on operating engine within 6 seconds after engine failure. The minimum go speed for a maximum thrust takeoff will be less than that for a military thrust takeoff due to the greater acceleration with maximum thrust up to and including the 3-second decision time.

MAXIMUM ABORT SPEED CHART

NOTE

- The maximum abort speed chart does not include the capability of any arrestment gear which may be installed, and takes into account only aircraft stopping performance for the given field conditions.

- Lower weight aircraft are often shown to have lower maximum abort speeds than higher weight aircraft due to the greater acceleration of the lighter aircraft during the abort decision period used in the calculations.

These charts (figures A3-3, A3-7) provide a means of determining the maximum speed at which an abort may be started and the aircraft stopped within the remaining runway length. Separate plots are provided for maximum and military thrust, and for aircraft with and without CFT's installed. Allowances included in this data are based on a 3-second decision period (with both engines operating at the initial thrust setting) followed by a 2-second period to apply wheel brakes and a 5-second period to reach idle thrust (these two abort procedures are initiated simultaneously).

USE

Enter applicable plot with the prevailing density ratio, and project horizontally to intersect the available runway length curve. From this point, descend further to intersect the computed takeoff gross weight, then horizontally to read the corresponding maximum abort speed.

SAMPLE MAXIMUM ABORT SPEED

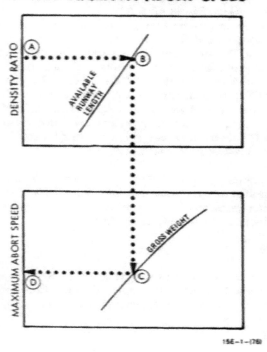

15E–1–(76)

Sample Problem

Maximum Thrust Takeoff, Hard Dry Runway, With CFT (with fuel tanks or A/G stores on wing pylons)

A. Density ratio	0.90
B. Available runway length	9000 Ft
C. Gross weight	75,000 Lb
D. Maximum abort speed	125 KCAS

TAKEOFF DISTANCE CHARTS

These charts (figures A3-4, A3-5, A3-8, A3-9) are used to determine the no wind ground run distance, wind adjusted ground run and the total distance required to clear a 50-foot obstacle. Separate charts are provided for maximum and military thrust, and for aircraft with and without CFT's installed. The without CFT charts (figures A3-8, A3-9) are based on CG's representative of each gross weight. With CFTs, the CG's used for each gross weight are noted on the chart. Takeoff distances will be reduced for aft CG's and increased for forward CG's.

The notes regarding CG effect on ground roll on the takeoff charts are based on conservative performance estimates based on data generated at typical weight, altitude, and temperature conditions.

USE

Enter the chart with existing temperature and project vertically to intersect the applicable pressure altitude curve. From that point, proceed horizontally to the right and intersect the takeoff weight line. Then descend vertically to read no wind ground run distance. Parallel the appropriate wind guideline (headwind or tailwind) to intersect the takeoff wind velocity. From this point project vertically down to read the ground run adjusted for wind effects. To find the total distance required to clear a 50-foot obstacle, continue downward to the reflector line and project horizontally to the left scale.

SAMPLE TAKEOFF DISTANCE

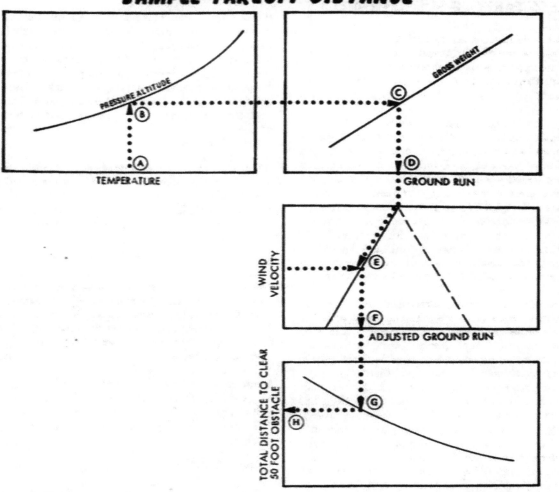

Sample Problem

Maximum Thrust With CFT (with fuel tanks or A/G stores on wing pylons)

A. Temperature	20°C
B. Pressure altitude	2000 Ft

A. Temperature		20°C
C. Gross weight		75,000 Lb
D. No wind Ground run distance		4050 Ft
E. Effective headwind		25 Kt
F. Ground run (wind corrected)		3100 Ft
G. Intersect reflector line		
H. Total distance required to clear 50-foot obstacle		5400 Ft

NOSEWHEEL LIFTOFF SPEED/TAKEOFF SPEED CHART

These charts (figures A3-10 and A3-11) are used to determine nosewheel liftoff speed and aircraft takeoff speed for various gross weights in either maximum or military thrust for aircraft with and without CFTs installed

With CFTs installed, rotation speeds along with the corresponding nosewheel liftoff and takeoff speeds are presented for standard two-engine takeoffs as a function of CG and gross weight. At the indicated rotation speed one-half aft stick should be applied and the aircraft rotated to 12°. Rotation speeds increase at forward CGs to prevent nosewheel bouncing. Rotation speeds are also presented for continued takeoffs after an engine failure during ground roll. For continued takeoffs one-half aft stick should be applied at the rotation speed, but the aircraft should only be rotated to 10° for improved acceleration.

Without CFTs, the speeds are based on CGs representative of each gross weight. The chart provides data for either a normal or maximum performance takeoff. A normal takeoff is accomplished by applying 1/2 aft stick over a period of 1 second as the aircraft is accelerating through 120 knots, and then holding 10° of pitch throughout the takeoff roll. A maximum performance takeoff is accomplished by applying full aft stick at a low speed and when the nose rotates, holding 12° of pitch throughout the takeoff roll. Aircraft rotation will be more rapid with the maximum performance takeoff technique. Rotation speeds are also presented for continued takeoffs after an engine failure during ground roll. For continued takeoffs one-half aft stick should be applied at the rotation speed, with a 10° pitch attitude held throughout the takeoff roll.

The difference in nosewheel lift-off speeds between military and maximum thrust are due to the thrust effects on pitching moment. The differences in takeoff speeds are due to the thrust support in lift and the time required to rotate the aircraft to takeoff attitude.

SINGLE ENGINE RATE OF CLIMB

These charts (figures A3-12 thru A3-16) provide the means of determining single engine rate of climb for takeoff planning purposes for existing conditions of temperature, pressure altitude, gross weight, airspeed, and Drag Index. Separate plots are provided for gross weights from 60,000 lb to 81,000 lb. The data are for one engine operating at maximum A/B thrust and the other engine windmilling. Out-of-ground-effects aero data were used in construction of these charts. Gear and flaps are extended.

These charts can be used to determine if single engine rate of climb is adequate at the single engine takeoff speeds obtained from figure A3-10 for the continued takeoff technique. The change in rate of climb due to increasing or decreasing takeoff speed can also be determined.

USE

Enter the applicable chart with existing temperature and project vertically to intersect the applicable pressure altitude curve. From this point, project horizontally to the right and intersect the applicable with or without wing stores line. Then descend vertically to intersect the baseline velocity of 210 KCAS. Parallel the guidelines to intersect the takeoff velocity in question. From this point descend vertically to intersect the baseline Drag Index. Parallel the appropriate velocity guideline to intersect the takeoff Drag Index. Descend vertically again to read the single engine rate of climb.

Sample Problem

Gross Weight 75,000 Lb

A. Temperature	5°C
B. Pressure Altitude	Sea Level
C. Wing Tanks or A/G Weapons Installed	
D. Takeoff Velocity	204 KCAS
E. Drag Index	100
F. Single Engine Rate of Climb	+1200 ft/ min

SAMPLE SINGLE ENGINE RATE OF CLIMB

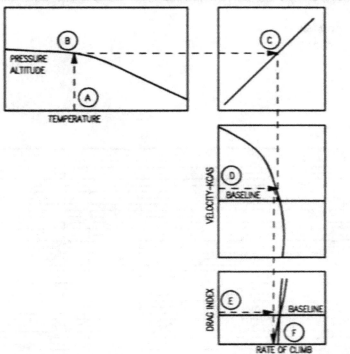

DENSITY RATIO

AIRPLANE CONFIGURATION
ALL DRAG INDEXES

GUIDE

DATE: 1 AUGUST 1986
DATA BASIS: ESTIMATED

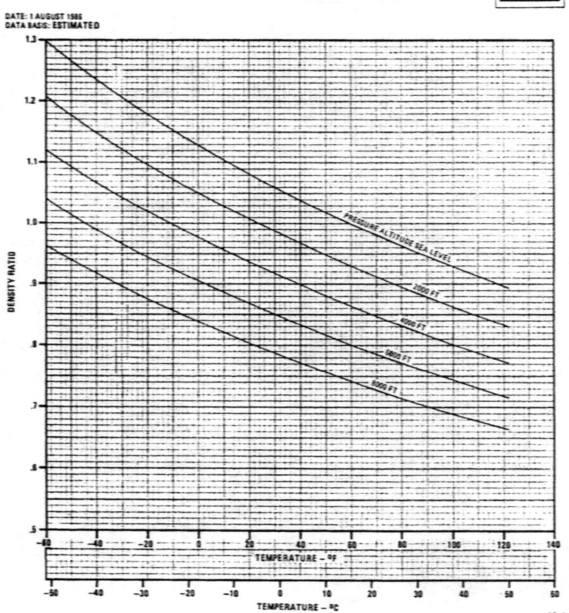

Figure A3-1

MINIMUM GO SPEEDS
WITH CFT
(WITH SINGLE ENGINE FAILURE)

AIRPLANE CONFIGURATION
GEAR AND FLAPS DOWN
ALL DRAG INDEXES

REMARKS
ENGINE(S): (2) F100-PW-220
U.S. STANDARD DAY, 1966

GUIDE

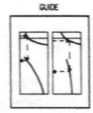

DATE:15 JUNE 1988
DATA BASIS: ESTIMATED

NOTE
- FOLLOWING ENGINE FAILURE WITH MILITARY THRUST, THE AFTERBURNER IS IGNITED ON THE OPERATING ENGINE.
- HALF AFT STICK APPLIED AT THE ROTATION SPEED FROM FIG A3-10 AND A 10 DEGREE PITCH ATTITUDE HELD AFTER ROTATION.
- DASHED LINES TO BE USED WHEN CARRYING AIR-TO-GROUND WEAPONS OR FUEL TANKS ON WING STATIONS.
- SOLID LINES TO BE USED WHEN CARRYING NO STORES OR ONLY AIR-TO-AIR WEAPONS ON WING STATIONS.

MAXIMUM THRUST TAKEOFF

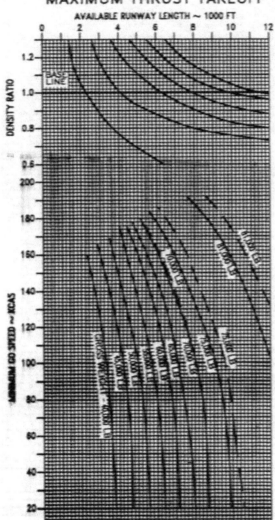

MILITARY THRUST TAKEOFF

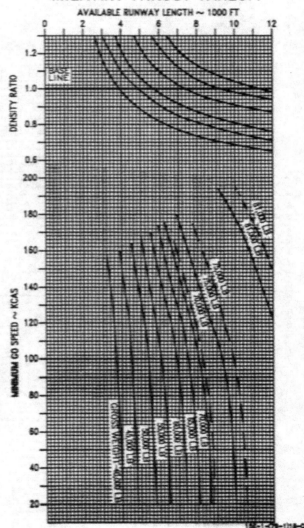

Figure A3-2

MAXIMUM ABORT SPEED
WITH CFT
MAXIMUM THRUST
HARD DRY RUNWAY

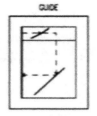

GUIDE

AIRPLANE CONFIGURATION
FLAP AND GEAR DOWN
ALL DRAG INDEXES

REMARKS
ENGINE(S): (2) F100-PW-220
U.S. STANDARD DAY, 1966

DATE: 15 JUNE 1968
DATA BASIS: ESTIMATED

NOTE
- TO OBTAIN MAXIMUM ABORT SPEED FOR RCR 15 RUNWAY (WET) REDUCE RCR 23 (DRY) BY 20%.
- DATA IS FOR NO-WIND CONDITION. ADD HEADWIND OR SUBTRACT TAILWIND TO DETERMINE ACTUAL MAXIMUM ABORT SPEED.
- HALF AFT STICK APPLIED AT THE ROTATION SPEED FROM FIG A3-10 AND A 12 DEGREE PITCH ATTITUDE HELD AFTER ROTATION UNTIL ALTERED BY ABORT PROCEDURES.

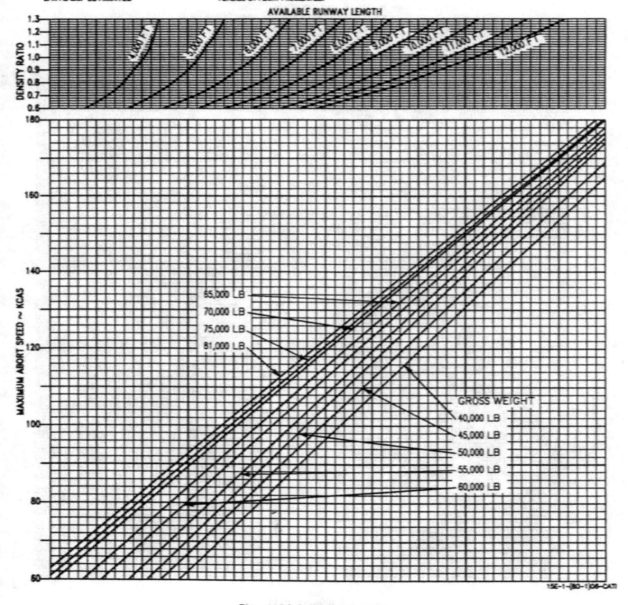

Figure A3-3 (Sheet 1 of 2)

15E-1-(80-1)06-CATI

MAXIMUM ABORT SPEED
WITH CFT
MILITARY THRUST
HARD DRY RUNWAY

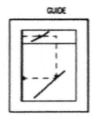

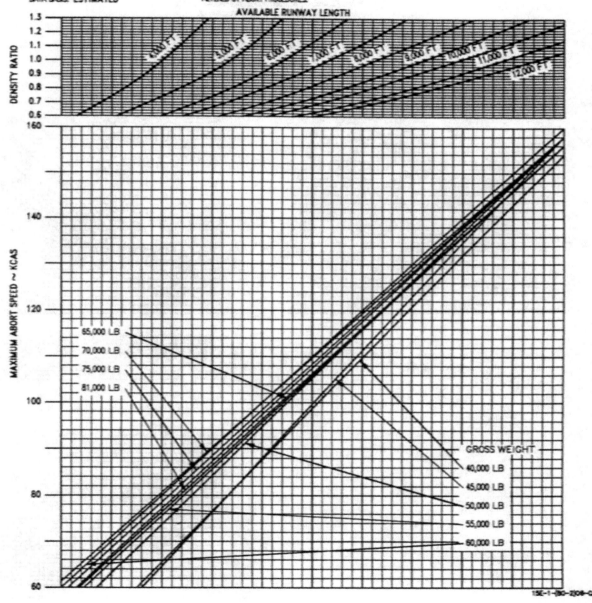

Figure A3-3 (Sheet 2)

TAKEOFF DISTANCE
WITH CFT
MAXIMUM THRUST
HARD DRY RUNWAY

AIRPLANE CONFIGURATION
FLAPS AND GEAR DOWN
ALL DRAG INDEXES

DATE: 15 JUNE 1988
DATA BASIS: ESTIMATED

REMARKS
ENGINE(S): (2) F100-PW-220
U.S. STANDARD DAY, 1966

NOTE
● THIS DATA BASED ON HALF AFT STICK APPLIED AT THE
ROTATION SPEED FROM FIG A3-10 AND A 12 DEGREE PITCH
ATTITUDE HELD AFTER ROTATION.
● DASHED LINES TO BE USED WHEN CARRYING AIR-TO-GROUND
WEAPONS OR FUEL TANKS ON THE WING STATIONS.
● SOLID LINES TO BE USED WHEN NO STORES OTHER THEN AIR-
TO-AIR WEAPONS ARE INSTALLED ON THE WING STATIONS.
● FOR EVERY 1% CG SHIFT FORWARD OF THE REFERENCE CG,
INCREASE THE ZERO WIND GROUND ROLL DISTANCE BY 5%.
FOR EVERY 1% CG SHIFT AFT OF THE REFERENCE CG, DECREASE
THE ZERO WIND GROUND ROLL DISTANCE BY 1%. THEN APPLY
WIND EFFECTS AND DETERMINE DISTANCE TO 50 FT. USING
NORMAL PROCEDURES.

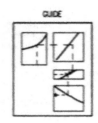
GUIDE

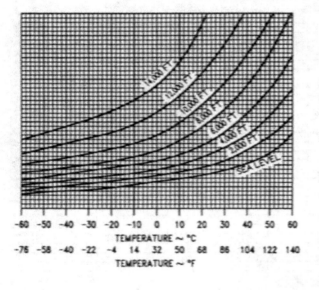

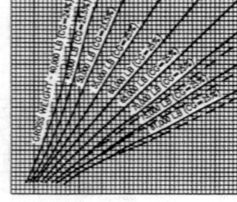

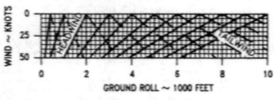

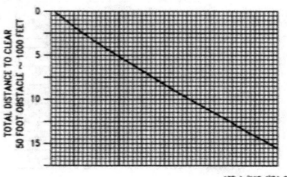

15E-1-(112-1)04-CAT1

Figure A3-4

TAKEOFF DISTANCE
WITH CFT
MILITARY THRUST
HARD DRY RUNWAY

AIRPLANE CONFIGURATION
FULL FLAPS, GEAR DOWN
ALL DRAG INDEXES

DATE: 15 JUNE 1988
DATA BASIS: ESTIMATED

REMARKS
ENGINE(S): (2) F100-PW-220
U.S. STANDARD DAY, 1966

NOTE
● THIS DATA BASED ON HALF AFT STICK APPLIED AT THE ROTATION SPEED FROM FIG A3-10 AND A 12 DEGREE PITCH ATTITUDE HELD AFTER ROTATION.
● DASHED LINES TO BE USED WHEN CARRYING AIR-TO-GROUND WEAPONS OR FUEL TANKS ON THE WING STATIONS.
● SOLID LINES TO BE USED WHEN NO STORES OTHER THEN AIR-TO-AIR WEAPONS ARE INSTALLED ON THE WING STATIONS.
● FOR EVERY 1% CG SHIFT FORWARD OF THE REFERENCE CG, INCREASE THE ZERO WIND GROUND ROLL DISTANCE BY 3%. FOR EVERY 1% CG SHIFT AFT OF THE REFERENCE CG, DECREASE THE ZERO WIND GROUND ROLL DISTANCE BY 1%. THEN APPLY WIND EFFECTS AND DETERMINE DISTANCE TO 50 FT. USING NORMAL PROCEDURES.

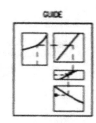

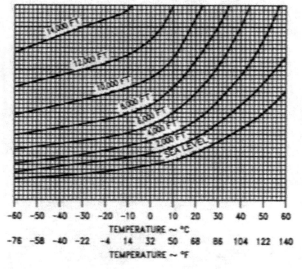

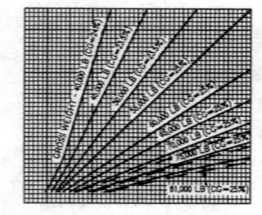

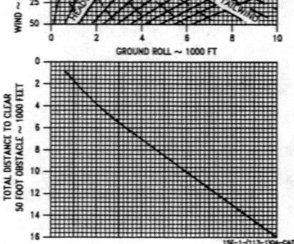

Figure A3-5

MINIMUM GO SPEED
WITHOUT CFT
(WITH SINGLE ENGINE FAILURE)

AIRPLANE CONFIGURATION
GEAR AND FLAPS DOWN
ALL DRAG INDEXES

REMARKS
ENGINE(S): (2) F100-PW-220
U.S. STANDARD DAY, 1966

NOTE
- FOLLOWING ENGINE FAILURE WITH MILITARY THRUST, THE AFTERBURNER IS IGNITED ON THE OPERATING ENGINE.
- HALF AFT STICK APPLIED AT THE ROTATION SPEED FROM FIG A3-11 AND A 10 DEGREE PITCH ATTITUDE HELD AFTER ROTATION.

DATE: 15 NOV 1988
DATA BASIS: ESTIMATED

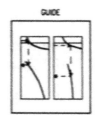
GUIDE

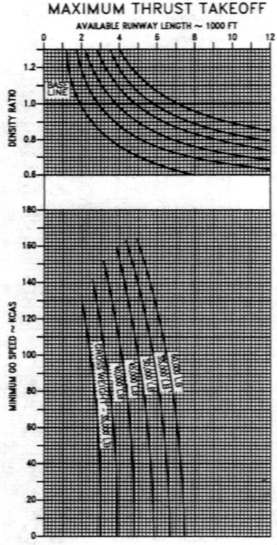

MAXIMUM THRUST TAKEOFF

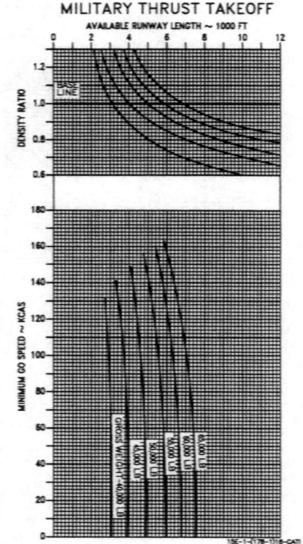

MILITARY THRUST TAKEOFF

Figure A3-6

15E-1-(178-1)18-CATI

MAXIMUM ABORT SPEED
WITHOUT CFT
MAXIMUM THRUST
HARD DRY RUNWAY

AIRPLANE CONFIGURATION
FLAPS AND GEAR DOWN
ALL DRAG INDEXES

REMARKS
ENGINES: (2) F100-PW-220
U.S. STANDARD DAY, 1968

DATE:15 NOV 1988
DATA BASIS: ESTIMATED

NOTE
- TO OBTAIN MAXIMUM ABORT SPEED FOR RCR 16 RUNWAY (WET) REDUCE RCR 23 (DRY) BY 25%.
- DATA IS FOR NO-WIND CONDITION. ADD HEADWIND OR SUBTRACT TAILWIND TO DETERMINE ACTUAL MAXIMUM ABORT SPEED.
- FULL AFT STICK APPLIED AT LOW SPEED AND A 12 DEGREE PITCH ATTITUDE HELD AFTER ROTATION UNTIL ALTERED BY ABORT PROCEDURES.

GUIDE

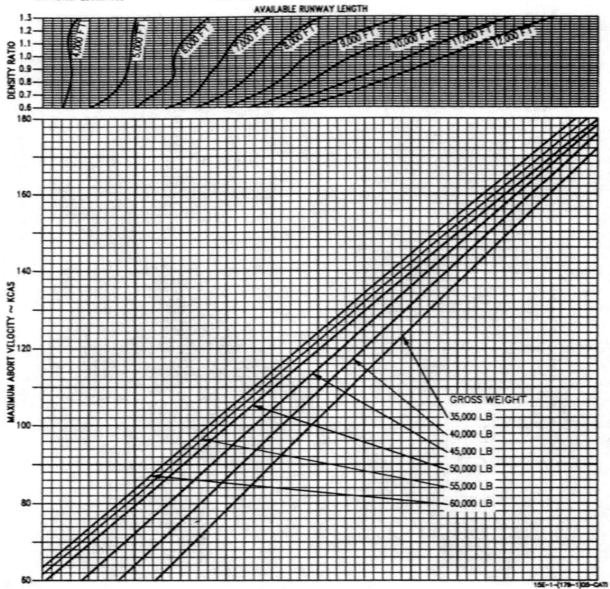

Figure A3-7 (Sheet 1 of 2)

MAXIMUM ABORT SPEED
WITHOUT CFT
MILITARY THRUST
HARD DRY RUNWAY

GUIDE

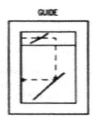

AIRPLANE CONFIGURATION
FLAPS AND GEAR DOWN
ALL DRAG INDEXES

REMARKS
ENGINE[S]: (2) F100-PW-220
U.S. STANDARD DAY, 1966

DATE: 15 NOV 1988
DATA BASIS: ESTIMATED

NOTE
● TO OBTAIN MAXIMUM ABORT SPEED FOR RCR 16 RUNWAY (WET) REDUCE RCR 23 (DRY) BY 25%.
● DATA IS FOR NO-WIND CONDITION. ADD HEADWIND OR SUBTRACT TAILWIND TO DETERMINE ACTUAL MAXIMUM ABORT SPEED.
● FULL AFT STICK APPLIED AT LOW SPEED AND A 12 DEGREE PITCH ATTITUDE HELD AFTER ROTATION UNTIL ALTERED BY ABORT PROCEDURES.

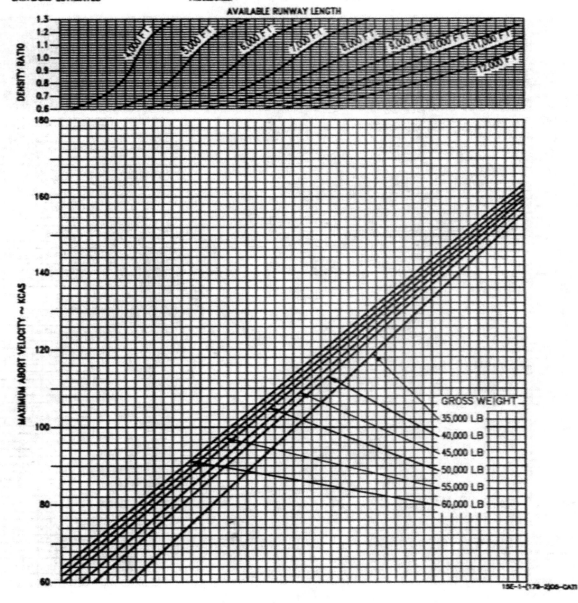

Figure A3-7 (Sheet 2)

15E-1-(178-2)06-CAT1

TAKEOFF DISTANCE
WITHOUT CFT
MAXIMUM THRUST
HARD DRY RUNWAY

AIRPLANE CONFIGURATION
FULL FLAPS, GEAR DOWN
ALL DRAG INDEXES

DATE: 1 AUGUST 1986
DATA BASIS: ESTIMATED

REMARKS
ENGINE(S): (2) F100-PW-220
U.S. STANDARD DAY, 1966

NOTE
THESE DATA BASED ON MAXIMUM PERFORMANCE TAKEOFF PROCEDURES:
FULL AFT STICK APPLIED AT LOW SPEED AND A 12 DEGREE
ATTITUDE IS HELD AFTER ROTATION.

GUIDE
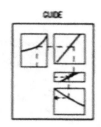

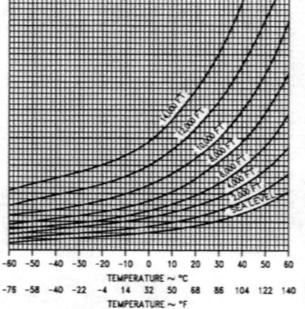
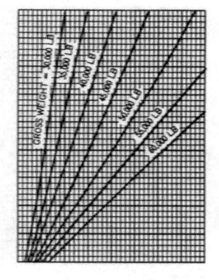
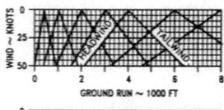
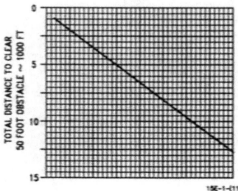

15E-1-(115-1)06-CATI

Figure A3-8

TAKEOFF DISTANCE
WITHOUT CFT
MILITARY THRUST
HARD DRY RUNWAY

AIRPLANE CONFIGURATION
FULL FLAPS, GEAR DOWN
ALL DRAG INDEXES

DATE: 1 AUGUST 1986
DATA BASIS: ESTIMATED

REMARKS
ENGINE(S): (2) F100-PW-220
U.S. STANDARD DAY, 1966

NOTE
THESE DATA BASED ON MAXIMUM PERFORMANCE TAKEOFF PROCEDURES:
FULL AFT STICK APPLIED AT LOW SPEED AND A 12 DEGREE
ATTITUDE IS HELD AFTER ROTATION.

GUIDE

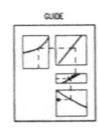

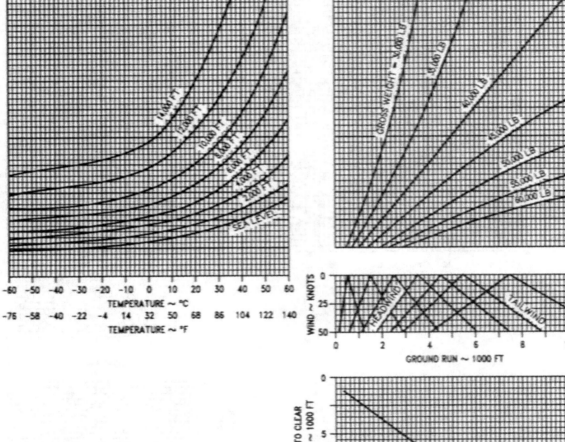

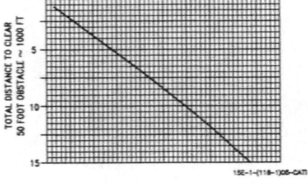

15E-1-(118-1)06-CATI

Figure A3-9

ROTATION SPEED/NOSEWHEEL LIFT-OFF SPEED/ TAKEOFF SPEED

WITH CFT

AIRPLANE CONFIGURATION
FULL FLAPS, GEAR DOWN
ALL DRAG INDEXES

REMARKS
ENGINE(S): (2) F100–PW–220
U.S. STANDARD DAY, 1966

NORMAL TAKEOFF
ONE–HALF AFT STICK APPLIED OVER A PERIOD OF 1 SECOND
STARTING AT THE ROTATION SPEED LISTED BELOW AND 12°
ATTITUDE HELD AFTER ROTATION.

DATE: 15 JUNE 1988
DATA BASIS: ESTIMATED

GROSS WEIGHT–LB	CG (–%)	ROTATION/NOSEWHEEL LIFT–OFF/TAKEOFF SPEEDS (KCAS)	
		MAXIMUM THRUST	MILITARY THRUST
40,000	28	——	——
	26	110 / 124 / 149	115 / 123 / 141
	24	110 / 128 / 152	115 / 125 / 143
	22	110 / 130 / 154	120 / 130 / 146
45,000	28	——	——
	26	115 / 130 / 154	120 / 127 / 144
	24	115 / 132 / 156	120 / 129 / 146
	23.5	115 / 133 / 156	120 / 129 / 148
	22	118 / 137 / 159	125 / 134 / 150
50,000	28	——	——
	26	120 / 134 / 158	125 / 132 / 148
	24	120 / 136 / 159	125 / 134 / 150
	23.5	120 / 137 / 160	125 / 134 / 150
	22	125 / 142 / 163	130 / 139 / 154
55,000	28	——	——
	26	125 / 138 / 161	130 / 137 / 155
	25	125 / 139 / 162	130 / 138 / 155
	24	125 / 141 / 163	135 / 142 / 156
	22		
60,000	28	——	——
	26	130 / 143 / 165	135 / 141 / 163
	25	130 / 144 / 166	135 / 142 / 163
	24	133 / 148 / 169	140 / 147 / 163
	22		——
65,000	28	140 / 150 / 171	145 / 150 / 169
	26	140 / 152 / 172	145 / 151 / 170
	25	140 / 154 / 173	145 / 151 / 170
	24	145 / 159 / 177	150 / 156 / 170
	22	——	——
70,000	28	155 / 164 / 183	155 / 159 / 180
	26	155 / 166 / 184	155 / 160 / 181
	25	155 / 167 / 185	155 / 161 / 181
	24	160 / 172 / 190	160 / 166 / 182
	22	——	——
75,000	28	160 / 169 / 187	160 / 164 / 186
	26	160 / 171 / 189	160 / 165 / 188
	25	160 / 173 / 190	160 / 166 / 188
	24	165 / 177 / 194	155 / 171 / 189
	22		
81,000	28	167 / 176 / 192	167 / 171 / 194
	26	167 / 177 / 194	167 / 171 / 195
	25	167 / 179 / 195	167 / 172 / 196
	24	172 / 184 / 199	172 / 177 / 197
	22		

15E-1-(114-1)04-CATI

Figure A3-10 (Sheet 1 of 2)

SINGLE ENGINE
ROTATION SPEED/NOSEWHEEL LIFT-OFF SPEED/
TAKEOFF SPEED

WITH CFT

AIRPLANE CONFIGURATION
FULL FLAPS, GEAR DOWN
ALL DRAG INDEXES
ALL CG LOCATIONS

REMARKS
ENGINE(S): (2) F100-PW-220
U.S. STANDARD DAY, 1966

NOTE
NOSEWHEEL BOUNCING MAY OCCUR DURING ONE-ENGINE-OUT
TAKEOFF AT GROSS WEIGHTS OF 65,000 LBS AND LESS.

DATE: 15 JUNE 1988
DATA BASIS: ESTIMATED

CONTINUED (SINGLE ENGINE) TAKEOFF
ONE-HALF AFT STICK APPLIED OVER A PERIOD OF 1 SECOND
STARTING AT THE ROTATION SPEED LISTED BELOW AND 10°
ATTITUDE HELD AFTER ROTATION.

GROSS WEIGHT-LB	ROTATION/NOSEWHEEL LIFT-OFF/TAKEOFF SPEEDS (KCAS)	
	MAXIMUM THRUST	
40,000	170 / 171 / 177	
45,000	180 / 181 / 187	
50,000	185 / 186 / 192	
55,000	190 / 191 / 196	
60,000	190 / 191 / 196	TO BE USED WHEN NO STORES OTHER THAN AIR-TO-AIR WEAPONS ARE IN-STALLED ON THE WING STATIONS.
65,000	190 / 192 / 197	
70,000	190 / 192 / 197	
75,000	190 / 192 / 199	
81,000	190 / 192 / 207	
70,000	190 / 192 / 198	TO BE USED WHEN CARRYING AIR-TO-GROUND WEAPONS OR FUEL TANKS ON THE WING STATIONS.
75,000	190 / 193 / 204	
81,000	190 / 193 / 213	

15E-1-(114-2)04-CAT1

Figure A3-10 (Sheet 2)

NOSEWHEEL LIFT-OFF SPEED/TAKEOFF SPEED

WITHOUT CFT

AIRPLANE CONFIGURATION	REMARKS
FULL FLAPS, GEAR DOWN ALL DRAG INDEXES	ENGINE(S): (2) F100-PW-220 U.S. STANDARD DAY, 1966

DATE: 1 AUGUST 1986
DATA BASIS: ESTIMATED

NORMAL TAKEOFF

ONE-HALF AFT STICK APPLIED OVER A PERIOD OF
1 SECOND STARTING AT 120 KNOTS AND 10°
ATTITUDE HELD AFTER ROTATION

GROSS WEIGHT – LB	NOSEWHEEL LIFT-OFF/TAKEOFF SPEEDS (KCAS)	
	MAXIMUM THRUST	MILITARY THRUST
30,000	129/143	124/135
35,000	134/150	128/141
40,000	136/153	129/142
45,000	137/155	130/148
50,000	129/158	133/161
55,000	150/166	144/169
60,000	158/173	161/177

MAXIMUM PERFORMANCE TAKEOFF

FULL AFT STICK APPLIED AT LOW SPEED AND
12° ATTITUDE HELD AFTER ROTATION

GROSS WEIGHT – LB	NOSEWHEEL LIFT-OFF/TAKEOFF SPEEDS (KCAS)	
	MAXIMUM THRUST	MILITARY THRUST
30,000	83/110	94/108
35,000	91/121	102/119
40,000	102/131	110/129
45,000	115/142	119/139
50,000	127/151	129/148
55,000	138/159	140/157
60,000	143/166	148/165

15E-1-(117-1)04

Figure A3-11 (Sheet 1 of 2)

SINGLE ENGINE
ROTATION SPEED/NOSEWHEEL LIFT-OFF SPEED/
TAKEOFF SPEED

AIRPLANE CONFIGURATION
FULL FLAPS, GEAR DOWN
ALL DRAG INDEXES
ALL CG LOCATIONS

WITHOUT CFT
REMARKS
ENGINES: (2) F100-PW-220
U.S. STANDARD DAY, 1966

DATE: 1 FEBRUARY 1989
DATA BASIS: ESTIMATED

CONTINUED (SINGLE ENGINE) TAKEOFF
ONE - HALF AFT STICK APPLIED OVER A PERIOD OF 1 SECOND
STARTING AT THE ROTATION SPEED LISTED BELOW AND 10°
ATTITUDE HELD AFTER ROTATION

GROSS WEIGHT – LB	ROTATION/NOSEWHEEL LIFT – OFF/TAKEOFF SPEEDS (KCAS)
	MAXIMUM THRUST
35000	160/163/169
40000	170/173/179
45000	180/183/188
50000	185/189/195
55000	190/194/199
60000	190/194/200

15E-1-(117-2)04

Figure A3-11 (Sheet 2)

SINGLE-ENGINE RATE OF CLIMB
GROSS WEIGHT – 60,000 POUNDS
WITH CFT
OUT OF GROUND EFFECT
MAXIMUM THRUST

AIRPLANE CONFIGURATION
FLAPS AND GEAR DOWN
SPEEDBRAKE RETRACTED

GUIDE

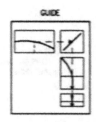

REMARKS
ENGINE(S): (2) F100–PW–220
U.S. STANDARD DAY, 1966

DATE: 15 JUNE 1968
DATA BASIS: ESTIMATED

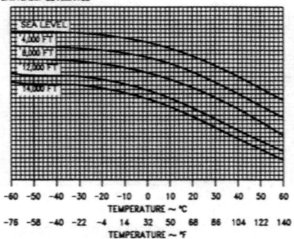

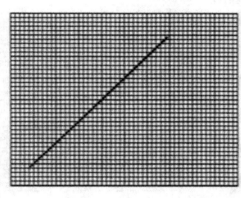

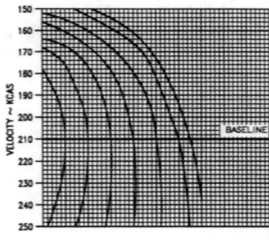

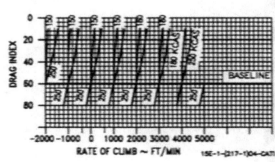

15E-1-(217-1)04-CAT1

Figure A3-12

SINGLE-ENGINE RATE OF CLIMB

GROSS WEIGHT – 65,000 POUNDS
WITH CFT
OUT OF GROUND EFFECT
MAXIMUM THRUST

AIRPLANE CONFIGURATION
FLAPS AND GEAR DOWN
SPEEDBRAKE RETRACTED

REMARKS
ENGINE(S): (2) F100-PW-220
U.S. STANDARD DAY, 1966

GUIDE

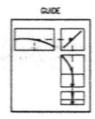

DATE:15 JUNE 1988
DATA BASS: ESTIMATED

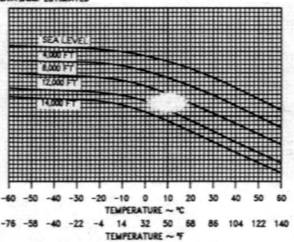

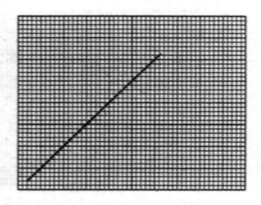

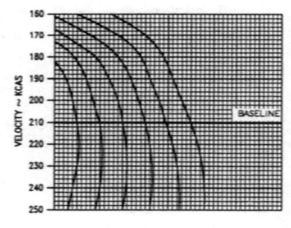

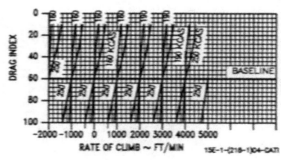

1SE-1-(218-1)04-CAT)

Figure A3-13

SINGLE-ENGINE RATE OF CLIMB

GROSS WEIGHT – 70,000 POUNDS
WITH CFT
OUT OF GROUND EFFECTS
MAXIMUM THRUST

AIRPLANE CONFIGURATION
FLAPS AND GEAR DOWN
SPEEDBRAKE RETRACTED

REMARKS
ENGINE(S): (2) F100-PW-220
U.S. STANDARD DAY, 1966

NOTE
● DASHED LINES TO BE USED WHEN CARRYING AIR-TO-GROUND WEAPONS OR FUEL TANKS ON THE WING STATIONS.
● SOLID LINES TO BE USED WHEN NO STORES OTHER THAN AIR-TO-AIR WEAPONS ARE INSTALLED ON THE WING STATIONS.

DATE:15 JUNE 1988
DATA BASIS: ESTIMATED

GUIDE

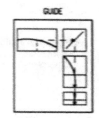

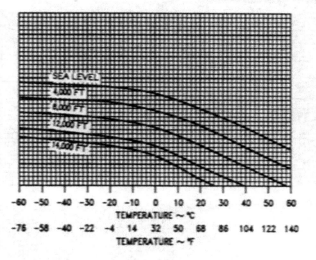

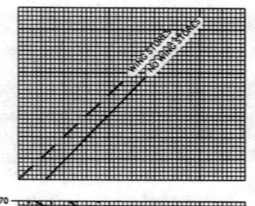

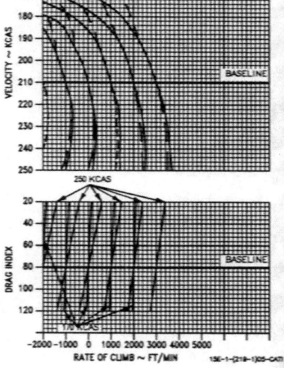

Figure A3-14

15E-1-(21B-1)05-CAT1

SINGLE-ENGINE RATE OF CLIMB
GROSS WEIGHT – 75,000 POUNDS
WITH CFT
OUT OF GROUND EFFECT
MAXIMUM THRUST

AIRPLANE CONFIGURATION
FLAPS AND GEAR DOWN
SPEEDBRAKE RETRACTED

DATE:15 JUNE 1988
DATA BASIS: ESTIMATED

GUIDE

REMARKS
ENGINE(S): (2) F100-PW-220
U.S. STANDARD DAY, 1966

NOTE
● DASHED LINES TO BE USED WHEN CARRYING AIR-TO-GROUND WEAPONS OR FUEL TANKS ON THE WING STATIONS.
● SOLID LINES TO BE USED WHEN NO STORES OTHER THAN AIR-TO-AIR WEAPONS ARE INSTALLED ON THE WING STATIONS.

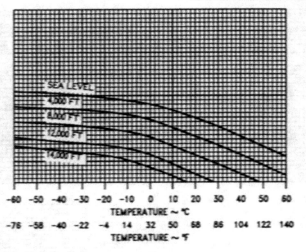

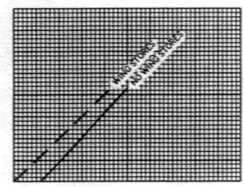

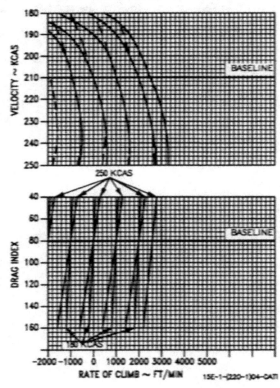

15E-1-(220-1)04-CAT1

Figure A3-15

SINGLE-ENGINE RATE OF CLIMB

GROSS WEIGHT – 81,000 POUNDS
WITH CFT
OUT OF GROUND EFFECT
MAXIMUM THRUST

GUIDE

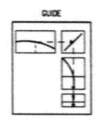

AIRPLANE CONFIGURATION
FLAPS AND GEAR DOWN
SPEEDBRAKE RETRACTED

REMARKS
ENGINE(S): (2) F100-PW-220
U.S. STANDARD DAY, 1966

DATE: 15 JUNE 1988
DATA BASIS: ESTIMATED

NOTE
- DASHED LINES TO BE USED WHEN CARRYING AIR-TO-GROUND WEAPONS OR FUEL TANKS ON THE WING STATIONS.
- SOLID LINES TO BE USED WHEN NO STORES OTHER THAN AIR-TO-AIR WEAPONS ARE INSTALLED ON THE WING STATIONS.

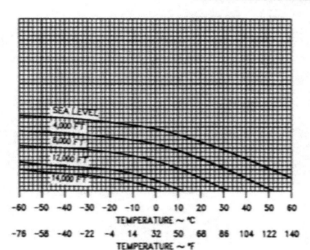

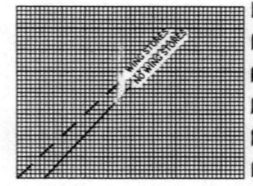

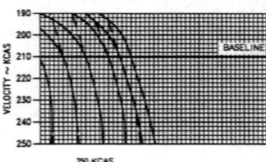

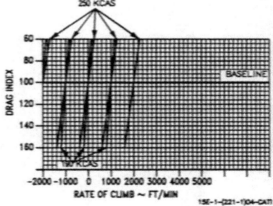

15E-1-(221-1)04-CATI

Figure A3-16

PART 4

CLIMB

TABLE OF CONTENTS

Charts

Climb A4-3
Combat Ceiling A4-9

CLIMB CHARTS

The Climb charts (figures A4-1 thru A4-6) are used to determine time, fuel used, and distance covered while in the climb. Each chart is based on a military or maximum thrust climb for individual drag index configurations. The climb speed schedule and pre-climb data are noted on each chart.

USE

The method of presenting data on the time, fuel and distance charts is identical, and the use of all three charts will be undertaken simultaneously here. Enter the charts with the initial climb gross weight and project horizontally right to intersect the assigned cruise altitude or the optimum cruise altitude for the computed drag index, then vertically down to intersect the applicable drag index curve. From this point project horizontally left to the temperature baseline and parallel the nearest temperature guideline to read time, fuel or distance. Time, fuel or distance required to accelerate to climb speed must be added to the chart values.

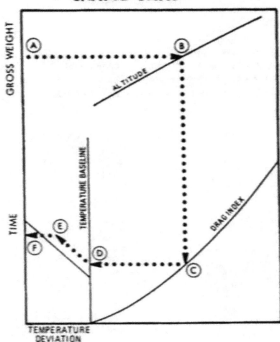

SAMPLE CLIMB

15E-1-(81)04

Sample Problem

Military Thrust

A. Gross weight	60,000 Lb
B. Cruise altitude	20,000 Ft
C. Drag Index	120
D. Temperature baseline	
E. Temperature deviation	+10°C
F. Time	6.0 Min
G. Fuel (from Fuel Required To Climb Chart)	1700 Lb
H. Distance (from Distance Required to Climb Chart)	35 NM

COMBAT CEILING CHARTS

These charts (figures A4-7 and A4-8) present the military and maximum thrust subsonic combat ceiling for both single engine and normal two engine operation. The variable of gross weight and pressure altitude are taken into consideration for a range of drag indexes.

USE

Enter the applicable graph with estimated gross weight at end of climb. Project vertically up to intersect applicable configuration curve, then horizontally to the left to read combat ceiling.

Sample Problem

Combat Ceiling - Maximum Thrust - (2) Engines

Configuration: -4 CFTs + (4) AIM-7F missiles

A. Gross weight at end of climb	55,000 Lb
B. Drag index	18.6
C. Combat ceiling	49,700 Ft

TIME TO CLIMB
MILITARY THRUST

REMARKS
ENGINE(S): (2) F100-PW-220
U.S. STANDARD DAY, 1966

AIRPLANE CONFIGURATION
INDIVIDUAL DRAG INDEXES

NOTES
- CLIMB SPEED SCHEDULE FOR DRAG INDEXES UP TO 40 IS .350 KCAS UNTIL INTERCEPTION OF .88 MACH, THEN MAINTAINING MACH TO CRUISE ALTITUDE. FOR DRAG INDEXES BETWEEN 40 AND 100, USE 330 KCAS/.83 MACH. GREATER THAN 100, USE 310 KCAS/.74 MACH.
- TIME FROM BRAKE RELEASE TO INITIAL CLIMB SPEED IS 1.0 MINUTES MILITARY THRUST TAKEOFF AND 0.5 MINUTES MAX THRUST TAKEOFF.

DATE: 15 JUNE 1988
DATA BASIS: ESTIMATED

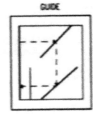

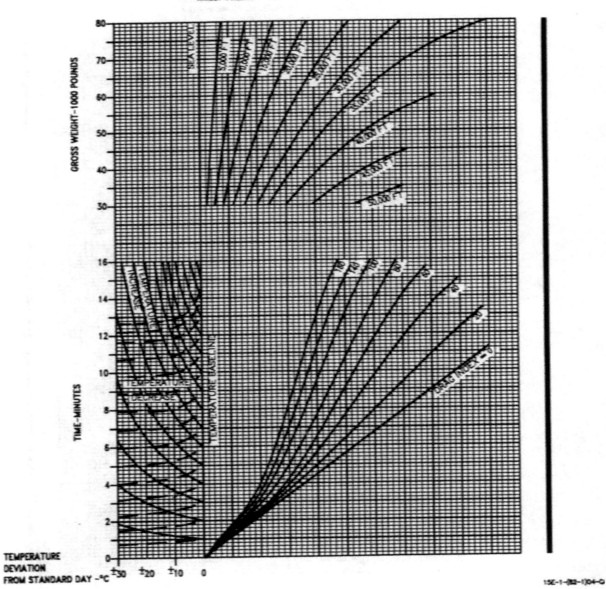

Figure A4-1

FUEL REQUIRED TO CLIMB
MILITARY THRUST

REMARKS
ENGINE(S): (2) F100–PW–220
U.S. STANDARD DAY, 1966

AIRPLANE CONFIGURATION
INDIVIDUAL DRAG INDEXES

GUIDE

NOTES
- CLIMB SPEED SCHEDULE FOR DRAG INDEXES UP TO 40 IS .350 KCAS
  UNTIL INTERCEPTION OF .88 MACH, THEN MAINTAINING MACH TO
  CRUISE ALTITUDE. FOR DRAG INDEXES BETWEEN 40 AND 100, USE
  .330 KCAS/.83 MACH. GREATER THAN 100, USE .310 KCAS/.74 MACH.
- PRETAKEOFF FUEL CONSUMPTION IS AS FOLLOWS:
  START– .32 LB/ENG; MIL RUNUP– 82 LB/ENG; TAXI 23 LB/MIN/ENG.
- FUEL REQUIRED FROM BRAKE RELEASE TO INITIAL CLIMB SPEED IS
  300 POUNDS MILITARY THRUST AND 550 POUNDS MAXIMUM THRUST.

DATE: 15 JUNE 1988
DATA BASIS: ESTIMATED

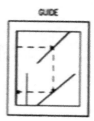

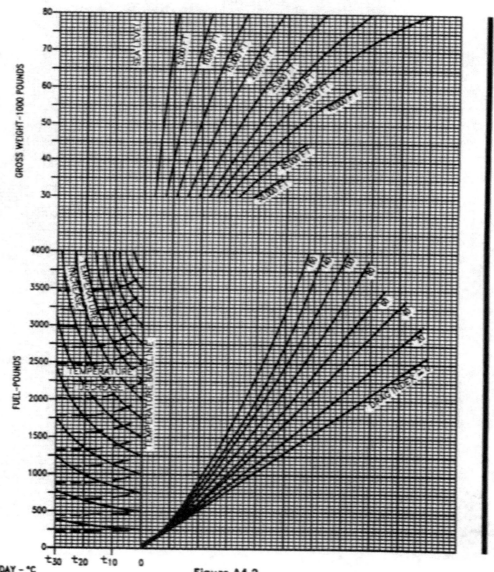

TEMPERATURE
DEVIATION
FROM STANDARD DAY – °C

Figure A4-2

15E-1-(83-1)04-CAT1

DISTANCE REQUIRED TO CLIMB
MILITARY THRUST

REMARKS
ENGINE(S): (2) F100-PW-220
U.S. STANDARD DAY, 1966

AIRPLANE CONFIGURATION
INDIVIDUAL DRAG INDEXES

DATE: 15 JUNE 1988
DATA BASIS: ESTIMATED

NOTES
- CLIMB SPEED SCHEDULE FOR DRAG INDEXES UP TO 40 IS 350 KCAS UNTIL INTERCEPTION OF .88 MACH, THEN MAINTAINING MACH TO CRUISE ALTITUDE. FOR DRAG INDEXES BETWEEN 40 AND 100, USE 330 KCAS/.83 MACH. GREATER THAN 100, USE 310 KCAS/.74 MACH.
- DISTANCE FROM BRAKE RELEASE TO INITIAL CLIMB SPEED IS 2.0 NAUTICAL MILES MILITARY THRUST TAKEOFF AND 1.0 NAUTICAL MILES MAXIMUM THRUST TAKEOFF.

GUIDE

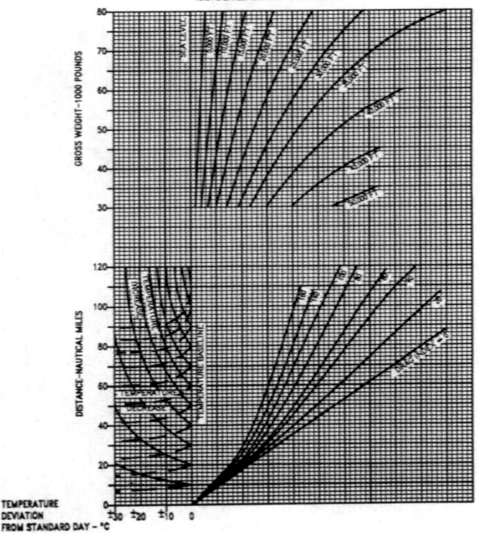

TEMPERATURE
DEVIATION
FROM STANDARD DAY – °C

15E-1-(84-1)04-CATI

Figure A4-3

TIME TO CLIMB
MAXIMUM THRUST

AIRPLANE CONFIGURATION
INDIVIDUAL DRAG INDEXES

REMARKS
ENGINE(S): (2) F100-PW-220
U.S. STANDARD DAY, 1966

NOTES
- TIME FROM BRAKE RELEASE TO INITIAL CLIMB SPEED IS 1.0 MINUTES MILITARY THRUST TAKEOFF AND 0.5 MINUTES MAX THRUST TAKEOFF.
- CLIMB SPEED SCHEDULE FOR DRAG INDEX OF 50 OR LESS IS 350 KCAS UNTIL INTERSECTION OF .95 MACH. FOR HIGHER DRAG INDEXES, USE 350 KCAS/.92 MACH.

DATE: 15 JUNE 1988
DATA BASIS: ESTIMATED

GUIDE

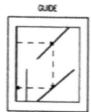

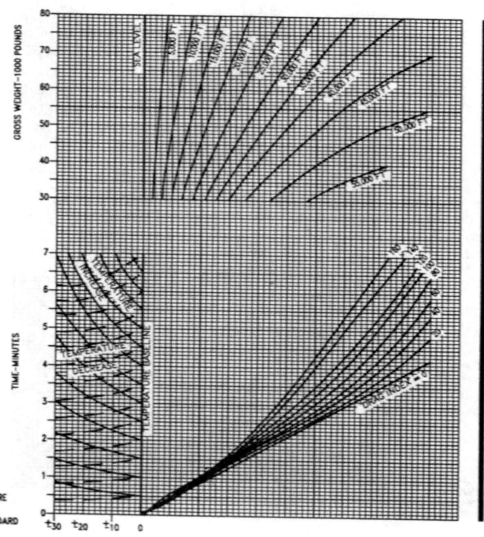

Figure A4-4

15E-1-(85-1)04-CATI

FUEL REQUIRED TO CLIMB
MAXIMUM THRUST

AIRPLANE CONFIGURATION
INDIVIDUAL DRAG INDEXES

REMARKS
ENGINE(S): (2) F100-PW-220
U.S. STANDARD DAY, 1966

NOTE
- CLIMB SPEED SCHEDULE FOR DRAG INDEXES OF UP TO 60 IS 350 KCAS UNTIL INTERSECTION OF .95 MACH. FOR HIGHER DRAG INDEXES, USE 350 KCAS/.92 MACH.
- FUEL REQUIRED FROM BRAKE RELEASE TO INITIAL CLIMB SPEED IS 300 POUNDS MILITARY THRUST AND 550 POUNDS MAXIMUM THRUST.
- PRETAKEOFF FUEL CONSUMPTION IS AS FOLLOWS: START- 32 LB/ENG; MIL RUNUP- 82 LB/ENG; TAXI 23 LB/MIN/ENG.

DATE: 15 JUNE 1988
DATA BASIS: ESTIMATED

GUIDE

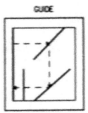

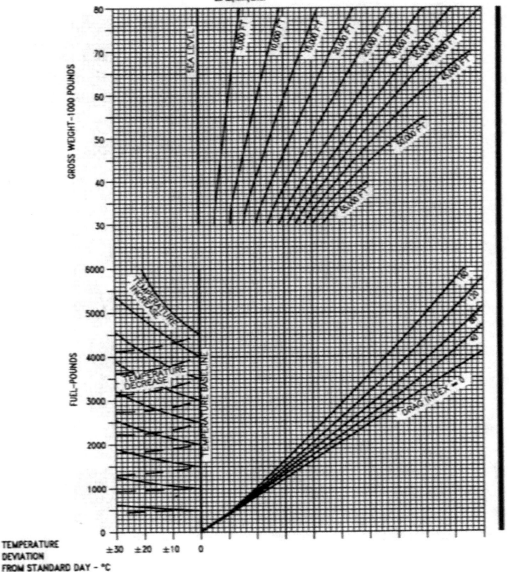

TEMPERATURE
DEVIATION
FROM STANDARD DAY - °C

15E-1-(B6-1)04-CAT)

Figure A4-5

DISTANCE REQUIRED TO CLIMB
MAXIMUM THRUST

GUIDE

AIRPLANE CONFIGURATION
INDIVIDUAL DRAG INDEXES

REMARKS
ENGINE(S): (2) F100-PW-220
U.S. STANDARD DAY, 1966

NOTES
● DISTANCE FROM BRAKE RELEASE TO INITIAL CLIMB SPEED
IS 2.0 NAUTICAL MILES MILITARY THRUST TAKEOFF AND
1.0 NAUTICAL MILES MAXIMUM THRUST TAKEOFF.

● CLIMB SPEED SCHEDULE FOR DRAG INDEX OF 60 OR LESS
IS 350 KCAS UNTIL INTERSECTION OF .95 MACH. FOR HIGHER
DRAG INDEXES, USE 350 KCAS/.92 MACH.

DATE: 15 JUNE 1988
DATA BASIS: ESTIMATED

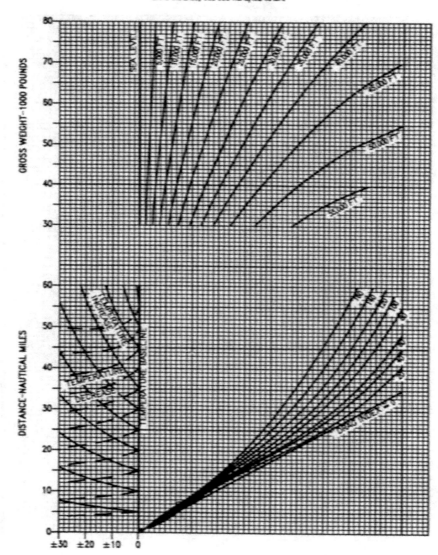
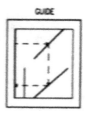

15E-1-(87-1)06-CATI

Figure A4-6

COMBAT CEILING

AIRPLANE CONFIGURATION
INDIVIDUAL DRAG INDEXES

REMARKS
ENGINE(S): (2) F100-PW-220
U.S. STANDARD DAY, 1966

NOTE
COMBAT CEILING IS THE PRESSURE ALTITUDE AT WHICH THE
AIRCRAFT CAN CLIMB AT A MAXIMUM RATE OF 500 FEET PER MINUTE.

DATE: 15 JUNE 1988
DATA BASIS: ESTIMATED

GUIDE

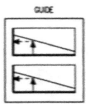

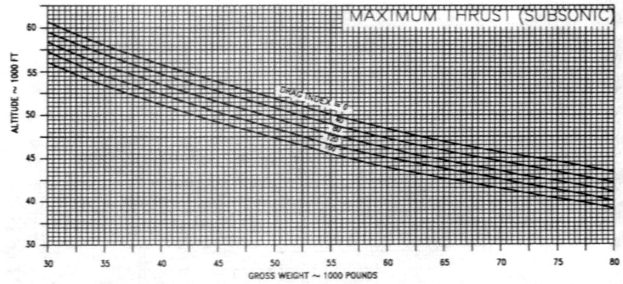

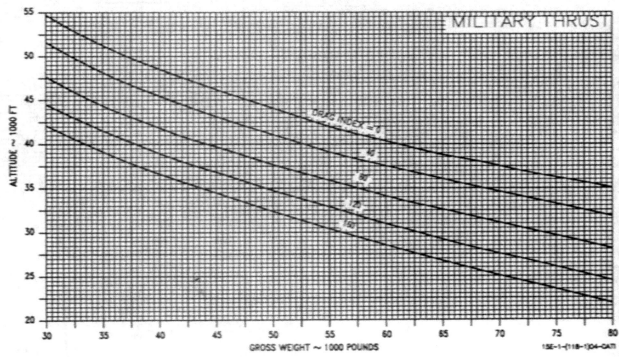

Figure A4-7

COMBAT CEILING
ONE ENGINE OPERATING

AIRPLANE CONFIGURATION
INDIVIDUAL DRAG INDEXES

REMARKS
ENGINE(S): (2) F100-PW-220
U.S. STANDARD DAY, 1966

NOTE
● COMBAT CEILING IS THE PRESSURE
ALTITUDE AT WHICH THE AIRCRAFT
CAN CLIMB AT A MAXIMUM RATE
OF 500 FEET PER MINUTE.

● INOPERATIVE ENGINE WINDMILLING.

DATE: 15 JUNE 1988
DATA BASIS: ESTIMATED

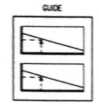

GUIDE

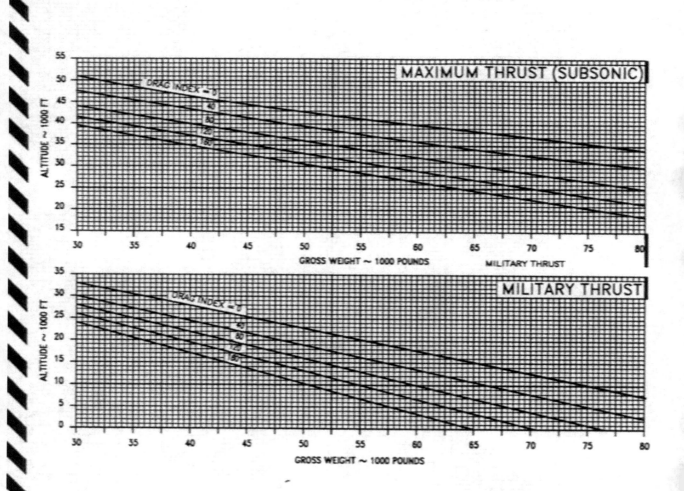

Figure A4-8

15E-1-(11P-1)04-CAT1

PART 5

RANGE

TABLE OF CONTENTS

Charts

Optimum Long Range Cruise.......................A5-5
Constant Altitude/Long Range Cruise A5-7
Constant Altitude Cruise..........................A5-17
Low Altitude Cruise..............................A5-18
High Altitude Cruise.............................A5-28
Constant Altitude Cruise-Landing Gear
Extended..A5-38

OPTIMUM LONG RANGE CRUISE

These charts (figures A5-1 and A5-2) present cruise data for twin-engine and single engine operation. These charts depict cruise altitude, specific range (nautical miles per pound) and cruise Mach number for various gross weights and drag indexes.

USE

Enter the chart with the applicable gross weight and project vertically up to intersect the appropriate drag index curves in each plot. From the intersection of the appropriate drag index curve, reflect horizontally left and read cruise Mach number, specific range in nautical miles per pound and cruise altitude.

SAMPLE OPTIMUM LONG RANGE CRUISE

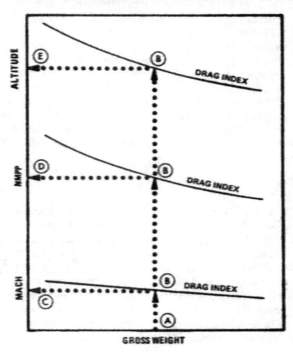

15E-1-(139)04

Sample Problem

A. Gross weight	60,000 Lb
B. Drag index	120
C. Mach number	0.765 Mach
D. Specific range	0.051 NMPP
E. Cruise altitude	31,200 Ft

CONSTANT ALTITUDE/LONG RANGE CRUISE

These charts (figures A5-3 thru A5-12) present the necessary planning data to set up optimum cruise schedules for normal two-engine operation at a constant altitude. The charts depict specific range (nautical miles per pound of fuel) for various Mach numbers, gross weights and individual drag indexes at altitudes of sea level thru 45,000 feet in increments of 5000 feet. The recommended procedure is to use an average gross weight for a given leg of the mission. One way to find the average gross weight is to divide the mission into weight segments. With this method, readjust the cruise schedule each time a given amount of fuel is used. Subtract one-half of the fuel weight allotted for the first leg from the initial cruise gross weight. The remainder is the average gross weight for the leg. It is possible to obtain instantaneous data if desired.

USE

Enter the chart with the desired gross weight and project vertically upward to intersect the appropriate drag index curve, then horizontally to the left to determine optimum cruise Mach number. From the optimum airspeed-gross weight intersection project vertically up to intersect the appropriate drag index curve, then horizontally left to determine the specific range. These charts are applicable for any temperature day. Use following paragraph to determine true airspeed and total fuel flow.

Sample Problem

Configuration - -4 CFT + (4)AIM-7F Missiles, Altitude - 30,000 feet

A. Gross weight	55,000 Lb
B. Drag index	18.6
C. Cruise Mach number	0.850
D. Drag index	18.6
E. Specific range	0.078 NMPP

CONSTANT ALTITUDE CRUISE CHARTS

This chart (A5-13) presents the necessary planning data to set up optimum cruise schedules for normal two engine operation at a constant altitude at various flight-level temperatures.

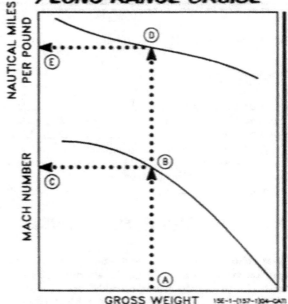

SAMPLE CONSTANT ALTITUDE /LONG RANGE CRUISE

USE

Enter the left side of the chart with the optimum cruise Mach number and project horizontally right to intersect the predicted flight-level temperature. Then, project vertically up to obtain the corresponding true airspeed. Project vertically down to intersect the interpolated specific range, then project horizontally left to obtain total fuel flow required in pounds per hour.

Sample Problem

Configuration - -4 CFT + (4) AIM-7F Missiles, Altitude - 30,000 feet, Temperature - −40°C

A. True Mach number	0.855
B. Temperature	−40°C
C. True airspeed	510 KTAS
D. Specific range	0.078 NMPP
E. Total fuel flow	6600 PPH

SAMPLE CONSTANT ALTITUDE CRUISE

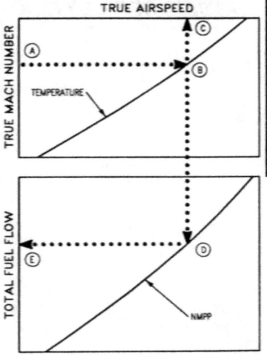

15E-1-(15B-1)04-CAT)-31

the non-standard day temperature correction factor obtained from the appropriate TEMP. EFFECTS column. Enter the table with the equivalent standard day true airspeed and project horizontally to the applicable drag index column and read total fuel flow for a standard day. To obtain the total fuel flow at the desired true airspeed, multiply the total fuel flow for a standard day by the nonstandard day temperature correction factor.

Sample Problem

Gross weight 35,000 lbs, 15,000 ft (−15°C)

A.	Desired airspeed	535 KTAS
B.	Drag Index	20
C.	Nonstandard day temperature	0°C
D.	Correction factor	1.029
E.	Equivalent standard day true airspeed (A ÷D)	520 Kt
F.	Standard day total fuel flow	9894 PPH
G.	Total fuel flow at desired true airspeed (F X D)	10181 PPH
H.	Standard day V_{max}	614.2 KTAS
J.	Standard day Mil. Pwr. total fuel flow	18,716 PPH

HIGH ALTITUDE CRUISE TABLES

These tables (figures A5-24 thru A5-33) present total fuel flow values for various combinations of cruise airspeed and drag index at altitudes of 25,000 feet thru 45,000 feet in 5000 foot increments. Also included for each altitude are the total fuel flow values and resultant V_{max} (maximum attainable TAS) for a MIL thrust setting. Separate charts are provided for gross weights of 35,000 thru 80,000 pounds. Fuel flow values are tabulated for U.S. Standard Day; however, correction factors are given for nonstandard temperatures. The standard day temperature is listed with the altitude. If the actual temperature at a particular altitude differs from the standard day temperature, refer to the TEMP. EFFECTS column to determine the appropriate temperature correction factor.

USE

After selecting the applicable table for gross weight and altitude, determine the equivalent standard day true airspeed by dividing the desired true airspeed by the nonstandard day temperature correction factor obtained from the appropriate TEMP EFFECTS column. Enter the table with the equivalent standard

LOW ALTITUDE CRUISE TABLES

These tables (figures A5-14 thru A5-23) present total fuel flow values for various combinations of cruise airspeed and drag index at altitudes of Sea Level, 5000, 10,000, 15,000 and 20,000 feet. Also included for each altitude are the total fuel flow values and resultant V_{max} (maximum attainable TAS) for a MIL thrust setting. Separate tables are provided for gross weights of 35,000 thru 80,000 pounds. Fuel flow values are tabulated for U.S. Standard Day; however, correction factors are given for non-standard temperatures. The standard day temperature is listed with the altitude. If the actual temperature at a particular altitude differs from the standard day temperature, refer to the TEMP. EFFECTS column to determine the appropriate temperature correction factor.

USE

After selecting the applicable table for gross weight and altitude, determine the equivalent standard day true airspeed by dividing the desired true airspeed by day true airspeed and project horizontally to the applicable drag index column and read total fuel flow for a standard day. To obtain the total fuel flow at the desired true airspeed, multiply the total fuel flow for a standard day by the nonstandard day temperature correction factor.

CONSTANT ALTITUDE CRUISE - LANDING GEAR EXTENDED

This chart (figure A5-34) presents data to set up constant altitude cruise schedules when landing gear cannot be retracted. The chart contains specific range (nautical miles per pound of fuel) data for various combinations of gross weight, drag index, and altitude for a cruise speed of 250 KCAS.

USE

Enter the chart at the gross weight scale and project horizontally right to intersect with the applicable drag index. From this point, project downward to intersect with the desired cruise altitude and project horizontally left to read the specific range.

Sample Problem

A. Gross weight	40,000 Lb
B. Drag index (external stores)	30
Drag index (all gear extended)	90
Total drag index	120
C. Altitude	10,000 Ft
D. Specific range	0.046 NMPP

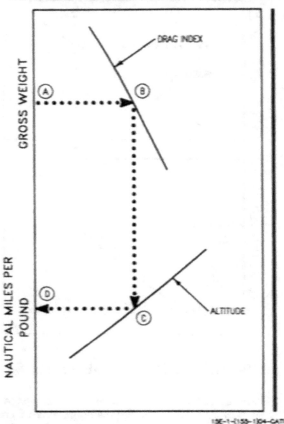

SAMPLE CONSTANT ALTITUDE CRUISE, LANDING GEAR EXTENDED

15E-1-(155-1)04-CATI

OPTIMUM LONG RANGE CRUISE
MILITARY THRUST

AIRPLANE CONFIGURATION
INDIVIDUAL DRAG INDEXES

REMARKS
ENGINE(S): (2) F100-PW-220
U.S. STANDARD DAY, 1966

NOTE
DATA IS FOR ALL FREE
AIR TEMPERATURES

DATE:15 JUNE 1988
DATA BASIS: ESTIMATED

GUIDE

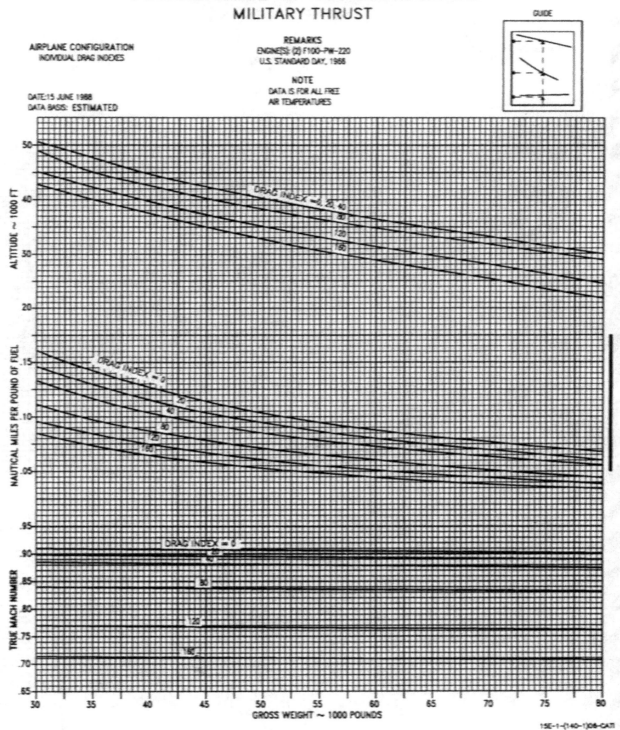

Figure A5-1

15E-1-(140-1)06-CATI

A5-5

OPTIMUM LONG RANGE CRUISE
ONE ENGINE OPERATING

AIRPLANE CONFIGURATION
INDIVIDUAL DRAG INDEXES

REMARKS
ENGINE(S): (2) F100-PW-220
U.S. STANDARD DAY, 1966

GUIDE

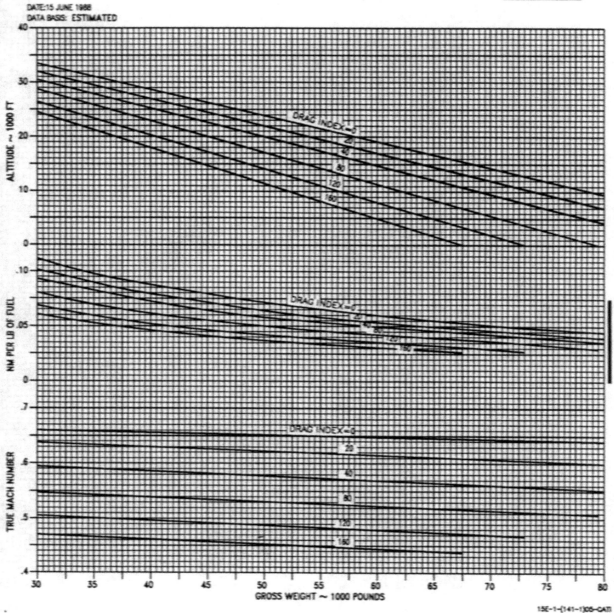

DATE:15 JUNE 1988
DATA BASIS: ESTIMATED

Figure A5-2

15E-1-(141-1)05-CAT1

CONSTANT ALTITUDE/LONG RANGE CRUISE
SEA LEVEL

AIRPLANE CONFIGURATION
INDIVIDUAL DRAG INDEXES

SPECIFIC RANGE, TRUE MACH NUMBER

REMARKS
ENGINE(S): (2) F100-PW-220
U.S. STANDARD DAY, 1966

GUIDE

DATE: 15 JUNE 1968
DATA BASIS: ESTIMATED

NOTE
DATA IS FOR ALL FREE
AIR TEMPERATURES

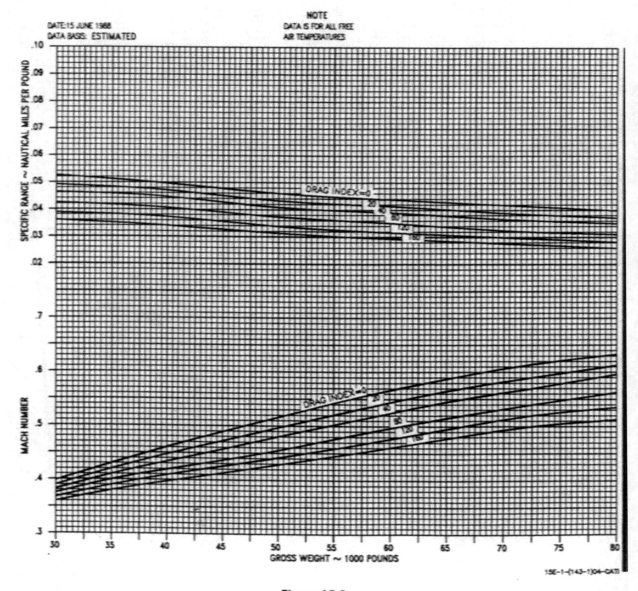

Figure A5-3

15E-1-(143-1)04-OATII

CONSTANT ALTITUDE/LONG RANGE CRUISE
5,000 FEET

GUIDE

SPECIFIC RANGE, TRUE MACH NUMBER

AIRPLANE CONFIGURATION
INDIVIDUAL DRAG INDEXES

REMARKS
ENGINE(S): (2) F100-PW-220
U.S. STANDARD DAY, 1966

NOTE
DATA IS FOR ALL FREE
AIR TEMPERATURES

DATE:15 JUNE 1988
DATA BASIS: ESTIMATED

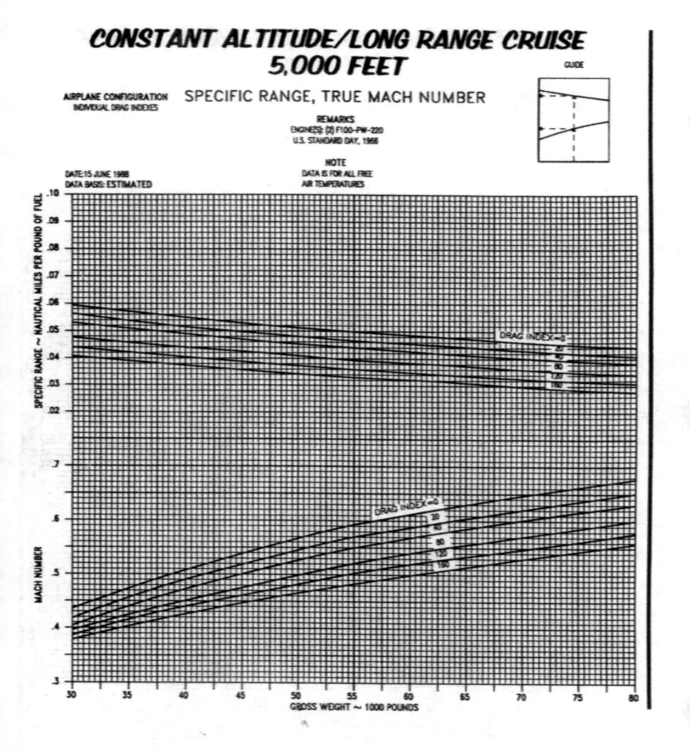

Figure A5-4

15E-1-(144-1)04-CATI

CONSTANT ALTITUDE/LONG RANGE CRUISE
10,000 FEET

AIRPLANE CONFIGURATION
INDIVIDUAL DRAG INDEXES

SPECIFIC RANGE, TRUE MACH NUMBER

REMARKS
ENGINE(S): (2) F100-PW-220
U.S. STANDARD DAY, 1966

NOTE
DATA IS FOR ALL FREE
AIR TEMPERATURES

GUIDE

DATE: 15 JUNE 1988
DATA BASIS: ESTIMATED

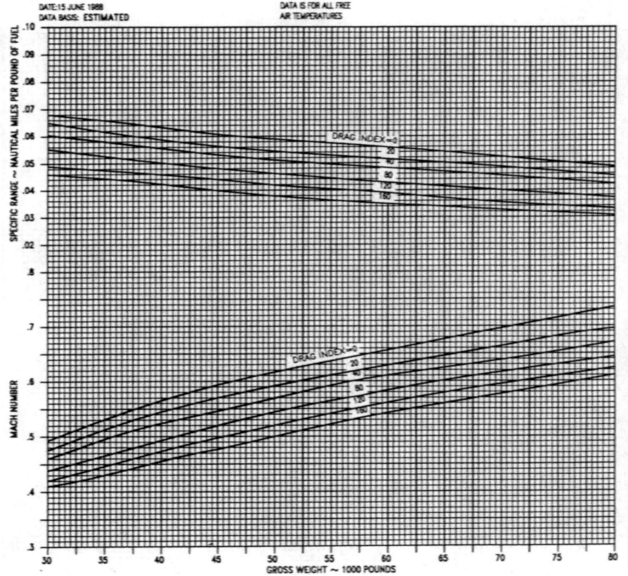

Figure A5-5

15E-1-(148-1)04-CAT1

CONSTANT ALTITUDE/LONG RANGE CRUISE
15,000 FEET

AIRPLANE CONFIGURATION
INDIVIDUAL DRAG INDEXES

SPECIFIC RANGE, TRUE MACH NUMBER

GUIDE

REMARKS
ENGINE(S): (2) F100-PW-220
U.S. STANDARD DAY, 1968

DATE: 15 JUNE 1968
DATA BASIS: ESTIMATED

NOTE
DATA IS FOR ALL FREE
AIR TEMPERATURES

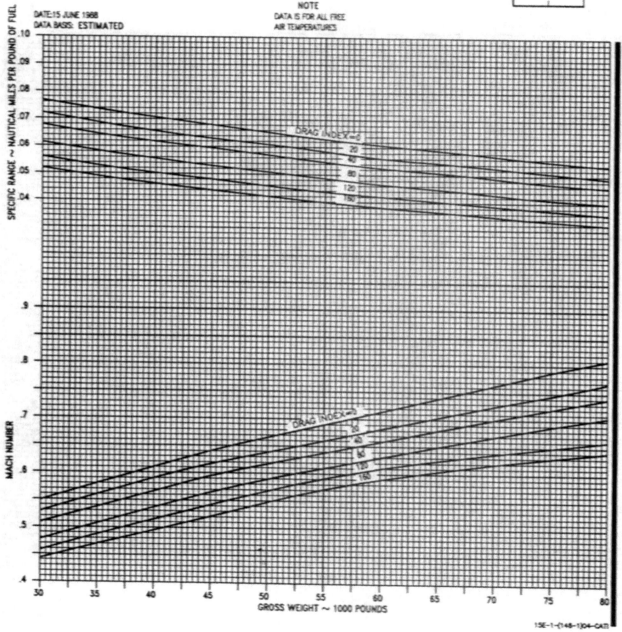

Figure A5-6

15E-1-(148-1)04-CAT)

CONSTANT ALTITUDE/LONG RANGE CRUISE
20,000 FEET

SPECIFIC RANGE, TRUE MACH NUMBER

AIRPLANE CONFIGURATION
INDIVIDUAL DRAG INDEXES

REMARKS
ENGINE(S): (2) F100-PW-220
U.S. STANDARD DAY, 1966

GUIDE

NOTE
DATA IS FOR ALL FREE
AIR TEMPERATURES

DATE: 15 JUNE 1988
DATA BASIS: ESTIMATED

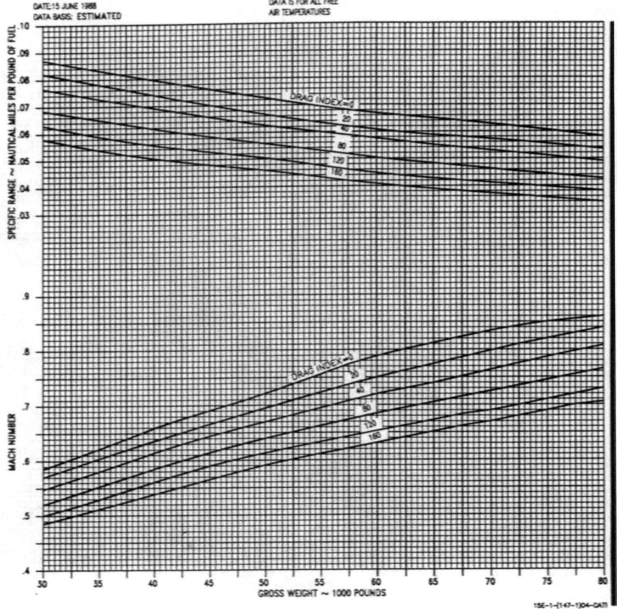

Figure A5-7

15E-1-(147-1)04-CATI

CONSTANT ALTITUDE/LONG RANGE CRUISE
25,000 FEET

AIRPLANE CONFIGURATION
INDIVIDUAL DRAG INDEXES

SPECIFIC RANGE, TRUE MACH NUMBER

REMARKS
ENGINE(S): (2) F100-PW-220
U.S. STANDARD DAY, 1966

GUIDE

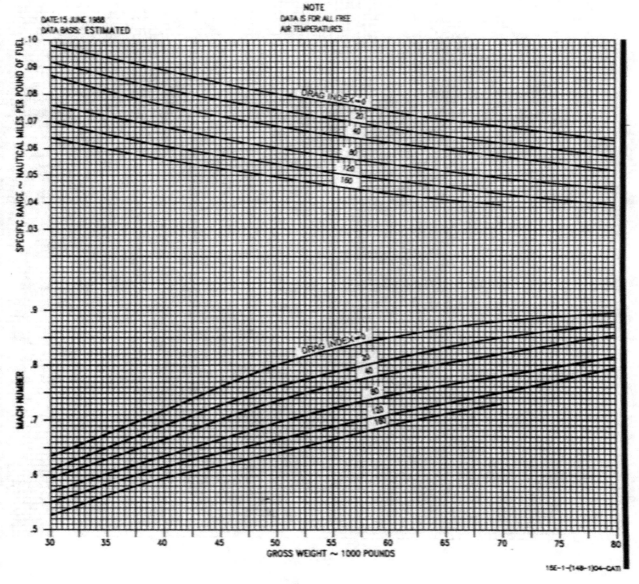

DATE: 15 JUNE 1988
DATA BASIS: ESTIMATED

NOTE
DATA IS FOR ALL FREE
AIR TEMPERATURES

Figure A5-8

15E-1-(148-1)04-CAT1

CONSTANT ALTITUDE/LONG RANGE CRUISE
30,000 FEET

SPECIFIC RANGE, TRUE MACH NUMBER

AIRPLANE CONFIGURATION
INDIVIDUAL DRAG INDEXES

REMARKS
ENGINE(S): (2) F100-PW-220
U.S. STANDARD DAY, 1966

GUIDE

NOTE
DATA IS FOR ALL FREE
AIR TEMPERATURES

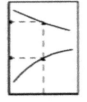

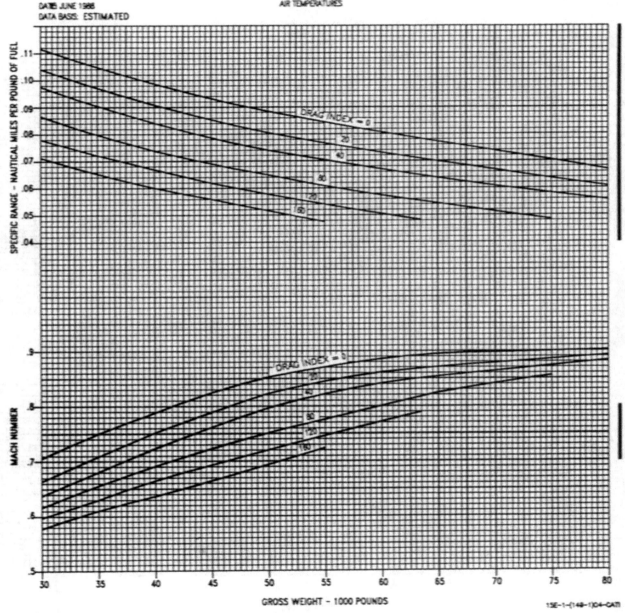

Figure A5-9

CONSTANT ALTITUDE/LONG RANGE CRUISE
35,000 FEET
SPECIFIC RANGE, TRUE MACH NUMBER

AIRPLANE CONFIGURATION
INDIVIDUAL DRAG INDEXES

REMARKS
ENGINE(S): (2) F100-PW-220
U.S. STANDARD DAY, 1966

GUIDE

NOTE
DATA IS FOR ALL FREE
AIR TEMPERATURES

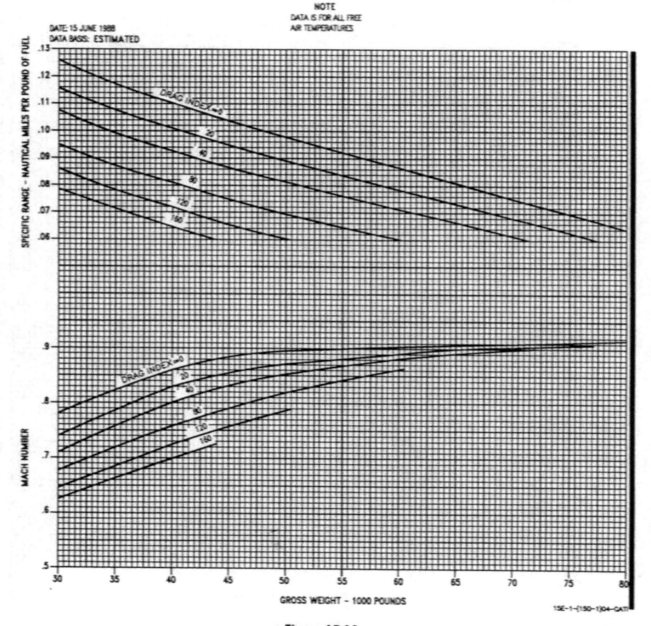

Figure A5-10

CONSTANT ALTITUDE/LONG RANGE CRUISE
40,000 FEET
SPECIFIC RANGE, TRUE MACH NUMBER

AIRPLANE CONFIGURATION
INDIVIDUAL DRAG INDEXES

REMARKS
ENGINE(S): (2) F100-PW-220
U.S. STANDARD DAY, 1966

GUIDE

NOTE
DATA IS FOR ALL FREE
AIR TEMPERATURES

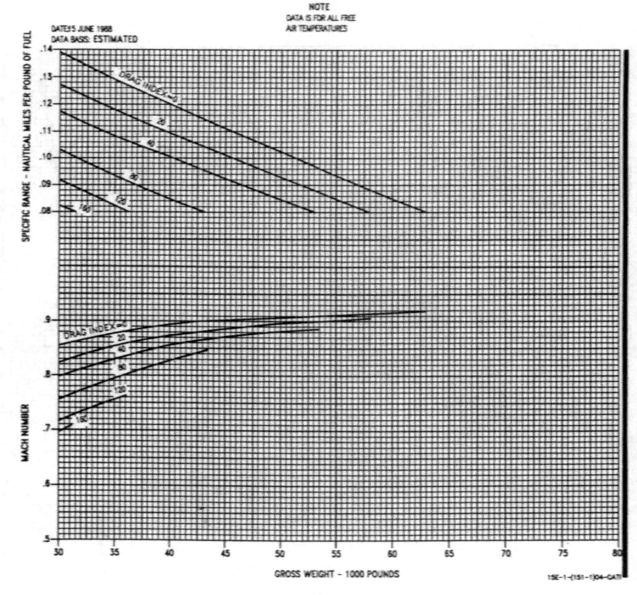

DATE:15 JUNE 1988
DATA BASIS: ESTIMATED

Figure A5-11

15E-1-(15)-1)04-CAT'

CONSTANT ALTITUDE/LONG RANGE CRUISE
45,000 FEET

AIRPLANE CONFIGURATION
INDIVIDUAL DRAG INDEXES

SPECIFIC RANGE, TRUE MACH NUMBER

REMARKS
ENGINE(S): (2) F100-PW-220
U.S. STANDARD DAY, 1966

GUIDE

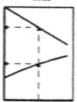

NOTE
DATA IS FOR ALL FREE
AIR TEMPERATURES

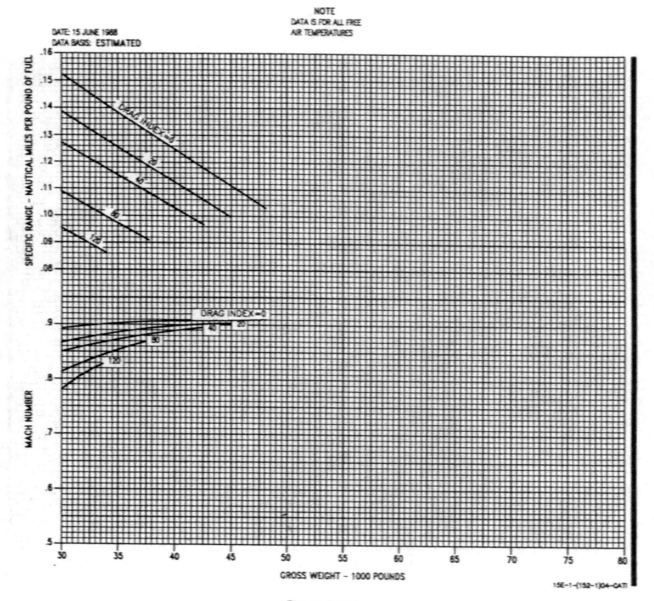

Figure A5-12

15E-1-(152-1)04-CATI

CONSTANT ALTITUDE CRUISE
TRUE AIRSPEED AND FUEL FLOW

AIRPLANE CONFIGURATION
ALL DRAG INDEXES

REMARKS
ENGINE(S): (2) F100-PW-220
U.S. STANDARD DAY, 1966

GUIDE

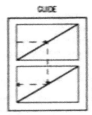

DATE:15 JUNE 1988
DATA BASIS: ESTIMATED

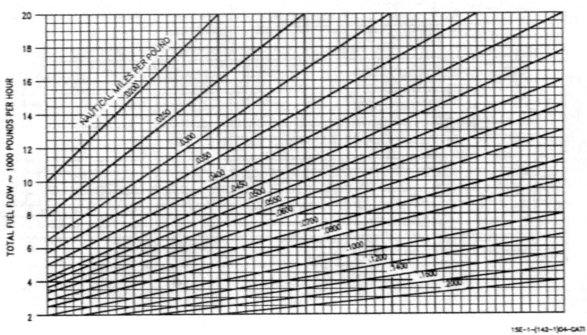

Figure A5-13

LOW ALTITUDE CRUISE
GROSS WEIGHT - 35,000 POUNDS

AIRPLANE CONFIGURATION
INDIVIDUAL DRAG INDEXES
DATE: 15 JUN 1988
DATA BASIS: ESTIMATED

REMARKS
ENGINES: (2) F100-PW-220

TOTAL FUEL FLOW - LB/HR

SEA LEVEL (15°C)

KTAS	0	20	40	60	80	100	120	140	160
360	7898	8335	8981	9642	10312	10982	11652	12350	13102
400	9013	9630	10682	11534	12388	13317	14271	15226	18196
440	10645	11629	12714	13873	15081	16289	17551	18823	20098
480	12270	13641	15153	16671	18248	19845	21459	23088	
520	14175	16073	17996	19999	22011	24038			
560	16437	18918	21440	23994					
600	20162	23518							
MIL	27165	26683	26270	25963	25643	25341	25023	24736	24485
VMAX	639.2	617.1	596.2	574.9	552.4	531.1	511.2	493.8	478.1

ACTUAL OAT DEG. C	CRUISE	MIL	VMAX
-40	.999	1.520	.975
-20	.937	1.330	.988
0	.974	1.140	.997
20	1.009	.960	1.000
40	1.042	.810	.999

6,000 FEET (8°C)

KTAS	0	20	40	60	80	100	120	140	160
360	6584	7121	7663	8219	8776	9334	9891	10528	11168
400	7624	8372	9085	9797	10538	11357	12177	12998	13848
440	8955	9868	10782	11809	12840	13883	14954	16025	17151
480	10414	11617	12909	14209	15554	16902	18362	19822	21289
520	12046	13656	15298	16974	18778	20614			
560	14114	16212	18407	20758					
600	17699	20851							
MIL	24312	24063	23708	23402	23013	22616	22260	21948	21676
VMAX	637.4	618.7	597.8	580.0	559.0	537.6	518.2	499.8	483.3

ACTUAL OAT DEG. C	CRUISE	MIL	VMAX
-40	.918	1.400	.976
-20	.954	1.225	.987
0	.991	1.050	.998
20	1.027	.885	1.000
40	1.061	.735	.998

10,000 FEET (-6°C)

KTAS	0	20	40	60	80	100	120	140	160
360	5830	6073	6548	7030	7515	7999	8511	9037	9662
400	6507	7131	7755	8379	9044	9721	10398	11100	11822
440	7613	8406	9225	10082	10940	11841	12751	13677	14648
480	8841	9895	10990	12116	13269	14459	15683	16947	18254
520	10273	11646	13061	14548	16084	17677	19311		
560	12077	13912	15841	17873	20002				
600	15484	18399							
MIL	21726	21419	21046	20748	20421	20020	19619	19302	19106
VMAX	633.5	617.8	597.5	580.0	562.8	542.8	522.8	504.9	488.5

ACTUAL OAT DEG. C	CRUISE	MIL	VMAX
-40	.932	1.300	.977
-20	.972	1.130	.992
0	1.006	.960	1.001
20	1.046	.800	1.003
40	1.081	.650	1.006

15,000 FEET (-15°C)

KTAS	0	20	40	60	80	100	120	140	160
360	4900	5285	5687	6090	6492	6910	7344	7777	8211
400	5638	6157	6676	7212	7771	8331	8899	9488	10077
440	6532	7181	7883	8609	9329	10082	10834	11640	12480
480	7630	8433	9341	10309	11281	12306	12343	14488	15628
520	8730	9894	11128	12399	13704	15137	16590		
560	10414	12018	13687	15508	17376				
600	13727	16293							
MIL	19013	18716	18288	17958	17679	17496	17303	17117	16962
VMAX	628.0	614.2	595.1	577.1	561.4	544.5	527.3	510.4	484.7

ACTUAL OAT DEG. C	CRUISE	MIL	VMAX
-40	.950	1.225	.985
-20	.990	1.045	.997
0	1.029	.880	1.007
20	1.066	.725	1.012
40	1.101	.560	1.017

20,000 FEET (-25°C)

KTAS	0	20	40	60	80	100	120	140	160
360	4204	4635	4965	5298	5641	5998	6357	6715	7089
400	4898	5324	5758	6220	6694	7182	7645	8138	8637
440	5607	6189	6761	7364	7982	8611	9270	9944	10629
480	6423	7190	7987	8758	9593	10460	11358	12283	13337
520	7418	8414	9452	10550	11691	12888	14230		
560	9049	10607	12041	13684	15458				
600	12371	14566							
MIL	16591	16389	16157	15872	15768	15631	15508	15390	15257
VMAX	622.5	609.6	594.0	571.6	561.9	548.5	533.1	517.7	502.6

ACTUAL OAT DEG. C	CRUISE	MIL	VMAX
-40	.989	1.145	.982
-20	1.010	.965	1.003
0	1.049	.810	1.012
20	1.087	.655	1.017
40	1.123	.500	1.023

15E1-52004

Figure A5-14

LOW ALTITUDE CRUISE
GROSS WEIGHT - 40,000 POUNDS
REMARKS

AIRPLANE CONFIGURATION
INDIVIDUAL DRAG INDEXES
DATE: 15 JUN 1988
DATA BASIS: ESTIMATED

ENGINES: (2) F100-PW-220

TOTAL FUEL FLOW - LB/HR

	KTAS	DRAG INDEX									ACTUAL OAT DEG. C	TEMP EFFECTS-FACTORS		
		0	20	40	60	80	100	120	140	160		CRUISE	MIL	V$_{MAX}$
SEA LEVEL (15°C)	360	7780	8418	9056	9716	10382	11048	11715	12416	13163.	-40	.899	1.520	.975
	400	9069	9886	10733	11581	12430	13360	14310	16261	18228	-20	.937	1.330	.586
	440	10677	11687	12738	13895	15098	16301	17559	18826	20098	0	.974	1.140	.997
	480	12296	13663	15172	16685	18254	19850	21457	23079		20	1.009	.960	1.000
	520	14178	16071	17988	19986	21993	24014				40	1.042	.810	.999
	560	16501	18916	21431	23980									
	600	20132	23480											
	MIL	27175	26691	26275	25965	25645	25345	25027	24729	24486				
	VMAX	639.7	617.5	596.4	575.1	562.5	531.3	511.5	493.9	478.2				
5,000 FEET (5°C)	360	6690	7224	7765	8318	8871	9424	9987	10623	11259	-40	.916	1.400	.978
	400	7750	8448	9158	9864	10609	11425	12241	13056	12904	-20	.954	1.225	.987
	440	9014	9923	10836	11862	12887	12928	14994	16061	17184	0	.991	1.050	.998
	480	10448	11647	12934	14230	15570	16914	18389	19824	21285	20	1.027	.885	1.000
	520	12072	13877	15314	16985	18782	20614				40	1.061	.735	.998
	560	14118	16208	18398	20743									
	600	17680	20823											
	MIL	24315	24058	23711	23407	23017	22820	22261	21948	21676				
	VMAX	637.5	616.9	598.0	580.3	569.2	537.8	518.2	499.6	483.4				
10,000 FEET (-5°C)	360	5759	6199	6679	7159	7639	8120	8537	9158	9679	-40	.932	1.300	.977
	400	6611	7230	7850	8470	9139	9811	10483	11186	11902	-20	.972	1.130	.992
	440	7689	8477	9297	10149	11002	11902	12807	13732	14697	0	1.009	.960	1.001
	480	8899	9956	11042	12185	13313	14500	15718	16980	18280	20	1.046	.800	1.003
	520	10307	11876	13107	14570	16099	17587	19215			40	1.081	.650	1.006
	560	12103	12933	15857	17863	20004								
	600	15464	18368											
	MIL	21730	21423	21050	20752	20422	20018	19618	15302	15102				
	VMAX	633.7	618.0	597.8	580.2	562.8	542.7	522.8	504.6	488.3				
15,000 FEET (-15°C)	360	5060	5456	5853	6252	6650	7076	7506	7934	8363	-40	.950	1.225	.985
	400	5788	6283	6796	7326	7893	8444	9018	9603	10187	-20	.990	1.045	.997
	440	6628	7282	7987	8692	9419	10167	10916	11721	12525	0	1.029	.880	1.007
	480	7601	8504	9411	10375	11345	12363	13402	14540	15686	20	1.066	.725	1.012
	520	8790	9853	11182	12449	13753	15179	16626			40	1.101	.560	1.017
	560	10439	12037	13700	15615	17377								
	600	13757	16316											
	MIL	19016	18716	18293	17966	17679	17484	17239	17113	16958				
	VMAX	628.2	614.3	595.0	577.0	561.4	544.6	526.9	510.0	494.3				
20,000 FEET (-25°C)	360	4515	4841	5168	5498	5851	6206	6568	8917	7254	-40	.969	1.145	.992
	400	5067	5479	5921	6380	6839	7313	7801	8289	8795	-20	1.010	.965	1.003
	440	5728	6257	6885	7481	8104	8727	9389	10068	10758	0	1.048	.810	1.012
	480	6523	7275	8063	8849	9684	10636	11444	12363	13422	20	1.087	.665	1.017
	520	7432	8490	9526	10818	11757	12957	14291			40	1.123	.500	1.023
	560	9114	10570	12099	13741	15506								
	600	12379	14584											
	MIL	16588	16387	16155	15870	15762	15626	15502	15374	15250				
	VMAX	622.4	609.5	593.8	571.5	561.6	548.1	532.6	518.9	501.7				

1561-(12)004

Figure A5-15

LOW ALTITUDE CRUISE
GROSS WEIGHT - 45,000 POUNDS

AIRPLANE CONFIGURATION
INDIVIDUAL DRAG INDEXES
DATE: 15 JUN 1988
DATA BASIS: ESTIMATED

REMARKS
ENGINES: (2) F100-PW-220

TOTAL FUEL FLOW - LB/HR

SEA LEVEL (15°C)

KTAS	DRAG INDEX 0	20	40	60	80	100	120	140	160
360	7888	8520	9154	9814	10476	11138	11801	12508	13251
400	9143	9959	10803	11647	12491	13424	14369	15315	16280
440	10635	11711	12787	13945	15143	16342	17597	18858	20124
480	12229	13691	15138	16708	18275	19861	21464	23081	
520	14198	16088	18000	19992	21993	24008			
560	16505	18914	21423	23988					
600	20118	23459							
MIL	27182	26854	26278	25967	25648	25347	25028	24739	24487
VMAX	638.9	617.6	596.8	575.2	552.7	531.5	511.6	493.8	478.2

ACTUAL OAT DEG. C	TEMP EFFECTS-FACTORS CRUISE	MIL	VMAX
-40	.899	1.520	.975
-20	.937	1.330	.986
0	.974	1.140	.993
20	1.009	.960	1.000
40	1.042	.810	.999

5,000 FEET (5°C)

KTAS	DRAG INDEX 0	20	40	60	80	100	120	140	160
360	6819	7349	7890	8439	8988	9538	10112	10744	11375
400	7841	8539	9243	9947	10699	11510	12321	13135	13878
440	9082	9988	10903	11923	12944	13981	15043	16104	17225
480	10499	11700	12982	14274	15609	16950	18399	19849	21304
520	12106	13707	15340	17006	18799	20624			
560	14139	16226	18409	20747					
600	17681	20798							
MIL	24317	24059	23715	23411	23017	22818	22260	21948	21673
VMAX	637.7	619.1	598.2	580.5	589.2	537.7	518.2	499.6	483.2

ACTUAL OAT DEG. C	TEMP EFFECTS-FACTORS CRUISE	MIL	VMAX
-40	.918	1.400	.976
-20	.954	1.225	.987
0	.991	1.050	.988
20	1.027	.885	1.000
40	1.061	.735	.998

10,000 FEET (-5°C)

KTAS	DRAG INDEX 0	20	40	60	80	100	120	140	160
360	5912	6362	6838	7315	7791	8276	8752	9309	9826
400	6735	7351	7987	8588	9256	9923	10591	11296	12007
440	7778	8562	9384	10231	11079	11975	12879	13803	14763
480	8863	10020	11102	12222	13385	14549	15762	17020	18315
520	10363	11725	13154	14613	16137	17721	19342		
560	12135	12962	15881	17902	20017				
600	15484	18382							
MIL	21733	21428	21049	20752	20421	20018	19613	19297	19098
VMAX	633.8	618.1	597.7	580.1	582.8	542.6	522.5	504.4	487.9

ACTUAL OAT DEG. C	TEMP EFFECTS-FACTORS CRUISE	MIL	VMAX
-40	.932	1.300	.977
-20	.972	1.130	.992
0	1.009	.960	1.001
20	1.048	.800	1.003
40	1.081	.650	1.006

15,000 FEET (-15°C)

KTAS	DRAG INDEX 0	20	40	60	80	100	120	140	160
360	5261	5658	6060	6445	6850	7275	7699	8124	8556
400	5924	6434	6945	7493	8043	8593	9166	9746	10328
440	6744	7402	8103	8803	9532	10274	11026	11828	12625
480	7584	8592	9600	10458	11425	12441	13482	14615	15758
520	8858	10019	11242	12506	13810	15229	16671		
560	10489	12083	13729	15551	17406				
600	13790	16343							
MIL	19014	18717	18290	17963	17676	17489	17254	17106	16952
VMAX	628.1	614.3	594.9	576.9	581.1	544.2	526.5	509.4	493.5

ACTUAL OAT DEG. C	TEMP EFFECTS-FACTORS CRUISE	MIL	VMAX
-40	.950	1.225	.988
-20	.990	1.048	.997
0	1.029	.880	1.007
20	1.066	.735	1.012
40	1.101	.590	1.017

20,000 FEET (-25°C)

KTAS	DRAG INDEX 0	20	40	60	80	100	120	140	160
360	4788	5088	5412	5760	6110	6460	6810	7182	7555
400	5248	5684	6119	6574	7029	7509	7992	8475	8990
440	5878	6452	7036	7636	8253	8876	9529	10203	10611
480	6644	7391	8170	8961	9799	10644	11558	12484	13538
520	7582	8581	9617	10704	11842	13047	14374		
560	9187	10640	12165	13808	15565				
600	12431	14811							
MIL	18584	18383	18149	15869	15758	15623	15495	15368	15241
VMAX	622.1	609.3	583.4	571.3	581.2	547.5	531.7	515.9	500.5

ACTUAL OAT DEG. C	TEMP EFFECTS-FACTORS CRUISE	MIL	VMAX
-40	.989	1.148	.992
-20	1.010	.865	1.003
0	1.049	.810	1.012
20	1.087	.655	1.017
40	1.123	.500	1.023

1561-g1304

Figure A5-16

LOW ALTITUDE CRUISE
GROSS WEIGHT - 50,000 POUNDS

AIRPLANE CONFIGURATION
INDIVIDUAL DRAG INDEXES
DATE: 15 JUN 1988
DATA BASIS: ESTIMATED

REMARKS
ENGINES: (2) F100-PW-220

TOTAL FUEL FLOW – LB/HR

	KTAS	DRAG INDEX									ACTUAL OAT DEG. C	TEMP EFFECTS-FACTORS		
		0	20	40	60	80	100	120	140	160		CRUISE	MIL	VMAX
SEA LEVEL (15°C)	360	8010	8639	9273	9930	10688	11248	11904	12819	13358	-40	.899	1.520	.975
	400	9225	10042	10882	11722	12562	13499	14440	15381	16345	-20	.937	1.330	.986
	440	10695	11767	12838	13998	15192	16385	17838	18894	20158	0	.974	1.140	.997
	480	12373	13724	15237	16739	18304	19885	21483	23094		20	1.009	.960	1.000
	520	14231	16118	18027	20013	22009	24019				40	1.042	.810	.999
	560	16515	18919	21422	23558									
	600	20104	23437											
	MIL	27186	26897	26282	25989	25648	25348	25027	24739	24485				
	VMAX	640.1	617.8	595.8	575.4	552.7	531.4	511.5	493.7	478.1				
6,000 FEET (6°C)	360	6969	7495	8038	8583	9128	9673	10253	10690	11517	-40	.816	1.400	.976
	400	7947	8647	9347	10047	10810	11616	12423	13236	14074	-20	.954	1.225	.987
	440	9168	10069	10991	12007	13022	14068	15115	16172	17292	0	.991	1.050	.998
	480	10659	11761	13038	14328	15657	16998	18441	19885	21335	20	1.027	.885	1.000
	520	12152	13748	15375	17035	18824	20644				40	1.061	.725	.998
	560	14174	16257	18437	20768									
	600	17656	20781											
	MIL	24319	24061	23717	23410	23015	22616	22257	21942	21668				
	VMAX	637.9	619.3	598.3	580.5	559.1	537.6	518.0	499.2	482.9				
10,000 FEET (-5°C)	360	6091	6552	7025	7497	7970	8465	8977	9490	10002	-40	.932	1.300	.977
	400	6883	7493	8104	8733	9396	10069	10724	11430	12137	-20	.972	1.130	.982
	440	7894	8674	9500	10343	11192	12047	12982	13906	14863	0	1.009	.960	1.001
	480	9061	10111	11187	12306	13445	14629	15836	17094	18383	20	1.046	.800	1.003
	520	10426	11785	13211	14669	16186	17758	19363			40	1.081	.650	1.006
	560	12179	14002	15917	17933	20041								
	600	15520	18414											
	MIL	21733	21425	21047	20751	20418	20007	19603	19281	19090				
	VMAX	633.8	618.1	597.6	580.1	562.6	542.2	522.1	503.9	487.3				
15,000 FEET (-15°C)	360	5497	5887	6278	6668	7086	7506	7927	8347	8786	-40	.950	1.225	.985
	400	6106	6611	7128	7674	8230	8768	9343	9918	10493	-20	.990	1.045	.997
	440	6884	7549	8245	8941	9673	10411	11168	11962	12756	0	1.029	.880	1.007
	480	7815	8708	9618	10571	11541	12549	13596	14722	15861	20	1.066	.725	1.012
	520	8950	10113	11331	12593	13900	15313	16750			40	1.101	.560	1.017
	560	10546	12125	13785	15595	17444								
	600	13841	16390											
	MIL	19011	18715	18282	17945	17671	17483	17285	17097	16944				
	VMAX	627.9	614.2	594.5	576.5	560.7	543.8	525.6	508.8	492.5				
20,000 FEET (-26°C)	360	5048	5371	5715	6065	6415	6765	7134	7507	7880	-40	.969	1.145	.992
	400	5489	5900	6350	6800	7261	7740	8218	8707	9223	-20	1.010	.965	1.003
	440	6055	6634	7212	7818	8431	9061	9719	10377	11097	0	1.049	.810	1.012
	480	6793	7636	8317	9105	9948	10796	11703	12648	13693	20	1.087	.655	1.017
	520	7700	8703	9741	10821	11960	13175	14455			40	1.123	.500	1.023
	560	9276	10730	12253	13898	15648								
	600	12488	14660											
	MIL	16578	16378	16140	15868	15751	15616	15485	15354	15228				
	VMAX	621.5	606.9	592.8	571.0	560.8	548.7	530.6	514.5	499.0				

Figure A5-17

LOW ALTITUDE CRUISE
GROSS WEIGHT - 55,000 POUNDS

AIRPLANE CONFIGURATION
INDIVIDUAL DRAG INDEXES
DATE: 15 JUN 1988
DATA BASIS: ESTIMATED

REMARKS
ENGINES: (2) F100-PW-220

TOTAL FUEL FLOW - LB/HR

	KTAS	DRAG INDEX									ACTUAL OAT DEG. C	TEMP EFFECTS-FACTORS		
		0	20	40	60	80	100	120	140	160		CRUISE	MIL	VMAX
SEA LEVEL (15°C)	360	8150	8776	9411	10065	10718	11372	12026	12751	13485	-40	.899	1.520	.975
	400	9335	10153	10989	11824	12668	13504	14540	15476	16441	-20	.937	1.330	.988
	440	10782	11849	12916	14079	15268	16458	17707	18959	20217	0	.974	1.140	.997
	480	12434	13797	15294	16752	18354	19931	21524	23130		20	1.009	.960	1.000
	520	14265	16149	18064	20035	22025	24030				40	1.042	.810	.999
	560	16551	18951	21448	23978									
	600	20091	23416											
	MIL	27189	26700	26285	25968	25648	25345	25025	24735	24481				
	VMAX	640.2	617.9	596.9	575.3	552.8	531.3	511.4	493.5	477.3				
5,000 FEET (5°C)	360	7141	7688	8207	8748	9289	9830	10439	11062	11684	-40	.918	1.400	.976
	400	8084	8780	9476	10172	10949	11761	12652	13385	14199	-20	.954	1.225	.987
	440	9271	10187	11096	12107	13118	14153	15204	16256	17377	0	.991	1.060	.998
	480	10638	11843	13115	14402	15728	17067	18504	19942	21387	20	1.027	.885	1.000
	520	12215	13807	15433	17088	18877	20690				40	1.061	.735	.998
	560	14208	16288	18464	20789									
	600	17676	20796											
	MIL	24321	24060	23716	23409	23012	22611	22249	21936	21669				
	VMAX	636.0	619.2	598.3	580.4	559.0	537.3	517.5	498.8	482.4				
10,000 FEET (-5°C)	360	6304	6771	7239	7707	8176	8684	9192	9700	10207	-40	.932	1.300	.977
	400	7052	7659	8266	8904	9562	10221	10892	11584	12296	-20	.972	1.130	.992
	440	8028	8801	9632	10471	11323	12213	13103	14031	14981	0	1.009	.960	1.001
	480	9151	10213	11284	12404	13538	14720	15921	17178	18461	20	1.048	.800	1.003
	520	10611	11863	13288	14744	16255	17834	15443			40	1.081	.650	1.005
	560	12241	14062	15976	17589	20090								
	600	15558	18446											
	MIL	21731	21424	21044	20747	20409	19998	19630	19280	19079				
	VMAX	633.7	618.0	597.4	579.9	562.2	541.7	521.4	500.0	484.4				
15,000 FEET (-15°C)	360	5763	6152	6541	6948	7357	7788	8206	8634	9076	-40	.950	1.225	.985
	400	6312	6814	7342	7884	8425	9079	9649	10119	10703	-20	.990	1.045	.997
	440	7047	7720	8411	9106	9839	10672	11336	12125	12917	0	1.029	.880	1.007
	480	7950	8838	9751	10699	11670	12672	13728	14848	15983	20	1.066	.725	1.012
	520	9054	10219	11430	12691	14002	15408	16841			40	1.101	.560	1.017
	560	10628	12212	13855	15665	17508								
	600	12906	16462											
	MIL	19006	18707	18273	17936	17665	17474	17274	17063	16933				
	VMAX	627.6	612.8	594.0	576.0	560.1	542.8	524.8	507.3	491.2				
20,000 FEET (-25°C)	360	5368	5711	6061	6410	6760	7127	7500	7872	8245	-40	.969	1.145	.992
	400	5721	6188	6615	7063	7537	8012	8487	8993	9504	-20	1.010	.965	1.003
	440	6288	6841	7420	8028	8636	9276	9929	10699	11315	0	1.049	.810	1.012
	480	6364	7708	8488	9282	10118	10974	11875	12838	13878	20	1.087	.655	1.017
	520	7833	8840	9881	10956	12095	13324	14838			40	1.123	.500	1.023
	560	9379	10650	12350	13599									
	600	12638	14809											
	MIL	16568	16387	16123	15863	15744	15607	15474	15329	15212				
	VMAX	621.0	606.2	591.7	570.8	555.9	545.5	529.1	512.8	497.0				

1581-81804

Figure A5-18

LOW ALTITUDE CRUISE

GROSS WEIGHT - 60,000 POUNDS

AIRPLANE CONFIGURATION
INDIVIDUAL DRAG INDEXES
DATE: 15 JUN 1988
DATA BASIS: ESTIMATED

REMARKS
ENGINES: (2) F100-PW-220

TOTAL FUEL FLOW – LB/HR

	KTAS	0	20	40	60	80	100	120	140	160	ACTUAL OAT DEG. C	CRUISE	MIL	Vmax
		DRAG INDEX										TEMP EFFECTS-FACTORS		
SEA LEVEL (15 °C)	360	8312	8834	9572	10222	10871	11521	12180	12910	13839	-40	.899	1.520	.975
	400	9453	10273	11104	11936	12788	13719	14650	15582	16647	-20	.937	1.330	.986
	440	10870	11933	12996	14164	15348	16535	17782	19028	20283	0	.974	1.140	.997
	480	12495	13869	15352	16845	18405	19876	21568	23188		20	1.009	.960	1.000
	520	14325	16204	18105	20090	22065	24084				40	1.042	.810	.999
	560	16587	18983	21474	23999									
	600	20106	23424											
	MIL	27193	26702	26284	25586	25645	25342	25019	24729	24475				
	VMAX	640.4	618.0	596.9	575.2	552.5	531.2	511.0	493.2	477.5				
5,000 FEET (5 °C)	360	7334	7882	8399	8936	9472	10023	10641	11258	11876	-40	.918	1.400	.976
	400	8237	8925	9620	10912	11106	11902	12699	13513	14341	-20	.954	1.225	.987
	440	9385	10277	11216	12222	13228	14282	15309	16358	17480	0	.991	1.050	.998
	480	10728	11936	13203	14489	15808	17150	18682	20014	21453	20	1.027	.885	1.000
	520	12285	13868	15491	17141	18929	20737				40	1.061	.735	.998
	560	14266	16343	18517	20635									
	600	17700	20812											
	MIL	24321	24058	23715	23407	23005	22602	22241	21924	21647				
	VMAX	638.0	619.1	598.2	580.3	558.9	538.8	512.1	498.1	481.7				
10,000 FEET (-5 °C)	360	6553	7017	7480	7944	8429	8932	9435	9938	10451	-40	.932	1.300	.977
	400	7248	7850	8463	9102	9755	10409	11088	11785	12482	-20	.972	1.130	.992
	440	8172	8947	9781	10614	11470	12355	13239	14172	15116	0	1.009	.960	1.001
	480	9268	10334	11400	12522	13649	14834	16030	17288	18566	20	1.046	.800	1.003
	520	10607	11957	13378	14833	16339	17918	19520			40	1.081	.650	1.005
	560	12304	14123	16035	18045	20140								
	600	15528	18519											
	MIL	21729	21421	21037	20740	20400	19982	19572	19258	19065				
	VMAX	632.6	617.9	597.0	579.5	561.7	540.9	520.5	501.9	486.2				
15,000 FEET (-15 °C)	360	6062	6450	6849	7268	7686	8104	8528	8968	9409	-40	.950	1.225	.985
	400	6544	7047	7584	8120	8657	9219	9784	10343	10949	-20	.990	1.045	.997
	440	7230	7912	8599	9300	10028	10756	11528	12312	13122	0	1.029	.890	1.007
	480	8102	8986	9903	10845	11820	12817	13884	14998	16131	20	1.066	.725	1.012
	520	9176	10344	11550	12811	14129	15529	16958			40	1.101	.560	1.017
	560	10716	12238	13536	15746									
	600	13583	16527											
	MIL	19000	18499	18261	17925	17557	17482	17259	17068	16918				
	VMAX	627.3	612.4	593.3	575.4	559.4	541.7	523.3	505.9	488.4				
20,000 FEET (-25 °C)	360	5760	6109	6458	6806	7177	7548	7920	8292	8683	-40	.969	1.145	.992
	400	6021	6470	6918	7384	7860	8336	8832	9344	9857	-20	1.010	.965	1.003
	440	6507	7076	7663	8258	8874	9521	10168	10854	11567	0	1.049	.810	1.012
	480	7155	7906	8680	9481	10310	11177	12072	13068	14091	20	1.087	.655	1.017
	520	7990	8993	10038	11118	12250	13485	14800			40	1.123	.500	1.023
	560	9496	10938	12455	14109									
	600	12791	14960											
	MIL	16550	16354	16106	15860	15736	15535	15459	15321	15182				
	VMAX	620.0	607.3	590.4	570.5	556.1	544.0	527.4	510.4	494.8				

15E-1-(12)04

Figure A5-19

LOW ALTITUDE CRUISE
GROSS WEIGHT - 65,000 POUNDS
REMARKS

AIRPLANE CONFIGURATION
INDIVIDUAL DRAG INDEXES
DATE: 15 JUN 1988
DATA BASIS: ESTIMATED

ENGINES: (2) F100-PW-220

TOTAL FUEL FLOW - LB/HR

SEA LEVEL (15°C)

KTAS	0	20	40	60	80	100	120	140	180
360	8496	9113	9755	10401	11046	11692	12387	13092	13818
400	9689	10413	11240	12067	12930	13857	14784	15711	16878
440	10585	12043	13101	14276	15454	16642	17883	19125	20377
480	12585	13954	15441	16929	18488	20053	21638	23233	
520	14393	16287	18166	20135	22115	24108			
560	16523	19015	21500	24019					
600	20128	23440							
MIL	27194	26700	26283	25964	25641	25328	25013	24722	24488
VMAX	640.5	617.9	596.8	576.0	552.3	530.7	510.8	492.7	477.0

ACTUAL OAT DEG. C	CRUISE	MIL	VMAX
-40	.889	1.520	.975
-20	.937	1.330	.988
0	.974	1.140	.997
20	1.009	.960	1.000
40	1.042	.810	.999

5,000 FEET (6°C)

KTAS	0	20	40	60	80	100	120	140	180
360	7548	8080	8612	9146	9678	10256	10868	11480	12054
400	8406	9092	9779	10487	11279	12071	12863	13679	14503
440	9522	10410	11361	12362	13383	14397	15439	16488	17608
480	10831	12047	13309	14593	15907	17251	18877	20104	21538
520	12379	13958	15577	17221	19010	20812			
560	14332	16407	18581	20692					
600	17728	20834							
MIL	24320	24066	23713	23401	22996	22593	22227	21910	21633
VMAX	637.9	618.9	598.1	580.0	558.1	536.3	516.2	497.3	480.8

ACTUAL OAT DEG. C	CRUISE	MIL	VMAX
-40	.918	1.400	.978
-20	.954	1.225	.987
0	.991	1.050	.998
20	1.027	.885	1.000
40	1.061	.735	.998

10,000 FEET (-5°C)

KTAS	0	20	40	60	80	100	120	140	180
360	6830	7293	7758	8224	8726	9229	9731	10234	10767
400	7464	8082	8673	9322	9971	10620	11307	12000	12692
440	8344	9128	9957	10786	11648	12527	13407	14348	15285
480	9412	10473	11537	12658	13779	14957	16157	17418	18689
520	10719	12069	13485	14940	16439	18018			
560	12400	14214	16128	18126	20222				
600	15703	18595							
MIL	21726	21416	21029	20733	20385	19964	19548	19251	19048
VMAX	633.5	617.8	596.5	579.0	581.0	540.0	519.3	500.6	483.8

ACTUAL OAT DEG. C	CRUISE	MIL	VMAX
-40	.932	1.300	.977
-20	.972	1.130	.992
0	1.009	.980	1.001
20	1.048	.800	1.003
40	1.081	.650	1.006

15,000 FEET (-15°C)

KTAS	0	20	40	60	80	100	120	140	180
360	6352	6787	7204	7622	8040	8460	8900	9340	9780
400	6802	7322	7856	8390	8934	9456	10067	10828	11241
440	7464	8126	8807	9516	10239	10967	11745	12522	13354
480	8281	9159	10083	11020	11999	12990	14071	15178	16310
520	9316	10489	11694	12950	14276	15669	17094		
560	10825	12406	14048	15850					
600	14106	16653							
MIL	18992	18881	18264	17912	17647	17448	17242	17045	16900
VMAX	626.8	612.8	592.4	574.3	558.5	540.5	521.7	503.8	487.2

ACTUAL OAT DEG. C	CRUISE	MIL	VMAX
-40	.950	1.225	.985
-20	.990	1.045	.997
0	1.029	.880	1.007
20	1.068	.725	1.012
40	1.101	.560	1.017

20,000 FEET (-25°C)

KTAS	0	20	40	60	80	100	120	140	180
360	6230	6578	6933	7304	7674	8045	8426	8827	9229
400	6356	6806	7265	7742	8219	8706	9220	9733	10258
440	6772	7337	7936	8534	9155	9797	10441	11148	11851
480	7368	8124	8894	9704	10627	11406	12293	13307	14334
520	8179	9177	10227	11310	12437	13703	15001		
560	9627	11080	12556	14259					
600	13035	15208							
MIL	16523	16335	16082	15857	15724	15580	15441	15259	15158
VMAX	619.0	606.0	588.9	570.2	558.1	542.3	525.2	507.7	491.4

ACTUAL OAT DEG. C	CRUISE	MIL	VMAX
-40	.969	1.145	.992
-20	1.010	.965	1.003
0	1.049	.810	1.012
20	1.082	.655	1.017
40	1.123	.500	1.023

15E-1-(21)j04

Figure A5-20

LOW ALTITUDE CRUISE
GROSS WEIGHT - 70,000 POUNDS

AIRPLANE CONFIGURATION
INDIVIDUAL DRAG INDEXES
DATE: 15 JUN 1988
DATA BASIS: ESTIMATED

REMARKS
ENGINES: (2) F100-PW-220

TOTAL FUEL FLOW - LB/HR

SEA LEVEL (15°C)

KTAS	DRAG INDEX 0	20	40	60	80	100	120	140	180
360	8696	9315	9968	10597	11238	11880	12573	13293	14013
400	9747	10570	11393	12215	13092	14014	14936	15858	16827
440	11101	12156	13218	14392	15566	16756	17991	19227	20477
480	12675	14049	15531	17014	18572	20132	21713	23303	
520	14462	16330	18226	20190	22166	24153			
560	18650	19079	21558	24071					
600	20161	23456							
MIL	27192	26838	26281	25961	25635	25229	25004	24711	24458
VMAX	640.4	617.8	596.7	574.8	551.8	530.3	510.1	492.1	476.3

ACTUAL OAT DEG. C	CRUISE	MIL	VMAX
-40	.899	1.520	.975
-20	.937	1.330	.988
0	.974	1.140	.997
20	1.009	.950	1.000
40	1.042	.810	.999

6,000 FEET (9°C)

KTAS	0	20	40	60	80	100	120	140	180
360	7791	8320	8849	9378	9907	10513	11122	11730	12339
400	8698	9281	9864	10696	11483	12271	13068	13876	14695
440	9667	10550	11514	12510	13506	14541	15577	16631	17748
480	10948	12171	13428	14712	16020	17369	18790	20212	
520	12477	14049	15668	17307	19098	20895			
560	14398	15471	18544	20949					
600	17811	20916							
MIL	24315	24052	23706	23394	22988	22577	22211	21893	21614
VMAX	637.9	618.8	587.7	579.5	557.6	535.5	515.3	496.3	479.6

ACTUAL OAT DEG. C	CRUISE	MIL	VMAX
-40	.918	1.400	.976
-20	.954	1.225	.987
0	.991	1.050	.998
20	1.027	.885	1.000
40	1.061	.735	.998

10,000 FEET (6°C)

KTAS	0	20	40	60	80	100	120	140	180
360	7133	7596	8059	8552	9064	9556	10068	10678	11117
400	7701	8295	8921	9585	10209	10865	11551	12238	12925
440	8532	9327	10151	10975	11843	12717	13604	14537	15470
480	9589	10625	11692	12808	13931	15115	16300	17565	18830
520	10845	12187	13607	15064	16558	18137			
560	12499	14006	15219	18229	20309				
600	15790	18676							
MIL	21721	21411	21020	20722	20368	19941	19618	19232	19026
VMAX	633.2	617.4	596.0	578.4	560.1	538.9	517.8	499.0	482.0

ACTUAL OAT DEG. C	CRUISE	MIL	VMAX
-40	.932	1.300	.977
-20	.972	1.130	.992
0	1.009	.950	1.001
20	1.048	.800	1.003
40	1.081	.650	1.005

16,000 FEET (15°C)

KTAS	0	20	40	60	80	100	120	140	180
360	6767	7184	7601	8018	8438	8875	9314	9753	10192
400	7092	7627	8161	8695	9257	9819	10381	10981	11597
440	7684	8361	9038	9755	10473	11214	11987	12780	13616
480	8474	9347	10278	11210	12194	13179	14276	15377	16508
520	9488	10647	11853	13103	14440	15828			
560	10945	12525	14173	15968					
600	14228	16779							
MIL	18977	18658	18228	17898	17635	17431	17218	17018	16878
VMAX	625.1	611.8	591.5	574.0	557.4	538.9	519.8	501.4	484.8

ACTUAL OAT DEG. C	CRUISE	MIL	VMAX
-40	.950	1.225	.985
-20	.990	1.045	.997
0	1.029	.890	1.007
20	1.068	.725	1.012
40	1.101	.560	1.017

20,000 FEET (2°C)

KTAS	0	20	40	60	80	100	120	140	180
360	6791	7158	7527	7897	8268	8663	9063	9463	9863
400	6715	7170	7649	8127	8606	9123	9638	10153	10728
440	7065	7650	8251	8858	9601	10146	10828	11536	12255
480	7604	8368	9137	9955	10782	11664	12574	13593	14813
520	8384	9377	10433	11521	12641	13530	15221		
560	9776	11231	12747	14421					
600	13282	15458							
MIL	16512	16314	16061	15853	15712	15562	15420	15270	15094
VMAX	617.8	604.6	587.5	569.8	556.9	540.0	522.5	504.1	486.7

ACTUAL OAT DEG. C	CRUISE	MIL	VMAX
-40	.969	1.145	.992
-20	1.010	.965	1.003
0	1.049	.810	1.012
20	1.087	.655	1.017
40	1.123	.500	1.023

Figure A5-21

LOW ALTITUDE CRUISE
GROSS WEIGHT - 75,000 POUNDS

AIRPLANE CONFIGURATION
INDIVIDUAL DRAG INDEXES
DATE: 15 JUN 1988
DATA BASIS: ESTIMATED

REMARKS
ENGINES: (2) F100-PW-220

TOTAL FUEL FLOW - LB/HR

SEA LEVEL (15°C)

KTAS	DRAG INDEX								
	0	20	40	60	80	100	120	140	160
360	8914	9538	10175	10811	11448	12085	12799	13514	14230
400	9919	10737	11556	12375	13256	14183	15100	16025	16992
440	11244	12293	13366	14535	15704	16894	18125	19356	20604
480	12783	14162	15639	17120	18674	20229	21806	23390	
520	14560	16422	18318	20276	22245	24227			
560	16758	19145	21518	24126					
600	20175	23473							
MIL	27190	26695	28279	25955	25629	25321	24992	24700	24442
VMAX	640.3	617.7	595.6	574.4	551.4	529.7	509.3	491.3	475.5

ACTUAL OAT DEG. C	TEMP EFFECTS-FACTORS		
	CRUISE	MIL	VMAX
-40	.859	1.520	.975
-20	.937	1.330	.986
0	.974	1.140	.997
20	1.009	.960	1.000
40	1.042	.810	.999

5,000 FEET (5°C)

KTAS	DRAG INDEX								
	0	20	40	60	80	100	120	140	160
360	8062	8590	9118	9646	10213	10821	11428	12036	12645
400	8808	9487	10168	10923	11706	12488	13278	14092	14906
440	9837	10716	11696	12687	13684	14715	15747	16808	17918
480	11080	12311	13582	14847	16150	17503	18918	20035	
520	12588	14155	15773	17411	19200	20990			
560	14493	16565	18740	21038					
600	17894	20987							
MIL	24317	24047	23659	23386	22973	22561	22192	21872	21592
VMAX	637.7	618.3	597.3	579.1	558.8	534.5	514.1	495.1	478.3

ACTUAL OAT DEG. C	TEMP EFFECTS-FACTORS		
	CRUISE	MIL	VMAX
-40	.918	1.400	.976
-20	.954	1.225	.987
0	.991	1.050	.998
20	1.027	.885	1.000
40	1.061	.735	.998

10,000 FEET (-5°C)

KTAS	DRAG INDEX								
	0	20	40	60	80	100	120	140	160
360	7463	7926	8407	8908	9410	9912	10421	10960	11498
400	7959	8553	9193	9833	10473	11141	11823	12505	13200
440	8734	9541	10359	11184	12053	12923	13818	14746	15674
480	9751	10801	11873	12984	14111	15289	16479	17738	
520	10985	12339	13743	15201	16689	18270			
560	12815	14418	16330	18340					
600	15907	18792							
MIL	21716	21403	21009	20712	20347	19915	19484	19208	19001
VMAX	632.9	617.0	595.3	577.8	559.1	537.6	516.1	497.0	480.0

ACTUAL OAT DEG. C	TEMP EFFECTS-FACTORS		
	CRUISE	MIL	VMAX
-40	.932	1.300	.977
-20	.972	1.130	.992
0	1.009	.960	1.001
20	1.046	.800	1.003
40	1.081	.650	1.005

15,000 FEET (-15°C)

KTAS	DRAG INDEX								
	0	20	40	60	80	100	120	140	160
360	7230	7648	8062	8482	8920	9358	9798	10235	10721
400	7422	7957	8452	9043	9606	10169	10749	11365	11982
440	7952	8825	9312	10025	10738	11493	12250	13048	13913
480	8685	9587	10493	11431	12410	13411	14508	15606	16732
520	9645	10830	12039	13282	14532	16018			
560	11085	12666	14318	16107					
600	14392	18951							
MIL	18959	18632	18206	17883	17621	17411	17190	16993	16852
VMAX	625.2	610.4	590.4	573.2	556.1	537.1	517.0	498.5	481.4

ACTUAL OAT DEG. C	TEMP EFFECTS-FACTORS		
	CRUISE	MIL	VMAX
-40	.950	1.225	.985
-20	.990	1.045	.997
0	1.029	.880	1.007
20	1.066	.725	1.012
40	1.101	.560	1.017

20,000 FEET (-25°C)

KTAS	DRAG INDEX								
	0	20	40	60	80	100	120	140	160
360	7294	7763	8133	8520	8920	9321	9721	10150	10603
400	7142	7820	8098	8578	9093	9608	10123	10684	11268
440	7371	7976	8580	9212	9860	10518	11229	11940	12718
480	7881	8840	9422	10233	11076	11952	12899	13912	14925
520	8604	9606	10655	11751	12899	14181			
560	9942	11390	12907	14592					
600	13610	15795							
MIL	16488	16286	16040	15848	15697	15540	15388	15236	15007
VMAX	616.2	602.7	586.1	569.4	555.6	537.2	518.8	500.0	481.1

ACTUAL OAT DEG. C	TEMP EFFECTS-FACTORS		
	CRUISE	MIL	VMAX
-40	.969	1.145	.992
-20	1.010	.965	1.003
0	1.049	.810	1.012
20	1.087	.655	1.017
40	1.123	.500	1.023

16E1-(210)04

Figure A5-22

LOW ALTITUDE CRUISE

GROSS WEIGHT - 80,000 POUNDS

AIRPLANE CONFIGURATION
INDIVIDUAL DRAG INDEXES
DATE: 15 JUN 1988
DATA BASIS: ESTIMATED

REMARKS
ENGINES: (2) F100-PW-220

TOTAL FUEL FLOW - LB/HR

	KTAS	DRAG INDEX									ACTUAL OAT DEG. C	TEMP EFFECTS-FACTORS		
		0	20	40	60	80	100	120	140	160		CRUISE	MIL	V MAX
SEA LEVEL (15°C)	360	9154	9785	10418	11051	11684	12344	13065	13768	14476	-40	.899	1.520	.975
	400	10117	10531	11745	12560	13468	14381	15293	16223	17185	-20	.937	1.330	.988
	440	11289	12435	13518	14683	15847	17040	18266	19492	20738	0	.974	1.140	.997
	480	12901	14289	15761	17242	18792	20341	21915	23434		20	1.009	.960	1.000
	520	14661	16517	18412	20365	22330	24306				40	1.042	.810	.999
	560	16827	19211	21678	24181									
	600	20241	23534											
	MIL	27187	26692	26271	25949	25622	25309	24979	24585	24427				
	VMAX	640.1	617.5	596.2	574.0	550.9	528.9	508.5	490.4	474.5				
5,000 FEET (5°C)	360	8354	8882	9410	9941	10547	11154	11761	12368	12593	-40	.918	1.400	.976
	400	9033	9707	10390	11167	11944	12722	13517	14325	15133	-20	.954	1.225	.987
	440	10018	10902	11888	12874	13873	14889	15925	16994	18058	0	.991	1.060	.996
	480	11225	12466	13713	14958	16296	17657	19066	20479		20	1.027	.885	1.000
	520	12717	14278	15896	17541	19323	21108				40	1.061	.735	.998
	560	14590	16662	18839	21131									
	600	17877	21079											
	MIL	24315	24041	23691	23373	22957	22529	22189	21848	21566				
	VMAX	632.5	617.9	596.8	578.5	556.0	533.4	512.8	493.8	476.8				
10,000 FEET (-5°C)	360	7820	8252	8793	9294	9796	10297	10834	11372	11910	-40	.932	1.300	.977
	400	8240	8858	9458	10139	10786	11459	12151	12834	13554	-20	.972	1.130	.982
	440	8968	9782	10597	11431	12255	13160	14065	14988	15912	0	1.009	.960	1.001
	480	9929	10985	12061	13156	14299	15472	16569	17922		20	1.046	.800	1.003
	520	11143	12499	13896	15350	16850	18428				40	1.081	.650	1.005
	560	12747	14543	16457	18470									
	600	15024	18506											
	MIL	21706	21291	20997	20699	20321	19983	19442	19181	18972				
	VMAX	632.5	616.3	594.6	577.0	557.8	538.0	514.0	494.8	477.8				
15,000 FEET (-15°C)	360	7767	8181	8606	9043	9480	9917	10367	10851	11336	-40	.950	1.225	.985
	400	7783	8319	8861	9425	9989	10653	11170	11787	12406	-20	.990	1.045	.997
	440	8242	8915	9620	10332	11067	11823	12589	13416	14281	0	1.029	.880	1.007
	480	8922	9814	10735	11681	12654	13677	14765	15868		20	1.066	.725	1.012
	520	9838	11000	12232	13489	14832	16217				40	1.101	.560	1.013
	560	11238	12817	14481	16264									
	600	14562	17130											
	MIL	18935	18598	18184	17864	17604	17381	17158	16965	16822				
	VMAX	624.2	606.9	585.3	572.2	554.5	534.4	516.1	455.3	477.8				
20,000 FEET (-25°C)	360	8212	8599	8994	9389	9784	10215	10683	11110	11587	-40	.968	1.145	.992
	400	7641	8120	8603	9118	9634	10150	10726	11301	11876	-20	1.010	.965	1.003
	440	7740	8347	8964	9616	10267	10967	11681	12427	13236	0	1.049	.810	1.012
	480	8190	8935	9742	10554	11422	12297	13297	14306		20	1.087	.655	1.017
	520	8865	9866	10910	12014	13193	14449				40	1.123	.500	1.023
	560	10122	11571	13080	14778									
	600	13839	16132											
	MIL	16458	16258	16020	15839	15690	15611	15351	15197	14862				
	VMAX	614.3	600.7	584.7	568.8	554.0	533.7	516.1	496.1	471.6				

Figure A5-23

HIGH ALTITUDE CRUISE
GROSS WEIGHT - 35,000 POUNDS
REMARKS

AIRPLANE CONFIGURATION
INDIVIDUAL DRAG INDEXES
DATE: 15 JUN 1988
DATA BASIS: ESTIMATED

ENGINES: (2)F100-PW-220

TOTAL FUEL FLOW – LB/HR

	KTAS	DRAG INDEX										ACTUAL OAT DEG. C	TEMP EFFECTS-FACTORS		
		0	20	40	60	80	100	120	140	160			CRUISE	MIL	VMAX
26,000 FEET (-36°C)	360	3832	4102	4371	4651	4953	5245	5540	5850	6160		-80	.900	1.480	.959
	400	4274	4626	5008	5389	5776	6179	6583	6998	7429		-60	.945	1.250	.978
	440	4816	5210	5603	6318	6839	7376	7929	8498	9111		-40	.988	1.005	.996
	480	5486	6120	6787	7481	8162	8895	9664	10504	11375		-20	1.030	.880	1.007
	520	6331	7196	8098	9036	10016	11095	12228				-0	1.070	.720	1.018
	560	7938	9269	10671	12193										
	600	11874	13496												
	MIL	14698	14548	14349	14033	13843	13619	13411	13182	12953					
	VMAX	617.9	605.4	591.2	570.1	559.2	548.3	532.8	518.9	501.0					
30,000 FEET (-44°C)	360	3476	3713	3952	4192	4435	4688	4942	5195	5462		-80	.919	1.025	.936
	400	3778	4089	4399	4719	5047	5374	5717	6068	6415		-60	.966	1.010	.978
	440	4195	4602	5024	5451	5890	6338	6807	7309	7823		-40	1.010	.955	1.001
	480	4718	5260	5811	6385	6979	7616	8293	8993	9749		-20	1.052	.785	1.006
	520	5438	6169	6943	7756	8609	9541	10564				-0	1.043	.810	1.011
	560	6577	8170	9434											
	600	10952	12626												
	MIL	12731	12638	12513	12043	12025	11692	11387	11045	10689					
	VMAX	612.3	600.0	588.3	556.6	555.8	541.9	529.1	512.8	494.9					
36,000 FEET (-54°C)	360	3293	3491	3698	3906	4114	4333	4557	4782	5014		-80	.940	.930	.943
	400	3444	3704	3972	4240	4519	4803	5089	5409	5729		-60	.987	.980	.988
	440	3720	4067	4414	4724	5135	5533	5939	6377	6825		-40	1.032	.915	1.010
	480	4112	4583	5034	5622	6040	6594	7170	7794			-20	1.075	.740	1.018
	520	4707	5353	6023	6722	7493	8352					-0	1.117	.570	1.023
	560	6347	7342	8546											
	600	10293													
	MIL	10560	10252	10003	9352	9304	9023	8761	8421	8074					
	VMAX	603.3	588.1	572.9	543.1	540.7	528.9	513.1	492.9	472.3					
40,000 FEET (-57°C)	360	3484	3664	3844	4030	4234	4439	4644	4862	5082		-80	.944	.915	.945
	400	2364	3587	3818	4046	4304	4564	4831	5115	5400		-60	.992	.985	.992
	440	3444	3730	4021	4332	4660	5008	5272	5746			-40	1.037	.930	1.019
	480	3684	4056	4442	4849	5288	5748	6240				-20	1.081	.765	1.033
	520	4119	4649	5198	5763	6489						-0	1.122	.600	1.048
	560	5677	6538	7585											
	600														
	MIL	8186	7991	7714	7276	7179	6918	6586	6162	5852					
	VMAX	591.1	577.1	561.2	542.8	531.1	515.4	490.7	458.9	426.4					
46,000 FEET (-57°C)	360	4911	5080	5250	5420	5589						-80	.944	.915	.946
	400	3696	3812	4139	4366	4601						-60	.992	.985	.993
	440	3414	3685	3960	4258	4560						-40	1.037	.930	1.018
	480	3436	3770	4119	4485	4889						-20	1.081	.765	1.027
	520	3768	4203	4674	5218							-0	1.122	.600	1.037
	560	5311	6065												
	600														
	MIL	6242	6058	5888	5683	5420	2276	2276	2276	2276					
	VMAX	573.6	560.1	547.7	531.3	508.3									

1581-02A504

Figure A5-24

HIGH ALTITUDE CRUISE
GROSS WEIGHT - 40,000 POUNDS

AIRPLANE CONFIGURATION
INDIVIDUAL DRAG INDEXES
DATE: 15 JUN 1988
DATA BASIS: ESTIMATED

REMARKS
ENGINES: (2) F100-PW-220

TOTAL FUEL FLOW - LB/HR

26,000 FEET (-36°C)

KTAS	DRAG INDEX 0	20	40	60	80	100	120	140	160
360	4091	4359	4848	4936	5227	5518	5826	6134	6442
400	4472	4838	5215	5593	5986	6385	6784	7206	7635
440	4984	5473	5965	6481	6998	7529	8066	8667	9273
480	5618	6254	6915	7591	8286	9025	9788	10638	11504
520	6437	7298	8200	9137	10111	11193	12325		
560	8030	9362	10763	12286					
600	11737	13559							
MIL	14680	14542	14343	14032	13831	13609	13397	13163	12929
VMAX	617.3	604.9	590.8	570.1	558.5	546.7	531.8	615.6	499.3

ACTUAL OAT DEG. C	CRUISE	MIL	VMAX
-80	.900	1.480	.959
-60	.945	1.250	.978
-40	.988	1.035	.996
-20	1.030	.880	1.007
-0	1.070	.720	1.018

30,000 FEET (-44°C)

KTAS	DRAG INDEX 0	20	40	60	80	100	120	140	160
360	3815	4064	4294	4542	4796	5049	5303	5577	5851
400	4048	4358	4671	4997	5323	5660	6007	6354	6732
440	4408	4816	5228	5661	6104	6546	7035	7531	8060
480	4884	5430	5983	6552	7158	7789	8476	9182	9534
520	5574	6308	7081	7890	8744	9652	10710		
560	7102	8293	9555						
600	11168								
MIL	12722	12527	12495	12041	11995	11670	11360	10984	10581
VMAX	611.2	598.7	585.1	556.5	554.8	541.0	527.8	509.9	490.7

ACTUAL OAT DEG. C	CRUISE	MIL	VMAX
-80	.919	1.025	.536
-60	.966	1.010	.978
-40	1.010	.555	1.001
-20	1.052	.785	1.006
-0	1.043	.610	1.011

36,000 FEET (-54°C)

KTAS	DRAG INDEX 0	20	40	60	80	100	120	140	160
360	3752	3999	4209	4433	4657	4881	5126	5379	5633
400	3781	4061	4321	4608	4894	5194	5518	5839	6182
440	3898	4345	4701	5061	5449	5854	6281	6728	7184
480	4334	4789	5258	5758	6280	6840	7434	8061	
520	4880	5523	6193	6894	7691	8644			
560	6815	7621	8882						
600									
MIL	10498	10235	9927	3348	5258	8566	8662	8239	7895
VMAX	599.5	584.9	569.4	543.0	538.5	524.1	507.2	486.5	461.6

ACTUAL OAT DEG. C	CRUISE	MIL	VMAX
-80	.540	.930	.543
-60	.587	.580	.588
-40	1.032	.515	1.010
-20	1.076	.740	1.016
-0	1.117	.570	1.023

40,000 FEET (-57°C)

KTAS	DRAG INDEX 0	20	40	60	80	100	120	140	160
360	4506	4709	4925	5142	5362	5576	5754		
400	2921	4164	4425	4687	4988	5254	5543		
440	3797	4092	4417	4750	5113	5483	5868		
480	2968	4352	4766	5203	5659	6159			
520	4375	4908	5464	6094	6775				
560	6070	6989							
600									
MIL	9089	7884	7501	7273	7080	6737	6129	2806	2806
VMAX	584.1	570.4	555.2	542.7	525.2	501.9	455.5		

ACTUAL OAT DEG. C	CRUISE	MIL	VMAX
-80	.544	.315	.545
-60	.592	.385	.592
-40	1.037	.530	1.019
-20	1.081	.765	1.033
-0	1.122	.600	1.048

40,000 FEET (-57°C)

KTAS	DRAG INDEX 0	20	40	60	80	100	120	140	160
360	6965	7131	7297	7464					
400	5018	5249	5480	5710					
440	4127	4429	4748	5061					
480	3882	4250	4638	5061					
520	4151	4824	5182						
560	5953								
600									
MIL	6067	5932	5751	5258	2276	2276	2276	2276	2276
VMAX	572.3	560.9	538.8	506.1					

ACTUAL OAT DEG. C	CRUISE	MIL	VMAX
-80	.544	.915	.546
-60	.592	.585	.593
-40	1.037	.530	1.016
-20	1.081	.765	1.027
-0	1.122	.600	1.037

1561-(12)04

Figure A5-25

HIGH ALTITUDE CRUISE
GROSS WEIGHT - 45,000 POUNDS

AIRPLANE CONFIGURATION

INDIVIDUAL DRAG INDEXES
DATE: 15 JUN 1988
DATA BASIS: ESTIMATED

REMARKS

ENGINES: (2) F100-PW-220

TOTAL FUEL FLOW - LB/HR

26,000 FEET (-36°C)

KTAS	DRAG INDEX 0	20	40	60	80	100	120	140	160
360	4392	4582	4972	5282	5565	5863	6171	6479	6797
400	4713	5086	5458	5839	6233	6628	7034	7457	7880
440	5183	5668	6165	6676	7193	7726	8276	8873	9474
480	5727	6415	7071	7748	8439	9187	9950	10806	11673
520	6587	7421	8325	9264	10244	11320	12453		
560	8136	9468	10867	12389					
600	11859	13687							
MIL	14681	14533	14330	14031	13818	13595	13376	13137	12895
VMAX	618.5	604.1	589.9	570.0	557.7	544.9	530.3	513.8	497.0

ACTUAL OAT DEG. C	CRUISE	MIL	VMAX
-80	.900	1.480	.955
-60	.945	1.250	.978
-40	.988	1.035	.996
-20	1.030	.880	1.007
-0	1.070	.720	1.016

30,000 FEET (-44°C)

KTAS	DRAG INDEX 0	20	40	60	80	100	120	140	160
360	4244	4489	4742	4995	5247	5517	5790	6063	6344
400	4358	4673	5000	5327	5667	6015	6363	6744	7135
440	4656	5071	5488	5918	6356	6816	7306	7802	8345
480	5093	5633	6189	6752	7374	8014	8701	9418	10162
520	5738	6477	7253	8067	8913	9882	10896		
560	7240	8429	9709						
600	11401								
MIL	12711	12814	12462	12040	11558	11625	11318	10854	10464
VMAX	609.8	596.9	582.9	556.4	553.0	539.2	525.8	505.6	485.1

ACTUAL OAT DEG. C	CRUISE	MIL	VMAX
-80	.919	1.025	.536
-60	.966	1.010	.978
-40	1.010	.955	1.001
-20	1.052	.785	1.006
-0	1.043	.810	1.011

35,000 FEET (-54°C)

KTAS	DRAG INDEX 0	20	40	60	80	100	120	140	160
360	4402	4624	4848	5084	5335	5586	5839	6106	6378
400	4208	4450	4778	5065	5389	5713	6047	6401	6754
440	4300	4658	5023	5411	5821	8250	6702	7163	
480	4582	5064	5533	6038	6579	7138	7747		
520	5092	5738	6407	7106	7937				
560	6911	7959	9242						
600									
MIL	10421	10162	9932	9348	9201	8881	8523	9045	7560
VMAX	595.3	580.8	565.1	542.8	536.7	519.9	499.0	470.6	436.7

ACTUAL OAT DEG. C	CRUISE	MIL	VMAX
-80	.940	.930	.943
-60	.987	.980	.988
-40	1.002	.915	1.010
-20	1.025	.740	1.016
-0	1.117	.570	1.023

40,000 FEET (-57°C)

KTAS	DRAG INDEX 0	20	40	60	80	100	120	140	160
360	6274	6488	6702	6916	7129				
400	4685	4944	5230	5517	6812				
440	4250	4597	4948	5323	5706				
480	4277	4697	5137	5597	6105				
520	4588	5237	5827	6509					
560	5634	7578							
600									
MIL	7972	7726	7488	7223	6877	2806	2806	2806	2806
VMAX	575.8	561.9	549.1	533.8	512.4				

ACTUAL OAT DEG. C	CRUISE	MIL	VMAX
-80	.944	.915	.945
-60	.992	.985	.992
-40	1.037	.830	1.019
-20	1.081	.765	1.033
-0	1.122	.600	1.045

45,000 FEET (-57°C)

KTAS	DRAG INDEX 0	20	40	60	80	100	120	140	160
360	9502	9661							
400	8952	7181							
440	5241	5560							
480	4548	4948							
520	4854	5225							
560									
600									
MIL	5953	5817	2276	2276	2276	2276	2276	2276	2276
VMAX	582.4	542.2							

ACTUAL OAT DEG. C	CRUISE	MIL	VMAX
-80	.944	.915	.946
-60	.992	.985	.993
-40	1.037	.830	1.016
-20	1.081	.765	1.027
-0	1.122	.600	1.037

15E-1-81404

Figure A5-26

HIGH ALTITUDE CRUISE
GROSS WEIGHT - 50,000 POUNDS

AIRPLANE CONFIGURATION
INDIVIDUAL DRAG INDEXES
DATE: 15 JUN 1988
DATA BASIS: ESTIMATED

REMARKS
ENGINES: (2) F100-PW-220

TOTAL FUEL FLOW – LB/HR

	KTAS	DRAG INDEX									ACTUAL OAT DEG. C	TEMP EFFECTS–FACTORS		
		0	20	40	60	80	100	120	140	160		CRUISE	MIL	V_{MAX}
28,000 FEET (-36°C)	360	4772	5061	5350	5648	5955	6282	6589	6894	7228	-80	.900	1.480	.959
	400	5005	5379	5758	6152	6547	6948	7372	7796	8230	-60	.945	1.250	.978
	440	5415	5894	6399	6904	7430	7987	8523	9118	9713	-40	.988	1.035	.996
	480	5962	6604	7255	7937	8630	9361	10163	11014	11878	-20	1.030	.880	1.007
	520	6721	7573	8478	9421	10411	11480	12517			-0	1.070	.720	1.016
	560	8247	9574	10975	12499									
	600	12019	13858											
	MIL	14887	14520	14312	14031	13803	13578	13348	13104	12850				
	V_{MAX}	616.3	603.0	588.7	570.0	556.9	543.9	528.3	511.5	493.9				
30,000 FEET (-44°C)	360	4806	5067	5311	5583	5858	6128	6415	6722	7028	-80	.915	1.025	.935
	400	4709	5038	5388	5712	6062	6413	6802	7196	7592	-60	.968	1.010	.978
	440	4950	5371	5796	6238	6687	7180	7673	8212	8753	-40	1.010	.955	1.001
	480	5336	5874	6431	7012	7630	8288	8968	9700		-20	1.052	.785	1.006
	520	5926	6576	7486	8286	9115	10110	11121			-0	1.043	.610	1.011
	560	7388	8580	9684										
	600	11700												
	MIL	12894	12597	12423	12038	11916	11575	11223	10777	10296				
	V_{MAX}	607.5	584.6	580.2	556.3	551.3	537.1	521.3	500.0	477.1				
36,000 FEET (-54°C)	360	5433	5683	5942	6210	6479	6752	7018	7288		-80	.940	.530	.943
	400	4773	5061	5388	5711	6047	6402	6756	7115		-60	.987	.580	.988
	440	4651	5021	5413	5828	6254	6721	7189			-40	1.032	.915	1.010
	480	4876	5346	5860	6393	6954	7562	8181			-20	1.075	.740	1.018
	520	5344	5953	6656	7403	8235					-0	1.117	.570	1.023
	560	7283	8379	9684										
	600													
	MIL	10326	10066	9728	9343	9122	8779	8219	7384	4196				
	V_{MAX}	585.9	575.6	560.4	542.7	531.8	514.2	480.9	423.5					
40,000 FEET (-57°C)	360	6298	6506	6715	6925						-80	.944	.915	.945
	400	5509	6204	6499	6754						-60	.992	.585	.992
	440	4961	5340	5727	6126						-40	1.037	.530	1.019
	480	4712	5162	5631	6151						-20	1.081	.765	1.033
	520	5060	5636	6321							-0	1.122	.600	1.048
	560	7261												
	600													
	MIL	7809	7580	7387	6955	2806	2806	2806	2806	2806				
	V_{MAX}	566.4	554.0	543.5	517.8									
46,000 FEET (-57°C)	360	12227									-80	.944	.915	.945
	400	9153									-60	.992	.585	.992
	440	6892									-40	1.037	.530	1.015
	480	5601									-20	1.081	.765	1.027
	520	5404									-0	1.122	.600	1.037
	560													
	600													
	MIL	5810	2276	2276	2276	2276	2276	2276	2276	2276				
	V_{MAX}	541.6												

15E1-P2804

Figure A5-27

HIGH ALTITUDE CRUISE
GROSS WEIGHT - 55,000 POUNDS
REMARKS

AIRPLANE CONFIGURATION
INDIVIDUAL DRAG INDEXES
DATE: 15 JUN 1988
DATA BASIS: ESTIMATED

ENGINES: (2) F100-PW-220

TOTAL FUEL FLOW – LB/HR

ALT	KTAS	DRAG INDEX 0	20	40	60	80	100	120	140	160	ACTUAL OAT DEG C	CRUISE	MIL	V_MAX
28,000 FEET (-36°C)	360	5234	5524	5829	6135	6441	6754	7088	7417	7749	-80	.500	1.480	.953
	400	5334	5709	6106	6503	6902	7327	7752	8183	8658	-60	.545	1.250	.978
	440	5679	6168	6669	7175	7707	8239	8818	9407	10028	-40	.588	1.035	.996
	480	6176	6821	7475	8154	8881	9606	10411	11255	12121	-20	1.030	.880	1.007
	520	6903	7781	8680	9607	10611	11877	12815			-0	1.070	.720	1.018
	560	8390	9715	11119	12647									
	600	12243	14100											
	MIL	14650	14602	14288	14030	13782	13555	13306	13057	12780				
	VMAX	613.9	601.5	587.1	569.9	555.7	542.6	525.7	508.2	488.7				
30,000 FEET (-44°C)	360	5488	5735	6004	6274	6576	6879	7183	7493	7818	-80	.919	1.025	.936
	400	5175	5507	5859	6210	6576	6970	7385	7778	8206	-60	.966	1.010	.978
	440	5271	5697	6141	6585	7060	7577	8111	8657	9217	-40	1.010	.965	1.001
	480	5810	6158	6710	7318	7938	8613	9310	10040		-20	1.052	.785	1.008
	520	6155	6904	7688	8508	9390	10377				-0	1.043	.810	1.011
	560	7561	8758	10088										
	600	12082												
	MIL	12872	12676	12379	12035	11887	11507	11096	10695	10023				
	VMAX	604.5	591.8	577.2	558.2	549.2	534.2	516.2	491.4	481.8				
36,000 FEET (-54°C)	360	7105	7370	7635	7899	8165	8430				-80	.940	.930	.943
	400	5398	5723	6058	6412	6769	7137				-60	.987	.980	.988
	440	5096	5502	5921	6371	6834	7311				-40	1.032	.915	1.010
	480	5175	5681	6206	6775	7374	8002				-20	1.075	.740	1.016
	520	5638	6256	6589	7790	8628					-0	1.117	.570	1.023
	560	7743	8902											
	600													
	MIL	10208	9924	9615	9338	8964	8450	4196	4196	4196				
	VMAX	583.4	569.2	555.3	542.4	524.0	494.8							
40,000 FEET (-57°C)	360	10646	10653	11069							-80	.944	.918	.945
	400	7799	8088	8377							-60	.992	.986	.992
	440	5954	8350	8750							-40	1.037	.930	1.019
	480	5303	5796	6324							-20	1.081	.785	1.033
	520	5515	6188	6903							-0	1.122	.600	1.045
	560													
	600													
	MIL	7648	7454	7045	2806	2806	2806	2806	2806	2806				
	VMAX	557.7	547.2	523.1										

Figure A5-28

HIGH ALTITUDE CRUISE
GROSS WEIGHT - 60,000 POUNDS

AIRPLANE CONFIGURATION
INDIVIDUAL DRAG INDEXES
DATE: 15 JUN 1988
DATA BASIS: ESTIMATED

REMARKS
ENGINES: (2) F100-PW-220

TOTAL FUEL FLOW - LB/HR

	KTAS	DRAG INDEX										ACTUAL OAT DEG. C	TEMP EFFECTS-FACTORS		
		0	20	40	60	80	100	120	140	160			CRUISE	MIL	V_MAX
26,000 FEET (-36 °C)	360	5813	6118	6423	6733	7083	7394	7724	8071	8443		-80	.900	1.480	.959
	400	5688	6084	6482	6881	7308	7726	8167	8644	9121		-60	.945	1.250	.978
	440	5972	6477	6982	7511	8047	8609	9202	9805	10466		-40	.988	1.035	.996
	480	6426	7065	7728	8399	9125	9863	10696	11536	12400		-20	1.030	.880	1.007
	520	7107	7972	8883	9817	10838	11913	13042				-0	1.070	.720	1.018
	560	8540	9865	11273	12807										
	600	12491													
	MIL	14829	14476	14258	14016	13759	13529	13257	12987	12715					
	VMAX	612.1	599.8	585.0	569.1	554.3	541.0	522.1	503.4	484.5					
30,000 FEET (-44 °C)	360	6480	6781	7082	7383	7705	8029	8352	8676	9000		-80	.919	1.025	.936
	400	5748	6097	6450	6845	7240	7643	8072	8501	8938		-60	.966	1.010	.978
	440	5625	6072	6520	7012	7514	8047	8587	9180			-40	1.010	.955	1.001
	480	5901	6462	7049	7670	8336	9018	9758				-20	1.052	.785	1.006
	520	6410	7162	7944	8774	9694	10679					-0	1.043	.610	1.011
	560	7764	8962	10323											
	600	12533													
	MIL	12844	12548	12332	12033	11804	11418	10919	10203	9523					
	VMAX	600.8	588.5	574.1	556.1	548.6	530.5	506.8	472.7	431.2					
36,000 FEET (-54 °C)	360	8581	9244	9508	9771	10034						-80	.940	.930	.943
	400	6489	6845	7215	7577	7943						-60	.987	.980	.988
	440	5689	6118	6583	7063	7543						-40	1.032	.915	1.010
	480	5551	6079	6648	7241	7877						-20	1.075	.740	1.018
	520	5871	6658	7408	8253							-0	1.117	.570	1.023
	560	8298	9477												
	600														
	MIL	10075	9785	9497	9174	8712	4198	4198	4198	4198					
	VMAX	578.0	563.0	550.0	534.4	510.2									
40,000 FEET (-57 °C)	360	13440	13643									-80	.944	.915	.945
	400	9811	10095									-60	.992	.985	.992
	440	7285	7891									-40	1.037	.930	1.019
	480	6133	6689									-20	1.081	.765	1.033
	520	6142	6869									-0	1.122	.600	1.048
	560														
	600														
	MIL	7504	7141	2806	2806	2806	2806	2806	2806	2806					
	VMAX	548.9	528.9												

15E-1-(12E)04

Figure A5-29

HIGH ALTITUDE CRUISE
GROSS WEIGHT - 65,000 POUNDS

AIRPLANE CONFIGURATION
INDIVIDUAL DRAG INDEXES
DATE: 15 JUN 1988
DATA BASIS: ESTIMATED

REMARKS
ENGINES: (2) F100-PW-220

TOTAL FUEL FLOW - LB/HR

28,000 FEET (-36°C)

KTAS	DRAG INDEX									ACTUAL OAT DEG. C	TEMP EFFECTS-FACTORS		
	0	20	40	60	80	100	120	140	160		CRUISE	MIL	V_{MAX}
360	6437	6744	7071	7397	7723	8068	8434	8802	9170	-80	.900	1.480	.958
400	6158	6557	6962	7389	7815	8257	8735	9212	9705	-60	.948	1.250	.978
440	6299	6807	7329	7868	8415	9012	9608	10261	10928	-40	.988	1.035	.996
480	6703	7340	8007	8688	9420	10188	11018	11860		-20	1.030	.880	1.007
520	7333	8206	9112	10053	11092	12177				-0	1.070	.720	1.018
560	8685	10009	11420	12560									
600	12793												
MIL	14603	14440	14217	13987	13731	13490	13193	12903	12607				
VMAX	610.0	597.4	582.3	567.5	552.7	538.3	517.7	497.6	477.4				

30,000 FEET (-44°C)

KTAS	DRAG INDEX									ACTUAL OAT DEG. C	TEMP EFFECTS-FACTORS		
	0	20	40	60	80	100	120	140	160		CRUISE	MIL	V_{MAX}
360	9064	8360	8698	9016	9334	9651	9989			-80	.919	1.025	.906
400	6361	6738	7137	7536	7967	8400	8834			-60	.966	1.010	.978
440	6079	6530	7028	7532	8071	8625	9193			-40	1.010	.955	1.001
480	6207	6774	7402	8049	8739	9484	10212			-20	1.062	.785	1.006
520	6680	7445	8240	9072	10040	11030				-0	1.043	.610	1.011
560	8006	9207	10606										
600													
MIL	12813	12482	12279	12029	11716	11306	10538	5308	5308				
VMAX	596.8	584.2	570.5	556.0	542.9	525.2	488.5						

36,000 FEET (-54°C)

KTAS	DRAG INDEX									ACTUAL OAT DEG. C	TEMP EFFECTS-FACTORS		
	0	20	40	60	80	100	120	140	160		CRUISE	MIL	V_{MAX}
360	11115	11374	11633	11893						-80	.540	.930	.943
400	8018	8377	8738	9095						-60	.987	.980	.988
440	6446	6917	7408	7902						-40	1.032	.915	1.010
480	6034	6607	7205	7849						-20	1.075	.740	1.018
520	6379	7094	7942	8809						-0	1.117	.570	1.023
560	8904												
600													
MIL	9910	9652	9381	8885	4196	4196	4196	4196	4196				
VMAX	568.6	557.0	544.5	520.2									

40,000 FEET (-57°C)

KTAS	DRAG INDEX									ACTUAL OAT DEG. C	TEMP EFFECTS-FACTORS		
	0	20	40	60	80	100	120	140	160		CRUISE	MIL	V_{MAX}
360	16049									-80	.544	.915	.545
400	12140									-60	.992	.985	.992
440	9157									-40	1.037	.930	1.019
480	7333									-20	1.081	.765	1.033
520	6945									-0	1.122	.600	1.048
560													
600													
MIL	7128	2806	2806	2806	2806	2806	2806	2806	2806				
VMAX	528.1												

15E1-QO4804

Figure A5-30

HIGH ALTITUDE CRUISE
GROSS WEIGHT - 70,000 POUNDS

AIRPLANE CONFIGURATION
INDIVIDUAL DRAG INDEXES
DATE: 15 JUN 1988
DATA BASIS: ESTIMATED

REMARKS
ENGINES: (2) F100-PW-220

TOTAL FUEL FLOW - LB/HR

	KTAS	DRAG INDEX									ACTUAL OAT DEG. C	TEMP EFFECTS-FACTORS		
		0	20	40	60	80	100	120	140	150		CRUISE	MIL	V_{MAX}
26,000 FEET (-36°C)	360	7298	7723	8065	8432	8799	9187	9549	9947	10345	-80	.900	1.480	.959
	400	6698	7112	7540	7987	8428	8904	9382	9882	10418	-60	.945	1.250	.978
	440	6661	7178	7721	8264	8857	9458	10099	10759	11442	-40	.988	1.035	.996
	480	7008	7687	8340	9060	9798	10622	11459	12322		-20	1.000	.880	1.007
	520	7582	8463	9377	10334	11373	12471				-0	1.070	.720	1.016
	560	8867	10191	11608	13156									
	600	12169												
	MIL	14675	14400	14181	13954	13690	13422	13116	12777	12365				
	VMAX	607.6	594.7	579.9	565.6	550.4	533.5	512.3	488.8	482.2				
30,000 FEET (-44°C)	360	9917	10233	10550	10867	11185	11502				-80	.918	1.025	.935
	400	7293	7700	8128	8554	8996	9430				-60	.968	1.010	.978
	440	6594	7101	7609	8159	8718	9291				-40	1.010	.955	1.001
	480	6657	7168	7803	8454	9208	9964				-20	1.032	.785	1.006
	520	6980	7770	8598	9496	10486					-0	1.043	.810	1.011
	560	8292	9489	10947										
	600													
	MIL	12578	12411	12221	12025	11553	10947	5308	5308	5308				
	VMAX	592.1	579.4	568.6	555.8	536.2	506.1							
36,000 FEET (-64°C)	360	13502	13752	14007							-80	.940	.330	.343
	400	9907	10264	10621							-60	.987	.980	.588
	440	7521	8015	8508							-40	1.032	.915	1.010
	480	6655	7288	7918							-20	1.078	.740	1.016
	520	6828	7636	8513							-0	1.117	.540	1.023
	560	9645												
	600													
	MIL	9769	9506	8114	4196	4196	4196	4196	4196	4196				
	VMAX	582.3	550.4	531.4										

Figure A5-31

HIGH ALTITUDE CRUISE
GROSS WEIGHT - 75,000 POUNDS
REMARKS

AIRPLANE CONFIGURATION
INDIVIDUAL DRAG INDEXES
DATE: 15 JUN 1988
DATA BASIS: ESTIMATED

ENGINES: (2) F100-PW-220

TOTAL FUEL FLOW - LB/HR

26,000 FEET (-36°C)

KTAS	DRAG INDEX 0	20	40	60	80	100	120	140	160	ACTUAL OAT DEG. C	TEMP EFFECTS-FACTORS CRUISE	MIL	VMAX
360	8684	9042	9405	9794	10182	10571	10972	11348	11736	-80	.900	1.480	.959
400	7338	7767	8203	8683	9162	9652	10178	10705	11233	-60	.945	1.250	.978
440	7072	7616	8161	8748	9350	9980	10653	11328		-40	.988	1.035	.996
480	7301	7981	8673	9419	10200	11044	11902			-20	1.030	.880	1.007
520	7857	8731	9656	10637	11674	12781				-0	1.070	.720	1.018
560	9075	10400	11824	13383									
600	13588												
MIL	14542	14358	14148	13918	13640	13343	12985	12558	11571				
VMAX	604.8	581.7	577.5	563.4	547.5	528.0	503.2	474.4	437.4				

30,000 FEET (-44°C)

KTAS	DRAG INDEX 0	20	40	60	80	100	120	140	160	ACTUAL OAT DEG. C	CRUISE	MIL	VMAX
360	11941	12253	12568	12878	13190					-80	.919	1.025	.936
400	8519	8952	9391	9829	10268					-60	.966	1.010	.978
440	7295	7818	8380	8944	9535					-40	1.010	.955	1.001
480	6583	7624	8307	9011	9774					-20	1.052	.785	1.006
520	7327	8135	8988	9967	10981					-0	1.043	.610	1.011
560	8822	9887	11388										
600													
MIL	12521	12344	12166	11850	11351	5308	5308	5308	5308				
VMAX	586.8	574.9	562.9	548.5	527.4								

36,000 FEET (-54°C)

KTAS	DRAG INDEX 0	20	40	60	80	100	120	140	160	ACTUAL OAT DEG. C	CRUISE	MIL	VMAX
360	16325	16572								-80	.940	.930	.943
400	11882	12234								-60	.987	.980	.988
440	8841	9336								-40	1.032	.915	1.010
480	7459	8121								-20	1.075	.740	1.016
520	7425	8310								-0	1.117	.570	1.023
560													
600													
MIL	9629	9357	4198	4198	4198	4198	4198	4198	4198				
VMAX	555.9	543.4											

15E1-20704

Figure A5-32

HIGH ALTITUDE CRUISE
GROSS WEIGHT - 80,000 POUNDS

AIRPLANE CONFIGURATION
INDIVIDUAL DRAG INDEXES
DATE: 15 JUN 1988
DATA BASIS: ESTIMATED

REMARKS
ENGINES: (2) F100-PW-220

TOTAL FUEL FLOW - LB/HR

	KTAS	DRAG INDEX									ACTUAL OAT DEG C	TEMP EFFECTS-FACTORS		
		0	20	40	60	80	100	120	140	160		CRUISE	MIL	V$_{MAX}$
26,000 FEET (-36°C)	360	10510	10913	11284	11671	12057	12444	12831	13217		-80	.900	1.480	.959
	400	7975	8432	8908	9384	9892	10415	10938	11470		-60	.945	1.250	.978
	440	7568	8114	8699	9306	9937	10614	11292	11985		-40	.988	1.035	.998
	480	7645	8330	9062	9814	10654	11507	12386			-20	1.030	.880	1.007
	520	8145	9041	9975	10998	12067					-0	1.070	.720	1.016
	560	9317	10647	12083	13654									
	600	14135												
	MIL	14489	14306	14113	13868	13579	13224	12781	12016	7173				
	VMAX	801.4	588.3	575.2	560.6	543.8	519.8	489.1	440.3					
30,000 FEET (-44°C)	360	14182	14489	14796	15103	15410					-80	.919	1.025	.936
	400	10267	10698	11128	11559	11990					-60	.966	1.010	.976
	440	8033	8600	9180	9777	10368					-40	1.010	.955	1.001
	480	7487	8163	8875	9634	10407					-20	1.052	.785	1.006
	520	7709	8552	9468	10482						-0	1.043	.810	1.011
	560	8995	10350											
	600													
	MIL	12444	12276	12104	11831	10747	5308	5308	5308	5308				
	VMAX	581.7	570.3	559.1	539.4	498.6								
36,000 FEET (-54°C)	360	18897									-80	.940	.530	.943
	400	14103									-60	.987	.980	.988
	440	10578									-40	1.032	.915	1.010
	480	8563									-20	1.075	.740	1.016
	520	8162									-0	1.117	.570	1.023
	560													
	600													
	MIL	9448	4196	4196	4196	4196	4196	4196	4196	4196				
	VMAX	547.8												

Figure A5-33

CONSTANT ALTITUDE CRUISE
LANDING GEAR EXTENDED
CRUISE SPEED-250 KCAS

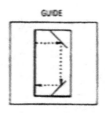

GUIDE

AIRPLANE CONFIGURATION
INDIVIDUAL DRAG INDEXES

DATE: 15 JUNE 1988
DATA BASIS: **ESTIMATED**

REMARKS
ENGINE(S): (2) F100-PW-220
DATA APPLICABLE FOR ANY TEMPERATURE

NOTE
- LANDING GEAR DRAG MUST ALSO BE INCLUDED
  WHEN CALCULATING TOTAL DRAG INDEX
- DI = 40 FOR NOSE GEAR DI = 25 FOR EACH MAIN GEAR
- SPEEDS RESTRICTED TO 250 KCAS WITH GEAR EXTENDED.

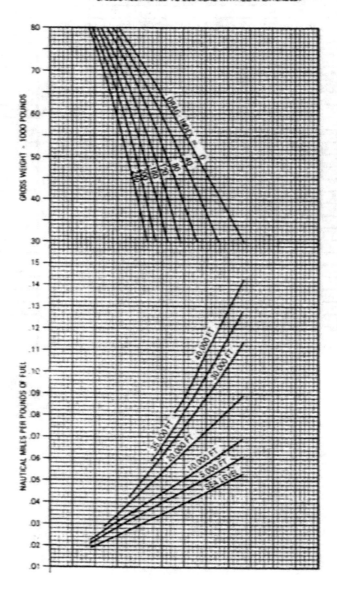

15E-1-(1154)04

Figure A5-34

PART 6

ENDURANCE

TABLE OF CONTENTS

Charts Maximum Endurance..................................A6-4
Endurance-Landing Gear Extended A6-6

MAXIMUM ENDURANCE CHARTS

These charts (figures A6-1 and A6-2) present optimum endurance altitude and maximum endurance specifics (fuel flow and Mach number) for various combinations of effective gross weight and altitude.

USE (ALTITUDE AND BANK ANGLE CHART)

Enter the Altitude and Bank Angle chart with the average gross weight. If bank angles are to be considered, follow the gross weight curve until it intersects the bank angle to be used, then project horizontally right to obtain effective gross weight. (If bank angles are not to be considered, enter the chart at the effective gross weight scale.) From this point proceed horizontally right to intersect the applicable drag index curve, then project vertically down to read optimum endurance altitude.

Sample Problem

Altitude and Bank Angle

A. Gross weight	60,000Lb
B. Bank angle	20°
C. Effective gross weight	63,800 Lb
D. Drag index	120
E. Optimum endurance altitude	18,000 Ft

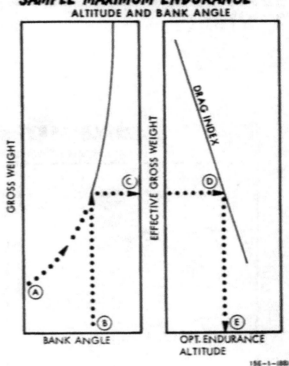

SAMPLE MAXIMUM ENDURANCE
ALTITUDE AND BANK ANGLE

USE (FUEL FLOW AND MACH NUMBER CHART)

Enter the fuel flow and Mach number plots on the
Fuel Flow and Mach Number chart with the effective
gross weight, then horizontally to intersect the optimum endurance altitude curve. From this point,
project vertically down to intersect the applicable
drag index curve, then horizontally to read fuel flow
or true Mach number.

Sample Problem

Fuel Flow

A. Effective gross weight	63,800 Lb	
B. Endurance altitude	18,000 Ft	
C. Drag index	120	
D. Fuel flow	8050 PPH	

Mach Number

A. Effective gross weight	63,800 Lb	
B. Endurance altitude	18,000 Ft	
C. Drag index	120	
D. True Mach number	0.589	

SAMPLE MAXIMUM ENDURANCE
FUEL FLOW AND TRUE MACH NUMBER

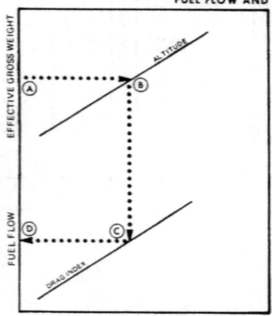
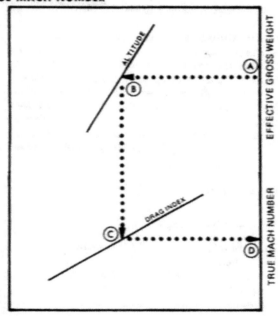

15E-1-189104

SAMPLE ENDURANCE, LANDING GEAR EXTENDED

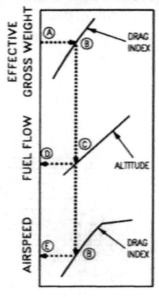 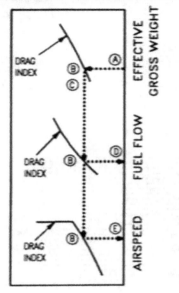

1SE-1-(154-1)04-CAT)

ENDURANCE-LANDING GEAR EXTENDED

This chart (figure A6-3) presents constant altitude endurance and maximum endurance specifics (fuel flow, calibrated airspeed, and altitude) for various combinations of gross weight and drag index.

USE

If bank angles are to be considered, utilize the method described in the previous problem to determine the effective gross weight. To obtain constant altitude endurance specifics, enter the left side of the chart at the effective gross weight scale. From this point, proceed horizontally right to intersect the applicable drag index curve, then project downward to intersect with the desired altitude. From this point, project horizontally left to read the fuel flow. To obtain the calibrated airspeed, project downward from the altitude-fuel flow intersection to intersect with the applicable drag index curves on the airspeed chart, project horizontally left from this point to read the calibrated airspeed.

To obtain maximum endurance specifics, the right side of the chart is used. Enter the chart at the effective gross weight and project horizontally left to

intersect with the applicable drag index curve. From this point, project downward to read the maximum endurance altitude from the horizontal scale. Project further downward to intersect with the applicable drag index curve and project horizontally right to read the fuel flow or the calibrated airspeed.

Sample Problem

Constant Altitude Endurance

A. Effective gross weight	42,500 Lb
B. Drag index (external stores)	30
Drag index (all gear extended)	90
Total drag index	120
C. Altitude	10,000 Ft
D. Fuel flow	5,400 PPH
E. Airspeed	203 KCAS

Maximum Endurance

A. Effective gross weight	42,500 Lb
B. Drag index	120
C. Altitude	28,000 Ft
D. Fuel flow	5,600 PPH
E. Airspeed	204 KCAS

A6-3

MAXIMUM ENDURANCE
ALTITUDE AND BANK ANGLE

AIRPLANE CONFIGURATION
INDIVIDUAL DRAG INDEXES

REMARKS
ENGINE(S): (2) F100-PW-220
U.S. STANDARD DAY, 1966

GUIDE

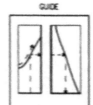

DATE:15 JUNE 1988
DATA BASIS: ESTIMATED

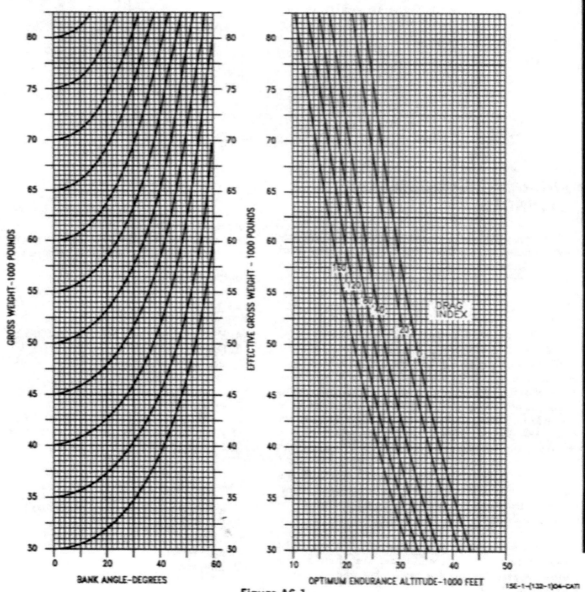

BANK ANGLE-DEGREES

OPTIMUM ENDURANCE ALTITUDE-1000 FEET

Figure A6-1

1SE-1-(132-1)04-CAT

MAXIMUM ENDURANCE
FUEL FLOW AND TRUE MACH NUMBER

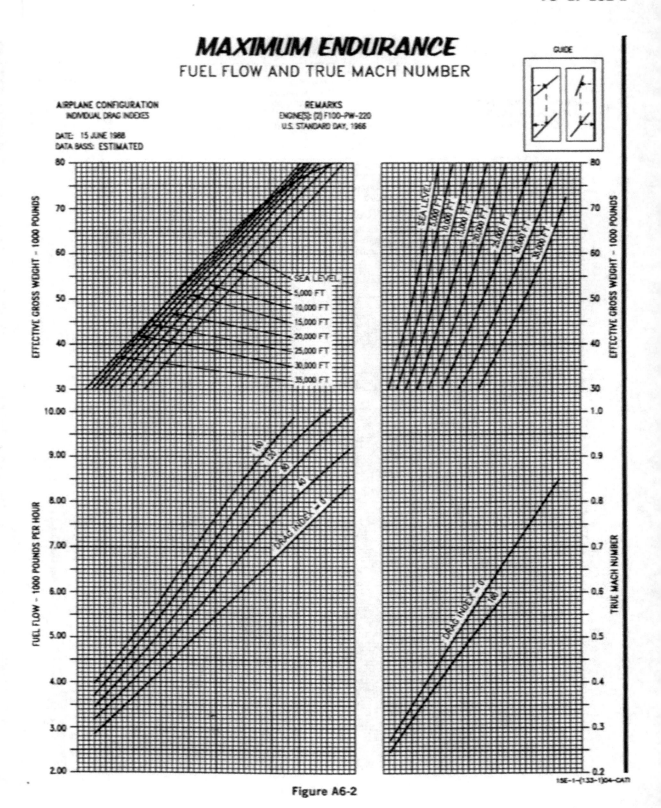

Figure A6-2

ENDURANCE
LANDING GEAR EXTENDED
REMARKS
ENGINE(S): (2) F100-PW-220
U.S. STANDARD DAY, 1968
NOTE
- LANDING GEAR DRAG MUST ALSO BE INCLUDED WHEN CALCULATING TOTAL DRAG INDEX.
- DI=40 NOSE GEAR DI=25 FOR EACH MAIN GEAR.
- SPEEDS RESTRICTED TO 250 KCAS WITH GEAR EXTENDED.
- USE FIGURE A6-1 TO DETERMINE EFFECTIVE GROSS WEIGHT FOR A BANKED TURN.

AIRPLANE CONFIGURATION
INDIVIDUAL DRAG INDEXES
FLAPS RETRACTED

DATE: 15 JUNE 1968
DATA BASIS: ESTIMATED

CONSTANT ALTITUDE ENDURANCE

MAXIMUM ENDURANCE

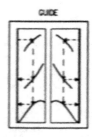

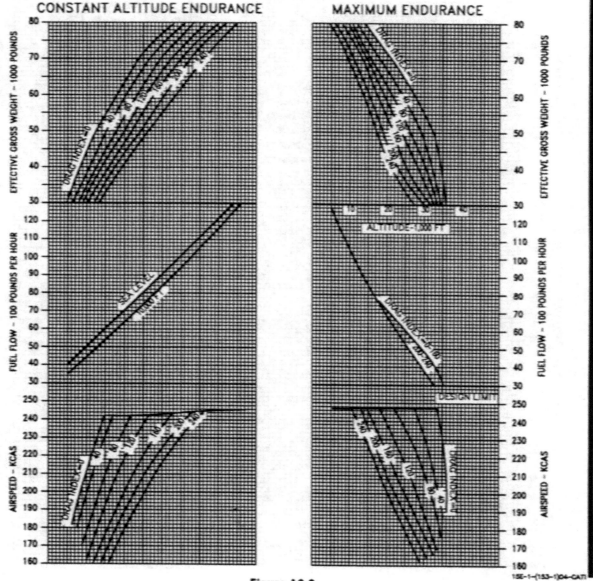

Figure A6-3

15E-1-(153-1)04-CAT3

PART 7

DESCENT

DESCENT CHARTS

The Descent charts (figures A7-1 thru A7-5) present distance, time, total fuel used and Mach number in the descent. Incremental data may be obtained for distance, time and fuel by subtracting data corresponding to level-off altitude from the data for the original cruising altitude.

USE

Enter the upper plot of the appropriate chart at the cruising altitude, project horizontally right to intersect both series of drag index curves. From the altitude - drag index intersection in the first series, project vertically down to read distance. From the altitude - drag index intersection in the second series, project vertically down to read time to descend. Enter the lower plot at the cruising altitude and project horizontally right to intersect the applicable drag index curve on the fuel graph. Continue horizontally right and intersect the curve on the Mach number graph. From the altitude - drag index intersection on the fuel graph, descend vertically and read total fuel used in the descent. From the intersection on the Mach number graph, project vertically down to read true Mach number.

Sample Problem

Maximum Range Descent, 220 KCAS, Idle Thrust, Speed Brake Retracted, F-15 without CFT

A. Altitude	30,000 Ft
B. Drag index	40

C. Distance	55 NM
D. Drag index	40
E. Time required	11.7 Min
F. Altitude	30,000 Ft
G. Drag index	40
H. Total fuel used	395 Lb
I. Drag reflector	
J. True Mach number	0.59 Mach

SAMPLE DESCENT

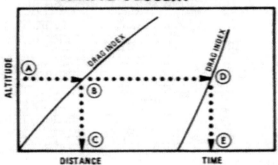

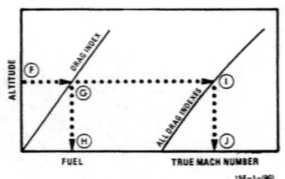

15E-1-(90)

A7-1

DESCENT
WITH CFT
MAXIMUM RANGE
220 KCAS – IDLE THRUST

AIRPLANE CONFIGURATION
SPEED BRAKE RETRACTED

REMARKS
ENGINE(S): (2) F100-PW-220
U.S. STANDARD DAY, 1966

DATE: 15 JUNE 1988
DATA BASIS: ESTIMATED

NOTE
DO NOT INCLUDE CFT OR CFT PYLON DRAG
WHEN CALCULATING DRAG INDEX.

GUIDE

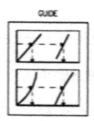

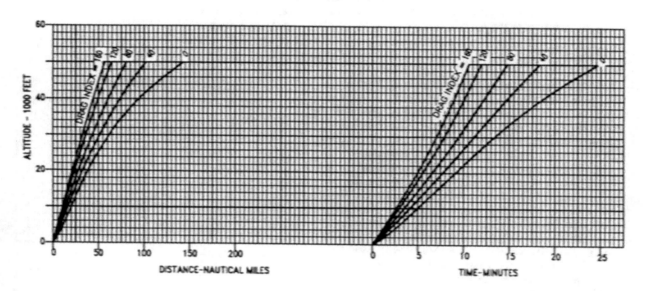

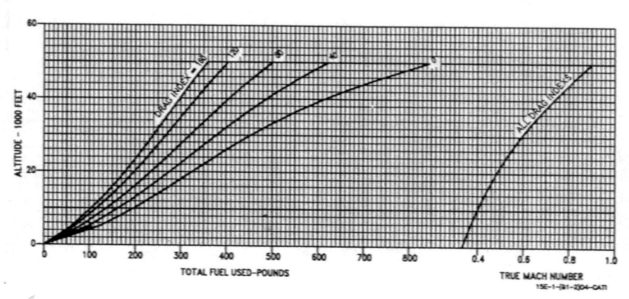

Figure A7-1

DESCENT
WITH CFT
MAXIMUM RANGE
300 KCAS – IDLE THRUST

AIRPLANE CONFIGURATION
SPEED BRAKE RETRACTED

REMARKS
ENGINE(S): (2) F100-PW-220
U.S. STANDARD DAY, 1966

DATE: 15 JUNE 1988
DATA BASIS: ESTIMATED

NOTE
DO NOT INCLUDE CFT OR CFT PYLON DRAG
WHEN CALCULATING DRAG INDEX.

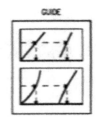

GUIDE

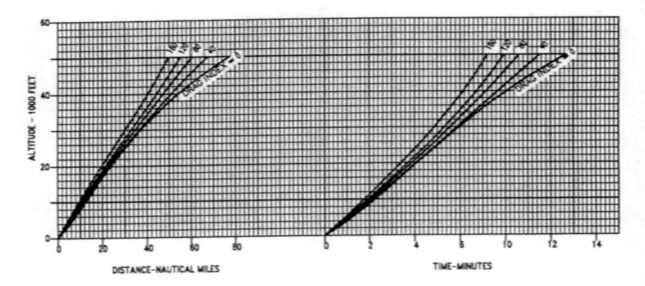

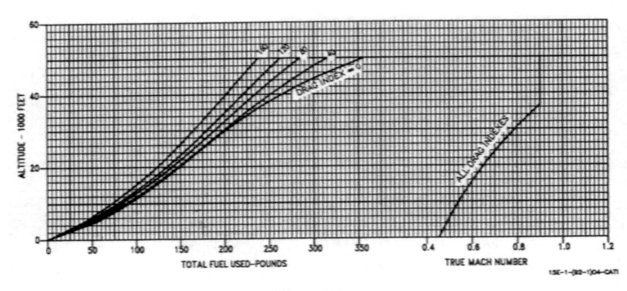

Figure A7-2

DESCENT

WITHOUT CFT
MAXIMUM RANGE
220 KCAS – IDLE THRUST

GUIDE

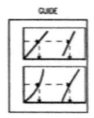

AIRPLANE CONFIGURATION
SPEED BRAKE RETRACTED

REMARKS
ENGINE(S): (2) F100-PW-220
U.S. STANDARD DAY, 1966

DATE: 15 JUNE 1988
DATA BASIS: ESTIMATED

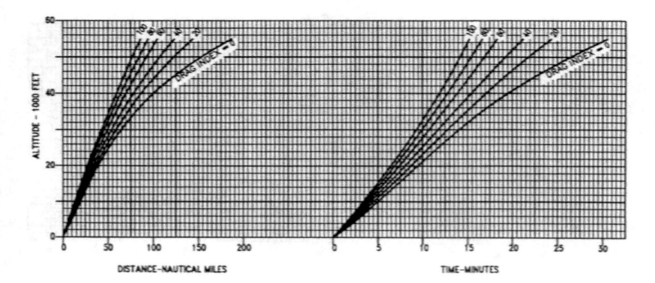

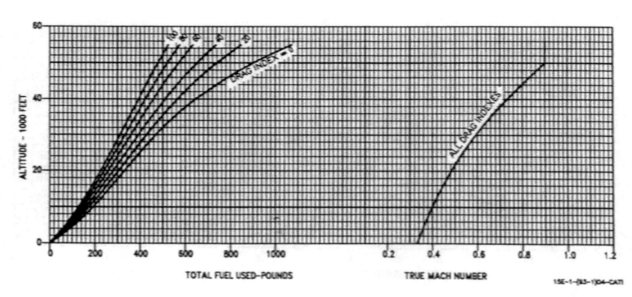

Figure A7-3

15E-1-(A3-1)04-CAT)

DESCENT

WITHOUT CFT
MAXIMUM RANGE
300 KCAS – IDLE THRUST

GUIDE

AIRPLANE CONFIGURATION
SPEED BRAKE RETRACTED

REMARKS
ENGINE(S): (2) F100–PW–220
U.S. STANDARD DAY, 1966

DATE: 15 JUNE 1988
DATA BASIS: ESTIMATED

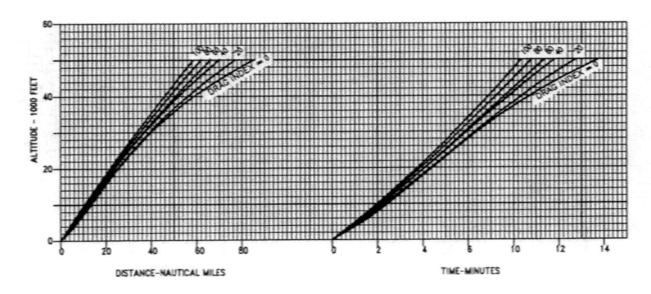

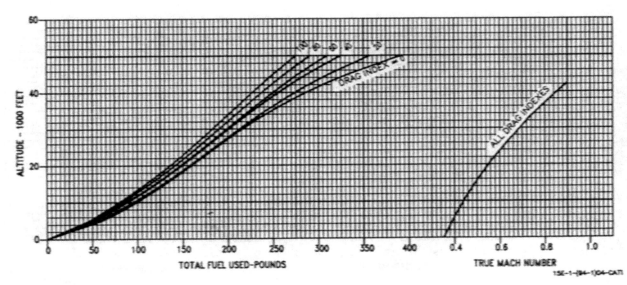

15E-1-(84-1)04-CAT1

Figure A7-4

DESCENT
WITH OR WITHOUT CFT
MAXIMUM RANGE
220 KCAS – IDLE THRUST

AIRPLANE CONFIGURATION
INDIVIDUAL DRAG INDEXES
SPEED BRAKE EXTENDED

REMARKS
ENGINE(S): (2) F100-PW-220
U.S. STANDARD DAY, 1968

DATE: 15 JUNE 1988
DATA BASIS: ESTIMATED

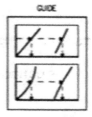

GUIDE

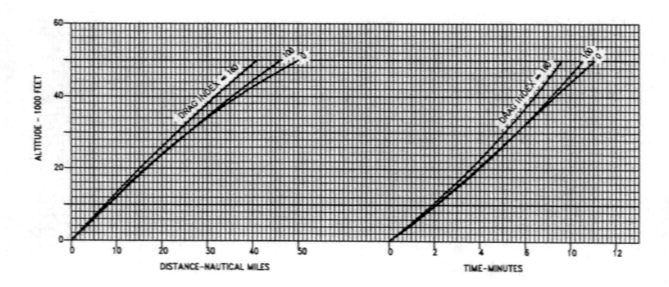

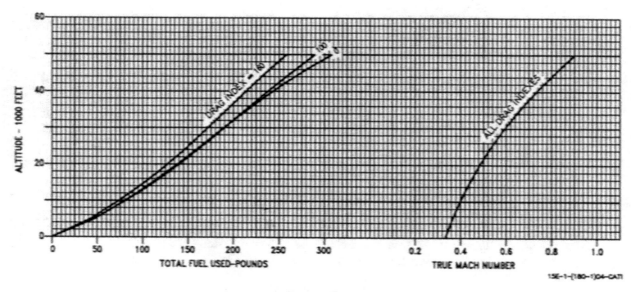

15E-1-(180-1)04-CAT1

Figure A7-5

PART 8

APPROACH AND LANDING

TABLE OF CONTENTS

Charts

Landing Approach Speed.................................... A8-5
Maximum Approach Gross Weight..................A8-6
Landing Distance A8-7

LANDING APPROACH SPEED CHART

The Landing Approach Speed chart (figure A8-1) provides recommended approach speed for various gross weights of the aircraft. The data is plotted for flaps either up or down.

USE

Enter the chart at the estimated landing gross weight and project vertically up to the appropriate flap reflector line. From this point, project horizontally left to read recommended approach speed.

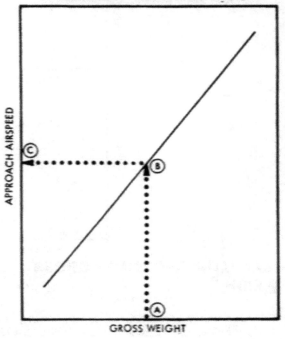

SAMPLE APPROACH SPEEDS

15E-1-051

Sample Problem

Configuration: Flaps Down

A. Estimated landing gross weight	50,000 Lb
B. Flaps down reflector line	
C. Landing approach speed	174.1 Kt

SAMPLE MAXIMUM APPROACH GROSS WEIGHT
(SINGLE ENGINE)

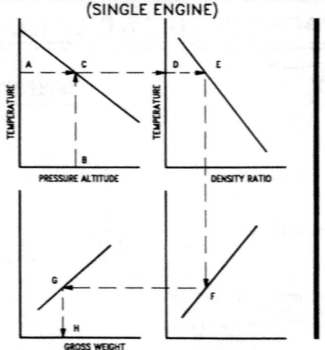

15E-1-(230-1)03-CAT1

MAXIMUM APPROACH GROSS WEIGHT

The Maximum Approach Gross Weight chart (figure A8-2) provides the maximum gross weight at which the aircraft can peform a single engine maximum power climb after experiencing an engine failure. The data presented are based on the requirement that the aircraft be able to climb at a rate of 500 ft/min at approach speed at the existing ambient temperature and pressure altitude.

USE

Enter the chart at the existing ambient temperature and ambient pressure. Project horizontally right at the existing ambient temperature and project vertically up at the existing ambient pressure. The intersection of the two projections represents existing conditions with respect to a standard day. From this point, project horizontally right to the existing ambient pressure altitude and then descend vertically to determine the appropriate density ratio. Continue descending vertically to intersect existing ambient temperature. From this point, project horizontally left to the effective Drag Index and then descend vertically to read gross weight.

Sample Problem

A. Temperature	21°C
B. Pressure Altitude	2000 Ft
C. Type Day	STD +10°C
D. Temperature	21°C
E. Pressure Altitude	2000 Ft
F. Type Day Reflector	STD +10°C
G. Drag Index Reflector	190
H. Gross Weight	77,500 Lb

LANDING DISTANCE CHART

These charts (figures A8-3 thru A8-5) provide landing roll distance information. One chart provides data for a normal landing using aerodynamic braking. The other provides data for a landing roll utilizing the technique of lowering the nose immediately after touchdown and applying maximum anti-skid braking. The variables of temperature, altitude, gross weight, effective wind, and runway condition are taken into consideration.

USE

Enter the chart with the runway temperature and project vertically up to the applicable pressure altitude. From this point, proceed horizontally right to the landing gross weight, then descend vertically to the wind baseline. Parallel the nearest guideline down to the effective headwind or tailwind for the appropriate runway condition. From this point, project vertically down to the appropriate runway condition reflector, then horizontally left to read ground roll. Continue further left to the appropriate runway condition reflector, then vertically down to read total distance required when landing over a 50 foot obstacle.

Sample Problem

Normal Landing - Aerodynamic Braking

A. Temperature	20°C
B. Pressure altitude	2000 Ft
C. Gross weight	40,000 Lb
D. Effective headwind (DRY)	15 Kt
E. RCR reflector (DRY)	23
F. Landing distance	4500 Ft
G. RCR Reflector (DRY)	
H. Total distance required over a 50-foot obstacle	5600 Ft

SAMPLE LANDING DISTANCE

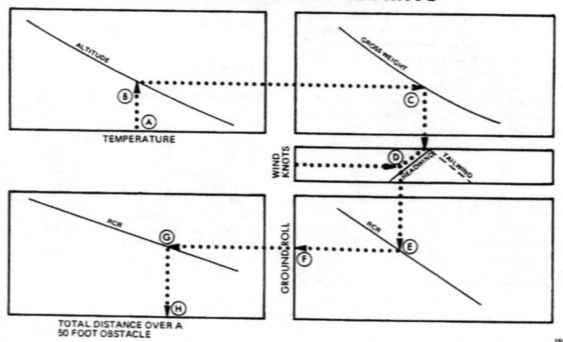

15E-1-(96)

LANDING APPROACH SPEED

WITH OR WITHOUT CFT

AIRPLANE CONFIGURATION
ALL DRAG INDEXES
21 UNITS AOA

REMARKS
ENGINE(S): (2) F100-PW-220
U.S. STANDARD DAY, 1966

GUIDE

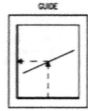

DATE:15 JUNE 1988
DATA BASIS: ESTIMATED

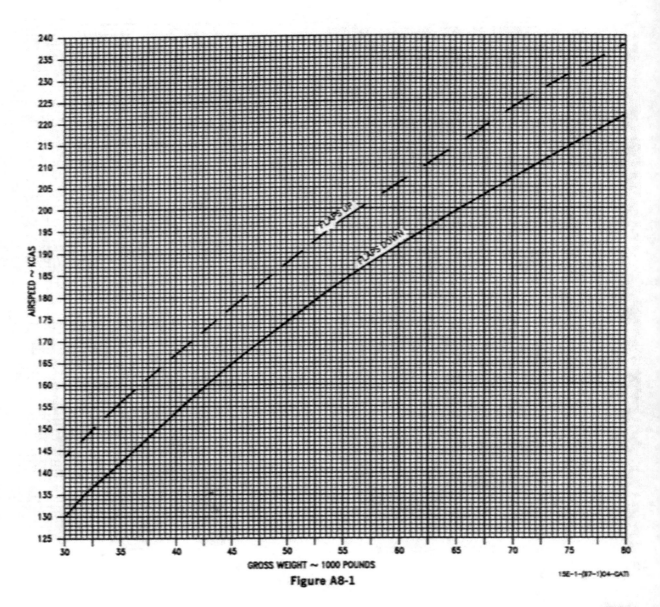

Figure A8-1

15E-1-(87-1)04-CAT1

MAXIMUM APPROACH GROSS WEIGHT
SINGLE ENGINE OPERATING

GUIDE

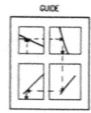

AIRPLANE CONFIGURATION
GEAR AND FLAPS EXTENDED
INDIVIDUAL DRAG INDEXES

REMARKS
ENGINE(S): (2) F100-PW-220
U.S. STANDARD DAY, 1966
NOTE
- LANDING GEAR DRAG MUST ALSO BE INCLUDED WHEN CALCULATING TOTAL DRAG INDEX
- Di=40 NOSE GEAR, Di=25 FOR EACH MAIN GEAR
- INOPERATIVE ENGINE WINDMILLING
- SPEEDBRAKE RETRACTED

DATE: 15 JUNE 1988
DATA BASIS: ESTIMATED

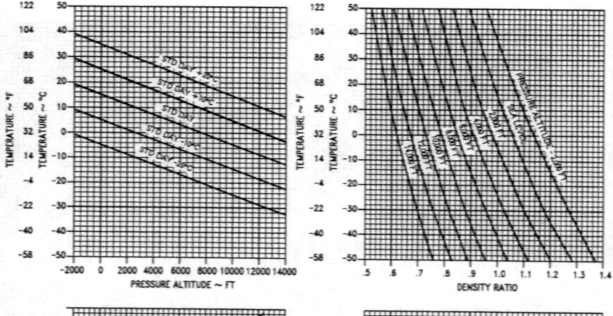

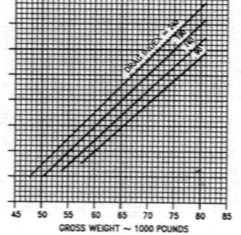

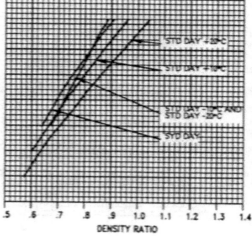

Figure A8-2

15E-1-(M8-1)04-CAT1

LANDING DISTANCE
WITH OR WITHOUT CFT
AERODYNAMIC BRAKING
IDLE THRUST
GROSS WEIGHT 35,000 TO 55,000 POUNDS

GUIDE

AIRPLANE CONFIGURATION
FLAPS DOWN GEAR DOWN
ALL DRAG INDEXES

REMARKS
ENGINE(S): (2) F100-PW-220

NOTE
- DATA IS BASED ON THE USE OF AERODYNAMIC BRAKING BY RAISING THE NOSE TO A 12° PITCH ATTITUDE AFTER TOUCHDOWN AND MAINTAINING AS LONG AS POSSIBLE.
- SPEED BRAKE IS EXTENDED AT TOUCHDOWN.

DATE: 15 JUNE 1988
DATA BASIS: ESTIMATED

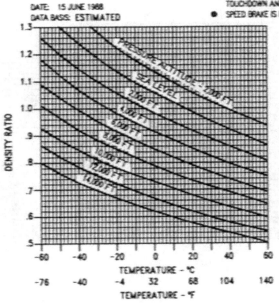

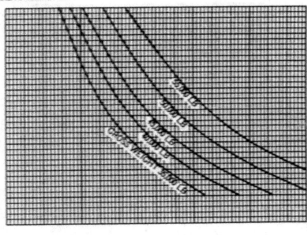

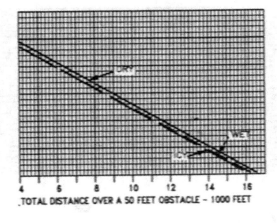

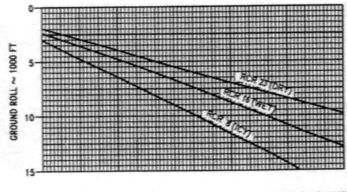

TOTAL DISTANCE OVER A 50 FEET OBSTACLE – 1000 FEET

Figure A8-3

15E-1-(99-1)04-CAT)

LANDING DISTANCE
WITH OR WITHOUT CFT
AERODYNAMIC BRAKING
IDLE THRUST
GROSS WEIGHT 55,000 TO 80,000 POUNDS

GUIDE

AIRPLANE CONFIGURATION
FLAPS DOWN
GEAR DOWN
ALL DRAG INDEXES

DATE: 15 JUNE 1988
DATA BASIS: ESTIMATED

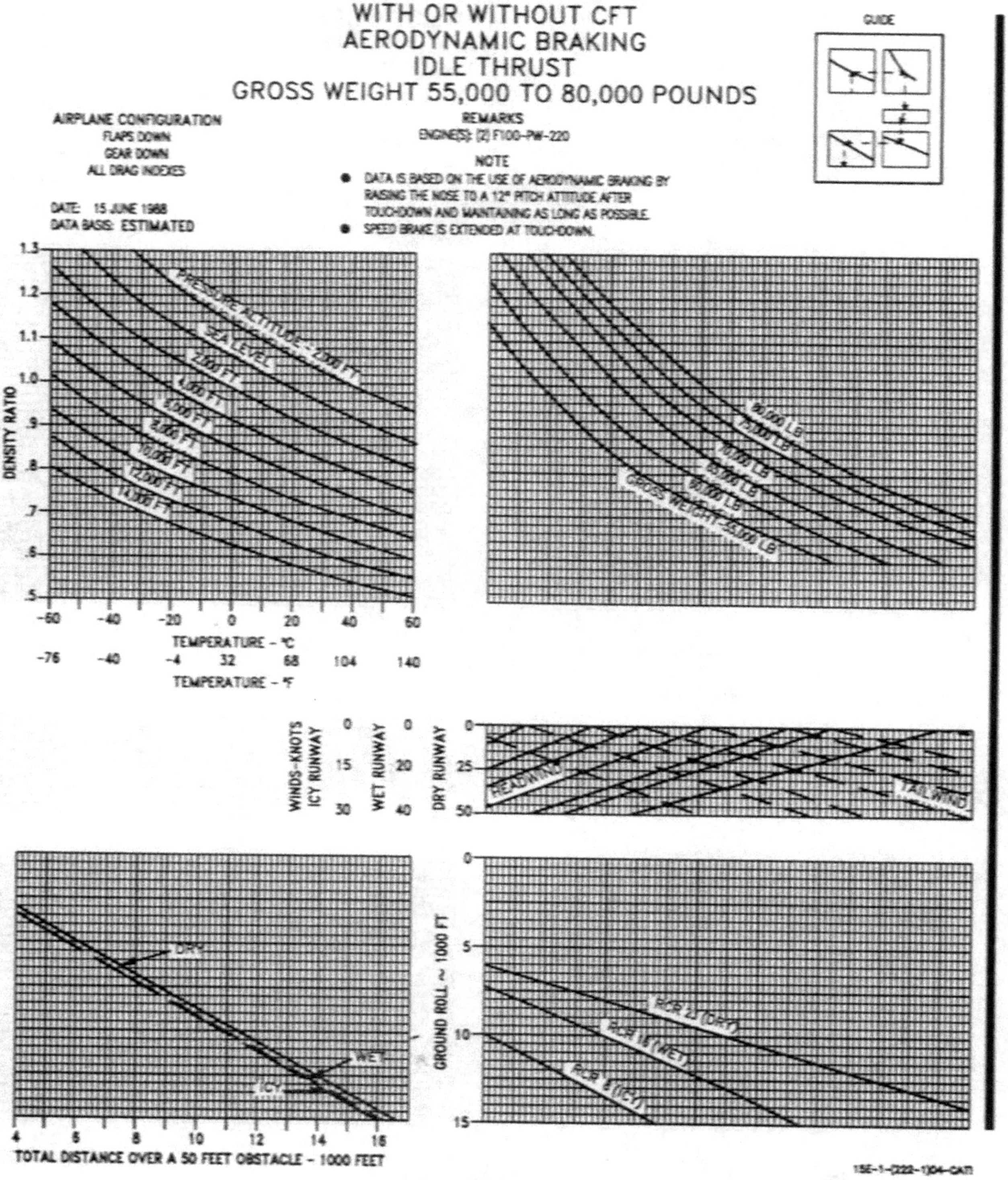

REMARKS
ENGINE(S): [2] F100-PW-220

NOTE
- DATA IS BASED ON THE USE OF AERODYNAMIC BRAKING BY RAISING THE NOSE TO A 12° PITCH ATTITUDE AFTER TOUCHDOWN AND MAINTAINING AS LONG AS POSSIBLE.
- SPEED BRAKE IS EXTENDED AT TOUCHDOWN.

Figure A8-4

15E-1-(222-1)04-CATI

LANDING DISTANCE

WITH OR WITHOUT CFT
MAXIMUM ANTI–SKID BRAKING
IDLE THRUST

AIRPLANE CONFIGURATION
FLAPS DOWN GEAR DOWN
ALL DRAG INDEXES

DATE: 15 JUNE 1988
DATA BASIS: ESTIMATED

REMARKS
ENGINE(S): (2) F100-PW-220

NOTE
- DATA IS BASED ON LOWERING THE NOSE IMMEDIATELY AFTER TOUCHDOWN AND APPLYING MAXIMUM ANTI-SKID BRAKING.
- SPEED BRAKE IS EXTENDED AT TOUCHDOWN.

GUIDE

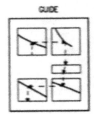

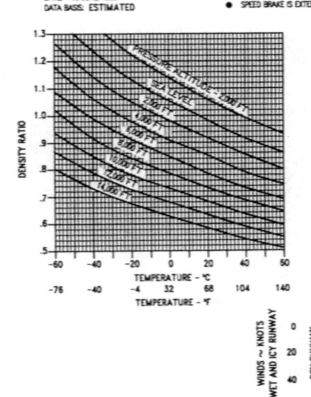

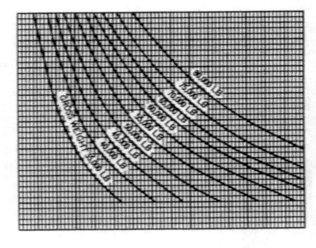

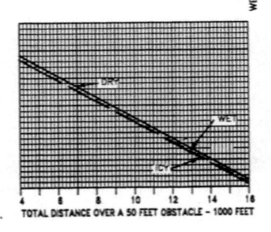

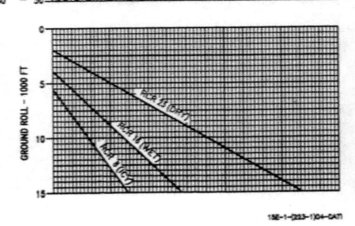

15E-1-(203-1)04-CAT1

Figure A8-5

PART 9

COMBAT PERFORMANCE

TABLE OF CONTENTS

Charts

Level Flight Envelope.................................. A9-7
Dive Recovery A9-23
Low Altitude Combat Performance................A9-25
Combat Fuel Management........................A9-26
Combat Fuel Flow A9-27
Overload Warning System
  Symmetrical Allowable Load Factor A9-32
Level Flight Acceleration A9-44
Sustained Level Turns................................A9-53

LEVEL FLIGHT ENVELOPE

These charts (figures A9-1 thru A9-14) present the aircraft level flight speed envelope for various configurations and average combat gross weights. Parameters of the envelopes extend from the maximum lift coefficient to maximum thrust Mach number at 0g acceleration throughout the altitude range. For each configuration, envelopes are presented for a standard day and standard day ±10°C. In addition to the maximum attainable Mach number at 0g acceleration, each standard day curve indicates Mach number at .03g acceleration. Figure A9-14 shows the relationship between maximum Mach number and Vmax for a selected configuration.

USE

Enter the chart with the desired combat altitude and project horizontally to intersect the applicable standard day .03g and 0g acceleration power curves. From these points, proceed vertically down to read the .03g Mach number and the maximum attainable Mach number in level flight.

SAMPLE LEVEL FLIGHT ENVELOPE

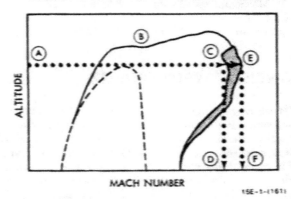

MACH NUMBER

15E-1-(1161)

Sample Problem

Configuration: -4 CFT + (4) AIM-7 + (4) AIM-9; 52,500 Pounds Gross Weight.

A. Combat altitude	35,000 Ft
B. Curve	Std Day
C. .03g Acceleration Curve	
D. .03g Acceleration Mach number	1.44
E. 0g Acceleration curve	
F. 0g Acceleration Mach number	1.52

MAXIMUM SPEED-LEVEL FLIGHT

This chart (figure A9-15 and A9-16) presents level flight maximum speed at military power for drag indexes from 0 to 160 for gross weight with 50% internal fuel remaining. The maximum speeds are listed by Mach/KCAS at 0g acceleration and 0.03g (0.5 knots per second) acceleration for various altitudes. For a given altitude, maximum speeds are provided for standard temperature, and ten degrees above and below standard temperature.

USE

Enter chart at nearest computed drag index and read maximum speeds for 0g and 0.03g accelerations at selected altitude with applicable temperature. For most accurate results, use standard interpolation techniques to determine maximum speeds.

Sample Problem

A. Drag index	40
B. Altitude	30,000 Ft
C. Temperature	-44.4°C
D. Maximum speed - 0g KCAS	0.99 Mach/383
E. Maximum speed - 0.03g KCAS	0.96Mach/374

DIVE RECOVERY CHARTS

These charts, (figures A9-17 and A9-18) present the airplanes dive recovery capability for various speeds (subsonic and supersonic), altitudes, and dive angles. The supersonic chart (figure A9-18) includes airplane structural limit curves to determine the maximum dive angle that can be achieved without exceeding the structural limit speed during dive recovery.

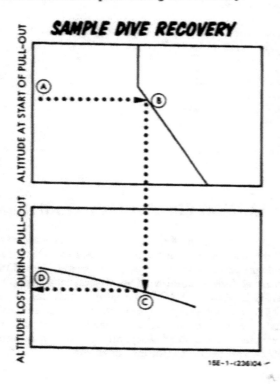

SAMPLE DIVE RECOVERY

15E-1-(236)04

USE

Enter the applicable chart with the altitude at the start of the pull-out and project horizontally right to intersect the curve for the Mach number at the start of the pull-out. From this point, project vertically down to intersect the dive angle at the start of pull-out, then horizontally left to read altitude lost during pull-out.

Sample Problem

Configuration: (4) AIM-9 Launchers; Supersonic

A. Altitude at start of pull out	40,000 Ft
B. Mach number at start of pull-out	1.5
C. Dive angle at start of pull-out	70°
D. Altitude loss during pull-out	11,800 Ft

LOW ALTITUDE COMBAT PERFORMANCE CHART

This table (figure A9-19) presents specific fuel flow values (pounds per minute) for maximum thrust operation at constant calibrated airspeeds of 300, 400, 500, 600, and 700 knots. The data are for altitudes of sea level, 5000 and 10,000 feet. Fuel flow values are computed for U.S. Standard Day; however, correction factors are given for nonstandard day temperatures. The standard day temperature is listed with the altitude. If the actual temperature at a particular altitude differs from the standard day temperature, refer to the TEMP. EFFECTS column to determine the appropriate temperature correction factor.

USE

Enter the table with the desired altitude and calibrated airspeed and project horizontally right to the specific fuel flow column to read specific fuel flow for a standard day. To obtain the specific fuel flow for a nonstandard day, mulitply the specific fuel flow for a standard day by the nonstandard day temperature correction factor obtained from the TEMP. EFFECTS column.

Sample Problem

A. Desired altitude	**5000 Ft**
B. Desired constant airspeed	600 KCAS
C. Specific fuel flow for a standard day	2113 Lb/Min
D. Nonstandard day temperature	0°C
E. Nonstandard day temperature correction factor	1.03
F. Nonstandard day specific fuel flow (C X E)	2176 Lb/Min

COMBAT FUEL MANAGEMENT CHART

This chart (figure A9-20) presents a relative comparison between engine power setting and fuel usage in pounds per minute. The chart emphasizes the effect of power setting on combat fuel management. Data presented are for engine power settings of military power, mid-range afterburner and maximum afterburner at altitudes from sea level to 40,000 feet and airspeeds between Mach 0.8 and Mach 1.1.

USE

Enter the chart at the desired altitude and project horizontally right to the selected Mach/engine power setting. From this point project vertically down to read fuel usage in pounds per minute.

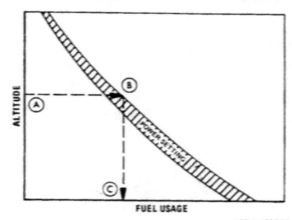

SAMPLE COMBAT FUEL MANAGEMENT

15E-1-(237)03

Sample Problem

A. Desired altitude	25,000 Ft
B. Mach/power setting	0.9/Max AB
C. Fuel usage	1020 PPM

COMBAT FUEL FLOW CHART

These charts (figures A9-21 thru A9-25) present a relative comparison between high airspeeds at stabilized level flight and fuel flow in pounds per minute. Data presented are for two non-CFT configurations and seven CFT configurations, based on F100-PW-220 engines.

USE

Enter the chart at the desired altitude and project horizontally right to the selected Mach number curve. From this point project vertically down to read fuel flow in pounds per minute.

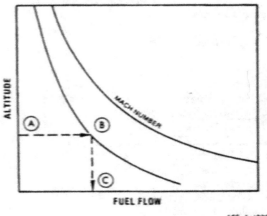

SAMPLE COMBAT FUEL FLOW

15E-1-(238)03

Sample Problem

Configuration: -4 CFT + (4) AIM-7 + (4) AIM-9

A. Desired altitude	30,000 Ft
B. Mach number	1.1
C. Fuel flow	660 PPM

A9-3

OVERLOAD WARNING SYSTEM SYMMETRICAL ALLOWABLE LOAD FACTOR CHARTS

These charts (Figures A9-26 thru A9-37) present the overload warning system symmetrical allowable load factor capability for various Mach numbers, altitudes, and airplane gross weights.

USE

Enter the chart (Figures A9-26 or A9-27) with the desired Mach number and project horizontally to the desired altitude. From this point, descend vertically to the applicable gross weight then project horizontally left to read the airplane symmetrical allowable load factor given by OWS. When CFT's are installed, enter the applicable CFT/Aircraft interface charts based on CFT fuel quantity (Figures A9-28 thru A9-37) with the desired Mach number and project horizontally to the desired altitude. From this point, descend vertically to the applicable aircraft gross weight, then project horizontally left to read the CFT/airplane symmetrical allowable load factor. The combined allowable load factor is the less of the two (airplane and CFT/airplane interface).

Sample Problem

Configuration: Full CFTS

A. Mach number	0.8
B. Altitude	Sea Level
C. Gross Weight	45,000 Lb
D. Airplane Symmetrical Load Factor	8.6 g
E. CFT fuel/CFT	4875 Lb
F. CFT/Airplane interface symmetrical allowable load factor	8.0 g
G. Combined Symmetrical allowable load factor	8.0 g

SAMPLE OVERLOAD WARNING SYSTEM SYMMETRICAL ALLOWABLE LOAD FACTORS

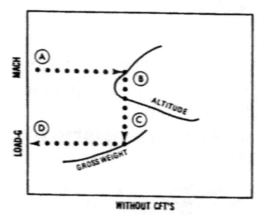

WITHOUT CFT'S

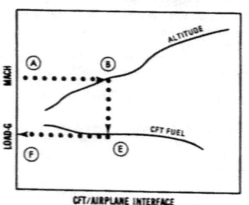

CFT/AIRPLANE INTERFACE

15E-1-(268)18

LEVEL FLIGHT ACCELERATION CHARTS

These charts (figures A9-38 thru A9-46) are used to determine time to accelerate in level flight between two Mach numbers. The curves are presented for various configurations with initial gross weights. Each chart shows maximum and military thrust accelerations at 10,000 feet and maximum thrust acceleration at 40,000 feet. The curves are presented for a standard day and standard day ±10°C. The origin for each curve is 250 KCAS and .03g acceleration points are indicated on each curve.

USE

Enter applicable configuration chart with initial Mach number and altitude, and project horizontally to appropriate thrust/standard day curve. Project vertically down to initial Mach time reference. Enter chart again with final Mach number, project horizontally to the same curve, and project vertically down to the final Mach time reference. To determine time to accelerate, subtract initial Mach number time reference from final Mach number time reference.

SAMPLE LEVEL FLIGHT ACCELERATION

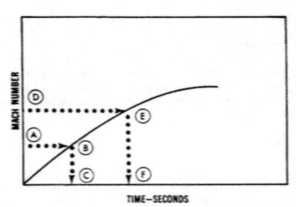

15E-1-(240)03

Sample Problem

Configuration: -4 CFT + (4) AIM-7 + (40 AIM-9; 58,100 Pounds Initial Gross Weight: Maximum Thrust, Altitude 10,000 Feet.

A.	Initial Mach number	0.8 Mach
B.	Maximum thrust/ standard day curve	STD −10° C
C.	Initial Mach number time reference	21 Seconds
D.	Final Mach number	0.9 Mach
E.	Maximum thrust/ standard day curve	STD −10° C
F.	Final Mach number time reference	27 Seconds
G.	Time to accelerate (F. minus C.)	6 Seconds

A9-5

SUSTAINED LEVEL TURNS

These charts (figures A9-47 thru A9-55) present the maximum sustained level rate of turn and corresponding maximum sustained load factor for a given Mach number and altitude. The charts are based on maximum thrust for various aircraft configurations. Bank angles are shown for corresponding load factors, and a formula is provided to calculate radius of turn.

USE

Enter chart with Mach number and project vertically up to applicable rate of turn and load factor altitude curves. Project horizontally left from rate of turn altitude curve to maximum sustained rate of turn. Project horizontally left from load factor altitude curve to the maximum sustained load factor corresponding to the maximum sustainable turn rate. Project horizontally right from the load factor altitude curve to bank angle corresponding to the maximum sustained load factor.

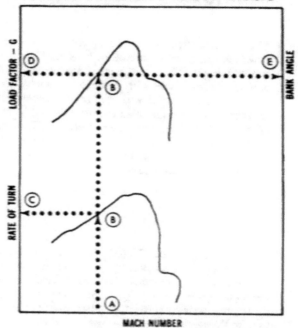

SAMPLE SUSTAINED LEVEL TURNS

15E-1-(239)03

Sample Problem

Configuration: -4 CFT + (4) AIM-7 + (4) AIM-9
52,500 Pounds Gross Weight

A. Mach number	0.9
B. Altitude	40,000 Ft
C. Maximum sustained turn rate	2.9°/SEC
D. Maximum sustained load factor	1.7g
E. Bank angle	53°

LEVEL FLIGHT ENVELOPE
GROSS WEIGHT – 39,500 POUNDS
MAXIMUM THRUST

AIRPLANE CONFIGURATION
CLEAN AIRPLANE

REMARKS
ENGINE(S): (2) F100-PW-220
U.S. STANDARD DAY, 1966

NOTE
CAPABILITY REMAINING: MAXIMUM SPEEDS, ACCELERATION OF
0 AND 0.03g; CEILINGS AND LOW SPEED, RATE OF CLIMB OF
500 FEET PER MINUTE. q/g = 0.03 REPRESENTS AN
ACCELERATION OF 0.5 KNOTS/SEC

DATE: 15 APRIL 1990
DATA BASIS: FLIGHT TEST

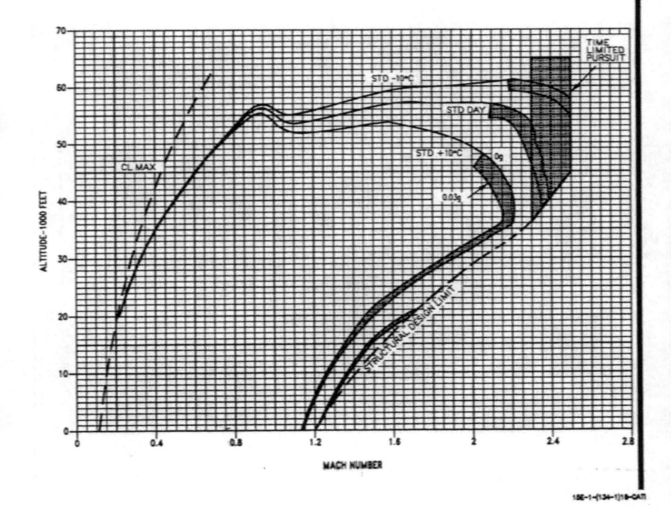

Figure A9-1

15E-1-(134-1)18-CATI

LEVEL FLIGHT ENVELOPE
GROSS WEIGHT – 41,500 POUNDS
MAXIMUM THRUST

AIRPLANE CONFIGURATION
(4)AIM-7

REMARKS
ENGINE(S): (2) F100-PW-220
U.S. STANDARD DAY, 1966

NOTE
CAPABILITY REMAINING: MAXIMUM SPEEDS, ACCELERATION OF
0 AND 0.03g; CEILINGS AND LOW SPEED, RATE OF CLIMB OF
500 FEET PER MINUTE. q/g = 0.03 REPRESENTS AN
ACCELERATION OF 0.5 KNOTS/SEC

DATE:15 APRIL 1990
DATA BASIS: FLIGHT TEST

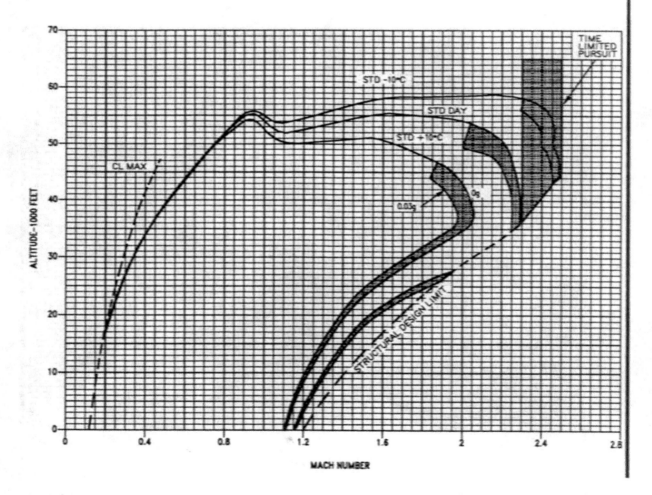

MACH NUMBER

ALTITUDE–1000 FEET

15E-1-(138-1)16-CAT)

Figure A9-2

LEVEL FLIGHT ENVELOPE
GROSS WEIGHT – 52,500 POUNDS
MAXIMUM THRUST

AIRPLANE CONFIGURATION
–4CFT, (4)AIM-9, (4)AIM-7

REMARKS
ENGINE(S): (2) F100-PW-220
U.S. STANDARD DAY, 1966

NOTE
CAPABILITY REMAINING: MAXIMUM SPEEDS, ACCELERATION OF
0 AND 0.03g; CEILINGS AND LOW SPEED, RATE OF CLIMB OF
500 FEET PER MINUTE. a/g = 0.03 REPRESENTS AN
ACCELERATION OF 0.5 KNOTS/SEC

DATE: 15 APRIL 1990
DATA BASIS: (STORES) ESTIMATED
(AIRCRAFT/CFT) FLIGHT TEST

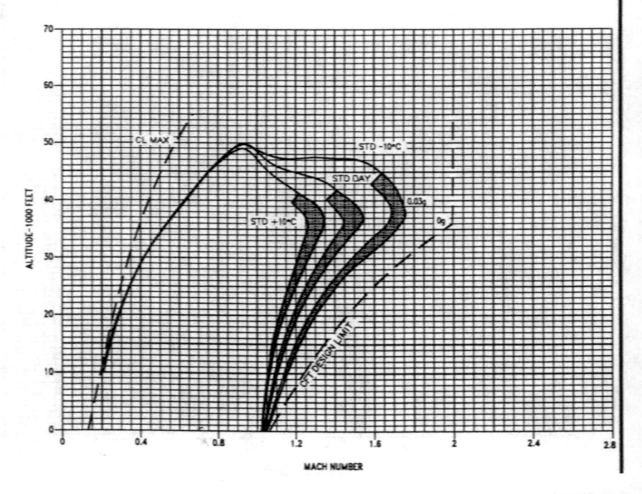

Figure A9-3

LEVEL FLIGHT ENVELOPE
GROSS WEIGHT – 53,700 POUNDS
MAXIMUM THRUST

AIRPLANE CONFIGURATION
–40FT, LANTIRN, (4)AIM-9,
(4)AIM-7

REMARKS
ENGINE(S): (2) F100–PW–220
U.S. STANDARD DAY, 1966

NOTE
CAPABILITY REMAINING: MAXIMUM SPEEDS, ACCELERATION OF
0 AND 0.03g; CEILINGS AND LOW SPEED, RATE OF CLIMB OF
500 FEET PER MINUTE. q/g = 0.03 REPRESENTS AN
ACCELERATION OF 0.5 KNOTS/SEC

DATE:15 APRIL 1990
DATA BASIS: (STORES) ESTIMATED
(AIRCRAFT/CFT) FLIGHT TEST

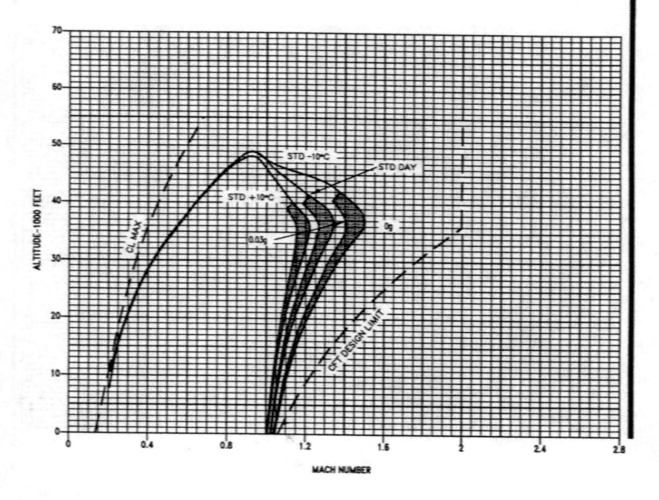

Figure A9-4

15E-1-(1-37-1)18-CA31

LEVEL FLIGHT ENVELOPE
GROSS WEIGHT – 55,600 POUNDS
MAXIMUM THRUST

AIRPLANE CONFIGURATION
–4CFT, LANTIRN, (4)AIM-9,
(2)MK-84

REMARKS
ENGINE(S): (2) F100-PW-220
U.S. STANDARD DAY, 1966

NOTE
CAPABILITY REMAINING: MAXIMUM SPEEDS, ACCELERATION OF
0 AND 0.03g, CEILINGS AND LOW SPEED, RATE OF CLIMB OF
500 FEET PER MINUTE. q/g = 0.03 REPRESENTS AN
ACCELERATION OF 0.5 KNOTS/SEC.

DATE:15 APRIL 1990
DATA BASIS: (STORES) ESTIMATED
(AIRCRAFT/CFT) FLIGHT TEST

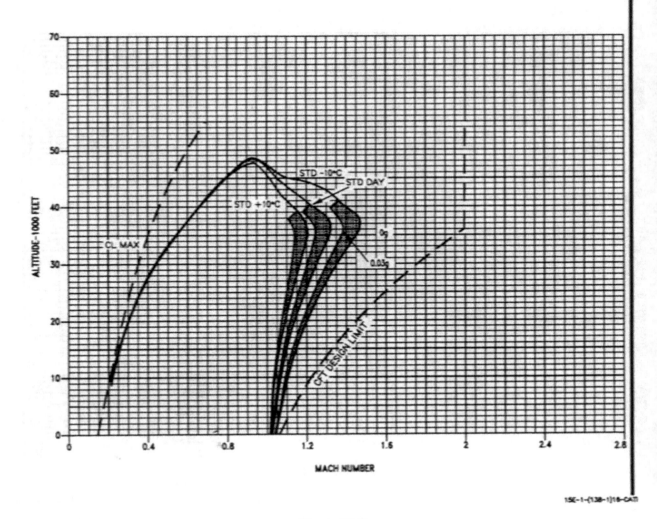

Figure A9-5

LEVEL FLIGHT ENVELOPE
GROSS WEIGHT – 55,900 POUNDS
MAXIMUM THRUST

AIRPLANE CONFIGURATION
–4CFT, LANTIRN, (4)AIM–9,
(6)CBU–89

REMARKS
ENGINE(S): (2) F100–PW–220
U.S. STANDARD DAY, 1966

NOTE
CAPABILITY REMAINING: MAXIMUM SPEEDS, ACCELERATION OF
0 AND 0.03g; CEILINGS AND LOW SPEED, RATE OF CLIMB OF
500 FEET PER MINUTE. q/g = 0.03 REPRESENTS AN
ACCELERATION OF 0.5 KNOTS/SEC

DATE:15 APRIL 1990
DATA BASIS: (STORES) ESTIMATED
(AIRCRAFT/CFT) FLIGHT TEST

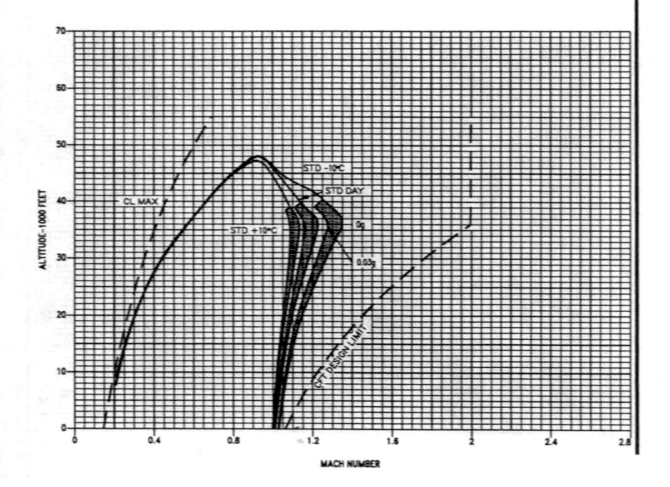

Figure A9-6

15E-1-(15B-1)16-CAT)

LEVEL FLIGHT ENVELOPE

GROSS WEIGHT – 57,700 POUNDS
MAXIMUM THRUST

AIRPLANE CONFIGURATION
–4CFT, LANTIRN, (4)AIM-9,
(12)MK-82

REMARKS
ENGINE(S): (2) F100-PW-220
U.S. STANDARD DAY, 1966

NOTE
CAPABILITY REMAINING: MAXIMUM SPEEDS, ACCELERATION OF
0 AND 0.03g; CEILINGS AND LOW SPEED, RATE OF CLIMB OF
500 FEET PER MINUTE. q/g = 0.03 REPRESENTS AN
ACCELERATION OF 0.5 KNOTS/SEC

DATE:15 APRIL 1990
DATA BASIS: (STORES) ESTIMATED
(AIRCRAFT/CFT) FLIGHT TEST

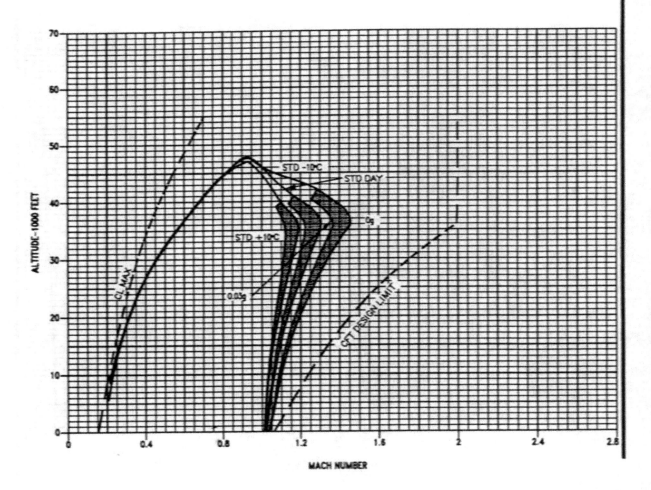

LEVEL FLIGHT ENVELOPE
GROSS WEIGHT – 59,500 POUNDS
MAXIMUM THRUST

AIRPLANE CONFIGURATION
-4CFT, LANTIRN, (4)AIM-9,
(4)MK-84

REMARKS
ENGINE(S): (2) F100-PW-220
U.S. STANDARD DAY, 1966

NOTE
CAPABILITY REMAINING: MAXIMUM SPEEDS, ACCELERATION OF
0 AND 0.03g; CEILINGS AND LOW SPEED, RATE OF CLIMB OF
500 FEET PER MINUTE. a/g = 0.03 REPRESENTS AN
ACCELERATION OF 0.5 KNOTS/SEC

DATE:15 APRIL 1990
DATA BASIS: (STORES) ESTIMATED
(AIRCRAFT/CFT) FLIGHT TEST

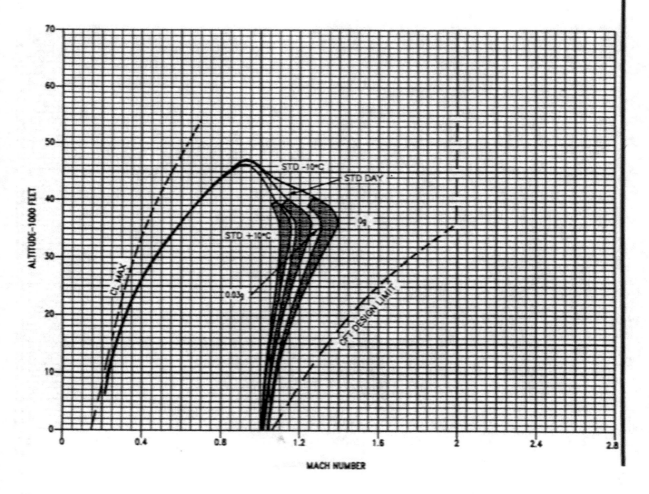

Figure A9-8

15E-1-(173-1)16-CATI

LEVEL FLIGHT ENVELOPE
GROSS WEIGHT – 60,300 POUNDS
MAXIMUM THRUST

AIRPLANE CONFIGURATION
–4CFT, LANTIRN, CL TANK,
(4)ASM-9, (12)MK-82

REMARKS
ENGINE(S): (2) F100-PW-220
U.S. STANDARD DAY, 1966

NOTE
CAPABILITY REMAINING: MAXIMUM SPEEDS, ACCELERATION OF
0 AND 0.03g; CEILINGS AND LOW SPEED, RATE OF CLIMB OF
500 FEET PER MINUTE. a/g = 0.03 REPRESENTS AN
ACCELERATION OF 0.5 KNOTS/SEC

DATE: 15 APRIL 1990
DATA BASIS: (STORES) ESTIMATED
(AIRCRAFT/CFT) FLIGHT TEST

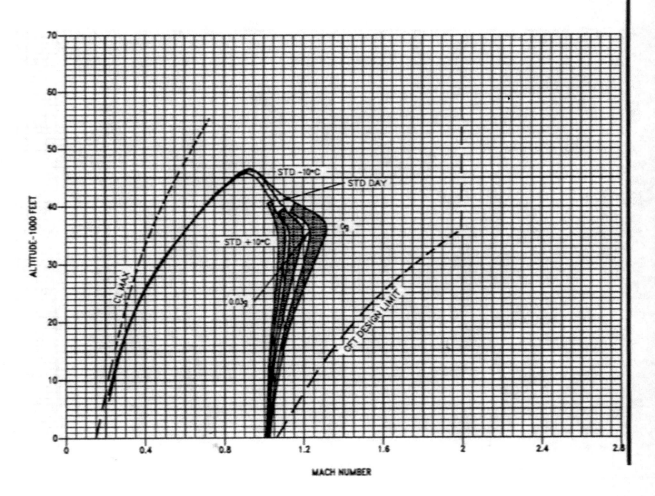

Figure A9-9

15E-1-(173-1)16-CATI

LEVEL FLIGHT ENVELOPE
MILITARY THRUST
GROSS WEIGHT – 40,000 POUNDS

AIRPLANE CONFIGURATION
INDIVIDUAL DRAG INDEXES

REMARKS
ENGINE(S): (2) F100-PW-220
U.S. STANDARD DAY, 1966

NOTE
- CAPABILITY REMAINING: MAXIMUM SPEEDS, ACCELERATION OF 0g; CEILINGS AND LOW SPEED, RATE OF CLIMB OF 500 FEET PER MINUTE.
- CFT DRAG MUST BE INCLUDED WHEN TOTAL DRAG INDEX IS CALCULATED.

DATE:15 JUNE 1988
DATA BASIS: ESTIMATED

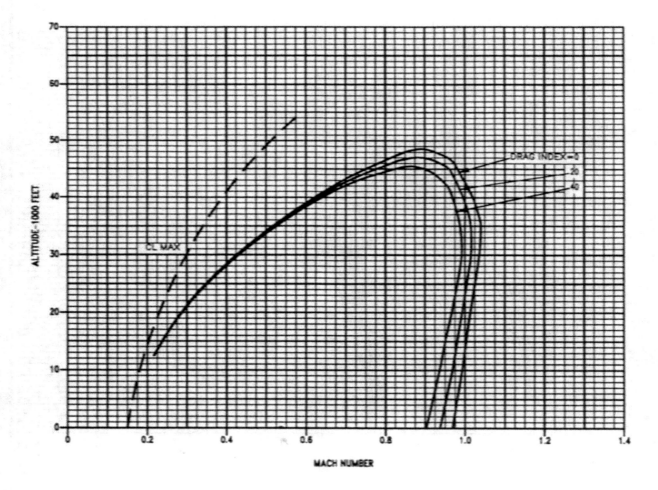

15E-1-(242-1)04-CATI

Figure A9-10

LEVEL FLIGHT ENVELOPE
MILITARY THRUST
GROSS WEIGHT – 50,000 POUNDS

AIRPLANE CONFIGURATION
INDIVIDUAL DRAG INDEXES

REMARKS
ENGINE(S): (2) F100-PW-220
U.S. STANDARD DAY, 1966

NOTES
- CAPABILITY REMAINING: MAXIMUM SPEEDS, ACCELERATION OF 0g; CEILINGS AND LOW SPEED, RATE OF CLIMB OF 500 FEET PER MINUTE.
- CFT DRAG MUST BE INCLUDED WHEN TOTAL DRAG INDEX IS CALCULATED.

DATE: 15 JUNE 1988
DATA BASIS: ESTIMATED

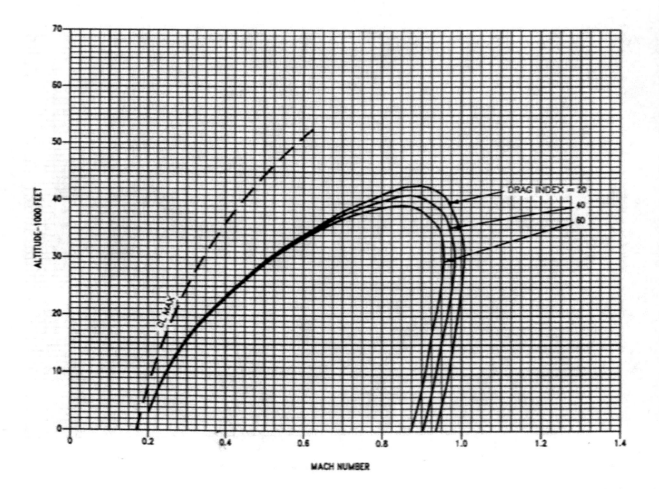

Figure A9-11

15E-1-(162-1)04-CATI

LEVEL FLIGHT ENVELOPE
MILITARY THRUST
GROSS WEIGHT – 60,000 POUNDS

AIRPLANE CONFIGURATION
INDIVIDUAL DRAG INDEXES

REMARKS
ENGINE(S): (2) F100-PW-220
U.S. STANDARD DAY, 1966

NOTES
- CAPABILITY REMAINING: MAXIMUM SPEEDS, ACCELERATION OF 0g; CEILINGS AND LOW SPEED, RATE OF CLIMB OF 500 FEET PER MINUTE.
- CFT DRAG MUST BE INCLUDED WHEN TOTAL DRAG INDEX IS CALCULATED

DATE: 15 JUNE 1988
DATA BASIS: ESTIMATED

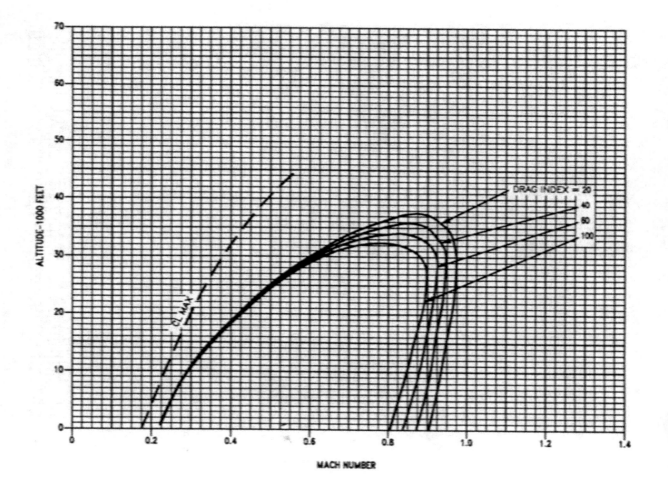

15E-1-(174-1)04-CAT)

Figure A9-12

LEVEL FLIGHT ENVELOPE
MILITARY THRUST
GROSS WEIGHT – 70,000 POUNDS

AIRPLANE CONFIGURATION
INDIVIDUAL DRAG INDEXES

REMARKS
ENGINE(S): (2) F100-PW-220
U.S. STANDARD DAY, 1966

NOTES
- CAPABILITY REMAINING: MAXIMUM SPEEDS, ACCELERATION OF 0g; CEILINGS AND LOW SPEED, RATE OF CLIMB OF 500 FEET PER MINUTE.
- CFT DRAG MUST BE INCLUDED WHEN TOTAL DRAG INDEX IS CALCULATED.

DATE: 15 JUNE 1988
DATA BASIS: ESTIMATED

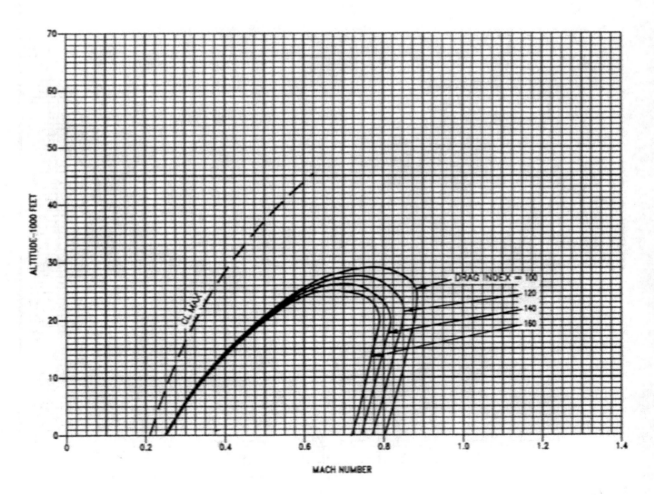

Figure A9-13

15E-1-(175-1)04-CAT1

LEVEL FLIGHT ENVELOPE
GROSS WEIGHT – 41,500 POUNDS

AIRPLANE CONFIGURATION
(4)AIM-7

REMARKS
ENGINE(S): (2) F100-PW-220
U.S. STANDARD DAY, 1966

NOTE
CAPABILITY REMAINING: MAXIMUM SPEEDS, ACCELERATION OF
0g; CEILINGS AND LOW SPEED, RATE OF CLIMB OF
500 FEET PER MINUTE.

DATE: 15 APRIL 1990
DATA BASIS: FLIGHT TEST

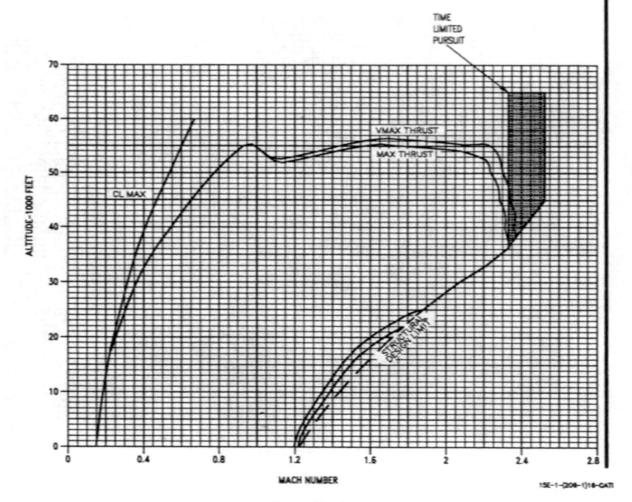

Figure A9-14

MAXIMUM SPEED - LEVEL FLIGHT
MILITARY POWER - DRAG INDEX 0 TO 60

REMARKS

AIRPLANE CONFIGURATION
INDIVIDUAL DRAG INDEXES

ENGINES: (2) F100-PW-220
U.S. STANDARD DAY, 1966

DATE: 15 JUNE 1988
DATA BASIS: **ESTIMATED**

NOTE

- CFT DRAG MUST BE INCLUDED WHEN TOTAL DRAG INDEX IS CALCULATED
- a/g=0.03 REPRESENTS AN ACCELERATION OF 0.5 KNOTS/SEC

		MAXIMUM SPEED MACH/KCAS							
		GROSS WEIGHT = 40,000 POUNDS				GROSS WEIGHT = 50,000 POUNDS			
DRAG INDEX		0	0	20	20	40	40	60	60
ALTITUDE (FT)	TEMP °C	a/g=0.0	a/g=0.03	a/g=0.0	a/g=0.03	a/g=0.0	a/g=0.03	a/g=0.0	a/g=0.03
S.L.	5.0	0.99/651	0.98/648	0.96/633	0.95/629	0.93/612	0.92/605	0.90/594	0.89/586
	15.0	0.97/641	0.96/636	0.93/618	0.93/612	0.90/598	0.89/589	0.87/576	0.86/566
	25.0	0.95/630	0.94/623	0.91/604	0.90/598	0.88/581	0.86/569	0.84/554	0.82/541
5000	-4.9	1.00/610	0.99/607	0.97/596	0.96/591	0.94/576	0.93/569	0.91/559	0.90/553
	5.1	0.98/602	0.98/599	0.95/584	0.94/578	0.92/564	0.91/556	0.89/547	0.88/537
	15.1	0.97/592	0.96/586	0.93/569	0.92/562	0.90/550	0.88/539	0.86/528	0.84/516
10000	-14.8	1.01/570	1.00/567	0.99/558	0.98/554	0.96/541	0.95/534	0.93/524	0.92/517
	-4.8	0.99/562	0.99/558	0.97/548	0.96/542	0.94/529	0.92/521	0.91/513	0.90/506
	5.2	0.98/554	0.97/549	0.95/536	0.94/528	0.92/517	0.90/508	0.89/499	0.86/486
20000	-34.6	1.03/490	1.02/485	1.01/479	1.00/475	0.98/467	0.97/461	0.95/449	0.94/444
	-24.6	1.01/482	1.00/477	0.99/471	0.98/466	0.97/458	0.95/447	0.94/442	0.92/433
	-14.6	1.00/475	1.00/470	0.98/464	0.96/457	0.94/446	0.92/436	0.92/432	0.90/422
30000	-54.4	1.05/412	1.03/404	1.02/401	1.01/393	0.99/385	0.97/375	0.95/368	0.94/361
	-44.4	1.04/407	1.02/400	1.02/397	1.00/391	0.99/383	0.96/374	0.95/368	0.91/312
	-34.4	1.02/398	1.00/392	1.00/389	0.98/382	0.97/375	0.94/364	0.94/364	0.91/352
35000	-64.3	1.04/368	1.02/358	1.02/356	0.99/347	0.97/339	0.94/327	0.95/330	0.91/312
	-54.3	1.04/366	1.02/357	1.02/356	0.99/348	0.97/339	0.94/328	0.95/330	0.91/312
	-44.3	1.02/360	1.01/353	1.00/352	0.98/344	0.97/337	0.94.326	0.95/329	0.90/312
40000	-66.5	1.02/320	0.99/309	1.00/311	0.97/300	0.95/295	—	0.90/278	—
	-56.5	1.02/319	0.99/309	1.00/311	0.97/300	0.95/295	—	0.91/278	—
	-46.5	1.01/315	0.98/306	0.99/307	0.96/298	0.94/292	—	0.90/278	—

Figure A9-15

MAXIMUM SPEED - LEVEL FLIGHT
MILITARY POWER - DRAG INDEX 80 TO 160

REMARKS

AIRPLANE CONFIGURATION
INDIVIDUAL DRAG INDEXES

ENGINES: (2) F100-PW-220
U.S.STANDARD DAY, 1966

DATE: 15 JUNE 1988
DATA BASIS: ESTIMATED

NOTE

- CFT DRAG MUST BE INCLUDED WHEN TOTAL DRAG INDEX IS CALCULATED
- a/g=0.03 REPRESENTS AN ACCELERATION OF 0.5 KNOTS/SEC

		MAXIMUM SPEED MACH/KCAS									
		GROSS WEIGHT = 60,000 POUNDS				GROSS WEIGHT = 70,000 POUNDS					
DRAG INDEX		80	80	100	100	120	120	140	140	160	160
ALTITUDE (FT)	TEMP °C	a/g=0.0	a/g=0.03	a/g=0.0	a/g=0.03	a/g=0.0	a/g=0.03	a/g=0.0	a/g=0.03	a/g=0.0	a/g=0.03
S.L.	5.0	0.87/573	0.85/561	0.83/551	0.81/538	0.80/531	0.78/514	0.77/512	0.75/496	0.75/495	0.73/480
	15.0	0.84/553	0.81/539	0.80/532	0.78/517	0.77/510	0.75/493	0.74/492	0.72/476	0.72/477	0.70/460
	25.0	0.80/529	0.77/512	0.77/507	0.74/491	0.74/487	0.71/468	0.71/470	0.68/452	0.69/455	0.66/436
5000	-4.9	0.89/543	0.87/531	0.86/524	0.84/511	0.83/505	0.80/488	0.80/488	0.77/469	0.77/470	0.74/453
	5.1	0.86/526	0.84/510	0.83/505	0.80/489	0.79/484	0.76/464	0.76/466	0.73/447	0.74/450	0.71/431
	15.1	0.83/505	0.80/489	0.80/485	0.77/467	0.76/463	0.73/442	0.73/446	0.70/426	0.71/431	0.67/410
10000	-14.8	0.91/510	0.89/499	0.88/494	0.85/480	0.85/475	0.81/455	0.82/457	0.78/438	0.79/441	0.75/422
	-4.8	0.88/496	0.86/481	0.85/477	0.82/459	0.81/455	0.77/433	0.78/438	0.75/417	0.76/423	0.72/402
	5.2	0.85/478	0.82/457	0.81/456	0.78/436	0.78/435	0.73/410	0.75/418	0.71/395	0.72/403	0.68/380
20000	-34.6	0.93/439	0.91/430	0.91/429	0.89/417	0.88/414	0.83/389	0.85/399	0.79/370	0.82/383	0.75/360
	-24.6	0.91/429	0.88/415	0.89/417	0.85/399	0.85/399	0.80/373	0.82/384	0.76/353	0.79/370	0.72/335
	-14.6	0.89/417	0.85/397	0.86.401	0.81/378	0.81.379	0.74/345	0.78/363	0.71/327	0.75/348	0.67/309
30000	-54.4	0.93/359	0.87/331	0.90/347	—	—	—	—	—	—	—
	-44.4	0.93/359	0.87/332	0.90/348	—	—	—	—	—	—	—
	-34.4	0.91/350	0.83/317	0.88/336	—	—	—	—	—	—	—
35000	-64.3	0.88/304	—	—	—	—	—	—	—	—	—
	-54.3	0.89/305	—	—	—	—	—	—	—	—	—
	-44.3	0.89/304	—	—	—	—	—	—	—	—	—
40000	-66.5	—	—	—	—	—	—	—	—	—	—
	-56.5	—	—	—	—	—	—	—	—	—	—
	-46.5	—	—	—	—	—	—	—	—	—	—

Figure A9-16

DIVE RECOVERY-6.0 G PULL-OUT
SUBSONIC-SPEEDBRAKE RETRACTED
GROSS WEIGHT 37,400 POUNDS-MAX POWER

AIRPLANE CONFIGURATION
(2) WING PYLONS,
(4) LAU-128 LAUNCHERS,
CENTERLINE 610 GAL. FUEL TANK

REMARKS
ENGINE(S): (2) F100-PW-220
U.S. STANDARD DAY, 1966

NOTE
PULL-OUT BASED ON 2.0 g PER SECOND ACCELERATION
BUILDUP TO MAXIMUM USABLE STABILATOR LIMIT OR
6.0 g WHICHEVER OCCURS FIRST.

DATE: 15 JUNE 1988
DATA BASIS: ESTIMATED

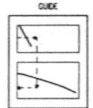

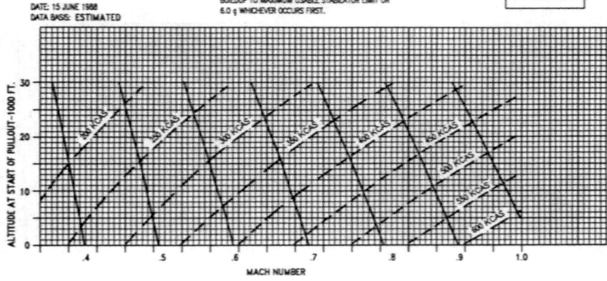

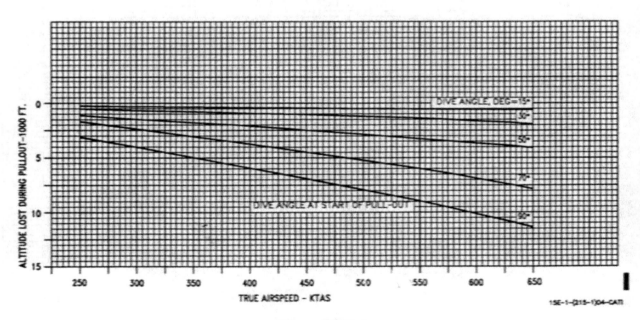

Figure A9-17

15E-1-(215-1)04-CAT1

DIVE RECOVERY-6.0 G PULL-OUT

SUPERSONIC-SPEEDBRAKE RETRACTED
GROSS WEIGHT 37,400 POUNDS-MAX POWER

GUIDE

AIRPLANE CONFIGURATION
(2) WING PYLONS,
(4) LAU-128 LAUNCHERS

REMARKS
ENGINE(S): (2) F100-PW-220
U.S. STANDARD DAY, 1966

NOTE
PULL-OUT BASED ON 2.0 g PER SECOND ACCELERATION
BUILDUP TO MAXIMUM USABLE STABILATOR LIMIT OR
6.0 g WHICHEVER OCCURS FIRST.

DATE: 15 JUNE 1988
DATA BASIS: ESTIMATED

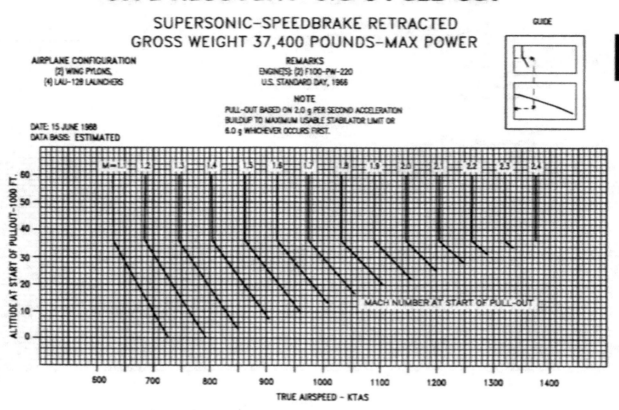

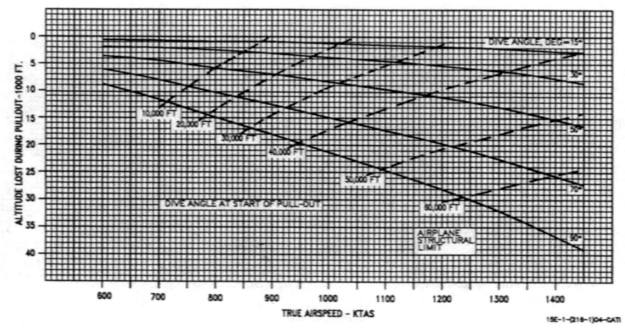

Figure A9-18

15E-1-(21E-1)04-CAT1

DIVE RECOVERY-6.0G PULL-OUT

SUBSONIC–SPEEDBRAKE RETRACTED
GROSS WEIGHT–45,000 POUNDS

AIRPLANE CONFIGURATION
(4)AIM-7+(2)WING PYLONS
+(4)LAUNCHERS/ADAPTERS
+(4)AIM-9

DATE: 15 MARCH 1991
DATA BASIS: ESTIMATED

REMARKS
ENGINE: (2)F100-PW-220
U.S. STANDARD DAY, 1966

NOTE
● ALTITUDE LOSS WITH MAXIMUM THRUST IS
ESSENTIALLY THE SAME WITH MILITARY THRUST
● PULL-OUT BASED ON 2.0G PER SECOND
ACCELERATION BUILDUP TO MAXIMUM USABLE
NORMAL FORCE STABILATOR LIMIT OR 6.0G,
WHICHEVER OCCURS FIRST

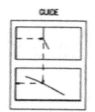

GUIDE

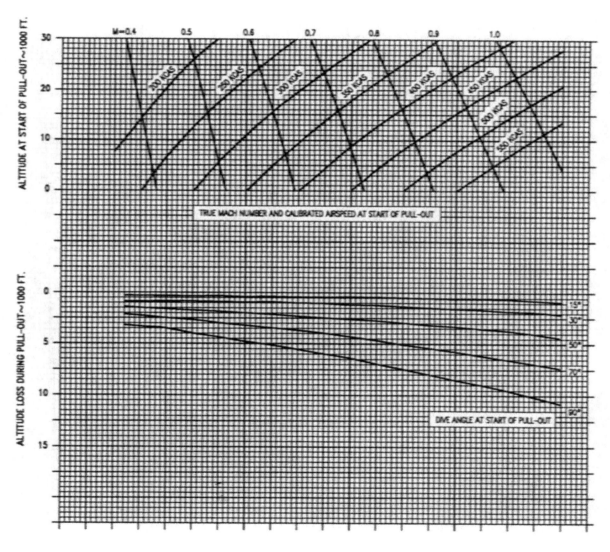

Figure A9-18A (Sheet 1 of 7)

15E-1-(2)78-1)21-CAT!!

DIVE RECOVERY-6.0G PULL-OUT
SUPERSONIC-SPEEDBRAKE RETRACTED
GROSS WEIGHT-45,000 POUNDS

AIRPLANE CONFIGURATION
(4)AIM-7 +(2)WING PYLONS
+(4)LAUNCHERS/ADAPTERS
+(4)AIM-9

DATE: 15 MARCH 1991
DATA BASIS: ESTIMATED

REMARKS
ENGINE: (2)F100-PW-220
U.S. STANDARD DAY, 1966

NOTE
- ALTITUDE LOSS WITH MAXIMUM THRUST IS ESSENTIALLY THE SAME WITH MILITARY THRUST
- PULL-OUT BASED ON 2.0G PER SECOND ACCELERATION BUILDUP TO MAXIMUM USABLE NORMAL FORCE STABILATOR LIMIT OR 6.0G, WHICHEVER OCCURS FIRST

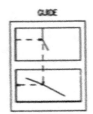
GUIDE

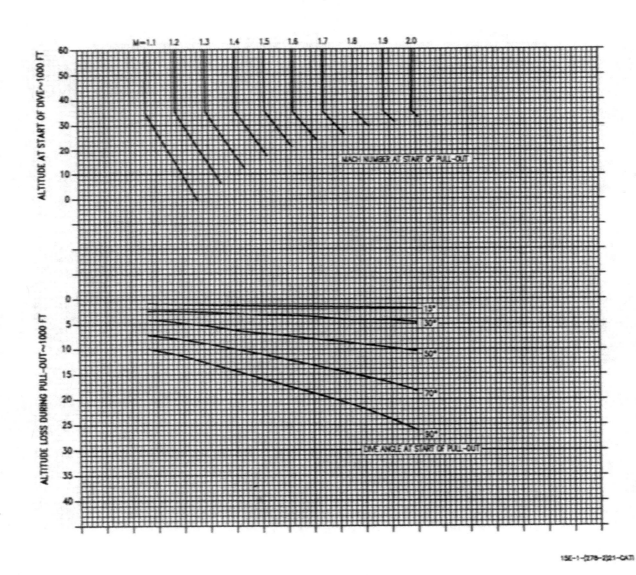

Figure A9-18A (Sheet 2)

DIVE RECOVERY-6.0G PULL-OUT
SUBSONIC–SPEEDBRAKE RETRACTED
GROSS WEIGHT–55,000 POUNDS

AIRPLANE CONFIGURATION
–4CFT+(4)AIM-7
+(2)WING PYLONS
+(4)LAUNCHERS/ADAPTERS
+(4)AIM-9

DATE: 15 MARCH 1991
DATA BASIS: ESTIMATED

REMARKS
ENGINE: (2)F100-PW-220
U.S. STANDARD DAY, 1966

NOTE
● ALTITUDE LOSS WITH MAXIMUM THRUST IS
   ESSENTIALLY THE SAME WITH MILITARY THRUST
● PULL-OUT BASED ON 2.0G PER SECOND
   ACCELERATION BUILDUP TO MAXIMUM USABLE
   NORMAL FORCE STABILATOR LIMIT OR 6.0G,
   WHICHEVER OCCURS FIRST
● SHADED AREA INDICATES POSSIBLE STRUCTURAL
   OVERLOAD AT 6G's. RECOVERIES IN THIS REGION
   SHOULD BE LIMITED TO Nz ALLOWABLE BASED ON
   OVERLOAD WARNING SYSTEM OR OWS INOPERATIVE
   CHARTS

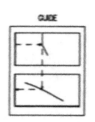

GUIDE

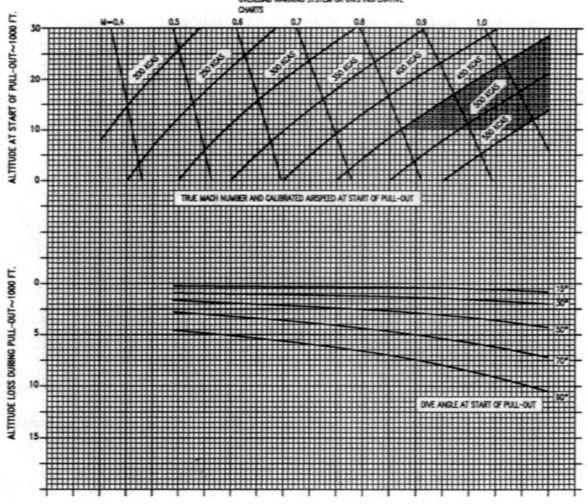

15E-1-(27B-3)21-CAT1

Figure A9-18A (Sheet 3)

DIVE RECOVERY-6.0G PULL-OUT
SUPERSONIC-SPEEDBRAKE RETRACTED
GROSS WEIGHT-55,000 POUNDS

AIRPLANE CONFIGURATION
-4CFT+(4)AIM-7
+(2)WING PYLONS
+(4)LAUNCHERS/ADAPTERS
+(4)AIM-9

DATE: 15 MARCH 1991
DATA BASIS: ESTIMATED

REMARKS
ENGINE: (2)F100-PW-220
U.S. STANDARD DAY, 1966

NOTE
● ALTITUDE LOSS WITH MAXIMUM THRUST IS
ESSENTIALLY THE SAME WITH MILITARY THRUST
● PULL-OUT BASED ON 2.0G PER SECOND
ACCELERATION BUILDUP TO MAXIMUM USABLE
NORMAL FORCE STABILATOR LIMIT OR 6.0G,
WHICHEVER OCCURS FIRST
● SHADED AREA INDICATES POSSIBLE STRUCTURAL
OVERLOAD AT 6G's. RECOVERIES IN THIS REGION
SHOULD BE LIMITED TO Nz ALLOWABLE BASED ON
OVERLOAD WARNING SYSTEM OR OWS INOPERATIVE
CHARTS

GUIDE

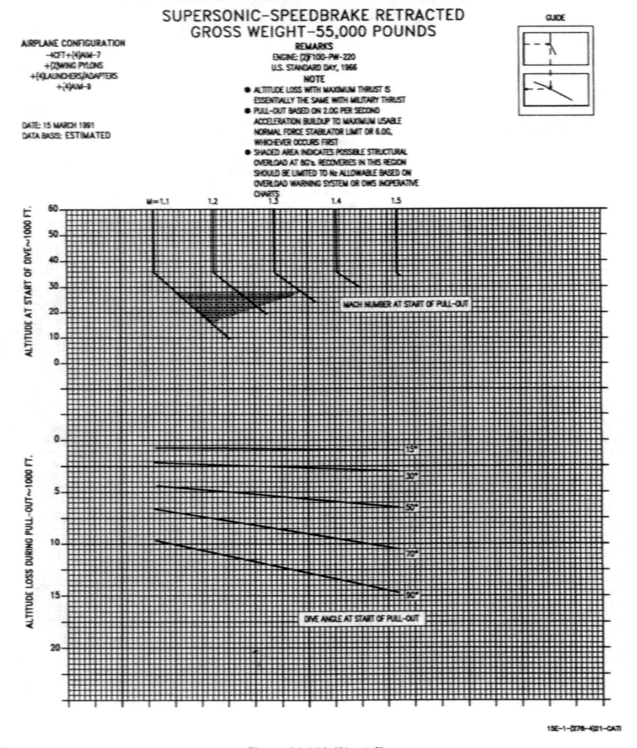

Figure A9-18A (Sheet 4)

15E-1-(1)76-(4)21-CATI

DIVE RECOVERY-6.0G PULL-OUT
SUBSONIC–SPEEDBRAKE RETRACTED
GROSS WEIGHT–65,000 POUNDS

GUIDE

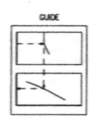

AIRPLANE CONFIGURATION
–4CFT+LANTIRN PODS
+(12)MK-82+(2)WING PYLONS
+(4)LAUNCHERS/ADAPTERS
+(4)AIM-9

DATE: 15 MARCH 1991
DATA BASIS: ESTIMATED

REMARKS
ENGINE: (2)F100-PW-220
U.S. STANDARD DAY, 1966

NOTE
- ALTITUDE LOSS WITH MAXIMUM THRUST IS ESSENTIALLY THE SAME WITH MILITARY THRUST
- PULL-OUT BASED ON 2.0G PER SECOND ACCELERATION BUILDUP TO MAXIMUM USABLE NORMAL FORCE STABILATOR LIMIT OR 6.0G, WHICHEVER OCCURS FIRST
- SHADED AREA INDICATES POSSIBLE STRUCTURAL OVERLOAD AT 6G's. RECOVERIES IN THIS REGION SHOULD BE LIMITED TO Nz ALLOWABLE BASED ON OVERLOAD WARNING SYSTEM OR OWS INOPERATIVE CHARTS

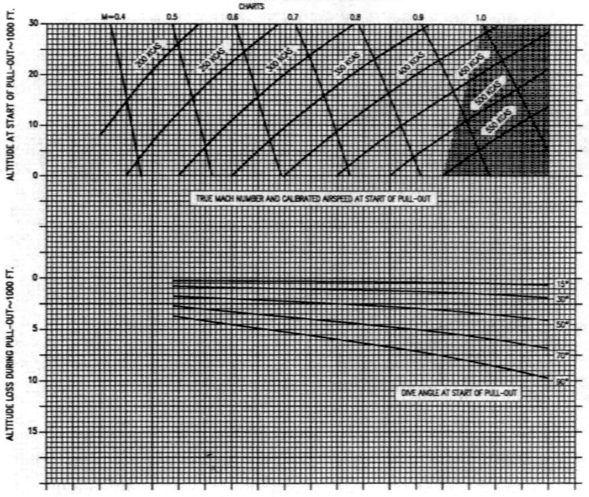

Figure A9-18A (Sheet 5)

Change 2   A9-24E

DIVE RECOVERY-6.0G PULL-OUT
SUPERSONIC-SPEEDBRAKE RETRACTED
GROSS WEIGHT-65,000 POUNDS

AIRPLANE CONFIGURATION
-4CTF+LANTIRN PODS
+(12)MK-82+(2)WING PYLONS
+(4)LAUNCHERS/ADAPTERS
+(4)AIM-9

DATE: 15 MARCH 1991
DATA BASIS: ESTIMATED

REMARKS
ENGINE: (2)F100-PW-220
U.S. STANDARD DAY, 1966

NOTE
● ALTITUDE LOSS WITH MAXIMUM THRUST IS
ESSENTIALLY THE SAME WITH MILITARY THRUST
● PULL-OUT BASED ON 2.0G PER SECOND
ACCELERATION BUILDUP TO MAXIMUM USABLE
NORMAL FORCE STABILATOR LIMIT OR 6.0G,
WHICHEVER OCCURS FIRST
● SHADED AREA INDICATES POSSIBLE STRUCTURAL
OVERLOAD AT 6G's. RECOVERIES IN THIS REGION
SHOULD BE LIMITED TO N_Z ALLOWABLE BASED ON
OVERLOAD WARNING SYSTEM OR OWS INOPERATIVE
CHARTS

GUIDE

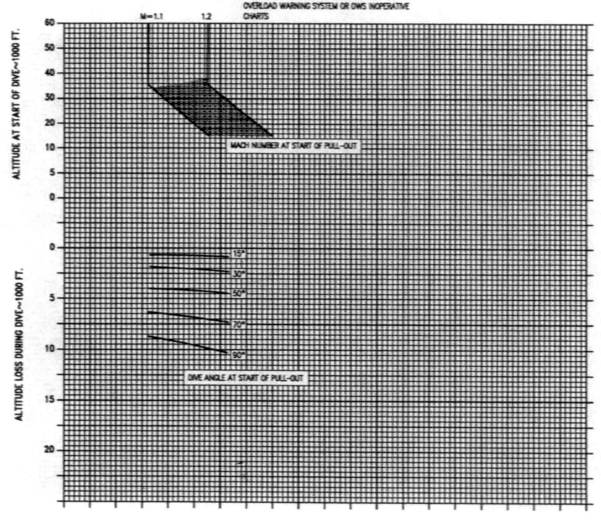

Figure A9-18A (Sheet 6)

DIVE RECOVERY-6.0G PULL-OUT

SUBSONIC-SPEEDBRAKE RETRACTED
GROSS WEIGHT-70,000 POUNDS

AIRPLANE CONFIGURATION
-4CFT+LANTIRN PODS
+(12)MK-82+(2)WING PYLONS
+(4)LAUNCHERS/ADAPTERS
+(4)AIM-9+CENTERLINE PYLON/TANK

DATE: 15 MARCH 1991
DATA BASIS: ESTIMATED

REMARKS
ENGINE: (2)F100-PW-220
U.S. STANDARD DAY, 1966

NOTE
- ALTITUDE LOSS WITH MAXIMUM THRUST IS ESSENTIALLY THE SAME WITH MILITARY THRUST
- PULL-OUT BASED ON 2.0G PER SECOND ACCELERATION BUILDUP TO MAXIMUM USABLE NORMAL FORCE STABILATOR LIMIT OR 6.0G, WHICHEVER OCCURS FIRST
- SHADED AREA INDICATES POSSIBLE STRUCTURAL OVERLOAD AT 6G's. RECOVERIES IN THIS REGION SHOULD BE LIMITED TO Nz ALLOWABLE BASED ON OVERLOAD WARNING SYSTEM OR OWS INOPERATIVE CHARTS

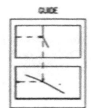

GUIDE

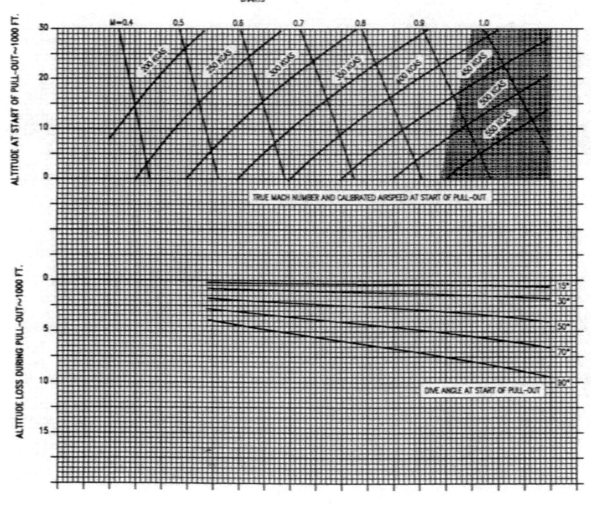

TRUE MACH NUMBER AND CALIBRATED AIRSPEED AT START OF PULL-OUT

DIVE ANGLE AT START OF PULL-OUT

15E-1-(27B-7)21-CAT1

Figure A9-18A (Sheet 7)

DIVE RECOVERY-EMERGENCY PULL-OUT

GROSS WEIGHT OF 40,000 TO 45,000 POUNDS
APPLICABLE ONLY FOR
RECOVERIES BELOW 10,000 FEET

AIRPLANE CONFIGURATION
(4)AIM-7+(2)WING PYLONS
+(4)LAUNCHERS/ADAPTERS
+(4)AIM-9

DATE: 15 MARCH 1991
DATA BASIS: ESTIMATED

REMARKS
ENGINE: (2)F100-PW-220
U.S. STANDARD DAY, 1966

NOTE
● RETRACT SPEEDBRAKE AT AIRSPEEDS BELOW
350 KCAS, EXTEND ABOVE 350 KCAS
● CAS ON OR OFF

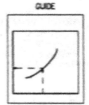

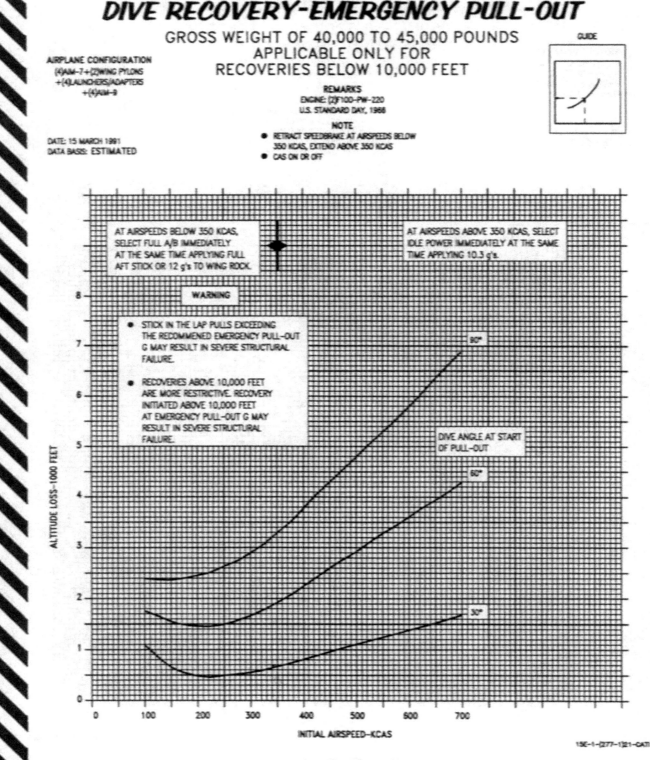

AT AIRSPEEDS BELOW 350 KCAS,
SELECT FULL A/B IMMEDIATELY
AT THE SAME TIME APPLYING FULL
AFT STICK OR 12 g's TO WING ROCK.

AT AIRSPEEDS ABOVE 350 KCAS, SELECT
IDLE POWER IMMEDIATELY AT THE SAME
TIME APPLYING 10.3 g's.

WARNING

● STICK IN THE LAP PULLS EXCEEDING
THE RECOMMENED EMERGENCY PULL-OUT
G MAY RESULT IN SEVERE STRUCTURAL
FAILURE.

● RECOVERIES ABOVE 10,000 FEET
ARE MORE RESTRICTIVE. RECOVERY
INITIATED ABOVE 10,000 FEET
AT EMERGENCY PULL-OUT G MAY
RESULT IN SEVERE STRUCTURAL
FAILURE.

DIVE ANGLE AT START
OF PULL-OUT

90°

60°

30°

ALTITUDE LOSS-1000 FEET

INITIAL AIRSPEED-KCAS

15E-1-(277-1)21-CATI

Figure A9-18B (Sheet 1 of 4)

DIVE RECOVERY-EMERGENCY PULL-OUT

GROSS WEIGHT OF 40,000 TO 45,000 POUNDS
APPLICABLE ONLY FOR
RECOVERIES BELOW 10,000 FEET

AIRPLANE CONFIGURATION
-4CFT+(4)AIM-7+(2)WING PYLONS
+(4)LAUNCHERS/ADAPTERS
+(4)AIM-9

DATE: 15 MARCH 1991
DATA BASIS: ESTIMATED

REMARKS
ENGINE: (2)F100-PW-220
U.S. STANDARD DAY, 1966

NOTE
● RETRACT SPEEDBRAKE AT AIRSPEEDS BELOW
  350 KCAS, EXTEND ABOVE 350 KCAS
● CAS ON OR OFF

GUIDE

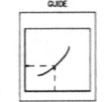

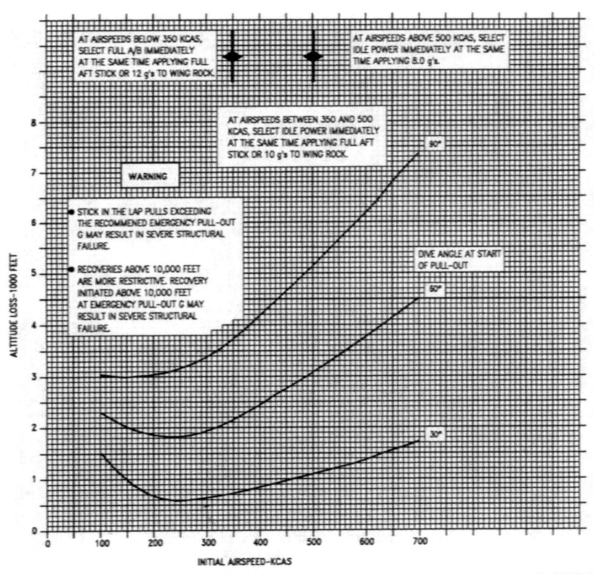

Figure A9-18B (Sheet 2)

DIVE RECOVERY-EMERGENCY PULL-OUT

GROSS WEIGHT OF 65,000 POUNDS
APPLICABLE ONLY FOR
RECOVERIES BELOW 10,000 FEET

AIRPLANE CONFIGURATION
-4CFT+LANTIRN PODS+(12)MK-82
+(2)WING PYLONS
+(4)LAUNCHERS/ADAPTERS
+(4)AIM-9

DATE: 15 MARCH 1991
DATA BASIS: ESTIMATED

REMARKS
ENGINE: (2)F100-PW-220
U.S. STANDARD DAY, 1966

NOTE
● RETRACT SPEEDBRAKE AT AIRSPEEDS BELOW
  350 KCAS, EXTEND ABOVE 350 KCAS
● CAS ON

GUIDE

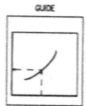

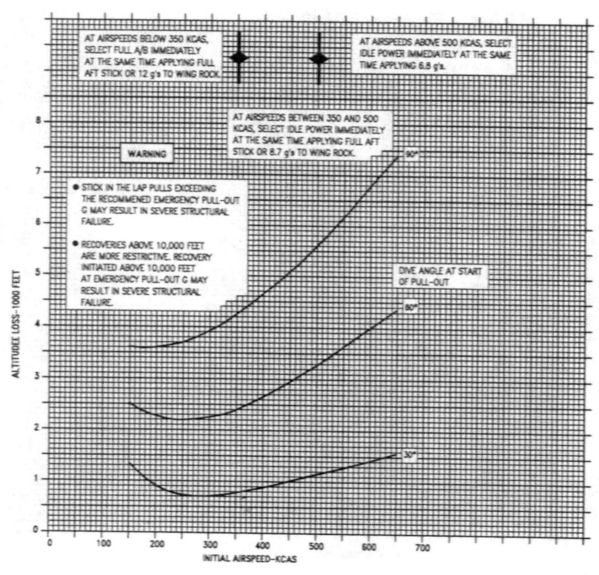

AT AIRSPEEDS BELOW 350 KCAS, SELECT FULL A/B IMMEDIATELY AT THE SAME TIME APPLYING FULL AFT STICK OR 12 g's TO WING ROCK.

AT AIRSPEEDS ABOVE 500 KCAS, SELECT IDLE POWER IMMEDIATELY AT THE SAME TIME APPLYING 6.8 g's.

AT AIRSPEEDS BETWEEN 350 AND 500 KCAS, SELECT IDLE POWER IMMEDIATELY AT THE SAME TIME APPLYING FULL AFT STICK OR 8.7 g's TO WING ROCK.

WARNING

● STICK IN THE LAP PULLS EXCEEDING THE RECOMMENED EMERGENCY PULL-OUT G MAY RESULT IN SEVERE STRUCTURAL FAILURE.

● RECOVERIES ABOVE 10,000 FEET ARE MORE RESTRICTIVE. RECOVERY INITIATED ABOVE 10,000 FEET AT EMERGENCY PULL-OUT G MAY RESULT IN SEVERE STRUCTURAL FAILURE.

DIVE ANGLE AT START OF PULL-OUT

90°
60°
30°

ALTITUDEE LOSS-1000 FEET

INITIAL AIRSPEED-KCAS

15E-1-(277-3)21-CATI

Figure A9-18B (Sheet 3)

DIVE RECOVER-EMERGENCY PULL-OUT

GROSS WEIGHT OF 70,000 POUNDS
APPLICABLE ONLY FOR RECOVERIES
BELOW 10,000 FEET

GUIDE

AIRPLANE CONFIGURATION
-4CFT+LANTIRN PODS+
(12)MK-82+(2)WING PYLONS
+(4)LAUNCHERS/ADAPTERS+
(4)AIM-9+CENTER LINE PYLON/TANK

REMARKS
ENGINE: (2)F100-PW-220
U.S. STANDARD DAY, 1966

DATE: 15 MARCH 1991
DATA BASIS: ESTIMATED

NOTE
● RETRACT SPEEDBRAKE AT AIRSPEEDS BELOW
350 KCAS, EXTEND ABOVE 350 KCAS
● CAS ON

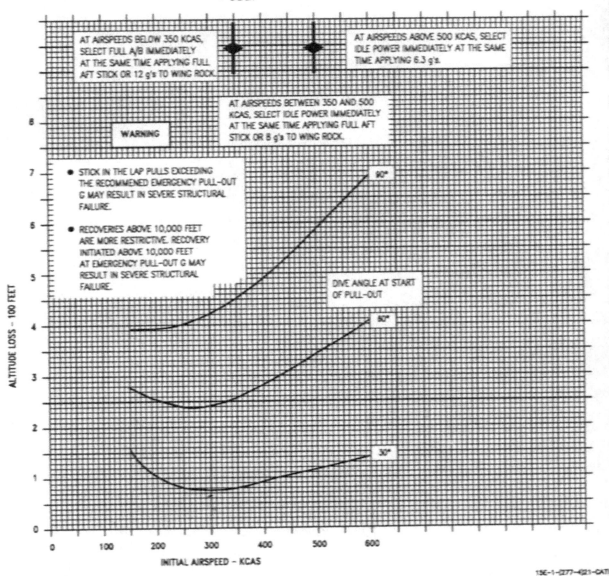

AT AIRSPEEDS BELOW 350 KCAS,
SELECT FULL A/B IMMEDIATELY
AT THE SAME TIME APPLYING FULL
AFT STICK OR 12 g's TO WING ROCK.

AT AIRSPEEDS ABOVE 500 KCAS, SELECT
IDLE POWER IMMEDIATELY AT THE SAME
TIME APPLYING 6.3 g's.

AT AIRSPEEDS BETWEEN 350 AND 500
KCAS, SELECT IDLE POWER IMMEDIATELY
AT THE SAME TIME APPLYING FULL AFT
STICK OR 8 g's TO WING ROCK.

WARNING

● STICK IN THE LAP PULLS EXCEEDING
THE RECOMMENED EMERGENCY PULL-OUT
G MAY RESULT IN SEVERE STRUCTURAL
FAILURE.

● RECOVERIES ABOVE 10,000 FEET
ARE MORE RESTRICTIVE. RECOVERY
INITIATED ABOVE 10,000 FEET
AT EMERGENCY PULL-OUT G MAY
RESULT IN SEVERE STRUCTURAL
FAILURE.

DIVE ANGLE AT START
OF PULL-OUT

90°

60°

30°

ALTITUDE LOSS – 100 FEET

INITIAL AIRSPEED – KCAS

15E-1-0277-4(2)-CATI

Figure A9-18B (Sheet 4)

LOW ALTITUDE COMBAT PERFORMANCE
MAXIMUM THRUST

AIRPLANE CONFIGURATION
ALL DRAG INDEXES

REMARKS
ENGINE(S): (2) F100-PW-220
U.S. STANDARD DAY, 1966

DATE:15 JUNE 1988
DATA BASIS: ESTIMATED

	CONSTANT KCAS	SPECIFIC FUEL FLOW–LB/MIN	TEMPERATURE EFFECTS	
			ACTUAL OAT DEG C	CORRECTION FACTOR
SEA LEVEL (15°C)	300	1793	-40	1.19
	400	1936	-20	1.17
	500	2103	0	1.07
	600	2196	20	.98
	700	2526	40	.90

5000 FEET (5.1°C)	300	1579	-40	1.21
	400	1724	-20	1.14
	500	1901	0	1.03
	600	2113	20	.94
	700	2341	40	.86

10,000 FEET (-4.8°C)	300	1388	-40	1.18
	400	1540	-20	1.08
	500	1722	0	.97
	600	1934	20	.88
	700	2208	40	.81

15E-1-(205-1)03-CAT1

Figure A9-19

COMBAT FUEL MANAGEMENT

AIRPLANE CONFIGURATION
ALL DRAG INDEXES

REMARKS
ENGINES: (2) F100-PW-220
U.S. STANDARD DAY, 1966

GUIDE

DATE: 15 JUNE 1988
DATA BASIS: ESTIMATED

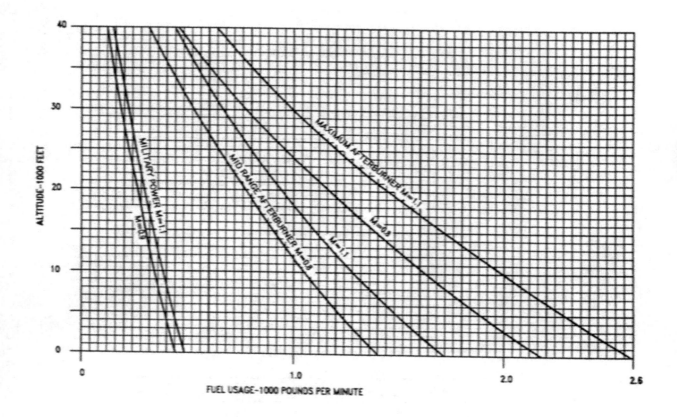

Figure A9-20

COMBAT FUEL FLOW
STABILIZED LEVEL FLIGHT

AIRPLANE CONFIGURATION
F-15E

REMARKS
ENGINE(S): (2) F100-PW-220
U.S. STANDARD DAY, 1966

GUIDE

DATE: 15 APRIL 1990
DATA BASIS: FLIGHT TEST

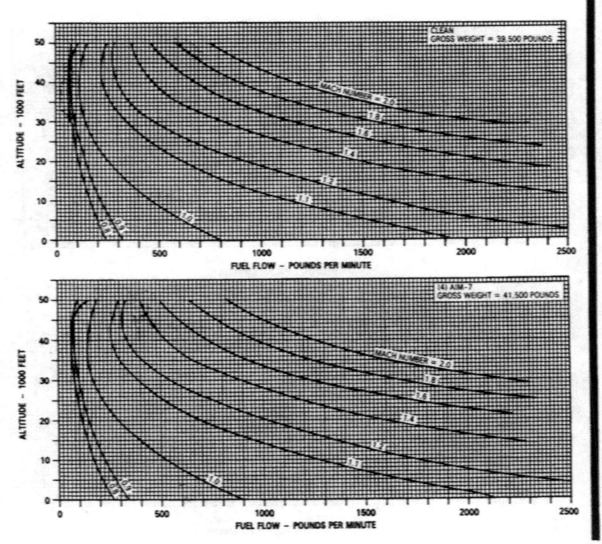

Figure A9-21

15E-1-(203)16

COMBAT FUEL FLOW

STABILIZED LEVEL FLIGHT

GUIDE

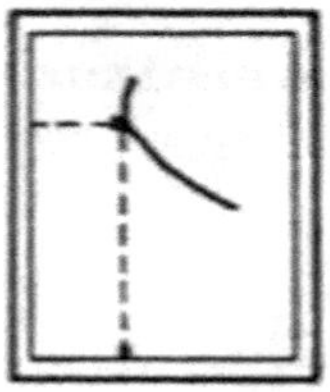

AIRPLANE CONFIGURATION

F-15E

REMARKS

ENGINE(S): (2) F100-PW-220
U.S. STANDARD DAY, 1966

DATE: 15 APRIL 1990
DATA BASIS: (STORES) ESTIMATED
(AIRCRAFT/CFT) FLIGHT TEST

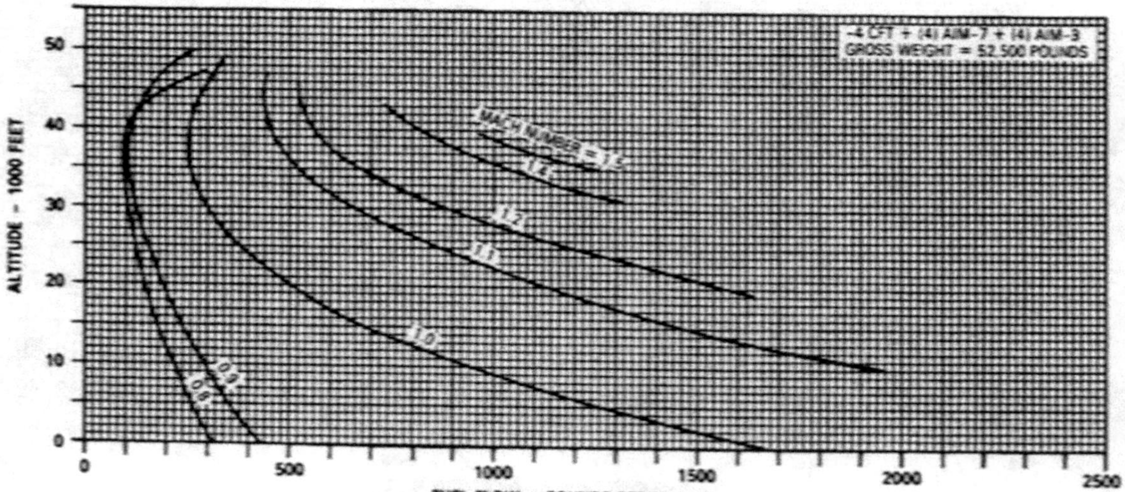

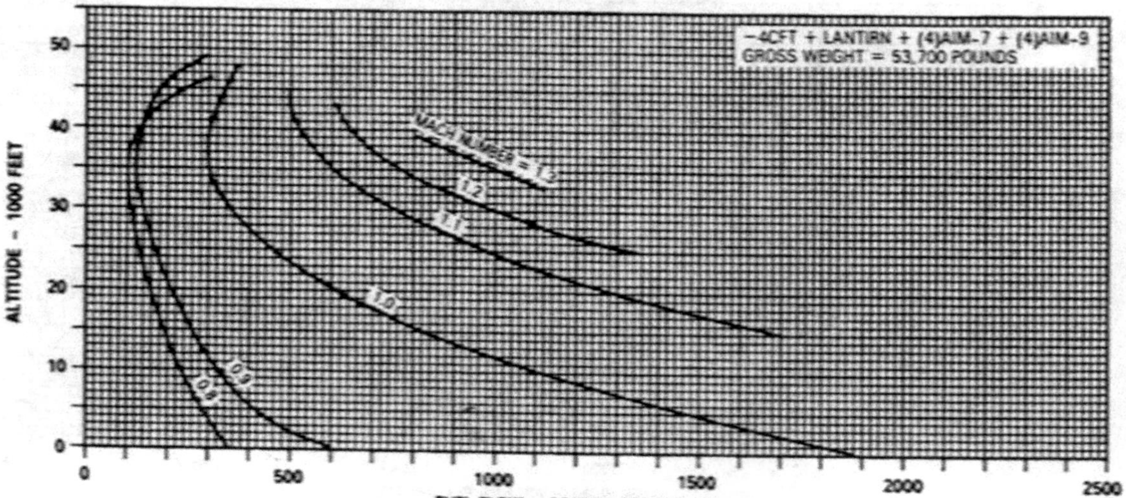

15E-1-(202)16

Figure A9-22

COMBAT FUEL FLOW
STABILIZED LEVEL FLIGHT

GUIDE

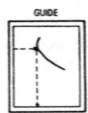

AIRPLANE CONFIGURATION
F-15E

REMARKS
ENGINE(S): (2) F100-PW-220
U.S. STANDARD DAY, 1966

DATE: 15 APRIL 1990
DATA BASIS: (STORES) ESTIMATED
(AIRCRAFT/CFT) FLIGHT TEST

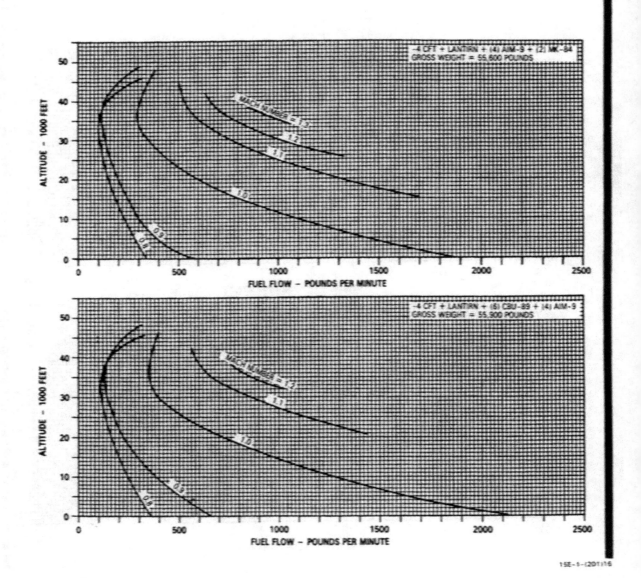

Figure A9-23

COMBAT FUEL FLOW
STABILIZED LEVEL FLIGHT

GUIDE

AIRPLANE CONFIGURATION

F-15E

REMARKS

ENGINE(S): (2) F100-PW-220
U.S. STANDARD DAY, 1966

DATE: 15 APRIL 1990
DATA BASIS: (STORES) ESTIMATED
(AIRCRAFT/CFT) FLIGHT TEST

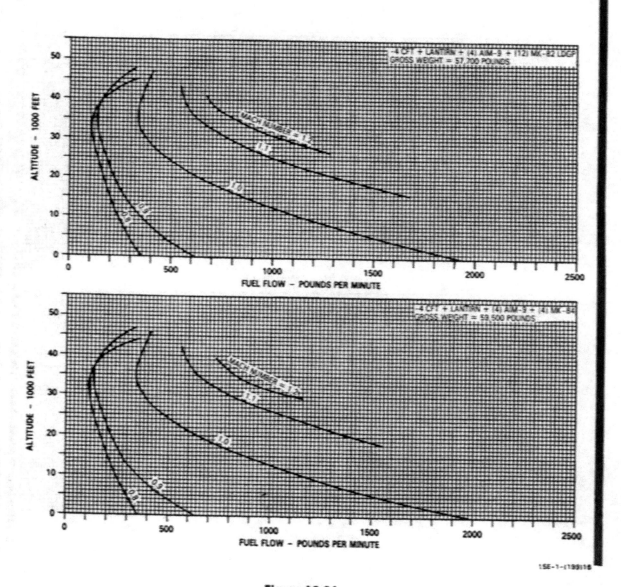

15E-1-(199)16

Figure A9-24

COMBAT FUEL FLOW
STABILIZED LEVEL FLIGHT

GUIDE

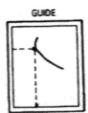

AIRPLANE CONFIGURATION

F-15E

REMARKS

ENGINE(S): (2) F100-PW-220
U.S. STANDARD DAY, 1966

DATE: 15 APRIL 1990
DATA BASIS: (STORES) ESTIMATED
(AIRCRAFT/CFT) FLIGHT TEST

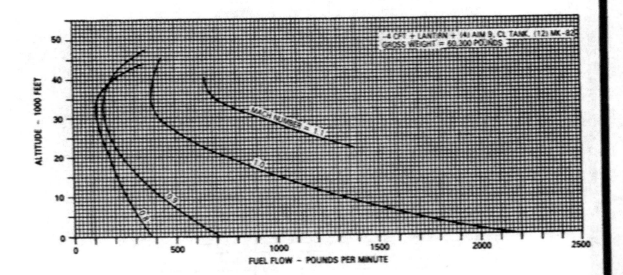

15E-1-(200)16

Figure A9-25

OVERLOAD WARNING SYSTEM SYMMETRICAL ALLOWABLE LOAD FACTORS

NOTE
1. NO WING TANKS OR STORES
2. CFT NOT INSTALLED

GUIDE

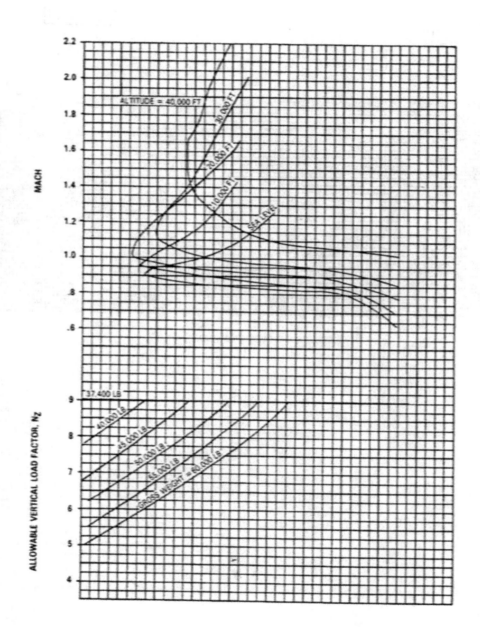

Figure A9-26

15E-1-(258)18

OVERLOAD WARNING SYSTEM SYMMETRICAL ALLOWABLE LOAD FACTORS - CFT/AIRCRAFT INTERFACE

TANKS OR STORES ON WING STATIONS 2 AND 8

NOTE
1. CFT NOT INSTALLED

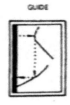

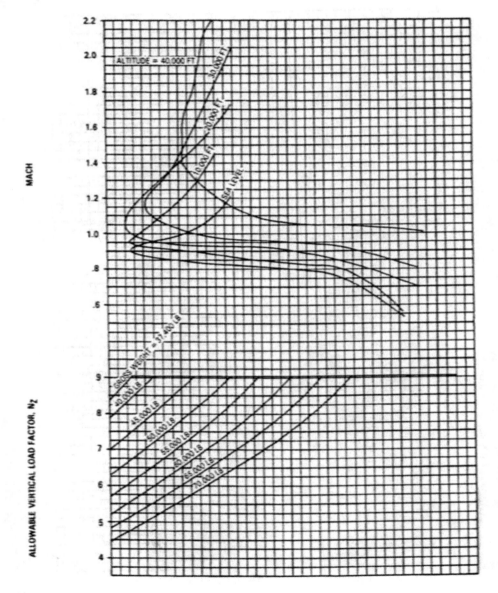

Figure A9-27

OVERLOAD WARNING SYSTEM SYMMETRICAL ALLOWABLE LOAD FACTORS - CFT/AIRCRAFT INTERFACE

CFT STORE STATIONS CLEAN

NOTE

1. NO WING TANKS OR STORES
2. BASED ON CFT WEIGHT = 2106 LB + FUEL PER SIDE

GUIDE

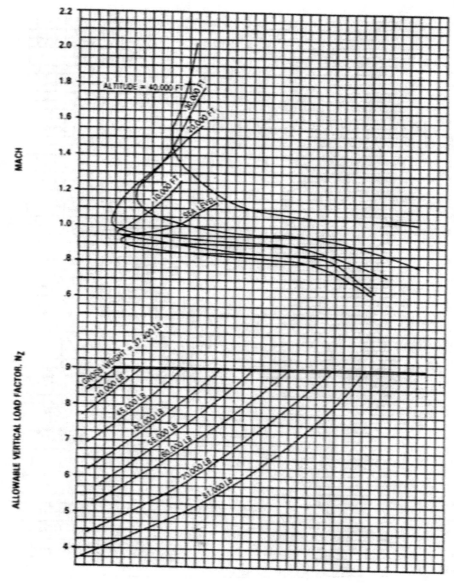

15E-1-(258)18

Figure A9-28

OVERLOAD WARNING SYSTEM SYMMETRICAL ALLOWABLE LOAD FACTORS - CFT/AIRCRAFT INTERFACE

TANKS OR STORES ON WING STATIONS 2 AND 8
CFT STORE STATIONS CLEAN

NOTE
1. BASED ON CFT WEIGHT = 2106 LB + FUEL PER SIDE

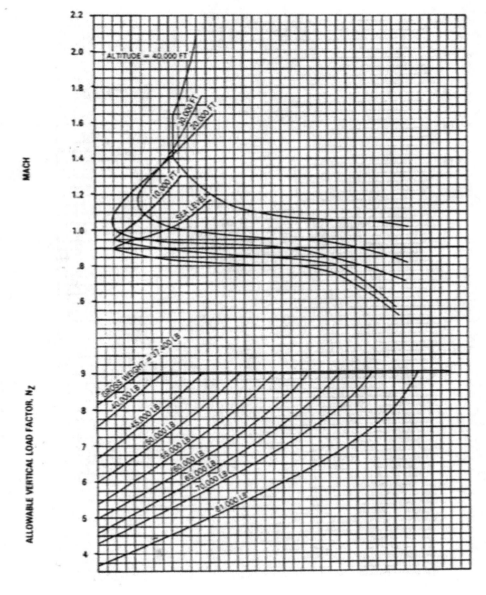

Figure A9-29

15E-1-(259)18

OVERLOAD WARNING SYSTEM SYMMETRICAL ALLOWABLE LOAD FACTORS - CFT/AIRCRAFT INTERFACE

AIM-7 MISSILES ON CFT STORE STATIONS

NOTE
1. NO WING TANKS OR STORES
2. BASED ON CFT WEIGHT = 3126 LB + FUEL PER SIDE

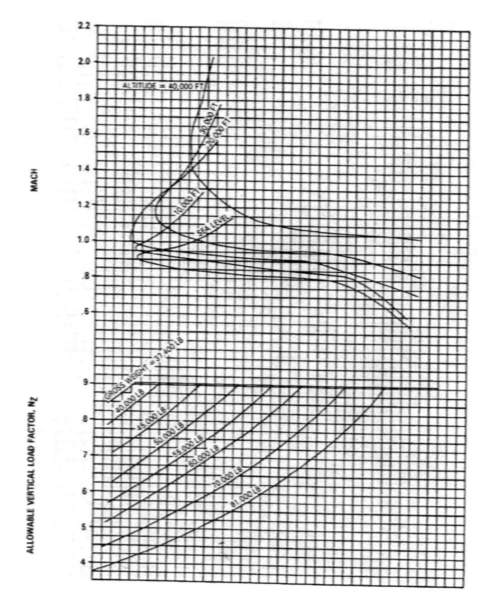

Figure A9-30

15E - 1 - (260)18

OVERLOAD WARNING SYSTEM SYMMETRICAL ALLOWABLE LOAD FACTORS - CFT/AIRCRAFT INTERFACE

AIM-7 MISSILES ON CFT STORE STATIONS
TANKS OR STORES ON WING STATIONS 2 AND 8

NOTE

1. BASED ON CFT WEIGHT = 3126 LB + FUEL PER SIDE

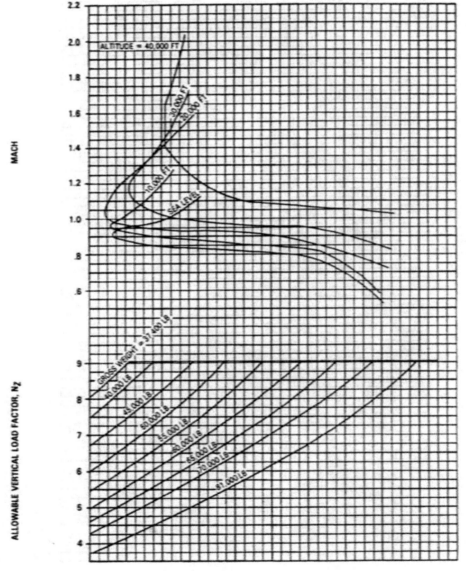

15E-1-(261)1B

Figure A9-31

OVERLOAD WARNING SYSTEM SYMMETRICAL ALLOWABLE LOAD FACTORS - CFT/AIRCRAFT INTERFACE

STORE ON CENTER INBOARD CFT STORE STATION

NOTE

1. NO WING TANKS OR STORES
2. EXTERNAL STORES LIMITATIONS MAY BE MORE RESTRICTIVE
3. BASED ON CFT WEIGHT = 4406 LB + FUEL PER SIDE

GUIDE

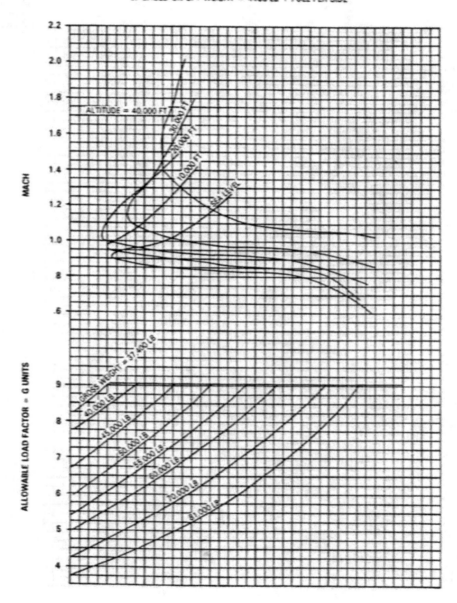

15E-1-(262)18

Figure A9-32

OVERLOAD WARNING SYSTEM SYMMETRICAL ALLOWABLE LOAD FACTORS - CFT/AIRCRAFT INTERFACE

TANKS OR STORES ON WING STATIONS 2 AND 8 STORE ON CENTER INBOARD CFT STORE STATION

NOTE
1. EXTERNAL STORES LIMITATIONS MAY BE MORE RESTRICTIVE
2. BASED ON CFT WEIGHT = 4406 LB + FUEL PER SIDE

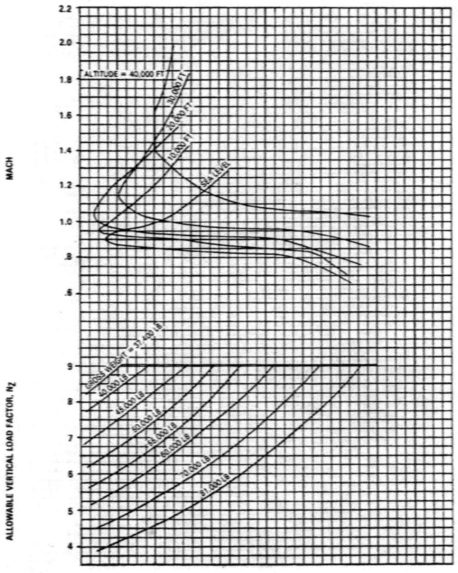

Figure A9-33

156-1-(263)18

OVERLOAD WARNING SYSTEM SYMMETRICAL ALLOWABLE LOAD FACTORS - CFT/AIRCRAFT INTERFACE

STORES ON FWD AND AFT INBOARD CFT STORE STATIONS

NOTE

1. NO WING TANKS OR STORES
2. EXTERNAL STORES LIMITATIONS MAY BE MORE RESTRICTIVE
3. BASED ON CFT WEIGHT = 6306 LB + FUEL PER SIDE

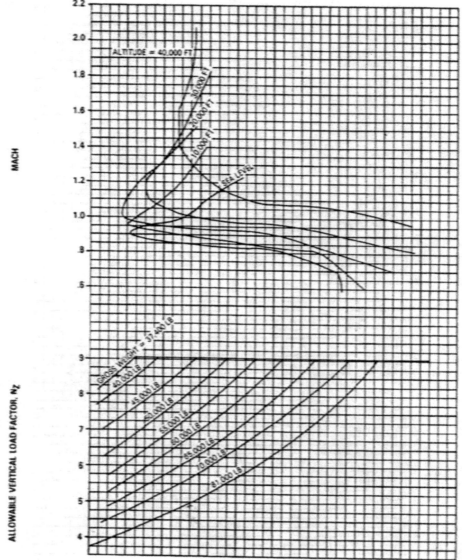

15E-1-(264)18

Figure A9-34

OVERLOAD WARNING SYSTEM SYMMETRICAL ALLOWABLE LOAD FACTORS - CFT/AIRCRAFT INTERFACE

TANKS OR STORES ON WING STATIONS 2 AND 8
STORES ON FWD AND AFT INBOARD CFT STORE STATIONS

NOTE

1. EXTERNAL STORES LIMITATIONS MAY BE MORE RESTRICTIVE
2. BASED ON CFT WEIGHT = 6306 LB + FUEL PER SIDE

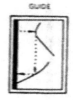

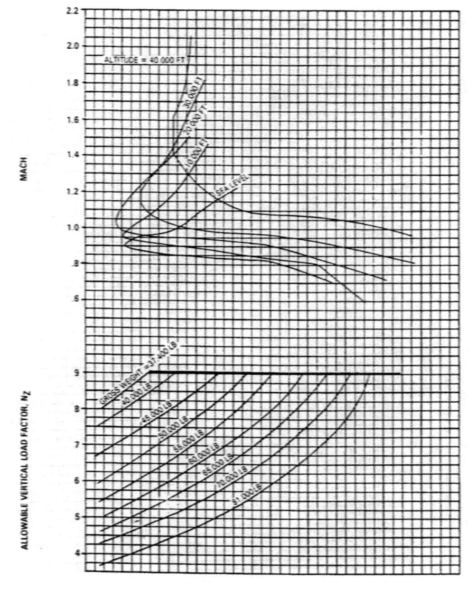

15E-1-(265)18

Figure A9-35

OVERLOAD WARNING SYSTEM SYMMETRICAL ALLOWABLE LOAD FACTORS - CFT/AIRCRAFT INTERFACE

STORES ON ALL CFT STORE STATIONS

NOTE

1. NO WING TANKS OR STORES
2. EXTERNAL STORES LIMITATIONS MAY BE MORE RESTRICTIVE
3. BASED ON CFT WEIGHT = 7806 LB + FUEL PER SIDE

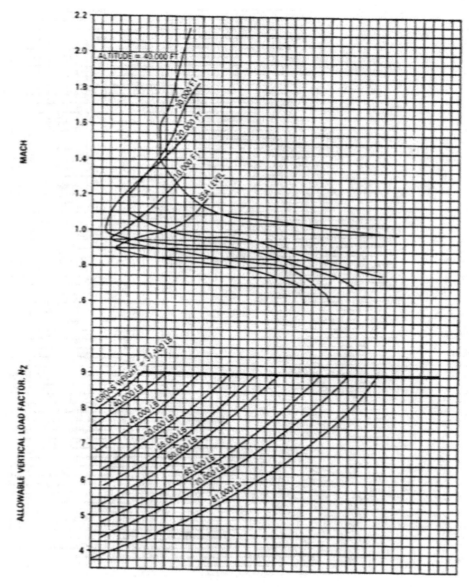

Figure A9-36

15E-1-(286)/18

OVERLOAD WARNING SYSTEM SYMMETRICAL ALLOWABLE LOAD FACTORS - CFT/AIRCRAFT INTERFACE

TANKS OR STORES ON WING STATIONS 2 AND 8
STORES ON ALL CFT STORE STATIONS

NOTE
1. EXTERNAL STORES LIMITATIONS MAY BE MORE RESTRICTIVE
2. BASED ON CFT WEIGHT = 7806 LB + FUEL PER SIDE

GUIDE

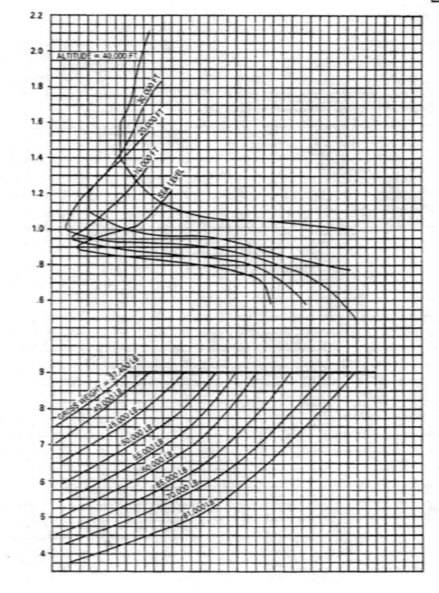

15E 1 (267)18

Figure A9-37

LEVEL FLIGHT ACCELERATION
INITIAL GROSS WEIGHT - 42,800 POUNDS

AIRPLANE CONFIGURATION
CLEAN

REMARKS
ENGINE(S): (2)F100-PW-220
1g LOAD FACTOR

GUIDE

DATE: 15 APRIL 1990
DATA BASIS: FLIGHT TEST

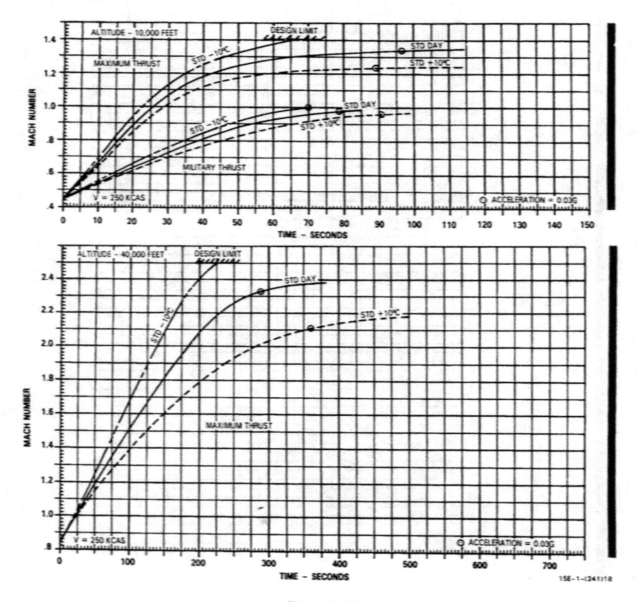

Figure A9-38

15E-1-(241)1B

LEVEL FLIGHT ACCELERATION
INITIAL GROSS WEIGHT – 44,000 POUNDS

AIRPLANE CONFIGURATION
(4) AIM-7

REMARKS
ENGINE(S): (2) F100-PW-220
1g LOAD FACTOR

GUIDE

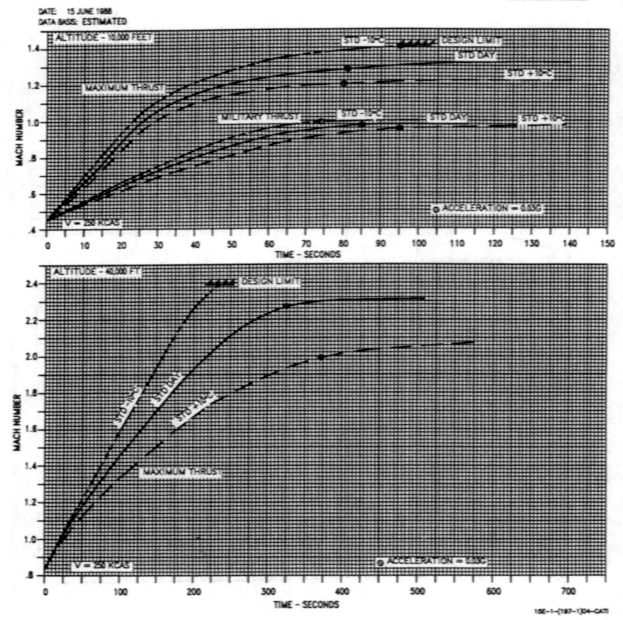

Figure A9-39

LEVEL FLIGHT ACCELERATION
INITIAL GROSS WEIGHT - 58,100 POUNDS

AIRPLANE CONFIGURATION
-4 CFT
(4) AIM-9, (4) AIM-7

REMARKS
ENGINE(S): (2) F100-PW-220
1g LOAD FACTOR

GUIDE

DATE: 15 APRIL 1990
DATA BASIS: (STORES) ESTIMATED
(AIRCRAFT/CFT) FLIGHT TEST

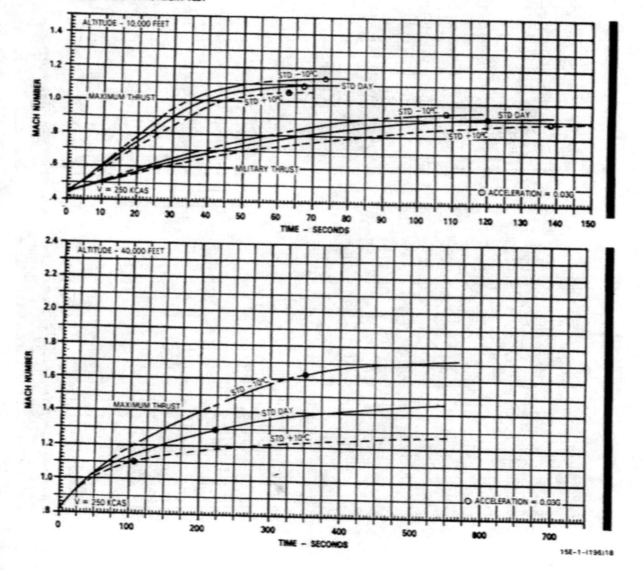

15E-1-(1196)18

Figure A9-40

LEVEL FLIGHT ACCELERATION
GROSS WEIGHT - 59,300 POUNDS

AIRPLANE CONFIGURATION
-4 CFT
LANTIRN
(4) AIM-7, (4) AIM-9

REMARKS
ENGINE(S) (2)F100-PW-220
1g LOAD FACTOR

GUIDE

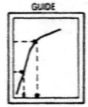

DATE   15 APRIL 1990
DATA BASIS: (STORES) ESTIMATED
(AIRCRAFT/CFT) FLIGHT TEST

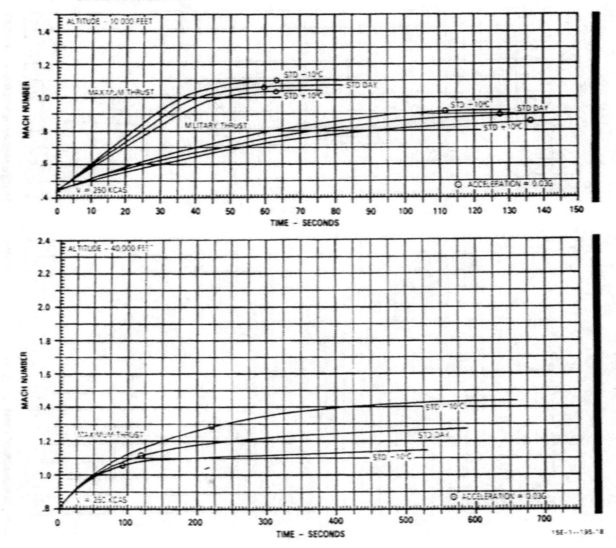

Figure A9-41

LEVEL FLIGHT ACCELERATION
GROSS WEIGHT - 61,200 POUNDS

AIRPLANE CONFIGURATION
-4 CFT
LANTIRN
(4) AIM-9, (2) MK-84

REMARKS
ENGINE(S): (2)F100-PW-220
1g LOAD FACTOR

GUIDE

DATE. 15 APRIL 1990
DATA BASIS: **(STORES) ESTIMATED**
(AIRCRAFT/CFT) FLIGHT TEST

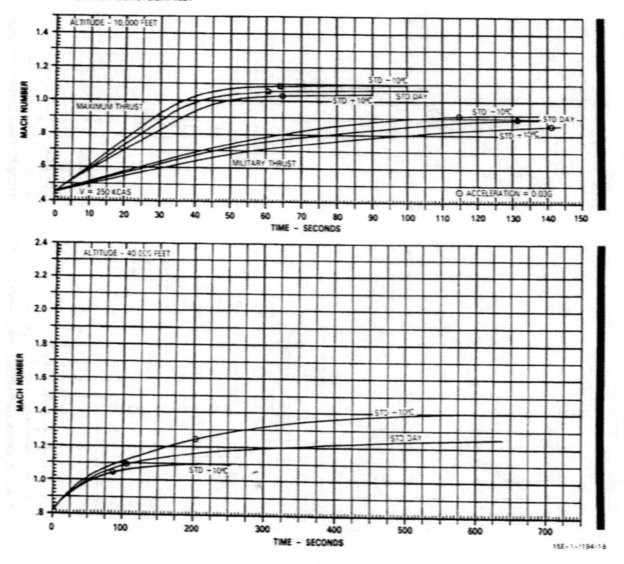

Figure A9-42

15E-1-1794-18

LEVEL FLIGHT ACCELERATION
INITIAL GROSS WEIGHT - 61,500 POUNDS

AIRPLANE CONFIGURATION
-4 CFT
(4) AIM-9, (6) CBU-89

REMARKS
ENGINE(S): (2) F100-PW-220
1g LOAD FACTOR

GUIDE

DATE: 15 APRIL 1990
DATA BASIS (STORES) ESTIMATED
(AIRCRAFT/CFT) FLIGHT TEST

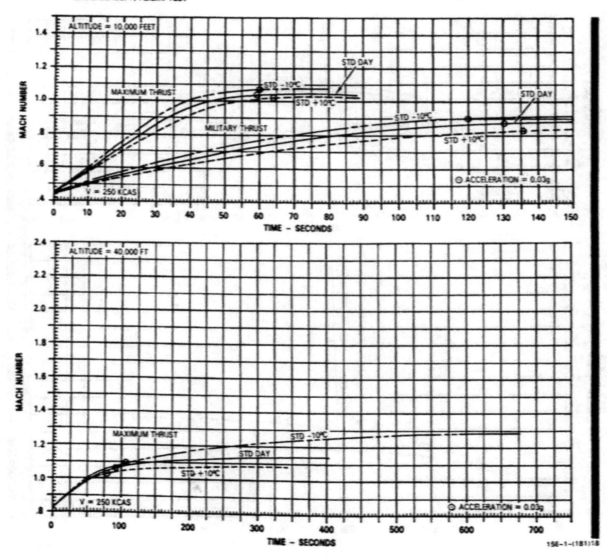

Figure A9-43

15E-1-(181)18

LEVEL FLIGHT ACCELERATION
INITIAL GROSS WEIGHT - 63,300 POUNDS

AIRPLANE CONFIGURATION
-4 CFT
LANTIRN
(4) AIM-9, (12) MK-82

REMARKS
ENGINE(S): (2) F100-PW-220
1g LOAD FACTOR

GUIDE

DATE: 15 APRIL 1990
DATA BASIS (STORES) ESTIMATED
(AIRCRAFT/CFT) FLIGHT TEST

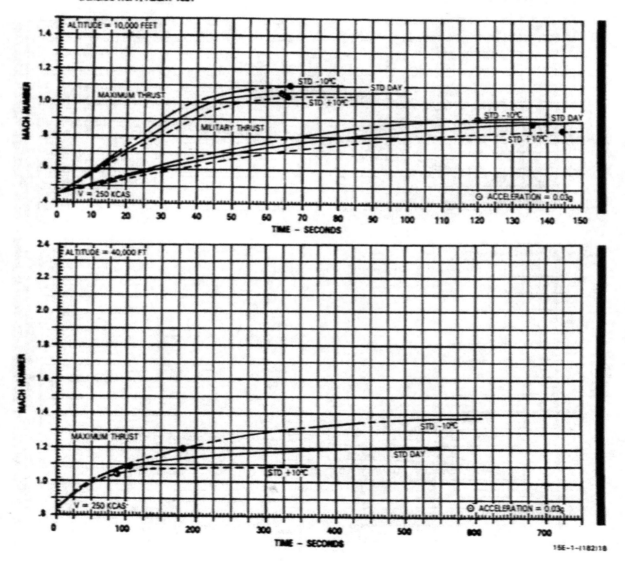

15E-1-(1182)18

Figure A9-44

LEVEL FLIGHT ACCELERATION
INITIAL GROSS WEIGHT - 65,100 POUNDS

AIRPLANE CONFIGURATION
-4 CFT
LANTIRN
(4) AIM-9, (4) MK-84

REMARKS
ENGINE(S): (2) F100-PW-220
1g LOAD FACTOR

GUIDE

DATE: 15 APRIL 1990
DATA BASIS: (STORES) ESTIMATED
(AIRCRAFT/CFT) FLIGHT TEST

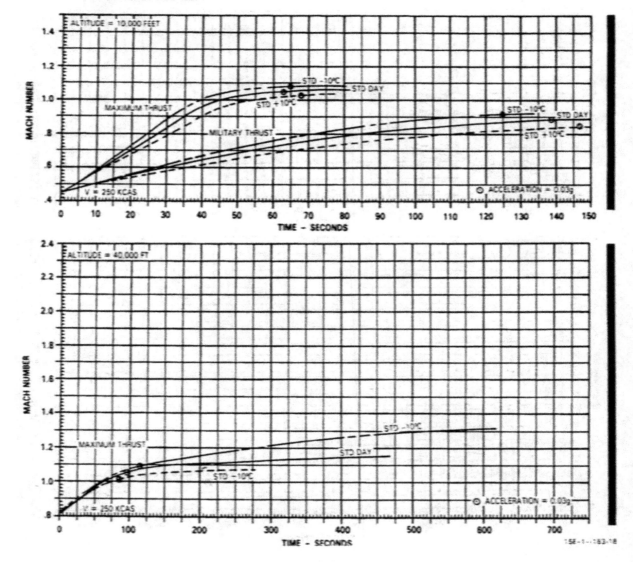

Figure A9-45

LEVEL FLIGHT ACCELERATION

INITIAL GROSS WEIGHT - 66,900 POUNDS

AIRPLANE CONFIGURATION
~4 CFT
LANTIRN
CL TANK
(4) AIM-9, (12) MK-82

REMARKS
ENGINE(S): (2)F100-PW-220
lg LOAD FACTOR

GUIDE

DATE: 15 APRIL 1990
DATA BASIS: (STORES) ESTIMATED
(AIRCRAFT/CFT) FLIGHT TEST

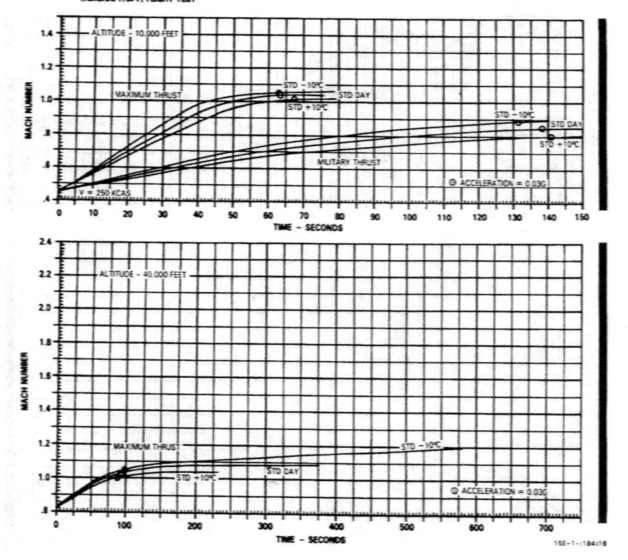

Figure A9-46

SUSTAINED LEVEL TURNS
GROSS WEIGHT - 39,500 POUNDS
MAXIMUM THRUST

AIRPLANE CONFIGURATION
F-15E CLEAN

REMARKS
ENGINE(S): (2) F100-PW-220
U.S. STANDARD DAY, 1966

GUIDE

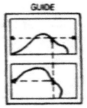

NOTE
MAXIMUM CAPABILITY MAY BE REDUCED
BY OVERLOAD WARNING SYSTEM.

DATE 15 APRIL 1990
DATA BASIS: FLIGHT TEST

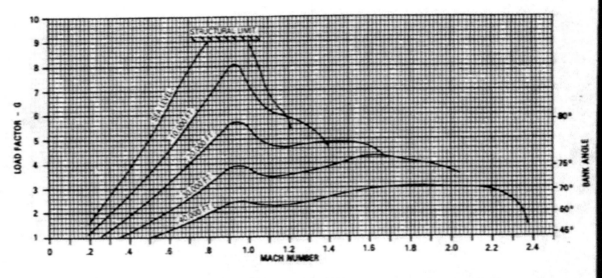

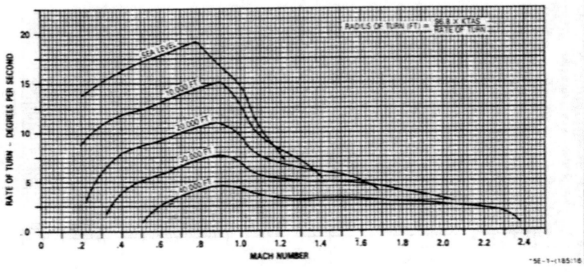

Figure A9-47

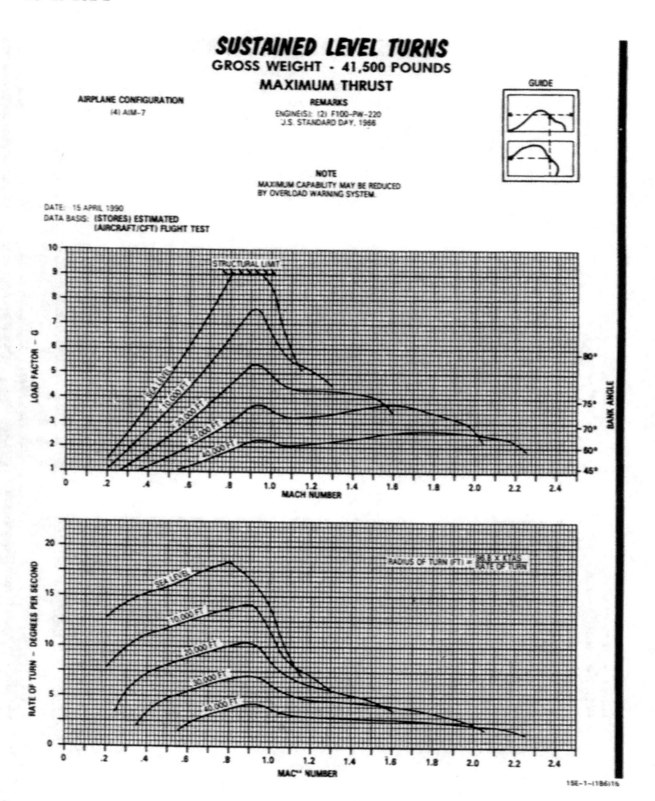

SUSTAINED LEVEL TURNS
GROSS WEIGHT - 41,500 POUNDS
MAXIMUM THRUST

AIRPLANE CONFIGURATION
(4) AIM-7

REMARKS
ENGINE(S): (2) F100-PW-220
U.S. STANDARD DAY, 1966

GUIDE

NOTE
MAXIMUM CAPABILITY MAY BE REDUCED
BY OVERLOAD WARNING SYSTEM.

DATE: 15 APRIL 1990
DATA BASIS: (STORES) ESTIMATED
(AIRCRAFT/CFT) FLIGHT TEST

$$\text{RADIUS OF TURN (FT)} = \frac{96.6 \times \text{KTAS}}{\text{RATE OF TURN}}$$

15E-1-(1B6)76

Figure A9-48

SUSTAINED LEVEL TURNS
GROSS WEIGHT - 52,500 POUNDS
MAXIMUM THRUST

AIRPLANE CONFIGURATION
-4 CFT
(4) AIM-7, (4) AIM-9

REMARKS
ENGINE(S): (2) F100-PW-220
U.S. STANDARD DAY, 1966

GUIDE

NOTE
MAXIMUM CAPABILITY MAY BE REDUCED
BY OVERLOAD WARNING SYSTEM.

DATE: 15 APRIL 1990
DATA BASIS: (STORES) ESTIMATED
(AIRCRAFT/CFT) FLIGHT TEST

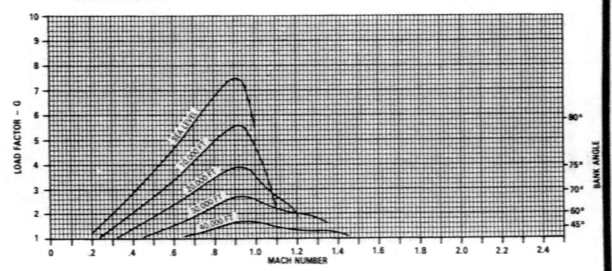

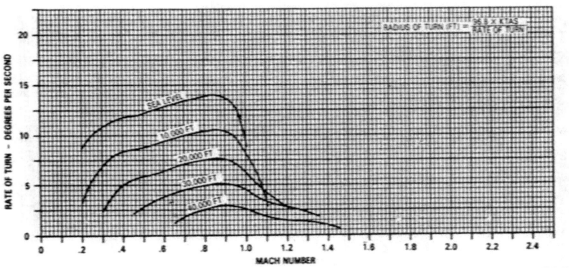

15E-1-(1)87(16)

Figure A9-49

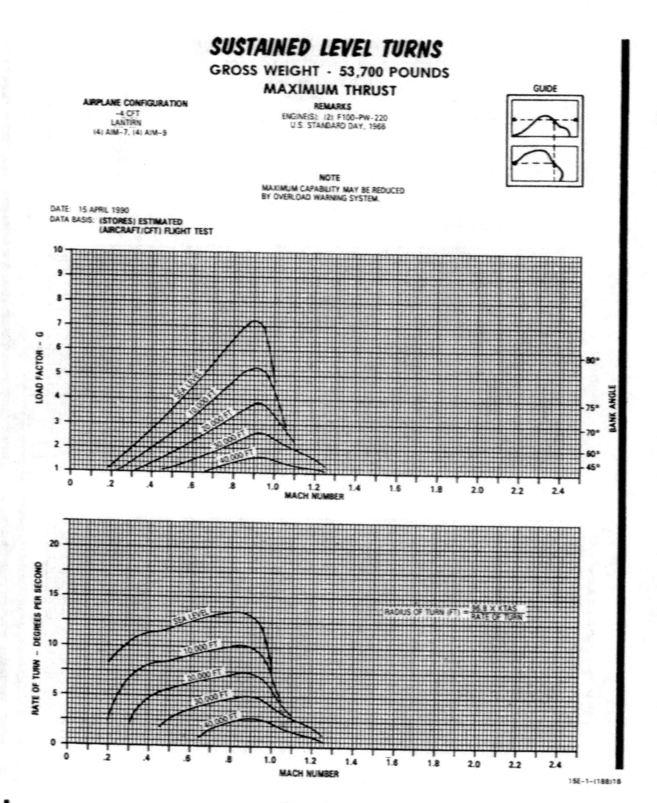

SUSTAINED LEVEL TURNS
GROSS WEIGHT - 53,700 POUNDS
MAXIMUM THRUST

AIRPLANE CONFIGURATION
-4 CFT
LANTIRN
(4) AIM-7, (4) AIM-9

REMARKS
ENGINE(S): (2) F100-PW-220
U.S. STANDARD DAY, 1966

GUIDE

NOTE
MAXIMUM CAPABILITY MAY BE REDUCED
BY OVERLOAD WARNING SYSTEM.

DATE: 15 APRIL 1990
DATA BASIS: (STORES) ESTIMATED
(AIRCRAFT/CFT) FLIGHT TEST

$$\text{RADIUS OF TURN (FT)} = \frac{96.8 \times \text{KTAS}}{\text{RATE OF TURN}}$$

15E-1-(188)16

Figure A9-50

SUSTAINED LEVEL TURNS
GROSS WEIGHT - 55,600 POUNDS
MAXIMUM THRUST

AIRPLANE CONFIGURATION
-4 CFT
LANTIRN
(4) AIM-9, (2) MK-84

REMARKS
ENGINE(S): (2) F100-PW-220
U.S. STANDARD DAY, 1966

GUIDE

NOTE
MAXIMUM CAPABILITY MAY BE REDUCED
BY OVERLOAD WARNING SYSTEM.

DATE: 15 APRIL 1990
DATA BASIS: (STORES) ESTIMATED
(AIRCRAFT/CFT) FLIGHT TEST

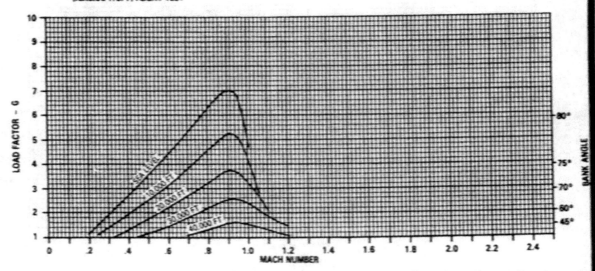

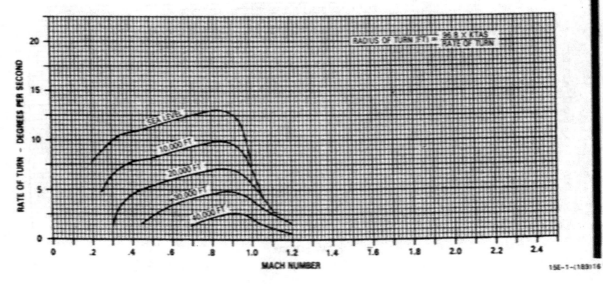

$$\text{RADIUS OF TURN (FT)} = \frac{96.8 \times \text{KTAS}}{\text{RATE OF TURN}}$$

15E-1-(18)9116

Figure A9-51

SUSTAINED LEVEL TURNS
GROSS WEIGHT - 55,900 POUNDS
MAXIMUM THRUST

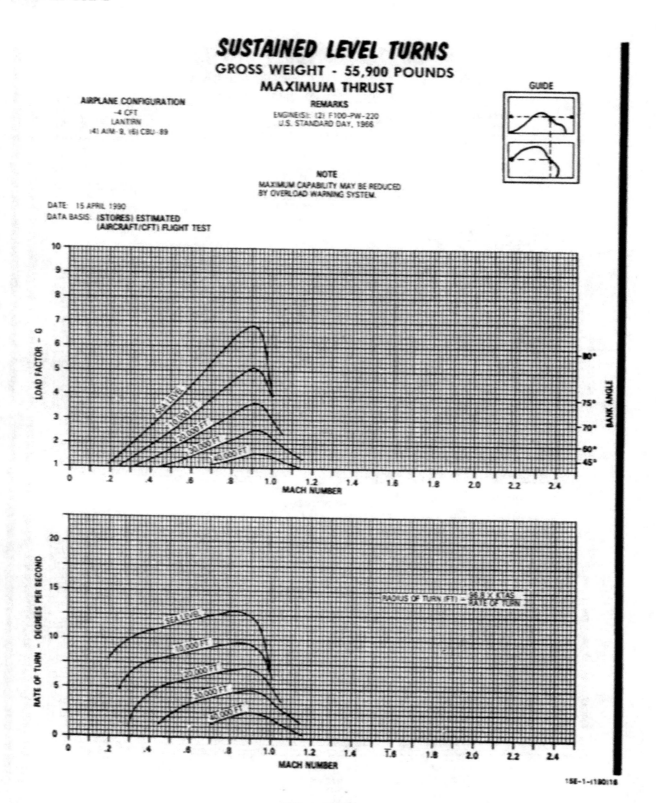

Figure A9-52

SUSTAINED LEVEL TURNS
GROSS WEIGHT - 57,700 POUNDS
MAXIMUM THRUST

AIRPLANE CONFIGURATION
-4 CFT
LANTIRN
(4) AIM-9, (12) MK 82

REMARKS
ENGINE(S): (2) F100-PW-220
U.S. STANDARD DAY, 1966

GUIDE

NOTE
MAXIMUM CAPABILITY MAY BE REDUCED
BY OVERLOAD WARNING SYSTEM.

DATE: 15 APRIL 1990
DATA BASIS: (STORES) ESTIMATED
(AIRCRAFT/CFT) FLIGHT TEST

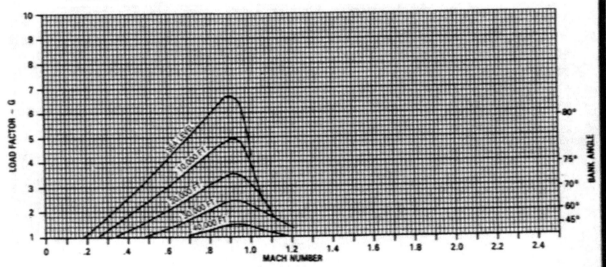

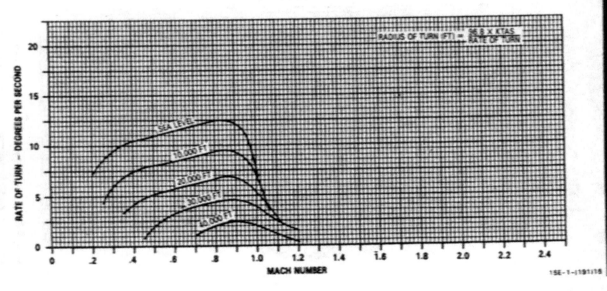

Figure A9-53

SUSTAINED LEVEL TURNS
GROSS WEIGHT - 59,500 POUNDS
MAXIMUM THRUST

AIRPLANE CONFIGURATION
-4 CFT
LANTIRN
(4) AIM-9, (4) MK-84

REMARKS
ENGINE(S): (2) F100-PW-220
U.S. STANDARD DAY, 1966

GUIDE
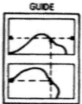

NOTE
MAXIMUM CAPABILITY MAY BE REDUCED
BY OVERLOAD WARNING SYSTEM.

DATE: 15 APRIL 1990
DATA BASIS: (STORES) ESTIMATED
(AIRCRAFT/CFT) FLIGHT TEST

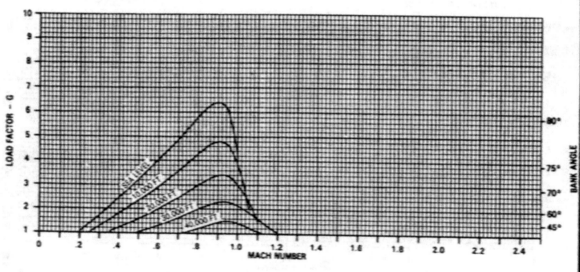

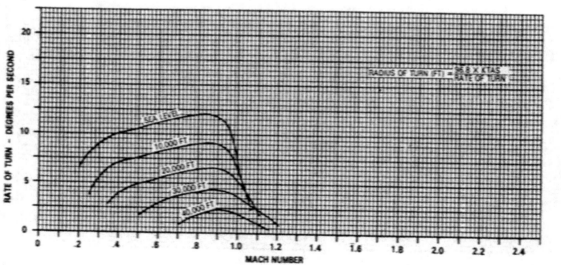

15E-1-(192)16

Figure A9-54

SUSTAINED LEVEL TURNS
GROSS WEIGHT - 60,300 POUNDS
MAXIMUM THRUST

AIRPLANE CONFIGURATION
-4 CFT
LANTIRN
CL TANK
(4) AIM-9, (12) MK-82

REMARKS
ENGINE(S): (2) F100-PW-220
U.S. STANDARD DAY, 1966

NOTE
MAXIMUM CAPABILITY MAY BE REDUCED
BY OVERLOAD WARNING SYSTEM.

DATE: 15 APRIL 1990
DATA BASIS: (STORES) ESTIMATED
(AIRCRAFT/CFT) FLIGHT TEST

GUIDE

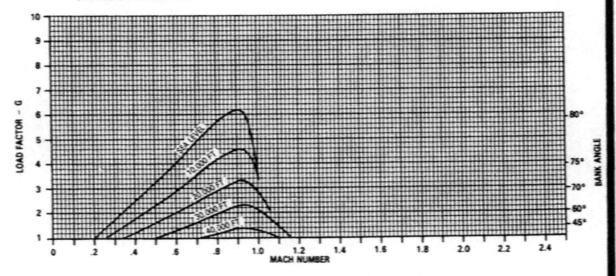

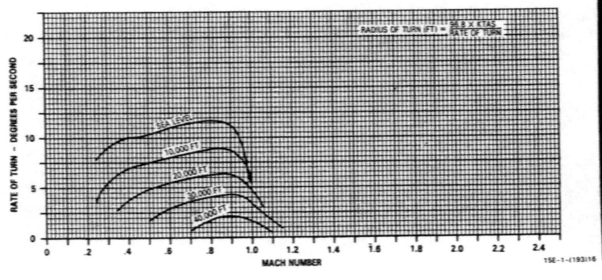

$$\text{RADIUS OF TURN (FT)} = \frac{96.8 \times \text{KTAS}}{\text{RATE OF TURN}}$$

15E-1-(193)16

Figure A9-55

APPENDIX B

PERFORMANCE DATA
WITH F100-PW-229 ENGINES

PART 1 INTRODUCTION B1-1

PART 2 ENGINE DATA B2-1

PART 3 TAKEOFF B3-1

PART 4 CLIMB B4-1

PART 5 RANGE B5-1

PART 6 ENDURANCE B6-1

PART 7 DESCENT B7-1

PART 8 APPROACH AND LANDING B8-1

PART 9 COMBAT PERFORMANCE B9-1

PART 1

INTRODUCTION

TABLE OF CONTENTS

Charts

Station Loading B1-5
F-15E Gross Weights (Lbs) and
  CG Location (%MAC) .... TBS
Standard Atmosphere Table B1-9
Stall Speeds.. B1-11
Airspeed Conversion B1-12
Airspeed Position Error Correction B1-13
Altimeter Position Error Correction B1-14
Wind Components... B1-15

NOTE

- All performance data are based on JP-4 fuel and are also applicable for JP-8 fuel.
- Performance charts for the PW-229 engines are currently being developed. The references to figures have been retained even if the chart is not available. The actual charts will be added as they become available.

DRAG INDEX SYSTEM

Most of the charts use the drag index system to effectively present the many combinations of weight/drag effects on performance. The Airplane Loading chart (figure B1-1) contains the drag number and weight of each externally carried store. The weight and drag number for external store suspension equipment are listed separately. The drag index for a specific configuration may be found by multiplying the number of stores carried by its drag number, and adding the drag number of the applicable suspension equipment. The total drag index may then be used to enter the planning data charts. The F-15E Gross Weights and CG Location (%MAC) chart (figure B1-2) contains the weight and % CG for certain "typical" load configurations. Charts applicable for all loads and configuration are labeled ALL DRAG INDEXES. Charts labeled INDIVIDUAL DRAG INDEXES contain data for a range of drag numbers; i.e., individual curves/columns for a specific drag

number. Supersonic data is not compatible to the drag index system; therefore, each chart is labeled for a specific configuration.

STALL SPEEDS CHARTS

The Stall Speeds charts (figures B1-4 thru B1-7) present stall speeds for various combinations of gross weight, bank angle, power setting and altitude. The data is based on having the gear and flaps down (figures B1-4, B1-5) or gear and flaps up (figures B1-6, B1-7).

USE

Enter the appropriate chart with the applicable gross weight and proceed horizontally to the right to intersect the applicable bank angle. From this intersection, descend vertically and intersect the applicable altitude curve. Then project horizontally left to read the stall speed.

Sample Problem

Configuration: Flaps Down, Gear Down, Maximum Thrust

A. Gross weight	40,000 Lb
B. Bank angle	15°
C. Altitude	10,000 Ft
D. Stall speed	107 Kt

AIRSPEED CONVERSION

The Airspeed Conversion charts, (figures B1-8 and B1-9) provide a means of converting calibrated airspeed to true Mach number and true airspeed.

INDICATED AIRSPEED

Indicated airspeed (IAS) is the uncorrected airspeed read directly from the indicator.

CALIBRATED AIRSPEED

Calibrated airspeed (CAS) is indicated airspeed corrected for static source error.

SAMPLE STALL SPEEDS

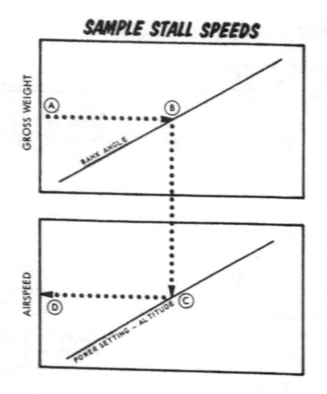

15E-1-1630

EQUIVALENT AIRSPEED

Equivalent airspeed (EAS) is calibrated airspeed corrected for compressibility. There is no provision made for reading equivalent airspeed.

TRUE AIRSPEED

True airspeed (TAS) is equivalent airspeed corrected for density altitude. Refer to the Airspeed Conversion charts (figures B1-8 and B1-9).

AIRSPEED POSITION ERROR CORRECTION CHART

Under normal conditions, the air data computer compensates for the static source position error. If an air data computer malfunction occurs, the primary airspeed/Mach indicator becomes inoperative and airspeed is read from the standby indicator. The indicated airspeed read on this indicator may be corrected to calibrated airspeed by utilizing the Airspeed Position Error Correction chart (figure B1-10).

USE

Enter the appropriate chart with the indicated airspeed read from the standby indicator. In the flaps down, gear down configuration at 10,000 feet and below read the calibrated airspeed from the tabulated chart. In the flaps up, gear up configuration, enter the chart with the indicated airspeed and project vertically up to the appropriate altitude reflector curve. From this point, project horizontally left to read the calibrated airspeed.

Sample Problem

Configuration: Flaps Up, Gear Up

A. Indicated airspeed	300 Kt
B. Altitude reflector line	40,000 Ft
C. Calibrated airspeed	312 Kt

Configuration: Flaps Down, Gear Down (10,000 Ft and below)

A. Indicated airspeed	200 Kt
B. Gross weight	40,000 Lb
C. Calibrated airspeed	198.5 Kt

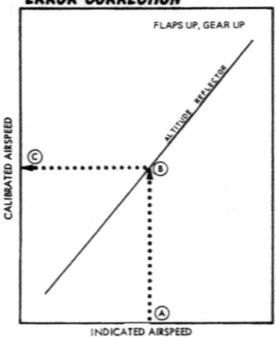

SAMPLE AIRSPEED POSITION ERROR CORRECTION

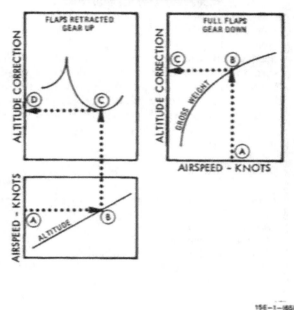

SAMPLE ALTIMETER POSITION ERROR CORRECTION

ALTIMETER POSITION ERROR CORRECTION CHART

Under normal conditions, the ADC compensates for the static source position error. If an ADC malfunction occurs, the primary altitude indicator becomes inoperative and altitude is read from the standby indicator. The indicated altitude read on this indicator may be corrected to calibrated altitude by utilizing the Altimeter Position Error Correction chart (figure B1-11).

USE

Enter the appropriate chart with indicated airspeed. In the flaps retracted, gear up configuration project horizontally right to the assigned altitude reflector. From this point, project vertically up to the reflector line. From this point, project horizontally left to read the ΔH altitude correction. In the full flaps, gear down configuration project vertically up to the appropriate gross weight curve. From this point project horizontally left to read the ΔH altitude correction. In either case apply the ΔH altitude correction to the altimeter and fly indicated altitude.

Sample Problem

Configuration: Flaps up, Gear Up

A. Indicated airspeed	400 Kt
B. Assigned altitude	55,000 Ft
C. Reflector line	
D. ΔH correction	+375 Ft
E. Indicated altitude necessary to maintain assigned altitude (B+D)	55,375 Ft

Configuration: Flaps Down, Gear Down

A. Indicated airspeed	155 Kt
B. Gross weight	40,000 Lb
C. ΔH correction	+60 Ft

WIND COMPONENTS CHART

A standard Wind Components chart (figure B1-12) is included. It is used primarily for breaking a forecast wind down into crosswind and headwind components for takeoff computations. It may, however, be used whenever wind component information is desired. It is not to be used as a ground controllability chart.

USE

Determine the effective wind velocity by adding one-half the gust velocity (incremental wind factor) to the steady state velocity; e.g., reported wind 050/30 G40, effective wind is 050/35. Reduce the reported wind direction to a relative bearing by determining the wind direction and runway heading. Enter the chart with the relative bearing. Move along the relative bearing to intercept the effective wind speed arc. From this point, descend vertically down to read the crosswind component. From the intersection of bearing and wind speed, project horizontally left to read headwind component.

Sample Problem

Reported wind 050/35, runway heading 030.

A. Relative bearing	20°
B. Intersect windspeed arc	35 Kt
C. Crosswind component	12 Kt
D. Headwind component	33 Kt

STATION LOADING

OPERATING WEIGHT (Basic airplane weight plus crew)

F-15E ....33,898 pounds

BASIC TAKEOFF WEIGHT (Operating weight plus full internal fuel and ammunition)

F-15E ....47,310 pounds

NOTE

FOR PRECISE AIRPLANE BASIC WEIGHT, REFER TO WEIGHT AND BALANCE DATA HANDBOOK, TO 1-1B-40, FOR THE PARTICULAR AIRPLANE

CONFIGURATION DRAG

ITEM	WEIGHT (POUNDS)	DRAG NUMBER
F-15E		0
Two -4 CFTs	E 4,286	20.1
(F-15E Production Model)	F 13,747	
LANTIRN Navigation Pod (AN/AAQ-13) and Adapter (ADU-576/A)	520	9.5
LANTIRN Targeting Pod (AN/AAQ-14) and Adapter (ADU-577/A)	621	7.4

ITEM	WEIGHT PER ITEM (POUNDS)	DRAG NUMBER WITHOUT CFT		DRAG NUMBER WITH CFT			
		CENTER-LINE STATION	OTHER STATIONS	CENTER-LINE STATION	WING STATIONS	CFT STATIONS WITHOUT BOMBS/TANKS ON WING STATIONS	CFT STATIONS WITH BOMBS/TANKS ON WING STATIONS
Air-to-Air Missiles							
AIM-7F, -7M	510	-	1.8	-	-	2.3	2.3
AIM-9L, 9M	195	-	2.1	-	2.1	-	-
AIM-9P/P-1	170	-	2.1	-	2.1	-	-
AIM-9P-2/P-3	180	-	2.1	-	2.1	-	-
AIM-120A	338	-	1.3	-	2.3	1.7	1.7
CATM-9L/M-1	195	-	2.1	-	2.1	-	-
Air-to-Ground Missiles							
AGM-65A, B	481	-	3.7	-	3.7	-	-
AGM-65D	485	-	3.7	-	3.7	-	-
AGM-65G	687	-	3.7	-	3.7	-	-
AGM-130A,B	2962	-	TBD	-	TBD	-	-

Figure B1-1 (Sheet 1 of 4)

STATION LOADING (CONT)

ITEM	WEIGHT PER ITEM (POUNDS)	DRAG NUMBER WITHOUT CFT		DRAG NUMBER WITH CFT			
		CENTER-LINE STATION	OTHER STATIONS	CENTER-LINE STATION	WING STATIONS	CFT STATIONS WITHOUT BOMBS/ TANKS ON WING STATIONS	CFT STATIONS WITH BOMBS/ TANKS ON WING STATIONS
Pylons, Launchers and Adapters							
SUU-73/A Center-line Pylon with BRU-47/A	316	3.3	-	3.3	-	-	-
SUU-59C/A Wing Pylon with BRU-47/A	371	-	3.3	-	3.3	-	-
LAU-128/A Launcher and AIM-9/AIM-120 Adapter (ADU-552/A)	111	-	1.1	-	1.1	-	-
LAU-88A/A Launcher (Triple Rail) and AGM-65 Adapter (ADU-578/A)	573	-	9.6	-	9.6	-	-
LAU-117/A Launcher (Single Rail) for AGM-65	135	-	1.4	-	1.4	-	-
LAU-114/A Launcher and AIM-9 Adapter (ADU-407/A)	79	-	1.2	-	1.2	-	-
General Purpose Weapons							
MK-82 LDGP	505	-	-	-	-	0.8	0.9
MK-82 SE	550	-	-	-	-	1.4	1.5
MK-82 AIR (With BSU-49 Fin)	540	-	-	-	-	1.1	1.2
MK-84 LDGP	1970	3.0	2.1	3.0	2.3	2.8	3.0
MK-84 AIR (With BSU-50 Fin)	2010	5.4	3.9	5.4	4.2	5.1	5.6

Figure B1-1 (Sheet 2)

STATION LOADING (CONT)

ITEM	WEIGHT PER ITEM (POUNDS)	DRAG NUMBER WITHOUT CFT		DRAG NUMBER WITH CFT			
		CENTER-LINE STATION	OTHER STATIONS	CENTER-LINE STATION	WING STATIONS	CFT STATIONS WITHOUT BOMBS/TANKS ON WING STATIONS	CFT STATIONS WITH BOMBS/TANKS ON WING STATIONS
Guided Weapons							
GBU-10A/B	2053	10.5	7.5	10.5	7.5	9.8	10.7
GBU-10C/B, D/B	2081	10.5	7.5	10.5	7.5	9.8	10.7
GBU-12B/B, C/B	610	-	-	-	-	3.9	4.3
GBU-15(V)-4/B	2502	-	5.6	-	5.6	-	-
GBU-24/B	2323	7.8	5.6	7.8	5.6	5.6	6.2
Dispensers/Rockets							
CBU-52B/B	785	-	-	-	-	4.6	5.0
CBU-58/B	810	-	-	-	-	4.6	5.0
CBU-71/B	810	-	-	-	-	4.6	5.0
CBU-87/B (TMD)	950	-	-	-	-	2.9	3.2
CBU-89/B (TMD)	706	-	-	-	-	2.9	3.2
MK-20 Rockeye	486	-	-	-	-	1.5	1.6
TMU-28/B Spray Tank	E 567 F 1935	-	4.9	-	4.9	-	-
Special Weapons							
B61	716	2.5	1.8	2.5	1.8	1.8	2.0
Miscellaneous Stores							
610 Gallon Fuel Tank	E 320 F 4285	12.2	5.5	12.2	6.0	-	-
610 Gallon Fuel Tank (With Bombs on Inboard CFT Station)	E 320 F 4285	-	-	12.2	8.2	-	-
610 Gallon Fuel Tank (With Bombs on Outboard CFT Station)	E 320 F 4285	-	-	12.2	12.3	-	-
SUU-20B/A Practice Dispenser (Empty)	276	5.0	3.6	5.0	3.9	3.9	3.9
MK-106 PB (Incl)	F 306	4.2	3.0	4.2	3.3	3.3	3.3
BDU-33 PB (Incl)	F 414	4.2	3.0	4.2	3.3	3.3	3.3
BDU-48 PB (Incl)	F 336	4.2	3.0	4.2	3.3	3.3	3.3

E - Empty   F - Full   PB - Practice Bomb

Figure B1-1 (Sheet 3)

STATION LOADING (CONT)

ITEM	WEIGHT PER ITEM (POUNDS)	DRAG NUMBER WITHOUT CFT		DRAG NUMBER WITH CFT			
		CENTER-LINE STATION	OTHER STATIONS	CENTER-LINE STATION	WING STATIONS	CFT STATIONS WITHOUT BOMBS/TANKS ON WING STATIONS	CFT STATIONS WITH BOMBS/TANKS ON WING STATIONS
BDU-38 (B61 Training Shape)	716	2.6	1.8	2.5	1.8	1.8	2.0
AN/AXQ-14 Data Link Pod (for GBU-15)	450	3.3	-	3.3	-	-	-
P-4A/AX AIS Pod	160	-	2.1	-	2.1	-	-
AN/ASQ-T17 AIS Pod	122	-	2.1	-	2.1	-	-
AN/ASQ-T20 AIS Pod	123	-	2.1	-	2.1	-	-
AN/ASQ-T21 AIS Pod	124	-	2.1	-	2.1	-	-
AN/ASQ-T25 AIS Pod	122	-	2.1	-	2.1	-	-
BLU-107 Durandal	494	-	-	-	-	1.2	1.4
MXU-648A/A-50 Cargo Pod	E 98 F 398	3.6	3.6	3.6	3.6	-	-
Ammunition (512 Live Rounds)	289	-	-	-	-	-	-
(Spent Cartridges)	136	-	-	-	-	-	-

E - Empty   F - Full

Figure B1-1 (Sheet 4)

STANDARD ATMOSPHERE TABLE

STANDARD SEA LEVEL AIR:
T = 59°F (15°C)
P = 29.921 IN. OF HG

W = 0.076475 LB/CU FT = 0.0023769 SLUGS/CU FT
1 IN. OF HG = 70.732 LB/SQ FT = 0.4912 LB/SQ IN
a_0 = 116.5 FT/SEC = 661.5 KNOTS

U.S. STANDARD ATMOSPHERE, 1966

ALTITUDE FEET	DENSITY RATIO ρ/ρ_0	$1/\sqrt{\sigma}$	AIR TEMPERATURE		SPEED OF SOUND RATIO a/a_0	PRESSURE	
			DEG. F	DEG. C		IN. OF HG	RATIO $P/P_0 = \delta$
-2.000	1.0598	0.9714	66.132	18.962	1.0068	32.15	1.0745
-1.000	1.0296	0.9855	62.566	16.981	1.0034	31.02	1.0368
0	1.0000	1.0000	59.000	15.000	1.0000	29.92	1.0000
1.000	0.9711	1.0148	55.434	13.019	0.9966	28.86	0.9644
2.000	0.9482	1.0299	51.868	11.038	0.9931	27.82	0.9298
3.000	0.9151	1.0454	48.302	9.057	0.9896	26.82	0.8962
4.000	0.8881	1.0611	44.735	7.075	0.9862	25.84	0.8637
5.000	0.8617	1.0773	41.169	5.094	0.9827	24.90	0.8320
6.000	0.8359	1.0938	37.603	3.113	0.9792	23.98	0.8014
7.000	0.8106	1.1107	34.037	1.132	0.9756	23.09	0.7716
8.000	0.7860	1.1279	30.471	-0.849	0.9721	22.22	0.7428
9.000	0.7620	1.1456	26.905	-2.831	0.9686	21.39	0.7148
10.000	0.7385	1.1637	23.338	-4.812	0.9650	20.58	0.6877
11.000	0.7156	1.1822	19.772	-6.793	0.9614	19.79	0.6614
12.000	0.6932	1.2011	16.206	-8.74	0.9579	19.03	0.6360
13.000	0.6713	1.2205	12.640	-10.756	0.9543	18.29	0.6113
14.000	0.6500	1.2403	9.074	-12.737	0.9507	17.58	0.5875
15.000	0.6292	1.2606	5.508	-14.718	0.9470	16.83	0.5643
16.000	0.6090	1.2815	1.941	-16.699	0.9434	16.22	0.5420
17.000	0.5892	1.3028	-1.625	-18.681	0.9397	15.57	0.5203
18.000	0.5699	1.3246	-5.191	-20.662	0.9361	14.94	0.4994
19.000	0.5511	1.3470	-8.757	-22.643	0.9324	14.34	0.4791
20.000	0.5328	1.3700	-12.323	-24.624	0.9827	13.75	0.4593
21.000	0.5150	1.3935	-15.889	-26.605	0.9250	13.18	0.4406
22.000	0.4976	1.4176	-19.456	-28.587	0.9213	12.64	0.4223
23.000	0.4807	1.4424	-23.022	-30.568	0.9175	12.11	0.4046
24.000	0.4642	1.4678	-26.588	-32.549	0.9138	11.60	0.3876
25.000	0.4481	1.4938	-30.154	-34.530	0.9100	11.10	0.3711
26.000	0.4325	1.5206	-33.720	-36.511	0.9062	10.63	0.3552
27.000	0.4173	1.5480	-37.286	-38.492	0.9024	10.17	0.3398
28.000	0.4025	1.5762	-40.852	-40.473	0.8986	9.725	0.3250
29.000	0.3881	1.6052	-44.419	-42.455	0.8948	9.297	0.3107
30.000	0.3741	1.6349	-47.985	-44.436	0.8909	8.885	0.2970
31.000	0.3605	1.6654	-51.551	-46.417	0.8871	8.488	0.2837
32.000	0.3473	1.6968	-55.117	-48.398	0.8832	8.106	0.2709
33.000	0.3345	1.7291	-58.683	-50.379	0.8793	7.737	0.2586
34.000	0.3220	1.7623	-62.249	-52.361	0.8754	7.382	0.2467
35.000	0.3099	1.7964	-65.816	-54.342	0.8714	7.041	0.2353
36.000	0.2981	1.8315	-69.382	-56.323	0.8675	6.712	0.2243
37.000	0.2844	1.8753	-69.700	-56.500	0.8671	6.397	0.2138
38.000	0.2710	1.9209	-69.700	-56.500	0.8671	6.097	0.2038
39.000	0.2583	1.9677	-69.700	-56.500	0.8671	5.811	0.1942
40.000	0.2462	2.0165	-69.700	-56.500	0.8671	5.538	0.1851
41.000	0.2346	2.0645	-69.700	-56.500	0.8671	5.278	0.1764
42.000	0.2236	2.1148	-69.700	-56.500	0.8671	5.030	0.1681
43.000	0.2131	2.1662	-69.700	-56.500	0.8671	4.794	0.1602
44.000	0.2031	2.2189	-69.700	-56.500	0.8671	4.569	0.1527
45.000	0.1936	2.2728	-69.700	-56.500	0.8671	4.355	0.1455
46.000	0.1845	2.3281	-69.700	-56.500	0.8671	4.151	0.1387
47.000	0.1758	2.3848	-69.700	-56.500	0.8671	3.956	0.1322
48.000	0.1676	2.4428	-69.700	-56.500	0.8671	3.770	0.1260
49.000	0.1597	2.5022	-69.700	-56.500	0.8671	3.593	0.1201
50.000	0.1522	2.5630	-69.700	-56.500	0.8671	3.425	0.1145
51.000	0.1451	2.6254	-69.700	-56.500	0.8671	3.264	0.1091
52.000	0.1383	2.5892	-69.700	-56.500	0.8671	3.111	0.1040
53.000	0.1318	2.7545	-69.700	-56.500	0.8671	2.965	0.09909
54.000	0.1256	2.8216	-69.700	-56.500	0.8671	2.826	0.09444
55.000	0.1197	2.8903	-69.700	-56.500	0.8671	2.693	0.09001
56.000	0.1141	2.9605	-69.700	-56.500	0.8671	2.567	0.08176
57.000	0.1087	3.0326	-69.700	-56.500	0.8671	2.446	0.07792
58.000	0.1036	3.1063	-69.700	-56.500	0.8671	2.331	0.07792
59.000	0.09877	3.1819	-69.700	-56.500	0.8671	2.222	0.07426

STANDARD ATMOSPHERE TABLE

STANDARD SEA LEVEL AIR:
T = 59°F (15°C)
P = 29.921 IN. OF HG

W = 0.076475 LB/CU FT = 0.0023769 SLUGS/CU FT
1 IN. OF HG = 70.732 LB/SQ FT = 0.4912 LB/SQ IN
a_0 = 116.5 FT/SEC = 661.5 KNOTS

60.000	0.09414	3.2593	-69.700	-56.500	0.8671	2.118	0.07078
61.000	0.08972	3.3386	-69.700	-56.500	0.8671	2.018	0.06746
62.000	0.08551	3.4198	-69.700	-56.500	0.8671	1.924	0.06429
63.000	0.08150	3.5029	-69.700	-56.500	0.8671	1.833	0.06127
64.000	0.07767	3.5881	-69.700	-56.500	0.8671	1.747	0.05840
65.000	0.07403	3.6754	-69.700	-56.500	0.8671	1.665	0.05566

AIRSPEED CONVERSION
LOW MACH

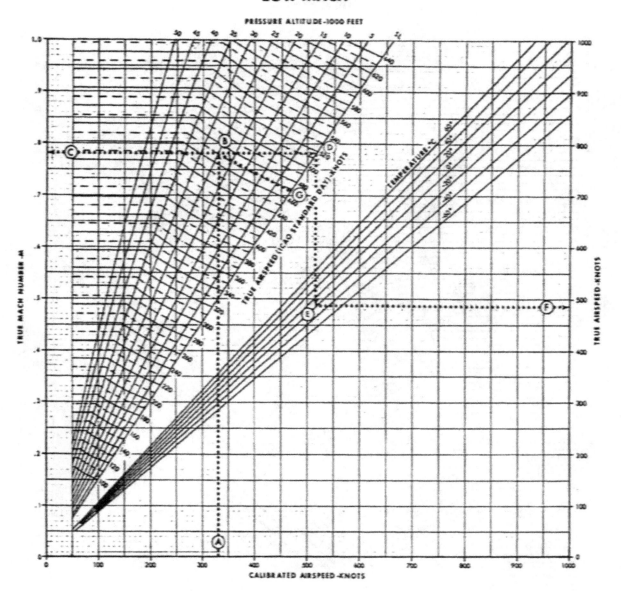

EXAMPLE

A = CAS = 330 KNOTS
B = ALTITUDE = 25,000 FEET
C = MACH = .782
D = SEA LEVEL LINE
E = TEMPERATURE = –20°C
F = TAS = 486 KNOTS
G = TAS (STANDARD DAY) = 472 KNOTS

1SE–1–1891

Figure B1-8

AIRSPEED CONVERSION

HIGH MACH

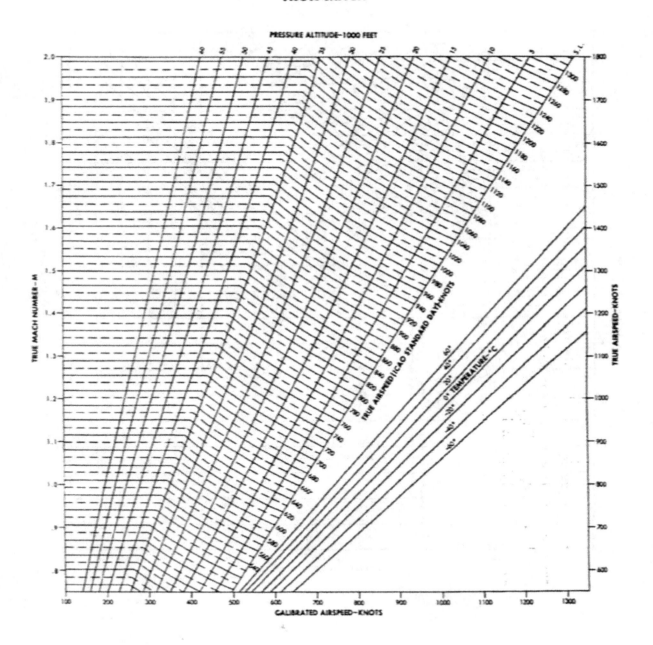

Figure B1-9

AIRSPEED POSITION ERROR CORRECTION
1G FLIGHT

AIRPLANE CONFIGURATION

FLAPS AND GEAR AS NOTED

REMARKS
ENGINE(S): (2) F100-PW 229
U.S. STANDARD DAY, 1966

GUIDE

DATE: 15 MARCH 1991
DATA BASIS: ESTIMATED

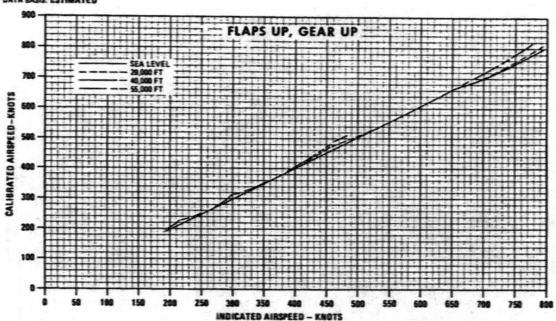

FLAPS DOWN, GEAR DOWN
10,000 FT AND BELOW

INDICATED AIRSPEED—KTS	CALIBRATED AIRSPEED-KTS		
	GW 30,000	GW 40,000	GW 50,000
140	137	–	–
160	158	157	–
180	178.5	178	177
200	198.5	198.5	198
220	219	218.5	218.5
240	239	239	239

15E-1-(274)21

Figure B1-10

ALTIMETER POSITION ERROR CORRECTION
STANDBY ALTIMETER ONLY

AIRPLANE CONFIGURATION
ALL DRAG INDEXES
FLAPS AND GEAR AS NOTED

REMARKS
ENGINE(S): (2) F100–PW 229
U.S. STANDARD DAY, 1966

NOTE
ASSIGNED ALTITUDE + ΔH = INDICATED
ALTITUDE. FLY INDICATED ALTITUDE.

DATE: 15 MARCH 1991
DATA BASIS: ESTIMATED

GUIDE

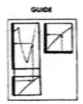

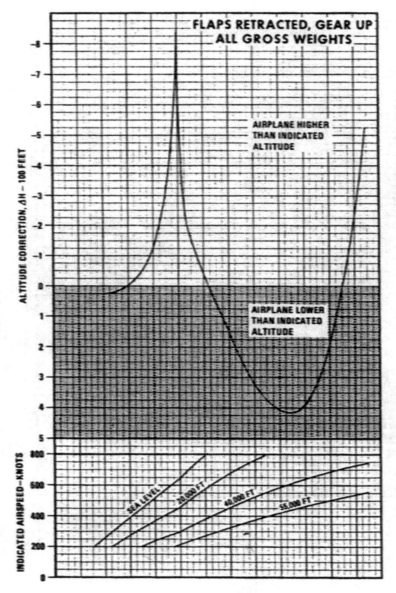

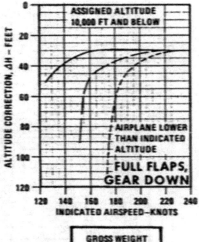

15E-1-(275)21

Figure B1-11

WIND COMPONENTS

- DETERMINE THE EFFECTIVE WIND VELOCITY BY ADDING ONE-HALF THE GUST VELOCITY (INCREMENTAL WIND FACTOR) TO THE STEADY STATE VELOCITY: E.G. REPORTED WIND 050/30 G40, EFFECTIVE WIND IS 050/35.

- CROSSWIND LIMITS FOR RCR VALUES, 12-16 AND 16-23 MAY BE OBTAINED BY INTERPOLATING BETWEEN THE LIMITS SHOWN.

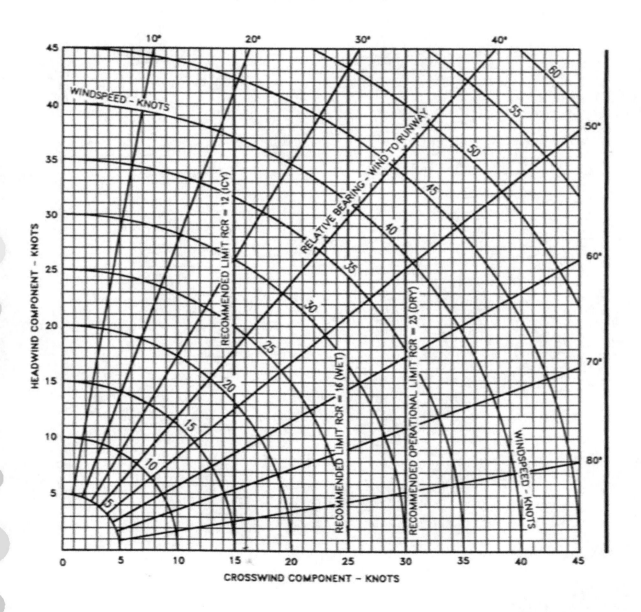

15E-1-073-1)18-CATI

Figure B1-12

PART 2

ENGINE DATA

This part not applicable.

PART 3

TAKEOFF

TABLE OF CONTENTS

Charts

Density Ratio B3-8
Minimum Go Speeds-With CFT .... TBS
Maximum Abort Speed-With CFT .... TBS
Takeoff Distance-With CFT .... TBS
Minimum Go Speeds-Without CFT .... TBS
Maximum Abort Speed-Without CFT .... TBS
Takeoff Distance-Without CFT .... TBS
Rotation Speed/Nosewheel Liftoff Speed/
Takeoff Speed-With CFT .... TBS
Nosewheel Liftoff Speed/Takeoff Speed
-Without CFT .... TBS
Single Engine Rate of Climb .... TBS

NOTE

Performance charts for the PW-229 engines are currently being developed. The references to figures have been retained even if the chart is not available. The actual charts will be added as they become available.

DENSITY RATIO CHART

This chart (figure B3-1) provides a means of obtaining a single factor (density ratio) that may be used to represent a combination of temperature and pressure altitude. Density ratio must be determined before the Minimum Go Speed and Maximum Abort Speed charts can be utilized.

USE

Enter the chart with existing temperature, and project vertically to intersect the applicable pressure altitude curve. From this point, project horizontally to the left scale to read density ratio.

SAMPLE DENSITY RATIO

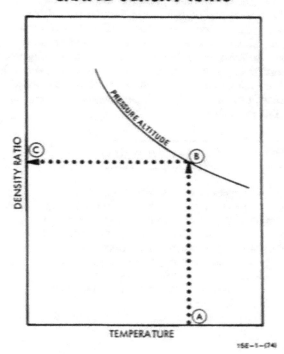

15E-1-(74)

Sample Problem

A. Temperature	60°F
B. Pressure Altitude	2000 Ft
C. Density ratio	0.93

MINIMUM GO SPEED CHART

These charts (figures B3-2, B3-6) provide the means of determining the minimum speed at which the aircraft can experience an engine failure and still take off under existing conditions of temperature, pressure altitude, gross weight, and the runway length remaining. Separate plots are provided for maximum and military thrust conditions, and for aircraft with and without CFT's installed. The data is based on an engine failure occurring at the minimum go speed and allows for a 3-second decision period with one engine operating at its initial thrust setting. In the case of a military thrust takeoff, an additional 3-second period is allowed for advancing the operating engine throttle to maximum thrust.

WARNING

If an engine is lost above the maximum abort speed but below the minimum go speed, the pilot can neither abort nor take off safely on the runway length remaining without considering such factors as reducing gross weight or engaging the overrun end arrestment cable. Refer to Engine Failure During Takeoff, section III.

USE

Enter the applicable plot with the prevailing density ratio, and project horizontally to the available runway length grid line. Parallel the nearest guideline up or down to intersect the baseline. From this point descend vertically to intersect the applicable takeoff gross weight curve, then horizontally to read minimum go speed. If this projected line lies entirely to the right of the gross weight curve single engine failure can be tolerated at any speed between zero and the highest speed shown with the ground roll being within the available runway length. If the above projected line lies entirely to the left of the gross weight curve, single engine failure takeoff cannot be accomplished with the available runway length. With CFTs, the recommended rotation speeds are given in figure B3-10. Without CFTs, with an engine failure before nose rotation at high gross weights, , the ground roll will be shortened if aft stick is relaxed until 10 to 15 knots below takeoff speed. This situation will be obvious to the pilot.

SAMPLE MINIMUM GO SPEED

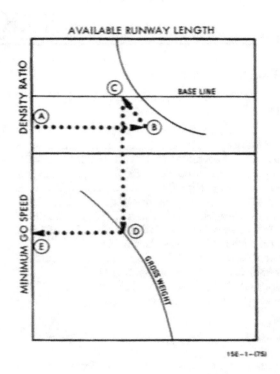

15E-1-(75)

Sample Problem

Maximum Thrust Takeoff With CFT (with fuel tanks or A/G stores on wing pylons)

A. Density ratio	0.90
B. Available runway length	9000 Ft
C. Parallel guideline to base-line	
D. Takeoff gross weight	75,000 Lb
E. Minimum go speed	172 KCAS

NOTE

This problem assumes maximum thrust on operating engine within 6 seconds after engine failure. The minimum go speed for a maximum thrust takeoff will be less than that for a military thrust takeoff due to the greater acceleration with maximum thrust up to and including the 3-second decision time.

MAXIMUM ABORT SPEED CHART

NOTE

- The maximum abort speed chart does not include the capability of any arrestment gear which may be installed, and takes into account only aircraft stopping performance for the given field conditions.

- Lower weight aircraft are often shown to have lower maximum abort speeds than higher weight aircraft due to the greater acceleration of the lighter aircraft during the abort decision period used in the calculations.

These charts (figures B3-3, B3-7) provide a means of determining the maximum speed at which an abort may be started and the aircraft stopped within the remaining runway length. Separate plots are provided for maximum and military thrust, and for aircraft with and without CFT's installed. Allowances included in this data are based on a 3-second decision period (with both engines operating at the initial thrust setting) followed by a 2-second period to apply wheel brakes and a 5-second period to reach idle thrust (these two abort procedures are initiated simultaneously).

USE

Enter applicable plot with the prevailing density ratio, and project horizontally to intersect the available runway length curve. From this point, descend further to intersect the computed takeoff gross weight, then horizontally to read the corresponding maximum abort speed.

SAMPLE MAXIMUM ABORT SPEED

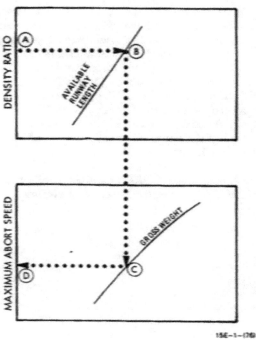

15E-1-(76)

Sample Problem

Maximum Thrust Takeoff, Hard Dry Runway, With CFT (with fuel tanks or A/G stores on wing pylons)

A. Density ratio	0.90
B. Available runway length	9000 Ft
C. Gross weight	75,000 Lb
D. Maximum abort speed	125 KCAS

TAKEOFF DISTANCE CHARTS

These charts (figures B3-4, B3-5, B3-8, B3-9) are used to determine the no wind ground run distance, wind adjusted ground run and the total distance required to clear a 50-foot obstacle. Separate charts are provided for maximum and military thrust, and for aircraft with and without CFT's installed. The without CFT charts (figures B3-8, B3-9) are based on CG's representative of each gross weight. With CFTs, the CG's used for each gross weight are noted on the chart. Takeoff distances will be reduced for aft CG's and increased for forward CG's.

The notes regarding CG effect on ground roll on the takeoff charts are based on conservative performance estimates based on data generated at typical weight, altitude, and temperature conditions.

USE

Enter the chart with existing temperature and project vertically to intersect the applicable pressure altitude curve. From that point, proceed horizontally to the right and intersect the takeoff weight line. Then descend vertically to read no wind ground run distance. Parallel the appropriate wind guideline (headwind or tailwind) to intersect the takeoff wind velocity. From this point project vertically down to read the ground run adjusted for wind effects. To find the total distance required to clear a 50-foot obstacle, continue downward to the reflector line and project horizontally to the left scale.

SAMPLE TAKEOFF DISTANCE

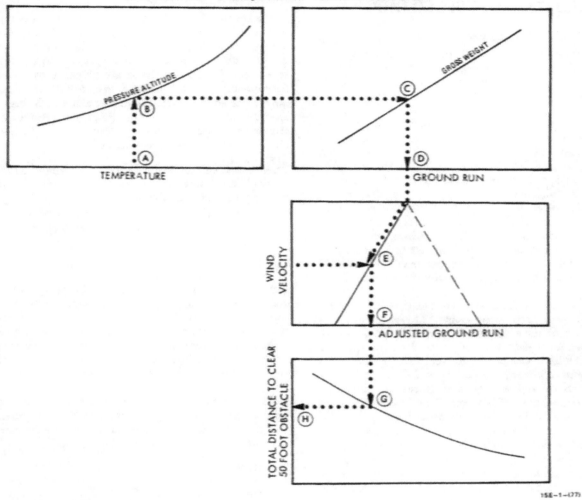

15E-1-(77)

Sample Problem

Maximum Thrust With CFT (with fuel tanks or A/G stores on wing pylons)

A. Temperature	20°C	
B. Pressure altitude	2000 Ft	
C. Gross weight	75,000 Lb	

D. No wind Ground run distance	4050 Ft	
E. Effective headwind	25 Kt	
F. Ground run (wind corrected)	3100 Ft	
G. Intersect reflector line		
H. Total distance required to clear 50-foot obstacle	5400 Ft	

NOSEWHEEL LIFTOFF SPEED/TAKEOFF SPEED CHART

These charts (figures B3-10 and B3-11) are used to determine nosewheel liftoff speed and aircraft takeoff speed for various gross weights in either maximum or military thrust for aircraft with and without CFTs installed

With CFTs installed, rotation speeds along with the corresponding nosewheel liftoff and takeoff speeds are presented for standard two-engine takeoffs as a function of CG and gross weight. At the indicated rotation speed one-half aft stick should be applied and the aircraft rotated to 12°. Rotation speeds increase at forward CGs to prevent nosewheel bouncing. Rotation speeds are also presented for continued takeoffs after an engine failure during ground roll. For continued takeoffs one-half aft stick should be applied at the rotation speed, but the aircraft should only be rotated to 10° for improved acceleration.

Without CFTs, the speeds are based on CGs representative of each gross weight. The chart provides data for either a normal or maximum performance takeoff. A normal takeoff is accomplished by applying 1/2 aft stick over a period of 1 second as the aircraft is accelerating through 120 knots, and then holding 10° of pitch throughout the takeoff roll. A maximum performance takeoff is accomplished by applying full aft stick at a low speed and when the nose rotates, holding 12° of pitch throughout the takeoff roll. Aircraft rotation will be more rapid with the maximum performance takeoff technique. Rotation speeds are also presented for continued takeoffs after an engine failure during ground roll. For continued takeoffs one-half aft stick should be applied at the rotation speed, with a 10° pitch attitude held throughout the takeoff roll.

The difference in nosewheel lift-off speeds between military and maximum thrust are due to the thrust effects on pitching moment. The differences in takeoff speeds are due to the thrust support in lift and the time required to rotate the aircraft to takeoff attitude.

SINGLE ENGINE RATE OF CLIMB

These charts (figures B3-12 thru B3-16) provide the means of determining single engine rate of climb for takeoff planning purposes for existing conditions of temperature, pressure altitude, gross weight, airspeed, and Drag Index. Separate plots are provided for gross weights from 60,000 lb to 81,000 lb. The data are for one engine operating at maximum A/B thrust and the other engine windmilling. Out-of-ground-effects aero data were used in construction of these charts. Gear and flaps are extended.

These charts can be used to determine if single engine rate of climb is adequate at the single engine takeoff speeds obtained from figure B3-10 for the continued takeoff technique. The change in rate of climb due to increasing or decreasing takeoff speed can also be determined.

USE

Enter the applicable chart with existing temperature and project vertically to intersect the applicable pressure altitude curve. From this point, project horizontally to the right and intersect the applicable with or without wing stores line. Then descend vertically to intersect the baseline velocity of 210 KCAS. Parallel the guidelines to intersect the takeoff velocity in question. From this point descend vertically to intersect the baseline Drag Index. Parallel the appropriate velocity guideline to intersect the takeoff Drag Index. Descend vertically again to read the single engine rate of climb.

Sample Problem

Gross Weight 75,000 Lb

A. Temperature	5°C
B. Pressure Altitude	Sea Level
C. Wing Tanks or A/G Weapons Installed	
D. Takeoff Velocity	204 KCAS
E. Drag Index	100
F. Single Engine Rate of Climb	+1200 ft/min

SAMPLE SINGLE ENGINE RATE OF CLIMB

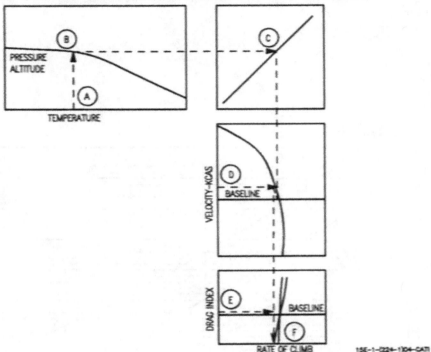

15E-1-(224-1)04-CAT1

DENSITY RATIO

AIRPLANE CONFIGURATION
ALL DRAG INDEXES

DATE: 15 MARCH 1991
DATA BASIS: **ESTIMATED**

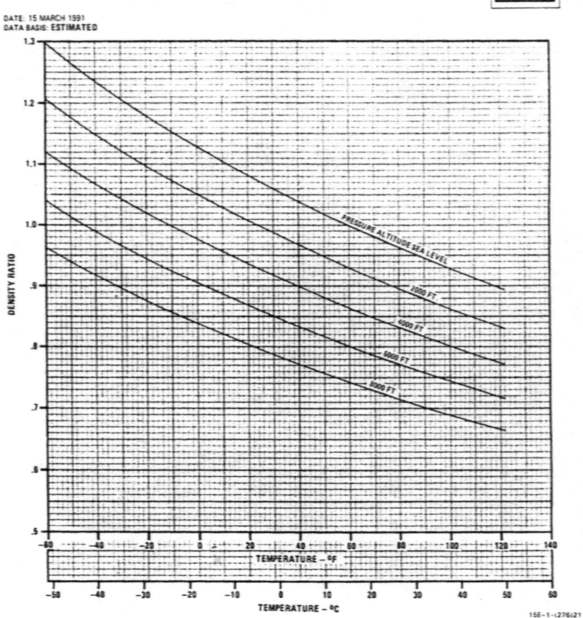

Figure B3-1

PART 4

CLIMB

TABLE OF CONTENTS

Charts

Climb ....TBS
Combat Ceiling ....TBS

NOTE

Performance charts for PW-229 engines are currently being developed. The references to figures have been retained even if the chart is not available. The actual charts will be added as they become available.

CLIMB CHARTS

The Climb charts (figures B4-1 thru B4-6) are used to determine time, fuel used, and distance covered while in the climb. Each chart is based on a military or maximum thrust climb for individual drag index configurations. The climb speed schedule and pre-climb data are noted on each chart.

USE

The method of presenting data on the time, fuel and distance charts is identical, and the use of all three charts will be undertaken simultaneously here. Enter the charts with the initial climb gross weight and project horizontally right to intersect the assigned cruise altitude or the optimum cruise altitude for the computed drag index, then vertically down to intersect the applicable drag index curve. From this point project horizontally left to the temperature baseline and parallel the nearest temperature guideline to read time, fuel or distance. Time, fuel or distance required to accelerate to climb speed must be added to the chart values.

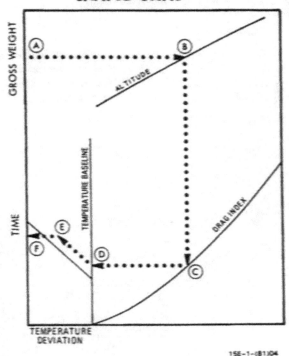

SAMPLE CLIMB

15E-1-081)04

Sample Problem

Military Thrust

A. Gross weight	60,000 Lb
B. Cruise altitude	20,000 Ft
C. Drag Index	120
D. Temperature baseline	
E. Temperature deviation	+10°C
F. Time	6.0 Min
G. Fuel (from Fuel Required To Climb Chart)	1700 Lb
H. Distance (from Distance Required to Climb Chart)	35 NM

COMBAT CEILING CHARTS

These charts (figures B4-7 and B4-8) present the military and maximum thrust subsonic combat ceiling for both single engine and normal two engine operation. The variable of gross weight and pressure altitude are taken into consideration for a range of drag indexes.

USE

Enter the applicable graph with estimated gross weight at end of climb. Project vertically up to intersect applicable configuration curve, then horizontally to the left to read combat ceiling.

Sample Problem

Combat Ceiling - Maximum Thrust - (2) Engines

Configuration: -4 CFTs + (4) AIM-7F missiles

A. Gross weight at end of climb	55,000 Lb
B. Drag index	18.6
C. Combat ceiling	49,700 Ft

PART 5

RANGE

TABLE OF CONTENTS

Charts

Optimum Long Range Cruise ....TBS
Constant Altitude/Long Range Cruise ....TBS
Constant Altitude Cruise ....TBS
Low Altitude Cruise ....TBS
High Altitude Cruise ....TBS
Constant Altitude Cruise-Landing Gear
Extended ....TBS

NOTE

Performance charts for the PW-229 engines are currently being developed. The references to figures have been retained even if the chart is not available. The actual charts will be added as they become available.

OPTIMUM LONG RANGE CRUISE

These charts (figures B5-1 and B5-2) present cruise data for twin-engine and single engine operation. These charts depict cruise altitude, specific range (nautical miles per pound) and cruise Mach number for various gross weights and drag indexes.

USE

Enter the chart with the applicable gross weight and project vertically up to intersect the appropriate drag index curves in each plot. From the intersection of the appropriate drag index curve, reflect horizontally left and read cruise Mach number, specific range in nautical miles per pound and cruise altitude.

SAMPLE OPTIMUM LONG RANGE CRUISE

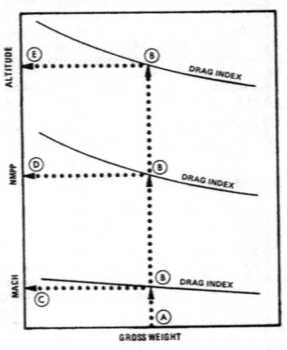

15E-1-(139)04

Sample Problem

A. Gross weight	60,000 Lb
B. Drag index	120
C. Mach number	0.765 Mach
D. Specific range	0.051 NMPP
E. Cruise altitude	31,200 Ft

CONSTANT ALTITUDE/LONG RANGE CRUISE

These charts (figures B5-3 thru B5-12) present the necessary planning data to set up optimum cruise schedules for normal two-engine operation at a constant altitude. The charts depict specific range (nautical miles per pound of fuel) for various Mach numbers, gross weights and individual drag indexes at altitudes of sea level thru 45,000 feet in increments of 5000 feet. The recommended procedure is to use an average gross weight for a given leg of the mission. One way to find the average gross weight is to divide the mission into weight segments. With this method, readjust the cruise schedule each time a given amount of fuel is used. Subtract one-half of the fuel weight allotted for the first leg from the initial cruise gross weight. The remainder is the average gross weight for the leg. It is possible to obtain instantaneous data if desired.

USE

Enter the chart with the desired gross weight and project vertically upward to intersect the appropriate drag index curve, then horizontally to the left to determine optimum cruise Mach number. From the optimum airspeed-gross weight intersection project vertically up to intersect the appropriate drag index curve, then horizontally left to determine the specific range. These charts are applicable for any temperature day. Use following paragraph to determine true airspeed and total fuel flow.

Sample Problem

Configuration - -4 CFT + (4)AIM-7F Missiles, Altitude - 30,000 feet

A. Gross weight	55,000 Lb
B. Drag index	18.6
C. Cruise Mach number	0.850
D. Drag index	18.6
E. Specific range	0.078 NMPP

CONSTANT ALTITUDE CRUISE CHARTS

This chart (B5-13) presents the necessary planning data to set up optimum cruise schedules for normal two engine operation at a constant altitude at various flight-level temperatures.

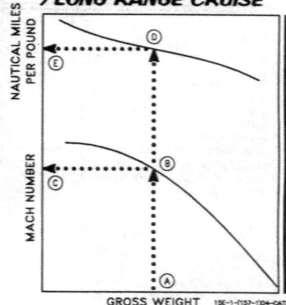

SAMPLE CONSTANT ALTITUDE /LONG RANGE CRUISE

USE

Enter the left side of the chart with the optimum cruise Mach number and project horizontally right to intersect the predicted flight-level temperature. Then, project vertically up to obtain the corresponding true airspeed. Project vertically down to intersect the interpolated specific range, then project horizontally left to obtain total fuel flow required in pounds per hour.

Sample Problem

Configuration - -4 CFT + (4) AIM-7F Missiles, Altitude - 30,000 feet, Temperature - −40°C

A. True Mach number	0.855
B. Temperature	−40°C
C. True airspeed	510 KTAS
D. Specific range	0.078 NMPP
E. Total fuel flow	6600 PPH

SAMPLE CONSTANT ALTITUDE CRUISE

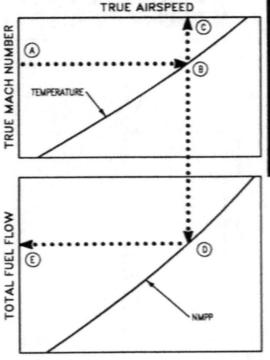

1SE-1-(1SB-1)04-OAT)-31

the non-standard day temperature correction factor obtained from the appropriate TEMP. EFFECTS column. Enter the table with the equivalent standard day true airspeed and project horizontally to the applicable drag index column and read total fuel flow for a standard day. To obtain the total fuel flow at the desired true airspeed, multiply the total fuel flow for a standard day by the nonstandard day temperature correction factor.

Sample Problem

Gross weight 35,000 lbs, 15,000 ft (−15°C)

A. Desired airspeed	535 KTAS
B. Drag Index	20
C. Nonstandard day temperature	0°C
D. Correction factor	1.029
E. Equivalent standard day true airspeed (A ÷ D)	520 Kt
F. Standard day total fuel flow	9894 PPH
G. Total fuel flow at desired true airspeed (F X D)	10181 PPH
H. Standard day V_{max}	614.2 KTAS
J. Standard day Mil. Pwr. total fuel flow	18,716 PPH

HIGH ALTITUDE CRUISE TABLES

These tables (figures B5-24 thru B5-33) present total fuel flow values for various combinations of cruise airspeed and drag index at altitudes of 25,000 feet thru 45,000 feet in 5000 foot increments. Also included for each altitude are the total fuel flow values and resultant V_{max} (maximum attainable TAS) for a MIL thrust setting. Separate charts are provided for gross weights of 35,000 thru 80,000 pounds. Fuel flow values are tabulated for U.S. Standard Day; however, correction factors are given for nonstandard temperatures. The standard day temperature is listed with the altitude. If the actual temperature at a particular altitude differs from the standard day temperature, refer to the TEMP. EFFECTS column to determine the appropriate temperature correction factor.

USE

After selecting the applicable table for gross weight and altitude, determine the equivalent standard day true airspeed by dividing the desired true airspeed by the nonstandard day temperature correction factor obtained from the appropriate TEMP EFFECTS column. Enter the table with the equivalent standard

LOW ALTITUDE CRUISE TABLES

These tables (figures B5-14 thru B5-23) present total fuel flow values for various combinations of cruise airspeed and drag index at altitudes of Sea Level, 5000, 10,000, 15,000 and 20,000 feet. Also included for each altitude are the total fuel flow values and resultant V_{max} (maximum attainable TAS) for a MIL thrust setting. Separate tables are provided for gross weights of 35,000 thru 80,000 pounds. Fuel flow values are tabulated for U.S. Standard Day; however, correction factors are given for non-standard temperatures. The standard day temperature is listed with the altitude. If the actual temperature at a particular altitude differs from the standard day temperature, refer to the TEMP. EFFECTS column to determine the appropriate temperature correction factor.

USE

After selecting the applicable table for gross weight and altitude, determine the equivalent standard day true airspeed by dividing the desired true airspeed by day true airspeed and project horizontally to the applicable drag index column and read total fuel flow for a standard day. To obtain the total fuel flow at the desired true airspeed, multiply the total fuel flow for a standard day by the nonstandard day temperature correction factor.

CONSTANT ALTITUDE CRUISE - LANDING GEAR EXTENDED

This chart (figure B5-34) presents data to set up constant altitude cruise schedules when landing gear cannot be retracted. The chart contains specific range (nautical miles per pound of fuel) data for various combinations of gross weight, drag index, and altitude for a cruise speed of 250 KCAS.

USE

Enter the chart at the gross weight scale and project horizontally right to intersect with the applicable drag index. From this point, project downward to intersect with the desired cruise altitude and project horizontally left to read the specific range.

Sample Problem

A. Gross weight	40,000 Lb
B. Drag index (external stores)	30
Drag index (all gear extended)	90
Total drag index	120
C. Altitude	10,000 Ft
D. Specific range	0.046 NMPP

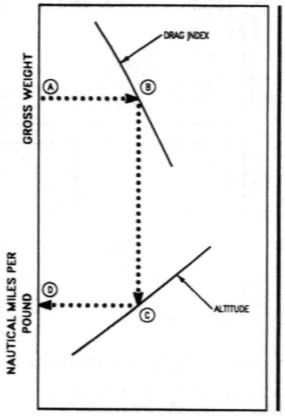

SAMPLE CONSTANT ALTITUDE CRUISE, LANDING GEAR EXTENDED

PART 6

ENDURANCE

TABLE OF CONTENTS

Charts Maximum Endurance.........................TBS
Endurance-Landing Gear Extended ....TBS

NOTE

Performance charts for the PW-229 engines are currently being developed. The references to figures have been retained even if the chart is not available. The actual charts will be added as they become available.

MAXIMUM ENDURANCE CHARTS

These charts (figures B6-1 and B6-2) present optimum endurance altitude and maximum endurance specifics (fuel flow and Mach number) for various combinations of effective gross weight and altitude.

USE (ALTITUDE AND BANK ANGLE CHART)

Enter the Altitude and Bank Angle chart with the average gross weight. If bank angles are to be considered, follow the gross weight curve until it intersects the bank angle to be used, then project horizontally right to obtain effective gross weight. (If bank angles are not to be considered, enter the chart at the effective gross weight scale.) From this point proceed horizontally right to intersect the applicable drag index curve, then project vertically down to read optimum endurance altitude.

Sample Problem

Altitude and Bank Angle

A. Gross weight	60,000 Lb
B. Bank angle	20°
C. Effective gross weight	63,800 Lb
D. Drag index	120
E. Optimum endurance altitude	18,000 Ft

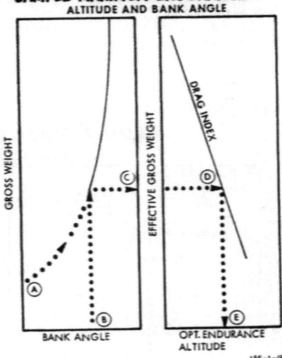

SAMPLE MAXIMUM ENDURANCE
ALTITUDE AND BANK ANGLE

156-1-(88)

USE (FUEL FLOW AND MACH NUMBER CHART)

Enter the fuel flow and Mach number plots on the Fuel Flow and Mach Number chart with the effective gross weight, then horizontally to intersect the optimum endurance altitude curve. From this point, project vertically down to intersect the applicable drag index curve, then horizontally to read fuel flow or true Mach number.

Sample Problem

Fuel Flow

A.	Effective gross weight	63,800 Lb
B.	Endurance altitude	18,000 Ft
C.	Drag index	120
D.	Fuel flow	8050 PPH

Mach Number

A.	Effective gross weight	63,800 Lb
B.	Endurance altitude	18,000 Ft
C.	Drag index	120
D.	True Mach number	0.589

SAMPLE MAXIMUM ENDURANCE
FUEL FLOW AND TRUE MACH NUMBER

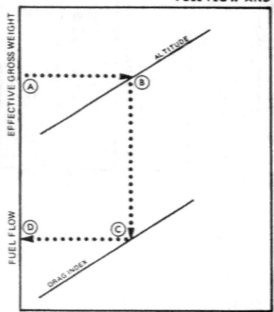
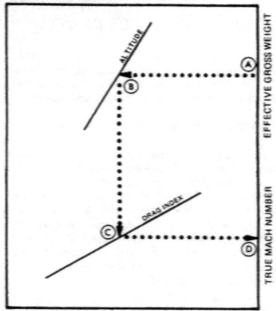

15E-1-(89)04

SAMPLE ENDURANCE, LANDING GEAR EXTENDED

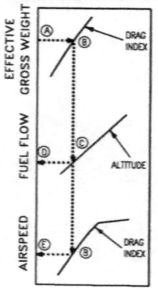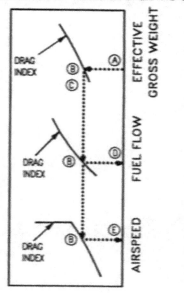

15E-1-(156-1)04-CAT)

ENDURANCE-LANDING GEAR EXTENDED

This chart (figure B6-3) presents constant altitude endurance and maximum endurance specifics (fuel flow, calibrated airspeed, and altitude) for various combinations of gross weight and drag index.

USE

If bank angles are to be considered, utilize the method described in the previous problem to determine the effective gross weight. To obtain constant altitude endurance specifics, enter the left side of the chart at the effective gross weight scale. From this point, proceed horizontally right to intersect the applicable drag index curve, then project downward to intersect with the desired altitude. From this point, project horizontally left to read the fuel flow. To obtain the calibrated airspeed, project downward from the altitude-fuel flow intersection to intersect with the applicable drag index curves on the airspeed chart, project horizontally left from this point to read the calibrated airspeed.

To obtain maximum endurance specifics, the right side of the chart is used. Enter the chart at the effective gross weight and project horizontally left to intersect with the applicable drag index curve. From this point, project downward to read the maximum endurance altitude from the horizontal scale. Project further downward to intersect with the applicable drag index curve and project horizontally right to read the fuel flow or the calibrated airspeed.

Sample Problem

Constant Altitude Endurance

A. Effective gross weight	42,500 Lb	
B. Drag index (external stores)	30	
Drag index (all gear extended)	90	
Total drag index	120	
C. Altitude	10,000 Ft	
D. Fuel flow	5,400 PPH	
E. Airspeed	203 KCAS	

Maximum Endurance

A. Effective gross weight	42,500 Lb
B. Drag index	120
C. Altitude	28,000 Ft
D. Fuel flow	5,600 PPH
E. Airspeed	204 KCAS

PART 7

DESCENT

NOTE

Performance charts for the PW-229 engines are currently being developed. The references to figures have been retained even if the chart is not available. The actual charts will be added as they become available.

DESCENT CHARTS

The Descent charts (figures B7-1 thru B7-5) present distance, time, total fuel used and Mach number in the descent. Incremental data may be obtained for distance, time and fuel by subtracting data corresponding to level-off altitude from the data for the original cruising altitude.

USE

Enter the upper plot of the appropriate chart at the cruising altitude, project horizontally right to intersect both series of drag index curves. From the altitude - drag index intersection in the first series, project vertically down to read distance. From the altitude - drag index intersection in the second series, project vertically down to read time to descend. Enter the lower plot at the cruising altitude and project horizontally right to intersect the applicable drag index curve on the fuel graph. Continue horizontally right and intersect the curve on the Mach number graph. From the altitude - drag index intersection on the fuel graph, descend vertically and read total fuel used in the descent. From the intersection on the Mach number graph, project vertically down to read true Mach number.

Sample Problem

Maximum Range Descent, 220 KCAS, Idle Thrust, Speed Brake Retracted, F-15 without CFT

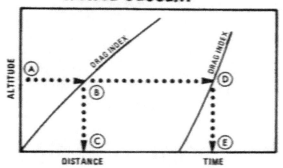

SAMPLE DESCENT

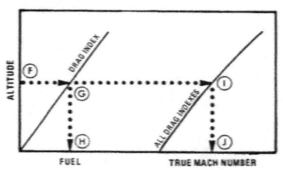

15E-1-(90)

A. Altitude	30,000 Ft
B. Drag index	40
C. Distance	55 NM
D. Drag index	40
E. Time required	11.7 Min
F. Altitude	30,000 Ft
G. Drag index	40
H. Total fuel used	395 Lb
I. Drag reflector	
J. True Mach number	0.59 Mach

PART 8

APPROACH AND LANDING

TABLE OF CONTENTS

Charts

Landing Approach Speed..................................... B8-5
Maximum Approach Gross Weight..................B8-6
Landing Distance B8-7

NOTE

Performance charts for the PW-229 engines are currently being developed. The references to figures have been retained even if the chart is not available. The actual charts will be added when they become available.

LANDING APPROACH SPEED CHART

The Landing Approach Speed chart (figure B8-1) provides recommended approach speed for various gross weights of the aircraft. The data is plotted for flaps either up or down.

USE

Enter the chart at the estimated landing gross weight and project vertically up to the appropriate flap reflector line. From this point, project horizontally left to read recommended approach speed.

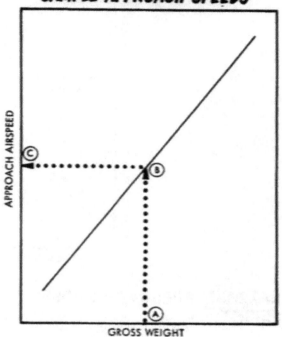

SAMPLE APPROACH SPEEDS

15E-1-059

Sample Problem

Configuration: Flaps Down

A. Estimated landing gross weight   50,000 Lb
B. Flaps down reflector line
C. Landing approach speed   174.1 Kt

SAMPLE MAXIMUM APPROACH GROSS WEIGHT
(SINGLE ENGINE)

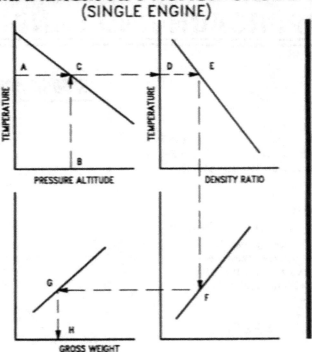

15E-1-(230-1)03-CATI

MAXIMUM APPROACH GROSS WEIGHT

The Maximum Approach Gross Weight chart (figure B8-2) provides the maximum gross weight at which the aircraft can peform a single engine maximum power climb after experiencing an engine failure. The data presented are based on the requirement that the aircraft be able to climb at a rate of 500 ft/min at approach speed at the existing ambient temperature and pressure altitude.

USE

Enter the chart at the existing ambient temperature and ambient pressure. Project horizontally right at the existing ambient temperature and project vertically up at the existing ambient pressure. The intersection of the two projections represents existing conditions with respect to a standard day. From this point, project horizontally right to the existing ambient pressure altitude and then descend vertically to determine the appropriate density ratio. Continue descending vertically to intersect existing ambient temperature. From this point, project horizontally left to the effective Drag Index and then descend vertically to read gross weight.

Sample Problem

A. Temperature	21°C
B. Pressure Altitude	2000 Ft
C. Type Day	STD +10°C
D. Temperature	21°C
E. Pressure Altitude	2000 Ft
F. Type Day Reflector	STD +10°C
G. Drag Index Reflector	190
H. Gross Weight	77,500 Lb

LANDING DISTANCE CHART

These charts (figures B8-3 thru B8-5) provide landing roll distance information. One chart provides data for a normal landing using aerodynamic braking. The other provides data for a landing roll utilizing the technique of lowering the nose immediately after touchdown and applying maximum anti-skid braking. The variables of temperature, altitude, gross weight, effective wind, and runway condition are taken into consideration.

USE

Enter the chart with the runway temperature and project vertically up to the applicable pressure altitude. From this point, proceed horizontally right to the landing gross weight, then descend vertically to the wind baseline. Parallel the nearest guideline down to the effective headwind or tailwind for the appropriate runway condition. From this point, project vertically down to the appropriate runway condition reflector, then horizontally left to read ground roll. Continue further left to the appropriate runway condition reflector, then vertically down to read total distance required when landing over a 50 foot obstacle.

Sample Problem

Normal Landing - Aerodynamic Braking

A. Temperature	20°C
B. Pressure altitude	2000 Ft
C. Gross weight	40,000 Lb
D. Effective headwind (DRY)	15 Kt
E. RCR reflector (DRY)	23
F. Landing distance	4500 Ft
G. RCR Reflector (DRY)	
H. Total distance required over a 50-foot obstacle	5600 Ft

SAMPLE LANDING DISTANCE

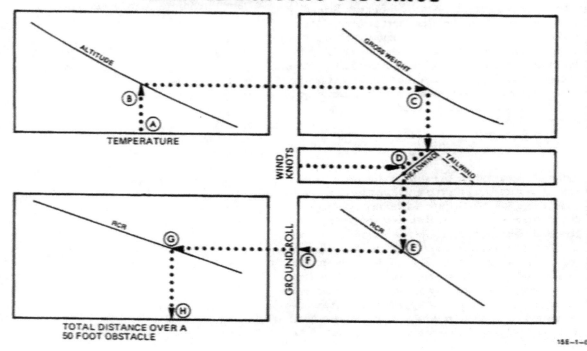

TEMPERATURE

ALTITUDE

GROSS WEIGHT

WIND KNOTS

HEADWIND   TAILWIND

RCR

GROUND ROLL

RCR

TOTAL DISTANCE OVER A
50 FOOT OBSTACLE

15E-1-(96)

LANDING APPROACH SPEED

WITH OR WITHOUT CFT

AIRPLANE CONFIGURATION
ALL DRAG INDEXES
21 UNITS AOA

REMARKS
ENGINE(S): (2) F100-PW-229
U.S. STANDARD DAY, 1966

GUIDE

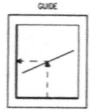

DATE:15 MARCH 1991
DATA BASIS: ESTIMATED

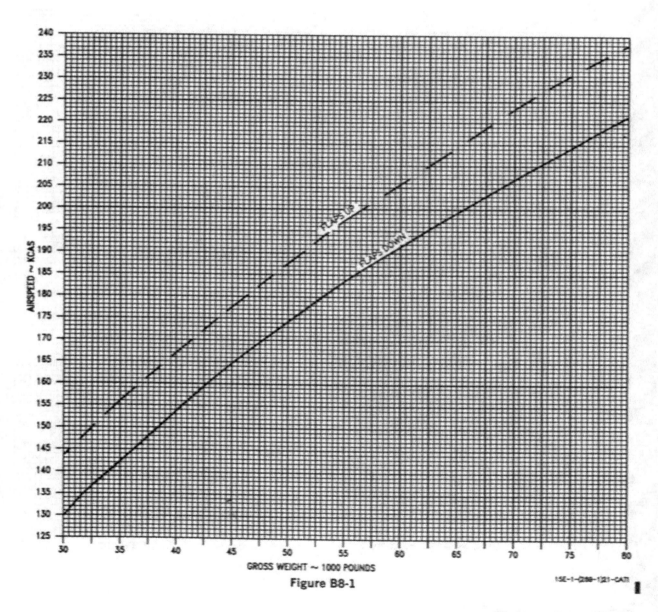

Figure B8-1

15E-1-(2)98-1(21-CA7)

MAXIMUM APPROACH GROSS WEIGHT
SINGLE ENGINE OPERATING

GUIDE

AIRPLANE CONFIGURATION
GEAR AND FLAPS EXTENDED
INDIVIDUAL DRAG INDEXES

REMARKS
ENGINE(S): (2) F100-PW-229
U.S. STANDARD DAY, 1966

NOTE
- LANDING GEAR DRAG MUST ALSO BE INCLUDED WHEN CALCULATING TOTAL DRAG INDEX
- DI=40 NOSE GEAR, DI=25 FOR EACH MAIN GEAR
- INOPERATIVE ENGINE WINDMILLING
- SPEEDBRAKE RETRACTED

DATE: 15 MARCH 1991
DATA BASIS: ESTIMATED

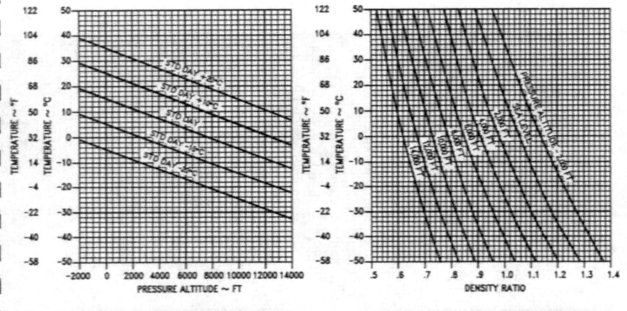

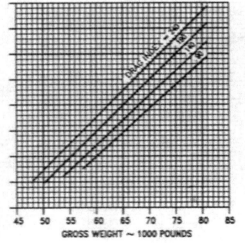

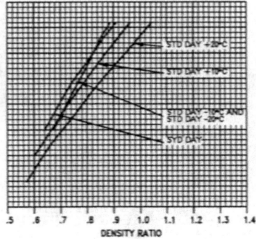

Figure B8-2

15E-1-(27D-1)21-CATI

LANDING DISTANCE
WITH OR WITHOUT CFT
AERODYNAMIC BRAKING
IDLE THRUST
GROSS WEIGHT 35,000 TO 55,000 POUNDS

GUIDE

AIRPLANE CONFIGURATION
FLAPS DOWN GEAR DOWN
ALL DRAG INDEXES

REMARKS
ENGINE(S): (2) F100-PW-229

NOTE
- DATA IS BASED ON THE USE OF AERODYNAMIC BRAKING BY RAISING THE NOSE TO A 12° PITCH ATTITUDE AFTER TOUCHDOWN AND MAINTAINING AS LONG AS POSSIBLE.
- SPEED BRAKE IS EXTENDED AT TOUCHDOWN.

DATE: 15 MARCH 1991
DATA BASIS: ESTIMATED

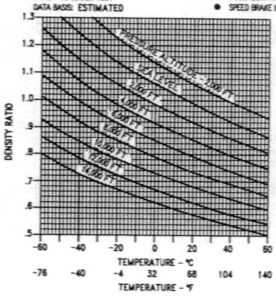

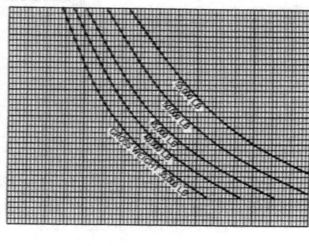

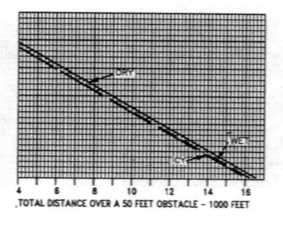

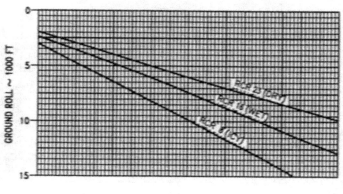

TOTAL DISTANCE OVER A 50 FEET OBSTACLE - 1000 FEET

Figure B8-3

15E-1-(271-1)21-CATI

LANDING DISTANCE
WITH OR WITHOUT CFT
AERODYNAMIC BRAKING
IDLE THRUST
GROSS WEIGHT 55,000 TO 80,000 POUNDS

GUIDE

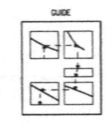

AIRPLANE CONFIGURATION
FLAPS DOWN
GEAR DOWN
ALL DRAG INDEXES

DATE: 15 MARCH 1991
DATA BASIS: ESTIMATED

REMARKS
ENGINE(S): (2) F100-PW-229

NOTE
- DATA IS BASED ON THE USE OF AERODYNAMIC BRAKING BY RAISING THE NOSE TO A 12° PITCH ATTITUDE AFTER TOUCHDOWN AND MAINTAINING AS LONG AS POSSIBLE.
- SPEED BRAKE IS EXTENDED AT TOUCHDOWN.

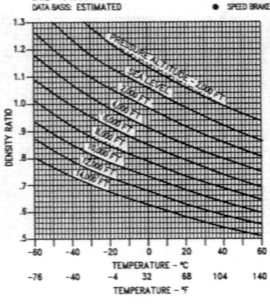

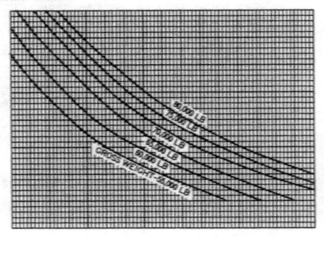

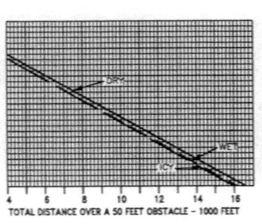

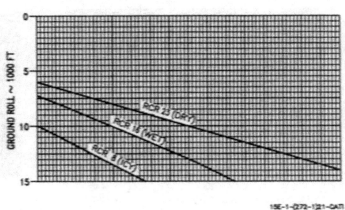

Figure B8-4

15E-1-(272-1)21-CATI

LANDING DISTANCE

WITH OR WITHOUT CFT
MAXIMUM ANTI–SKID BRAKING
IDLE THRUST

AIRPLANE CONFIGURATION
FLAPS DOWN GEAR DOWN
ALL DRAG INDEXES

DATE: 15 MARCH 1991
DATA BASIS: ESTIMATED

REMARKS
ENGINE(S): (2) F100-PW-229

NOTE
- DATA IS BASED ON LOWERING THE NOSE IMMEDIATELY AFTER TOUCHDOWN AND APPLYING MAXIMUM ANTI-SKID BRAKING.
- SPEED BRAKE IS EXTENDED AT TOUCHDOWN.

GUIDE

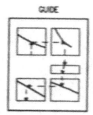

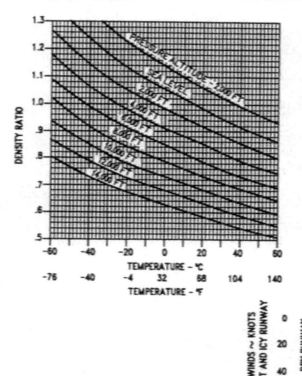

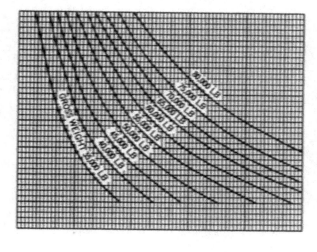

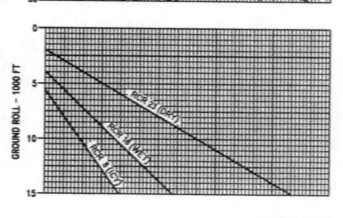

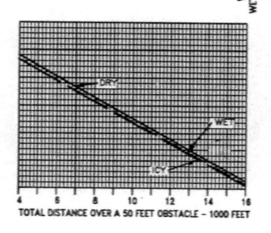

15E-1-(273-1)21-CATI

Figure B8-5

PART 9

COMBAT PERFORMANCE

TABLE OF CONTENTS

Charts

Level Flight Envelope................................ TBS
Dive Recovery .... TBS
Low Altitude Combat Performance......................TBS
Combat Fuel Management..............................TBS
Combat Fuel Flow....................................TBS
Overload Warning System
   Symmetrical Allowable Load Factor...................TBS
Level Flight Acceleration ....TBS
Sustained Level Turns..............................TBS

NOTE

> Performance charts are currently being developed for the PW-229 engines. The references to figures have been retained even if the chart is not available. The actual charts will be added as they become available.

LEVEL FLIGHT ENVELOPE

These charts (figures B9-1 thru B9-14) present the aircraft level flight speed envelope for various configurations and average combat gross weights. Parameters of the envelopes extend from the maximum lift coefficient to maximum thrust Mach number at 0g acceleration throughout the altitude range. For each configuration, envelopes are presented for a standard day and standard day ±10°C. In addition to the maximum attainable Mach number at 0g acceleration, each standard day curve indicates Mach number at .03g acceleration. Figure B9-14 shows the relationship between maximum Mach number and Vmax for a selected configuration.

USE

Enter the chart with the desired combat altitude and project horizontally to intersect the applicable standard day .03g and 0g acceleration power curves. From these points, proceed vertically down to read the .03g Mach number and the maximum attainable Mach number in level flight.

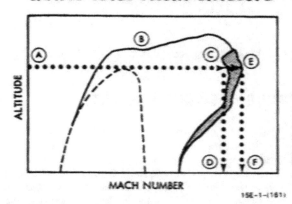

SAMPLE LEVEL FLIGHT ENVELOPE

15E-1-(161)

Sample Problem

Configuration: -4 CFT + (4) AIM-7 + (4) AIM-9; 52,500 Pounds Gross Weight.

A. Combat altitude	35,000 Ft
B. Curve	Std Day
C. .03g Acceleration Curve	
D. .03g Acceleration Mach number	1.44
E. 0g Acceleration curve	
F. 0g Acceleration Mach number	1.52

MAXIMUM SPEED-LEVEL FLIGHT

This chart (figure B9-15 and B9-16) presents level flight maximum speed at military power for drag indexes from 0 to 160 for gross weight with 50% internal fuel remaining. The maximum speeds are listed by Mach/KCAS at 0g acceleration and 0.03g (0.5 knots per second) acceleration for various altitudes. For a given altitude, maximum speeds are provided for standard temperature, and ten degrees above and below standard temperature.

USE

Enter chart at nearest computed drag index and read maximum speeds for 0g and 0.03g accelerations at selected altitude with applicable temperature. For most accurate results, use standard interpolation techniques to determine maximum speeds.

Sample Problem

A. Drag index	40
B. Altitude	30,000 Ft
C. Temperature	-44.4°C
D. Maximum speed - 0g KCAS	0.99 Mach/383
E. Maximum speed - 0.03g KCAS	0.96Mach/374

DIVE RECOVERY CHARTS

These charts, (figures B9-17 and B9-18) present the airplanes dive recovery capability for various speeds (subsonic and supersonic), altitudes, and dive angles. The supersonic chart (figure B9-18) includes airplane structural limit curves to determine the maximum dive angle that can be achieved without exceeding the structural limit speed during dive recovery.

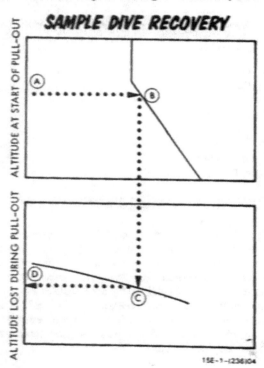

SAMPLE DIVE RECOVERY

15E-1-(238)04

USE

Enter the applicable chart with the altitude at the start of the pull-out and project horizontally right to intersect the curve for the Mach number at the start of the pull-out. From this point, project vertically down to intersect the dive angle at the start of pull-out, then horizontally left to read altitude lost during pull-out.

Sample Problem

Configuration: (4) AIM-9 Launchers; Supersonic

A. Altitude at start of pull out	40,000 Ft
B. Mach number at start of pull-out	1.5
C. Dive angle at start of pull-out	70°
D. Altitude loss during pull-out	11,800 Ft

LOW ALTITUDE COMBAT PERFORMANCE CHART

This table (figure B9-19) presents specific fuel flow values (pounds per minute) for maximum thrust operation at constant calibrated airspeeds of 300, 400, 500, 600, and 700 knots. The data are for altitudes of sea level, 5000 and 10,000 feet. Fuel flow values are computed for U.S. Standard Day; however, correction factors are given for nonstandard day temperatures. The standard day temperature is listed with the altitude. If the actual temperature at a particular altitude differs from the standard day temperature, refer to the TEMP. EFFECTS column to determine the appropriate temperature correction factor.

USE

Enter the table with the desired altitude and calibrated airspeed and project horizontally right to the specific fuel flow column to read specific fuel flow for a standard day. To obtain the specific fuel flow for a nonstandard day, mulitply the specific fuel flow for a standard day by the nonstandard day temperature correction factor obtained from the TEMP. EFFECTS column.

Sample Problem

A. Desired altitude	**5000 Ft**
B. Desired constant airspeed	600 KCAS
C. Specific fuel flow for a standard day	2113 Lb/Min
D. Nonstandard day temperature	0°C
E. Nonstandard day temperature correction factor	1.03
F. Nonstandard day specific fuel flow (C X E)	2176 Lb/Min

COMBAT FUEL MANAGEMENT CHART

This chart (figure B9-20) presents a relative comparison between engine power setting and fuel usage in pounds per minute. The chart emphasizes the effect of power setting on combat fuel management. Data presented are for engine power settings of military power, mid-range afterburner and maximum afterburner at altitudes from sea level to 40,000 feet and airspeeds between Mach 0.8 and Mach 1.1.

USE

Enter the chart at the desired altitude and project horizontally right to the selected Mach/engine power setting. From this point project vertically down to read fuel usage in pounds per minute.

SAMPLE COMBAT FUEL MANAGEMENT

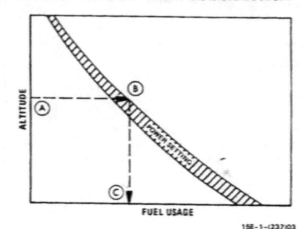

15E-1-(237)03

Sample Problem

A. Desired altitude	25,000 Ft
B. Mach/power setting	0.9/Max AB
C. Fuel usage	1020 PPM

COMBAT FUEL FLOW CHART

These charts (figures B9-21 thru B9-25) present a relative comparison between high airspeeds at stabilized level flight and fuel flow in pounds per minute. Data presented are for two non-CFT configurations and seven CFT configurations, based on F100-PW-229 engines.

USE

Enter the chart at the desired altitude and project horizontally right to the selected Mach number curve. From this point project vertically down to read fuel flow in pounds per minute.

SAMPLE COMBAT FUEL FLOW

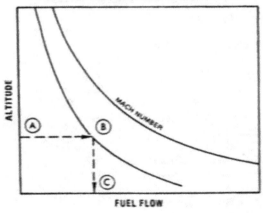

15E-1-(238)03

Sample Problem

Configuration: -4 CFT + (4) AIM-7 + (4) AIM-9

A. Desired altitude	30,000 Ft
B. Mach number	1.1
C. Fuel flow	660 PPM

OVERLOAD WARNING SYSTEM SYMMETRICAL ALLOWABLE LOAD FACTOR CHARTS

These charts (Figures B9-26 thru B9-37) present the overload warning system symmetrical allowable load factor capability for various Mach numbers, altitudes, and airplane gross weights.

USE

Enter the chart (Figures B9-26 or B9-27) with the desired Mach number and project horizontally to the desired altitude. From this point, descend vertically to the applicable gross weight then project horizontally left to read the airplane symmetrical allowable load factor given by OWS. When CFT's are installed, enter the applicable CFT/Aircraft interface charts based on CFT fuel quantity (Figures B9-28 thru B9-37) with the desired Mach number and project horizontally to the desired altitude. From this point, descend vertically to the applicable aircraft gross weight, then project horizontally left to read the CFT/airplane symmetrical allowable load factor. The combined allowable load factor is the less of the two (airplane and CFT/airplane interface).

Sample Problem

Configuration: Full CFTS

A. Mach number	0.8	
B. Altitude	Sea Level	
C. Gross Weight	45,000 Lb	
D. Airplane Symmetrical Load Factor	8.6 g	
E. CFT fuel/CFT	4875 Lb	
F. CFT/Airplane interface symmetrical allowable load factor	8.0 g	
G. Combined Symmetrical allowable load factor	8.0 g	

SAMPLE OVERLOAD WARNING SYSTEM SYMMETRICAL ALLOWABLE LOAD FACTORS

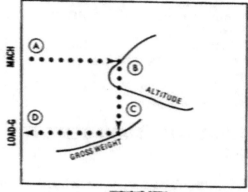

WITHOUT CFT'S

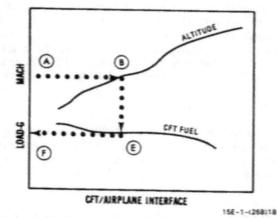

CFT/AIRPLANE INTERFACE

15E–1–(268)18

LEVEL FLIGHT ACCELERATION CHARTS

These charts (figures B9-38 thru B9-46) are used to determine time to accelerate in level flight between two Mach numbers. The curves are presented for various configurations with initial gross weights. Each chart shows maximum and military thrust accelerations at 10,000 feet and maximum thrust acceleration at 40,000 feet. The curves are presented for a standard day and standard day ±10°C. The origin for each curve is 250 KCAS and .03g acceleration points are indicated on each curve.

USE

Enter applicable configuration chart with initial Mach number and altitude, and project horizontally to appropriate thrust/standard day curve. Project vertically down to initial Mach time reference. Enter chart again with final Mach number, project horizontally to the same curve, and project vertically down to the final Mach time reference. To determine time to accelerate, subtract initial Mach number time reference from final Mach number time reference.

SAMPLE LEVEL FLIGHT ACCELERATION

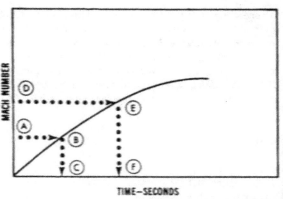

15E-1-(240)03

Sample Problem

Configuration: -4 CFT + (4) AIM-7 + (4) AIM-9; 58,100 Pounds Initial Gross Weight: Maximum Thrust, Altitude 10,000 Feet.

A.	Initial Mach number	0.8 Mach
B.	Maximum thrust/ standard day curve	STD −10° C
C.	Initial Mach number time reference	21 Seconds
D.	Final Mach number	0.9 Mach
E.	Maximum thrust/ standard day curve	STD −10° C
F.	Final Mach number time reference	27 Seconds
G.	Time to accelerate (F. minus C.)	6 Seconds

SUSTAINED LEVEL TURNS

These charts (figures B9-47 thru B9-55) present the maximum sustained level rate of turn and corresponding maximum sustained load factor for a given Mach number and altitude. The charts are based on maximum thrust for various aircraft configurations. Bank angles are shown for corresponding load factors, and a formula is provided to calculate radius of turn.

USE

Enter chart with Mach number and project vertically up to applicable rate of turn and load factor altitude curves. Project horizontally left from rate of turn altitude curve to maximum sustained rate of turn. Project horizontally left from load factor altitude curve to the maximum sustained load factor corresponding to the maximum sustainable turn rate. Project horizontally right from the load factor altitude curve to bank angle corresponding to the maximum sustained load factor.

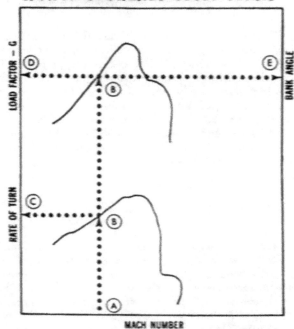

SAMPLE SUSTAINED LEVEL TURNS

15E-1-(239)03

Sample Problem

Configuration: -4 CFT + (4) AIM-7 + (4) AIM-9
52,500 Pounds Gross Weight

A. Mach number	0.9
B. Altitude	40,000 Ft
C. Maximum sustained turn rate	2.9°/SEC
D. Maximum sustained load factor	1.7g
E. Bank angle	53°

GLOSSARY

A

A/A - Air-to-air

AAI - Air-to-air interrogator

AB - Afterburner

AC - Alternating current

A/D - Air data

ADC - Air data computer

ADF - Automatic direction finding

AFC - Afterburner fuel control

AFCS - Automatic flight control system

A/G - Air-to-ground

AHRS - Attitude heading reference system

AIC - Air inlet controller

AIM - Air intercept missile

AIU - Avionics Interface Unit

ALTMTR - Altimeter

AMAD - Airframe mounted accessory drive

AMI - Airspeed Mach indicator

AOA - Angle-of-attack

ARI - Aileron rudder interconnect

ASP - Avionics status panel

ATDP - Asymmetric Thrust Departure Prevention

ATDPS - Asymmetric Thrust Departure Prevention System

ATF - Automatic Terrain Following

AUX - Auxiliary

B

BATH - Best available true heading

BCN - Beacon

BINGO - Return to this channel (radio). Return fuel state

BIT - Built-in-test

BOS - Backup Oxygen System

BST PMP - Boost pump

C

CAS - Control augmentation system. Calibrated airspeed

CC - Central computer

CCC - Central computer complex

CCW - Counterclockwise

CFT - Conformal fuel tank

CG - Center of gravity. Command groundspeed

CGB - Central gearbox

CIVV - Compressor Inlet variable vanes

C/M - Channel/manual

CMD - Countermeasures dispenser

COMM - Communication(s)

CSBPC - Control stick boost/pitch compensator

CSD - Constant speed drive

CSO - Control stick override

CSS - Control stick steering

CTR - Centerline tank. Center

CW - Clockwise

D

DART - Directional automatic realignment of trajectory

DC - Direct current

DEEC - Digital electronic engine control

DG - Directional gyro

DTM - Data transfer module

DTMR - Data transfer module receptacle

E

EADI - Electronic attitude director indicator

EAS - Equivalent airspeed

ECCM - Electronic counter-countermeasures

ECM - Electronic countermeasures

ECS - Environmental control system

EDU - Engine diagnostic unit

EHSI - Electronic horizontal situation indicator

EMD - Engine monitor display

EMI - Engine monitor indicator

EPR - Engine pressure ratio

EWW - Electronic warfare warning

EXCDNCE CNTR - Exceedance counter

EXT - External

F

FF - Fuel flow, Free fall

FLIR - Forward looking radar

FPM - Feet per minute

FRZ - Freeze

FTIT - Fan turbine inlet temperature

G

g - Unit of acceleration of gravity

GC - Gyrocompass

GCA - Ground control approach

GPM - Gallons per minute

GREC - Guard receiver

GT - Ground track

H

HOTAS - Hands on throttle and stick

HQ - Have quick

HRM - High resolution mapping

HUD - Head-up display

HYD - Hydraulic

HZ - Hertz

I

IAS - Indicated airspeed

IBS - Interference blanker set

ICS - Internal countermeasures set, Intercommunication system

IDG - Integrated drive generator

IFF - Identification friend or foe

ILS - Instrument landing system

INU - Inertial navigation unit

INS - Inertial navigation system

INV - (BTInvalid

I/P - Identification of position

J

JFS - Jet fuel starter

JTIDS - Joint tactical information display system

K

KT - Knot(s)

L

LANTIRN - Low altitude navigation targeting infrared for night

LAU - Launcher

LCG - Lead computing gyroscope

LDG GR - Landing gear

LE - Leading edge

LOD - Light-off detector

LOX - Liquid oxygen

M

MAC - Mean aerodynamic center

MAX - Maximum

MFC - Main fuel control

MIL - Military

MHz - Megahertz

MM - Millimeter

MN - Mission navigator

MPCD - Multi-purpose color display

MPD - Multi-purpose display

MPDP - Multipurpose Display Processor

MRM - Medium range missile

MSOGS - Molecular Sieve Oxygen Generating System

MUX BUS - Multiplex Bus

M/V - Magnetic variation

N

NM - Nautical mile(s)

NOZ POS - Nozzle position indicator

N_1 - Fan speed

N_2 - High compressor speed

O

OAT - Outside air temperature

OFLY - Overfly

OMNI - Omnidirectional range (VOR)

ORIDE - Override

O/S - Offset

OWS - Overload warning system

P

PACS - Programmable armament control set

PB - Pushbutton

PC - Power control

PC1, PC2 - Power control hydraulic system

PIO - Pilot Induced Oscillation

PMG - Permanent magnet generator

PP - Present position

PPH - Pounds per hour

PPM - Pounds per minute

PRESS - Pressure

PRCA - Pitch/roll channel assembly

PRF - Pulse repetition frequency

PSI - Pounds per square inch

PTC - Pitch trim compensator

PVU - Precision velocity update

Q

Q - Dynamic or impact pressure

QTY - Quantity

R

RADAR - Radio detection and ranging

RCVV - Rear compressor variable vanes

RLG - Ring laser gyro

RLS - Reservoir level sensing

RMR - Remote map reader

RPM - Revolutions per minute

R/T - Receiver transmitter

RWR - Radar warning receiver

S

SAI - Standby attitude indicator

SCP - Sensor control panel

SDR - Signal data recorder

SH - Stored heading

SHF - Shift

SIF - Selective identification feature

SOL - Solenoid

SPD BK - Speed brake

SRM - Short range missile

SRS - Short range search

SRU - Shop replaceable unit

STA/JETT - Station jettison

STBY - Standby

STBY ATTD - Standby attitude indicator

T

TAS - True airspeed

TCN - TACAN. Tactical air navigation

TDC - Target designator control

TE - Trailing edge

TEWS - Tactical electronic warfare system

TF - Terrain following

T/O - Takeoff

TOA - Time-of-arrival

TOD - Time-of-day

TOT - Time-on-target

TR - Transformer Rectifier(s)

TRANS - Transfer

TSD - Tactical situation display

U

UFC - Upfront control

UHF - Ultra high frequency

UTL - Utility hydraulic system

UTM - Universal transverse mercator

V

VTRS - Video tape recorder system

W

WOD - Word-of-the-day

X

XFER - Transfer

ALPHABETICAL INDEX

1

1 G STALLS 6-3

A

ABNORMAL ENGINE START 3-3
ABORT 3-7
AC ELECTRICAL POWER. 1-17
ACCELERATED STALLS. 6-3
ACCELERATION LIMITATIONS 5-10
ADC FAILURE. 3-26
ADI (BACK-UP MODE) DISPLAY. 1-107
ADVISORY LIGHTS. 1-38
AFCS PREFLIGHT INITIATED BIT 1-42
AFTER LANDING 2-17, 7-3, 7-4
AFTERBURNER BURN THRU 3-19
AFTERBURNER FAILURE. 3-8
AFTERBURNER OPERATION. 2-13
AFTERBURNER SYSTEM 1-4
AHRS INTERFACE 1-141
AIR DATA (A/D) MODE. 3-26
AIR DATA COMPUTER (ADC) 1-132
AIR FLOW SELECTOR SWITCH 1-153
AIR INLET SYSTEM MALFUNCTION. 3-17
AIR REFUELING SYSTEM. 1-16
AIR SOURCE KNOB 1-153
AIRCRAFT. 1-1
AIRCRAFT FUEL SYSTEM. 1-10
AIRCRAFT SETUP. 2-26
AIRCREW EGRESS (BOTH)
    (After TO 1F-15E-602) 2-18A
AIRFRAME MOUNTED ACCESSORY
    DRIVE (AMAD) 1-9
AIRSPEED LIMITATIONS 5-6
ALIGNMENT 3-27
ALTERNATE FUEL. 5-1
AMAD FAILURE. 3-24
AMAD FIRE DURING START 3-2A
AMAD FIRE INFLIGHT. 3-19
ANGLE-OF-ATTACK (AOA) INDICATOR . . . 1-88
ANGLE-OF-ATTACK (AOA) PROBES. 1-135
ANTI-G SYSTEM 1-154
ANTI-SKID MALFUNCTION 3-31
AOA TONE 1-28
APPENDIX A   PERFORMANCE DATA A-1
APPENDIX B PERFORMANCE DATA B-1
APPROACH END ARRESTMENT 3-35
ARRANGEMENT. iii
ARRESTING HOOK SYSTEM 1-23
ARRESTMENT GEAR DATA 3-37

ASYMMETRIC LOADS. 6-6A, 6-7
ASYMMETRIC THRUST DEPARTURE
    PREVENTION (ATDP) SYSTEM CAUTION
    (F-15E 90-233 AND UP). 3-20A,
ASYMMETRIC THRUST DEPARTURE
    PREVENTION SYSTEM (ATDPS) 1-6, 6-6A
ASYMMETRIC THRUST DEPARTURE
    PREVENTION SYSTEM (ATDPS) FAILURE
    (F-15E 90-0233 AND UP)(-229 engines) 3-8
ATTITUDE DIRECTOR INDICATOR
    (ADI) 1-89
ATTITUDE HEADING REFERENCE SET
    (AHRS) 1-141
AUDIO WARNING SYSTEM. 1-38
AUTO BIT. 1-40
AUTO-ACCELERATION ABOVE IDLE. 3-3
AUTOMATIC FLIGHT CONTROL SYSTEM
    (AFCS). 1-28A
AUTOPILOT FUNCTIONS 1-28A
AUTOROLLS 6-8
AVAILABLE FUNCTIONS WITH CC FAILURE
    3-28
AVIONICS INTERFACE UNIT FAILURE . . . 3-29
AVIONICS INTERFACE UNITS (AIU) 1-42
AVIONICS PRESSURIZATION AND
    TEMPERATURE. 1-153

B

BACK-UP MODE DISPLAYS 1-106
BEFORE ENTERING COCKPIT 7-4
BEFORE ENTERING FRONT COCKPIT 2-4
BEFORE ENTERING REAR COCKPIT. 2-12
BEFORE LEAVING AIRCRAFT. 7-5
BEFORE TAKEOFF 2-12C, 2-27
BEFORE TAXI. 2-26
BEFORE TAXIING. 2-27, 7-4
BEFORE TAXIING (FRONT COCKPIT). 2-8
BEFORE TAXIING (REAR COCKPIT) 2-12B
BIT. 1-152
BIT DISPLAY. 1-39
BLEED AIR CAUTION 3-20
BLEED AIR CAUTIONS 1-153
BLOWN MAIN TIRE DURING LANDING
    ROLLOUT 3-31
BLOWN TIRES 3-31
BOARDING STEPS 1-155
BOARDING STEPS EXTENDED 3-26
BOOST SYSTEM MALFUNCTION Caution . . 1-13

BOTH MAIN FUEL BOOST PUMPS AND
  EMERGENCY BOOST PUMP INOPERATIVE
  (TOTAL BOOST PUMP FAILURE) 3-20C
BRAKE OVERHEAT 3-5
BRAKE SYSTEM 1-22
BRAKES................................. 5-6
BREATHING REGULATOR 1-152B
BUILT - IN TEST (BIT) SYSTEM 1-39

C

CABIN PRESSURIZATION
  MALFUNCTION 3-6
CANOPY LOST 3-20
CANOPY SYSTEM 1-155
CANOPY UNLOCKED...................... 3-20
CANOPY UNLOCKED INFLIGHT/LOSS OF
  CANOPY............................. 3-20
CAS FUNCTIONAL FAILURE 1-33
CAS OFF.............................. 5-9
CAUTION LIGHTS...................... 1-37
CENTER OF GRAVITY LIMITATIONS 5-9
CENTRAL COMPUTER (CC) 1-42
CENTRAL COMPUTER FAILURE.......... 3-28
CENTRAL COMPUTER INTERFACE....... 1-42
CENTRAL GEARBOX (CGB) 1-9
CFT FAILS TO TRANSFER 3-21
CHANGE SYMBOL...................... iii
CHECKLISTS......................... iii
CIRCUIT BREAKERS 1-20
CLIMB TECHNIQUES 2-13
COCKPIT PRESSURE ALTIMETER 1-153
COCKPIT PRESSURIZATION 1-153
COCKPIT TEMPERATURE CONTROL 1-153
COLD WEATHER OPERATION 7-4
COMBAT JETTISON PROGRAMMING
  (BOTH)............................2-18A
COMPASS CONTROL PANEL 1-141
CONTROL AUGMENTATION
  SYSTEM (CAS) 1-28A
CONTROLLABILITY CHECK 3-30
CREW REQUIREMENTS.................. 5-1
CREWMEMBER IN COMMAND
  OF AIRCRAFT 4-1
CREWMEMBER IN CONTROL
  OF AIRCRAFT 4-1
CREWMEMBER NOT IN CONTROL
  OF AIRCRAFT 4-1
CROSSWIND LANDING.................. 2-17

D

DATA 1 DISPLAY...................... 1-104
DATA 2 DISPLAY...................... 1-105

DATA ENTRY/DISPLAY (BOTH)........... 2-20
DATA FORMATS 2-19
DATA TRANSFER MODULE SET (DTMS).. 1-44
DC ELECTRICAL POWER................ 1-18
DEPARTURE END ARRESTMENT......... 3-35
DEPARTURE WARNING................. 1-28
DEPARTURES......................... 6-6
DESCENT CHECK/BEFORE LANDING..... 2-16
DIMENSIONS......................... 1-2
DISPLAY FLOW LOW CAUTION 1-154, 3-5,
                                    3-20A
DISPLAY FORMAT ADVISORIES 1-116
DISPLAY FORMAT CHANGES WITH CC
  FAILURE........................... 3-28
DISPLAY FORMAT OPTIONS............. 1-115
DOUBLE ENGINE STALL/STAGNATION
  (-220 engines).................... 3-12
DOUBLE ENGINE STALL/STAGNATION
  (-229 engines).................... 3-13
DOUBLE ENGINE
  STALL/STAGNATION/FAILURE......... 3-12
DOUBLE GENERATOR FAILURE.......... 3-23
DUAL ENGINE OPERATION
  (ECS CAUTION ON) 3-4
DYNAMIC HYDROPLANING.............. 7-3

E

ECS CAUTION........................1-153, 3-20
ECS MALFUNCTIONS 3-4
EJECTION........................... 3-10
EJECTION SEAT SYSTEM............... 1-158
ELECTRICAL POWER SUPPLY SYSTEM .. 1-17
EMER BST ON AND/OR BST SYS MAL
  CAUTION...........................3-20B
EMERGENCY CANOPY SYSTEM 1-158
EMERGENCY FUEL TRANSFER/DUMP
  (EXTERNAL TANKS), GEAR DOWN 3-21
EMERGENCY GENERATOR 1-18
EMERGENCY GENERATOR NOT ON LINE ON
  START 3-3
EMERGENCY LANDING GEAR HANDLE .. 1-21
EMERGENCY OXYGEN SUPPLY 1-151
EMERGENCY VENT CONTROL........... 1-154
ENGINE AIR INDUCTION SYSTEM........ 1-2
ENGINE ANTI-ICE 1-5
ENGINE CONTROL MALFUNCTION
  (-220 engines..................... 3-17
ENGINE CONTROL MALFUNCTION
  (-229 engines).................... 3-17
ENGINE CONTROL SYSTEM 1-3
ENGINE CONTROLS AND INDICATORS.... 1-6
ENGINE FAILS TO ACCELERATE
  NORMALLY 3-3

ENGINE FAILS TO START 3-3
ENGINE FAILURE ON TAKEOFF 3-8
ENGINE FIRE DURING START 3-4
ENGINE FIRE INFLIGHT 3-18
ENGINE FIRE ON TAKEOFF 3-9
ENGINE FUEL SYSTEM 1-3
ENGINE LIMITATIONS. 5-1 5-3
ENGINE MASTER SWITCHES 1-6
ENGINE MONITOR DISPLAY (EMD) 1-8
ENGINE MONITORING SYSTEM 1-4
ENGINE OIL SYSTEM 1-3
ENGINE OPERATION DURING DEPARTURE
   AND SPIN 6-8
ENGINE SHUTDOWN 2-18
ENGINE STALL/STAGNATION 3-11
ENGINE START .2-7 2-26
ENGINE STARTING SYSTEM 1-2
ENGINES. 1-2
ENVIRONMENTAL CONTROL
   SYSTEM (ECS) 1-152C
EXCESSIVE GROUNDSPEED/POSITION
   ERROR 3-5
EXTERIOR INSPECTION 2-1
EXTERIOR LIGHTING 1-149
EXTERNAL ELECTRICAL POWER 1-19
EXTERNAL FUEL TRANSFER. 5-6
EXTERNAL POWER START
   (Following cockpit interior check) 2-25
EXTERNAL STORES JETTISON 3-7
EXTERNAL STORES LIMITATIONS 5-10
EXTERNAL TANK FAILS TO TRANSFER. . 3-21
EXTERNAL TANK JETTISON 1-16
External Wing and Centerline Tank Transfer . . 1-11
EXTREME COCKPIT TEMPERATURE. 3-20

F

FIRE LIGHTS. 1-8A
FIRE SENSOR CAUTION 1-9
FIRE TEST/EXTINGUISHER SWITCH 1-9
FIRE VOICE WARNINGS 1-8B
FIRE WARNING/EXTINGUISHING
   SYSTEM. 1-8A
FLAP MALFUNCTIONS. 3-31
FLAP SYSTEM 1-23
FLIGHT CONTROL SYSTEM 1-24
FLIGHT CONTROL SYSTEM
   MALFUNCTION 3-24
FLIGHT MANUAL BINDERS. iii
FLIGHT WITH ASYMMETRIC LOADS 6-4
FOLDOUT ILLUSTRATIONS . . . . FO 1
For Solo Flight - 2-4
FRONT COCKPIT CONTROLS 1-45
FRONT COCKPIT INTERIOR CHECK 2-4

FUEL BOOST PUMPS INOPERATIVE 3-20B
FUEL DUMP SYSTEM 1-15
FUEL FEED SYSTEM 1-12
FUEL MONITORING. 2-15
FUEL QUANTITY INDICATING SYSTEM . . 1-13
FUEL TANK PRESSURIZATION
   AND VENT 1-13
FUEL TRANSFER SYSTEM 1-11
FUEL TRANSFER SYSTEM MALFUNCTION
   . . . . .3-20C
FUNCTIONAL FAILURES. 1-42

G

GENERAL AIRCREW RESPONSIBILITIES . . 4-1
GENERATOR FAILURE. 3-23
GROSS WEIGHT LIMITATIONS 5-9
GROUND EGRESS 3-7
GROUND OPERATION. 3-4
GROUND REFUELING. 1-17
GYROCOMPASS AND STORED HEADING
   ALIGNMENT AND NAV 1-137

H

HAND CONTROLLERS 1-55
HANDLING CHARACTERISTICS. 6-1
HANDLING QUALITIES 6-1
HAVE QUICK II SYSTEM 1-129
HAVE QUICK SYSTEM 1-128
HEADING ERROR 3-27
HEAD-UP DISPLAY (HUD) 1-68
HEAVY GROSS WEIGHT 6-3
HIGH ANGLE OF ATTACK WARNING 1-28
HOLDING BRAKE. 5-6
HORIZONTAL SITUATION
   INDICATOR (HSI) 1-90
HOT REFUELING 2-18
HOT START. 3-3
HOT WEATHER/DESERT OPERATION 7-5
HOW TO BE ASSURED OF HAVING LATEST
   DATA. iii
HOW TO GET PERSONAL COPIES. iii
HUD BACK-UP MODE 1-81
HUD CONTROLS 1-68
HUD GUN MODE 1-81
HUD MRM MODE 1-81
HUD NAVIGATION DISPLAYS. 1-99
HUD SRM MODE 1-81
HUD SYMBOLS. 1-68
HUD WINDOWS 1-72
HYDRAULIC FAILURE 3-32
HYDRAULIC POWER SUPPLY SYSTEM . . . 1-20
HYDRAULIC PRESSURE INDICATORS 1-20

HYDRAULIC SYSTEMS CAUTION
LIGHTS 1-20
HYDROMECHANICAL FLIGHT CONTROL
SYSTEM 1-24
HYDROPLANING 7-3

I

IDENTIFICATION FRIEND OR FOE (IFF)
SYSTEM 1-130
IDENTIFICATION OF POSITION (IP) 1-131
IFF EMERGENCY OPERATION 1-131
IFF INTERROGATOR SET 1-132
IFF MODE 4 CAUTION 1-131
IFF SUBMENU 1-131
IFF TRANSPONDER SET 1-130
IGNITION SYSTEM 1-3
IN THE STORM 7-1
INERTIAL NAVIGATION DIGITAL
COMPUTER 1-135
INERTIAL NAVIGATION SYSTEM (INS) . . 1-135
INERTIAL SENSOR ASSEMBLY (ISA) 1-135
INFLIGHT 2-15, 3-9, 7-2
INFLIGHT FUEL LEAK 3-22
INLET LIGHT ON 3-17
INS ALIGNMENTS (BOTH) 2-22
INS FAILURE 3-26
INS INFLIGHT ALIGNMENT (IFA) 3-26
INS MODE KNOB 1-136
INS PROBLEMS 3-5
INS PROCEDURES 2-22
INS UPDATES 1-139, 2-24
INSTRUMENT APPROACHES 2-15
INSTRUMENT FLIGHT PROCEDURES 2-15
INSTRUMENT LANDING SYSTEM (ILS) . . 1-144
INSTRUMENT MARKINGS 5-1
Instrument Panel - 2-5
INSTRUMENTS 1-86
INTERCOM CONTROLS 1-124
INTERCOM SYSTEM 1-124
INTERCOMMUNICATIONS SET CONTROL
PANEL 1-124
INTERFERENCE BLANKER SYSTEM (IBS)
. . . . 1-164
INTERIOR CHECK 7-4
INTERIOR LIGHTING 1-150
INTERNAL TANK(S) FAIL TO TRANSFER
. . . . 3-20C
INVERTED SPINS 6-8

J

JET FUEL STARTER (JFS) 1-9
JFS ASSISTED RESTART 3-15

JFS FAILS TO ENGAGE OR ABNORMAL
ENGAGEMENT/DISENGAGEMENT 3-2A
JFS GENERATOR 1-18A
JFS LIMITATIONS 5-6
JFS READY LIGHT DOES NOT
COME ON 3-2A
JFS START 2-7, 2-26
JFS/ENGINE START 2-26

L

LANDING 3-30, 7-2
LANDING CONFIGURATION STALLS 6-4
LANDING GEAR CONTROL HANDLE 1-21
LANDING GEAR EMERGENCY
EXTENSION 3-34
LANDING GEAR FAILS TO RETRACT 3-9
LANDING GEAR SYSTEM 1-21
LANDING GEAR UNSAFE 3-32
LANDING TECHNIQUE 2-16
LANDING WITH ABNORMAL GEAR
CONFIGURATION 3-35
LANDING WITH KNOWN BLOWN
MAIN TIRE 3-31
LANTIRN NAVIGATION POD (NAV Pod) . . 1-164
LANTIRN OVERTEMPERATURE
CONDITION 3-29
LANTIRN RESTRICTIONS 5-9
LANTIRN TARGETING POD (TGT Pod) . . . 1-164
LAT STK LMT CAUTION 3-25
LATERAL CONTROL 1-27
LATERAL-DIRECTIONAL
CHARACTERISTICS 6-2
Left Console - 2-5
LIGHTING EQUIPMENT 1-149
LONGITUDINAL CONTROL 1-24
LOSS OF BRAKES 3-5
LOSS OF DIRECTIONAL CONTROL 3-6
LOW - ALTITUDE HIGH SPEED FLIGHT . . 6-10

M

Magnetic Variation (Mag Var) 2-20
MASTER CAUTION LIGHTS 1-38
MASTER MODE PROGRAMMING 1-85
MENU 1 DISPLAY 1-105
MENU 2 DISPLAY 1-105
MENU DISPLAY 1-83
MICROPHONE SWITCH 5-19
MINIMUM RUN LANDING 2-17
MISSED APPROACH/GO AROUND 2-16
MISSION NAVIGATOR (MN) 1-42

MOLECULAR SIEVE OXYGEN GENERATING SYSTEM (MSOGS) (F-15E 90-0233 AND UP AND F-15E 86-0183 THRU 90-0232 AFTER TO 1F-15E-561) 1-152
MSOGS CONCENTRATOR 1-152A
MULTIPLE-WORD-OF-DAY (MWOD) 1-129
MULTIPLEX BUS (MUX BUS) 1-42
MULTIPURPOSE DISPLAY PROCESSOR (MPDP) 1-81
MULTIPURPOSE DISPLAY PROCESSOR (MPDP) FAILURE 3-30
MULTI-PURPOSE DISPLAY/MULTI-PURPOSE COLOR DISPLAY (MPD/MPCD) 1-82

N

NAVIGATION DISPLAYS 1-99
NAVIGATION/STEERING MODES 1-90
NEGATIVE ANGLE-OF-ATTACK STALLS... 6-4
NEGATIVE G AUTOROLLS 6-9
NEGATIVE G FLIGHT 5-6
NEGATIVE G FLIGHT CHARACTERISTICS . 6-9
NO FLAP LANDING 2-17
NON-PROGRAMMED RECORDING 1-146
NORMAL CANOPY SYSTEM............... 1-155
NORMAL LANDING 2-16
NORMAL OXYGEN SUPPLY............... 1-151
NOSE GEAR STEERING SYSTEM 1-21
NOZZLE FAILURE........................... 3-18

O

OIL SYSTEM MALFUNCTION 3-20B
OPERATION OF UHF RADIOS 1-125
OPERATIONAL SUPPLEMENTS. iii
OUT-OF-CONTROL RECOVERY............. 3-9
OVERLOAD WARNING SYSTEM (OWS).... 1-35
OWS MATRIX DISPLAY (BOTH)........... 2-19
OXYGEN CAUTION (F-15E 90-0233 AND UP; ALSO F-15E 86-0183 THRU 90-232 AFTER TO 1F-15E-561) 3-20A
OXYGEN HOSE STOWAGE FITTING 1-152
OXYGEN QUANTITY GAGE 1-152
OXYGEN REGULATOR...................... 1-151
OXYGEN SYSTEM (F-15E 86-0183 THRU 90-0232 BEFORETO 1F-15E-561) 1-151

P

PC SYSTEMS............................... 1-20
PENETRATION.............................. 7-1
PENETRATION AIRSPEED 7-1
PERFORMANCE MONITOR DATA 2-25
PERMISSIBLE OPERATIONS............... iii

PITCH RATIO FAILURE 3-9
PITCH SYSTEM MALFUNCTION 3-25
PITOT-STATIC SYSTEM. 1-135
POSITIVE G AUTOROLLS 6-9
POWER UP OPERATION 1-83
PRECONDITION THE AHRS 3-27
PREFLIGHT CHECK........................ 2-1
PREPARATION FOR FLIGHT.............. 2-1
PRIMARY FUEL............................ 5-1
PROGRAMMABLE ARMAMENT CONTROL SET (PACS)............................... 1-164
PROGRAMMED RECORDING............. 1-148
PROHIBITED MANEUVERS 5-8

Q

QUICK TURN (BOTH) 2-27

R

RADAR ALTIMETER 1-88
RADAR SYSTEM 1-164
REAR COCKPIT CONTROLS............... 1-53
REAR COCKPIT INTERIOR CHECK 2-12
RECOMMENDED AIRSPEEDS 2-15
REMOTE INTERCOMMUNICATIONS CONTROL PANEL....................... 1-124
REMOTE MAP READER (RMR)........... 1-115
RESERVOIR LEVEL SENSING (RLS)....... 1-20
RESTART (-220 engines) 3-13
RESTART (-229 engines) 3-14
REVERTED RUBBER HYDROPLANING 7-3
Right Console - 2-6
ROLL RATIO and RUDR LMTR CAUTION ON - 3-17
ROLL SYSTEM MALFUNCTION 3-25
ROLLS 5-8
RUDDER SYSTEM MALFUNCTIONS 3-25
RUNAWAY TRIM........................... 3-24

S

SAFETY SUPPLEMENTS..................... iii
SCOPE..................................... iii
SCRAMBLE................................. 2-26
SECONDARY POWER SYSTEM 1-9
SECURE SPEECH SYSTEM (KY-58)....... 1-128
SEQUENCE POINTS 1-100, 1-113
SINGLE ENGINE OPERATION............. 3-20B
SINGLE ENGINE OPERATION............. 3-12
SINGLE ENGINE OPERATION (AUTOMATIC AVIONICS SHUTDOWN).................. 3-4
SINGLE ENGINE STALL/STAGNATION (-220 engines) 3-11

SINGLE ENGINE STALL/STAGNATION
(-229 engines) 3-12
SINGLE OR DOUBLE (ANY TWO) FUEL
BOOST PUMP FAILURE 3-20C
SINGLE-ENGINE OPERATION 3-30
SINGLE-ENGINE TAXI 2-17
SLOW SPEED FLIGHT 6-9
SMOKE, FUMES, OR FIRE IN COCKPIT ... 3-19
SNOW, ICE, RAIN AND SLUSH 7-2
SPEED BRAKE FAILURE 3-26
SPEED BRAKE SYSTEM 1-23
SPIN CHARACTERISTICS 6-6A
SPIN MODES 6-7
STALLS 6-3
STANDBY AIRSPEED INDICATOR 1-88
STANDBY ALTIMETER 1-88
STANDBY ATTITUDE INDICATOR 1-86
STANDBY MAGNETIC COMPASS 1-88
STARTING 3-2A
STARTING ENGINES 2-6, 7-4
STARTING JFS 7-4
STORES JETTISON SYSTEMS 1-163
SURVIVABILITY 1-11
SYMMETRIC LOADS 6-6A
SYSTEM POWER UP 1-68
SYSTEMS RESTRICTIONS 5-6

T

TACAN CONTROLS 1-142
TACAN (TACTICAL AIR NAVIGATION)
SYSTEM 1-142
TACTICAL ELECTRONIC WARFARE SYSTEM
(TEWS) 1-164
TACTICAL SITUATION DISPLAY (TSD) .. 1-113
TAKE COMMAND OPERATION 1-86
TAKEOFF 2-13, 3-7, 7-2, 7-4
TAKEOFF AND LANDING DATA CARD 2-1
TAKEOFF WITHOUT CFT 2-13
TAXIING 2-12C, 7-2, 7-4
TF (BACK-UP MODE) DISPLAY 1-107
THROTTLE QUADRANTS 1-6
THUNDERSTORM PENETRATION 7-1
TIME-OF-DAY (TOD) 1-129
TIRE FAILURE DURING TAKEOFF 3-9
TOTAL TEMPERATURE PROBE 1-135
TOTAL UTILITY SYSTEM FAILURE 3-32
TRANSPONDER CONTROLS 1-130
TSD (BACK-UP MODE) DISPLAY 1-107
TSD NAVIGATION 1-113
TSD SENSOR POSITIONING 1-117
TURBULENCE AND THUNDERSTORMS ... 7-1

U

UFC DISPLAYS 1-61
UFC NAVIGATION DISPLAYS 1-99
UFC PROCEDURES 2-19
UHF 1 AND UHF 2 SUBMENUS 1-128
UHF COMMUNICATIONS SYSTEM 1-124
UHF CONTROLS AND INDICATORS 1-124
UNCOMMANDED FUEL VENTING 3-22
UPFRONT CONTROLS (UFC) 1-60, 1-128
UTILITY SYSTEM 1-20
UTL A AND PC2 A FAILURE 3-32
UTL A FAILURE 3-32

V

VARIABLE AREA EXHAUST NOZZLE 1-5
VERIFY: 2-6
VERTICAL VELOCITY INDICATOR (VVI) .. 1-86
VIDEO TAPE RECORDER SET (VTRS) 1-146
VISCOUS HYDROPLANING 7-3
VTRS ADVISORY LIGHTS 1-146
VTRS CONTROL PANEL 1-146

W

WARNING/CAUTION/ADVISORY
LIGHTS 1-36
WEAPON SYSTEMS 1-164
WEIGHT AND BALANCE 2-1
WEIGHT LIMITS 6-4
WEIGHTS 1-2
WINDSHIELD ANTI-FOG 1-154
WINDSHIELD ANTI-ICE SWITCH 1-155
WITHOUT OPERATIVE OWS 5-8
WORD-OF-DAY (WOD) 1-129

Y

YAW CONTROL 1-129

U.S. GOVERNMENT PRINTING OFFICE: 1991-554-023-47171

FOLDOUT ILLUSTRATIONS

TABLE OF CONTENTS

General Arrangement FO-3
Front Cockpit FO-5
Rear Cockpit FO-7
Circuit Breaker Location FO-9
Airplane and Engine Fuel System FO-11

Electrical System FO-13
Hydraulic Systems FO-17
Flight Controls FO-19
Ejection Seat FO-21
Ejection Seat Performance Charts FO-23
Environmental Control System FO-25

LEFT CONSOLE

1. CONTROL AUGMENTATION SYSTEM CONTROL PANEL
2. NUC PANEL
3. BLANK
4. THROTTLE QUADRANT
5. EXTERIOR LIGHTS CONTROL PANEL
6. SENSOR PANEL
7. BLANK
8. BLANK
9. ANTI-G PANEL
10. BOARDING STEPS POSITION INDICATOR PANEL
11. GROUND POWER PANEL
12. ARMAMENT SAFETY OVERRIDE SWITCH
13. BLANK
13A. GND TEST MAINTENANCE DIAGNOSTIC TEST
14. EMERGENCY AIR REFUELING SWITCH
15. BLANK
16. REMOTE INTERCOMMUNICATIONS CONTROL PANEL
17. EWWS ENABLE SWITCH
18. IFF ANTENNA SELECT SWITCH
19. SEAT ADJUST SWITCH
20. FLYUP ENABLE SWITCH
21. BLANK
22. NON-COOPERATIVE TARGET RECOGNITION (NCTR) ENABLE SWITCH
23. VMAX SWITCH
24. FUEL CONTROL PANEL
25. MISCELLANEOUS CONTROL PANEL
26. CANOPY JETTISON HANDLE
27. COCKPIT COOLING VENT

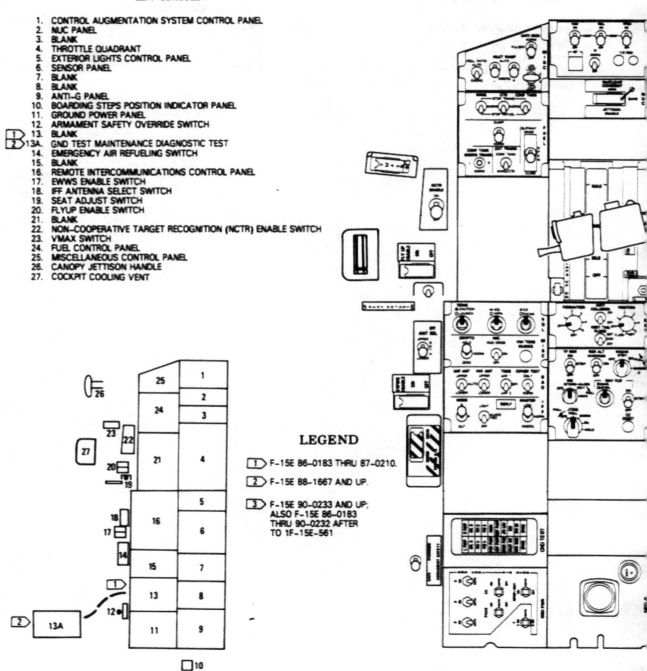

LEGEND

1. F-15E 86-0183 THRU 87-0210.

2. F-15E 88-1667 AND UP.

3. F-15E 90-0233 AND UP;
ALSO F-15E 86-0183
THRU 90-0232 AFTER
TO 1F-15E-561

Figure FO-2

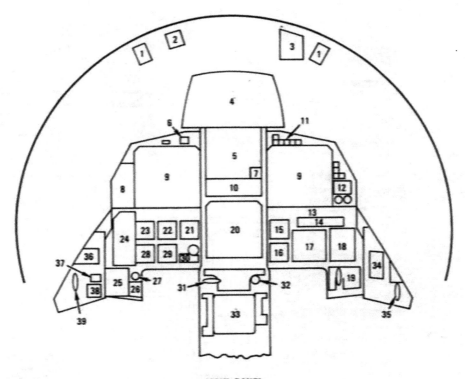

MAIN PANEL

1. LOCK / SHOOT LIGHTS
2. AIR REFUELING READY LIGHT
3. STANDBY MAGNETIC COMPASS
4. HEAD UP DISPLAY COMBINING GLASS
5. UPFRONT CONTROL PANEL
6. MASTER CAUTION LIGHT
7. EMISSION LIMIT SWITCH
8. FIRE WARNING / EXTINGUISHING PANEL
9. MULTI-PURPOSE DISPLAY (MPD)
10. HEAD UP DISPLAY CONTROL PANEL
11. WARNING / CAUTION / ADVISORY LIGHTS
12. HYDRAULIC PRESSURE INDICATORS
13. BLANK
14. DATA TRANSFER MODULE RECEPTACLE
15. EIGHT DAY CLOCK
16. CABIN PRESSURE ALTIMETER
17. ENGINE MONITOR INDICATOR
18. FUEL QUANTITY INDICATOR
19. JET FUEL STARTER CONTROL HANDLE / BRAKE HOLD SWITCH
20. MULTI-PURPOSE COLOR DISPLAY (MPCD)
21. ALTIMETER
22. STANDBY ATTITUDE INDICATOR
23. STANDBY AIRSPEED INDICATOR
24. ARMAMENT CONTROL PANEL
25. LANDING GEAR CONTROL HANDLE
26. PITCH RATIO SELECT SWITCH
27. PITCH RATIO INDICATOR
28. ANGLE OF ATTACK INDICATOR
29. VERTICAL VELOCITY INDICATOR
30. EMERGENCY JETTISON BUTTON
31. EMERGENCY BRAKE / STEERING CONTROL HANDLE
32. RUDDER PEDAL ADJUST RELEASE KNOB
33. COCKPIT COOLING AND PRESSURIZATION OUTLET
34. CAUTION LIGHTS PANEL
35. EMERGENCY VENT CONTROL HANDLE
36. ARRESTING HOOK CONTROL SWITCH
37. FLAP POSITION INDICATOR
38. RADIO CALL PANEL
39. EMERGENCY LANDING GEAR HANDLE

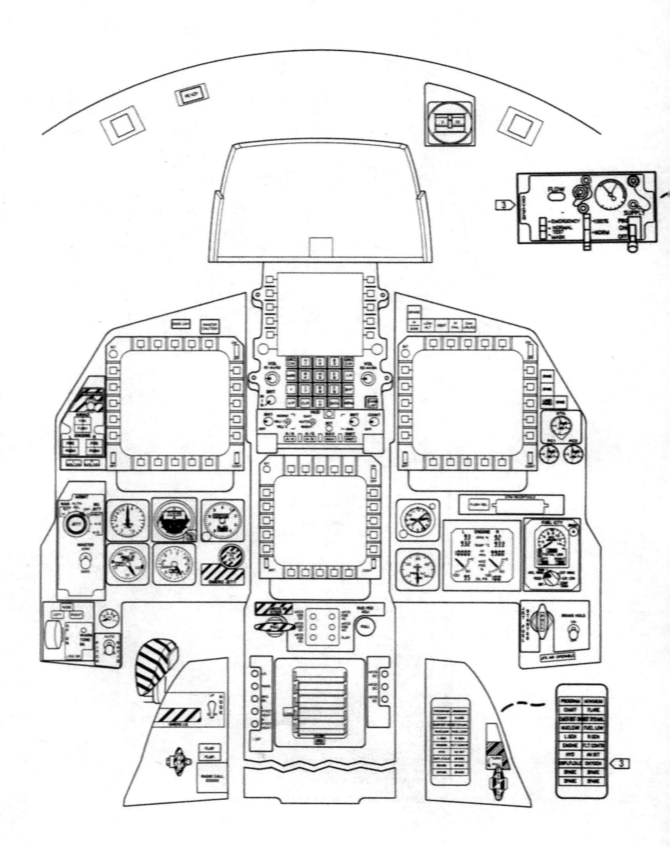

FRONT COCKPIT F-15E

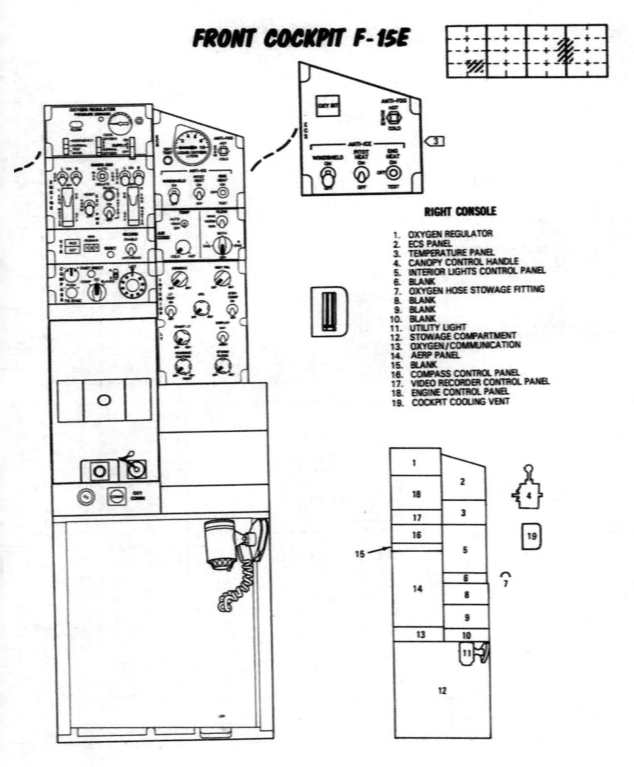

RIGHT CONSOLE

1. OXYGEN REGULATOR
2. ECS PANEL
3. TEMPERATURE PANEL
4. CANOPY CONTROL HANDLE
5. INTERIOR LIGHTS CONTROL PANEL
6. BLANK
7. OXYGEN HOSE STOWAGE FITTING
8. BLANK
9. BLANK
10. BLANK
11. UTILITY LIGHT
12. STOWAGE COMPARTMENT
13. OXYGEN/COMMUNICATION
14. AERP PANEL
15. BLANK
16. COMPASS CONTROL PANEL
17. VIDEO RECORDER CONTROL PANEL
18. ENGINE CONTROL PANEL
19. COCKPIT COOLING VENT

15E-1-(1)21

LEFT CONSOLE

1. NUC PANEL
2. BLANK PANEL
3. LEFT HAND CONTROLLER
4. SENSOR PANEL
5. EW CONTROL PANEL
6. INTERCOMMUNICATIONS SET CONTROL PANEL
7. AERP PANEL
8. ANTI-G PANEL
9. STOWAGE PROVISIONS
10. RELAY PANEL
11. THROTTLE QUADRANT
12. BLANK PANEL
13. SEAT ADJUST SWITCH
14. CIRCUIT BREAKER PANEL
15. COCKPIT COOLING VENT

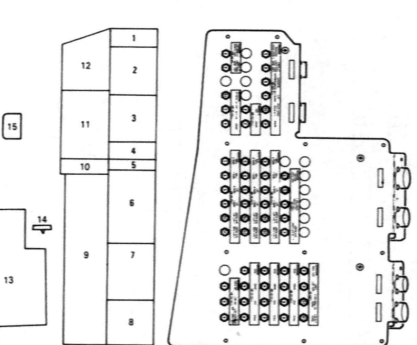

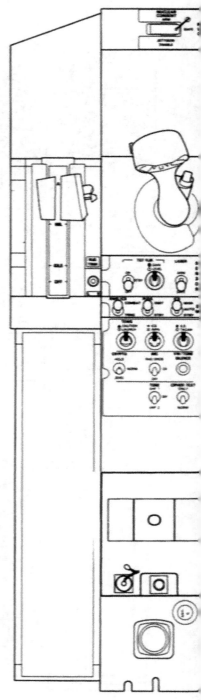

Figure FO-3

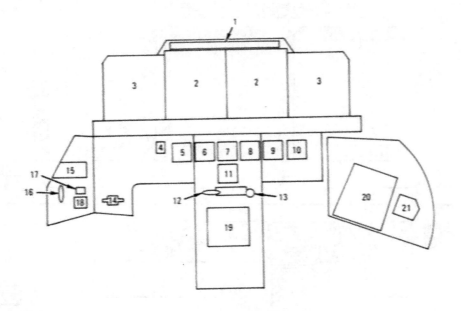

MAIN PANEL

1. WARNING/CAUTION/ADVISORY LIGHTS PANEL
2. MULTI-PURPOSE DISPLAY
3. MULTI-PURPOSE COLOR DISPLAY
4. MASTER MODE LIGHT PANEL
5. CABIN PRESSURE ALTIMETER
6. STANDBY AIRSPEED INDICATOR
7. STANDBY ATTITUDE INDICATOR
8. STANDBY ALTIMETER
9. FUEL QUANTITY INDICATOR
10. CLOCK
11. VERTICAL VELOCITY INDICATOR
12. EMERGENCY BRAKE/STEERING CONTROL HANDLE
13. RUDDER PEDAL ADJUST RELEASE KNOB
14. LANDING GEAR POSITION LIGHTS
15. ARRESTING HOOK CONTROL SWITCH
16. EMERGENCY LANDING GEAR HANDLE
17. FLAP POSITION INDICATOR
18. RADIO CALL PANEL
19. COCKPIT COOLING AND PRESSURIZATION OUTLET
20. UPFRONT CONTROL PANEL
21. COMMAND SELECTOR VALVE

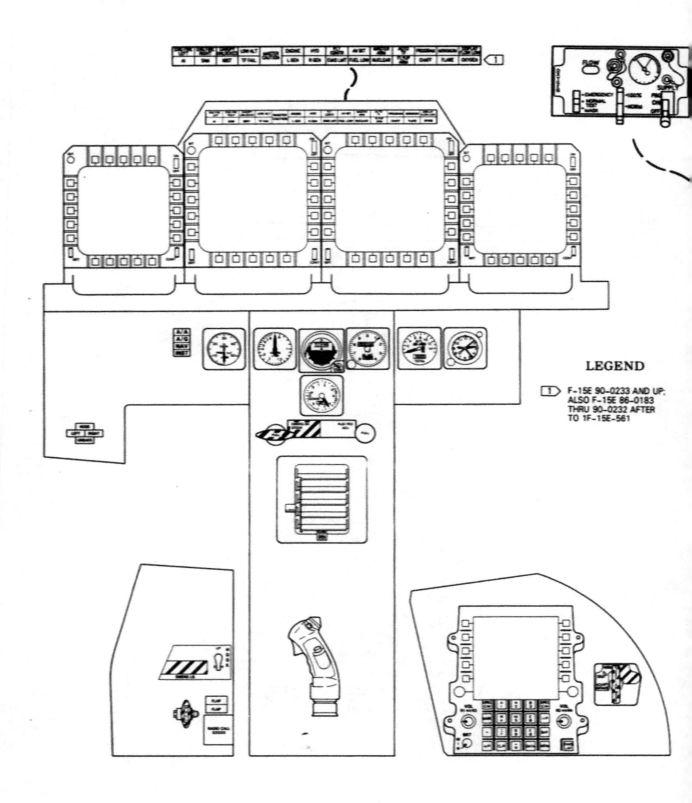

LEGEND

1 F-15E 90-0233 AND UP;
ALSO F-15E 86-0183
THRU 90-0232 AFTER
TO 1F-15E-561

REAR COCKPIT F-15E

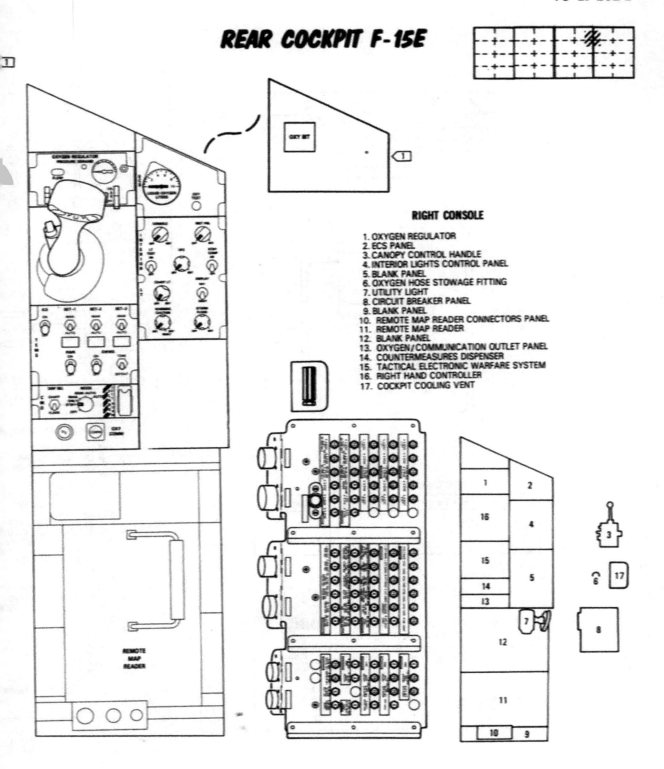

RIGHT CONSOLE

1. OXYGEN REGULATOR
2. ECS PANEL
3. CANOPY CONTROL HANDLE
4. INTERIOR LIGHTS CONTROL PANEL
5. BLANK PANEL
6. OXYGEN HOSE STOWAGE FITTING
7. UTILITY LIGHT
8. CIRCUIT BREAKER PANEL
9. BLANK PANEL
10. REMOTE MAP READER CONNECTORS PANEL
11. REMOTE MAP READER
12. BLANK PANEL
13. OXYGEN/COMMUNICATION OUTLET PANEL
14. COUNTERMEASURES DISPENSER
15. TACTICAL ELECTRONIC WARFARE SYSTEM
16. RIGHT HAND CONTROLLER
17. COCKPIT COOLING VENT

15E-1-(2)21

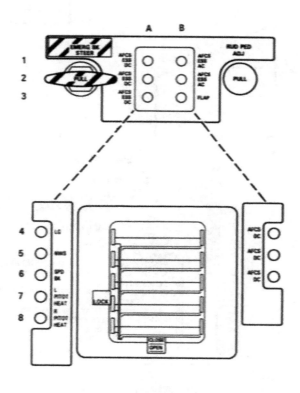

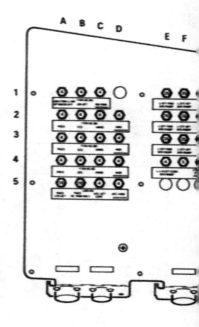

CENTER CIRCUIT BREAKER PANEL

NOMENCLATURE	ZONE(S)
AFCS ESSENTIAL AC	B1, B2,
AFCS ESSENTIAL DC	A1, A2, A3
FLAPS	B3

**COCKPIT CENTER INSTRUMENT PANEL
CIRCUIT BREAKER ASSEMBLY**

NOMENCLATURE	ZONE(S)
AFCS DC	B4, B5, B6
LANDING GEAR	A4
LEFT PITOT HEATER	A7
NOSEWHEEL STEERING	A5
RIGHT PITOT HEATER	A8
SPEED BRAKE	A6

LEFT CIRCUIT B

NOMENCLAT
ADC
AHRS
AOA (FWD) & AIR SP MACH (A
CCC
CFT LEVEL CONT NO. 1
1 ENGINE BURN THRU
HOT FUEL RECIRCULATION
HUD
HUD/UFC LIGHTS
INSTRUMENT LIGHTS (AFT)
INTERFERENCE BLANKER
INTERIOR LIGHTS
LEFT AIR INLET CONTROLLER
LAIC/RUDDER TRAVEL CAUTIO
LEFT CFT AFT TRANSFER PUM
LEFT CFT FWD TRANSFER PUM
LEFT DUCT PITOT HEATERS
LEFT MPD (AFT)
LEFT MPD (FWD)
L & R CFT CONT XFR PUMP
L & R PITOT MAST HEATERS
2 MAINTENANCE DIAGNOS
MPDP
PACS
PACS DC POWER NO. 2
PACS LIGHTS (AFT)
RIGHT MPD (AFT)
RIGHT MPD (FWD)
UFC CONT (AFT)
UFC (FWD)
UTILITY FLOOD LIGHT POWER
VSI (AFT)
VSI (FWD)

1 F-1
2 F-1

Figure FO-4

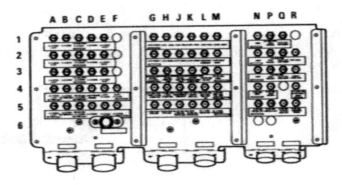

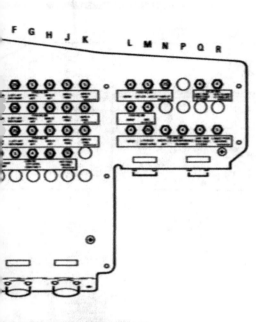

RIGHT CIRCUIT BREAKER PANEL NO. 3

NOMENCLATURE	ZONE(S)
A/A STATION 3 (L CFT)	A1, A2, A3
A/A STATION 3 (L CFT) DC POWER NO. 1	A4
A/A STATION 3 (L CFT) DC POWER NO. 2	A5
A/A STATION 4	B1, B2, B3
A/A STATION 4 DC POWER NO. 1	B4
A/A STATION 4 DC POWER NO. 2	B5
A/A STATION 6	D1, D2, D3
A/A STATION 7 (R CFT)	E1, E2, E3
A/G STATION 2	D5
A/G STATION 5	C1, C2, C3, E5
A/G STATION 5 ARMING POWER	G3
A/G STATION 5 DC POWER NO. 1	C4
A/G STATION 5 DC POWER NO. 2	C5
A/G STATION 8	F5
EMD/R FUEL FLOW IDICATOR	G4
EXCEEDANCE COUNTER	J4
GUN TRIGGER POWER	J3
HOLDING BRAKE	R5
ICE DETECTOR	K4, L3
LAST ROUND POWER	D4
LEFT CFT A/G STATION	E4
LEFT CFT AMAC	H2
LEFT CFT RACK	G2
LEFT ENGINE NOZZLE POSITION INDICATOR	G5
LEFT ENGINE OIL PRESSURE INDICATOR	J5
LEFT FUEL FLOW INDICATOR	H4
MASTER ARM LOGIC POWER	K3
MPCD (L AFT)	N5
MPCD (R CFT)	P5
NUCLEAR CONSENT	L2
OXYGEN GAGE	R2
PC-1 HYDRAULIC PRESSURE INDICATOR	L5
PC-2 HYDRAULIC PRESSURE INDICATOR	M5
PRC POSITION INDICATOR	L4
RIGHT AIR INLET CONTROLLER	M2, R4
RIGHT CFT AFT TRANSFER PUMP	Q1, Q2, Q3
RIGHT CFT A/G STATION	F4
RIGHT CFT AMAC	K2
RIGHT CFT RACK	J2
RIGHT DUCT PITOT HEATERS	R3
RIGHT ENGINE NOZZLE POSITION INDICATOR	H5
RIGHT ENGINE OIL PRESSURE INDICATOR	K5
REMOTE MAP READER	N1, N2, N3, N4
SEAT ADJUST	P1, P2, P3, P4
STATION 2 AMAC	H1
STATION 2 RACK	G1
STATION 5 AMAC	K1
STATION 5 RACK	J1
STATION 8 AMAC	M1
STATION 8 RACK	L1
UMBILICAL RETRACT POWER	H3
UTILITY HYDRAULIC PRESSURE INDICATOR	M4
VIDEO TAPE RECORDER SYSTEM	M3
WINDSHIELD ANTI-ICE	Q5

CIRCUIT BREAKER PANEL NO. 2

NOMENCLATURE	ZONE(S)
	M2
	C2, C3, C4
MACH (AFT)	A1
	B2, B3, B4
1	F4
THRU	H4
TION	G4
	D2, D3, D4
	N1
(AFT)	N3
KER	P3
	M1
ROLLER (LAIC)	Q3
CAUTION LIGHT CONTROL	Q1
FER PUMP	F1, F2, F3
FER PUMP	E1, E2, E3
ATERS	R3
	G1, G2, G3
	J1, J2, J3
PUMP	E4
ATERS	M3
DIAGNOSTIC PANEL	J4
	L1, L2, L3
	A2, A3, A4
2	B5
	A5
	H1, H2, H3
	K1, K2, K3
	C5
	D5
	R1
POWER (AFT)	B1
	C1

NOTE

1. F-15E 87-0201 AND UP.
2. F-15E 88-1667 AND UP.

15E-1-(250)06

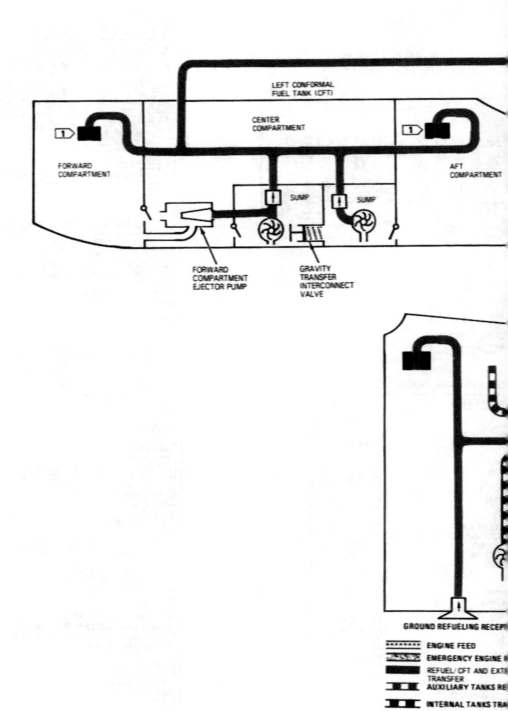

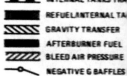

Figure FO-5

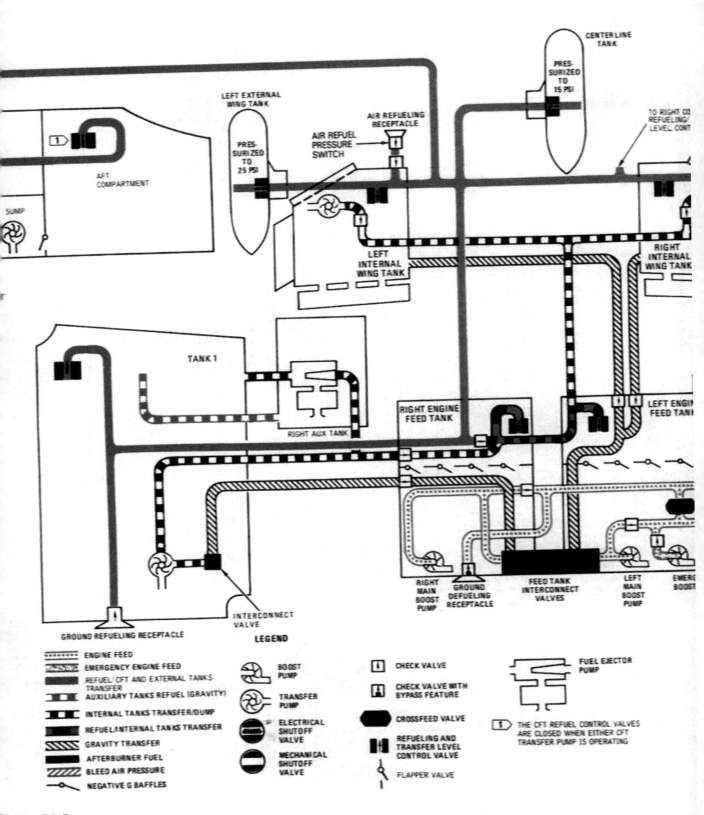

CENTER LINE TANK

PRESSURIZED TO 15 PSI

TO RIGHT CO REFUELING/ LEVEL CONT

LEFT EXTERNAL WING TANK

AIR REFUELING RECEPTACLE

AIR REFUEL PRESSURE SWITCH

PRESSURIZED TO 25 PSI

LEFT INTERNAL WING TANK

RIGHT INTERNAL WING TANK

AFT COMPARTMENT

SUMP

TANK 1

RIGHT AUX TANK

RIGHT ENGINE FEED TANK

LEFT ENGINE FEED TANK

INTERCONNECT VALVE

GROUND REFUELING RECEPTACLE

RIGHT MAIN BOOST PUMP

GROUND DEFUELING RECEPTACLE

FEED TANK INTERCONNECT VALVES

LEFT MAIN BOOST PUMP

EMERG BOOST

LEGEND

ENGINE FEED
EMERGENCY ENGINE FEED
REFUEL/CFT AND EXTERNAL TANKS TRANSFER
AUXILIARY TANKS REFUEL (GRAVITY)
INTERNAL TANKS TRANSFER/DUMP
REFUEL/INTERNAL TANKS TRANSFER
GRAVITY TRANSFER
AFTERBURNER FUEL
BLEED AIR PRESSURE
NEGATIVE G BAFFLES

BOOST PUMP

TRANSFER PUMP

ELECTRICAL SHUTOFF VALVE

MECHANICAL SHUTOFF VALVE

CHECK VALVE

CHECK VALVE WITH BYPASS FEATURE

CROSSFEED VALVE

REFUELING AND TRANSFER LEVEL CONTROL VALVE

FLAPPER VALVE

FUEL EJECTOR PUMP

1 THE CFT REFUEL CONTROL VALVES ARE CLOSED WHEN EITHER CFT TRANSFER PUMP IS OPERATING

Figure FO-5

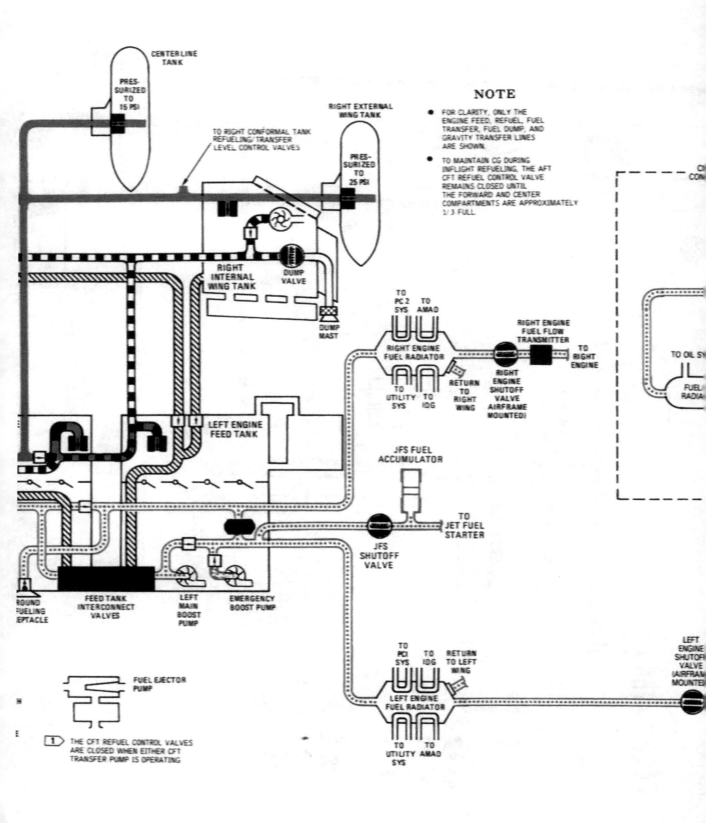

AIRPLANE & ENGINE FUEL SYSTEM F-15E

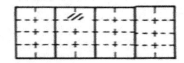

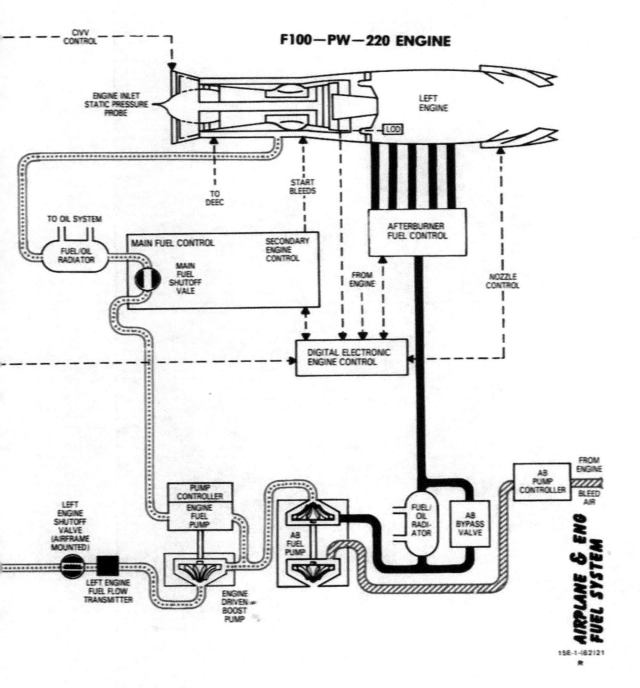

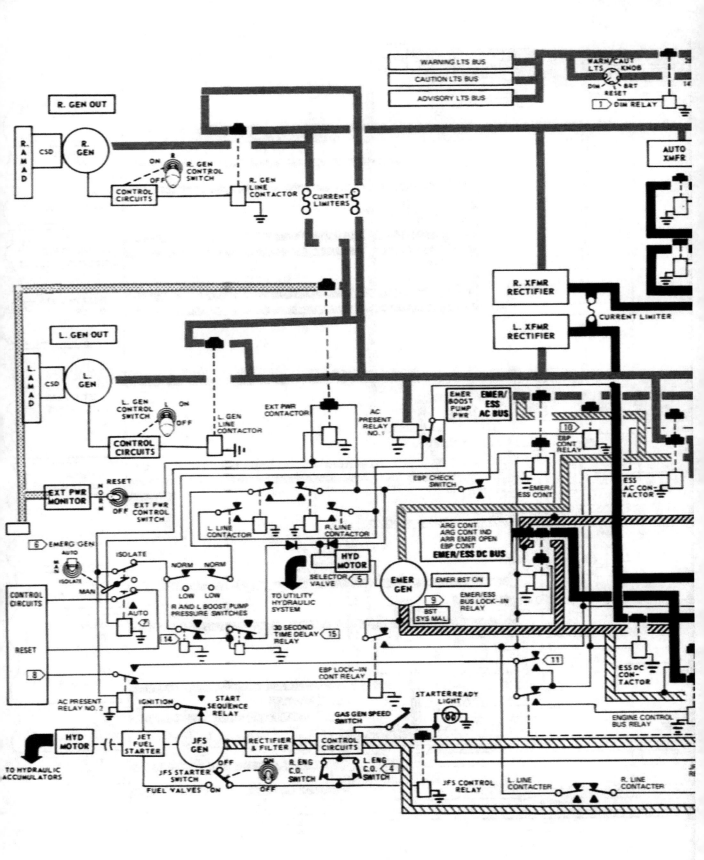

Figure FO-6 (Sheet 1 of 2)

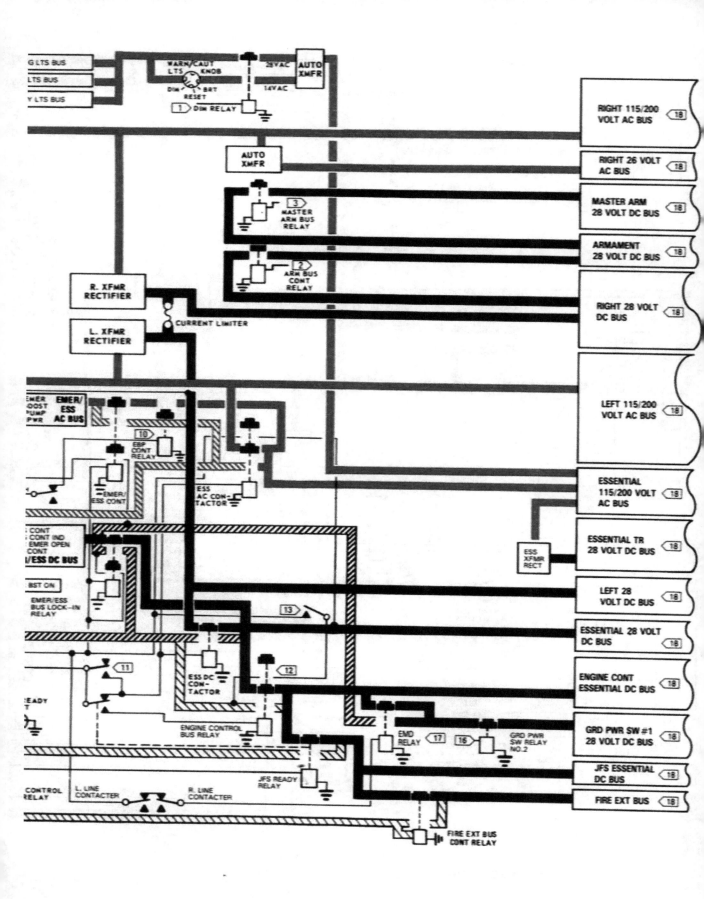

ELECTRICAL SYSTEM
EXTERNAL POWER APPLIED

NOTES

1 ⟩ DIMMING RELAY ENERGIZED WITH FLIGHT INSTRU–
MENT LIGHTS KNOB ON AND WARNING CAUTION
LIGHTS KNOB MOVED TEMPORARILY TO RESET.
RELAY IS DEENERGIZED BY TURNING FLIGHT
INSTRUMENTS LIGHT OFF OR TURNING STORM/
FLOODS KNOB TO FULL BRIGHT . OPERATION
TYPICAL FOR BOTH COCKPITS.

2 ⟩ ARMAMENT BUS CONTROL RELAY ENERGIZED WITH
GEAR HANDLE UP. WITH GEAR HANDLED DOWN,
RELAY IS ENERGIZED BY PLACING ARMAMENT
SAFETY OVERRIDES SWITCH TO OVERRIDE POSITION.

3 ⟩ MASTER ARM BUS RELAY IS ENERGIZED WITH THE
MASTER ARM SWITCH IN THE ARM POSITION,
PROVIDING ARAMENT BUS IS ENERGIZED.

4 ⟩ ENGINE CUTOUT SWITCHES OPEN AFTER THEIR
RESPECTIVE ENGINES START.

5 ⟩ WITH ELECTRICAL POWER AT SELECTED VALVE,
HYDRAULIC POWER IS SHUT OFF FROM
EMERGENCY GENERATOR (EG) TO PREVENT
OPERATION.

6 ⟩ EMERGENCY GENERATOR CONTROL SWITCH
SHOWN IN AUTO POSITION WITH EXTERNAL
POWER APPLIED. THE EG IS PREVENTED
FROM OPERATING BY A CONTACT OF THE EXT
PWR CONT RELAY ENERGIZING THE EG
SELECTOR VALVE. DURING NORMAL FLIGHT
CONDITIONS WITH THE SWITCH IN AUTO,THE
EG WILL OPERATE IF ONE OR MORE OF THE
FOLLOWING CONDITIONS OCCUR: A MAIN
GENERATOR GOES OFF THE LINE OR A MAIN
FUEL BOOST PUMP LOSES PRESSURE.
POSITIONING THE SWITCH TO MANUAL CAUSES
THE EG TO OPERATE. POSITIONING THE SWITCH
TO ISOLATE AFTER THE EG HAS OPERATED IN THE
MANUAL (OR AUTO) POSITION CAUSES THE EG
TO POWER ONLY THE EMER/ESS BUSES (EMERGENCY
BOOST PUMP (EBP), ARRESTING HOOK, FLIGHT CONTROL
COMPUTER AND EMERGENCY AIR REFUELING SWITCH).
THIS IS ACCOMPLISHED THRU THE LOCK–IN ACTION
OF THE EMER/ESS BUS LOCK–IN RELAY.

7 ⟩ ISOLATE POSITION IS ELECTRICALLY HELD THRU
LOCK–IN ACTION OF THE EMER/ESS CONTACTOR.

8 ⟩ CONTROL SIGNAL AVAILABLE AT THIS POINT WITH
EMERGENCY GENERATOR OPERATING AND
GENERATING POWER OF CORRECT VOLTAGE/
FREQUENCY, PROVIDED CONTROL SWITCH IS
OUT OF ISOLATE POSITION.

9 ⟩ THE FOLLOWING ELECTRICAL SYSTEM LOGIC
APPLIES TO EMER BST ON AND BST SYS MAL LIGHTS:

  (1) EMER BST ON AND AND BST SYS MAL
  LIGHT OFF – EMERGENCY GENERATOR
  ACTIVATED AND ELECTRICAL LOCK–UP
  CIRCUIT NORMAL.
  (2) EMER BST ON LIGHT OFF AND BST SYS MAL
  LIGHT ON–EMERGENCY GENERATOR
  EMERGENCY FUEL BOOST PUMP FAILED.
  (3) EMER BST ON LIGHT ON AND BST SYS MAL
  LIGHT ON–EMERGENCY FUEL BOOST PUMP
  OUTPUT PRESSURE NORMAL, BUT IS NOT
  BEING POWERED BY THE EMERGENCY
  GENERATOR. DO NOT PLACE THE EMER–
  GENCY GENERATOR SWITCH TO ISOLATE.

LEGEND

▬▬▬	AC POWER	⟋⟋⟋⟋ START POWER
▬▬▬	DC POWER	———— CONTROL POWER
▭▭▭▭	EXTERNAL AC POWER	– – – – MECHANICAL CONNECTION
⟋⟋⟋⟋	EMERG AC POWER	
⟋⟋⟋⟋	EMERG DC POWER	

10 ⟩ EBP CONTROL RELAY ENERGIZES TO PREVENT OPERATION
OF THE EBP WHENEVER POWER IS PRESENT AT
SELECTOR VALVE OF EG TO PREVENT EG OPERATION.
THE EBP CAN BE OPERATED UNDER THIS CONDITION BY
ACTUATING THE EBP CHECK SWITCH.
FOR ENGINE START WITHOUT EXTERNAL POWER,
RELAY REMAINS DE–ENERGIZED AFTER EG IS SHUTDOWN
30 SECONDS AFTER FIRST GENERATOR COMES ON
LINE,SO THAT RESULTING OPERATION OF EBP CAUSES
BST SYS MAL LIGHT TO COME ON AND EMER BST ON LIGHT
TO REMAIN ON UNTIL SECOND GENERATOR COMES ON LINE.

11 ⟩ CONTACT IS CLOSED (DUE TO OPERATION OF
WEIGHT ON WHEELS RELAY) WHILE AIRBORNE
TO ENSURE EG POWERS ALL ESSENTIAL BUSES DURING
INFLIGHT OPERATION OF THE JFS WITH BOTH MAIN GEN–
ERATORS OFF THE LINE.

12 ⟩ WHILE AIRBORNE WITH BOTH MAIN GENERATORS
OFF THE LINE AND JFS AND EG OPERATING,ENERGIZED CONTACT OF
ENGINE CONTROL BUS RELAY ENERGIZES EMER/ESS CONT AND EMER/ESS BUS
LOCK–IN RELAYS TO CONNECT OUTPUT OF THE EG TO THE EMR/ESS BUSES
(WHICH CAUSES OPERATION OF THE EMER BOOST PUMP).

13 ⟩ CONTACT IS CLOSED WHILE AIRBORNE. CONTACT IS OPEN ON THE
GROUND TO PREVENT OPERATION OF THE EMER BOOST PUMP.

14 ⟩ RELAY ENERGIZED ON GROUND BY WEIGHT ON WHEELS CIRCUIT

15 ⟩ WITH AIRCRAFT ON GROUND,RELAY CLOSES 30 SECONDS AFTER FIRST
GENERATOR COMES ON LINE,PROVIDING EMERGENCY GENERATOR
SWITCH IS IN AUTO DURING A START WITHOUT EXTERNAL POWER.

16 ⟩ EXCEPT ON EXTERNAL POWER WITH GROUND POWER SWITCH
NO. 1 IN AUTO, RELAY IS DE-ENERGIZED TO CLOSE
THE CONTACT.RELAY SHOWN DE–ENERGIZED WITH
GROUND POWER SWITCH NO. 1 IN ON POSITION (THIS
POSITION REQUIRED FOR ENGINE START ON EXTERNAL
POWER TO PROVIDE OPERATION OF ENGINE MONITOR INDICATOR).

17 ⟩ WITH EG OPERATING WHILE AIRBORNE AND BOTH MAIN GENERATORS OFF
THE LINE,EMD RELAY ENERGIZES TO PROVIDE POWER
TO GRD PWR SW #1 28 VOLT DC BUS WITH EG SWITCH
IN ANY POSITION.

18 ⟩ SEE SHEET 2 FOR CIRCUIT BREAKERS ON THIS BUS.

19 ⟩ F-15E 86-0183 THRU 87-0210.

20 ⟩ F-15E 86-0183 THRU 89-0496.

21 ⟩ F-15E 89-0497 AND UP.

R
15E-1–(57-1)23

ELECTRICAL SYSTEM

RIGHT 115/200 VOLT AC BUS	A/A STA 2A, 2B, 8A & 8B PWR A/A STA 3L & 7R CFT A/A STA 4 & 6 A/C UTIL PWR RECP A/G STA 2 & 8 A/G STA 5	EMO/R FUEL FLOW IND EXCEEDANCE COUNTER GUN POWER ICE DETECTOR J TIDS L FUEL FLOW IND	L WING XFR PUMP PWR OXY GAGE R AIR INLET CONT R AOA PROBE HTR R BOOST PUMP PWR R CONF TANK AFT XFR PUMP	R DUCT PITOT HT RH TEWS POD R DUCT PITOT HT RMR R TOTAL TEMP PR R WING XFR PUMP
RIGHT 26 VOLT AC BUS	L ENG ENP IND L ENG OIL PRESS IND	PC-1 HYD PRESS IND PC-2 HYD PRESS IND	PRC POS IND R ENG ENP IND	R ENG OIL PRESS UTL HYD PRESS IN
MASTER ARM 28 VOLT DC BUS	A/A STA 2A, 2B, 8A & 8B MASTER ARM PWR A/G STA 5 MASTER ARMING PWR A/A MSL MOTOR FIRE NO. 1	A/A MSL MOTOR FIRE NO. 2 GUN CONT DC PWR GUN TRIGGER PWR MASTER ARM LOGIC PWR	UMB RET PWR	
ARMAMENT 28 VOLT DC BUS	MASTER ARM BUS PWR MASTER ARM CONT			
RIGHT 28 VOLT DC BUS	A/A STA 3/L CFT DC PWR NO. 1 & 2 A/A STA 2A, 2B, 8A & 8B DC PWR NO. 1 & 2 A/A STA 6/R CFT DC PWR NO. 1 & 2 A/A STA CFT PWR NO. 1 & 2 A/A STA 4 PWR 1 & 2 AFCS CH A AFCS CH B	AFCS CH C A/G STA 2, 5 & 8 A/G STA DC PWR NO. 1 & 2 A/G STA 5 PWR NO. 1 & 2 ARM BUS CONT CSBPC HYD BYPASS DC PWR UTIL RECP	FUEL SYS CHK HOLDING BRAKE HYD PRESS ICE DETECTOR LANDING LT LANDING & TAXI LT LANTIRN NAV POD LANTIRN TARGET POD	LAST ROUND PWR L/R CFT A/G STA L WING XFR PUMP MODE SEL PWR MPCD L AFT MPCD R AFT NUCLEAR CONSEN R AIR INLET CONT
LEFT 115/200 VOLT AC BUS	AC PRESENT RLY ADC AHRS AIR INLET CONT AIU NO. 2 AOA IND-FWD CCC	EWWS HUD INMU INTRG RCVR/XMTR PWR INTRL NAV SET DSPL UNIT INTERIOR LTS INTR BLANKER IRE KIR KIT	L AIR INLET CONT L AOA PROBE HTR L BOOST PUMP PWR L CONF TANK AFT XFR PUMP L CONF TANK FWD XFR PUMP L DUCT PITOT HTR L & R PITOT MAST HTR 19 > LEAD COMP GYRO LH/CTR TEWS POD L TOTAL TEMP PROBE HTR	L XFMR/RECT MPD L AFT MPD L FWD MPDP MPD R AFT MPD R FWD PACS POS ANTI-COLLIS RADAR RADAR COOLANT RADAR XMTR
ESSENTIAL 115/200 VOLT AC BUS	AFCS AC AIU NO. 1 ARR FLOOD LIGHTS BLEED AIR LEAK DET	ESS TRU FUEL LEVEL SENS FUEL QTY IND PWR HORIZ SIT IND	INMU L & R PITOT HEAD HEAT L DUCT PITOT HTR L ENG LOW ENERGY IGN	MPDP MSOGS PWR R CONF TK FWD X R ENG LOW ENER STBY ATTD IND
ESSENTIAL TR 28 VOLT DC BUS	AFT CMD SW PWR CABIN AIR DUMP CAUT LT/MC RESET FLAP CONT	FUEL DUMP FWD CMD SW PWR 21 > MPCD-FWD SPEED BRAKE UHF RT NO. 1	WARN/CAUT/ADV LTS	
LEFT 28 VOLT DC BUS	AIU RELAY CONT ADF AV STATUS PANEL CARA CONF TANK LVL CONT VALVE	EMER GEN HYDR SOL EWWS GRD HOT FUEL RECIRC ILS	IRE LEAD COMP GYRO L A/C/RUD TRV CAUT LT CONT L BOOST PUMP	L CONF TK HT EXC L & R CONF TANK LH/CTR TEWS POD PACS PACS DC PWR NO. 2
ESSENTIAL 28 VOLT DC BUS	AERIAL REFUEL AFCS CH A AFCS CH B AFCS CH C	ARI SHUTOFF/ANTI-SKID CONT BLEED AIR LEAK DET/BK PULSER CFT/AG STORES RELEASE CFT LEVEL CONT NO. 2 ECS	ECS HEAT EXCHANGER EJECT PWR NO. 1 EJECT PWR NO. 2 EMER JETT NO. 1 EMER JETT NO. 2 FUEL LVL SENSING UNIT	FUEL PRESS REGU HOT FUEL/GRD RE IFF/TRANSPONDER INT COMM PANEL INT LTS TEST LDG GR POS WRN T
ENGINE CONT ESSENTIAL DC BUS	ENG FIRE EXT SYS ENG FIRE/OVHT DET SYS ENG EDU ENG FUEL SOV	NOSE LDG WOW PWR R ENG EDU R ENG FUEL SOV		
GRD PWR SW #1 28 VOLT DC BUS	EMD			
JFS ESSENTIAL DC BUS	AMAD FIRE DET SYS INTERCOM FWD	L AMAD SEL R AMAD SEL	UTILITY FLOODLIGHT FWD	
FIRE EXT BUS	AMAD F EXT SYS			

Figure FO-6 (Sheet 2)

ELECTRICAL SYSTEM
EXTERNAL POWER APPLIED

NOTE

NOMENCLATURE CALLOUTS ON THE INDIVIDUAL BUSES ARE CIRCUIT BREAKER NOMENCLATURES THESE NOMENCLATURES DO NOT NECESSARILY IDENTIFY EACH SYSTEM POWERED BY THE CIRCUIT BREAKERS.

UCT PITOT HTR
TEWS POD
UCT PITOT HTR
R
OTAL TEMP PROBE HTR
NING XFR PUMP

R XFMR R/RECT
RDR WARN RCVR
BWR PWR
SEAT ADJUST
26VAC AUTO XFMR

NG OIL PRESS IND
HYD PRESS IND

ST ROUND PWR
CFT A/G STA
NING XFR PUMP RLY
DE SEL PWR
CD L AFT
CD R AFT
CLEAR CONSENT
AIR INLET CONT

R BOOST PUMP RLY
R CONF TK HT EXCH DR ACTR
R IDLE NOZL RESET/ENG OIL PRESS
RH TEWS POD
BMR
RUDDER TRAVEL LMTR
R WG XFER PUMP
RDR WRN RCVR PWR

SEAT ADJUST CONT
STA 2, 5 & 8 AMAC
STA 2, 5 & 8 RACK
TAXI LT
TEWS POD CONT
UTILITY PWR RCPT
VTRS
WSHLD ANTI–ICE

XFMR/RECT
PD L AFT
PD L FWD
PDP
PD R AFT
PD R FWD
CS
S ANTI–COLLISION LTS
ADAR
ADAR COOLANT PUMP
ADAR XMTR

RDR XMTR & LVPS
SIGNAL DATA RCDR
TACAN RCVR/XMTR
TIS
TNK NO. 1 XFR PUMP PWR
VSI AFT
VSI FWD

PDP
SOGS PWR
CONF TK FWD XFR PUMP
ENG LOW ENERGY IGN
TBY ATTD IND

STORM FLOODS/CAUTION LTS
STORM FLOOD LTS FWD
UFC POWER
WARN/ADV/CAUT LTS PWR

CONF TK HT EXCH DR ACTR
& R CONF TANK CTR XFR PUMP
N/CTR TEWS POD
CS
CS DC PWR NO. 2

PSN ANTI–COLLISION LT CONT
RDR CONT & LVPS
RDR COOLANT PUMP
RDR LVPS POWER
TACAN/RCVR XMTR

TIS DC PWR
UFC–AFT
UFC–FWD
UHF RT NO. 2
UTIL FLOOD LT PWR – AFT

EL PRESS REGULATORS
T FUEL/GRD REFUEL
F/TRANSPONDER
T COMM PANEL
T LTS TEST
G GR POS WRN TONE

LG
LDG GR CONT
LG POS IND
L MAIN GEAR WOW PWR
L/R CFT AFT AFR PUMP
20 MPCD–FWD

NLG STEERING
PRAD CONT
R MAIN GEAR WOW PWR

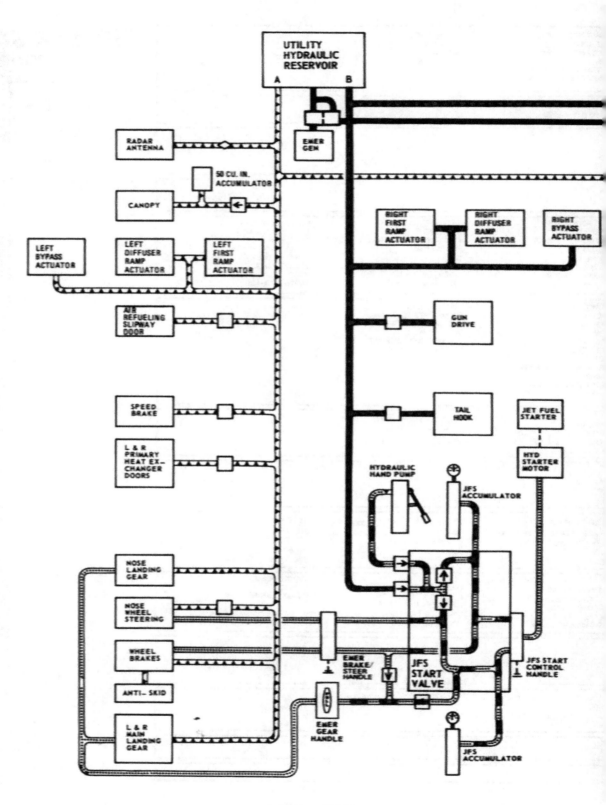

Figure FO-7

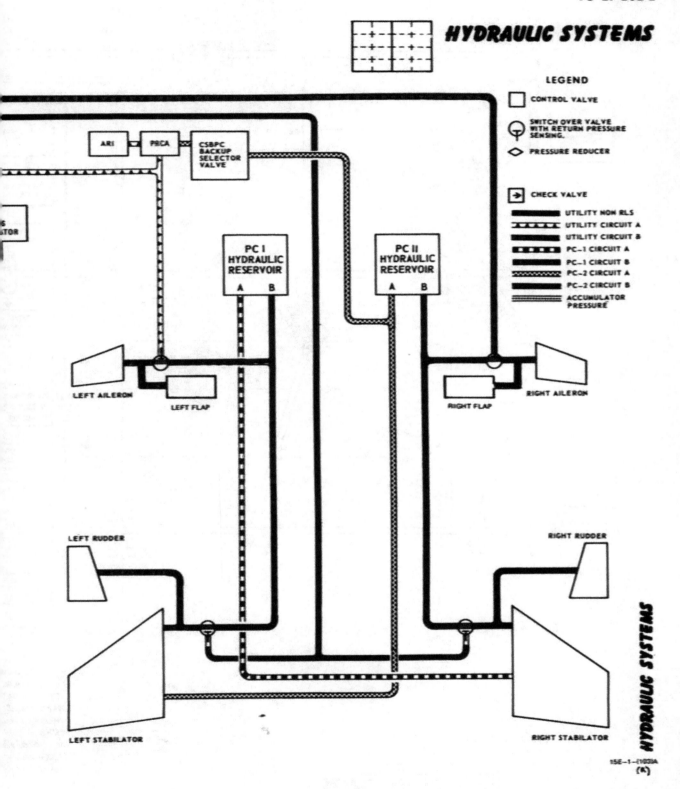

HYDRAULIC SYSTEMS

LEGEND

☐ CONTROL VALVE

⊖ SWITCH OVER VALVE WITH RETURN PRESSURE SENSING.

◇ PRESSURE REDUCER

→ CHECK VALVE

UTILITY NON RLS
UTILITY CIRCUIT A
UTILITY CIRCUIT B
PC-1 CIRCUIT A
PC-1 CIRCUIT B
PC-2 CIRCUIT A
PC-2 CIRCUIT B
ACCUMULATOR PRESSURE

ARI
PRCA
CSBPC BACKUP SELECTOR VALVE

PC I HYDRAULIC RESERVOIR
A   B

PC II HYDRAULIC RESERVOIR
A   B

LEFT AILERON

LEFT FLAP

RIGHT FLAP

RIGHT AILERON

LEFT RUDDER

RIGHT RUDDER

LEFT STABILATOR

RIGHT STABILATOR

HYDRAULIC SYSTEMS

15E-1-(103)A
(K)

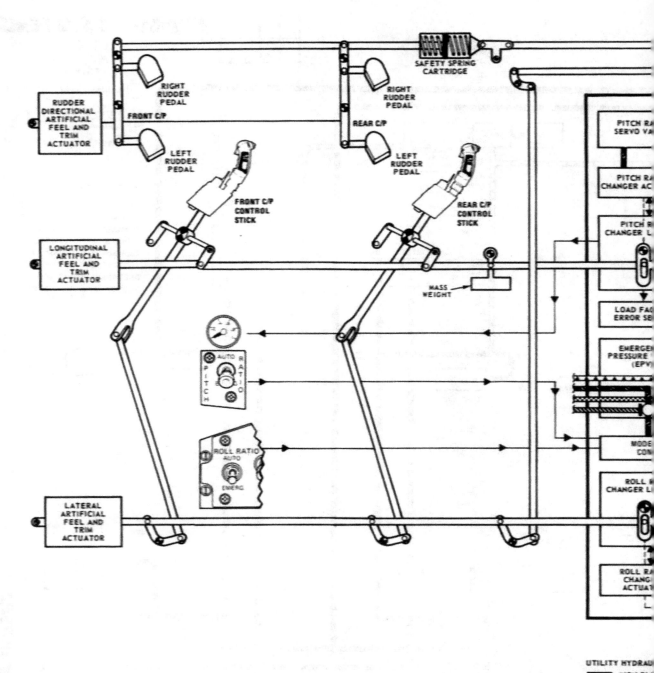

Figure FO-8

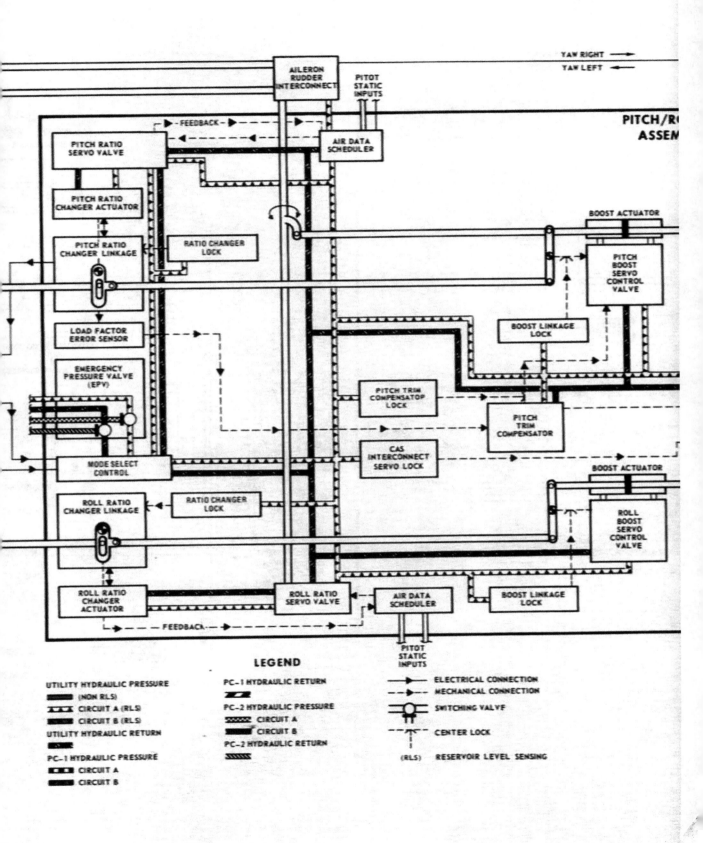

YAW RIGHT →
YAW LEFT ←

AILERON RUDDER INTERCONNECT

PITOT STATIC INPUTS

PITCH/R
ASSEM

PITCH RATIO SERVO VALVE

FEEDBACK

AIR DATA SCHEDULER

BOOST ACTUATOR

PITCH RATIO CHANGER ACTUATOR

PITCH RATIO CHANGER LINKAGE

RATIO CHANGER LOCK

PITCH BOOST SERVO CONTROL VALVE

LOAD FACTOR ERROR SENSOR

BOOST LINKAGE LOCK

EMERGENCY PRESSURE VALVE (EPV)

PITCH TRIM COMPENSATOR LOCK

PITCH TRIM COMPENSATOR

MODE SELECT CONTROL

CAS INTERCONNECT SERVO LOCK

BOOST ACTUATOR

ROLL RATIO CHANGER LINKAGE

RATIO CHANGER LOCK

ROLL BOOST SERVO CONTROL VALVE

ROLL RATIO CHANGER ACTUATOR

ROLL RATIO SERVO VALVE

AIR DATA SCHEDULER

BOOST LINKAGE LOCK

FEEDBACK

PITOT STATIC INPUTS

LEGEND

UTILITY HYDRAULIC PRESSURE
 (NON RLS)
 CIRCUIT A (RLS)
 CIRCUIT B (RLS)
UTILITY HYDRAULIC RETURN

PC-1 HYDRAULIC PRESSURE
 CIRCUIT A
 CIRCUIT B

PC-1 HYDRAULIC RETURN

PC-2 HYDRAULIC PRESSURE
 CIRCUIT A
 CIRCUIT B
PC-2 HYDRAULIC RETURN

→ ELECTRICAL CONNECTION
--→ MECHANICAL CONNECTION
 SWITCHING VALVE
 CENTER LOCK

(RLS) RESERVOIR LEVEL SENSING

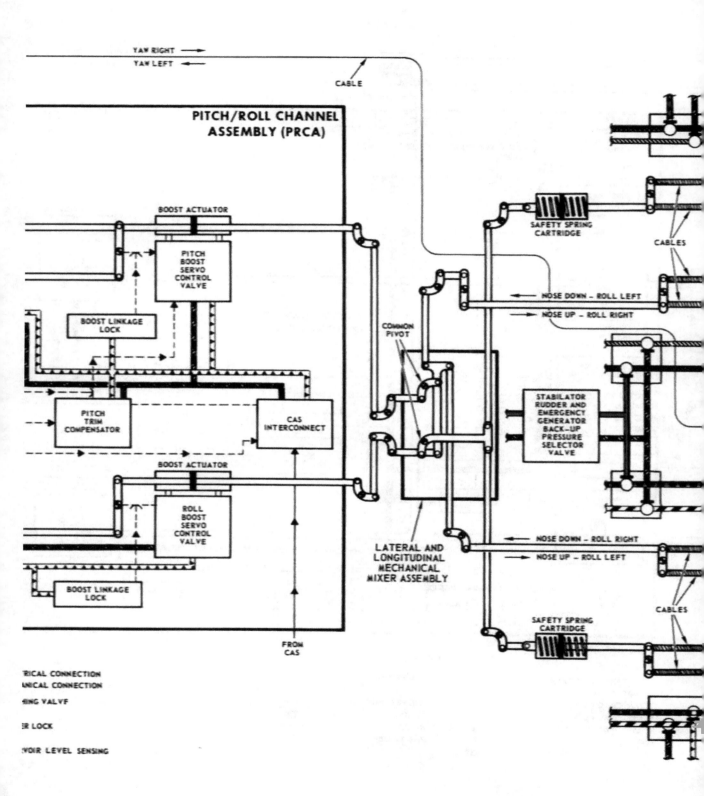

YAW RIGHT →
YAW LEFT ←

CABLE

PITCH/ROLL CHANNEL ASSEMBLY (PRCA)

BOOST ACTUATOR

PITCH BOOST SERVO CONTROL VALVE

BOOST LINKAGE LOCK

PITCH TRIM COMPENSATOR

CAS INTERCONNECT

BOOST ACTUATOR

ROLL BOOST SERVO CONTROL VALVE

BOOST LINKAGE LOCK

FROM CAS

COMMON PIVOT

LATERAL AND LONGITUDINAL MECHANICAL MIXER ASSEMBLY

SAFETY SPRING CARTRIDGE

CABLES

NOSE DOWN – ROLL LEFT ←
NOSE UP – ROLL RIGHT →

STABILATOR RUDDER AND EMERGENCY GENERATOR BACK–UP PRESSURE SELECTOR VALVE

NOSE DOWN – ROLL RIGHT ←
NOSE UP – ROLL LEFT →

CABLES

SAFETY SPRING CARTRIDGE

RICAL CONNECTION
ANICAL CONNECTION
SING VALVE
ER LOCK
VOIR LEVEL SENSING

FLIGHT CONTROLS

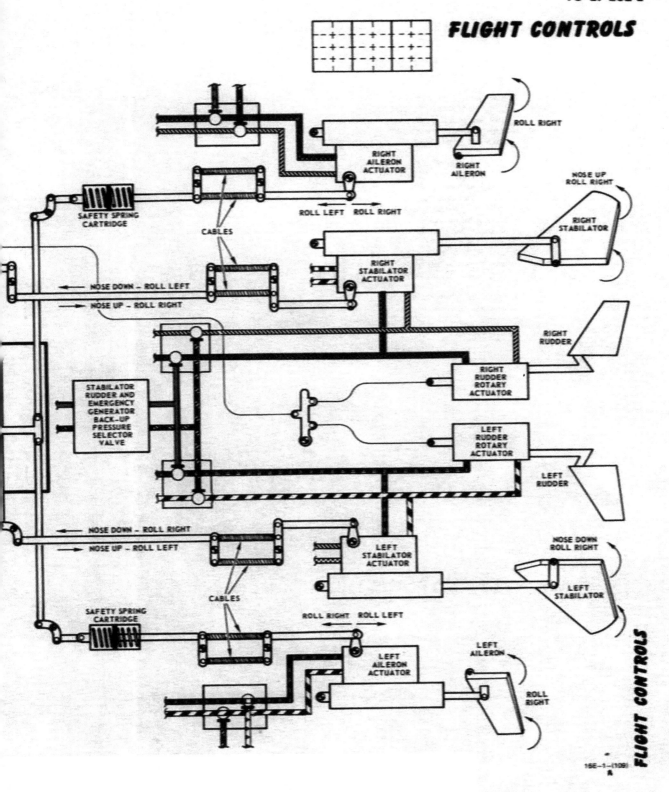

TIE DOWN PROCEDURE

1. After orienting the strap and labeled PARACHUTE CONNECTOR END toward top of seat, attach accessory rings to survival kit; center and tighten straps.

2. Install strap end labeled PARACHUTE CONNECTOR END through both parachute/shoulder harness connectors; buckle and fully tighten strap with the shoulder harness lock/unlock handle in forward position.

3. Loop the lower end of the strap around the seat torque tube; fasten and snug down.

4. Fasten and tighten lap belt on top of tie down.

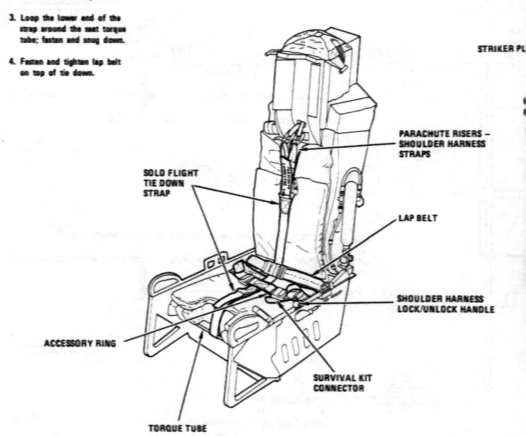

STRIKER PL

PARACHUTE RISERS – SHOULDER HARNESS STRAPS

SOLO FLIGHT TIE DOWN STRAP

LAP BELT

SHOULDER HARNESS LOCK/UNLOCK HANDLE

ACCESSORY RING

SURVIVAL KIT CONNECTOR

TORQUE TUBE

SOLO FLIGHT TIE DOWN STRAP INSTALLATION

Figure FO-9

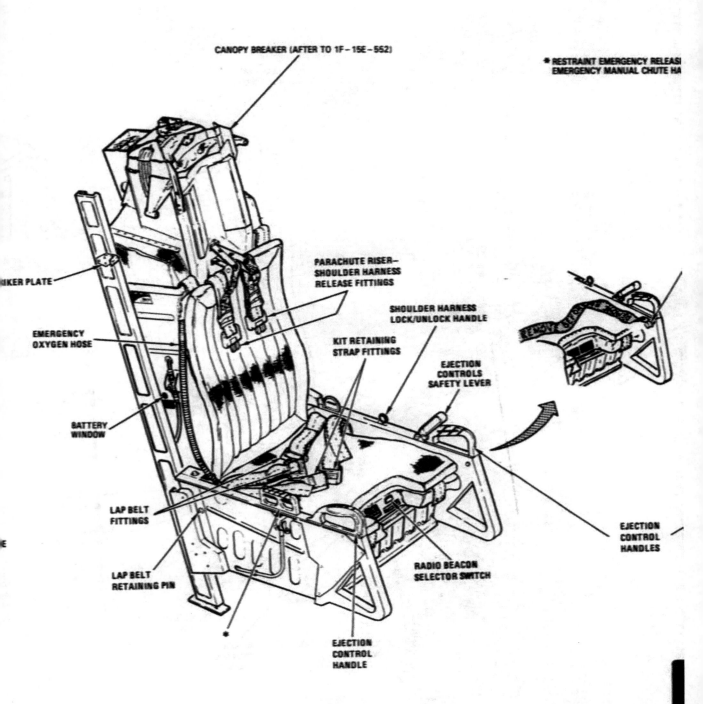

CANOPY BREAKER (AFTER TO 1F–15E–552)

* RESTRAINT EMERGENCY RELEAS
EMERGENCY MANUAL CHUTE HA

PARACHUTE RISER–
SHOULDER HARNESS
RELEASE FITTINGS

SHOULDER HARNESS
LOCK/UNLOCK HANDLE

KIT RETAINING
STRAP FITTINGS

EJECTION
CONTROLS
SAFETY LEVER

NKER PLATE

EMERGENCY
OXYGEN HOSE

BATTERY
WINDOW

LAP BELT
FITTINGS

EJECTION
CONTROL
HANDLES

LAP BELT
RETAINING PIN

RADIO BEACON
SELECTOR SWITCH

EJECTION
CONTROL
HANDLE

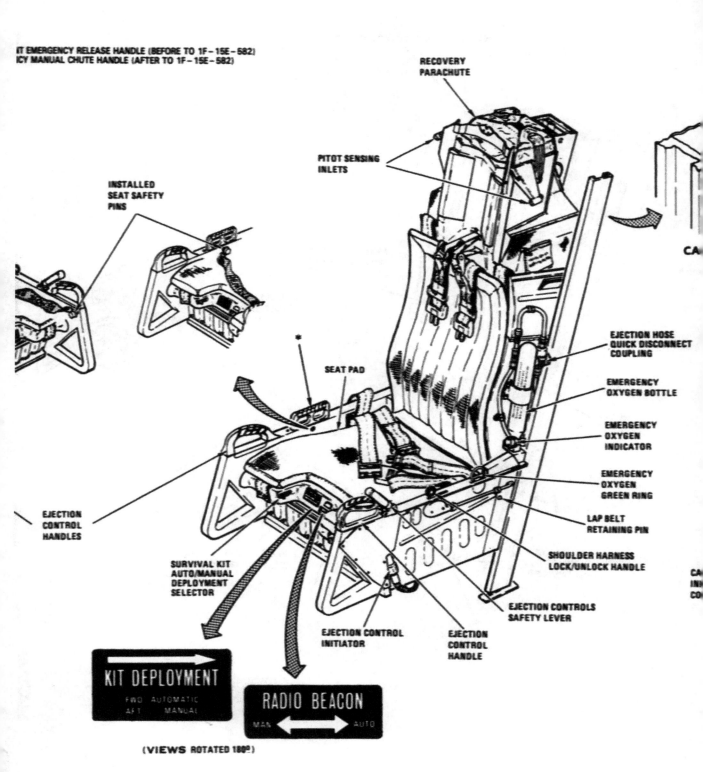

KIT EMERGENCY RELEASE HANDLE (BEFORE TO 1F–15E–582)
ICY MANUAL CHUTE HANDLE (AFTER TO 1F–15E–582)

RECOVERY
PARACHUTE

PITOT SENSING
INLETS

INSTALLED
SEAT SAFETY
PINS

EJECTION HOSE
QUICK DISCONNECT
COUPLING

EMERGENCY
OXYGEN BOTTLE

SEAT PAD

EMERGENCY
OXYGEN
INDICATOR

EMERGENCY
OXYGEN
GREEN RING

EJECTION
CONTROL
HANDLES

LAP BELT
RETAINING PIN

SHOULDER HARNESS
LOCK/UNLOCK HANDLE

SURVIVAL KIT
AUTO/MANUAL
DEPLOYMENT
SELECTOR

EJECTION CONTROLS
SAFETY LEVER

EJECTION CONTROL
INITIATOR

EJECTION
CONTROL
HANDLE

KIT DEPLOYMENT

FWD   AUTOMATIC
AFT   MANUAL

RADIO BEACON

MAN ←——→ AUTO

(VIEWS ROTATED 180°)

EJECTION SEAT

TYPICAL

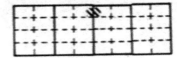

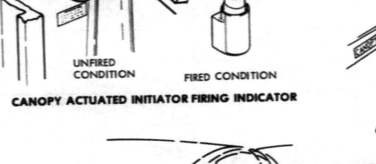

UNFIRED
CONDITION

FIRED CONDITION

CANOPY ACTUATED INITIATOR FIRING INDICATOR

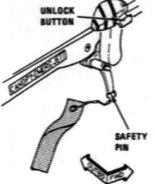

UNLOCK
BUTTON

SAFETY
PIN

CANOPY JETTISON HANDLE

EJECTION HOSE
QUICK DISCONNECT
COUPLING

EMERGENCY
OXYGEN BOTTLE

EMERGENCY
OXYGEN
INDICATOR

EMERGENCY
OXYGEN
GREEN RING

LAP BELT
RETAINING PIN

SHOULDER HARNESS
LOCK/UNLOCK HANDLE

CTION CONTROLS
ETY LEVER

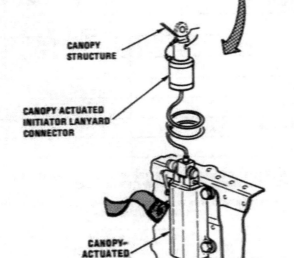

CANOPY
STRUCTURE

CANOPY ACTUATED
INITIATOR LANYARD
CONNECTOR

CANOPY-
ACTUATED
INITIATOR

EJECTION SEAT

15E-1-(51)18

MINIMUM EJECTION ALTITUDE VS. SINK RATE
SINGLE AND DUAL EJECTION

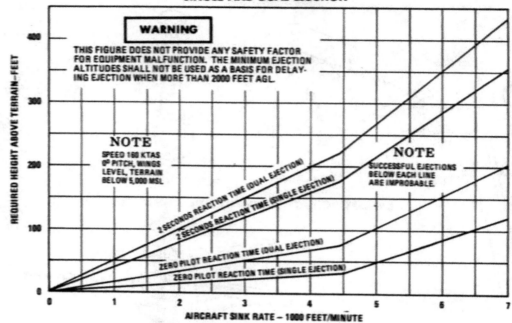

MINIMUM EJECTION ALTITUDE FOR SELECTED FLIGHT CONDITIONS

FLIGHT CONDITIONS	SINGLE EJECTION MINIMUM EJECTION ALT (FEET)	DUAL EJECTION MINIMUM EJECTION ALT (FEET)
ZERO SPEED, ZERO ALTITUDE – (CANOPY MUST BE CLOSED AND LOCKED OR COMPLETELY SEPARATED)	0	0
120 KNOTS, 0° PITCH, 60° BANK ☐1☐	0	0 ☐2☐
600 KNOTS, 0° PITCH, 0° BANK	0	0
150 KNOTS, 0° PITCH, 180° BANK	280	280
150 KNOTS, 0° PITCH, 0° BANK, 10,000 FPM SINK RATE	240	360
200 KNOTS, -60° PITCH, 0° BANK	600	810
450 KNOTS, -30° PITCH, 0° BANK	570	880
200 KNOTS, -60° PITCH, 60° BANK	650	880 ☐2☐
250 KNOTS, -45° PITCH, 180° BANK	780	1000

☐1☐ FOR THIS CASE, IMPACT OCCURS AT THE INSTANT OF SEAT/AIRCRAFT SEPARATION. IN ALL OTHER CASES, CONDITIONS ARE AT SYSTEM INITIATION.

☐2☐ FOR THESE CASES, RECOVERY PERFORMANCE IS BASED ON THE MOST CRITICAL (FRONT SEAT) ROLL/SEAT TRAJECTORY COMBINATION.

WARNING

THE FIGURE DOES NOT PROVIDE ANY SAFETY FACTOR FOR EQUIPMENT MALFUNCTION OR PILOT REACTION TIME. THE ABOVE MINIMUM EJECTION ALTITUDES SHALL NOT BE USED AS THE BASIS FOR DELAYING EJECTION MORE THAN 2000 FEET AGL.

Figure FO-10

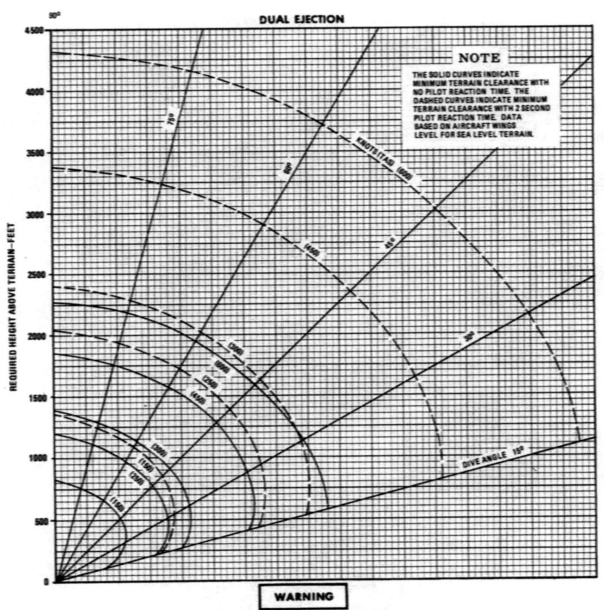

DUAL EJECTION

NOTE

THE SOLID CURVES INDICATE MINIMUM TERRAIN CLEARANCE WITH NO PILOT REACTION TIME. THE DASHED CURVES INDICATE MINIMUM TERRAIN CLEARANCE WITH 2 SECOND PILOT REACTION TIME. DATA BASED ON AIRCRAFT WINGS LEVEL FOR SEA LEVEL TERRAIN.

REQUIRED HEIGHT ABOVE TERRAIN—FEET

DIVE ANGLE 15°

WARNING

THE FIGURE DOES NOT PROVIDE ANY SAFETY FACTOR FOR EQUIPMENT MALFUNCTION. THE ABOVE MINIMUM EJECTION ALTITUDES SHALL NOT BE USED AS THE BASIS FOR DELAYING EJECTION WHEN MORE THAN 2000 FEET AGL.

EJECTION SEAT PERFORMANCE CHARTS

i. AIRSPEED AND DIVE ANGLE

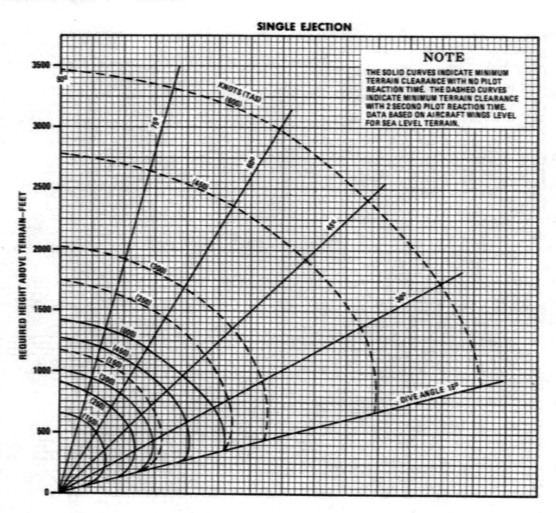

SINGLE EJECTION

NOTE

THE SOLID CURVES INDICATE MINIMUM TERRAIN CLEARANCE WITH NO PILOT REACTION TIME. THE DASHED CURVES INDICATE MINIMUM TERRAIN CLEARANCE WITH 2 SECOND PILOT REACTION TIME. DATA BASED ON AIRCRAFT WINGS LEVEL FOR SEA LEVEL TERRAIN.

WARNING

THE FIGURE DOES NOT PROVIDE ANY SAFETY FACTOR FOR EQUIPMENT MALFUNCTION. THE ABOVE MINIMUM EJECTION ALTITUDES SHALL NOT BE USED AS THE BASIS FOR DELAYING EJECTION WHEN MORE THAN 2000 FEET AGL.

15E—1—(55)

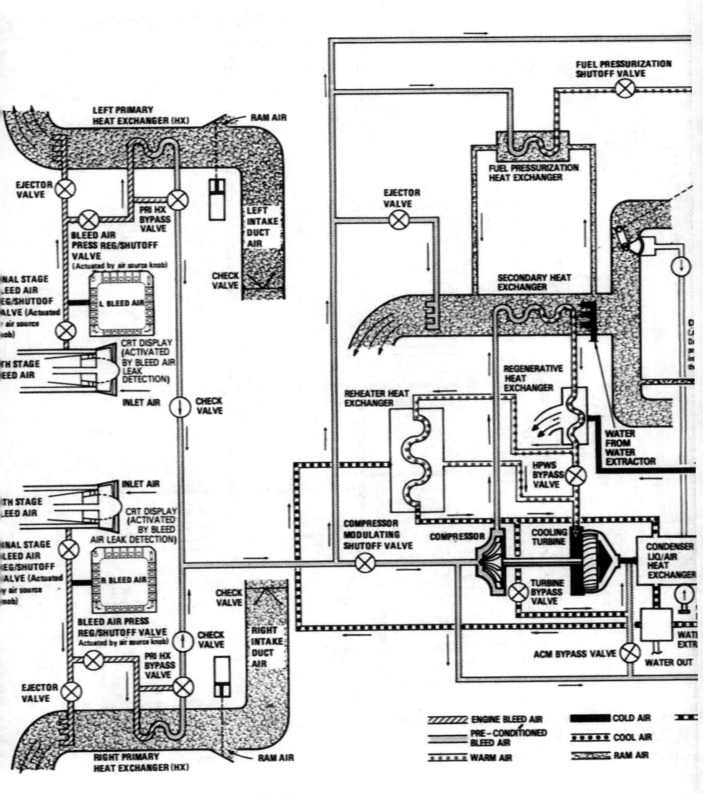

Figure FO-11

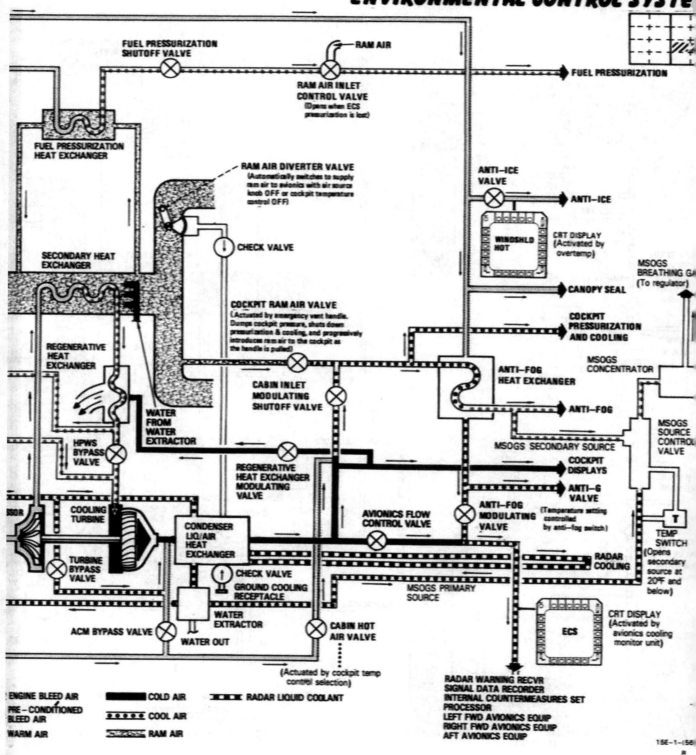

FUEL PRESSURIZATION SHUTOFF VALVE

RAM AIR

FUEL PRESSURIZATION

RAM AIR INLET CONTROL VALVE
(Opens when ECS pressurization is lost)

FUEL PRESSURIZATION HEAT EXCHANGER

RAM AIR DIVERTER VALVE
(Automatically switches to supply ram air to avionics with air source knob OFF or cockpit temperature control OFF)

ANTI–ICE VALVE

ANTI–ICE

SECONDARY HEAT EXCHANGER

CHECK VALVE

WINDSHLD HOT

CRT DISPLAY
(Activated by overtemp)

MSOGS BREATHING GA
(To regulator)

REGENERATIVE HEAT EXCHANGER

COCKPIT RAM AIR VALVE
(Actuated by emergency vent handle. Dumps cockpit pressure, shuts down pressurization & cooling, and progressively introduces ram air to the cockpit as the handle is pulled)

CANOPY SEAL

COCKPIT PRESSURIZATION AND COOLING

MSOGS CONCENTRATOR

ANTI–FOG HEAT EXCHANGER

WATER FROM WATER EXTRACTOR

CABIN INLET MODULATING SHUTOFF VALVE

ANTI–FOG

MSOGS SOURCE CONTROL VALVE

HPWS BYPASS VALVE

REGENERATIVE HEAT EXCHANGER MODULATING VALVE

MSOGS SECONDARY SOURCE

COCKPIT DISPLAYS

COOLING TURBINE

AVIONICS FLOW CONTROL VALVE

ANTI–FOG MODULATING VALVE

ANTI–G VALVE

(Temperature setting controlled by anti–fog switch)

TEMP SWITCH
(Opens secondary source at 20°F and below)

TURBINE BYPASS VALVE

CONDENSER LIQ/AIR HEAT EXCHANGER

CHECK VALVE

GROUND COOLING RECEPTACLE

MSOGS PRIMARY SOURCE

RADAR COOLING

ACM BYPASS VALVE

WATER EXTRACTOR

WATER OUT

CABIN HOT AIR VALVE

ECS

CRT DISPLAY
(Activated by avionics cooling monitor unit)

(Actuated by cockpit temp control selection)

RADAR WARNING RECVR
SIGNAL DATA RECORDER
INTERNAL COUNTERMEASURES SET
PROCESSOR
LEFT FWD AVIONICS EQUIP
RIGHT FWD AVIONICS EQUIP
AFT AVIONICS EQUIP

ENGINE BLEED AIR   COLD AIR   RADAR LIQUID COOLANT
PRE–CONDITIONED BLEED AIR   COOL AIR
WARM AIR   RAM AIR

15E–1–(56

R

WARSHIPS DVD SERIES

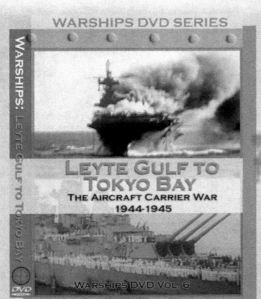
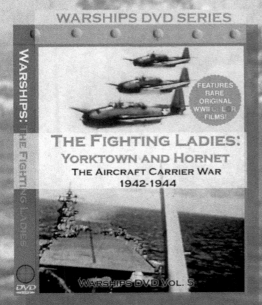
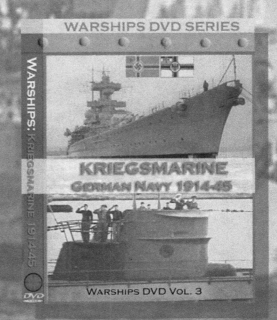

Aircraft At War
DVD Series

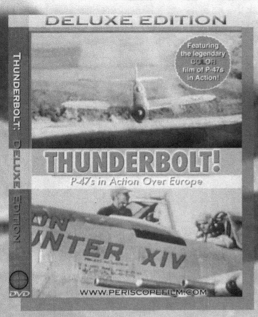

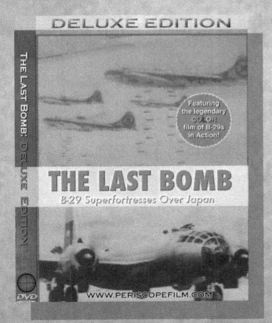

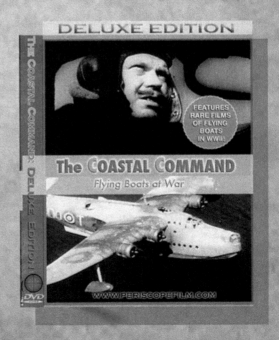

Now Available!

EPIC BATTLES
OF WWII

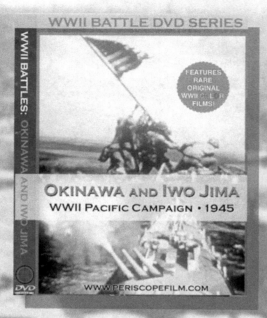
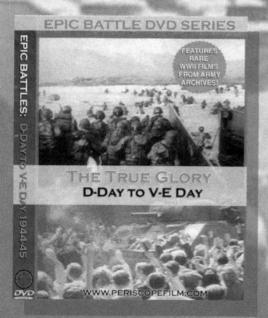

NOW AVAILABLE ON DVD!

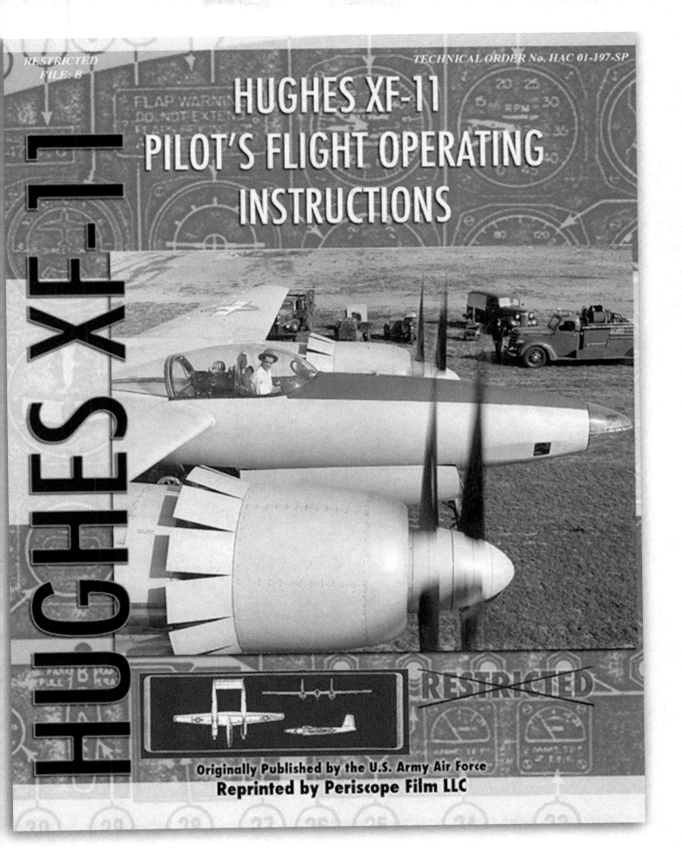

RESTRICTED
FILE-B

TECHNICAL ORDER No. HAC 01-197-SP

HUGHES XF-11
PILOT'S FLIGHT OPERATING
INSTRUCTIONS

HUGHES XF-11

Originally Published by the U.S. Army Air Force
Reprinted by Periscope Film LLC

NOW AVAILABLE!

SPRUCE GOOSE

HUGHES FLYING BOAT
MANUAL

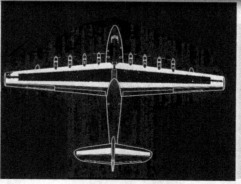

~~RESTRICTED~~

**Originally Published by the War Department
Reprinted by Periscope Film LLC**

NOW AVAILABLE!

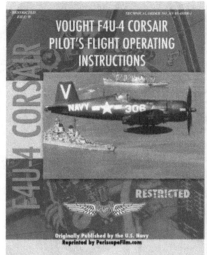
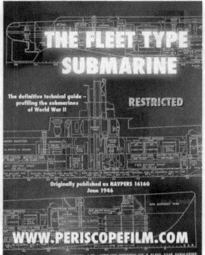

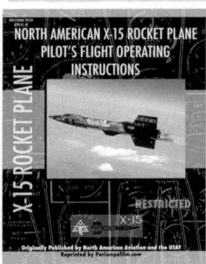
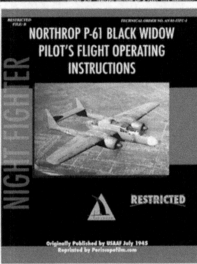
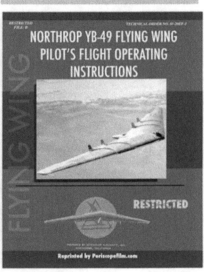

CPSIA information can be obtained
at www.ICGtesting.com
Printed in the USA
LVHW061153280523
748262LV00005B/261